AF496451

Queen Mary's
Photograph Albums

QUEEN MARY'S
PHOTOGRAPH ALBUMS

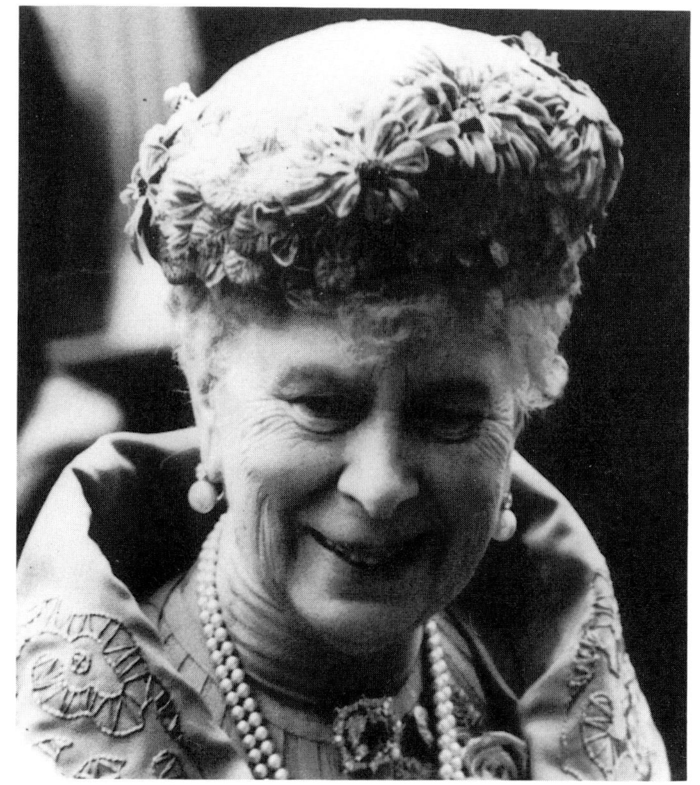

Edited by

CHRISTOPHER WARWICK

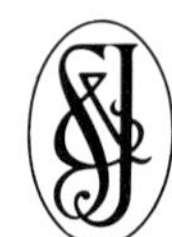

Sidgwick & Jackson

London

For Sylvia Pakenham-Beatty
with love

First published in Great Britain in 1989 by
Sidgwick & Jackson Limited

ISBN 0 283 99853 9

Photoset by Rowland Phototypesetting Limited
Bury St Edmunds, Suffolk
Printed and bound in Great Britain by
Butler and Tanner Limited, Frome and London
for Sidgwick & Jackson Limited
1 Tavistock Chambers, Bloomsbury Way
London WC1A 2SG

◆

History – or more precisely, historians – have handed down to us an image of Queen Mary which casts her in a distantly majestic, almost mystical light. There can be no doubt, of course, that Queen Mary was always as majestic as she was regal and dignified, yet she was no less human for all that. Indeed, the 'other side' of this legendary Queen Consort shines through the vast number of photographs – somewhere in the region of 10,000 – that are contained within the thirty-three albums she kept throughout her adult life and which span the years 1880 to 1952.

Each of these tall, weighty volumes, uniformly bound in scarlet cloth and leather and tooled in gold, is identical both in shape and size. Each of them contains sixty board-like pages and, on average, each page contains five or six photographs. As well as captioning the photographs in her own hand – many of those captions are reproduced here – Queen Mary invariably signed her albums on the inside front cover. The first signature, underlined with a flourish, reads 'Victoria Mary of Teck'. Later, as Duchess of York and subsequently as Princess of Wales, she signed herself 'Victoria Mary'. Once her husband had ascended the throne as King George V and she had become Queen Consort, the name 'Victoria' disappears altogether and the signatures read 'Mary R'. Finally, during her widowhood, Queen Mary sometimes dispensed with the 'R' and simply signed herself 'Mary'. This wasn't an especially common occurrence, but for this album, a fourth variation serves our purposes conveniently well; allowing us to reproduce the Queen's signatures as part openings.

Only in the last of Queen Mary's albums do we find evidence of a second hand at work. As her strength began to fail during the final months of her life, it seems probable that Queen Mary delegated the task of captioning her photographs, though doubtless under her direction, to one of her ladies-in-waiting.

As we studied each and every one of Queen Mary's albums at Windsor Castle, where they have been housed since her death in March 1953, my editor and I became acutely aware of the largely unsung warmth of the Queen's personality and, perhaps even more surprisingly, of her sense of humour, which is often so very apparent in some of the more private snapshots.

Although the majority of the photographs seen here tell their own stories sufficiently clearly, my publishers and I felt that the collection should be supplemented by a brief account of Queen Mary's life and times. However, in preparing this 'sketch', I wanted the Queen to speak for herself as often as possible and I have therefore drawn on some of the innumerable letters and diary entries that were originally quoted in James Pope-Hennessy's unsurpassable official biography of Queen Mary, published by Messrs George Allen and Unwin in 1959.

Of course, without the express permission of Her Majesty The Queen, this volume would not have been even remotely possible. I would like to acknowledge my debt of gratitude to Her Majesty, for granting me unrestricted access to the photograph albums of her late grandmother.

It also gives me pleasure to extend my very warmest thanks to each of the following: Frances Dimond, Curator of the Royal Photograph Collection, whose co-operation and guidance were invaluable; William Armstrong, Managing Director of Sidgwick & Jackson; my editor, Carey Smith, for all her advice and sheer hard work; Libby Joy, for her enthusiastic assistance; my agent, Doreen Montgomery of Rupert Crew Ltd; and Bob Hook, whose design has so surely added that extra something to an already unique album.

Christopher Warwick

Sunningdale, Berkshire

April 1989

THE ROYAL FAMILY TREE AS IT APPEARED
AT THE TIME OF QUEEN MARY'S
DEATH IN 1953

KING GEORGE III = QUEEN CHARLOTTE
1738–1820   1744–1818

King George IV
1762–1830

Edward, Duke of Kent
1767–1820
m. Victoria, Princess of
Saxe-Coburg 1786–1861

Augusta, = Adolphus, Duke
Princess of Hesse   of Cambridge
1797–1889   1774–1850

QUEEN VICTORIA = Albert of
1819–1901   Saxe-Coburg-Gotha
                 1819–1861

Victoria
Princess Royal
1840–1901
(Empress Frederick of
Germany)

King Edward VII = Alexandra, Princess
1841–1910   of Denmark
                   1844–1925

7 others

Albert Victor,
Duke of Clarence
and Avondale
1864–1892

Louise,
1867–1931
m. Duke of Fife
1849–1912

Victoria
1868–1935

Maud
1869–1938
m. Haakon VII,
King of Norway
1872–(1957)

Alexander
1871

Two daughters

Olav
1903–

Edward,
Duke of Windsor
King Edward VIII
(abdicated 1936)
1894–(1972)

= Wallis
Warfield
Simpson
1896–(1986)

Albert
King George VI
b. 1895; 1936–1952

= Lady Elizabeth
Bowes Lyon
1900–

Mary,
Princess Royal
1897–(1965)

= Henry, Viscount
Lascelles, 6th Earl of
Harewood
1882–1947

George,
7th Earl of
Harewood
1923–

Gerald
Lascelles
1924–

Queen Elizabeth II =
b. 1926; 1952–

Philip,
Duke of Edinburgh
1921–

Margaret
1930–

Charles,
Prince of Wales
1948–

Anne
1950–

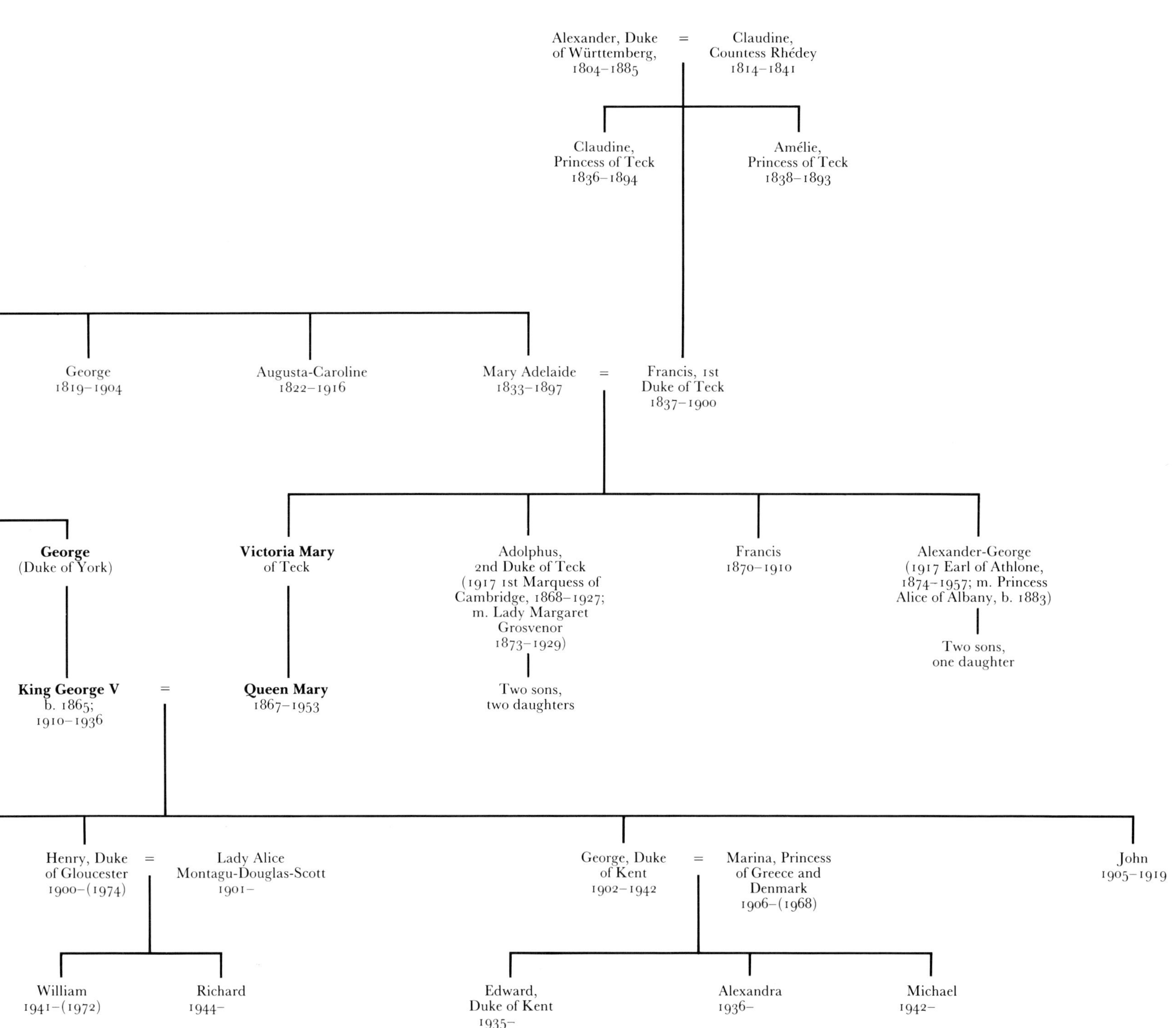

12 others

Alexander, Duke
of Württemberg,
1804–1885
=
Claudine,
Countess Rhédey
1814–1841

Claudine,
Princess of Teck
1836–1894

Amélie,
Princess of Teck
1838–1893

George
1819–1904

Augusta-Caroline
1822–1916

Mary Adelaide
1833–1897
=
Francis, 1st
Duke of Teck
1837–1900

George
(Duke of York)

Victoria Mary
of Teck

Adolphus,
2nd Duke of Teck
(1917 1st Marquess of
Cambridge, 1868–1927;
m. Lady Margaret
Grosvenor
1873–1929)

Francis
1870–1910

Alexander-George
(1917 Earl of Athlone,
1874–1957; m. Princess
Alice of Albany, b. 1883)

King George V
b. 1865;
1910–1936
=
Queen Mary
1867–1953

Two sons,
two daughters

Two sons,
one daughter

Henry, Duke
of Gloucester
1900–(1974)
=
Lady Alice
Montagu-Douglas-Scott
1901–

George, Duke
of Kent
1902–1942
=
Marina, Princess
of Greece and
Denmark
1906–(1968)

John
1905–1919

William
1941–(1972)

Richard
1944–

Edward,
Duke of Kent
1935–

Alexandra
1936–

Michael
1942–

Silver Wedding June 12th 1891.

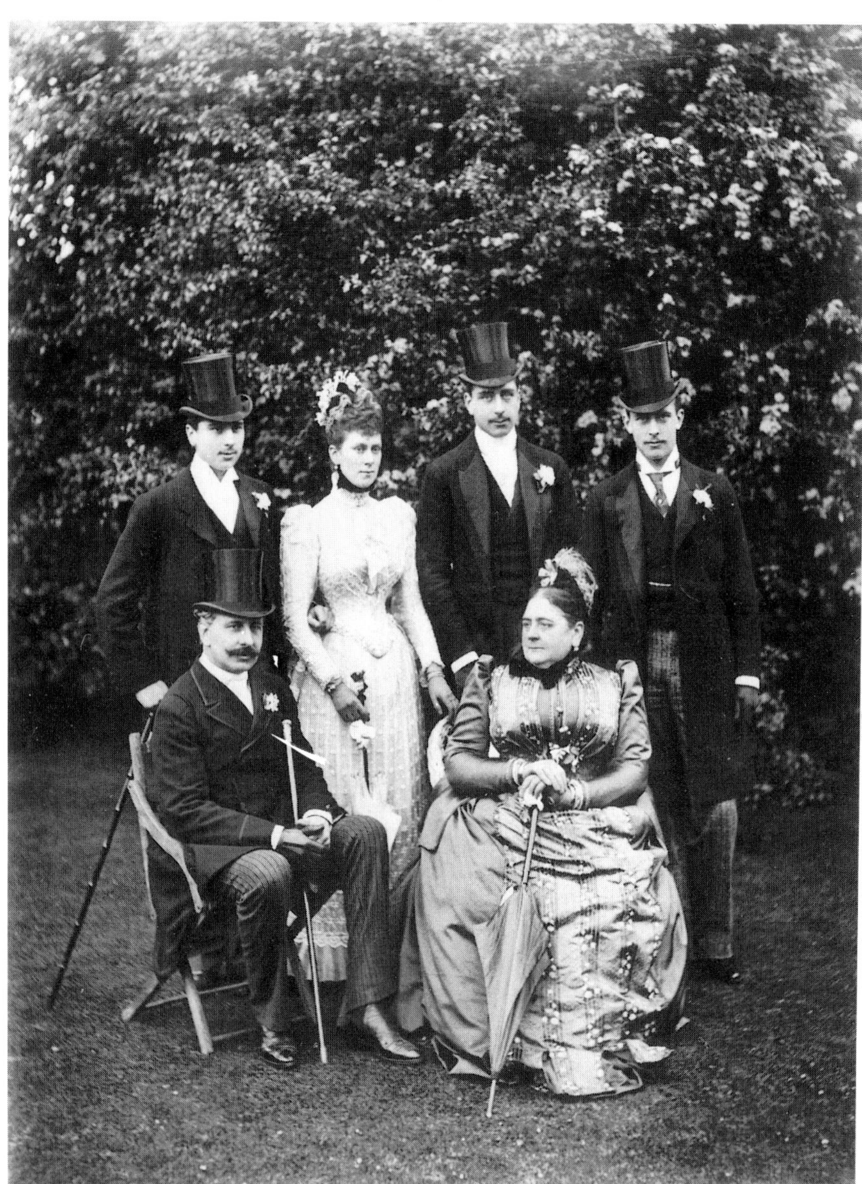

Alge
May
Francis
Frank
Dolly
Mary Adelaide

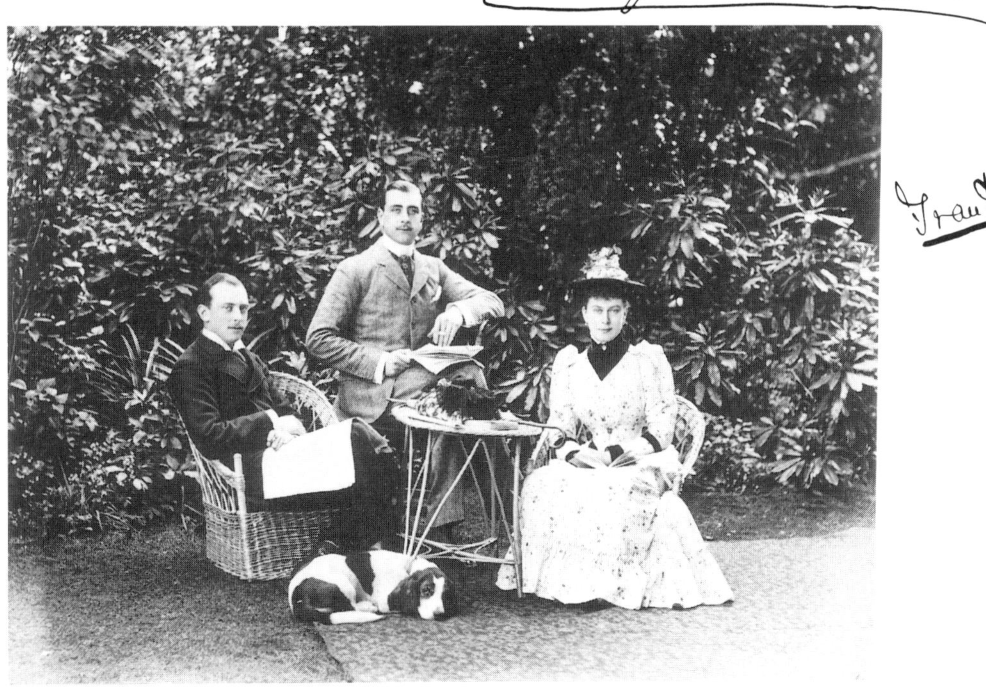

Dolly
Frank
In the garden
June 14th
1891.

PART ONE

Victoria Mary of Teck

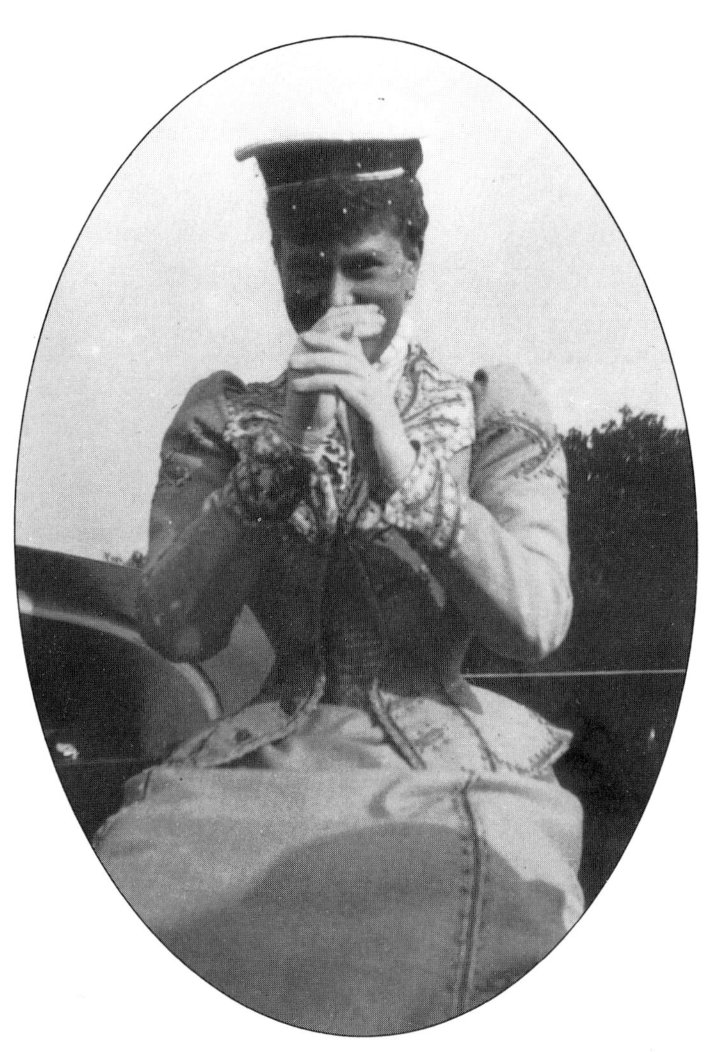

'ANNEFANNING' (A FORM OF WHISTLING); PRINCESS MAY, AS DUCHESS OF YORK, AT BEAULIEU IN AUGUST 1898

(*OPPOSITE*) THE DUKE AND DUCHESS OF TECK'S SILVER WEDDING ANNIVERSARY, 21 JUNE 1891. THESE FAMILY GROUPS WERE PHOTOGRAPHED AT WHITE LODGE, RICHMOND

Aperipheral member of the British royal family, Her Serene Highness Princess Victoria Mary Augusta Louise Olga Pauline Claudine Agnes of Teck, was born at Kensington Palace, in what was then a small village on the outskirts of London, on 26 May 1867. The formal announcement of the birth read: 'Her Royal Highness the Princess Mary Adelaide was safely delivered of a Princess at one minute before midnight on the 26th inst . . . Her Royal Highness and the infant Princess are doing perfectly well.'

To certain members of the royal family, not least the Princess's first cousin Queen Victoria and her eldest daughter Vicky, then Crown Princess of Prussia, the news that Mary Adelaide had come through the process of childbirth even remotely well seemed, for reasons that will be explained, nothing short of miraculous.

Born in 1833, the youngest child of Adolphus, Duke of Cambridge (seventh son and tenth child of King George III and Queen Charlotte), and Princess Augusta of Hesse, Princess Mary Adelaide became a colourful and flamboyant woman of – as the late James Pope-Hennessy gently put it – 'unusual girth'. The Victorian public, by whom this jovial, 18-, perhaps even 20-stone Princess was generally adored, put it more bluntly. To them she was simply 'Fat Mary'. Though she, too, was to to grow extremely stout in later life, the diminutive Queen Victoria once wrote of her cousin, 'her *size* is fearful! It is *really* a misfortune'.

Handicapped from youth by her immensity, there were those who, as the years passed by, seriously wondered whether Mary Adelaide would ever marry, even though Napoleon III once thought she would make an ideal wife for one of his more reckless cousins and despite the fact that, in 1856, the King of Sardinia offered to make her his queen. High-spirited, extravagant and full of life, the occasionally imperious Mary Adelaide would often poke fun at herself, even to the point of allowing younger friends to weigh her on a pair of velvet-covered scales. The Princess's weight, however, did nothing to diminish her confidence in herself or dent her love of jewels or her passion for brilliant, if at times unbecoming, costumes. Nor did it suppress her fondness for parties and dancing. Remarkably graceful though she was, there was one memorable occasion on which, while partnering the Comte de Paris, Princess Mary Adelaide collided with another young woman and sent her flying.

In the spring of 1866, when she was almost thirty-three, Princess Mary Adelaide's marital prospects suddenly blossomed with the arrival in London of His Serene Highness Prince Franz (Francis) of Teck. At twenty-nine this handsome – if penniless – young man, who was born in Vienna in 1837, seemed a suitable candidate for the hand of the equally handsome Princess Mary Adelaide. Championed by the Prince and Princess of Wales, who had met him in Vienna a year before and who were now his hosts in London, Prince Teck met, liked and almost immediately proposed to Mary Adelaide who, in her delight, was reported by her father, the Duke of Cambridge, to be found 'rushing about like an emancipated schoolgirl'.

Two months after the announcement of their engagement, Prince Teck and Princess Mary Adelaide were married by the Archbishop of Canterbury in the picturesque, red-brick church of St Anne on Kew Green. Leading a host of royal guests on that hot summer's day was Queen Victoria herself who, in the face of much teasing at his having taken on so great a responsibility, declared Prince Teck to be, 'very nice & amiable, thoroughly unassuming & very gentle-manlike'. One notable absentee, though he was officially represented at the wedding, was the bridegroom's sixty-two-year-old father, Alexander, Duke of Württemberg, to whom Prince Teck owed the one stigmatism which, despite his prestigious marriage, blighted his social horizons.

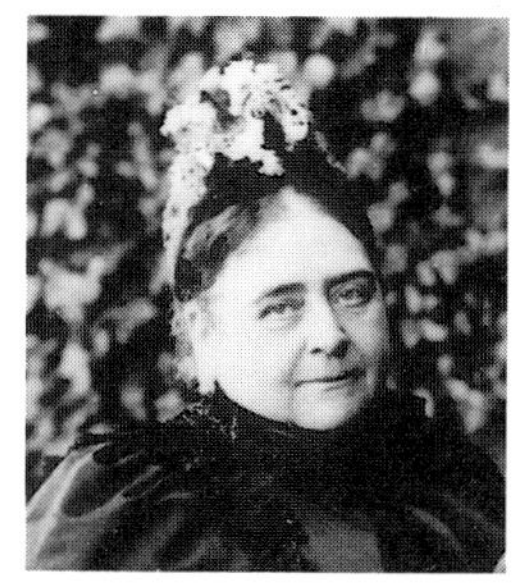

In 1835, when he was thirty-one, Duke Alexander – once heir apparent to the throne of Württemberg – had contracted a morganatic marriage with the Hungarian countess, Claudine Rhèdey. Only six years later she was killed in tragic circumstances when she was thrown from her horse at a military review and trampled to death by a squadron of cavalry. Had it not been for what was contemptuously regarded as his parents' misalliance, therefore, Prince Francis himself might one day have inherited the kingdom of Württemberg, then a small independent state sandwiched between Baden and Bavaria to the south of Prussia. As it was, the Prince's tainted blood prevented him from even using the Württemberg name and, in 1871, King Carl of Württemberg was finally prevailed upon to elevate his cousin from the rank of prince to the more important title in German terms of Duke of Teck.

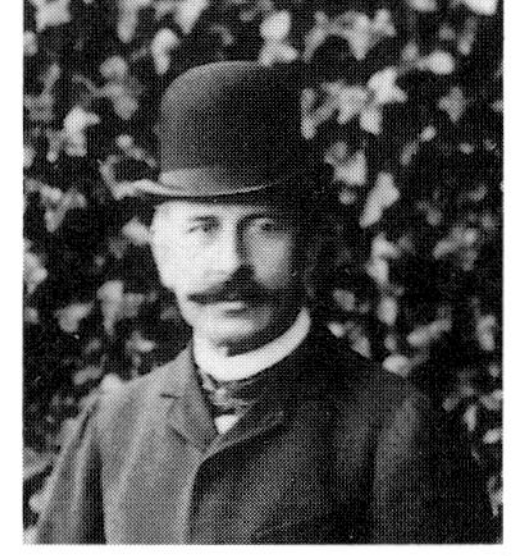

Almost a year after their marriage at Kew, Princess Mary Adelaide and her husband set up home at Kensington Palace in rooms given to them by Queen Victoria. This late-seventeenth-century building, west of Hyde Park, had been built for William and Mary by Sir Christopher Wren as a retreat from Whitehall, and it was in the very same suite that she now allocated to her cousin that Queen Victoria had been born in May 1819. It was there that she had also spent a strict and lonely childhood, under the watchful gaze of her widowed mother, the Duchess of Kent, and there, during the early hours of 20 June 1837, that the eighteen-year-old Princess had been roused from her sleep to be told of her accession to the throne.

By the time the Tecks took up residence at Kensington Palace thirty years later, Princess Mary Adelaide was already heavily pregnant, causing Vicky, the Crown Princess of Prussia, to write to her mother, 'Poor Mary . . . it seems most alarming – with her size – and at her age – her prospects must fill her with fear.'

To Queen Victoria – who had given birth to nine children of her own – her cousin's condition was of only marginal importance. In the spring of 1867 her thoughts were more closely focused on her widening circle of grandchildren. That February Alexandra, Princess of Wales, already the mother of two boys, Prince Albert Victor and Prince George, had given birth to her first daughter, Louise, by whom the Queen seemed decidedly unimpressed – declaring her not to 'look very strong'. Then, on 14 April, her third daughter, Helena, Princess

Christian of Schleswig-Holstein, had been delivered of a son. Known to his family as 'Christle', the infant Prince Christian Victor instantly captivated his illustrious grandmother, who pronounced him to be 'a splendid fellow'.

The birth of a daughter to Princess Mary Adelaide on 26 May did not, therefore, merit the Queen's immediate attention. Indeed, it was not until she made one of her infrequent visits to London from Windsor in June that Queen Victoria called upon her cousin to see little Victoria Mary of Teck, 'Princess May'. After her sickly granddaughter, Louise of Wales, Princess May met with the Queen's full approval; 'a *very* fine child,' she wrote, 'with quantities of hair – brushed up into a curl on the top of its head! – & very pretty features . . .'.

Six months after the birth of Princess May, the god-daughter Queen Victoria grew to admire so greatly in later years, Princess Mary Adelaide was again pregnant. Her eldest son, Adolphus, known as 'Dolly', was born on 13 August 1868. Two years later, on 9 January 1870, a second son, Francis ('Frank') was born. Each of these confinements was met by the same anxious sentiments that had preceded Princess May's nativity, but the chorus grew even louder and still more vociferous when, in 1873, the forty-year-old Princess Mary Adelaide, now Duchess of Teck, fell pregnant yet again. Her fourth and last child, Alexander George, known as 'Alge', was born on 14 April 1874. The following day an almost incredulous Queen Victoria noted, 'Mary Teck was safely confined yesterday with another & *still* bigger boy! That seems hardly possible'.

In his official biography of Queen Mary, James Pope-Hennessy wrote:

Thus was the general ground-plan for Princess May's youth prepared: the only girl in a family of four. Known as 'the Peacemaker' in nursery and, later, schoolboy squabbles, she early learned to exercise her native discretion, firmness and tact. Her eldest brother, Prince Dolly, fair-haired and blue-eyed like herself, was throughout his life the closest to her of the three. Prince Frank and the baby . . . Alexander George, were very dark, like their father. Prince Dolly and Prince Frank were startlingly handsome children; in the nursery their sister would refer to them as 'Beauty Boys'.

By far the greatest part of their charming, though conventional, childhood and youth was spent, not at Kensington Palace, but well away from London at White Lodge in Richmond Park, Surrey. Now the home of the Royal Ballet School, White Lodge was originally planned as a hunting-box for King George I, though he never lived to see it completed. Built in the Palladian style during the first half of the eighteenth-century, White Lodge was used frequently by Queen Caroline, consort of George II, and later, in her capacity as Ranger of Richmond Park, by the Duchess of Teck's aunt, Mary, Duchess of Gloucester. Later still the Prince and Princess of Wales had used the house, albeit briefly, as a weekend retreat. Now the Duchess of Teck agitated for the tenancy of White

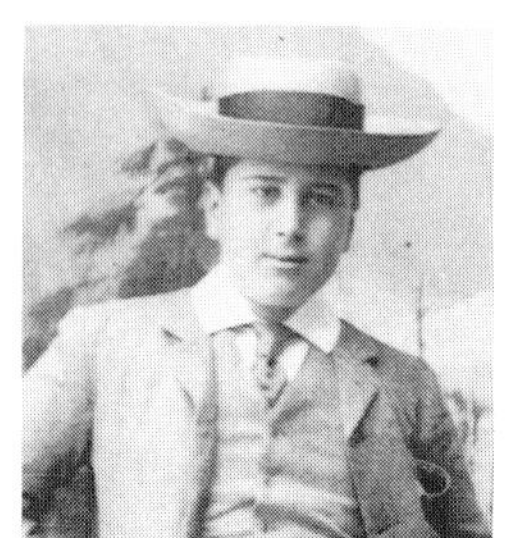

PRINCE ADOLPHUS OF
TECK ('DOLLY') IN 1887

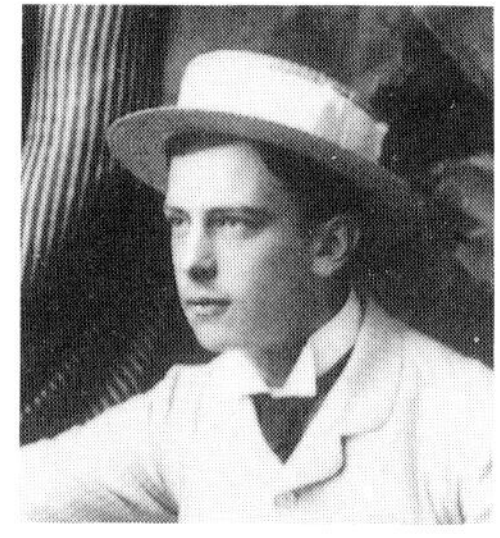

PRINCE ALEXANDER OF
TECK ('ALGE') IN 1887

Lodge and Queen Victoria, though very much against her better judgement, finally agreed.

Kind hearted though the Duchess of Teck was, she was also utterly reckless in her generosity. With no appreciation whatsoever of the value of money, but unashamedly enjoying a lifestyle that demanded plenty of it, she was permanently in debt; a state from which neither rich friends like Baroness Burdett-Coutts – who frequently provided financial aid – nor a long-suffering bank manager, could ever hope to permanently extricate her.

With an annual – and at that time not inconsiderable – income of £8,000, the Duchess of Teck invariably managed to spend twice as much, not only to the vexation of her immediate relations, the despair of her husband – to say nothing of that of her cousin, the Queen – but to the increasing impatience of her creditors who, in their exasperation, eventually threatened to take action. Under pressure from all sides to economize and to live within her means, the Duchess was virtually ordered to leave England until the dust had settled and her return seemed appropriate.

Protesting all the while that her parlous financial situation was not her fault, the Duchess of Teck nevertheless admitted defeat, shut up the newly-decorated White Lodge, surrendered her apartments at Kensington Palace – the contents of which were sold at a very public auction – to Queen Victoria and, with her family, prepared to leave London and all its temptations. The family's immediate, though short-term, destination was Rorschach on the Bodensee, where they were to stay with some German relations before settling into an indefinite period of exile in Florence. Travelling incognito as the family 'Hohenstein', the name by which the Duke of Teck had been known before his elevation to princely status, the 'Count', the 'Countess' and their four children, attended by a handful of servants, quietly departed from Victoria Station on the evening of 15 September 1883.

In later years, Queen Mary herself looked back on this episode in her young life with evident incomprehension. She told a friend, 'Even *I* used to sign myself Victoria Mary Hohenstein. Very ridiculous we must have seemed, I must say, this utterly English family, all talking English, and maintaining the artless fiction that we were the family Hohenstein.'

Before long the incorrigible Duchess of Teck's irresponsible habits had manifested themselves anew. In April 1884 the Tecks took up residence at the fifteenth-century Villa I Cedri on the banks of the Arno in Florence and the Duchess was soon to be seen in all the fashionable places: occupying the royal box at the Opera; hosting lavish dinner parties; and, modelling brand-new satin ballgowns set off by the jewels she resolutely refused to sell, even *in extremis*, attending the grandest balls and entertainments on offer. Not for nothing had Queen Victoria written to her cousin: 'It was with much regret that I heard you were gone to Florence for living in a town full of attractions & temptations to expense, made me very anxious. Some quieter & more retired spot would surely have been better.'

Some quieter spot might well have helped curb the Duchess of Teck's excesses, but at least for her teenaged daughter, Florence afforded a more profound renaissance. Surrounded by all the glories of living antiquity, Princess May's eyes were opened to the restrictive, but typical, education she and the majority of well-to-do girls in Victorian society received at home in England. Now, at the age of sixteen, she resolved to grasp every opportunity for self-improvement and thus embarked on a stringent round of sightseeing: visiting museums, art galleries, churches, monasteries, theatres and a myriad other places of cultural and historical significance. Tutors were engaged to teach her French and Italian and, with laudable enthusiasm, she not only threw herself into studying works of art, but Tuscan literature as well. At about this time she wrote to a friend, 'I have spent all my afternoons lately going to *Museums*, how much one learns & picks up, & how much nicer than going out to tea & gossip.'

Tea and gossip may have been pastimes in which the Duchess of Teck herself liked to indulge, but it must be said that the finer aspects of her Florentine exile did not entirely pass her by unnoticed. Accompanying Princess May, whose opinions, straightforwardness and good common sense she greatly admired, and whose counsel she soon came to rely on, the Duchess also exhibited genuine wonder when gazing upon the City's heritage. Of one visit to the Pitti Palace, for example, she wrote, '. . . we visited *five saloons* very carefully. Titians! Raphaels! Andrea del Sartos! Van Dycks! Rubenses! – gloriously beautiful! Quite beyond everything.'

At length, two years after the family 'Hohenstein' had left England, they were finally bidden to return. Their love affair with Florence, begun in a mood of near indifference, was suddenly over and it was with sincere regret and not a little sadness that, on 24 May 1885, they boarded the night express bound for London. Shortly after dawn on the 26th – which also happened to be Princess May's eighteenth birthday – the Teck family, free of their flimsy alias and now fully restored to grace in the eyes of their once disapproving relations, arrived back at Victoria Station. 'Nothing could have been kinder than our reception by one and all,' wrote Princess May's father, '. . . and indeed it does one good to see everyone smile their greetings from carriages and footpath . . .'.

Having spent the next two months luxuriating in the welcome all London accorded them, the Teck family vacated the house in Chester Square, temporarily loaned to them by Baroness Burdett-Coutts, and returned to the tranquillity of Richmond Park and White Lodge.

———————————

Though afflicted all her life by a painful shyness that she eventually learned to conceal, if not entirely to conquer, Princess May had returned from Italy wiser and more self-assured. Those who knew her insufficiently well or who failed to understand her sensitive, reserved nature, often tended to attribute the Princess's diffidence to dullness, remaining ignorant to the fact that, unlike her garrulous and extrovert mother – who was, after all, so very much larger than life – and some of her more immature royal contemporaries, Princess May operated on a higher and infinitely more refined level. Included among those who frequently ridiculed her or made stinging remarks were her distant cousins and future sisters-in-law, the Princesses Louise, Victoria and Maud of Wales. Overtly cosseted by their mother, Alexandra, Princess of Wales, these girls gleefully indulged in childish pursuits even when young adults.

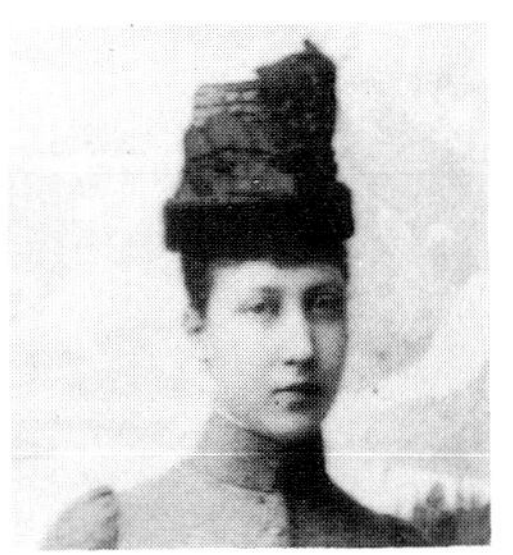

In February 1886, for example, Princess May wrote to her mother's sister Augusta, Grand Duchess of Mecklenberg-Strelitz, telling her of 'a *children's party*' held at Marlborough House (the Wales's London residence) to celebrate Princess Louise's *nineteenth* birthday. 'Does not that seem too ridiculous?' Princess May asked. 'Everybody seemed to enjoy themselves, but I was shy, & bored . . . Cousins like these juvenile entertainments, we [Princess May and her brothers] don't relish 'em!'

In many ways a kindred spirit, the Grand Duchess Augusta – who had been born and ever remained at heart 'an English Princess' – became something of a mentor to the niece she adored. It was she who did much to instil in Princess May an acute sense of pride at having been born into the British royal family and, more generally, a sense of pride at being *English*. Above all, the Grand Duchess understood Princess May and never failed to support and encourage all that she represented, in the most positive manner. On one occasion she wrote, 'What I love in you is the truth and straightness of your character . . . the charm of your being both serious and gay.'

These qualities, combined with Princess May's abilities as a 'peacemaker', her innate sense of responsibility and her ready humour – 'I always have to be so careful never to laugh,' she once said, 'because you see I have such a *vulgar* laugh!' – were all attributes that engendered the deepest loyalty and affection in those to whom she extended the hand of friendship.

In the spring of 1886, Princess May made her formal début in London society, attending her first Drawing-Room at Buckingham Palace and her first State Opening of Parliament, watching the Prince of Wales lay the foundation stone of Tower Bridge, and attending the opening by Queen Victoria of the Colonial and Indian Exhibition. Essentially, however, Princess May was to spend the next six years of her life sharing some of the limelight which fell upon her mother, to whom, in her own words, Princess May acted as 'daughter, secretary and lady-in-waiting combined'.

Tireless in her work for the poor and underprivileged, the Duchess of Teck had always been deeply involved with any number of charitable organizations, thousands of which flourished in Victorian England, and it now fell to Princess May to assist in these vitally important activities. Though hopelessly inept when it came to managing her own finances, the Duchess of Teck was curiously well able to direct and manage those of her charities: 'Her advice was sound and her experience invaluable,' one observer noted. 'Indeed, many a bazaar would have failed to pay its expenses, and probably have landed the promoters in debt, had it not been for [the Duchess of Teck's] timely aid and practical assistance.'

By sharing her mother's need to help relieve poverty and distress in the slums of Whitechapel and throughout the East End as a whole, Princess May served an invaluable apprenticeship for her future role as Queen; while her first-hand knowledge of hardship and human suffering aroused in her a profound respect, sympathy and compassion for the ordinary man that she was never to lose.

Apart from the charitable work she undertook and the assistance she continued to give to her mother, Princess May pursued her wish to broaden her mind. Under the guidance of her governess, Mademoiselle Hélène Bricka, she read historical memoirs and modern history, studied the writings of George Eliot, John Ruskin, Thomas Carlyle and James Froude, and the works of poets such as Alfred, Lord Tennyson and Robert Browning. On a less aesthetic level, she also began to delve into the more basic issues of industrial and social conditions. When in 1888, for instance, the House of Lords appointed a Select Committee to look into allegations of sweated labour, the enquiry found the Princess an appalled but attentive student. One of her earliest biographers wrote, 'Over Blue Books, with their sometimes horrifying evidence, she would bend her head for hours at a time, to rise from them with the fixed resolve to look down to the very root of the evil'.

Excluding interests such as these, Princess May was also expected to take part in a great many of the events which brought the royal family into the public arena *en masse*. By far the grandest occasion during the penultimate decade of the nineteenth-century was Queen Victoria's Golden Jubilee. Celebrated in June 1887, the fiftieth anniversary of the Queen's accession to the throne brought with it a punishing schedule of engagements for both the Sovereign and the majority of her relations, the high spots of which were the Empire's service of thanksgiving at Westminster Abbey, a jubilee luncheon at Windsor Castle, attended by over fifty Royal and Serene Highnesses, a party for 30,000 poor children in Hyde Park, an immense firework display (which the Queen witnessed from the balcony of Buckingham Palace), a military review of the army at Aldershot and the Royal Naval review at Spithead.

'We have all been so overworked . . . that we are nearly dead,' Princess May wrote to a friend that July. 'I really cannot describe all the fêtes. The excitement here in London was something not to be imagined & I believe it was this that kept us all up thro' that fatiguing time when we were on the go from morning till night . . . .'

The following March there was the much quieter celebration within the royal family of the Prince and Princess of Wales's Silver Wedding anniversary, which was followed a year later by the marriage of their eldest daughter, Louise, to Alexander Duff, Earl (and later 1st Duke) of Fife, at which Princess May was among the bridesmaids. Then, on 12 June 1891, it was the turn of the Duke and Duchess of Teck to occupy centre stage on the occasion of their own Silver Wedding. In celebration the Duke and Duchess gave two garden parties on consecutive days at White Lodge, to which were invited members of the royal family, most of their innumerable friends and a host of neighbours from Sheen and Richmond. In a commemorative photograph the Duke and Duchess of Teck are seated side by side in the garden at White Lodge with Princess May, in a flowery bonnet, and her three brothers, wearing morning coats and silk hats, standing behind. In Princess May's album, the photograph is surrounded by her family's signatures.

During this period in her life Princess May also had time in which to play with a will and, well away from London and out of the public eye, she gave free rein to the natural high spirits that her shyness always concealed when she was on show or whenever she felt ill at ease.

Joining country house parties, often for several days at a time, was the kind of social life Princess May adored for, as she once put it, 'one gets to know people better in a country house'. Of course these were the halcyon days when those who owned country estates could not only afford to live on them, ably supported by battalions of servants, but also had the wherewithal to entertain large numbers of guests in style and comfort. It was a time of tennis and boating parties, lavish picnics, tea and croquet on the lawn and indoor and outdoor pursuits of every description. In the evenings there were spendid dinner parties in resplendent dining-rooms, music and dancing, the rustle of silk, the flutter of fans and sometimes, one supposes, romance among the potted palms. Wentworth Woodhouse, Luton Hoo, Malvern Hall, Temple Newsam, Ashridge Park, Buckhurst, Normanton, Chillingham Castle and Hatfield House, were all houses where Princess May, her parents and often one or more of her brothers, were entertained during the late 1880s and early 1890s; guests-of-honour at house parties that might easily be composed of thirty or forty people at any one time.

Luton Hoo, rented by the Danish Minister de Falbe, especially was to carry lasting memories. It was there, for example, that she met Count Thaddeus Koziebrodzki, a young diplomat at the Austrian Embassy in London, who is said to have fallen in love with the fair-haired, blue-eyed Princess May and wished to marry her. On another occasion there the Princess, in cahoots with fellow guest Sir Thomas Lauder, played a trick on a certain Sir Hubert Miller that he undoubtedly remembered all his life. In her diary Princess May noted: 'After lunch . . . Mama & Sir T drove in the pony carriage, Sir H & I in the tandem Cantilupe . . . we drove . . . to Hartfield to see the church, Mama didnt [sic] get out, we did. Sir T & I locked Sir H into the church, he rang the bell, 2 people came to see what was the matter. Oh! I nearly died of laughing. . . .' Later on, in another instance that illustrates Princess May's sense of fun and appreciation of the absurd, she told her diary: 'After dinner we had an exhibition of wax figures, we were the figures, I was the sleeping beauty. Sir H the prince . . . it was too ridiculous, I laughed till I cried.'

For Princess May, Luton Hoo not only held vivid memories of lighthearted escapades such as these, but of something far more significant and far-reaching that occurred there in 1891.

Throughout the years 1890–91, one vexing question had been exercising the minds of senior members of the royal family, most notably those of Queen Victoria and the Prince and Princess of Wales. This was the future of Prince Albert Victor, Duke of Clarence and Avondale, elder son of the future Edward VII and Queen Alexandra, and heir presumptive to the throne.

Wayward, volatile and self-indulgent, this tall, good-looking young man was proving himself something of a liability, not simply to his family but to the future of the monarchy itself. Backward and listless, Prince Albert Victor, or 'Eddy' as he was known to his family, had been an apathetic student and had received little real education. His primary interest seemed to be the pursuit of pleasure, and this not infrequently led him into trouble.

In the words of Queen Mary's official biographer, Prince Albert Victor was 'as heedless and as aimless as a gleaming goldfish in a crystal bowl'. In August 1891, dismissing proposals that Prince 'Eddy' should be sent away on prolonged colonial tours, it was decided that he should be found a suitable wife, in the hope that marriage might have a corrective influence on the attitude and behaviour of England's future king.

Capable of falling in and out of love almost at will, Albert Victor had once proposed to his ill-fated cousin, Alix of Hesse, who was destined to become the last Tsarina of Russia. No sooner had she rejected him, however, than he had fallen for the Catholic Princess Hélène d'Orléans, daughter of the Comte de Paris. Yet while the French Princess reciprocated the Duke of Clarence's love, her father would not hear of Hélène converting to the Anglican faith – as she would need to have done under laws governing the British succession. Indeed, the Comte de Paris went so far as to forbid any marriage between his daughter and the Prince of Wales's elder son no matter what the circumstances.

So it was that Princess Victoria Mary of Teck, though unbeknown to her, was singled out as the most suitable candidate for the not altogether enviable role of Duchess of Clarence. This was, of course, a time when arranged marriages within royal families was still a common enough practice and, for his part, Prince Albert Victor offered no resistance to the suggestion that he should marry Princess May. But what of the prospective bride? From childhood the Princess had been brought up to revere the institution of monarchy and to take pride in the fact that she was a member of the British royal family, albeit not a terribly important one. Moreover, while she knew and liked Prince Eddy, she had a particularly highly-developed sense of duty, so that while there were certainly disadvantages attached to marrying a man as weak and vain as the Duke of Clarence, there were inescapable advantages too. Nor must we forget that the morganatic blood which flowed through Princess May's veins could have presented very real difficulties had it ever come to her marrying into some foreign royal house. None of the small Germanic states, for instance, would have accepted Princess May, with or without the strong personal aversion she felt towards their stiff and pompous ways.

One person who had no time for the prejudices morganatic blood aroused in others was Queen Victoria. In fact she wholeheartedly approved the idea that her Teck god-daughter should one day become Queen Consort of England, but in order to confirm her judgement she invited Princess May and her brother Prince Adolphus ('Dolly') to stay with her at Balmoral. That visit, in November 1891, lasted for ten days, during which the Queen and Princess May saw a good deal of one another.

In no time Queen Victoria was writing to her eldest daughter, by now Empress Frederick of Germany, 'We have seen a gt deal of May & Dolly Teck . . . & I cannot say enough good of them. May is a particularly nice girl, so quiet & yet cheerful & so vy carefully brought up & so sensible. She is grown very pretty.' In response, the Empress introduced an almost barbed note into her letter to her mother, remarking that there were those who thought Princess May shallow or superficial, 'but you know how little worth criticisms are in general'. Rattled by this, the Queen replied, 'You speak of May Teck . . . I think she is a superior girl – quiet & reserved *till* you know her well – but she is the reverse of [shallow or superficial]. She has no frivolous tastes, has been very carefully brought up & is well informed & always occupied.'

With Queen Victoria's blessing on the proposed marriage between her grandson and her god-daughter, we now return to Luton Hoo. For it was there, during a ball on 3 December, that Prince Albert Victor proposed to Princess May. 'Of course I said yes,' she noted in her diary. 'We are both very happy.'

The wedding of Prince Eddy and Princess May was to have taken place two months later on 27 February 1892, but at Sandringham on 7 January – the day before his twenty-eighth birthday – the bridegroom was put to bed with a high temperature. Influenza had already struck his sister 'Toria' (Princess Victoria) and had spread to other members of the Household, including his equerry. It now felled the Prince himself. Within two days, however, Albert Victor had developed inflammation of the lungs and the royal physician diagnosed incipient pneumonia. Three days later his condition had deteriorated alarmingly and, in his agonized delirium, he frequently shouted out the name 'Hélène'.

During the early hours of 14 January, the Prince of Wales's domestic chaplain was summoned to Prince Eddy's bedroom. There, surrounded by the grieving Prince and Princess of Wales, their younger son, Prince George, their three daughters, Louise, Duchess of Fife, Princess Victoria and Princess Maud, and the Duchess of Teck and Princess May, he began to recite prayers for the dying. At 9.35 that same morning, Prince Albert Victor died.

All over Britain mourning bells tolled, messages of sympathy flooded in on behalf of a shocked nation and magazines published black-bordered memorial portraits of the Duke of Clarence. Into her photograph album for 1892 a dazed

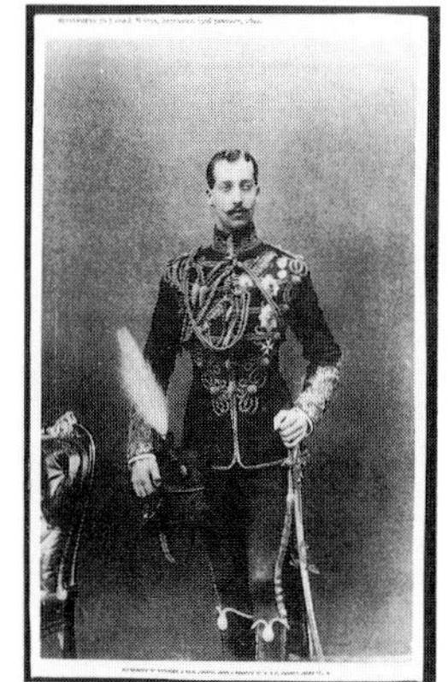

A MEMORIAL PORTRAIT OF
ALBERT VICTOR, DUKE OF
CLARENCE AND AVONDALE.
FROM *LAND AND WATER*,
23 JANUARY 1892

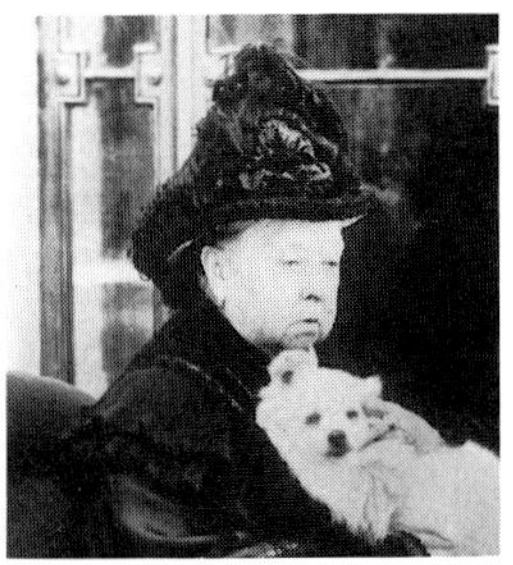

QUEEN VICTORIA IN 1899

Princess May pasted one such portrait, which she had clipped from a supplement to the journal *Land and Water*, published nine days after the death of her fiancé.

'The dear girl looks like a crushed flower [and] is grown thinner,' Queen Victoria noted after Princess May and her parents had arrived at Osborne House on the Isle of Wight, where they had been invited to spend a few days in the middle of February. Less than a month later, the Tecks decamped to the South of France where 'dear Lady Wolverton', friend as well as emergency cheque-book to the still debt-prone Duchess of Teck, had taken a lease on the Villa Clementine in Cannes. The Duchess herself had originally hoped to be put up at Menton to be coincidentally near the entire Wales family – and especially young Prince George – who just happened to be staying close by at Cap Martin. Having got wind of the Duchess's plan, however, both her brother, Prince George, Duke of Cambridge, and the Prince of Wales – who was never especially enamoured of his Amazonian cousin – insisted that the Tecks should settle further along the Riviera.

During this private holiday in the sun, well away from Sandringham and the bleak East Anglian coast, the two families inevitably came together. After all they had so recently experienced, how could they not? Towards the end of March, Prince George sent a note to Princess May, in which he told her that his father and he would be 'coming over to Cannes . . . for a few days & so I hope I shall see you then'. Expressing the wish that she might even give them 'a little dinner', he ended, 'Goodbye dear "Miss May" . . . ever yr loving old cousin, Georgie.'

As the months passed and the raw edge of their common sorrow began to dull, hopes grew that a marriage might now take place between Prince George, who had been created Duke of York in May 1892, and his 'dear Miss May'.

In character and temperament the Dukes of Clarence and York could not have been more different. 'The Duke of York,' wrote Pope-Hennessy, 'required neither stimulus nor dragooning. What he needed was a marriage with a woman of superior intelligence and superior education, who could untether him from his excessive adulation for his mother.' Princess May was that woman and, once more with the blessing of Queen Victoria and the Prince and Princess of Wales, Georgie became engaged to May on 3 May 1893.

Many years later, after he had succeeded to the throne as King George V, 'Georgie' wrote to his wife, 'We suit each other admirably & I thank God every day that he should have brought us together, especially under the tragic circumstances of dear Eddy's death, & people only said I married you out of pity & sympathy. That shows how little the world really knows what it is talking about.'

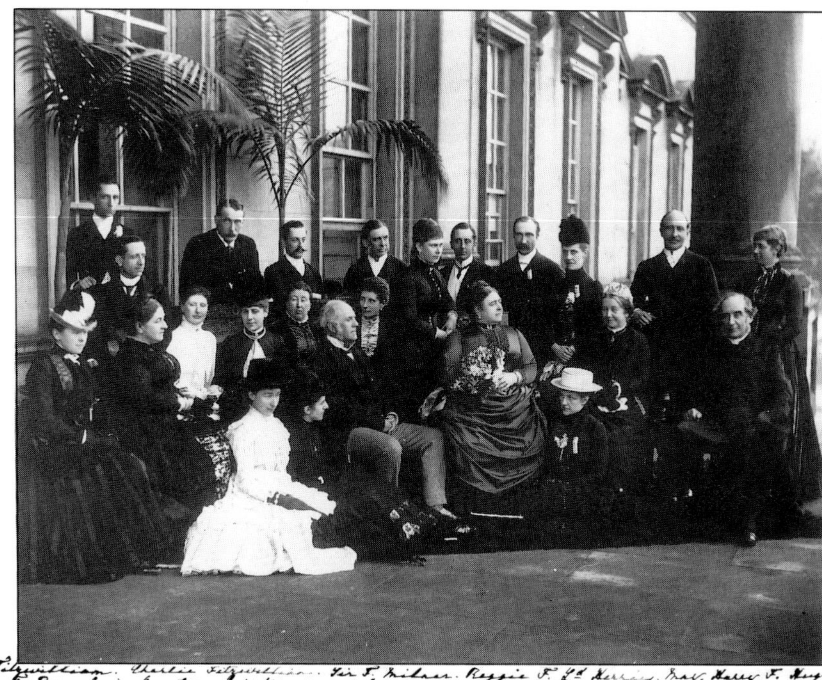

PRINCESS MAY (STANDING CENTRE, BACK ROW) AND HER MOTHER (THIRD FROM RIGHT, MIDDLE ROW) AT A HOUSE PARTY AT WENTWORTH IN 1886

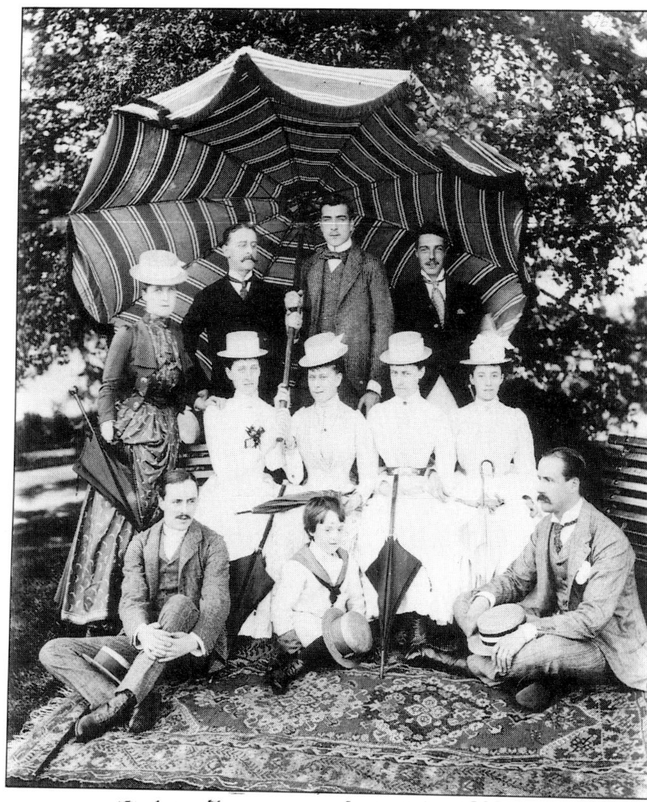

PRINCESS MAY (SEATED IN THE MIDDLE ROW, SECOND FROM LEFT) AND HER BROTHER PRINCE FRANK (BEHIND HER), STAYING AT LUTON HOO IN 1888

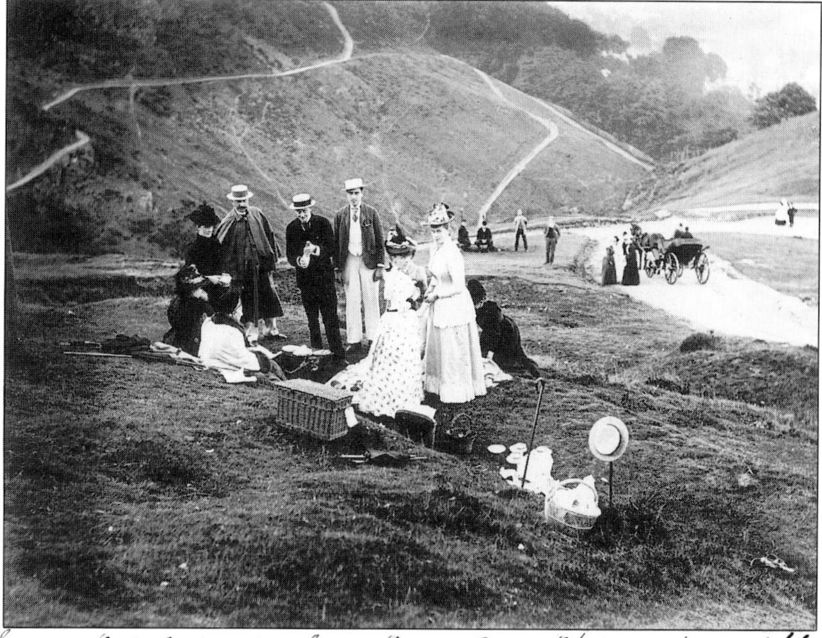

GUESTS ON A PICNIC AT MALVERN IN SEPTEMBER 1891. PRINCESS MAY IS STANDING IN THE CENTRE OF THIS PHOTOGRAPH

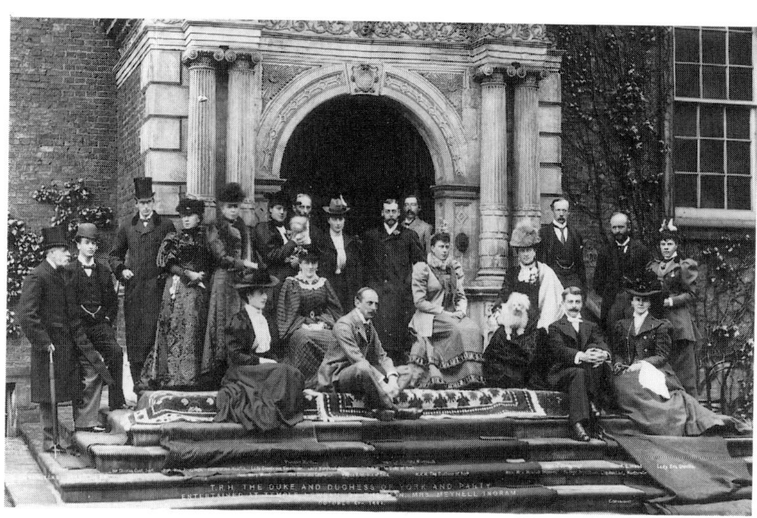

PRINCE GEORGE, DUKE OF YORK (STANDING IN THE CENTRE OF THE ARCH) AND PRINCESS MAY (SEATED IN FRONT OF HIM) IN A PARTY AT TEMPLE NEWSAM

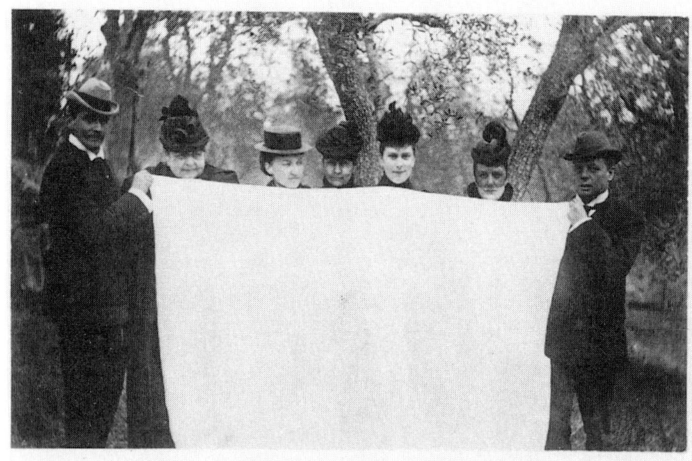

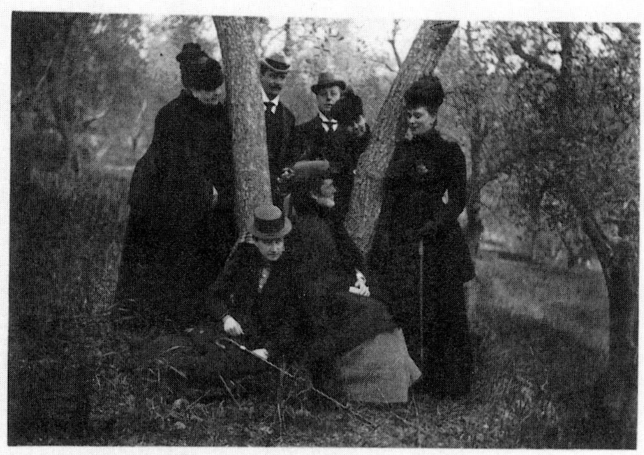

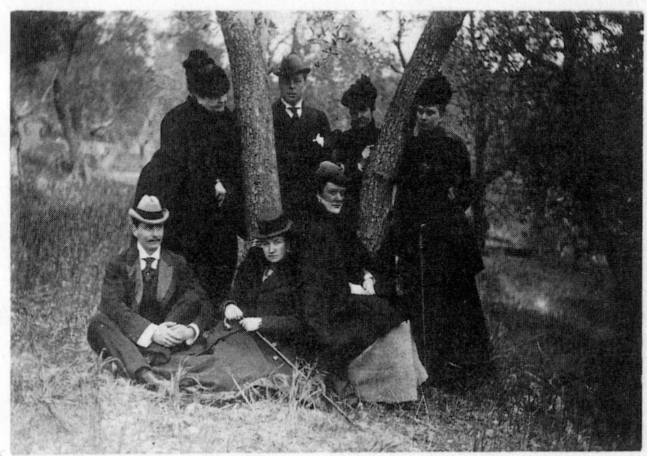

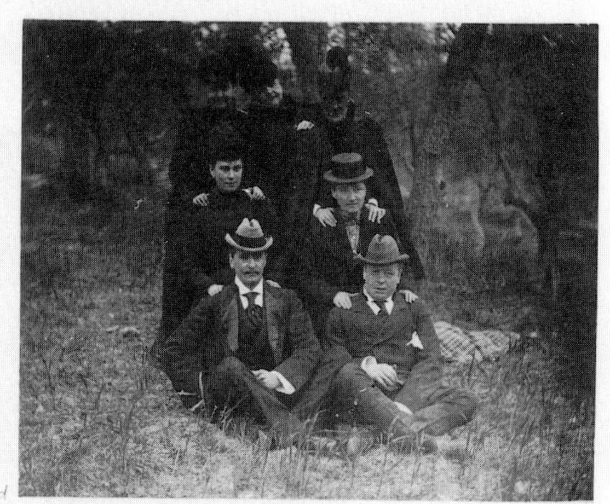

Mama. Mr Aubrey. Fitzclarence. Lady. K. Coke. Self
Count Gaf. Miss Tufnell. Lady Arran

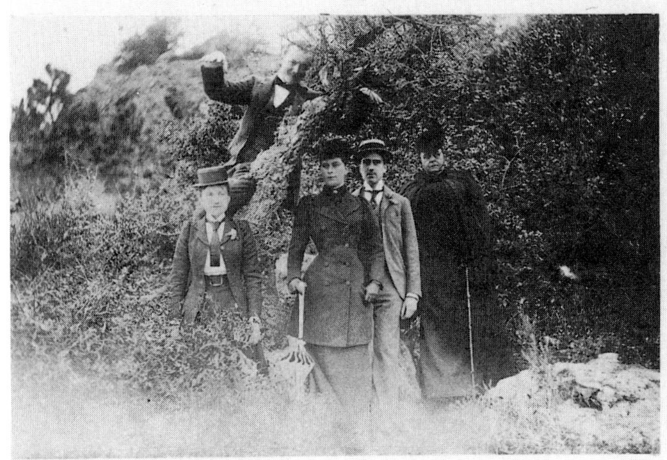

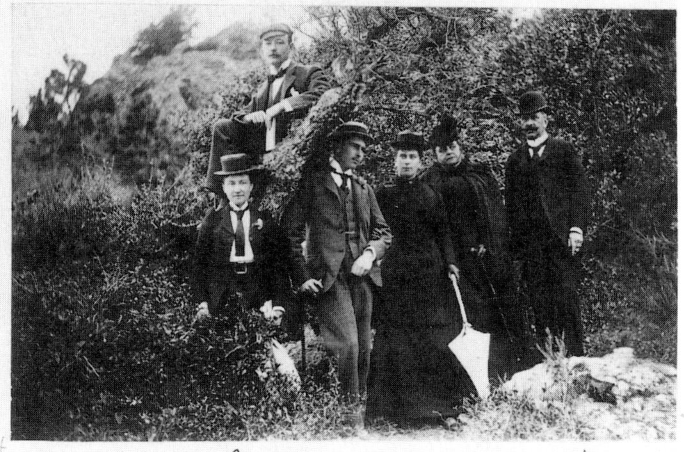

Mama. Papa. Alge. Self.   Mr Cecil Murray. Fina Tufnell

A PAGE OF SNAPSHOTS FROM PRINCESS MAY'S
ALBUM, TAKEN AT CANNES IN 1892. THE PRINCESS
AND HER FAMILY WERE STILL IN MOURNING FOR
THE DUKE OF CLARENCE

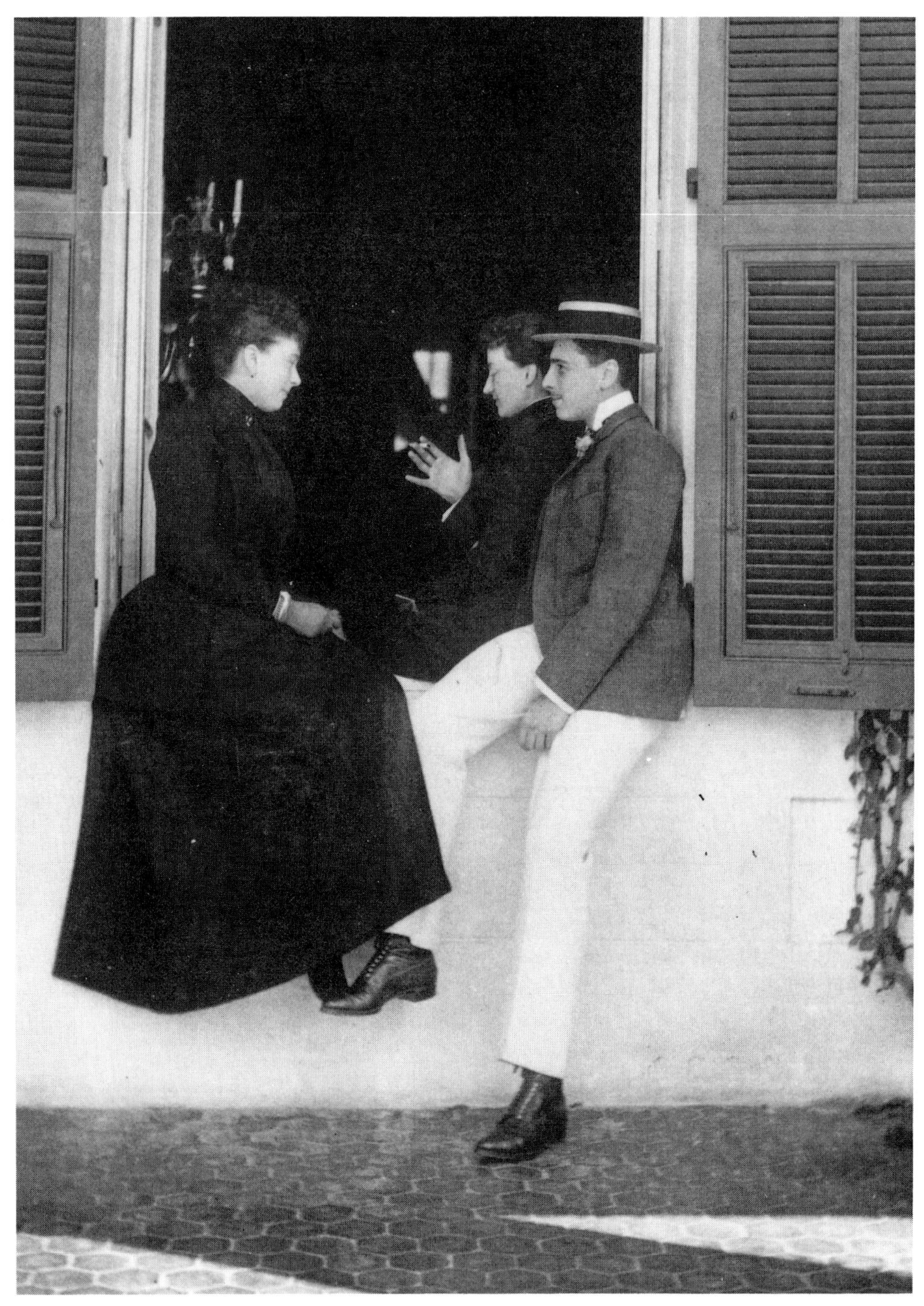

PRINCESS MAY AND HER BROTHER 'ALGE'
(PRINCE ALEXANDER OF TECK) AT
CANNES IN 1892

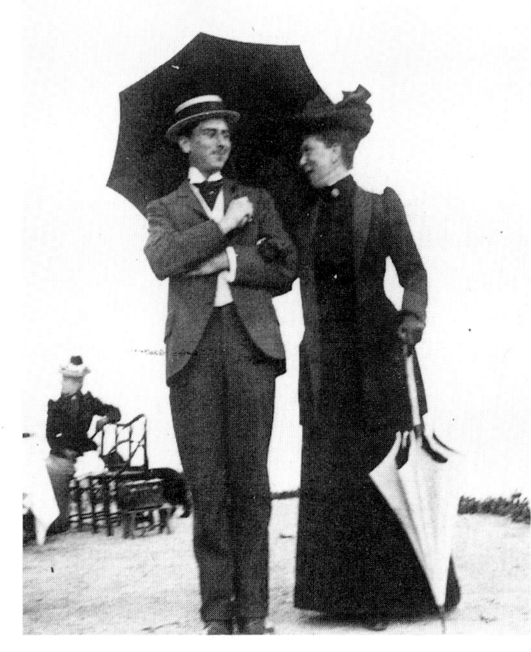

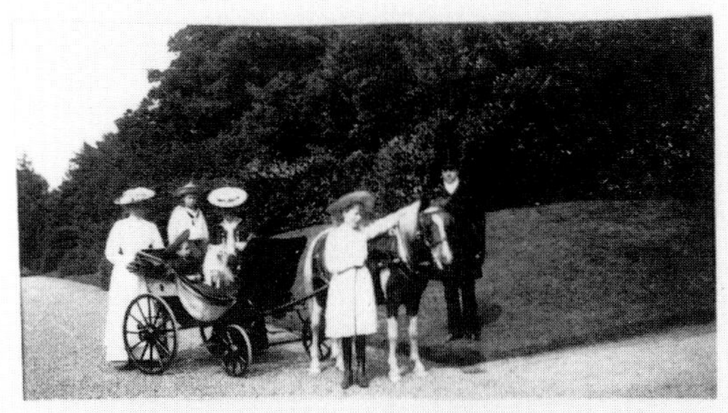
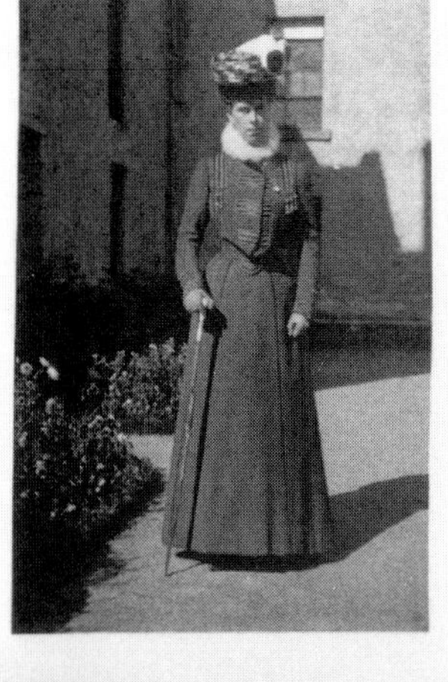
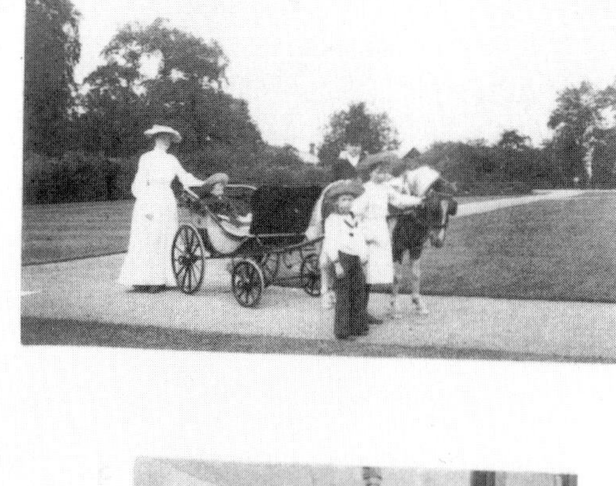
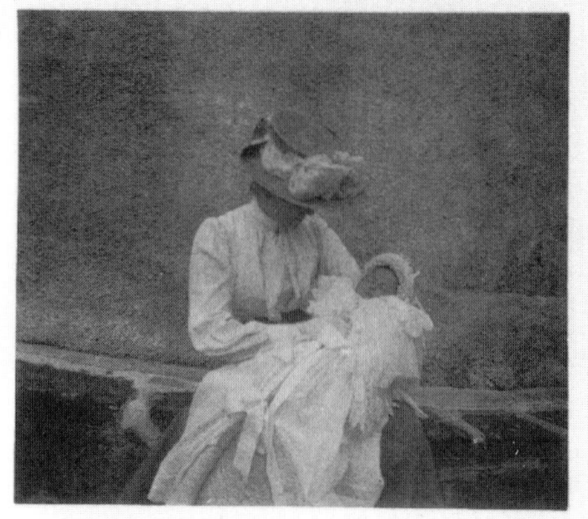
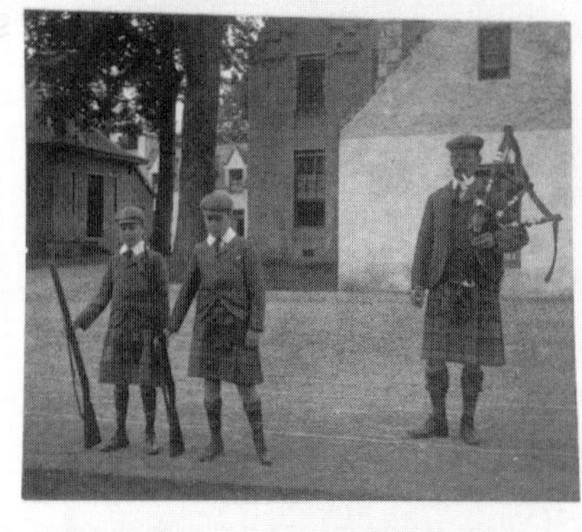
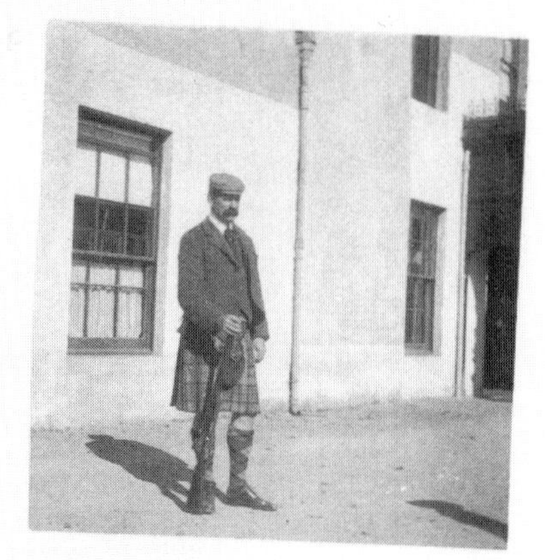
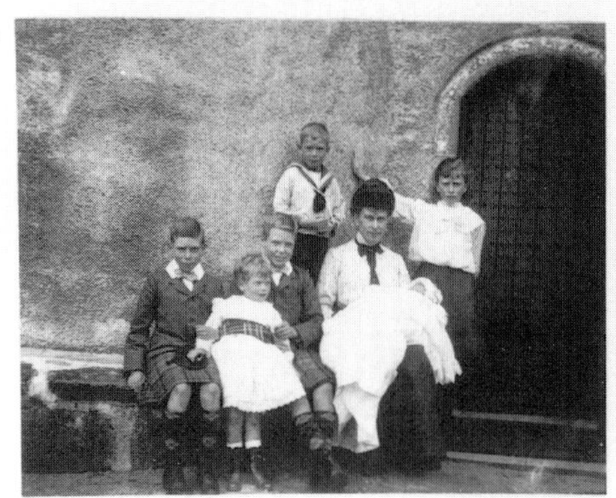
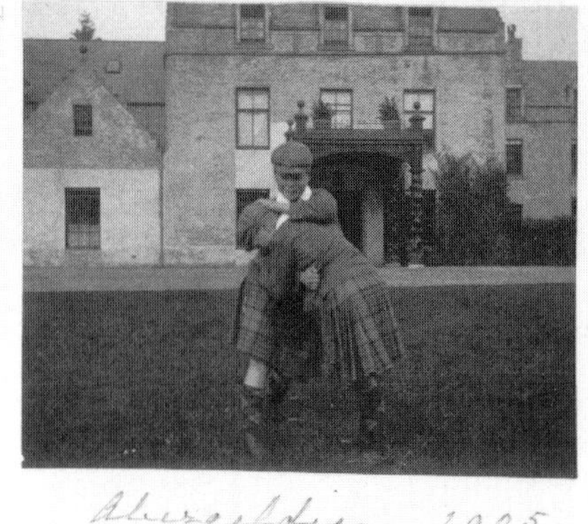
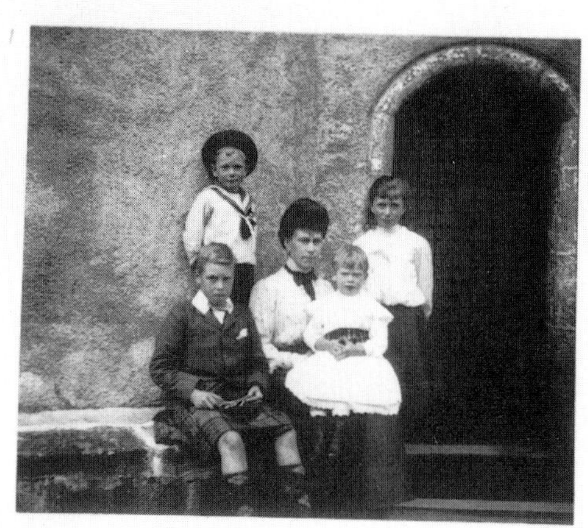

Abergeldie 1905.

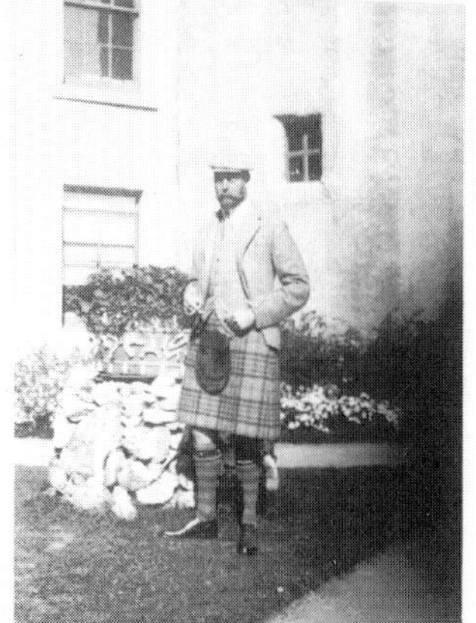
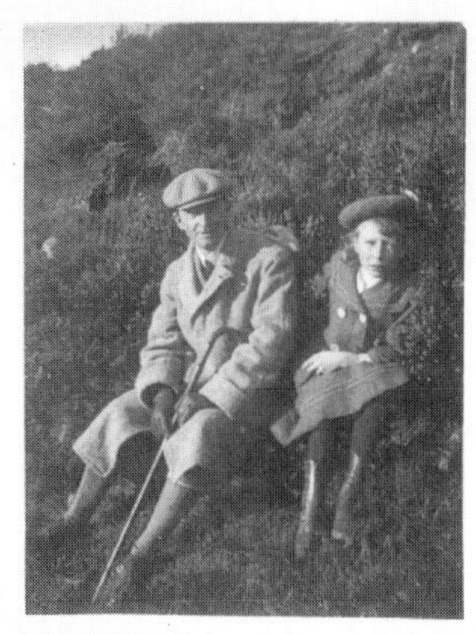
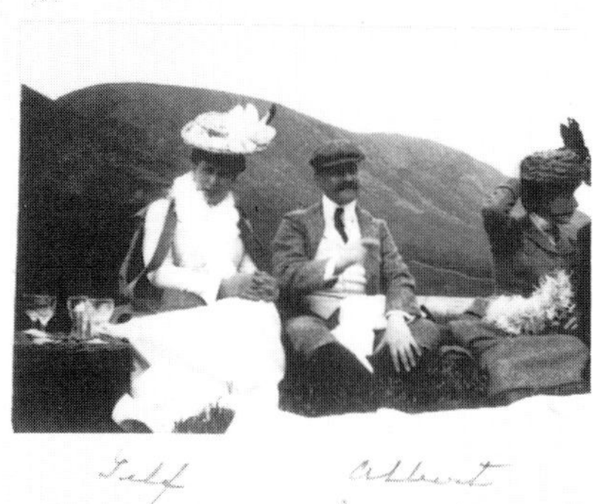

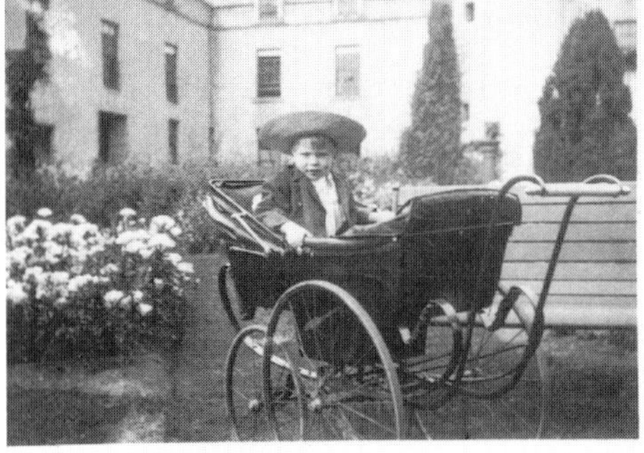

ABERGELDIE CASTLE, 1905. SNAPS OF THE PRINCE
AND PRINCESS OF WALES AND THEIR FAMILY. (THE
BABY IS THEIR SIXTH CHILD, 'JOHNNIE', BORN
THAT YEAR)

Victoria Mary

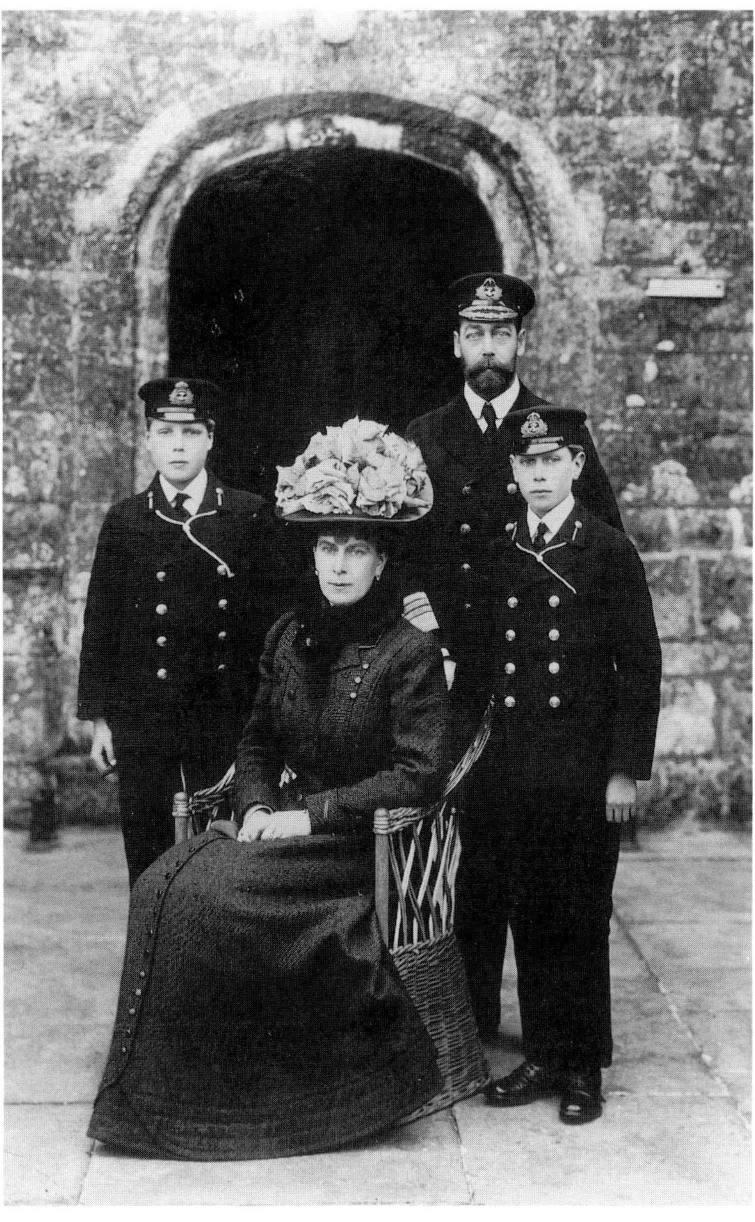

THE PRINCE AND PRINCESS
OF WALES WITH THEIR
ELDEST SONS 'DAVID' AND
'BERTIE', MARCH 1909

The marriage of the Duke of York and Princess Victoria Mary of Teck, was celebrated at the Chapel Royal, St James's Palace, during the early afternoon of 6 July 1893, a day of brilliant sunshine and intense heat. Dressed in a short-sleeved gown of white and silver brocade with an underskirt of tiered lace trimmed with orange blossom, and a diamond tiara securing a short lace veil, the twenty-six-year-old Princess May drove to her wedding through a multitude of cheering Londoners.

In the opinion of the usually vituperative Lady Geraldine Somerset, once lady-in-waiting to the bride's maternal grandmother, the late Duchess of Cambridge, who, for some reason best known to herself, was no admirer of the Teck family, the royal wedding was 'the greatest success ever seen or heard of!' 'The first to enter the Chapel was the Queen,' Lady Geraldine went on, 'followed by [the Duchess of Teck] who drove *in* the Queen's carriage from Buckingham Palace!! will her head be still on her shoulders tomorrow! I believe it will have expanded and blown to the moon!! – The Princess of Wales looked *more lovely* – than ever! . . . but I was sorry for her today. May with the Duke of York standing at the Altar!! and for the Princess [of Wales] *what pain.*'

It is unlikely that thoughts of Prince Albert Victor were far from the minds of anyone in the Chapel Royal that day, least of all the bride and bridegroom themselves. But in what appears to have been some kind of aberration on the part of the Duke of York – and even Queen Victoria thought it 'rather unlucky & sad' at the time – the bridal couple spent their honeymoon at York Cottage on the Sandringham estate, barely a five-minute walk away from the room in which they had witnessed the death of the Duke of Clarence less than eighteen months before.

Strangely, not one of the photographs taken of the Duke and Duchess of York's wedding appears in Queen Mary's albums. Whether this was because most of the prints are mounted on card as thick and inflexible as table mats (and therefore had always to be kept loose and separate) or due to more personal reasons, isn't known. Yet since Princess May – as she still was – included several photographs of the gifts she and Prince George received, the absence of Lafayette's now famous wedding-day portraits seems very curious.

There is, however, a photograph of the honeymoon house at Sandringham, which was taken by the Stereoscopic Company and beneath which the new Duchess of York added the caption, 'Our Cottage, July 6th 1893'. York Cottage, part Victorian Gothic, part mock-Tudor, stands at the edge of a pond, which the Yorks called 'the lake'. An unpretentious, if not very attractive house, composed of small, stuffy, rooms which the Duke very much liked, not least because they precluded entertaining, which he disliked, York Cottage was to remain the beloved country home of Georgie and May for the next thirty-three years. In London, their first official residence was York House, St James's Palace, virtually next door to the Chapel in which they were married.

Early married life for the Duchess of York was a relatively sedate affair, at least when compared to the pattern of things to come. One of the paramount causes of the Duchess's public inactivity was, of course, a series of pregnancies. It was a curious fact that neither the Duke nor the Duchess was ever able to articulate his or her love for the other – save for expressing it, as they frequently did, in writing – though they quite evidently had no trouble when it came to securing the line of succession. In the space of only six years the Duchess fell pregnant four times, and each time she regarded her condition with the same feeling of near contempt that she felt towards illness and infirmity. Never did she want the subject raised or discussed, much less even remarked upon.

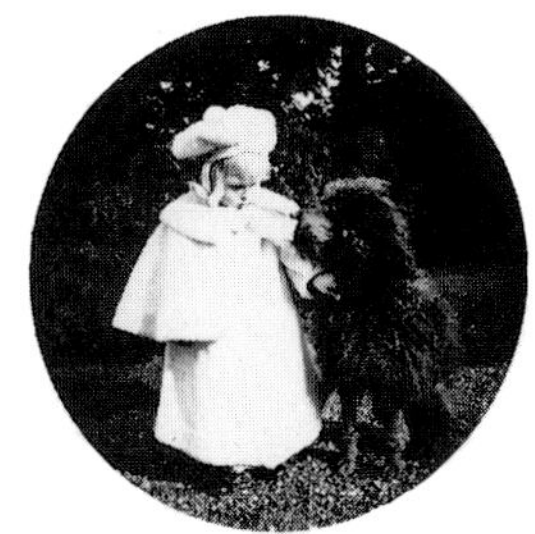

SANDRINGHAM, NOVEMBER 1896. DAVID AND BERTIE

The first of the Duke and Duchess of York's six children, a son, was born at White Lodge, Richmond, on 23 June 1894. At his christening one month later, the infant received the names Edward Albert Christian George Andrew Patrick David. Known to his family by the last of these names, this was the prince who was destined to ascend the throne as King Edward VIII.

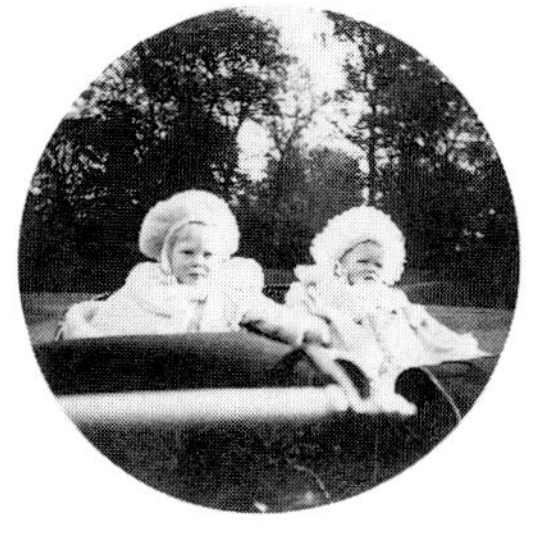

The Yorks' second child, who was to succeed his brother as King George VI, was Prince Albert Frederick Arthur George, known as 'Bertie', who was born at York Cottage on 14 December 1895. Two years later, on 25 April 1897, the Duchess of York gave birth to her only daughter, the Princess Victoria Alexandra Alice Mary. Like her eldest brother, the princess was known by the last of her four names. Prince Henry William Frederick Albert, later created Duke of Gloucester, and known as 'Harry', was born at York Cottage on 31 March 1900, to be followed by Prince George Edward Alexander Edmund, later Duke of Kent, on 20 December 1902, and Prince John Charles Francis, who was born on 12 July 1905.

The lives of these royal children are almost as well documented in the pages of their mother's photograph albums as that of the Duchess herself. The photographs are not only delightfully evocative vignettes of royal childhood during the reigns of Queen Victoria and King Edward VII, but represent private moments in the development and evolution of the royal family as we know it today. Perhaps even more importantly, these snapshots tend to give the lie to the prevalent belief that George V and Queen Mary saw little of their children during their early and most formative years.

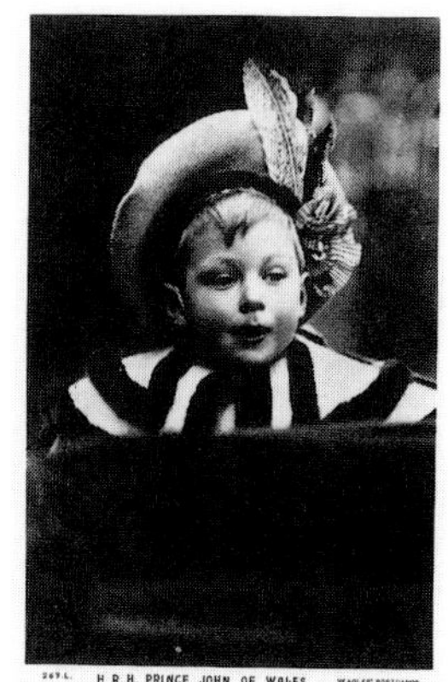

A POSTCARD OF PRINCE JOHN, DATED 1908

Outside the nucleus of family life, duty occasionally called the Duke and Duchess of York into the public eye. At this time their official schedules were less than demanding and the Duchess, with her charity work and other interests, found rather more to do than her husband. Inactivity always irked the Duke, but beyond sporting interests – and in particular an excessive, almost obsessive, love of shooting, deer-stalking and the like – he lacked the will and the self-motivation to fill his time more constructively.

As with Queen Victoria's Golden Jubilee in 1887, so the bigger and better celebration of her Diamond Jubilee ten years later, may be said to have crowned the final decade of the nineteenth century, and to have opened the final brief chapter of the Queen-Empress's epic reign. The Duke and Duchess of York both had their parts to play in the ceremonies marking the sixtieth anniversary of the Queen's accession in June 1897 and that August they undertook an official visit to Ireland as Her Majesty's representatives, the success of which was to be repeated in April 1899.

Yet while the year of the Diamond Jubilee had opened on a note of personal celebration for the Yorks, with the birth of Princess Mary, it was to end on a note of sorrow with the death of the Duchess's mother, Princess Mary Adelaide, Duchess of Teck. That April, as the Duchess of York lay in her cottage at Sandringham, recovering from the birth of her daughter, the Duchess of Teck had undergone an operation for a strangulated umbilical hernia. When strong enough to travel, she had gone abroad to recuperate, but upon her return that autumn had picked up her taxing schedule of social and charitable activities anew.

On 25 October, the Duchesses of York and Teck met at White Lodge to sort out piles of clothing which had been donated for the poor but, by the end of the day, the Duchess of Teck complained of feeling unwell. By the following evening her condition was so much worse that her doctors decided a second operation was necessary and this was begun shortly after midnight on 27 October. At 3a.m. the sixty-four-year-old Duchess of Teck died of heart failure.

For the young Duchess of York, the shock of her mother's death was made more agonizing by her father's already weakened state of mind, following a stroke in 1884: 'he, poor dear man, seems really to have softening of the brain', wrote the Empress Frederick, during one of her visits to Windsor early in 1897, 'and one does not quite understand what he means – he laughs about nothing & cannot find his words'. From the end of that year onwards, the Duchess of York had to take virtually all the decisions connected with her family, which added burden led her younger brother, Prince Alge, to remark, 'Dear Mama has left us at a very trying time . . .'

The spectre of death continued to haunt the royal family even as the new century began. On 21 January 1900 the Duke of Teck, whose mental deterioration had kept him in permanent seclusion at White Lodge, finally died at the early age of sixty-three. Almost exactly one year later to the very day, Queen Victoria died at Osborne House on 22 January 1901. The Duchess of York noted in her diary that evening, 'We got there at 5.30 only just in time to see beloved Grandmama alive for she passed away at 6.30p.m. surrounded by us all. It was too sad for words. . . . The thought of England without the Queen is dreadful even to think of.'

<hr>

'Uncle Wales', as the Duchess of York always referred to her father-in-law, was a corpulent, fifty-nine-year-old libertine, whose fast and colourful life-style had already become a part of popular legend by the time he finally succeeded his mother as King Edward VII.

As Prince of Wales, the new sovereign had long presided over a rival court, known as 'The Marlborough House Set'. Philistine both in outlook and deed, members of the Wales's coterie pursued pleasure with a fervour that made other royal circles, at home as well as abroad, look positively vapid. Wales himself was also a notorious womanizer, with a string of mistresses who were all paraded before his beautiful but long-suffering wife.

Born Princess Alexandra of Denmark, the eponymous heroine of Tennyson's ode, *The Sea-King's Daughter*, 'Motherdear', as she was known to her family, sought refuge from the hurt of her husband's infidelities in her children and later her grandchildren, all of whom she enjoyed spoiling to the utmost. After the death of her elder son, Prince Albert Victor, Prince George became the apple of his mother's eye, and although the Princess of Wales was undeniably very fond of her daughter-in-law, she resented losing her 'Georgie' to another woman. As a result she was, on occasion, as waspish towards Princess May as her daughters 'Loulou', 'Toria' and 'Harry' (the family's pet name for Princess Maud) were.

With the accession of Edward VII and Queen Alexandra the Duke of York became Heir Apparent, but for the best part of 1901 found himself denied the title synonymous with his new position, that of Prince of Wales. For her part, the Duchess of York greatly disapproved of this break with tradition, even though it proved to be no more than temporary. The change in Prince George's status wasn't overlooked entirely, however, and in the short term it was acknowledged by a revision of the title he already held. Then as now, one of the Heir Apparent's seven subsidiary titles is that of Duke of Cornwall, and thus, for the time being, the Duke and Duchess of York became known as the Duke and Duchess of Cornwall and York.

Despite the official period of court mourning for Queen Victoria, the Duke and Duchess were instructed to proceed with their first important overseas tour and, on 16 March, they set sail aboard the 7,000-ton liner *Ophir*, for Australia. In Melbourne the Duke of Cornwall and York, acting as the King's representative, was to open the first Federal Parliament of the Commonwealth of Australia. During the long voyage out, which took the *Ophir* via Gibraltar, Malta, Port Said, Colombo and Singapore, members of the royal party enjoyed themselves in the way of most travellers: playing deck games, taking part in gymnastics, spending time reading and writing, joining the crew in singsongs and taking part in the traditional, but comic, ceremony of Crossing the Line.

With his naval training, the Duke was well able to take the voyage comfortably in his stride, but for the Duchess, who was never a good sailor, the journey was not something she looked forward to at all. 'I *detest* the sea,' she had written to a friend. 'I like seeing the places & being on land, the rest of it is purgatory to me & makes me miserable & depressed, so please don't envy me.'

In Australia the royal couple, and in particular the Duchess, found themselves immensely popular, so much so that Princess May wrote home, 'You will see that your humble servant has found great favour with the Australians, rather different to at home where they always find fault with what I do or do not do.' Their duties discharged, the Duke and Duchess of Cornwall and York sailed on to New Zealand and Mauritius, returning to Britain, where they arrived on 1 November, via South Africa and Canada. Eight days later, on the King's sixtieth birthday, the Duke was at last created Prince of Wales.

On 4 April 1903, the new Prince and Princess of Wales bowed gracefully to another change in their lives when they moved from York House, St James's Palace, to Marlborough House, literally just around the corner. Built by Wren for the 1st Duke of Marlborough between 1709 and 1710, this imposing red-brick mansion, east of St James's Park and once the residence of the Dowager Queen Adelaide, widow of William IV, had been the home of Edward VII and Queen Alexandra for almost forty years. Indeed, it was only with the utmost reluctance that the latter finally accepted the fact that she had no choice but to move with her husband to the sovereign's official residence further down the Mall at Buckingham Palace.

Infinitely more palatial than York House, the Wales's new residence consisted of commodious state rooms, such as the two-storey Great Salon, hung with Flemish tapestries and frescoes of the Battle of Blenheim by Louis Laguerre; the magnificent state Drawing-Room, where pairs of columns helped support an ornate ceiling from which were hung three immense crystal chandeliers; and the state Dining-Room, dominated by an imposing mahogany table around which were placed twenty-four high-back red leather chairs. Even the private rooms were light and spacious, and in her first-floor bedroom a floor-to-ceiling canopy hung above the Princess of Wales's bed, while all around were sofas, tables, chairs, bookcases, vitrines, a brocaded day-bed and innumerable pictures, photographs, *objets d'art* and, as always wherever Princess May lived, vases of fresh cut flowers.

Much as the Prince of Wales disliked entertaining, he and Princess May now had no choice but to do just that. It is doubtful, though, whether any entertainment ever surpassed a ball they gave at Marlborough House in July 1903 for over a thousand guests and for which a sumptuously decorated ballroom was built out over the garden. During the reign of 'The Marlborough House Set' such a thing would not have been at all surprising, but for the more domesticated Prince George and Princess May, it was a rarity.

At about this time, the Prince and Princess of Wales were also given the small, Dee-side castle of Abergeldie. Not far from Balmoral this was to be their Scottish home until they inherited Balmoral Castle itself. Princess May was never fond of Abergeldie but, notwithstanding bouts of gloom and depression when Prince George was away shooting or perhaps sailing at Cowes, she accepted the situation for what it was and learned to make the most of it. Certainly, any number of photographs in Queen Mary's albums taken during their summer holidays at Abergeldie create an impression if not of utter contentment, then of peace and tranquillity. Outside Marlborough House, however, the Princess of Wales was probably happiest either at Sandringham or Frogmore, the latter enclosed by the private grounds of the Home Park at Windsor. Here the Wales family exchanged Highland dress for more casual

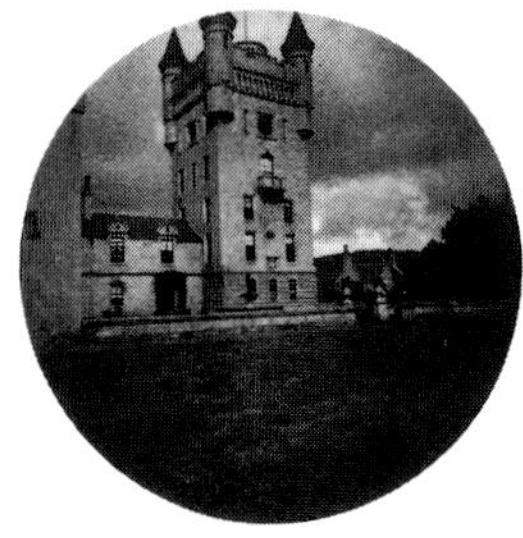

BALMORAL CASTLE, 1893

suits and straw boaters, light summer outfits or, for the most junior, the familiar navy and white sailor-suits, much favoured at the time.

Lingering over works of art, enjoying summer afternoons by the lake at Frogmore, rearranging her collections of family memorabilia or making endless inventories of their contents, concentrating on her needlework (for which she became justly famous) or, as a life-long, albeit moderate, smoker, relaxing with a book and a cigarette, writing letters or attending to her photograph albums, was much more the future Queen Mary's style than indulging in anything more radical or revolutionary. Yet she was by no means opposed to everything modern or progressive even if, to begin with, she did draw the line at something as innovatory as the motor car. This development she found disturbing, the machines themselves 'odious'. All the same, the Princess's first tentative step towards accepting automobiles as part of the modern world had been taken as early as October 1900 when, accompanied by her lady-in-waiting, Lady Eva Dugdale, she had been taken for a drive at The Hendre in Monmouth by the Hon. C. S. Rolls.

Three years later, both the Prince and Princess of Wales were passengers when Lord Shrewsbury drove them out to Hampton Court Palace in Middlesex. This excursion clearly had a greater impact on the Princess, for she lost no time in writing to her old aunt Augusta, Grand Duchess of Mecklenberg-Strelitz, to tell her all about it.

The Grand Duchess replied promptly, '. . . I very nearly had a fit and quite screamed out to myself . . . oh! dearest child, how could you? *38m.* too . . . It really actually took my breath away.'

Motoring evidently took the Wales's breath away, too, or at least created so favourable an impression on them that in July 1903 the Prince took delivery of the first of several Daimlers that were to become a permanent feature of royal travel. These vehicles ranged from a modest 50-hp model with open sides, traditional carriage lamps and flat-topped canopy, to a sophisticated 57-hp model, painted in the royal colours and built in 1910. Later still, Prince George (by now King) took delivery of an extraordinary six-wheel Crossley convertible, designed specifically for estate work or for use over rough terrain.

Early in 1904, carriages as opposed to cars were the mode of transport at an event which caused the Princess of Wales considerable personal happiness. On 10 February that year her youngest brother, Prince Alexander ('Alge') of Teck, was married at St George's Chapel, Windsor, to Princess Alice of Albany. The only daughter of Queen Victoria's favourite son, Prince Leopold, Duke of Albany, who had died in tragic circumstances in 1884 at the early age of only thirty-one, Princess Alice would one day achieve the distinction of becoming the longest-lived member of the British royal family. Better known as Princess Alice, Countess of Athlone, she died at her Kensington Palace home on 3 January 1981, seven weeks short of her ninety-eighth birthday.

Two months after the Teck–Albany wedding, at which the seven-year-old

Princess Mary of Wales had acted as one of the bridesmaids, Prince George and Princess May paid a four-day official visit to the aged Emperor Franz Josef of Austria. With her appreciation of history, the Princess of Wales was charmed by the old Emperor himself, fascinated and amused by the antiquated ways of Austrian Court life, and delighted that the visit meant she was able to see something of the eldest of her three brothers, Prince Adolphus, now the 2nd Duke of Teck. 'Dolly', who had married Lady Margaret Grosvenor, daughter of the 1st Duke of Westminster, in December 1894, had been appointed British Military Attaché to the Austrian Imperial Court, and he and his wife were among those waiting to greet the Prince and Princess of Wales upon their arrival in Vienna.

Save for their extended Antipodean tour, travel for the Princess of Wales had always been restricted to Europe; the Teck family's Florentine exile, visits to German relations at places such as Rumpenheim, Neu Strelitz and Reinthal, holidays in St Moritz, which she visited four times, and sojourns in the South of France, on occasion accompanying Queen Victoria to the Hotel Regina at Cimiez. Now the exotic prevailed and, on 19 October 1905 only three months after the birth of her sixth and last child, Prince John, the Princess of Wales accompanied her husband to India – the jewel of the British Empire.

In preparation for this six-month adventure, Princess May read voraciously about the great sub-continent. Her interest and diligence reaped their own rewards when Sir Walter Lawrence, Chief of Staff on the tour and private secretary to Lord Curzon when he was Viceroy of India, told her, 'I consider you have a very good grasp on Indian affairs, quite remarkable in a woman.' In those unenlightened days when women were not expected, much less encouraged, to have opinions or even minds of their own, such a remark was seen as complimentary and accepted as such. 'I felt much flattered & repeat this for yr ears only,' the Princess wrote to Hélène Bricka, 'as only you know what trouble I took to get the right books.'

This particular tour was the first of two the Prince and Princess of Wales undertook of the sub-continent. In 1905–06 they went as representatives of the Crown. When they returned, five years later, they did so as Emperor and Empress of India. Of her introduction to this land of the Mogul emperors, James Pope-Hennessy tells us that it was of 'cardinal importance' to Princess May's development: '. . . its manifold varieties of scenery, cultures and religions,' he wrote, 'was to her an astounding revelation'.

Indeed, so great were the impressions and memories of her visits that, over thirty years later (as Queen Mary), she was heard to remark, 'When I die, INDIA will be found written on my heart.'

The four remaining years left to Prince George and Princess May before the Empire passed into their custody, were spent in the manner we have already glimpsed. However, two events in particular provided highlights to the year 1906. In May the Prince and Princess of Wales travelled to Madrid for the wedding of Prince George's cousin 'Ena', Princess Victoria Eugenie of

Battenberg, to King Alfonso XIII of Spain. This occasion, which had already caused some little controversy over the bride having to adopt the Catholic faith, was otherwise made memorable by the drama of attempted assassination. As the King and his bride were returning to the Palacio Real from the church of St Hieronimo after the marriage ceremony on 31 May, a bomb was tossed at the bridal coach from a house in the Calle Mayor, along which the procession was passing. Horses, soldiers and onlookers were killed in the subsequent explosion, but King Alfonso and Queen Ena, their wedding clothes covered with blood, survived.

Infinitely less traumatic was the coronation in the cathedral at Trondheim that June of the new King and Queen of Norway. United with Sweden for almost a century, Norway had gained its independence in 1905, at which time it was decided that a constitutional monarch and not a President should be elected Head of State. Thus the Norwegian crown was offered to and accepted by Prince Carl (otherwise Charles), second son of King Frederick VIII of Denmark.

For the Prince and Princess of Wales, who set out for Norway one week after their return from Madrid, the coronation was of far greater importance than the Spanish royal wedding, for the simple reason that the new Queen of Norway was Prince George's youngest sister, Maud. Unlike the long and theatrical coronation rituals staged in England, that of King Haakon VII (as the new monarch chose to be known) and Queen Maud was a simple, almost cosy, affair, though the idea that they occupied a 'revolutionary' throne troubled the Princess of Wales, who considered an elected monarchy a contradiction in terms.

Of course, in the not so distant future, revolution would destroy, not create, many of the thrones of Europe, and in August 1909 the British royal family were visited by their Romanov kinsmen, arguably the most famous victims of any such revolution.

Russia's last Tsar, Nicholas II, and the Prince of Wales, to whom he bore a striking resemblance, were first cousins: their mothers, Queen Alexandra and the Dowager Empress Marie Feodorovna (born Princess Dagmar of Denmark) were sisters. The Prince of Wales and the Tsarina Alexandra Feodorovna – who, it will be remembered, had refused to marry the Duke of Clarence – were also first cousins: the Prince's father, Edward VII, and the Tsarina's mother, Princess Alice, Grand Duchess of Hesse, had been brother and sister.

The visit of the Russian imperial family to England, in what proved to be the last summer of Edward VII's life, is captured, somewhat poignantly, in Queen Mary's albums. Her photographs of the two families meeting aboard the imperial yacht *Standart* are a vivid reminder of a world that was soon to vanish forever.

———————————

Over the years, popular historians have led us to believe that Princess May became a connoisseur of fine art. This is not strictly true. Primarily her interests revolved around works of art that were connected directly or indirectly with the history of her family, and it was on that basis that she built up impressive collections of pictures and *objets d'art* which now form part of the much wider Royal Collection itself. It is nevertheless true that Princess May was a very keen *patron* of the arts, forever visiting galleries and museums, stately homes, churches, cathedrals and so on. She also had an appreciative eye for the decorative arts and had certainly inherited her mother's love of the theatre. Indeed, it was not unusual for her to attend the opera or to see a play or a show two or even three times a month.

It was in this already well-established way, combined with a variety of official functions, that the Princess of Wales passed the autumn and winter months of 1909. With the approach of spring, however, concern for the King's health became increasingly apparent as his attacks of bronchial trouble, breathlessness and fainting became more regular and prolonged. By the beginning of May, anxiety within immediate royal circles had risen to a point whereby a message was sent to Queen Alexandra, then holidaying on the island of Corfu with her middle daughter, Princess Victoria, asking her to return to London. On 5 May, the Queen arrived home to be met by her entire family at Victoria Station. Throughout the following day the Prince of Wales stayed beside the bed of his dying father at Buckingham Palace, whither Princess May was eventually summoned at seven o'clock that evening. Almost five hours later, at 11.45, King Edward VII died.

'I have lost my best friend & the best of fathers', lamented the Prince of Wales, '. . . I am heart-broken and overwhelmed with grief but God will help me in my great responsibilities & darling May will be my comfort as she always has been.'

(*OPPOSITE*) THE DUKE AND DUCHESS OF YORK SPENT THEIR HONEYMOON AT YORK COTTAGE AT SANDRINGHAM, AND IT WAS THEIR COUNTRY HOME FOR THIRTY-THREE YEARS. THE BOTTOM PHOTOGRAPH SHOWS THE DUKE OF YORK IN A CANOE ON THE LAKE THERE IN 1893

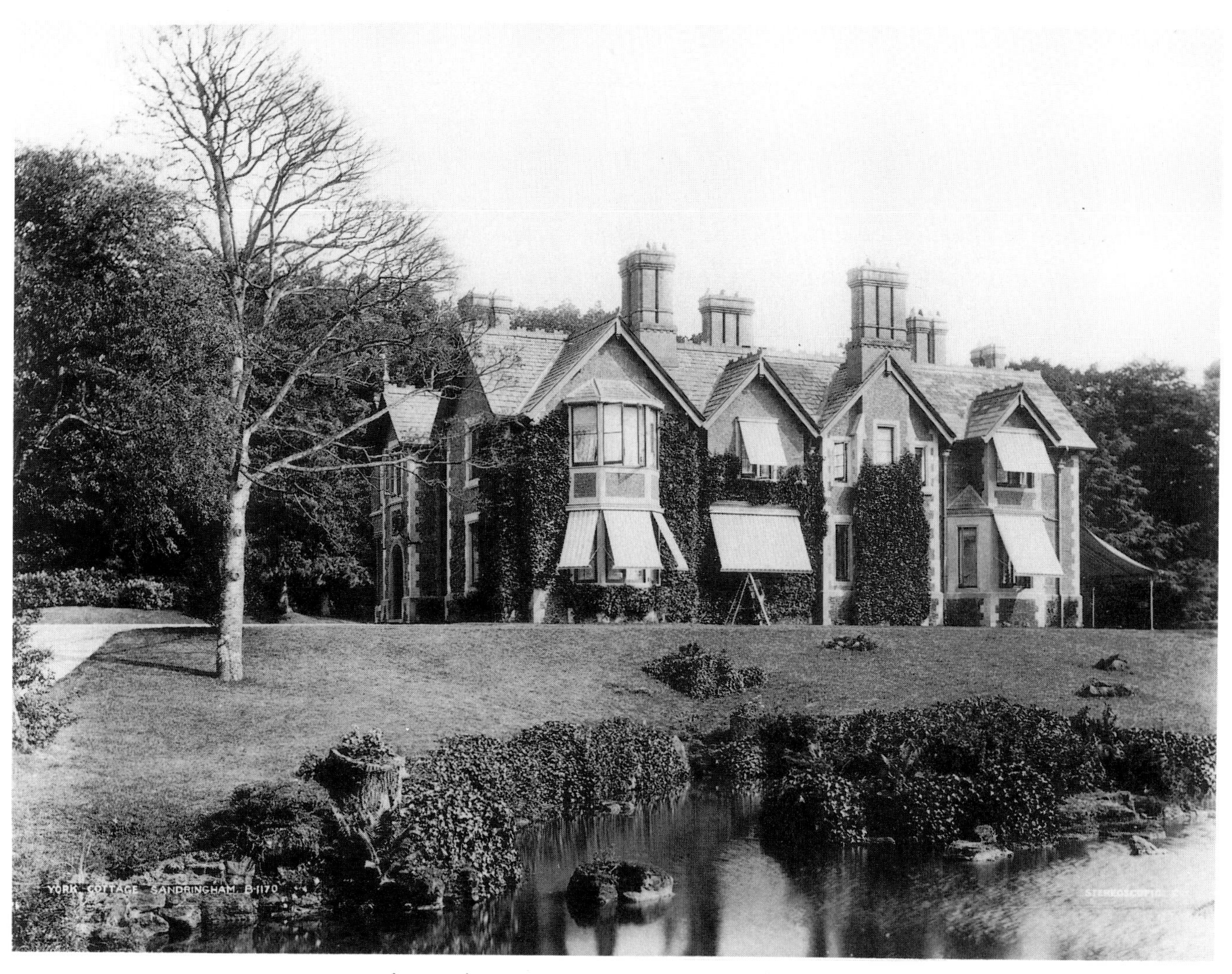

Our Cottage. July 6th 1893.

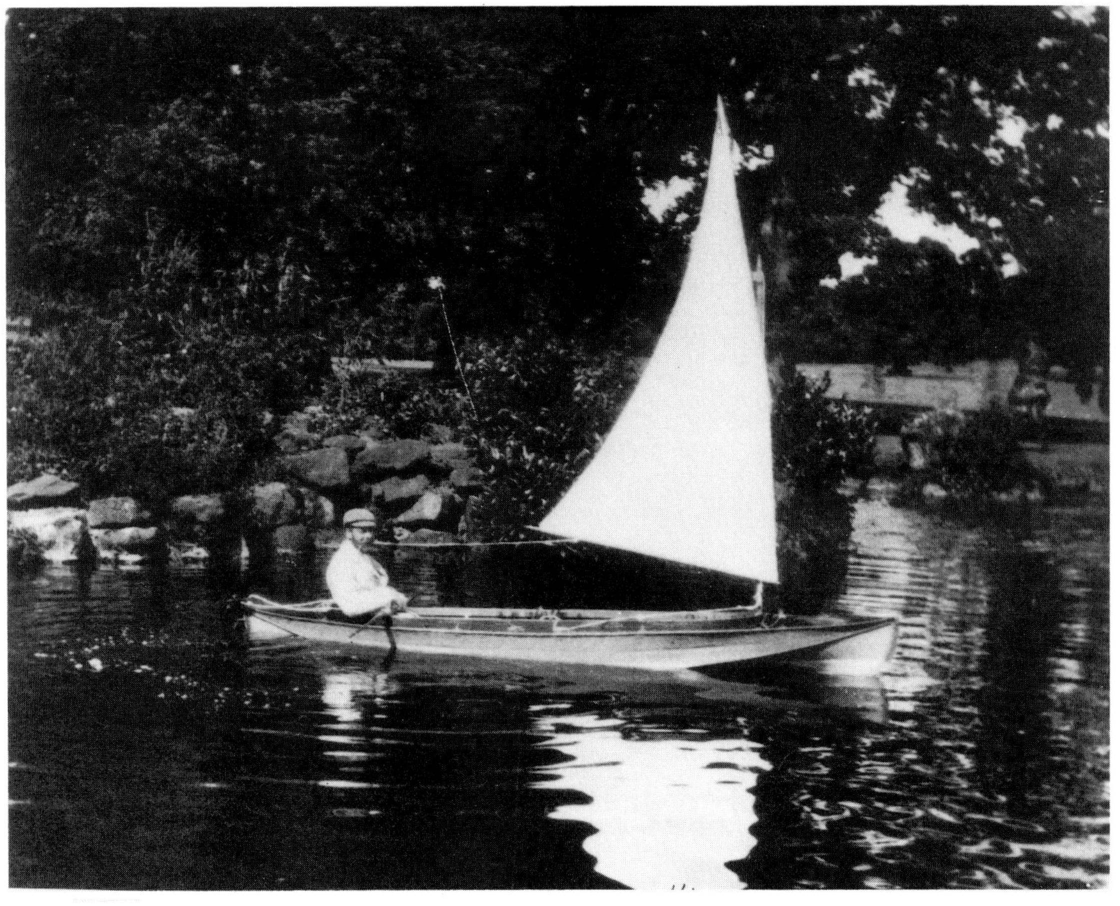

georgie in the canoe

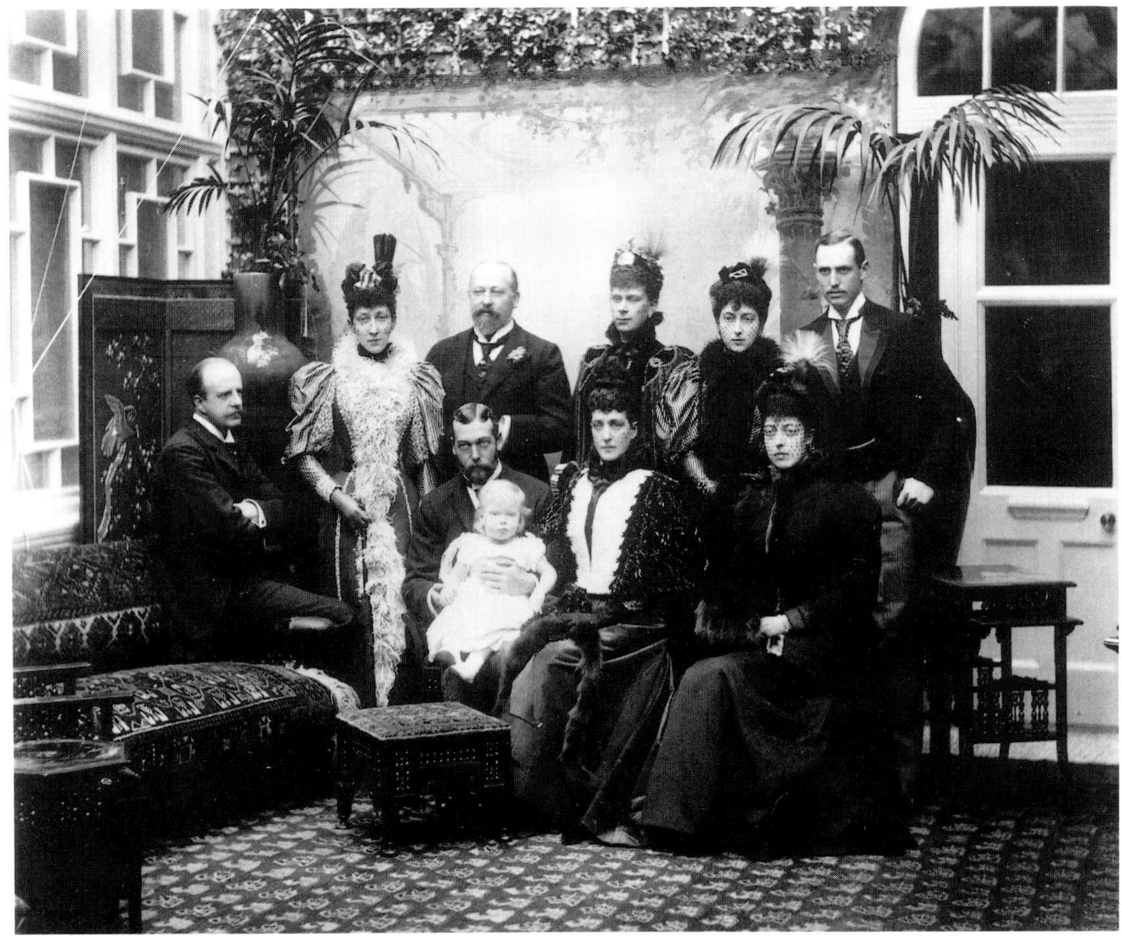

FAMILY GROUP, SANDRINGHAM 1895.
LEFT TO RIGHT, BACK: EARL OF FIFE AND
HIS WIFE PRINCESS LOUISE, THE PRINCE
OF WALES ('PAPA', LATER EDWARD VII),
THE DUCHESS OF YORK, PRINCESS MAUD
(LATER QUEEN OF NORWAY) AND PRINCE
CARL (CHARLES) OF DENMARK (LATER
KING HAAKON VII OF NORWAY); FRONT:
PRINCE GEORGE, DUKE OF YORK WITH
PRINCE EDWARD (DAVID), THE PRINCESS
OF WALES ('MAMA', LATER QUEEN
ALEXANDRA) AND PRINCESS VICTORIA

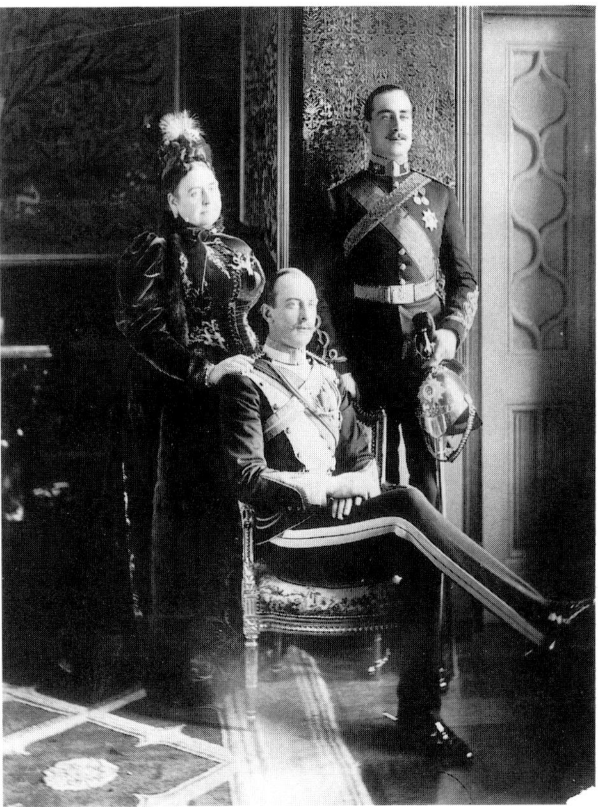

THE WEDDING DAY OF PRINCE
ADOLPHUS OF TECK ('DOLLY'), SEEN
HERE (SEATED) WITH THE DUCHESS
OF TECK AND PRINCE 'FRANK',
12 DECEMBER 1894

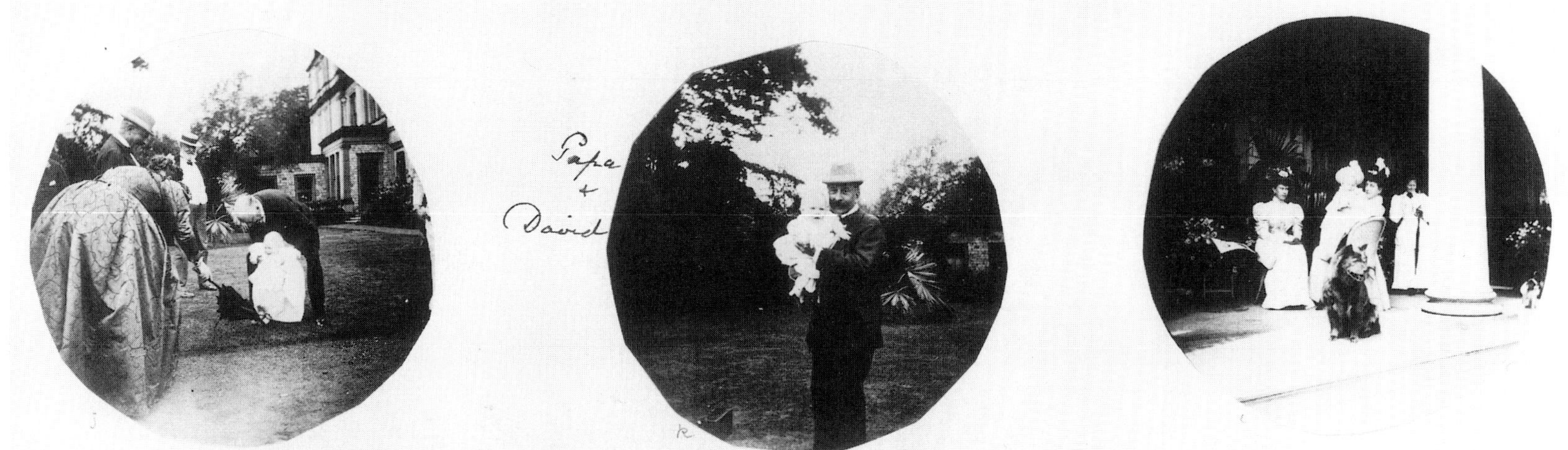

SNAPSHOTS TAKEN AT ST LEONARD'S HILL, WINDSOR, JUNE 1895. DAVID WITH THE DUKE AND DUCHESS OF TECK, THE DUCHESS OF YORK AND THE PRINCESS OF WALES

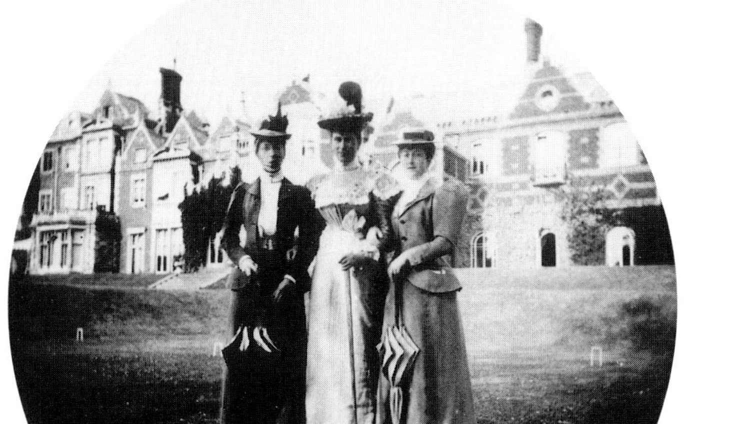

SANDRINGHAM 1896. THE DUCHESS OF YORK IS IN THE MIDDLE

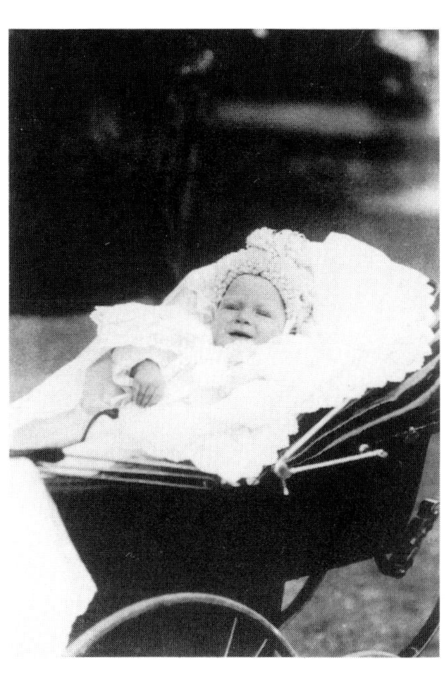

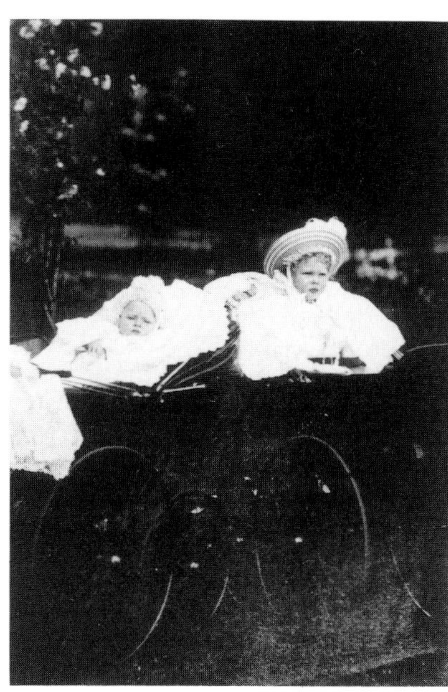

(*OVERLEAF LEFT*) SANDRINGHAM, 1898, INCLUDING THE DUCHESS OF YORK'S SITTING-ROOM AT YORK COTTAGE, AND DAVID WITH HIS GRANDMOTHER (THE PRINCESS OF WALES IS WEARING A LONG APRON) FEEDING THE DOGS IN THE SANDRINGHAM KENNELS

(*OVERLEAF RIGHT*) PRINCESS MAY, DUCHESS OF YORK, WITH FAMILY AND FRIENDS ABOARD THE *VICTORIA AND ALBERT* AT COWES IN AUGUST 1898, AND AT OSBORNE BAY, ON THE ISLE OF WIGHT

DAVID AND BERTIE AS INFANTS, JUNE 1896

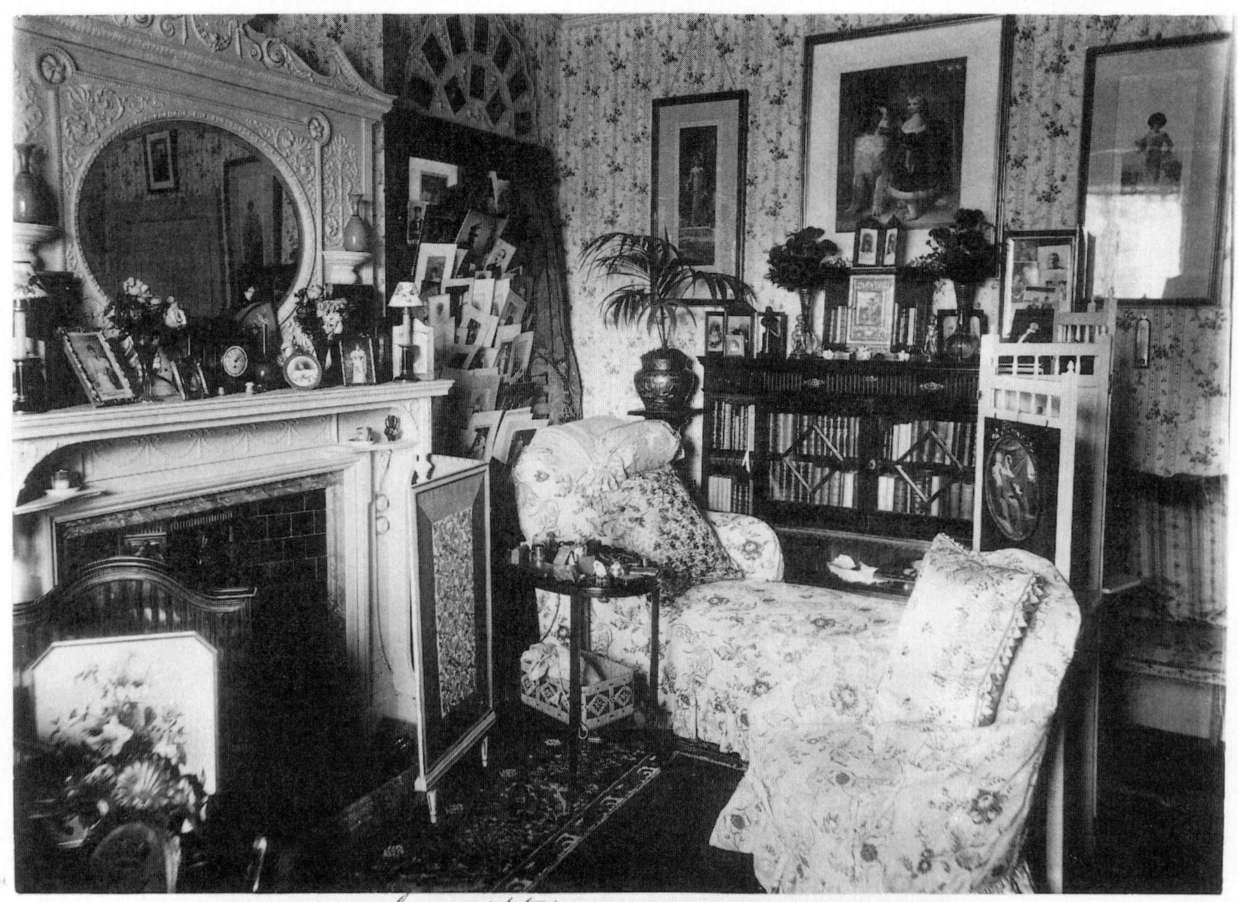

My sitting room

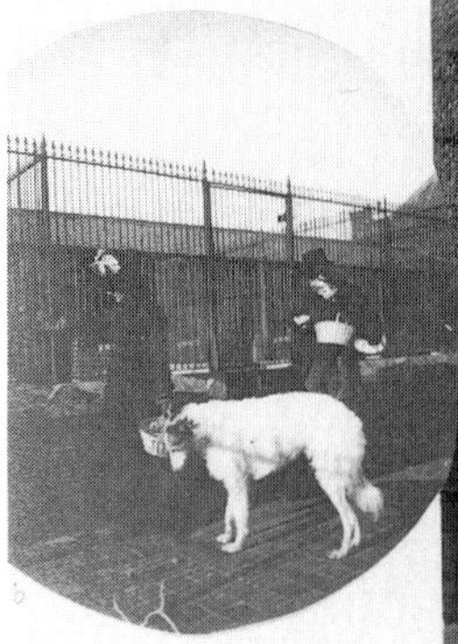

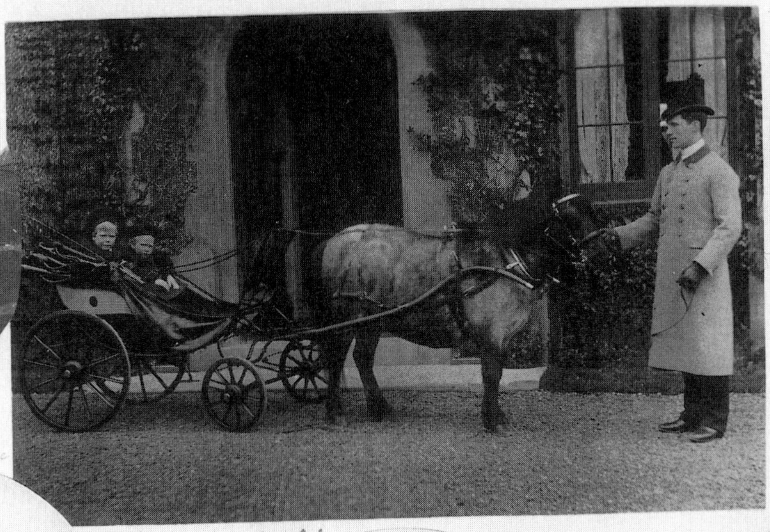

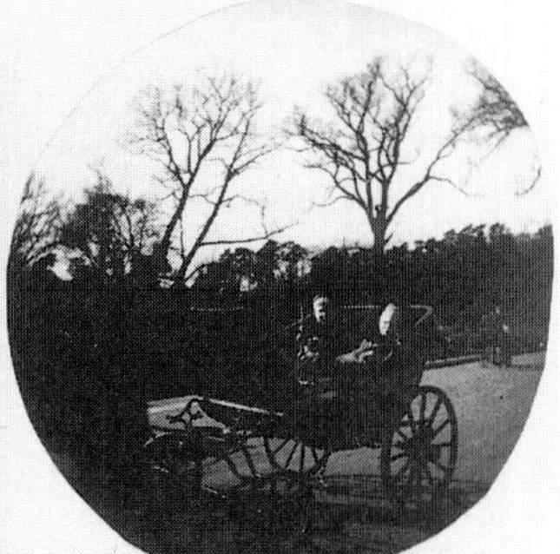

David & Bertie   1898.

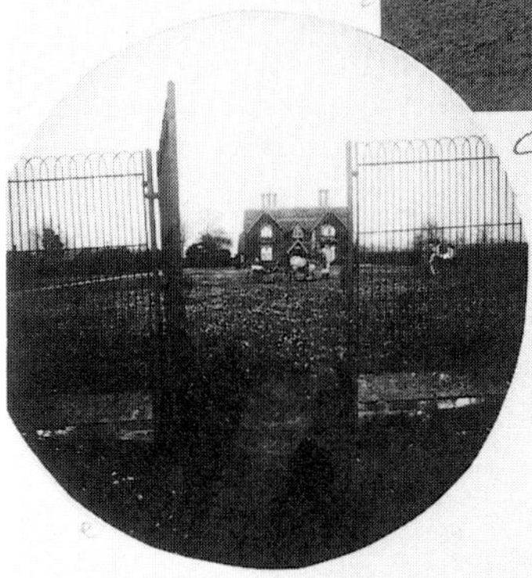

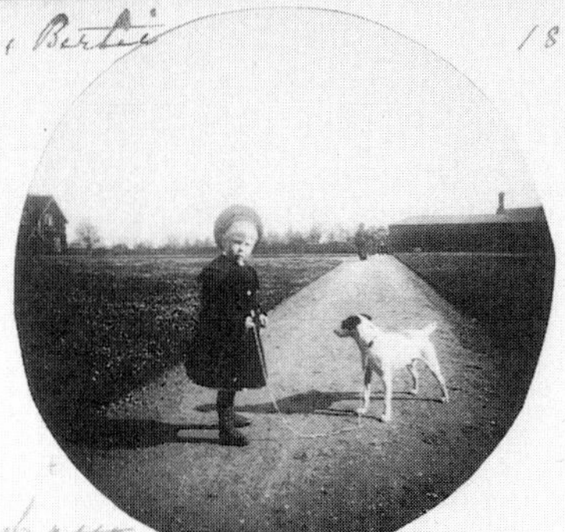

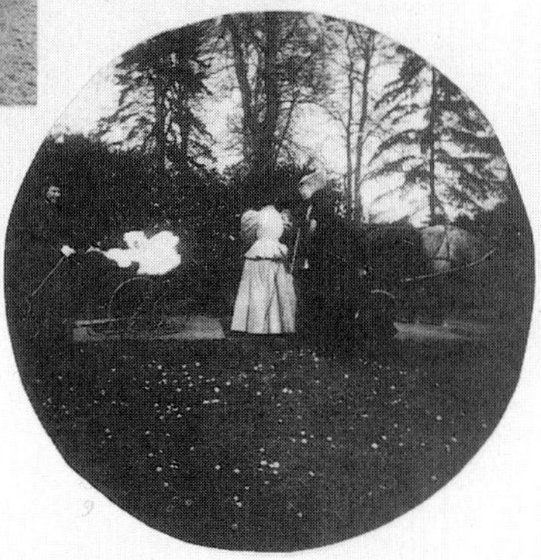

Sandringham

1898

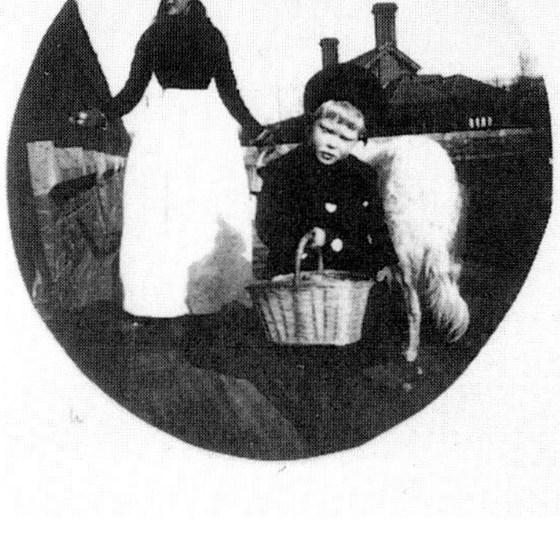

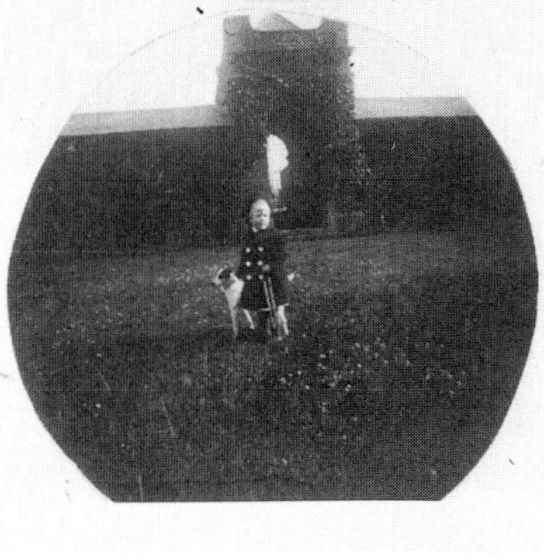

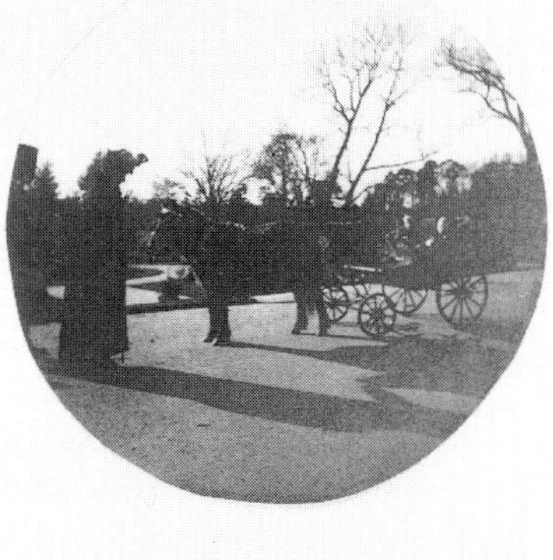

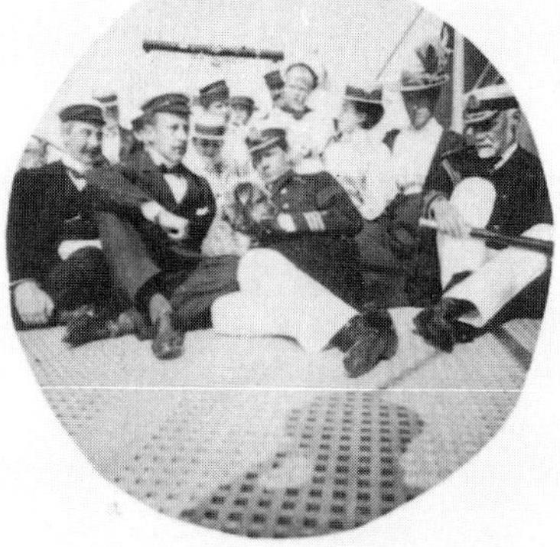

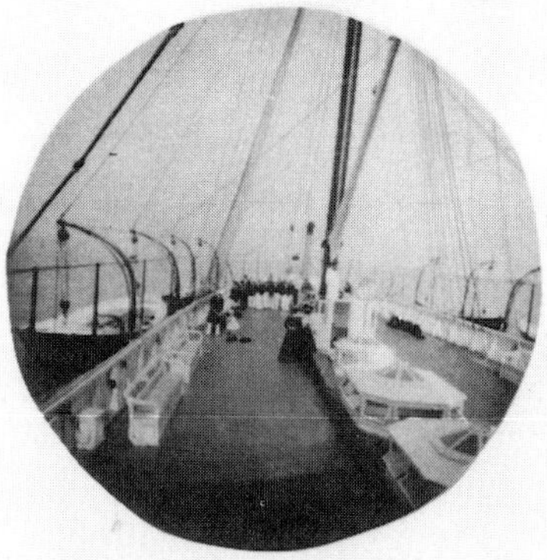

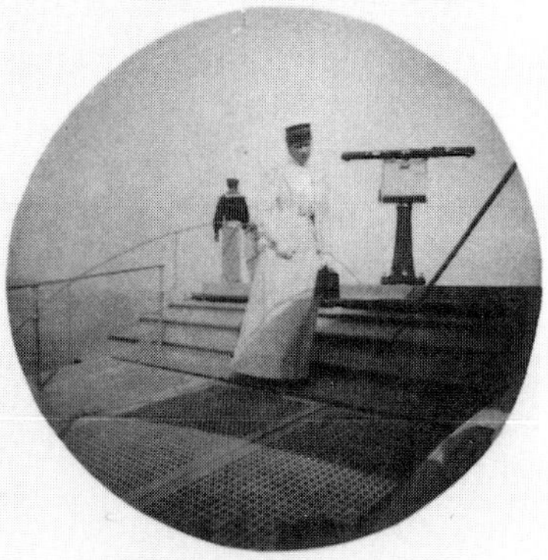

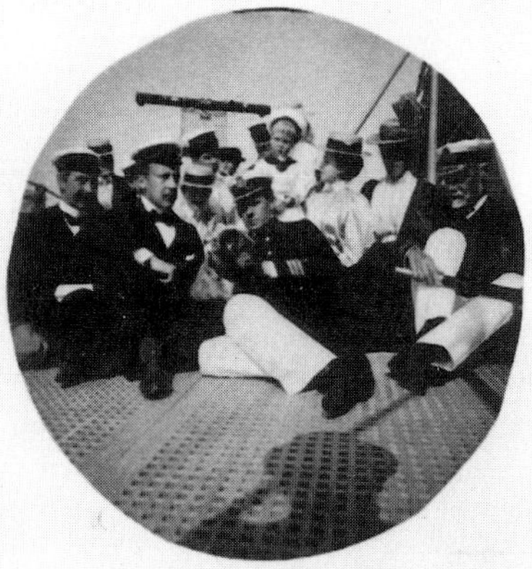

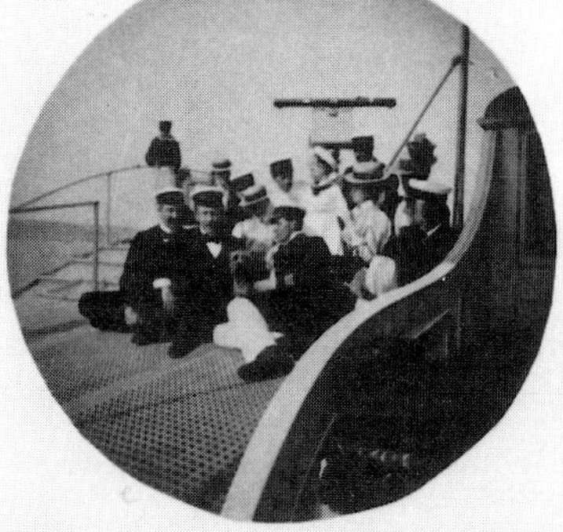

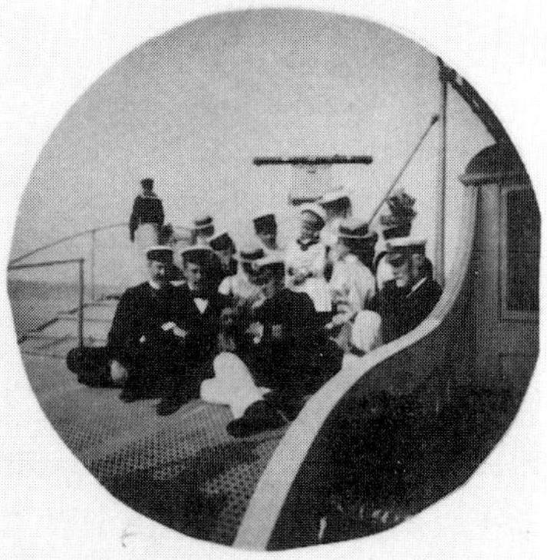

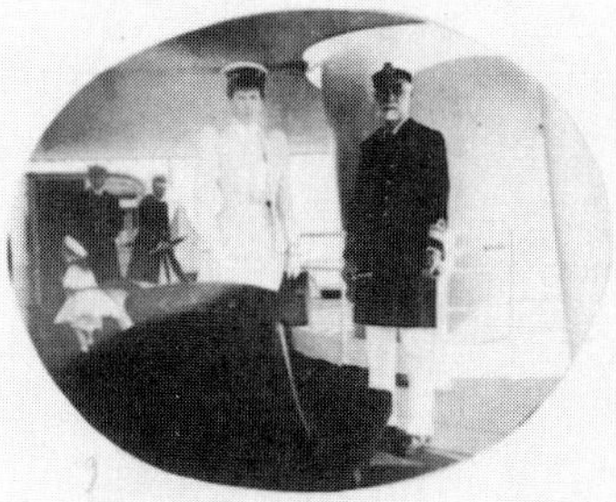

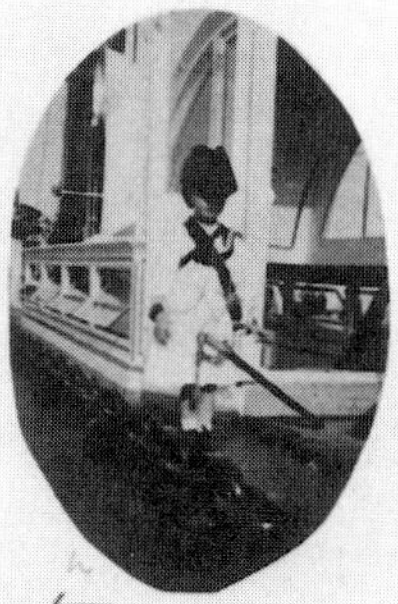

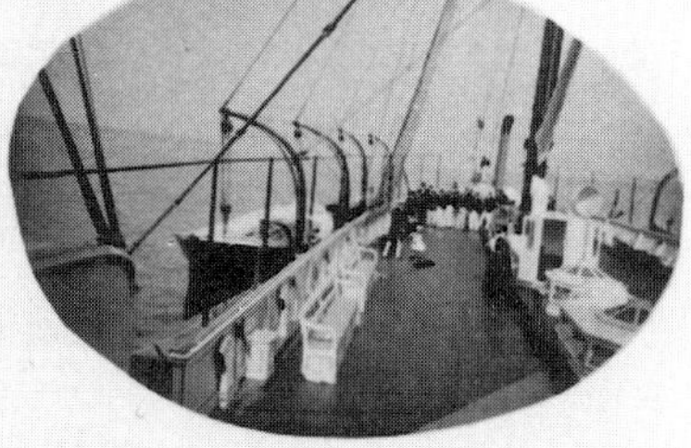

40

Victoria & Albert
Cowes Regt:
1898

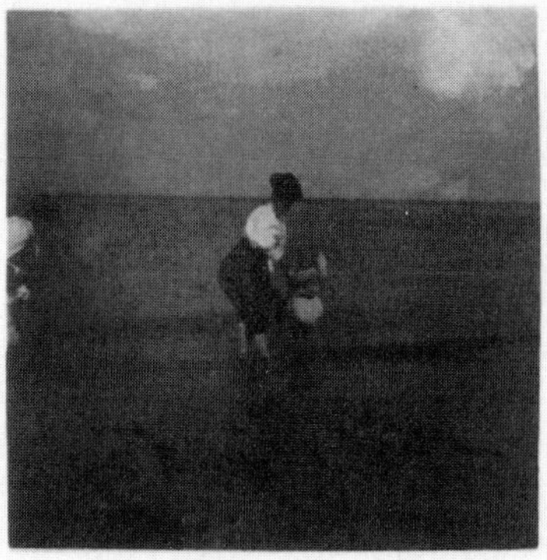

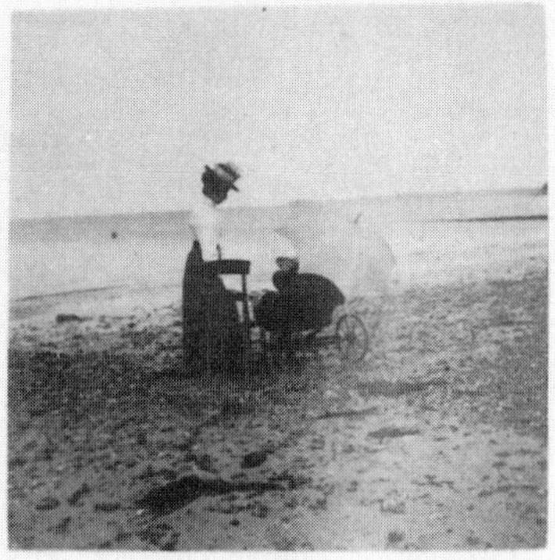

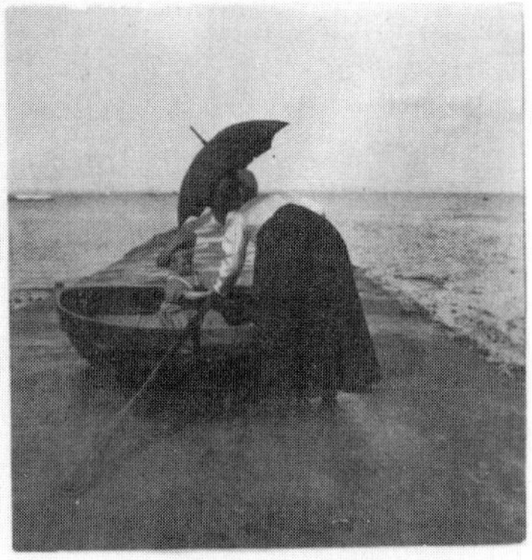

Osborne Bay
1898

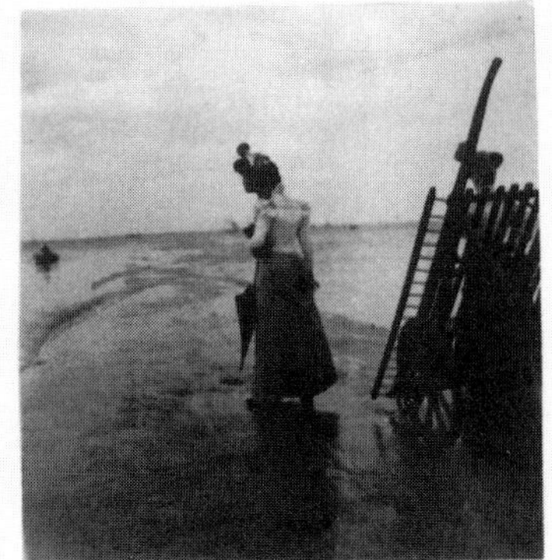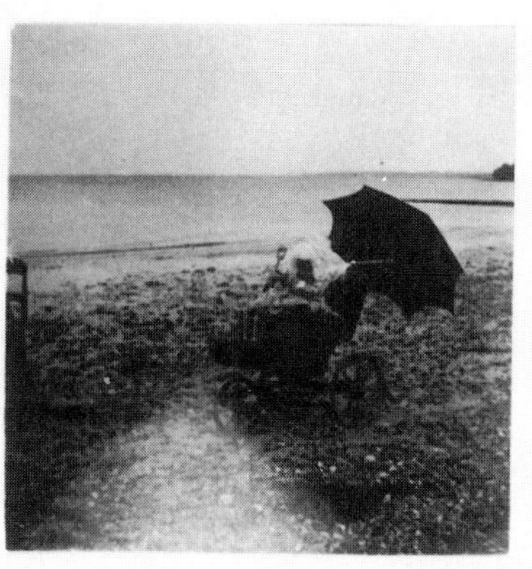

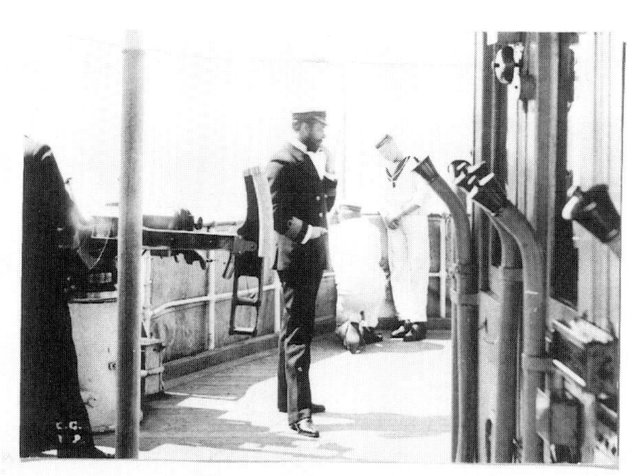

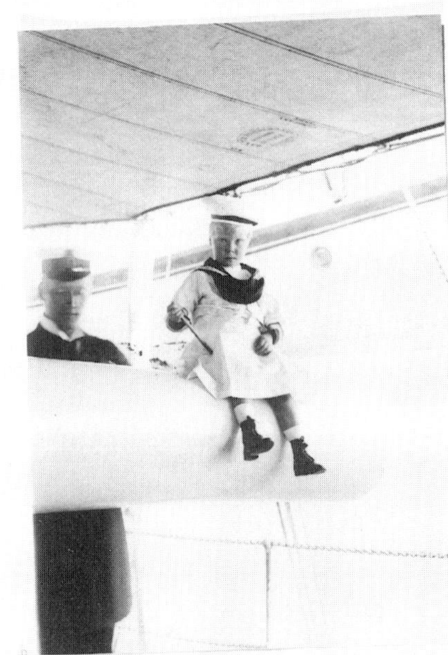

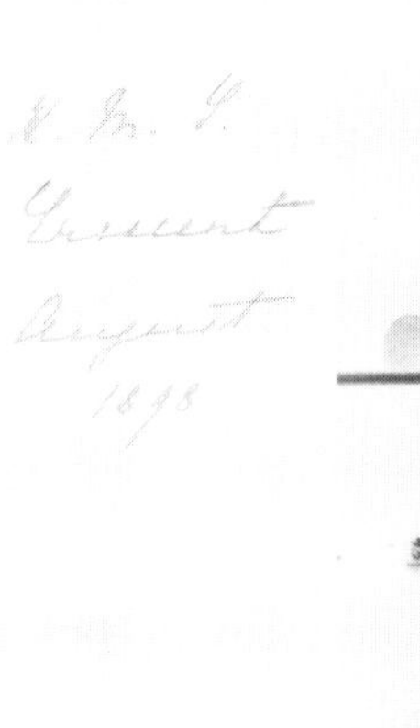
H. M. S.
Crescent
August
1898

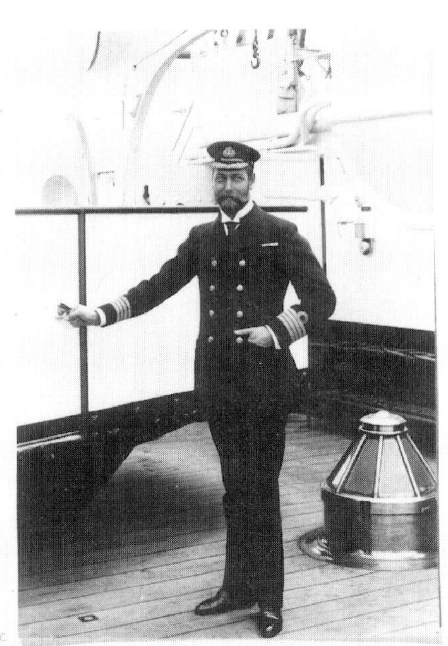

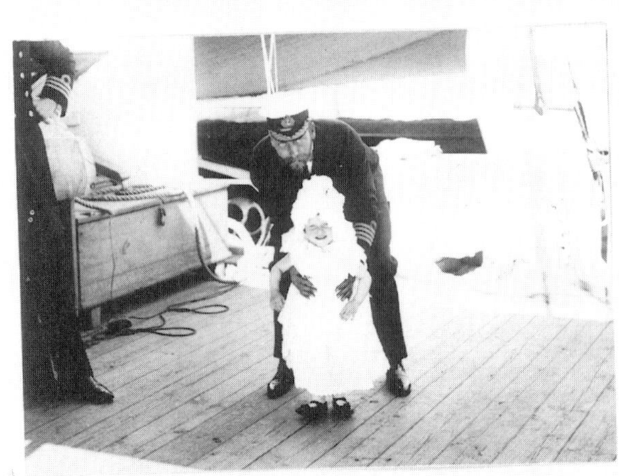

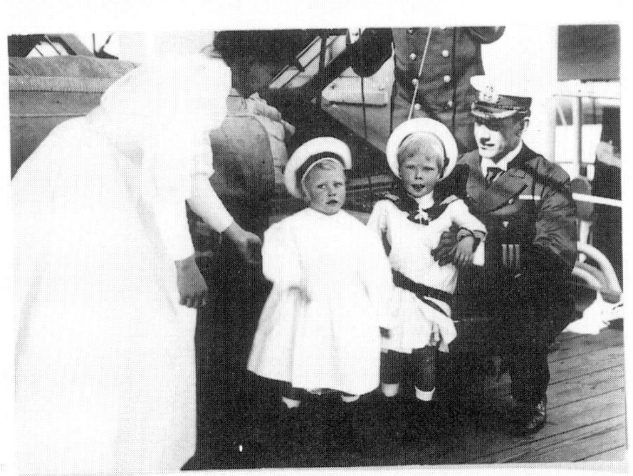

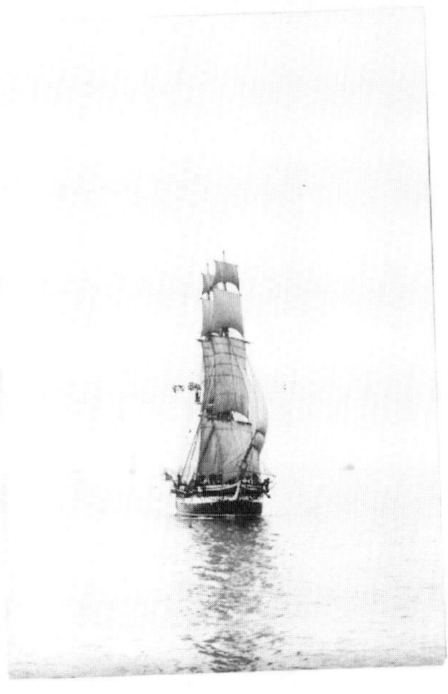

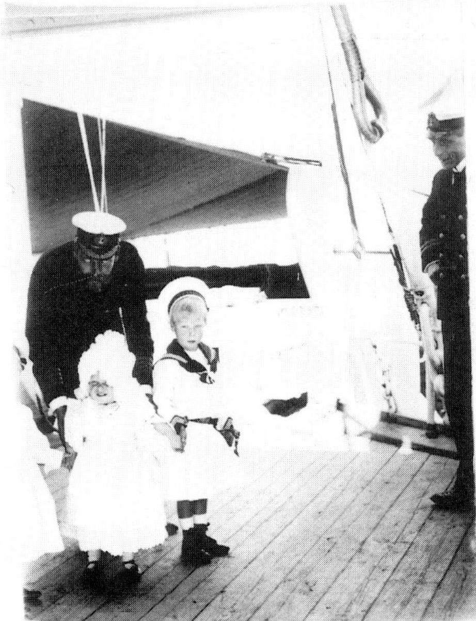

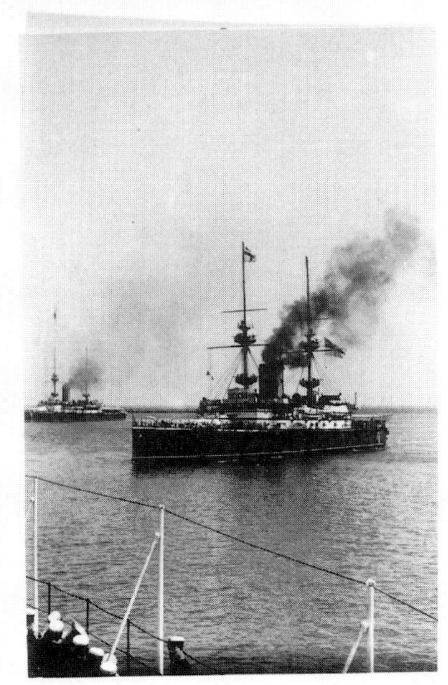

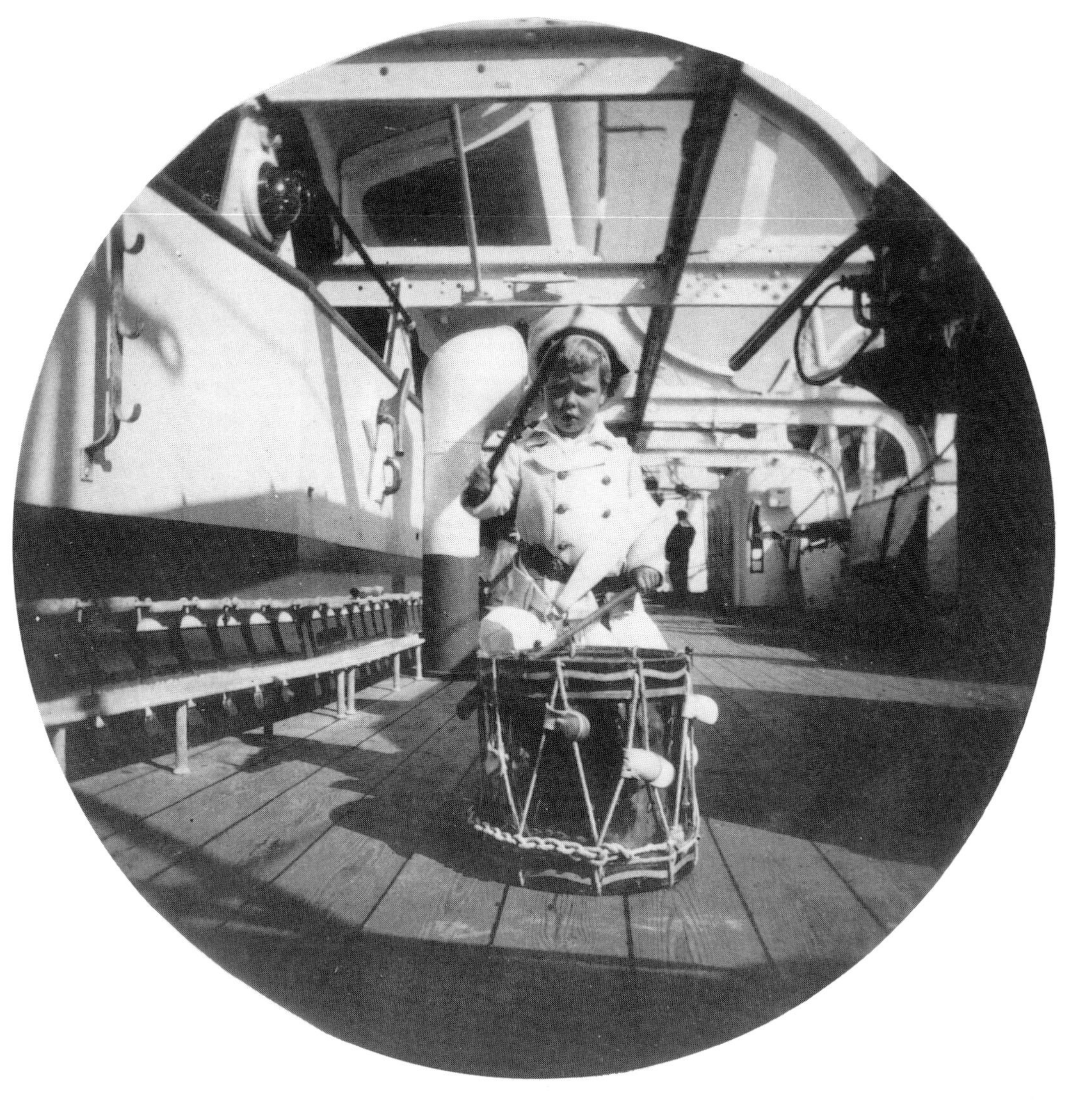

(*OPPOSITE*) A PAGE OF
SNAPS SHOWING THE DUKE
OF YORK AND HIS
CHILDREN ABOARD HMS
CRESCENT, AUGUST 1898

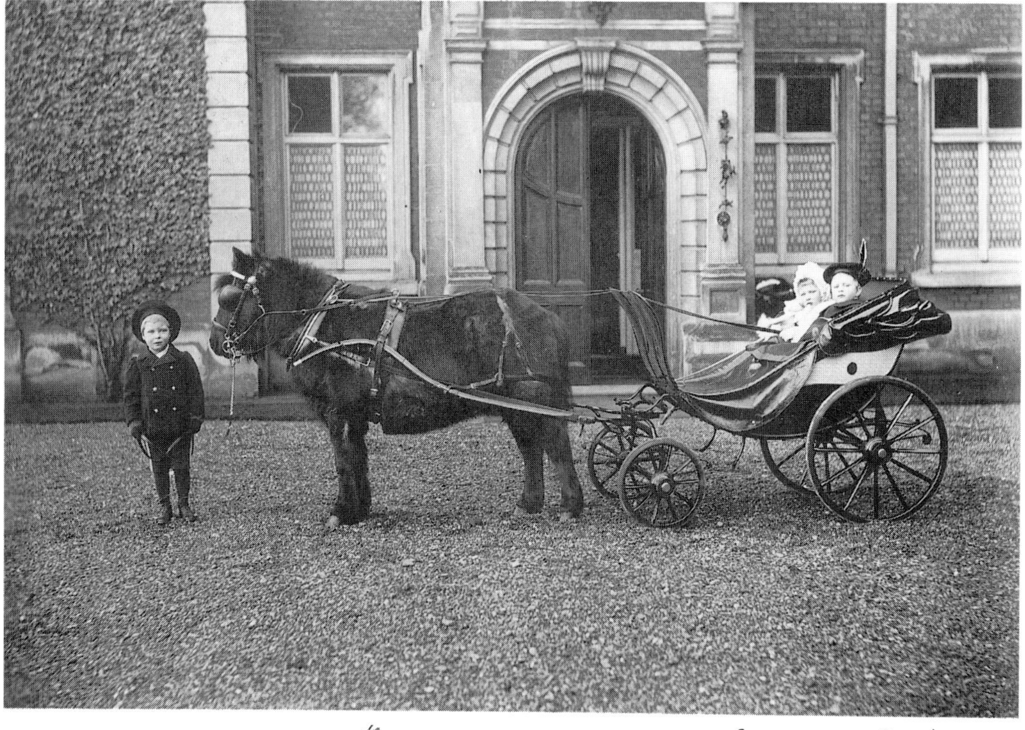

THE YORK CHILDREN,
DAVID, BERTIE AND MARY,
AT SANDRINGHAM IN
DECEMBER 1898

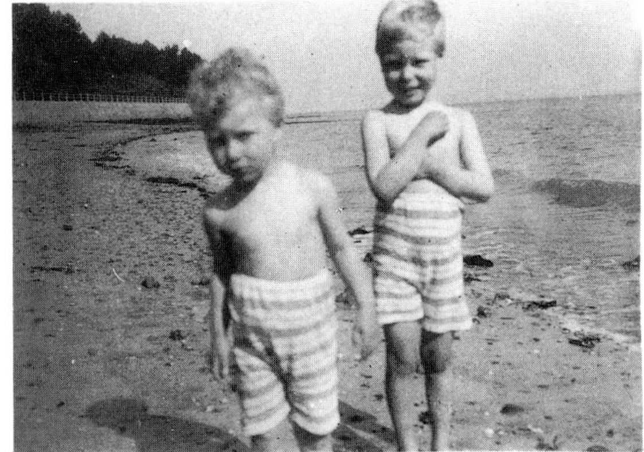

*Baby Mary. David
Osborne

August
1899.*

THE DUKE AND DUCHESS
OF YORK AND THEIR
CHILDREN VISITING
QUEEN VICTORIA AT
OSBORNE, AUGUST 1899

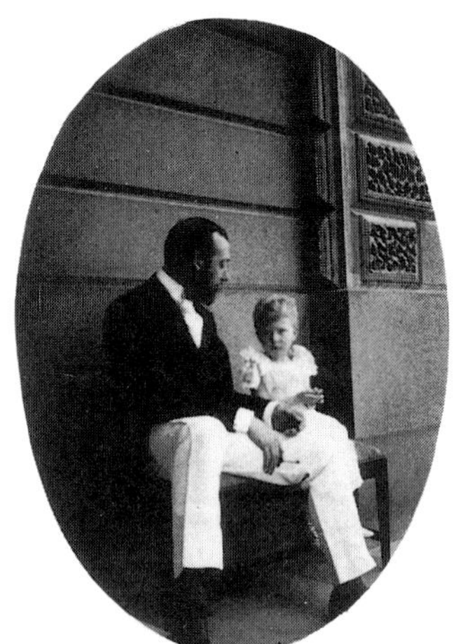

G. & Mary

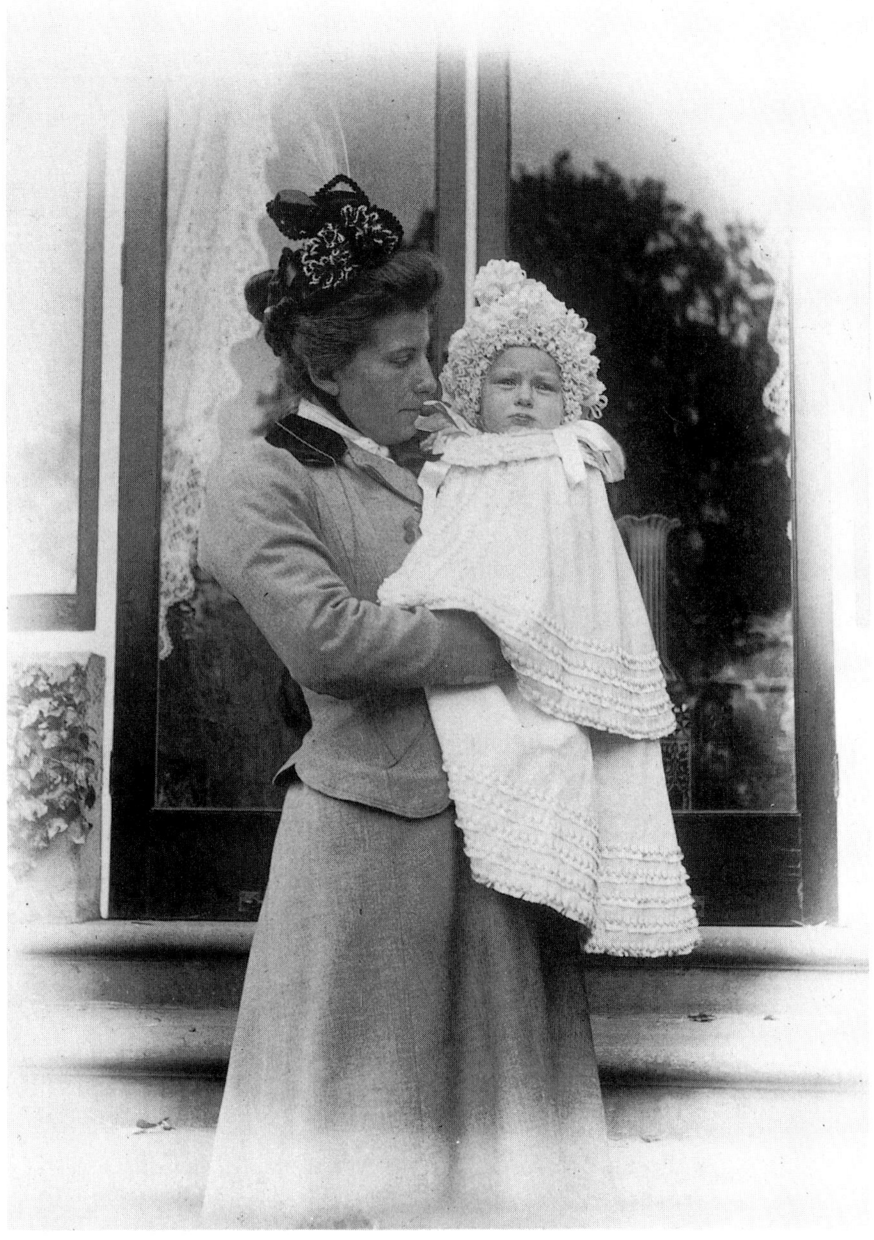

*Lalla & Baby Harry
Octr 1900*

MRS BILL ('LALLA'), NURSE
TO THE YORK CHILDREN,
WITH PRINCE HENRY
('HARRY') AT YORK
COTTAGE, OCTOBER 1900

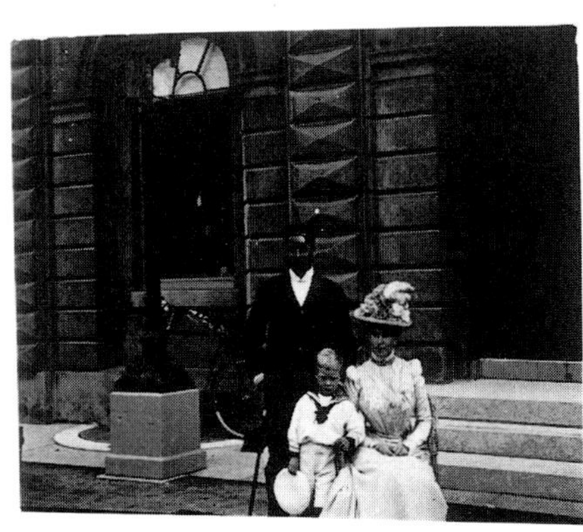

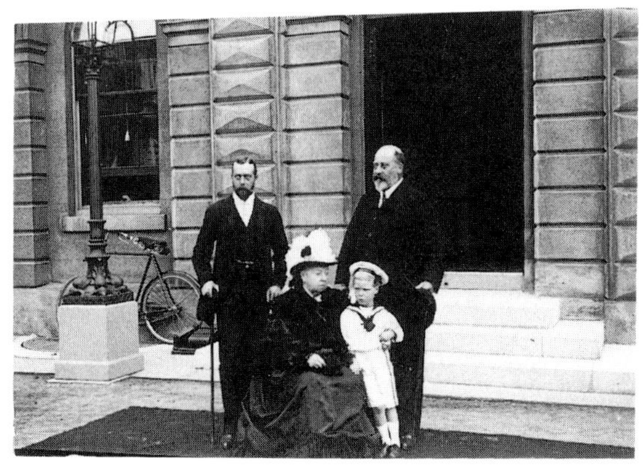

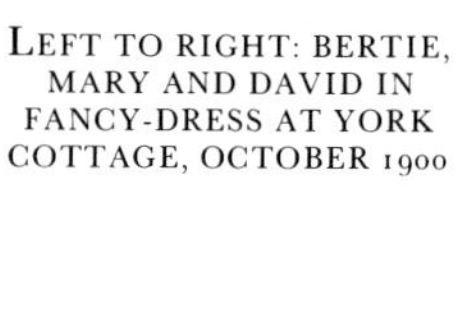

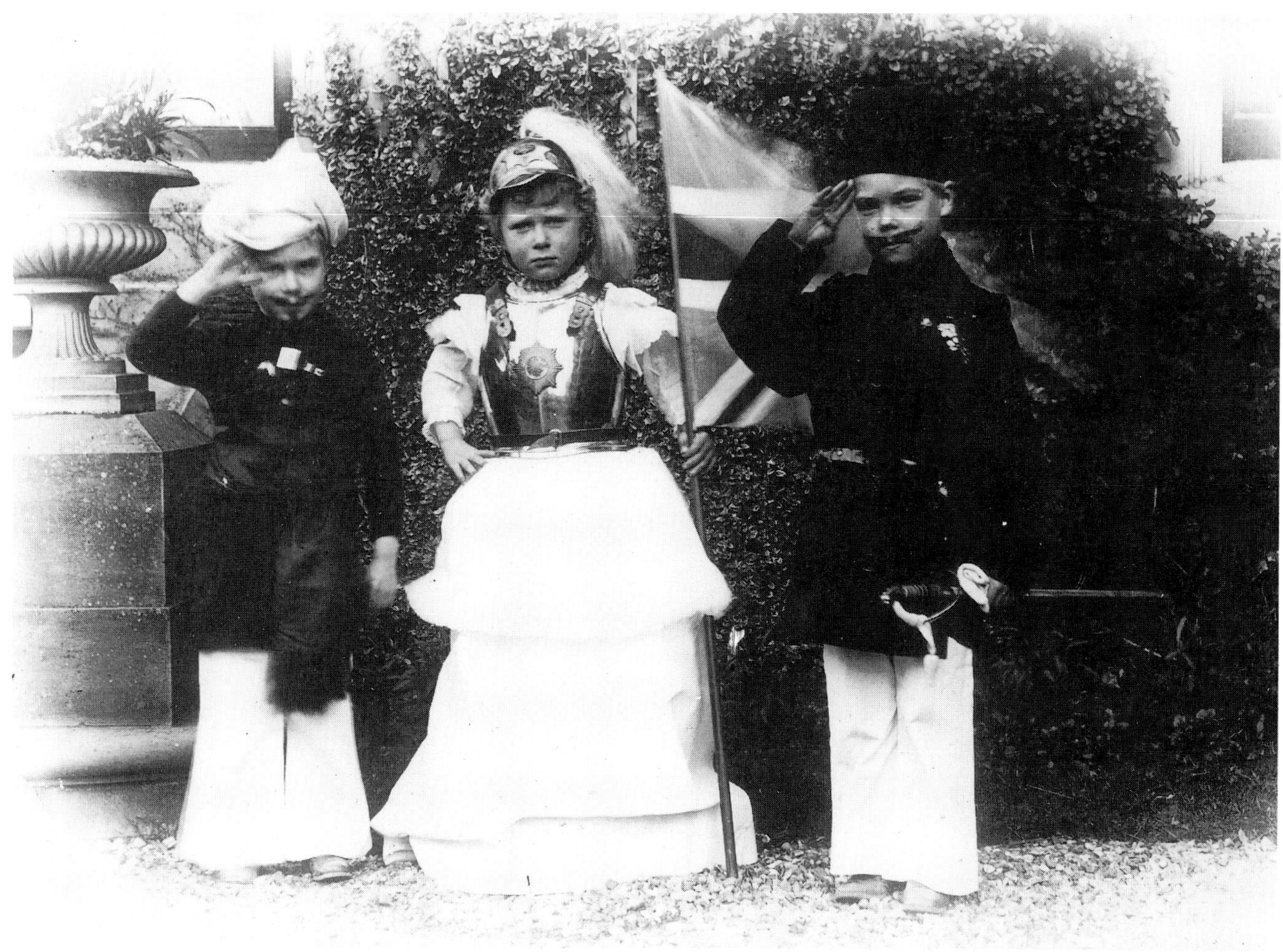

LEFT TO RIGHT: BERTIE, MARY AND DAVID IN FANCY-DRESS AT YORK COTTAGE, OCTOBER 1900

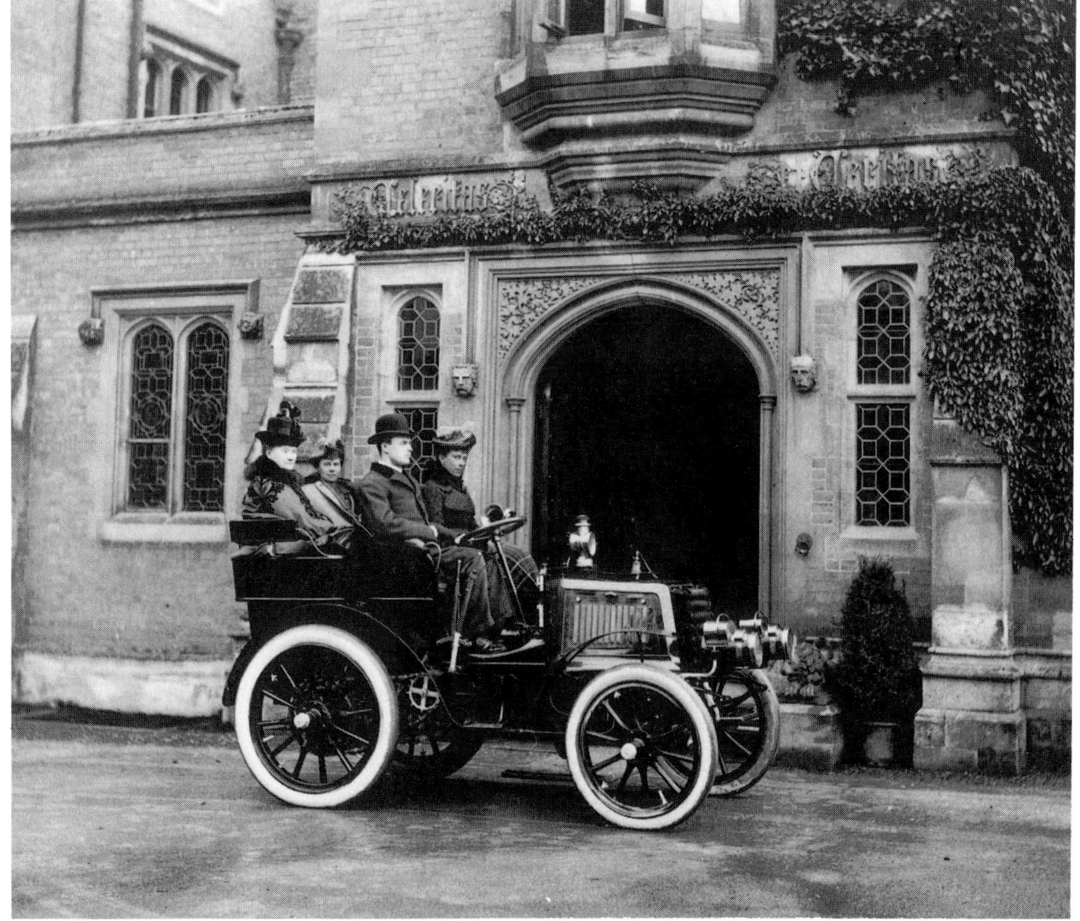

THE DUCHESS OF YORK TAKING HER FIRST DRIVE IN A MOTOR CAR AT THE HENDRE, OCTOBER 1900. SHE IS SEATED NEXT TO THE HON. C. S. ROLLS

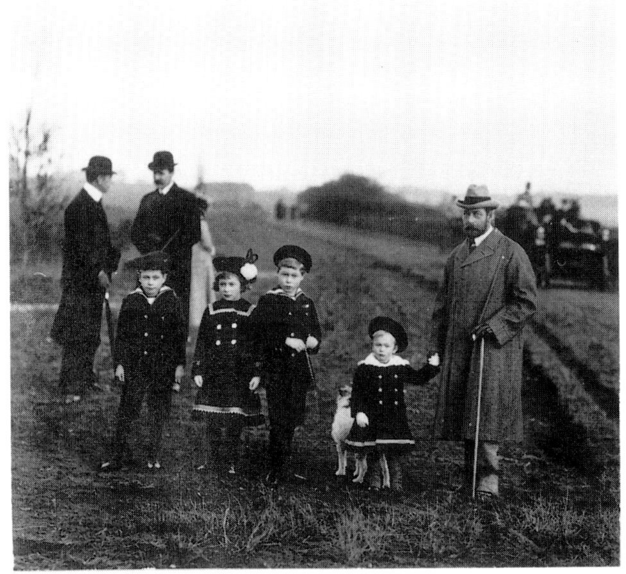

Bertie . Mary . David . Harry . G—

Capt. A. Campbell — Lt. E. Hansell

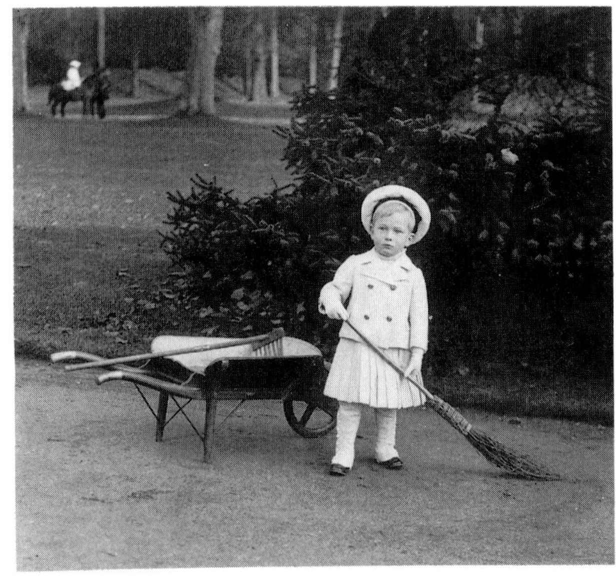

Harry

York Cottage
1902

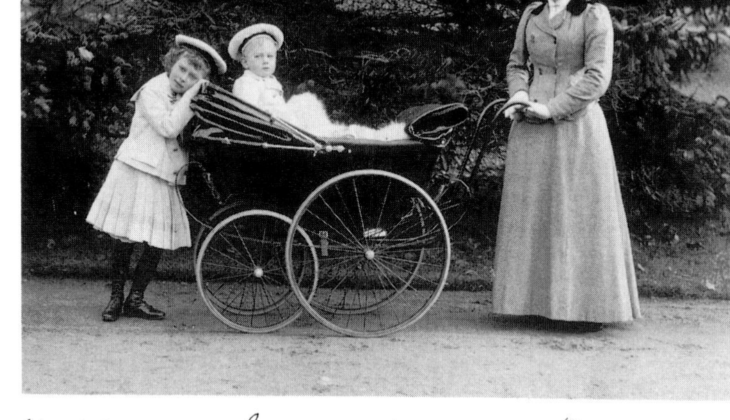

Bertie .   David .

Stratton

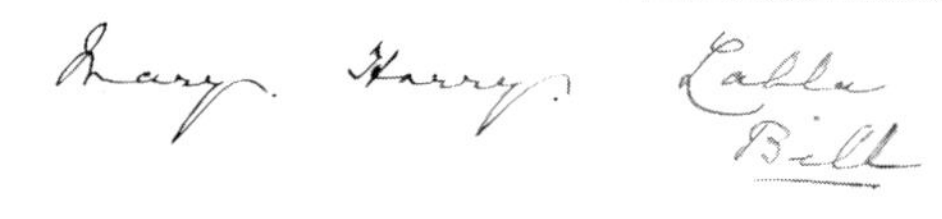

Mary . Harry . Lalla
Bill

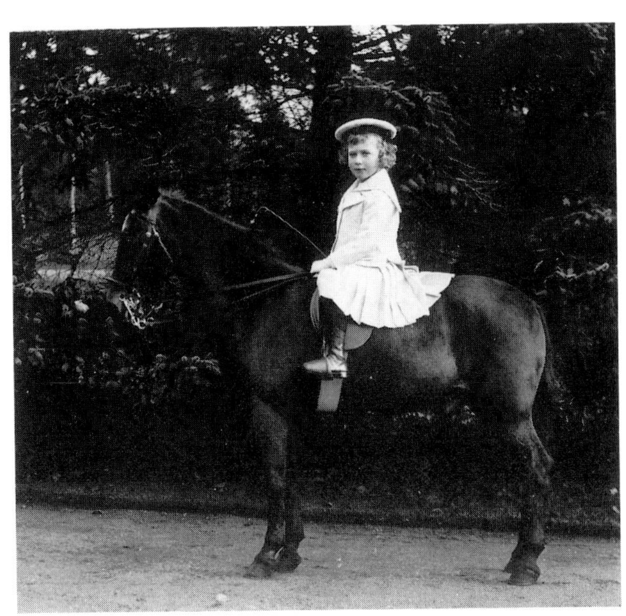

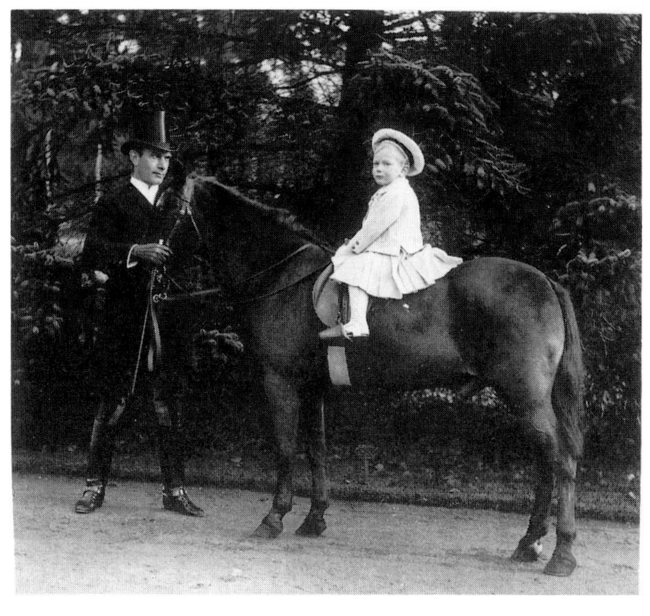

The children

1903

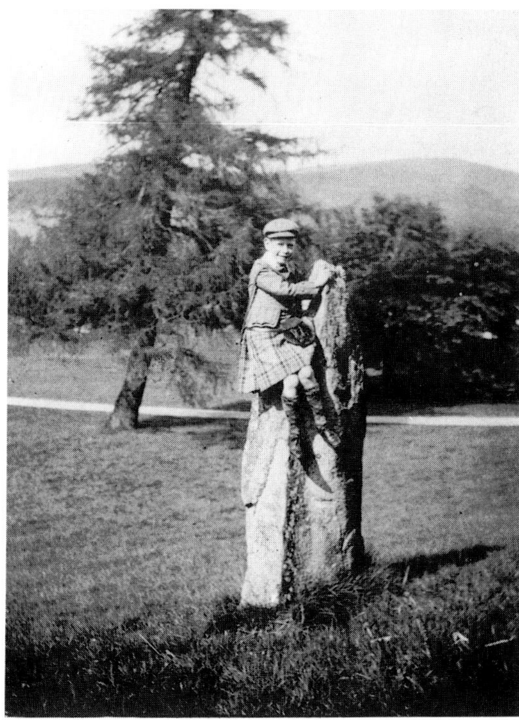

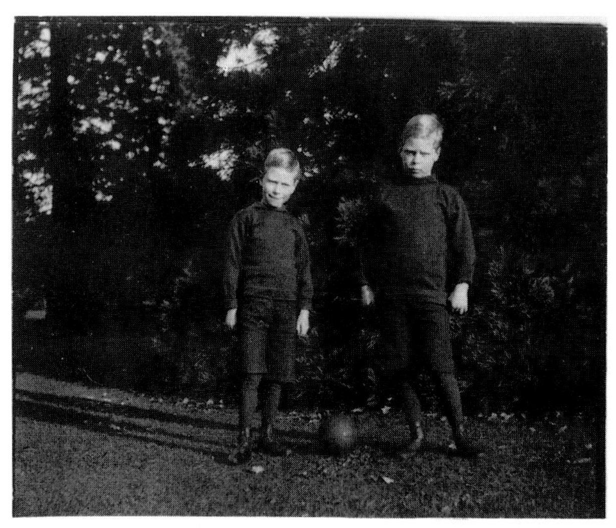

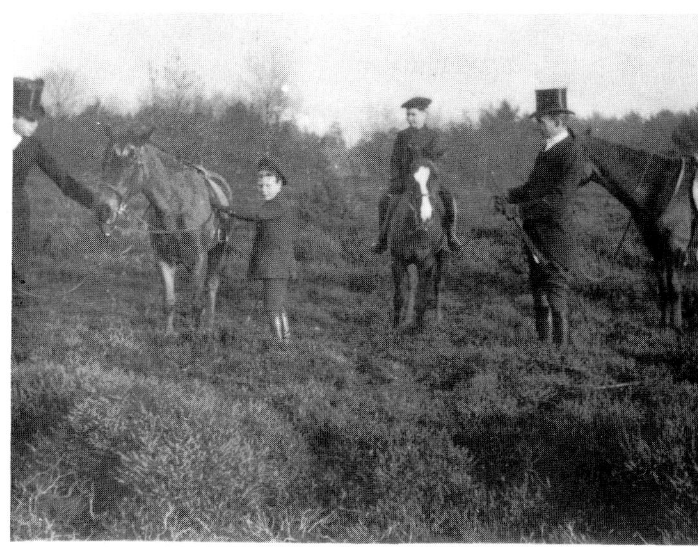

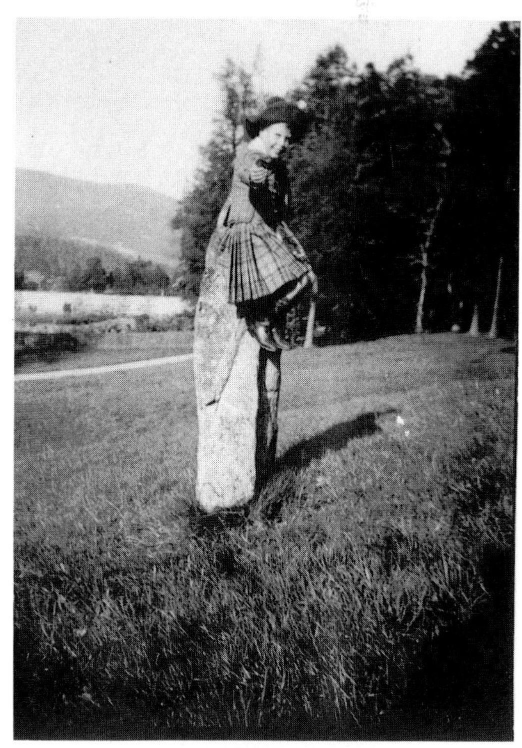

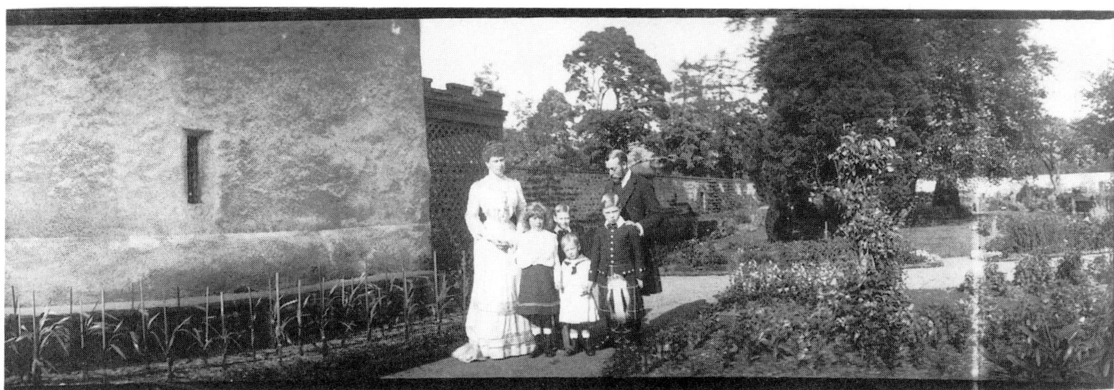

THE PRINCE AND PRINCESS
OF WALES WITH DAVID,
BERTIE, MARY AND HARRY
AT ABERGELDIE CASTLE,
1903

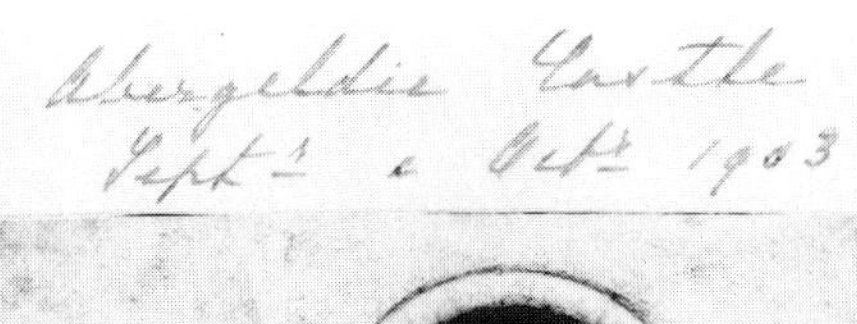

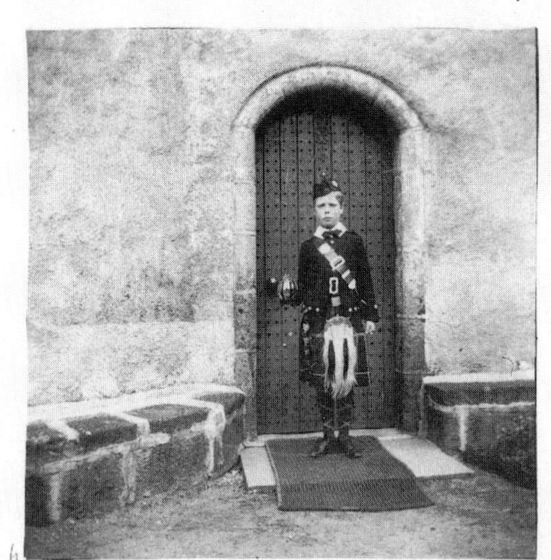

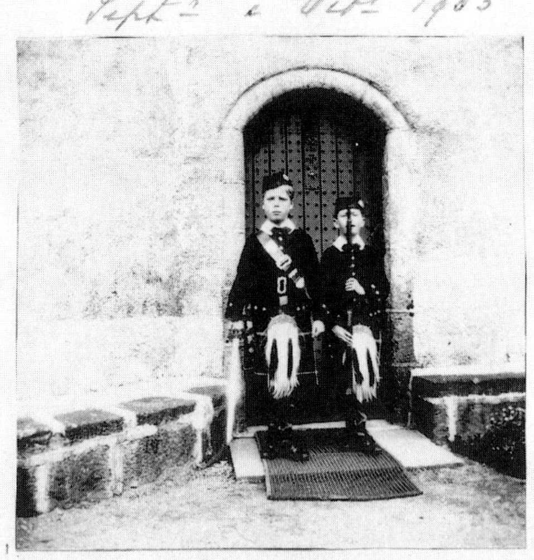

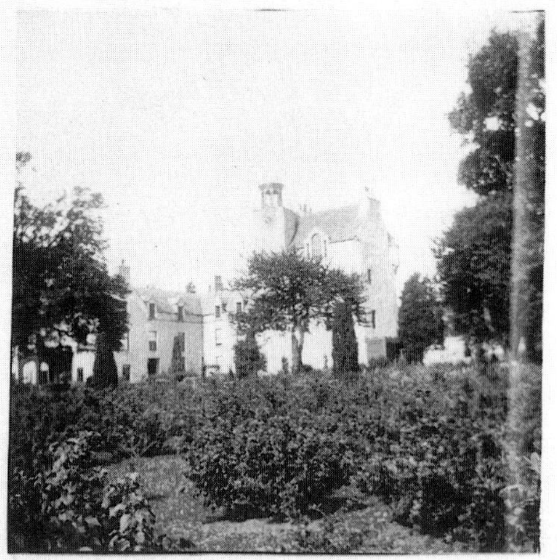

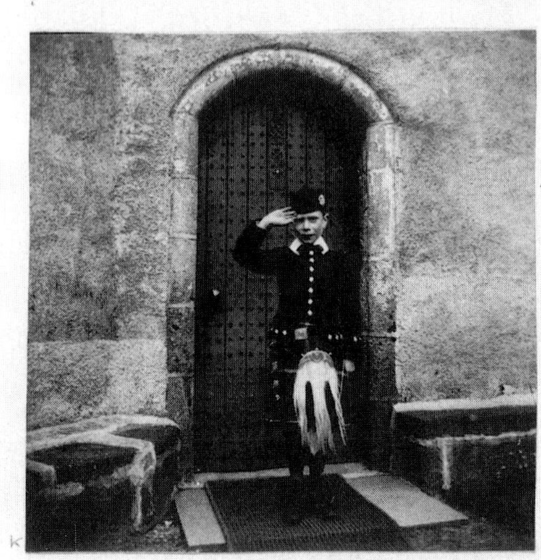

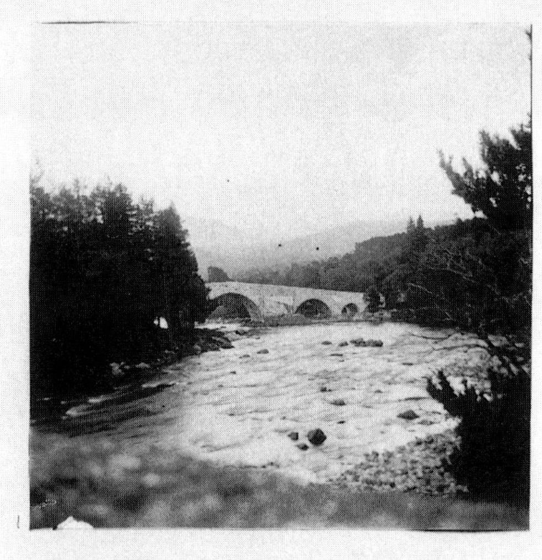

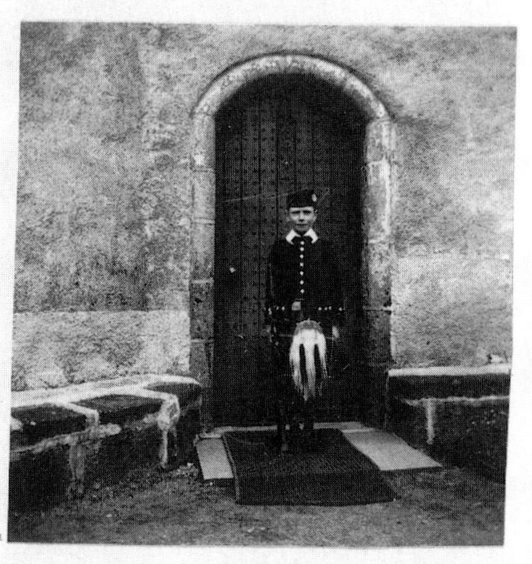

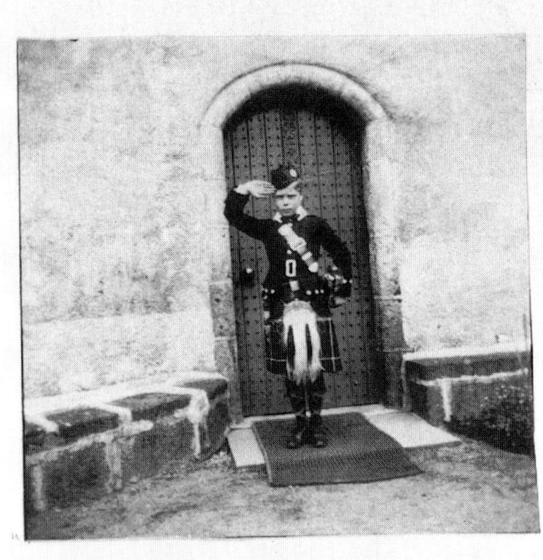

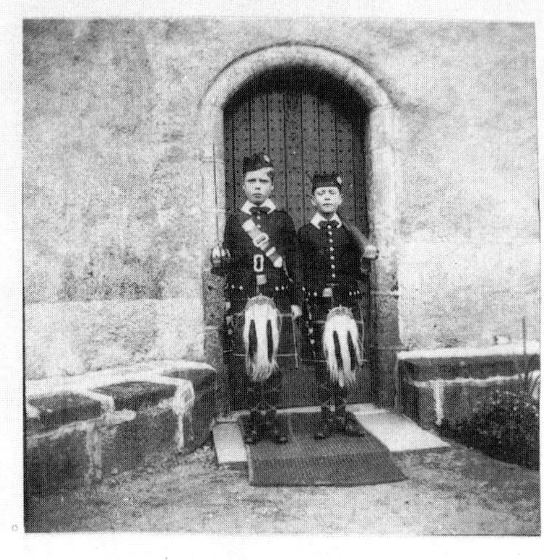

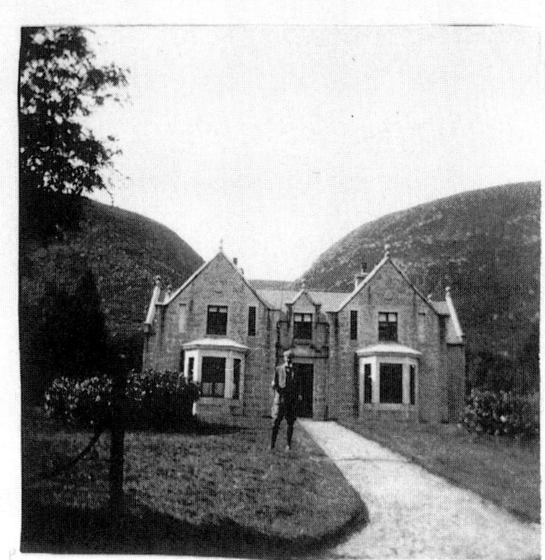

DAVID WITH BERTIE AT ABERGELDIE,
AUTUMN 1903

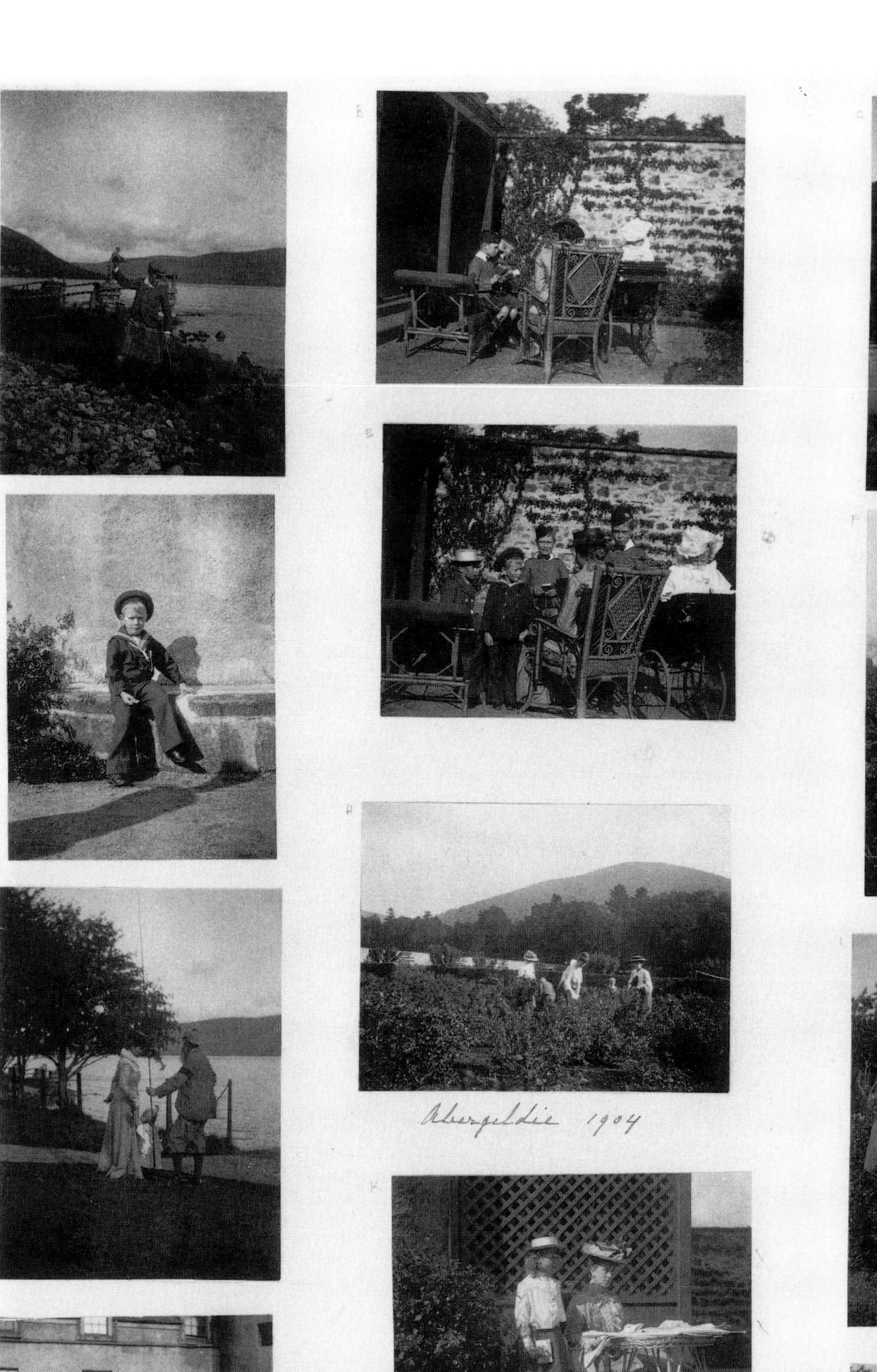

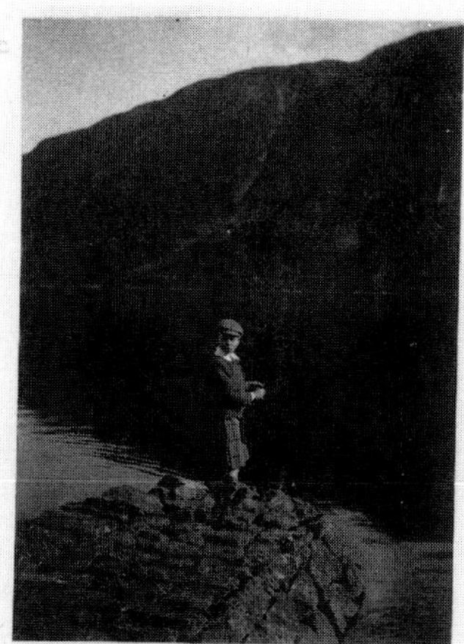

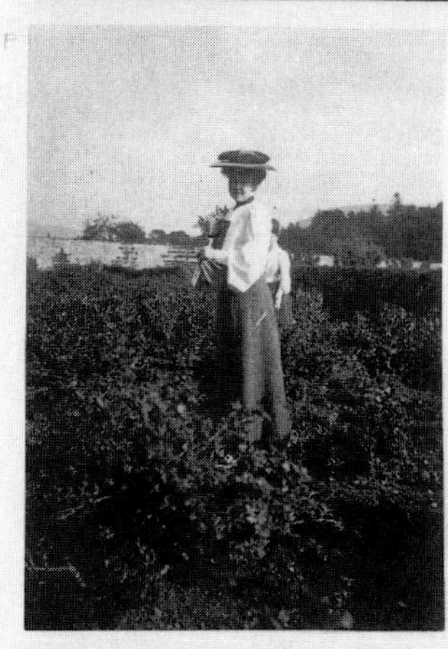

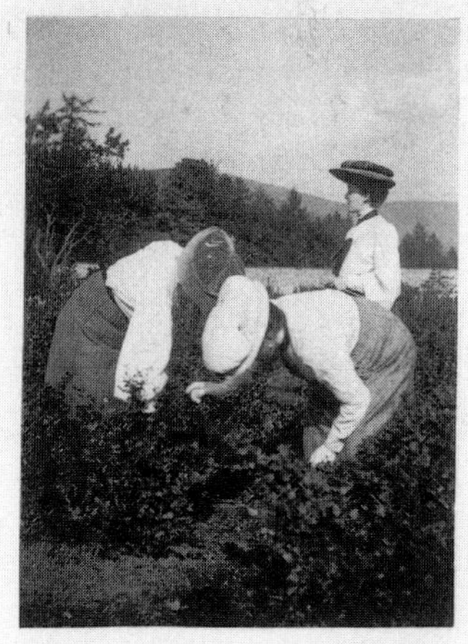

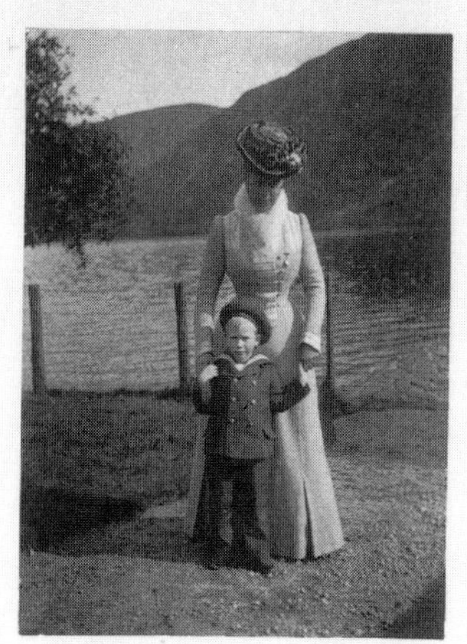

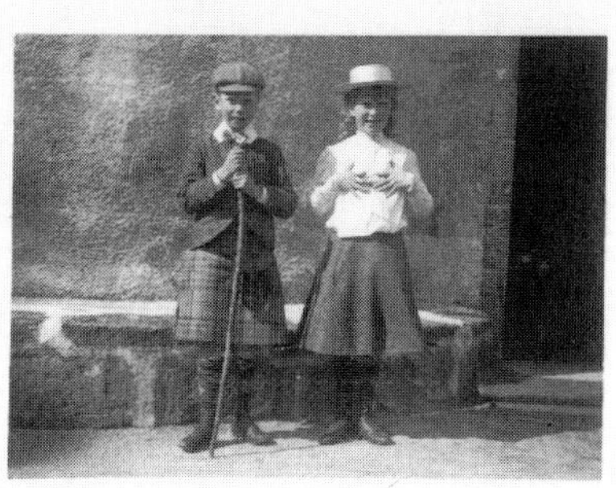

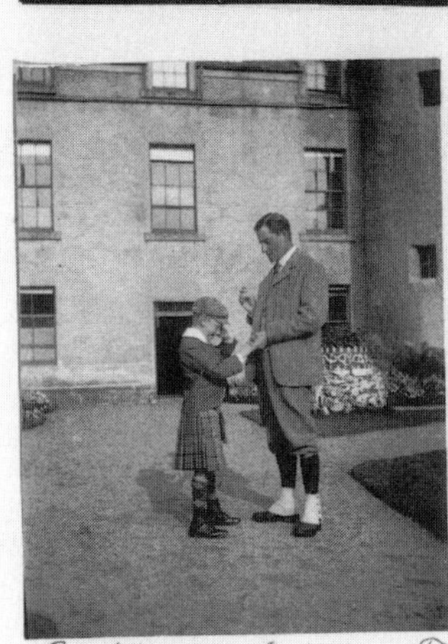

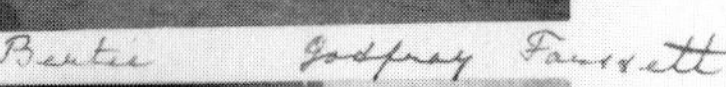

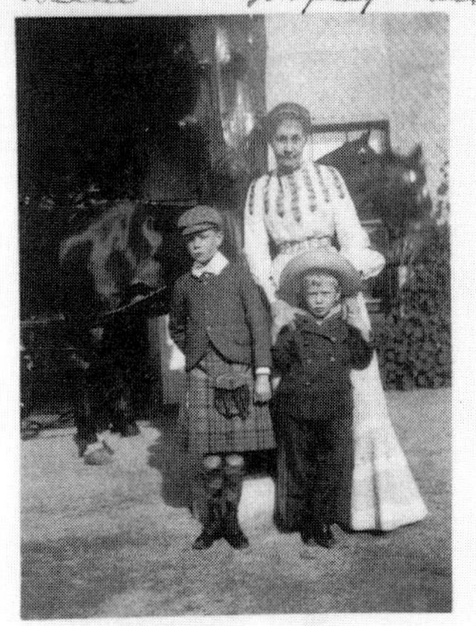

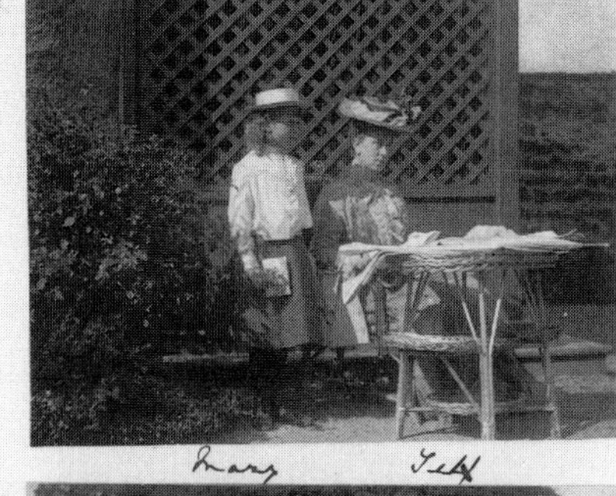

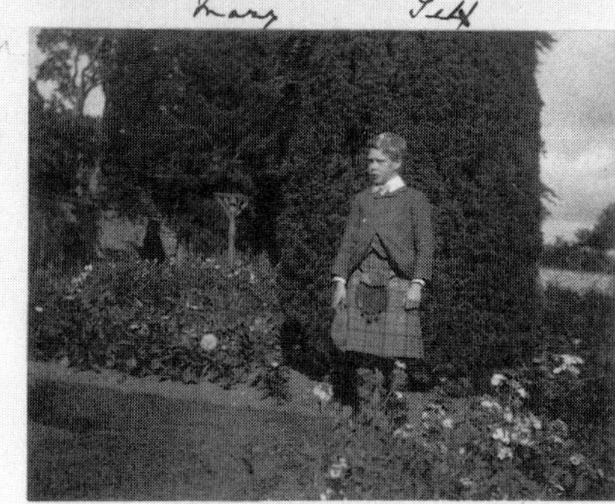

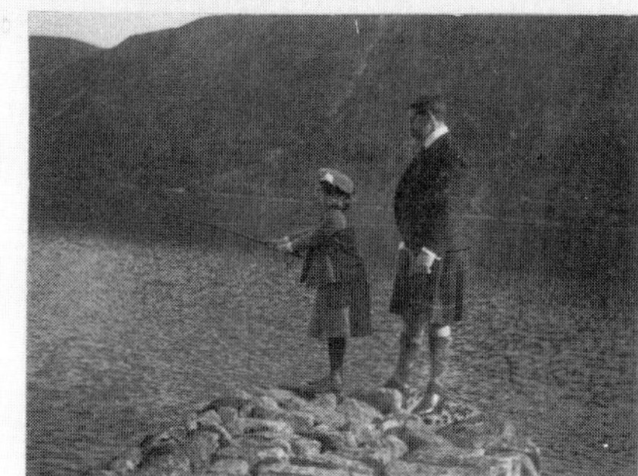

THE PRINCESS OF WALES WITH HER CHILDREN AT ABERGELDIE, 1904. (THE BABY, 'GEORGIE', WAS BORN IN 1902)

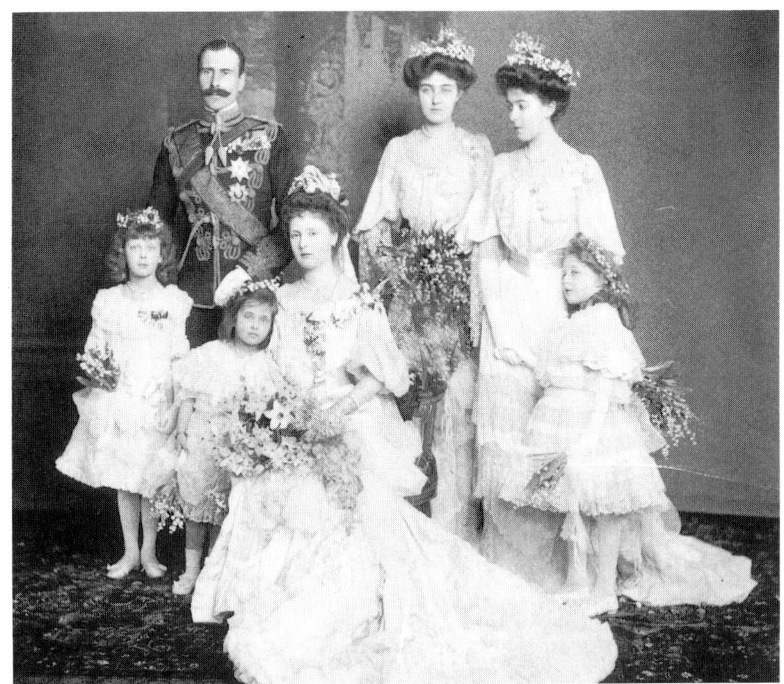

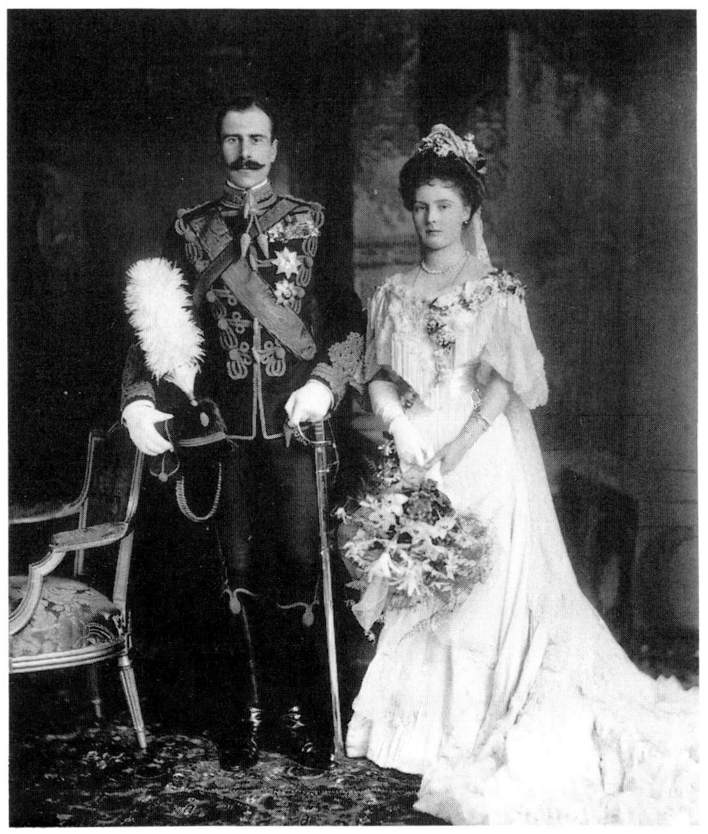

PRINCE ALEXANDER (ALGE) OF TECK'S
WEDDING TO PRINCESS ALICE OF
ALBANY, 10 FEBRUARY 1904. THE
BRIDESMAIDS INCLUDE PRINCESS MARY
OF WALES (STANDING LEFT) AND THE
PRINCESSES MARGARET AND PATRICIA OF
CONNAUGHT (RIGHT)

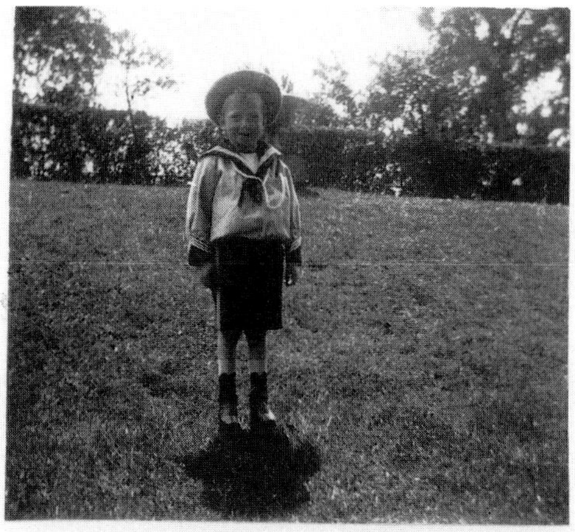

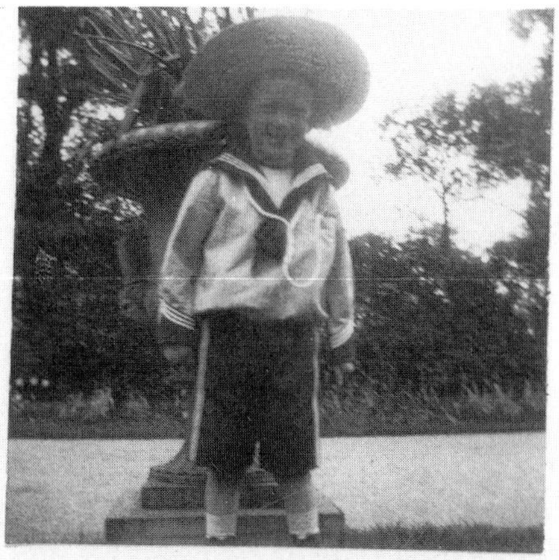

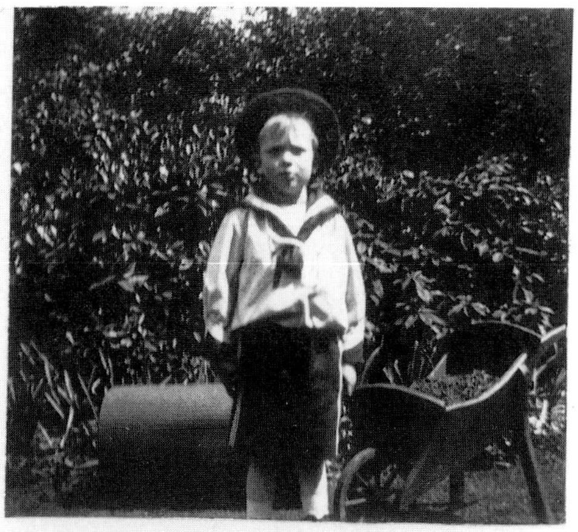

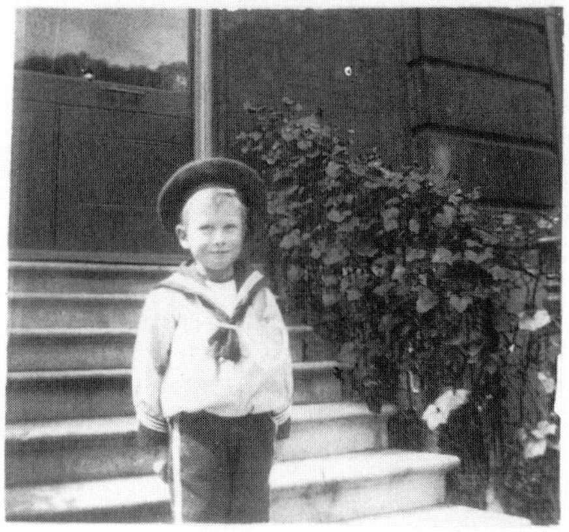

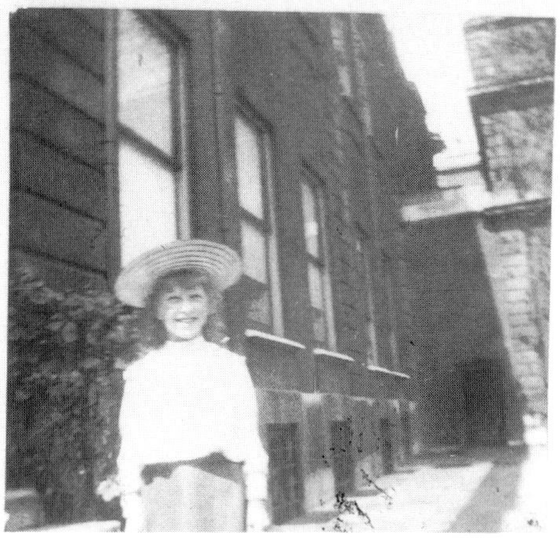

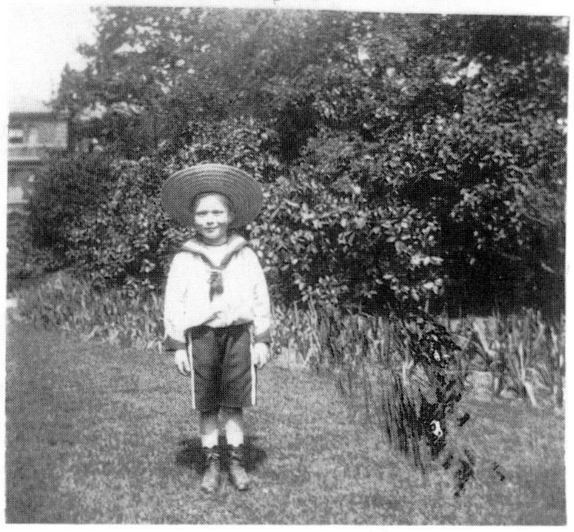

HARRY, GEORGIE AND MARY IN THE GARDENS
OF MARLBOROUGH HOUSE, 1905

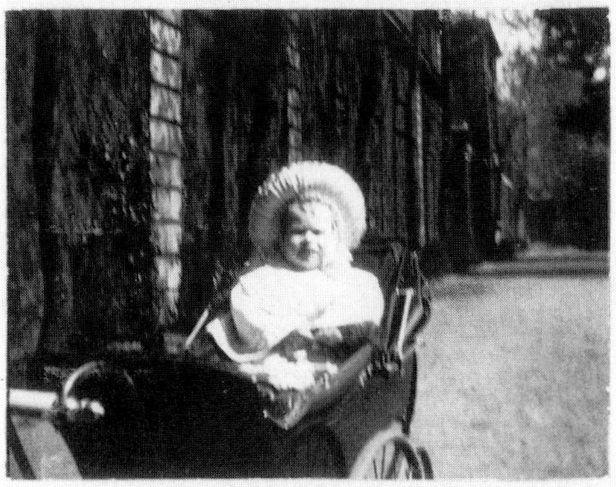

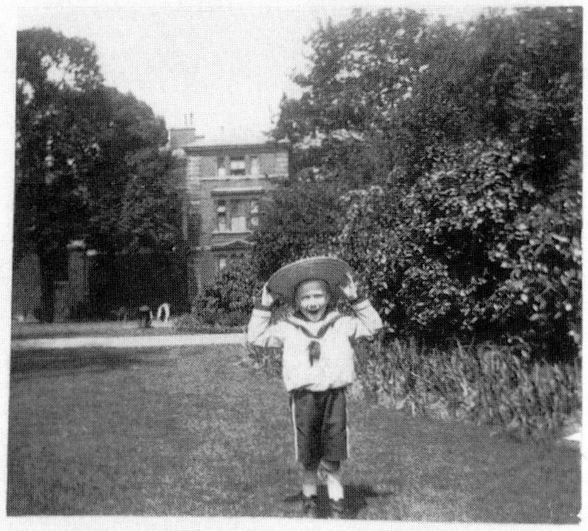

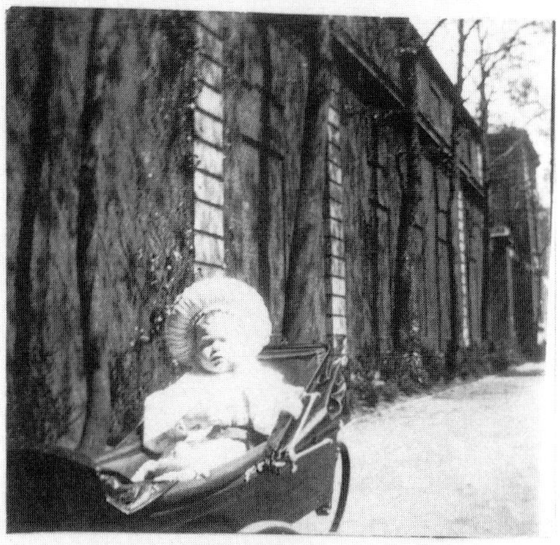

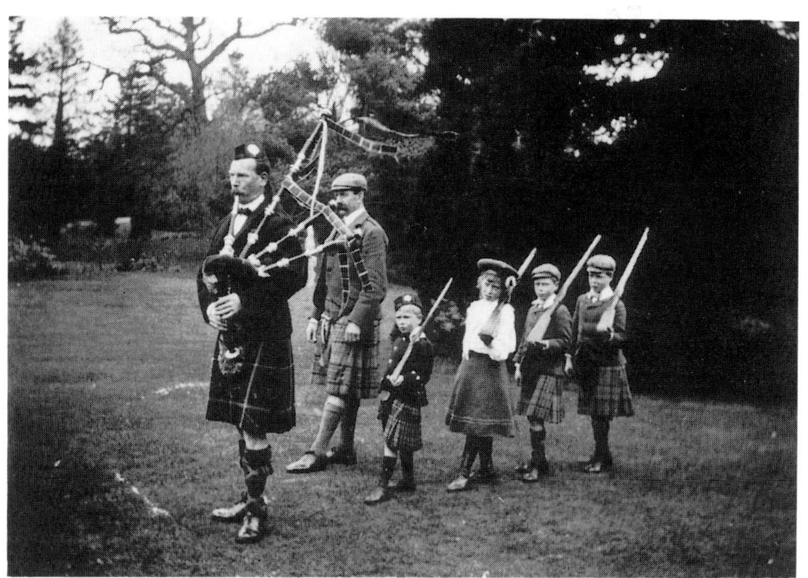

HARRY, MARY, BERTIE AND DAVID PLAYING
SOLDIERS WITH THE PIPER AT SANDRINGHAM,
APRIL 1905

Cowes

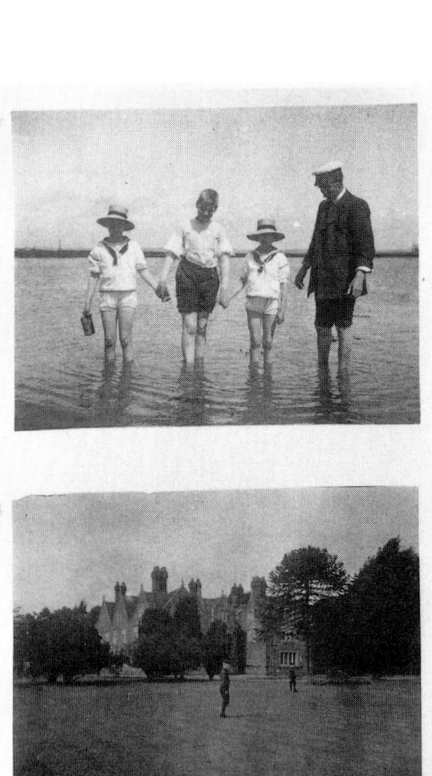

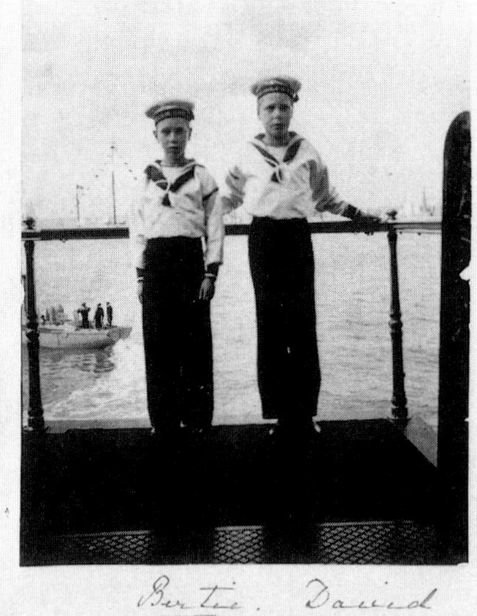

Bertie. David
Osborne
1905

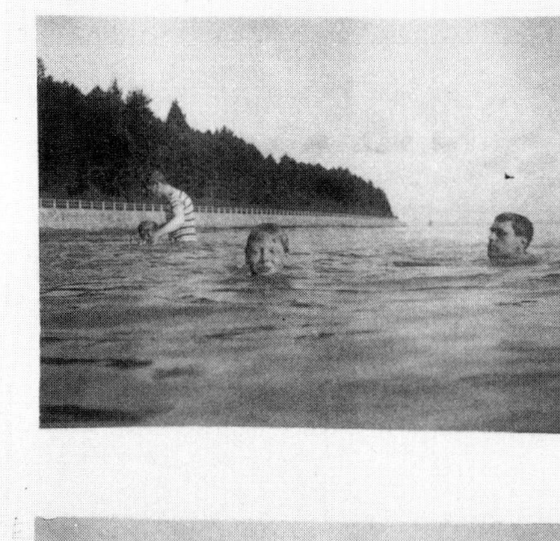

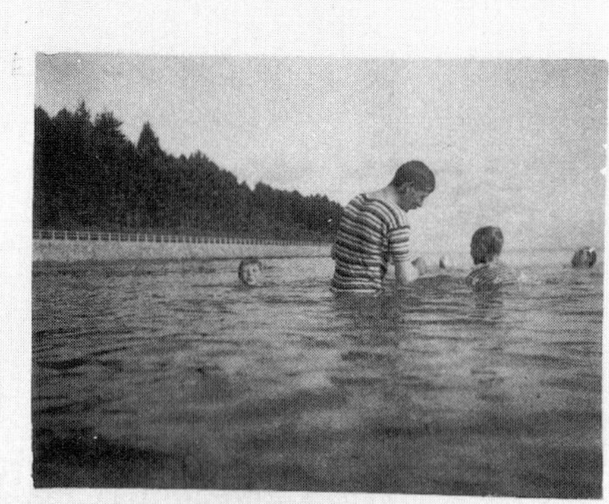

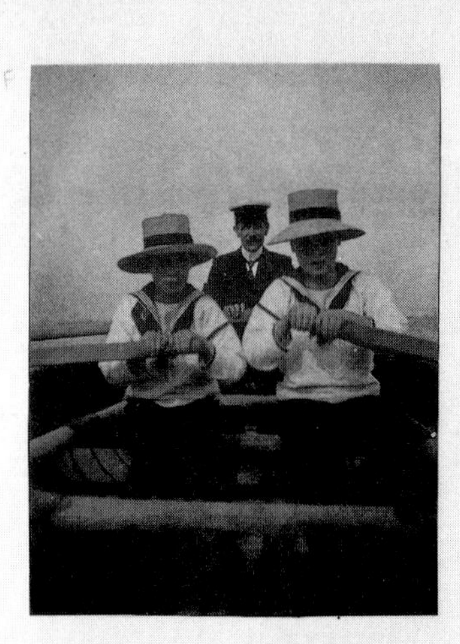

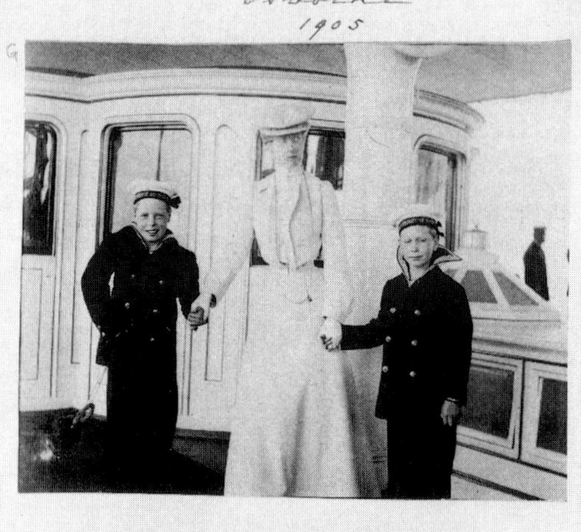

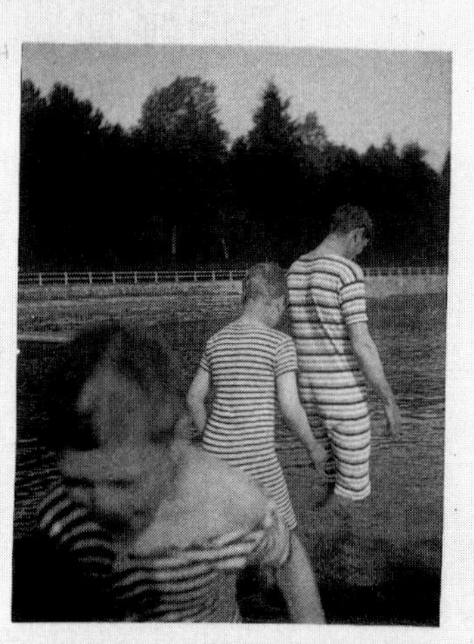

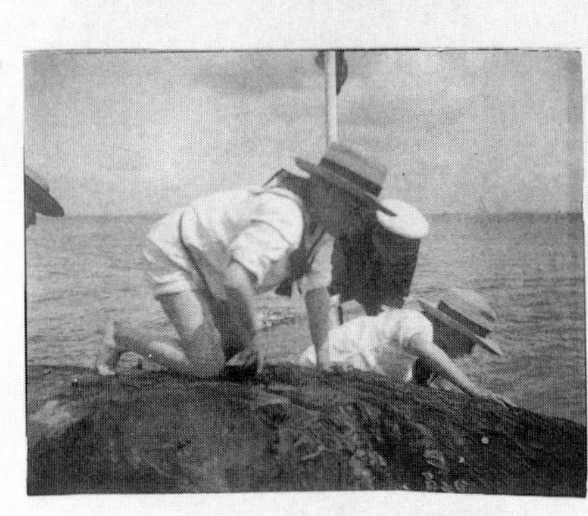

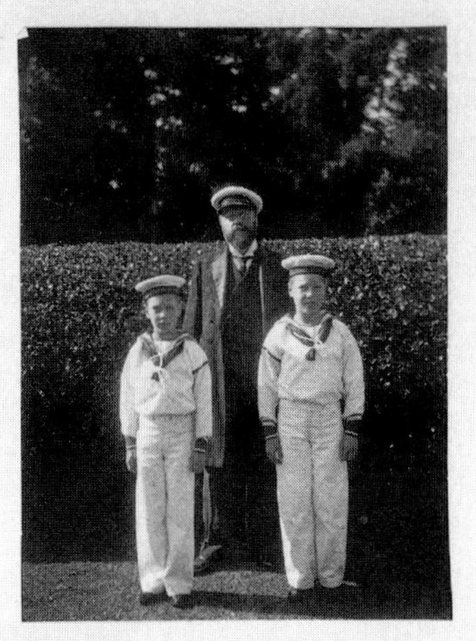

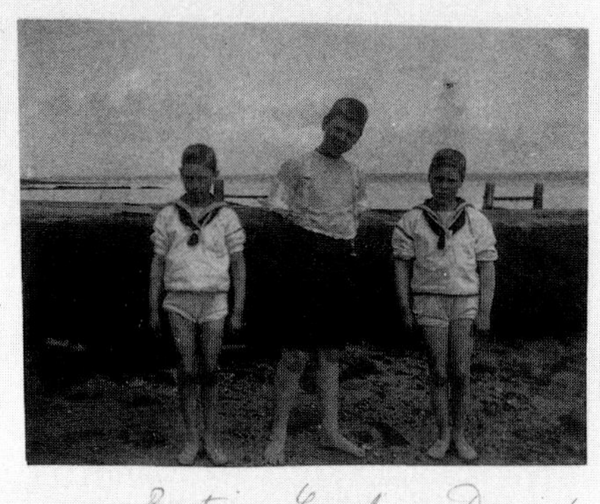

Bertie Carol David

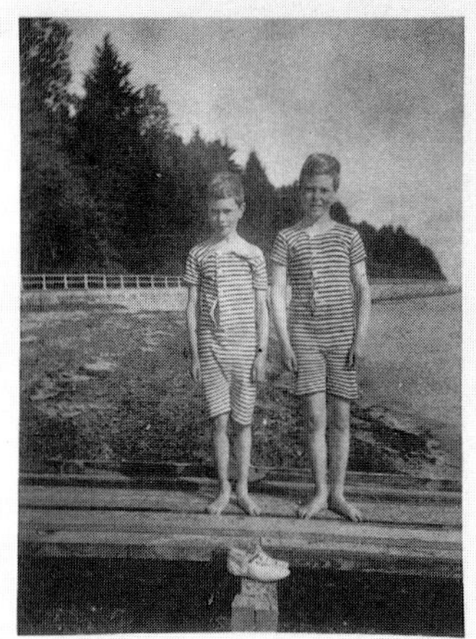

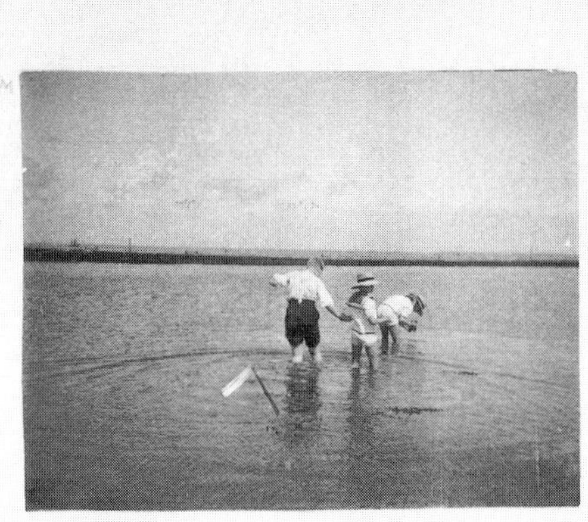

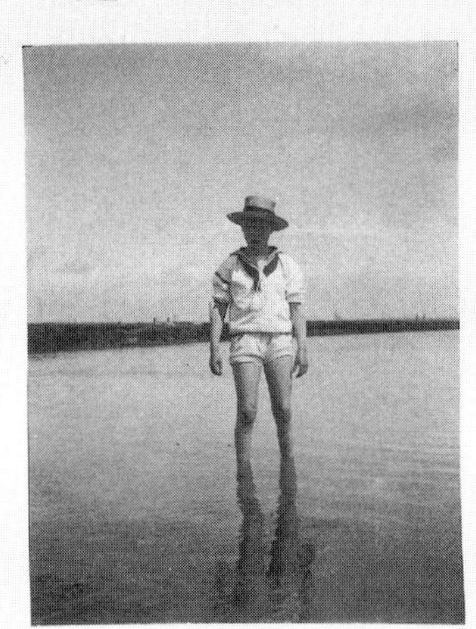

(*OPPOSITE*) SNAPSHOTS OF
DAVID AND BERTIE AT
OSBORNE IN 1905. IN ONE
OF THE PHOTOGRAPHS
THEY ARE SEEN WITH
THEIR AUNT TORIA,
PRINCESS VICTORIA, AND
IN OTHERS THE THIRD
TALLER BOY IS THEIR
COUSIN, CAROL OF
ROMANIA

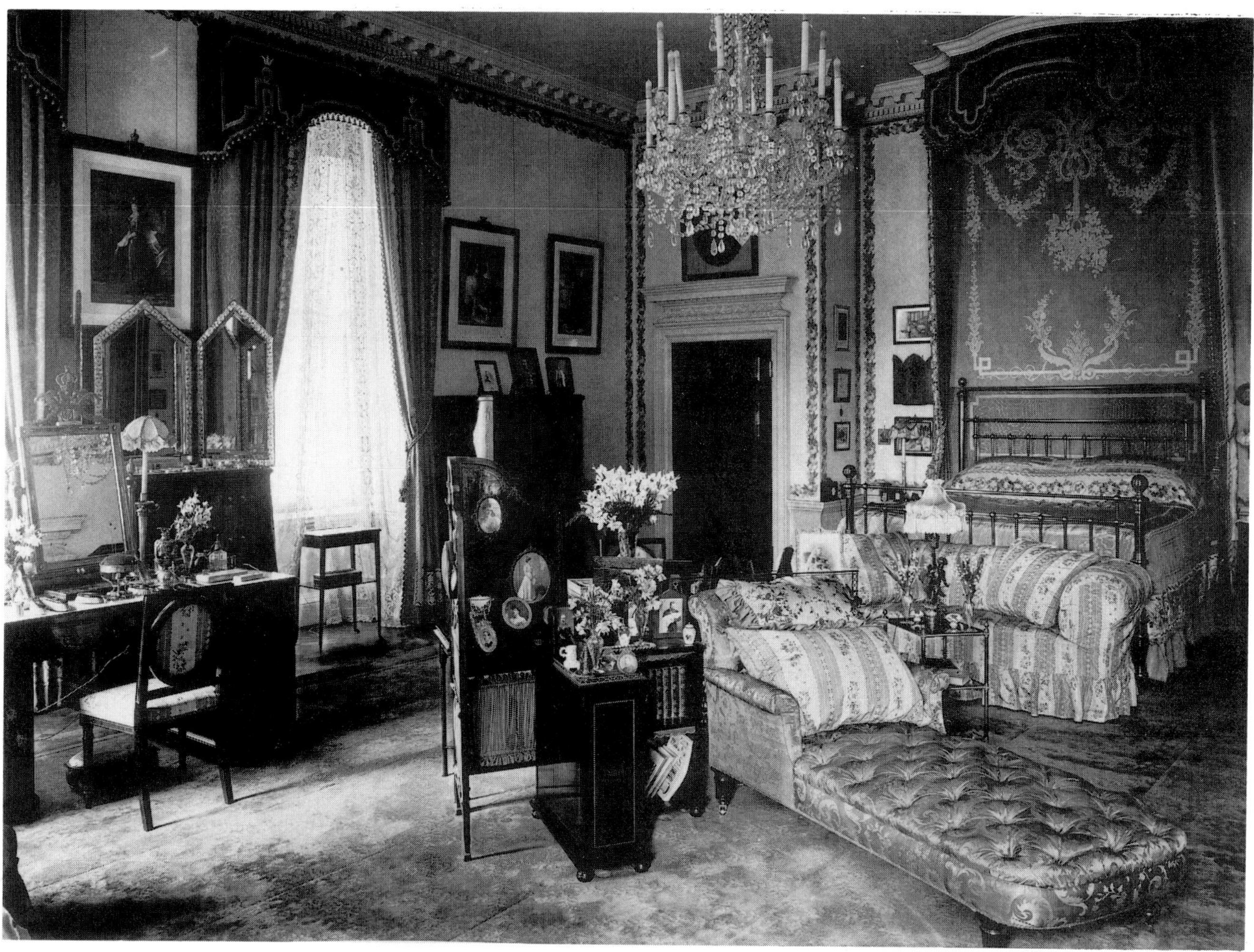

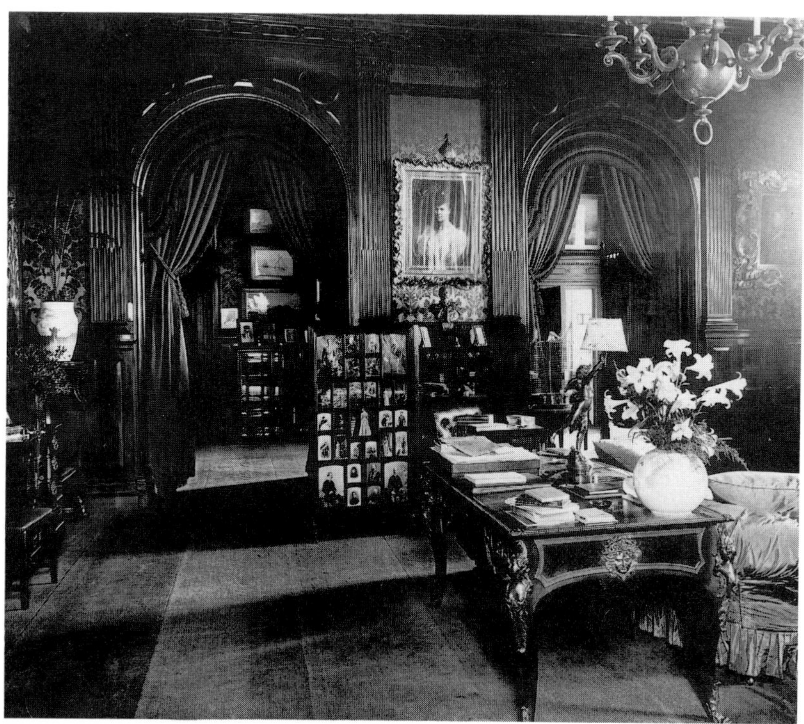

MARLBOROUGH HOUSE, 1905. THE
PRINCESS OF WALES'S BEDROOM
(ABOVE) AND THE PRINCE OF WALES'S
SITTING-ROOM (BELOW)

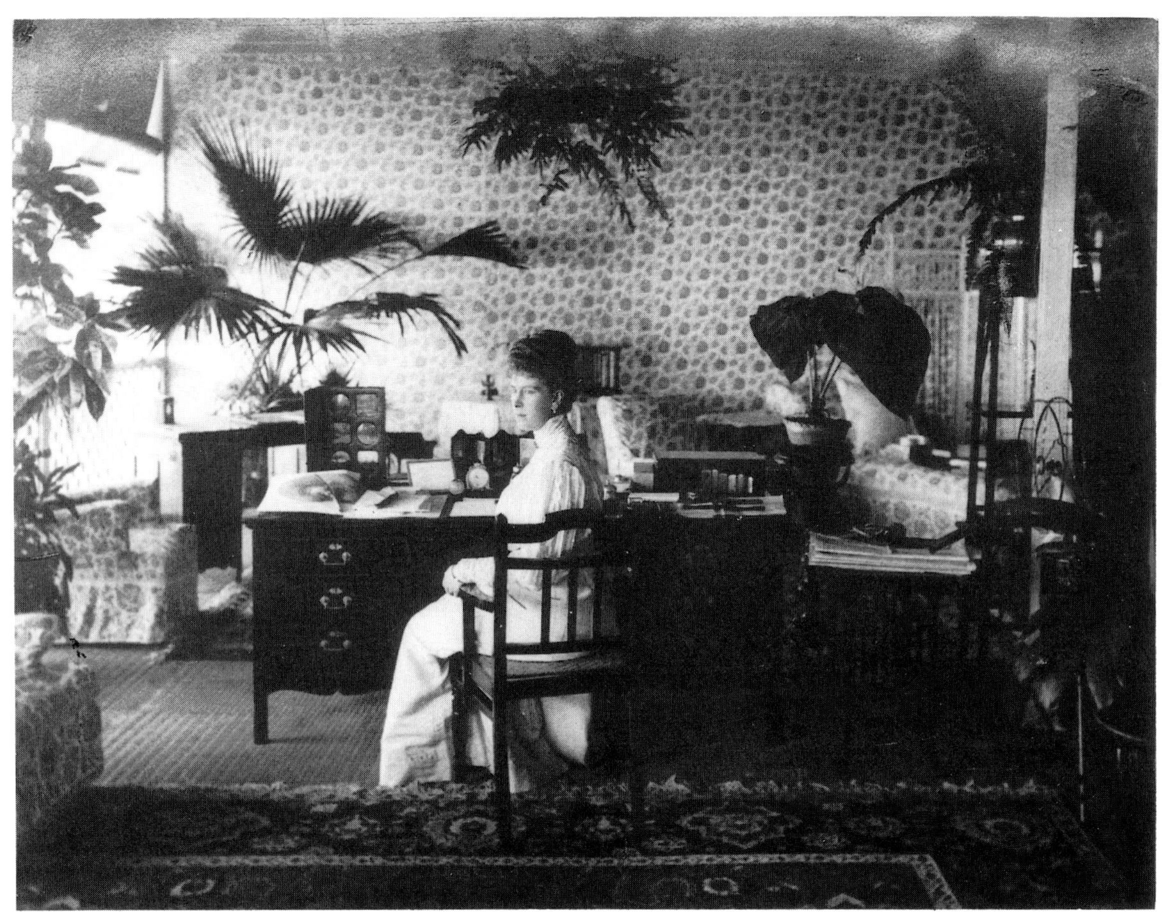

THE PRINCESS OF WALES
IN THE 'SITTING-ROOM' OF
HER TENT AT MALABAR
POINT, BOMBAY IN 1905

IN RESPLENDENT
HOWDAHS, THE PRINCE
AND PRINCESS OF WALES
ENTER GWALIOR DURING
THEIR TOUR OF INDIA,
DECEMBER 1905

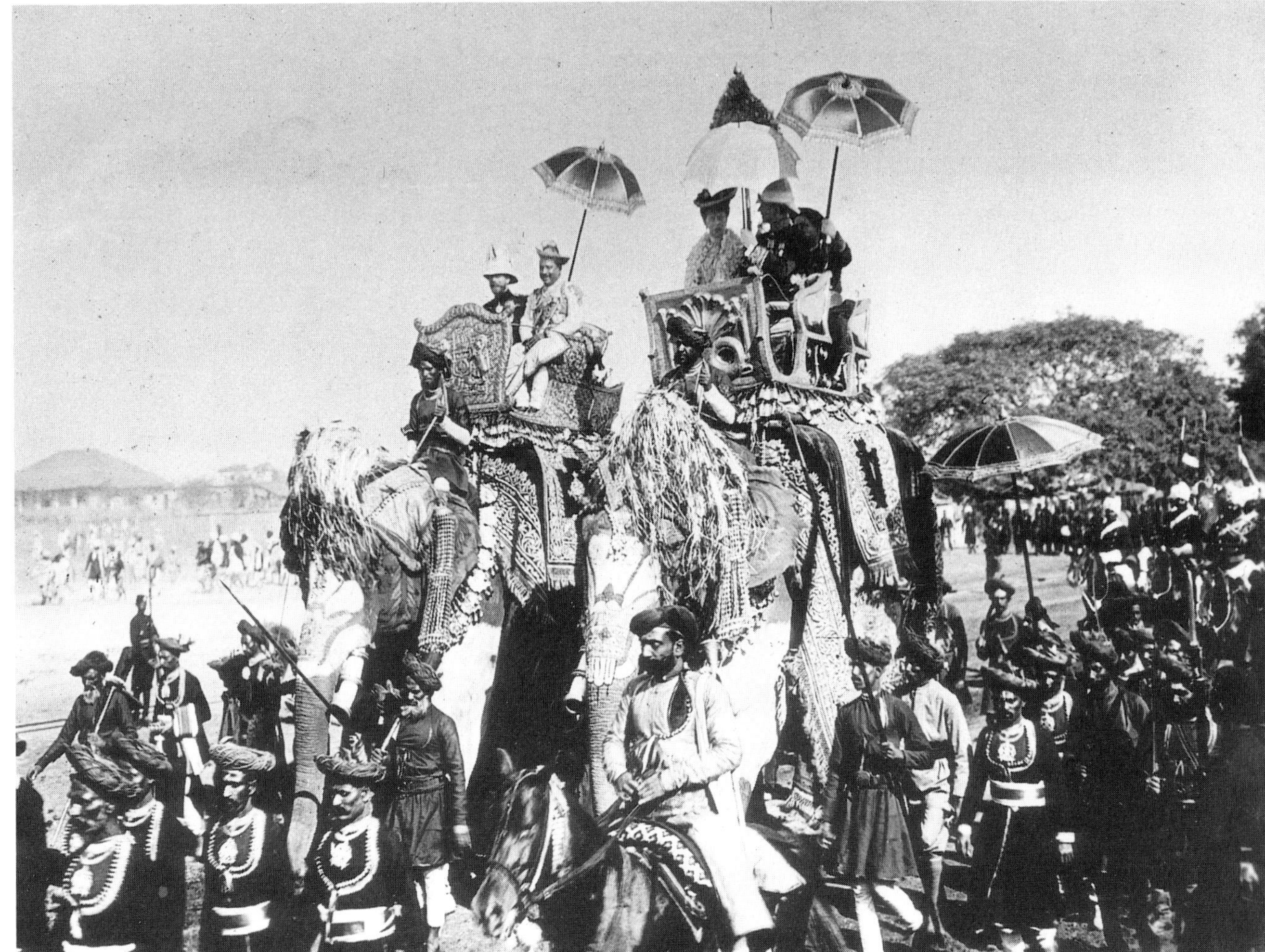

(*OPPOSITE*) THE PRINCE
AND PRINCESS OF WALES
AND MARY ABOARD THE
ROYAL YACHT *VICTORIA
AND ALBERT* IN NORWAY
FOR THE CORONATION OF
KING HAAKON AND QUEEN
MAUD, 1906

(*OVERLEAF*) THE WALES
FAMILY RELAXING AT
FROGMORE. BOTTOM
RIGHT: THE PRINCESS OF
WALES WITH DAVID AND
BERTIE AT ALDERSHOT

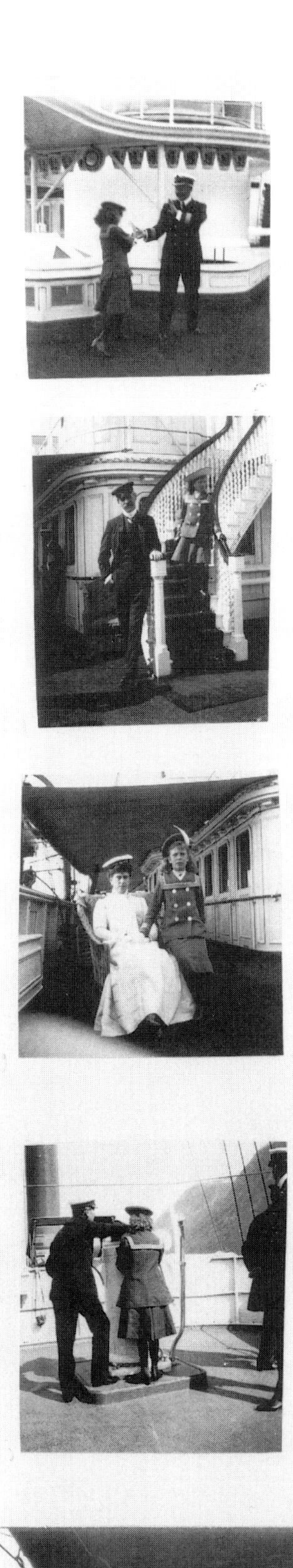

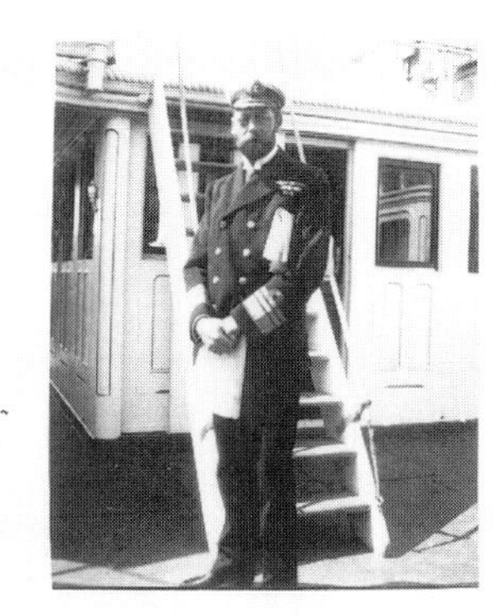

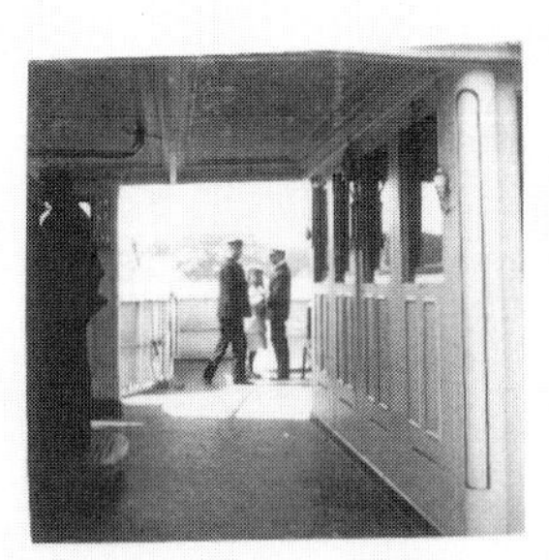

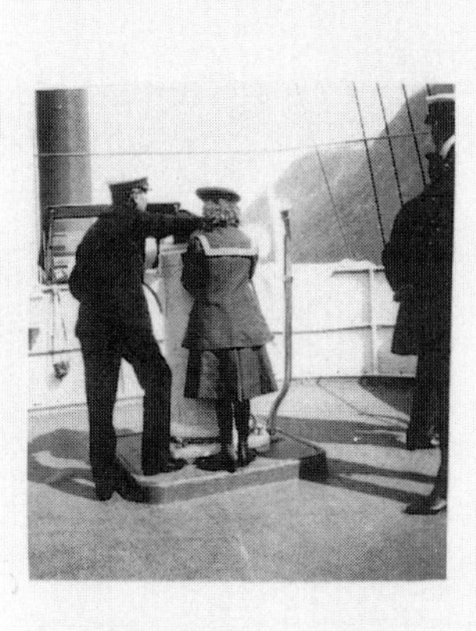

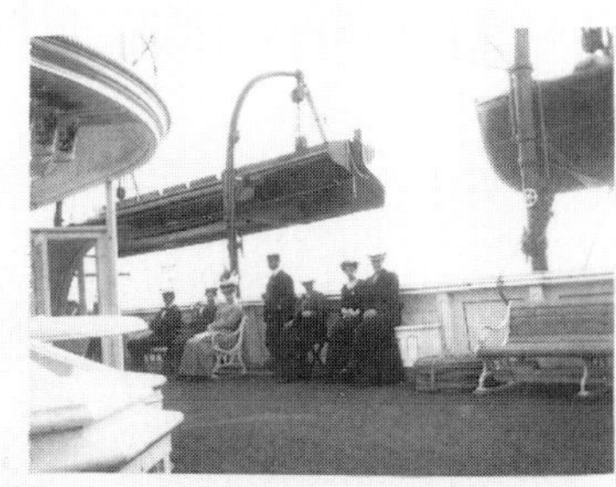

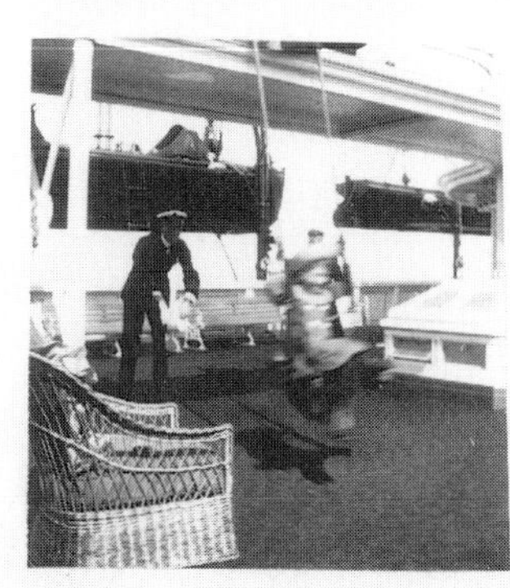

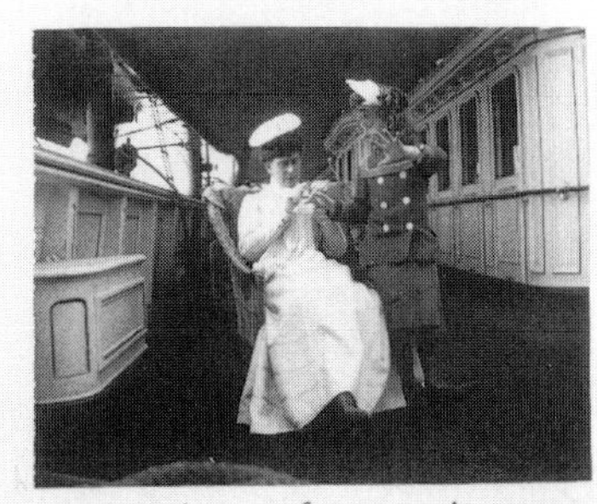

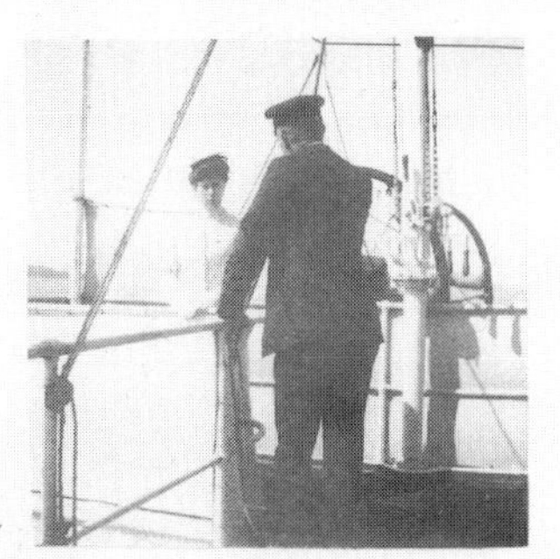

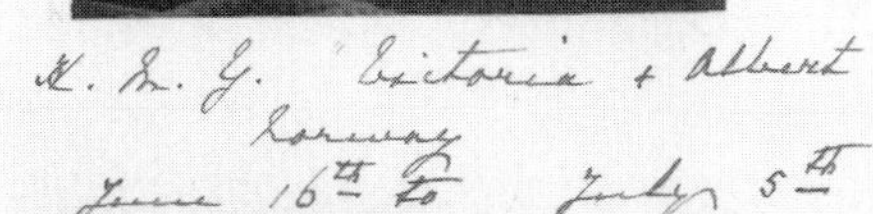

H. M. Y. "Victoria & Albert"
Norway
June 16th to   July 5th

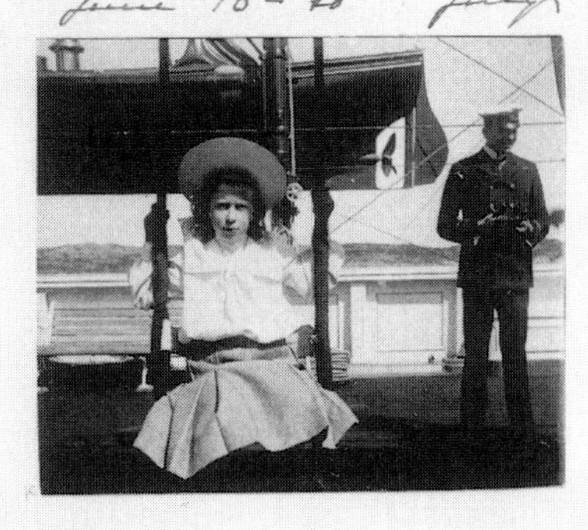

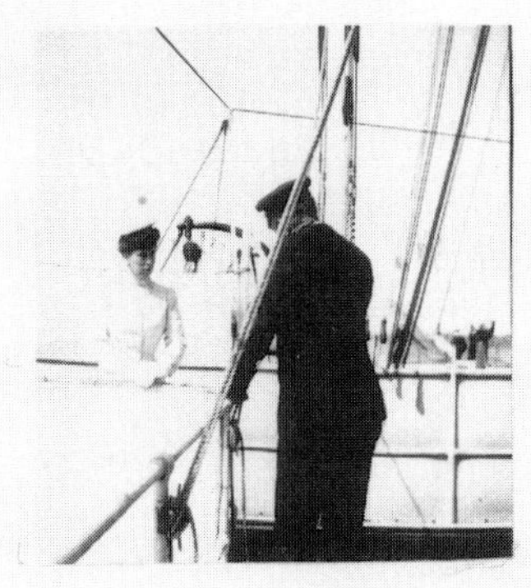

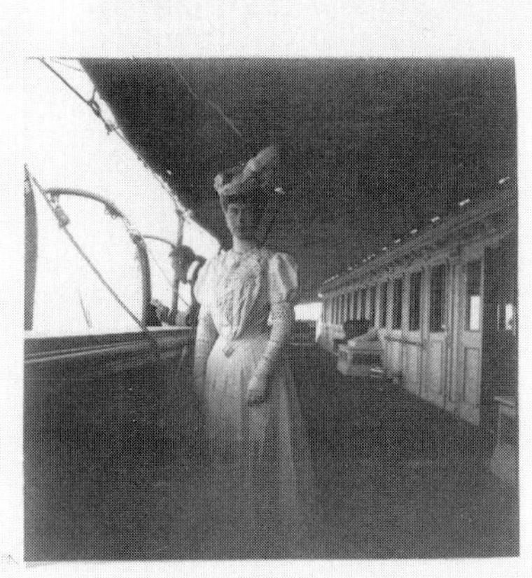

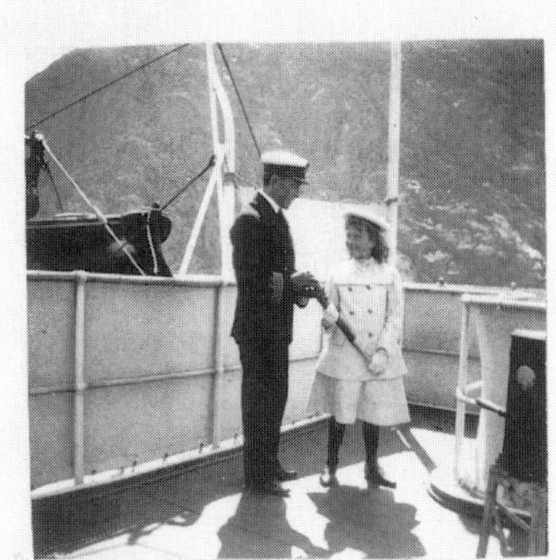

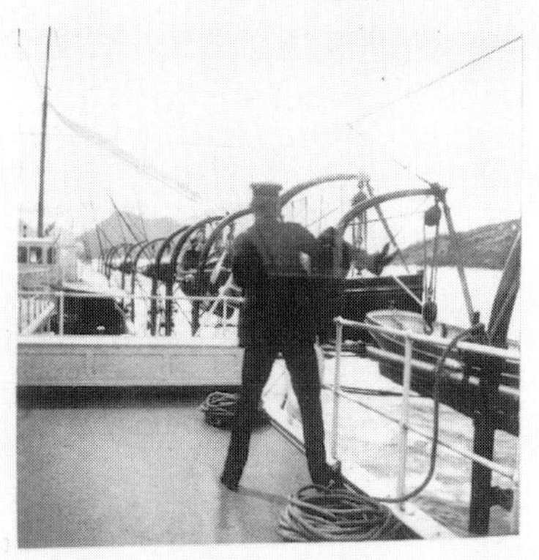

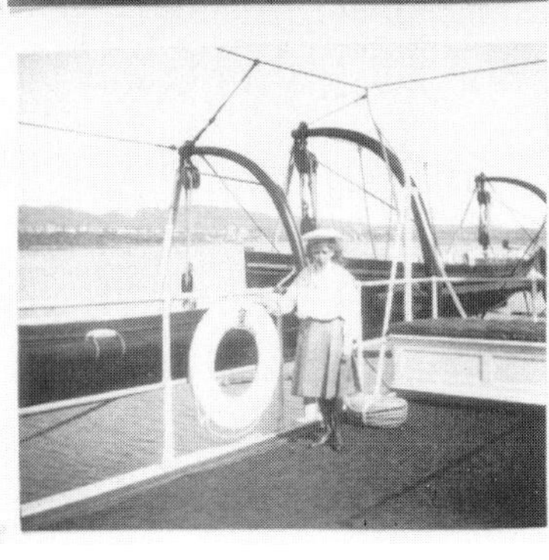

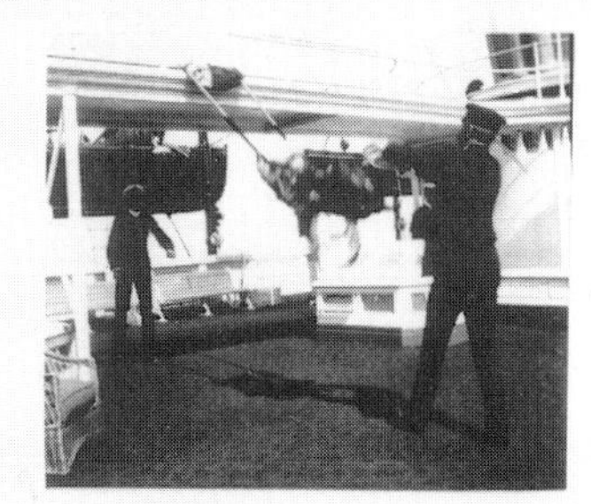

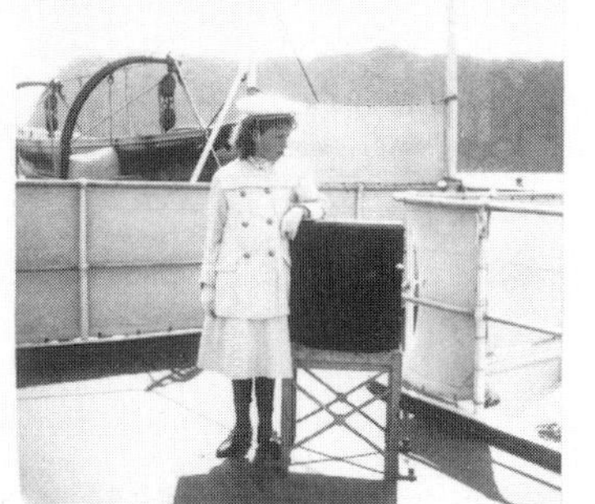

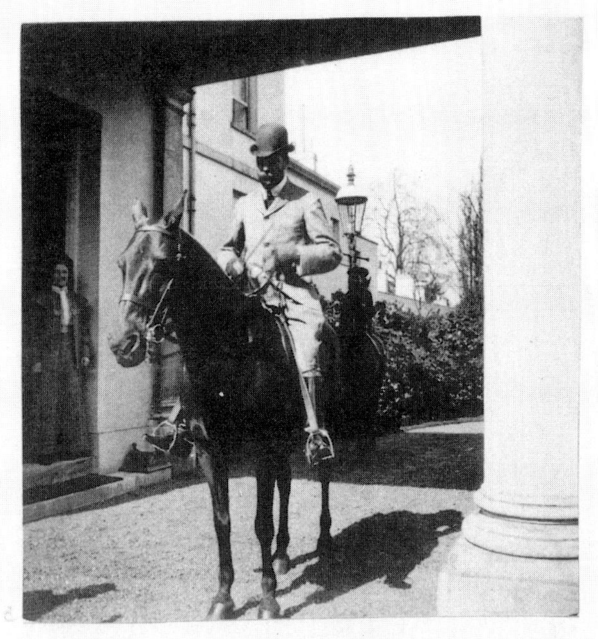

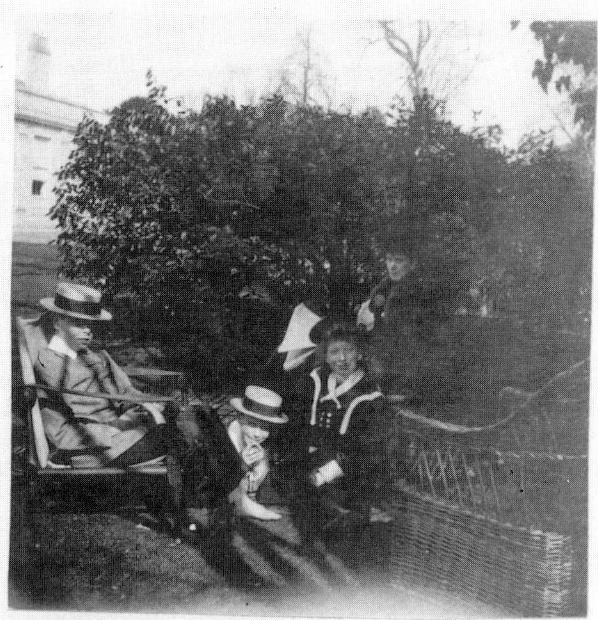

G.

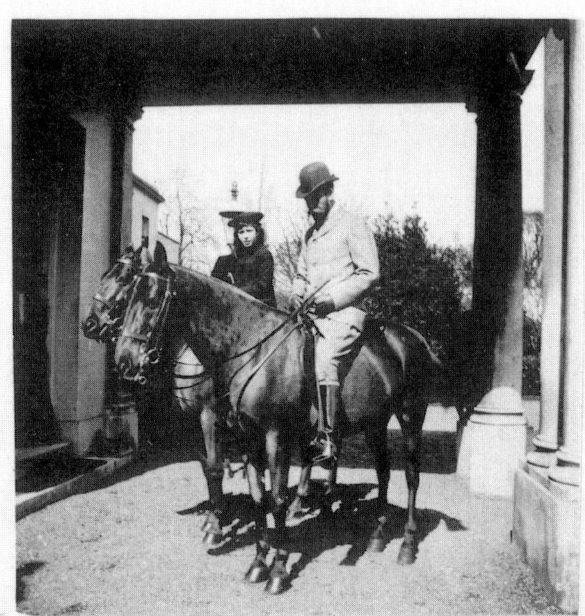

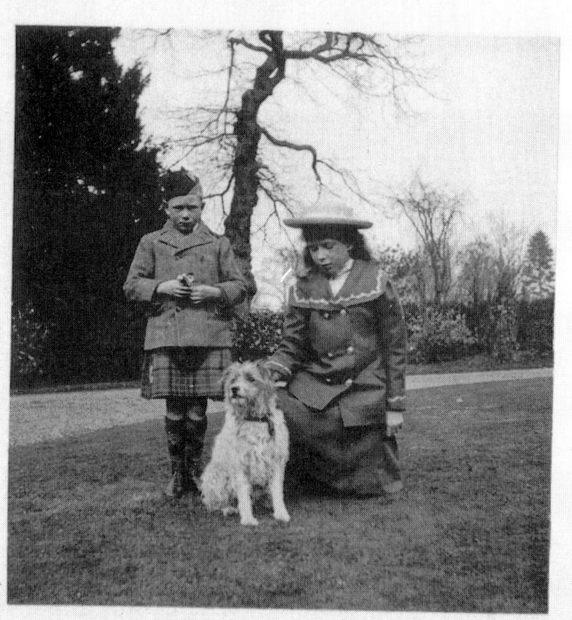

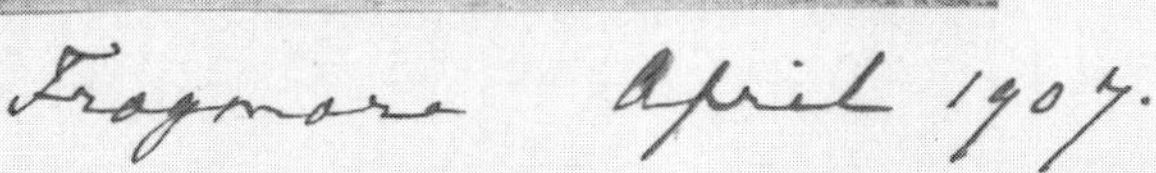

Frogmore April 1907.

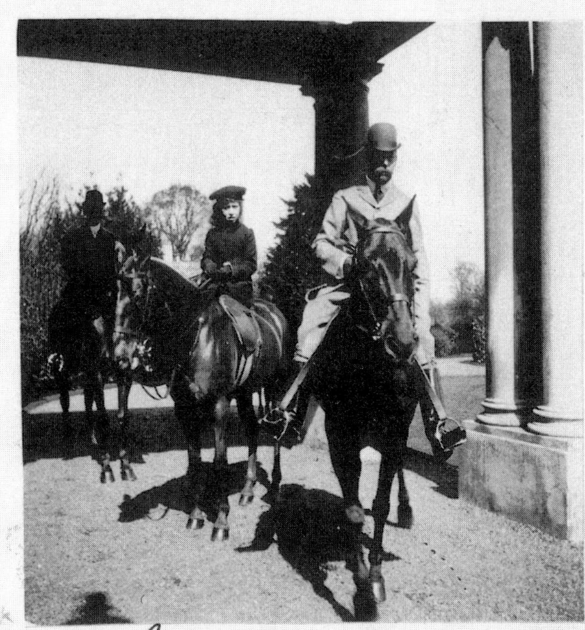

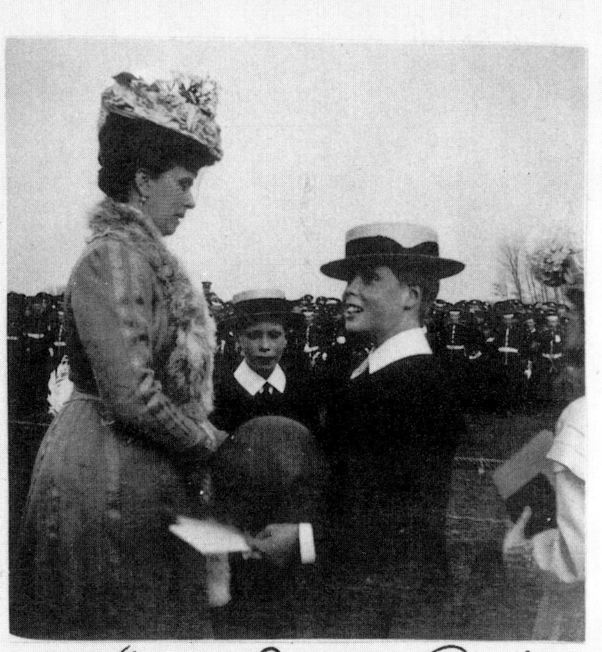

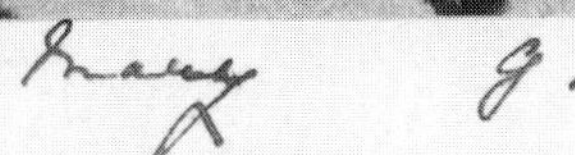

May G.

Self Bertie David

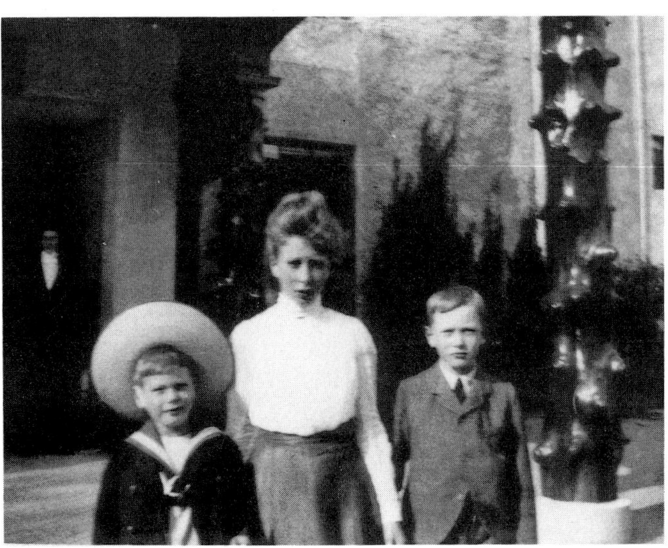

PRINCESS MARY WITH HARRY AND
GEORGIE AT ABERGELDIE, SUMMER
1907

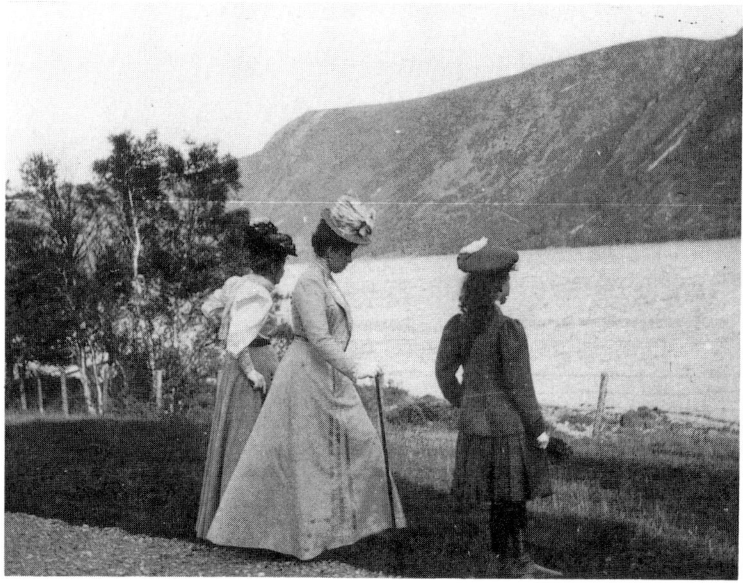

THE PRINCESS OF WALES AND HER
DAUGHTER AT THE EDGE OF LOCH
MUICK, SUMMER 1907

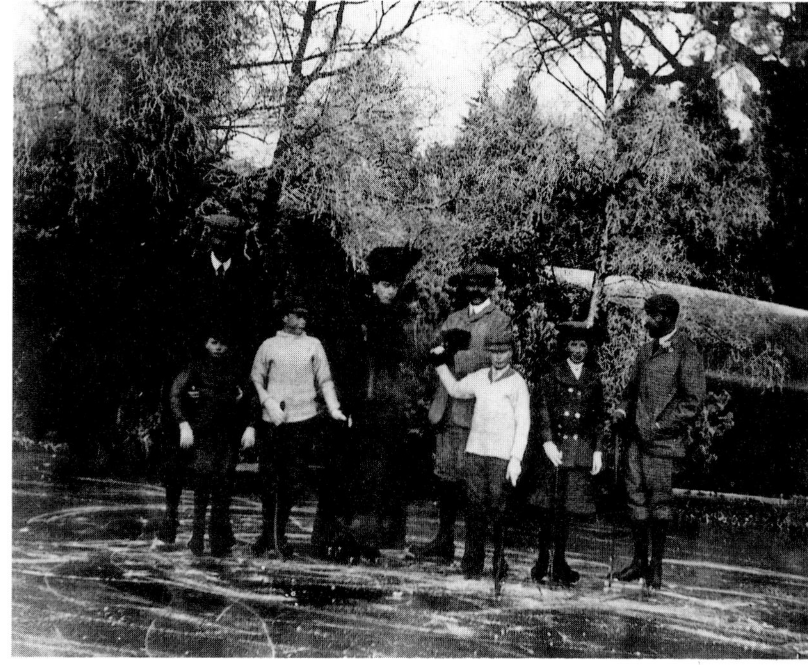

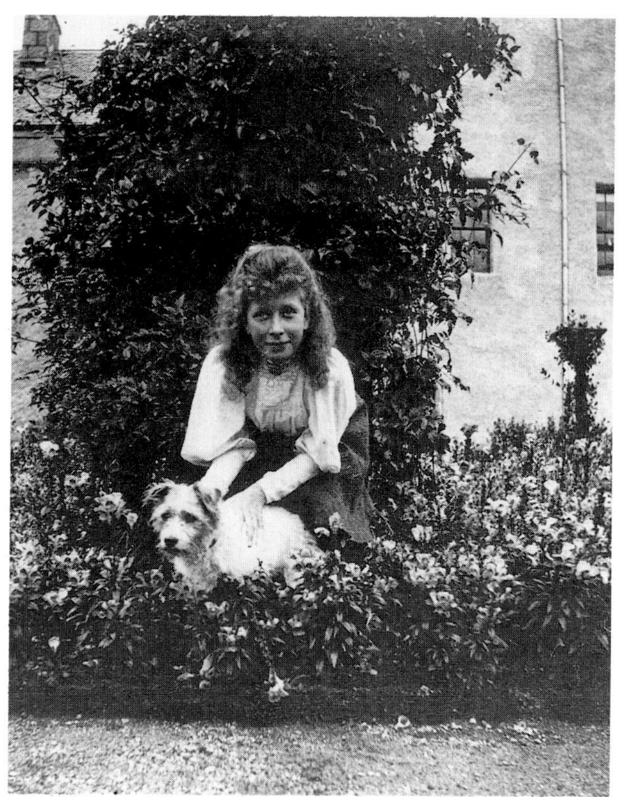

PRINCESS MARY AT
ABERGELDIE CASTLE IN
SEPTEMBER 1908

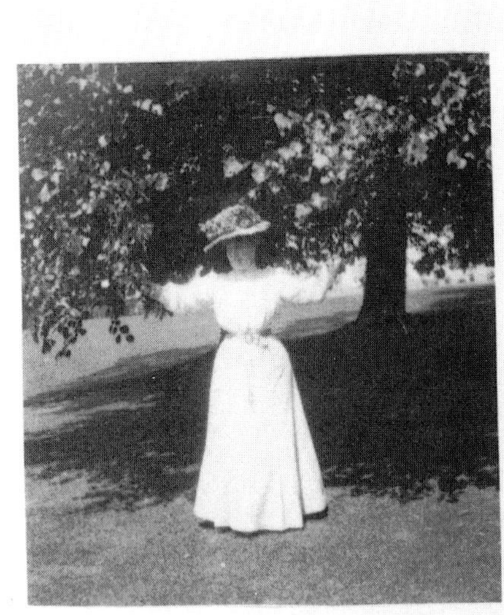
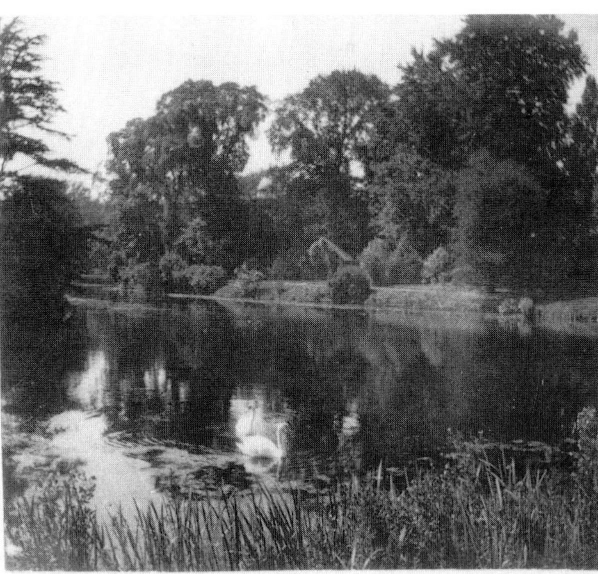
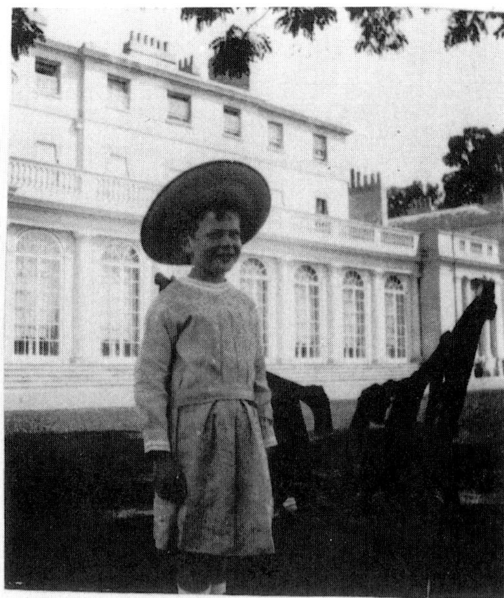

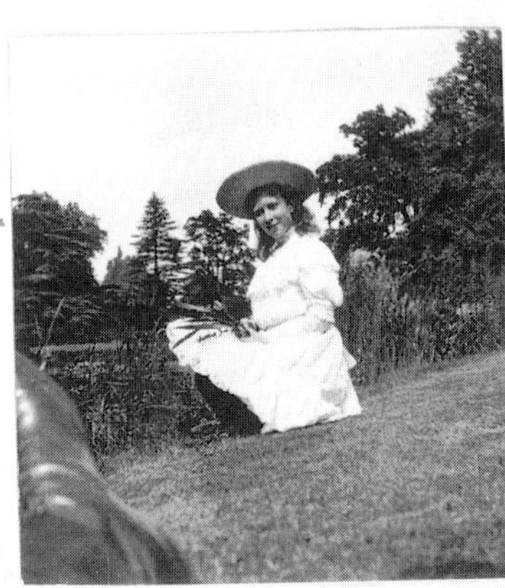
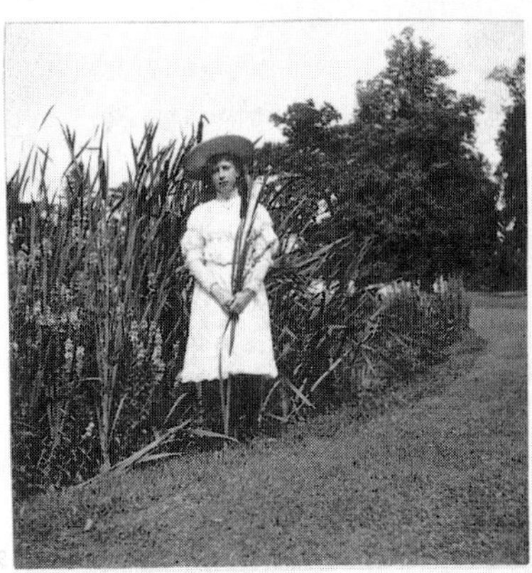
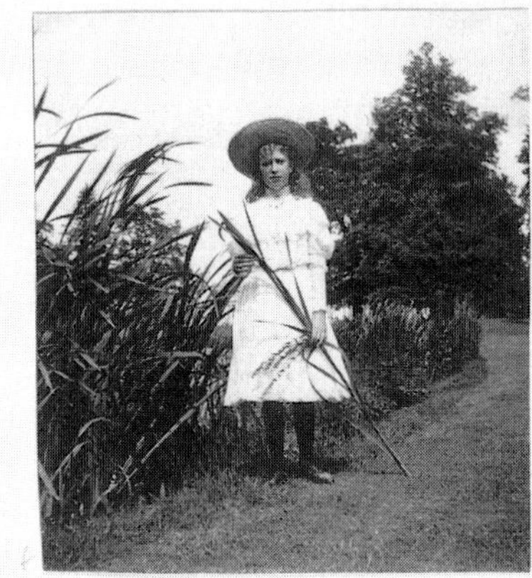
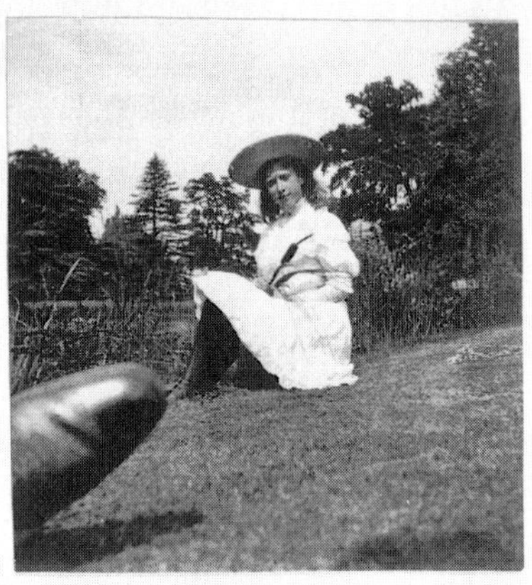

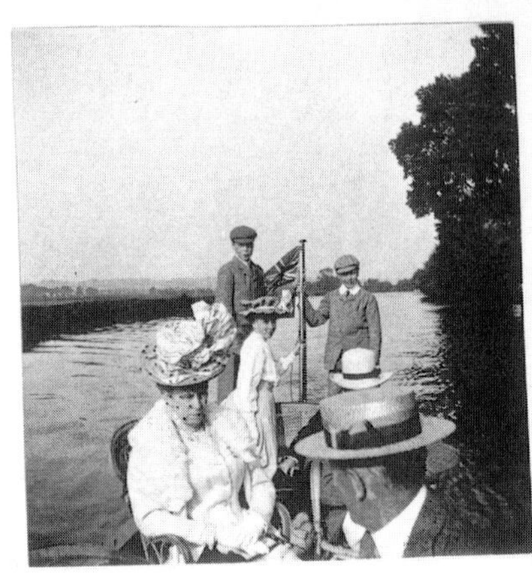
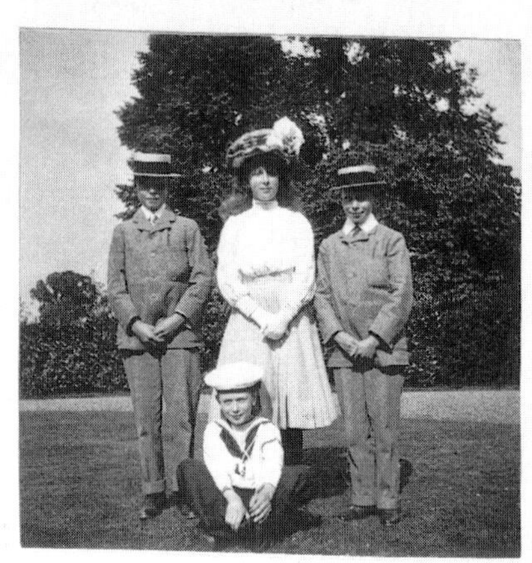
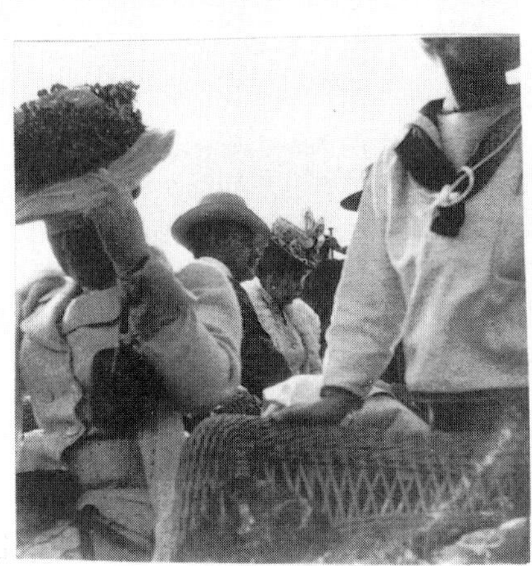

SNAPSHOTS TAKEN IN THE GROUNDS OF
FROGMORE DURING THE SUMMER OF 1908. GEORGIE
WEARS A WIDE-BRIMMED STRAW SUN-HAT WHILE
JOHNNIE, SEEN WITH HIS SISTER AND TWO OF HIS
BROTHERS, IN BOATERS OR CLOTH CAPS, WEARS A
SAILOR-SUIT

GEORGIE AND JOHNNIE WITH THEIR COUSIN,
PRINCE OLAV OF NORWAY, AT APPLETON HOUSE ON
THE SANDRINGHAM ESTATE. APPLETON,
BIRTHPLACE OF PRINCE OLAV, WAS THE ENGLISH
HOME OF HIS MOTHER MAUD, WHO IS SEEN HERE
RIDING WITH HER SISTER TORIA

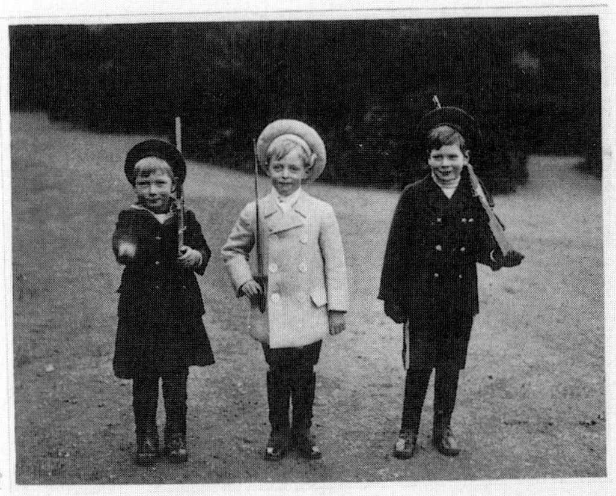

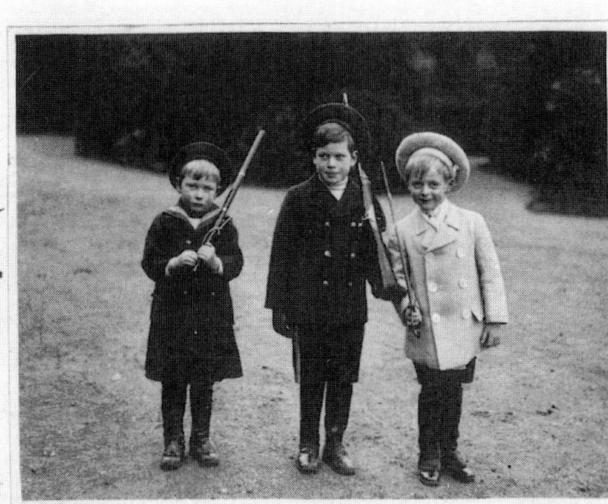

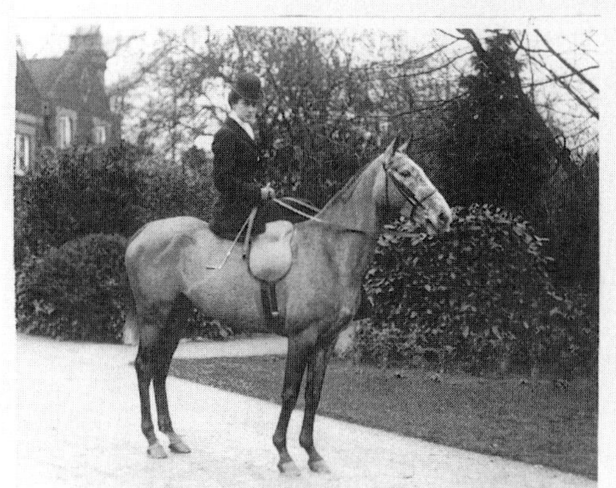

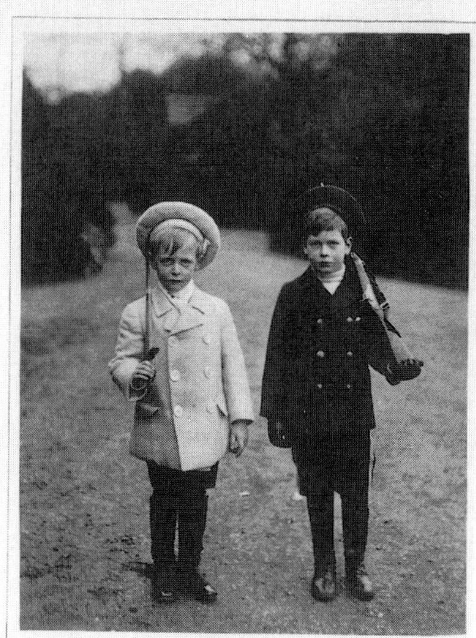

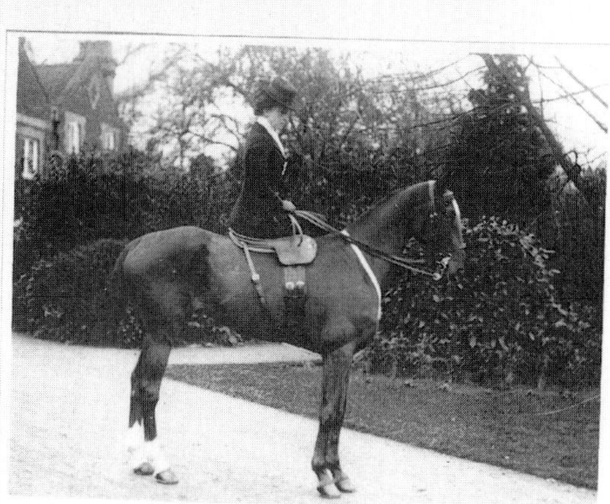

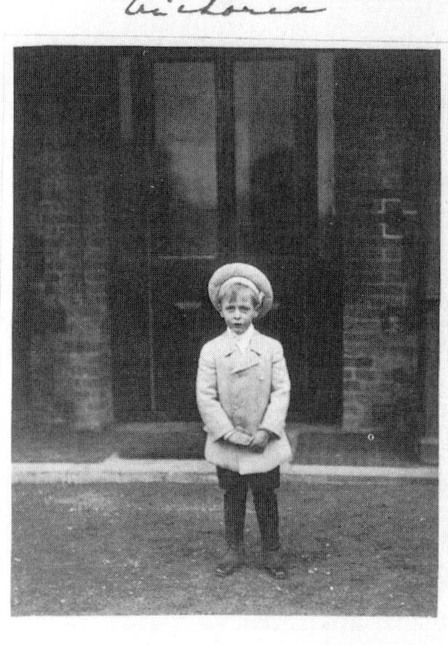

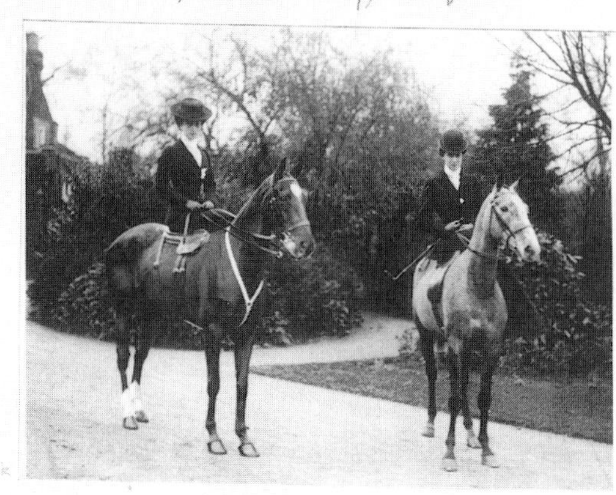

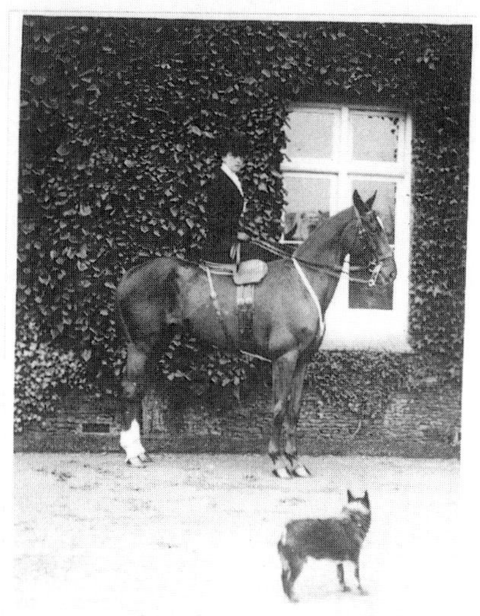

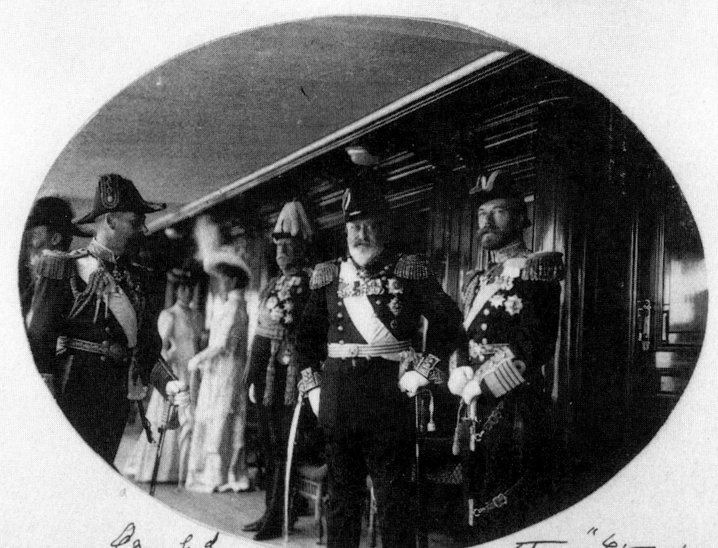

Mama
Alix
("Empress of
Russia")

George

Ed Grenfell
Papa

Nicky
("Emperor of
Russia")

Pa Ed   The "Standart"

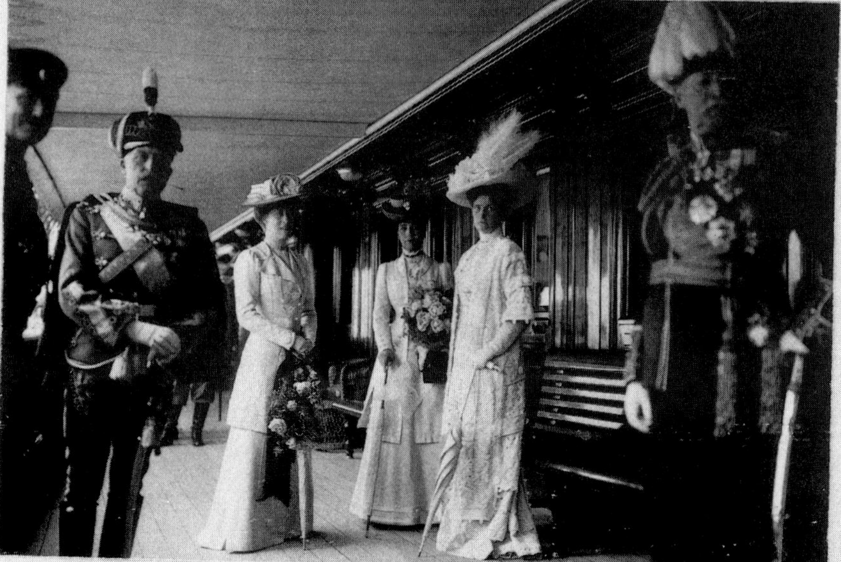

"Standart"
August
Ed. Arthur
Victoria

Ed
Grenfell
Cowes
1909
Mama
Alix

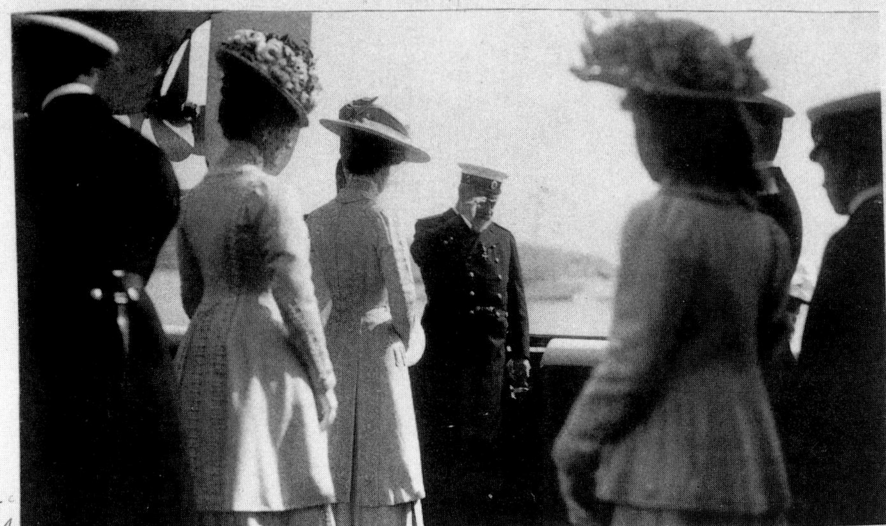

George
May
Victoria
Papa

Mary

David

Luncheon
on ed Standart

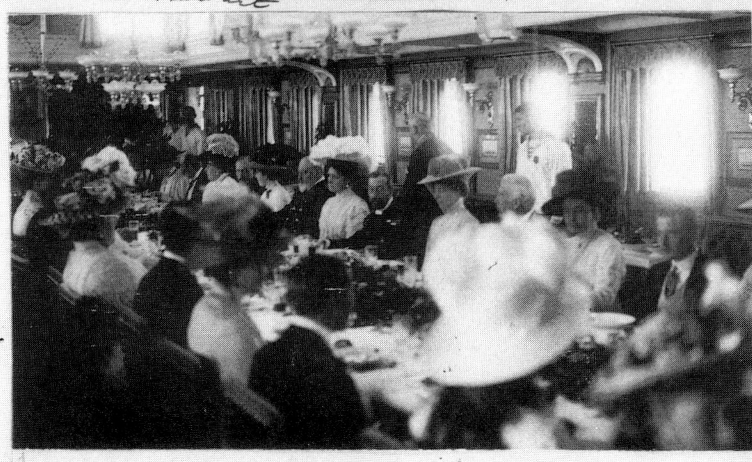

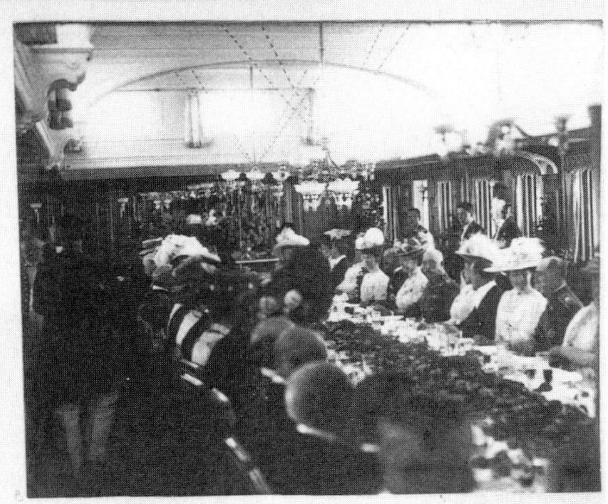

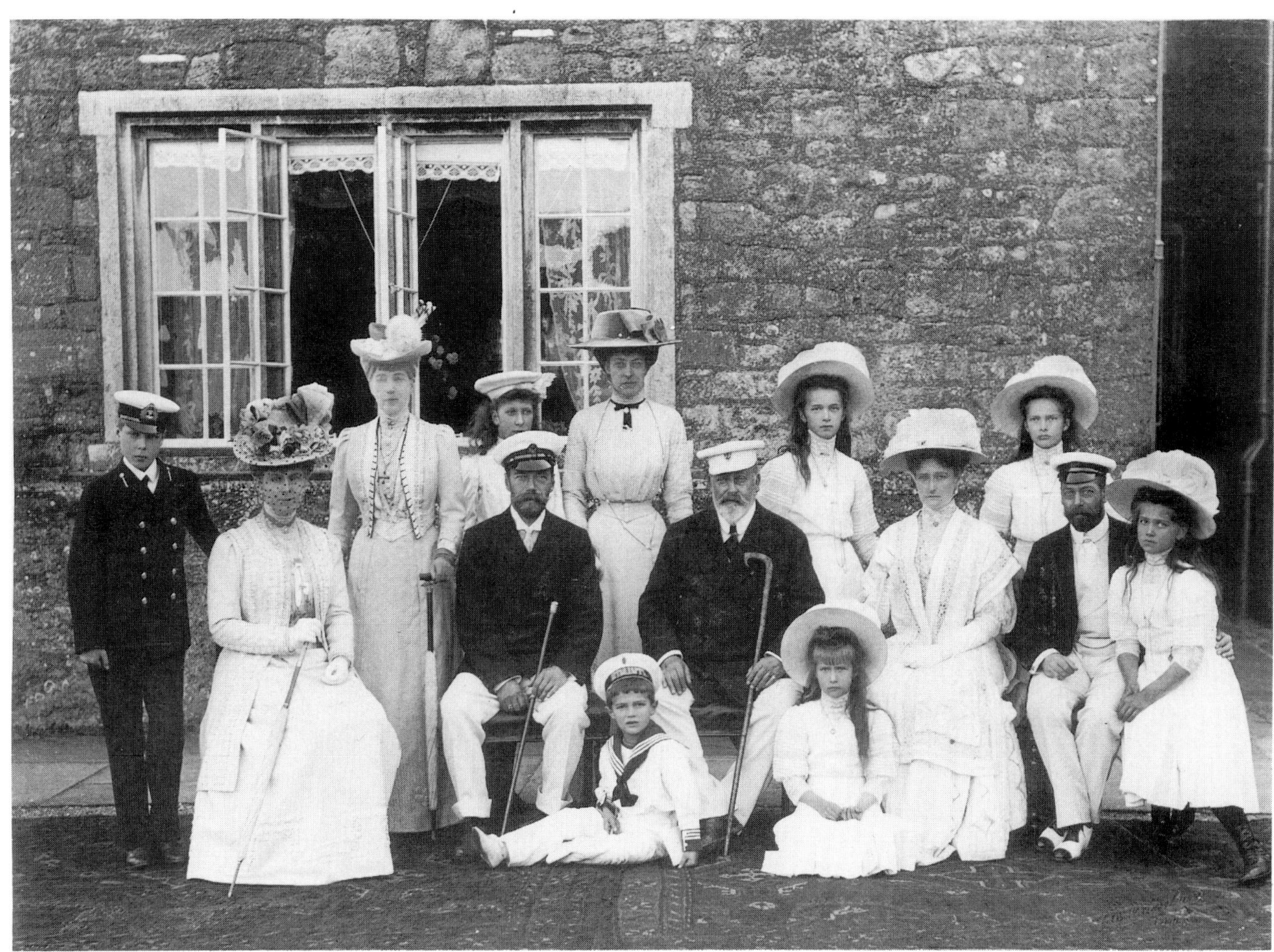

THE TWO FAMILIES AT BARTON MANOR ON THE ISLE OF WIGHT,
4 AUGUST 1909. THE GROUP SHOWS FROM LEFT TO RIGHT: DAVID
(PRINCE EDWARD), MARY, PRINCESS OF WALES, QUEEN ALEXANDRA
(STANDING), TSAR NICHOLAS II (PARTIALLY OBSCURING PRINCESS
MARY), PRINCESS VICTORIA, KING EDWARD VII, THE GRAND
DUCHESS OLGA, THE TSARINA ALEXANDRA FEODOROVNA, THE
GRAND DUCHESS TATIANA, GEORGE, PRINCE OF WALES AND THE
GRAND DUCHESS MARIE. THE TSAREVITCH ALEXIS AND THE GRAND
DUCHESS ANASTASIA ARE SEATED IN FRONT

(OVERLEAF LEFT) THE PRINCE AND PRINCESS OF WALES VISITING
PHOENIX MINES AT CHEESEWRING ON 10 JUNE 1909

(OVERLEAF RIGHT, TOP) THE DEATH OF KING EDWARD VII. HERE THE
KING'S COFFIN LIES IN STATE IN THE THRONE ROOM AT
BUCKINGHAM PALACE, 6 MAY 1910

(OVERLEAF RIGHT, BOTTOM) THE CONFIRMATION OF DAVID, NOW
PRINCE OF WALES, IN THE PRIVATE CHAPEL OF WINDSOR CASTLE,
24 JUNE 1910. ALL THE WOMEN WEAR DEEPEST MOURNING FOR
EDWARD VII

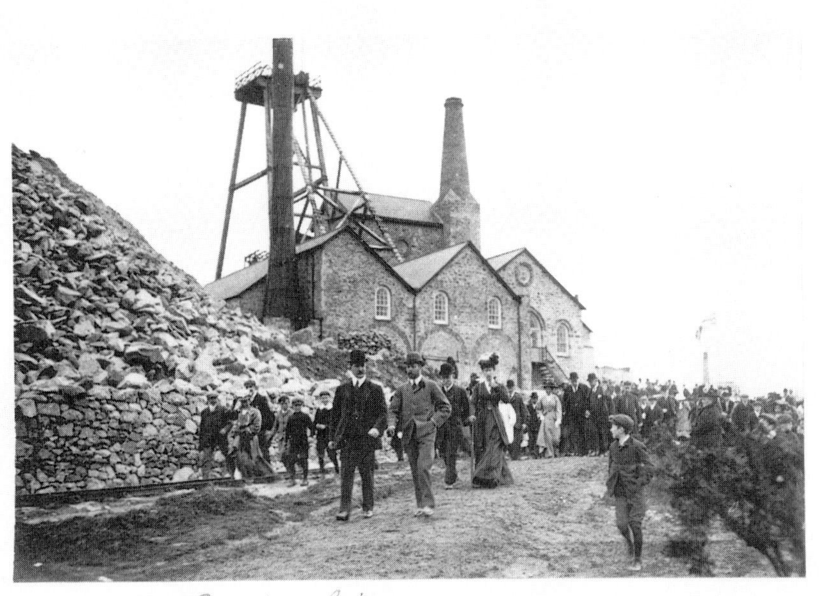

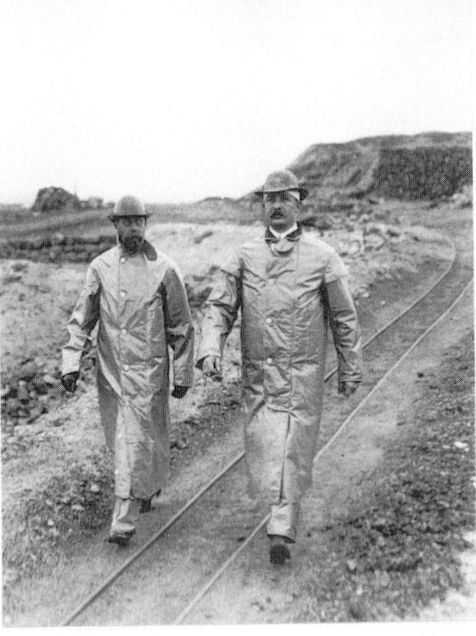

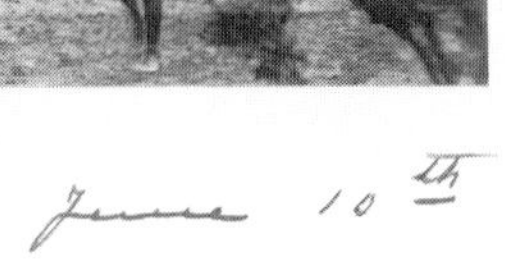

Phœnix Mines
Cheering   June 10th

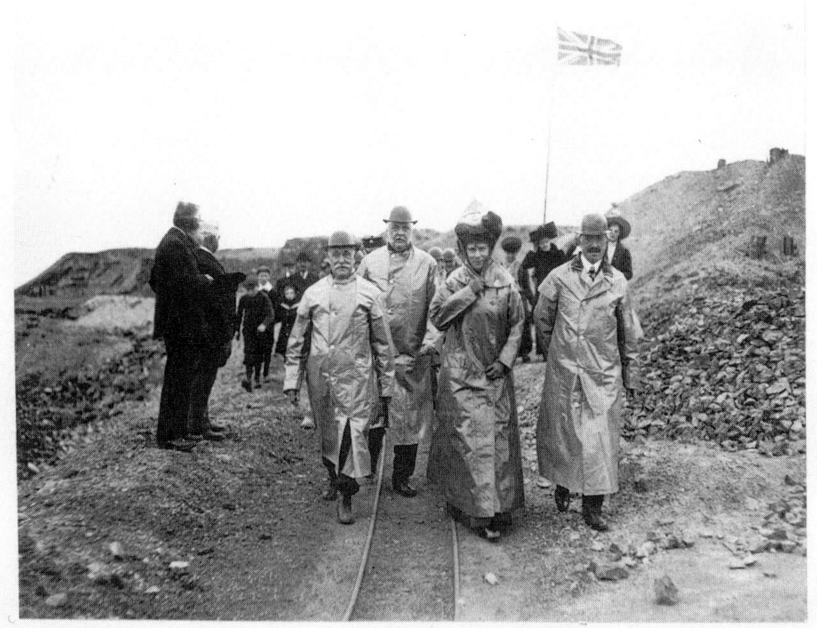

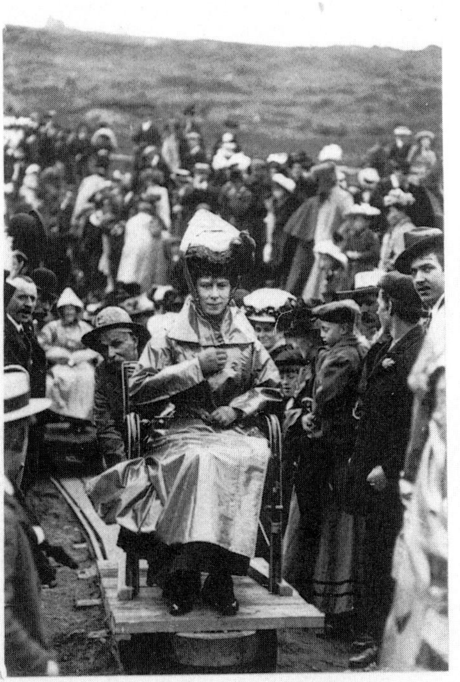

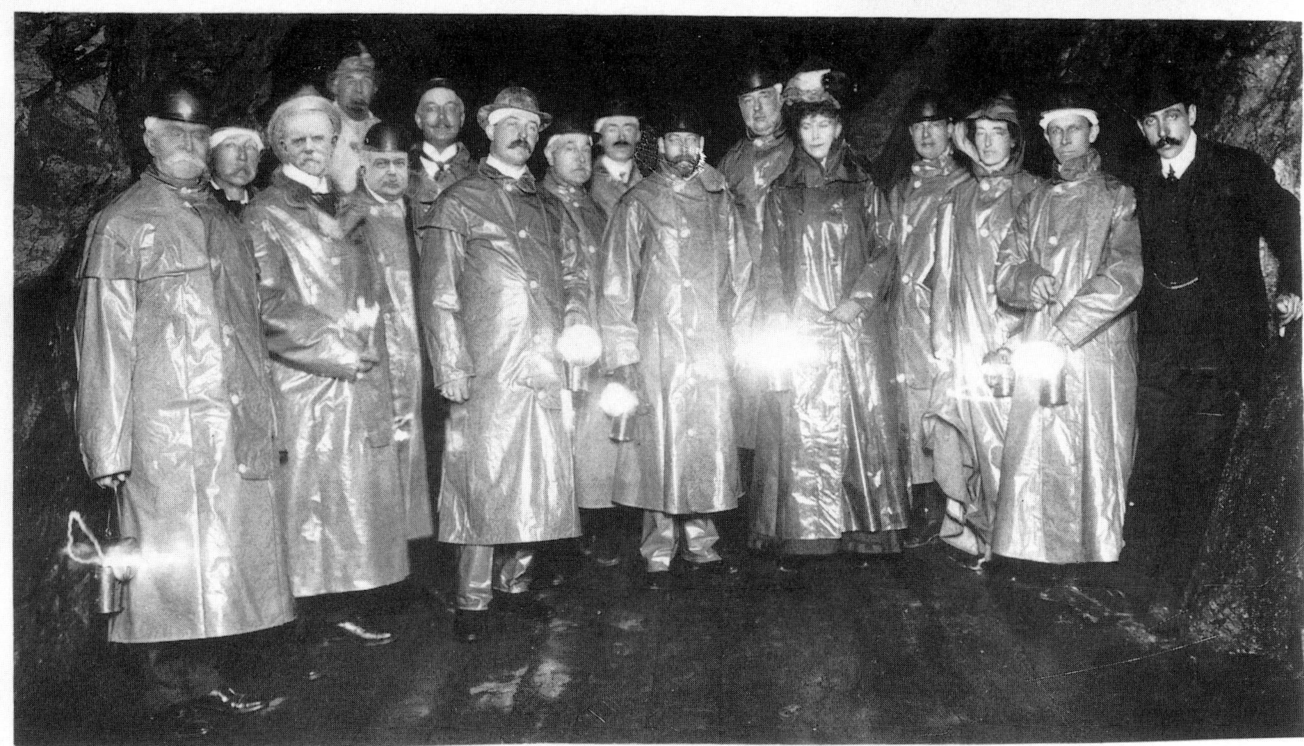

In the Mine

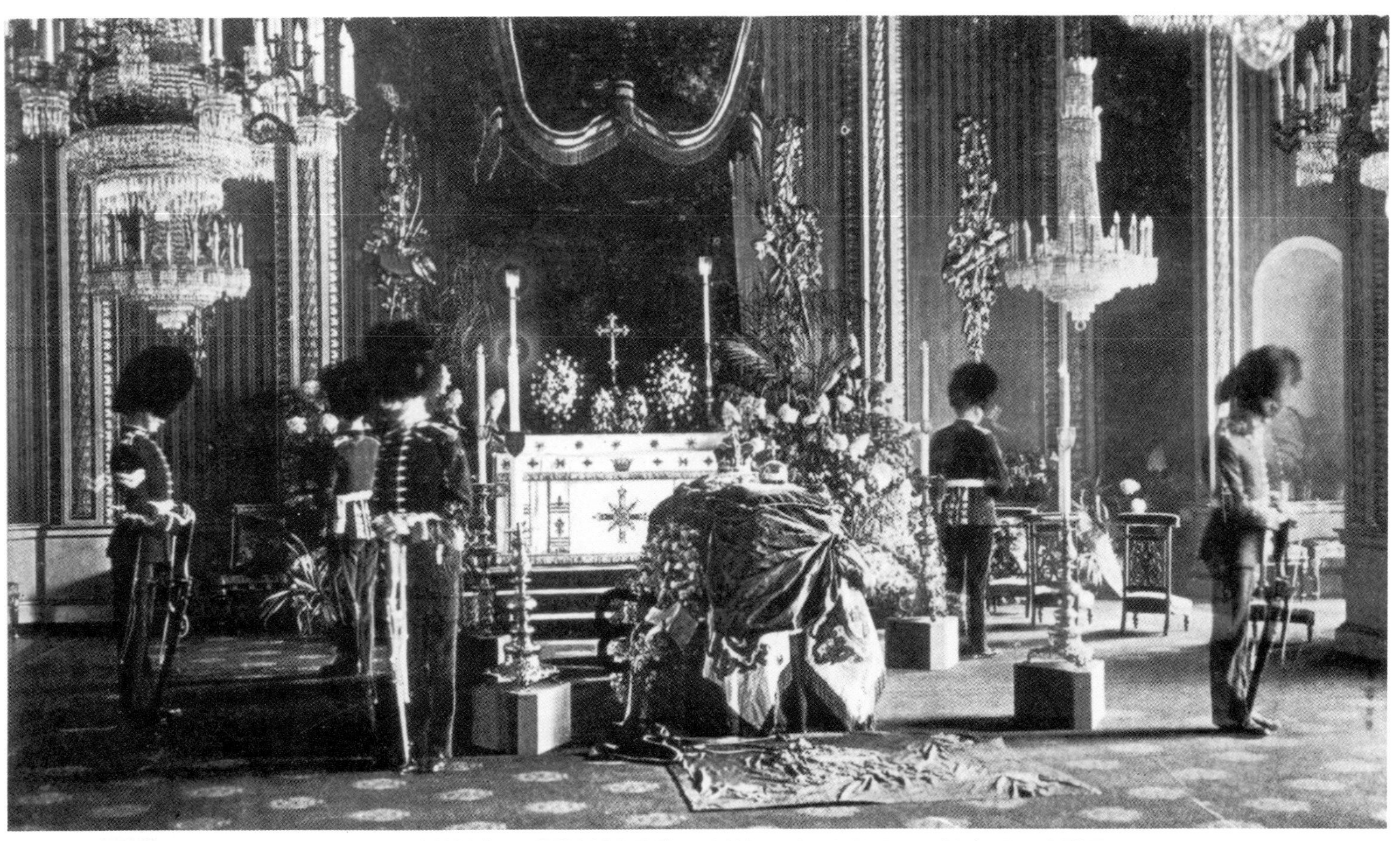

KING EDWARD VII. LYING IN STATE
In The Throne Room, Buckingham Palace, May 16th. 1910.
Photographed by Messrs. W. & D. Downey, Ebury Street, S.W.

Marion & Co., Ltd.

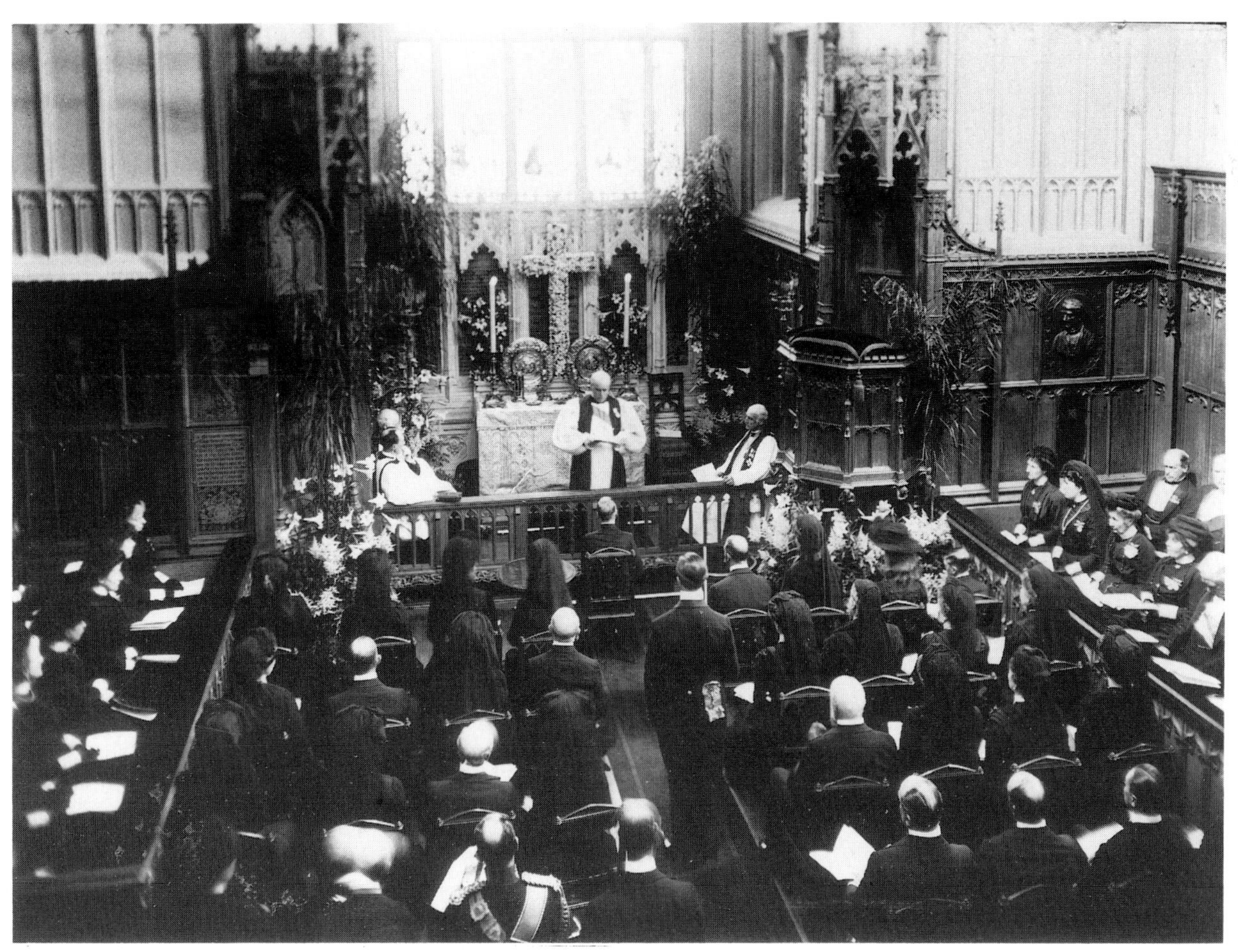

David's confirmation. Windsor Castle Chapel
June 24th 1910.

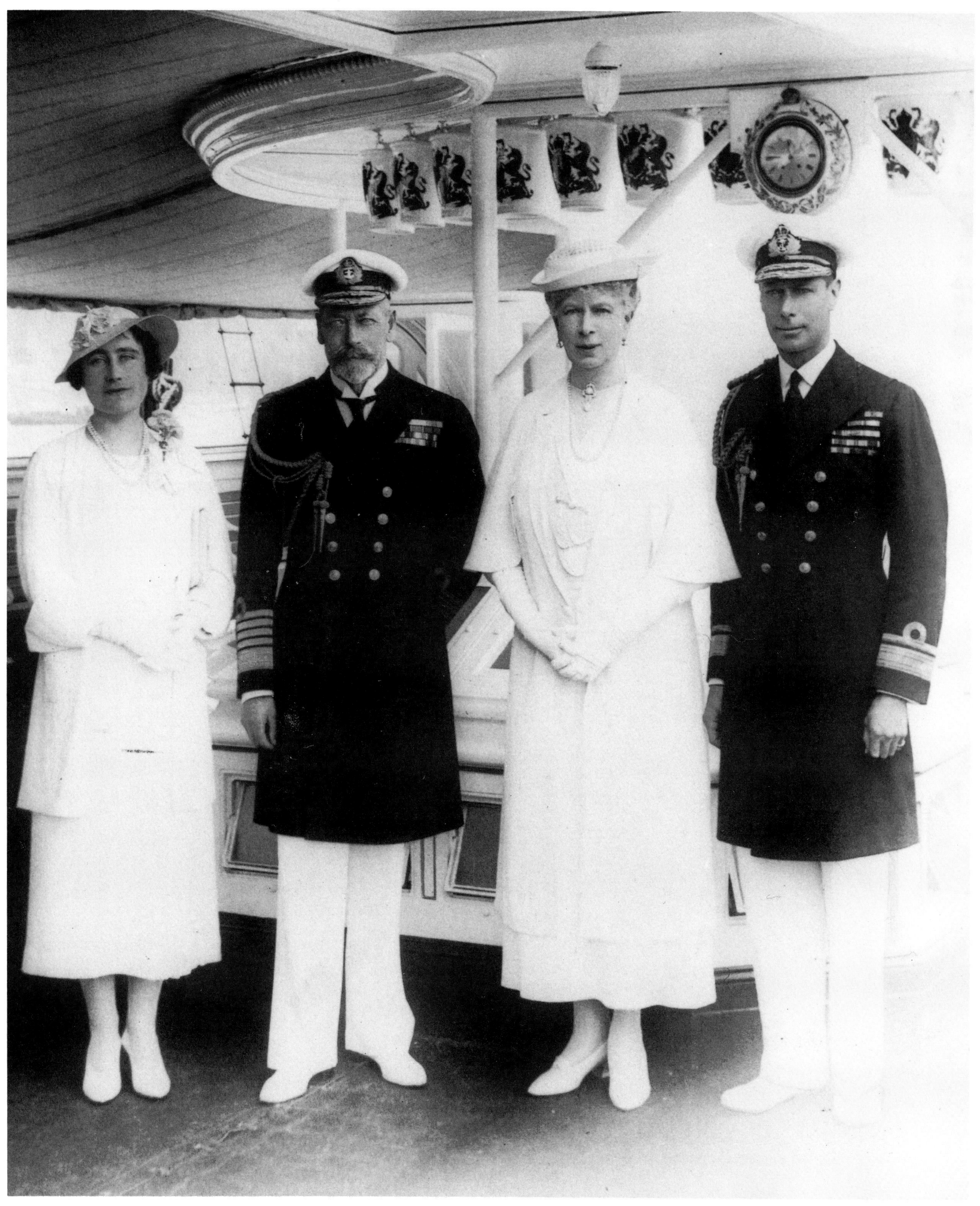

Cowes.   July 30

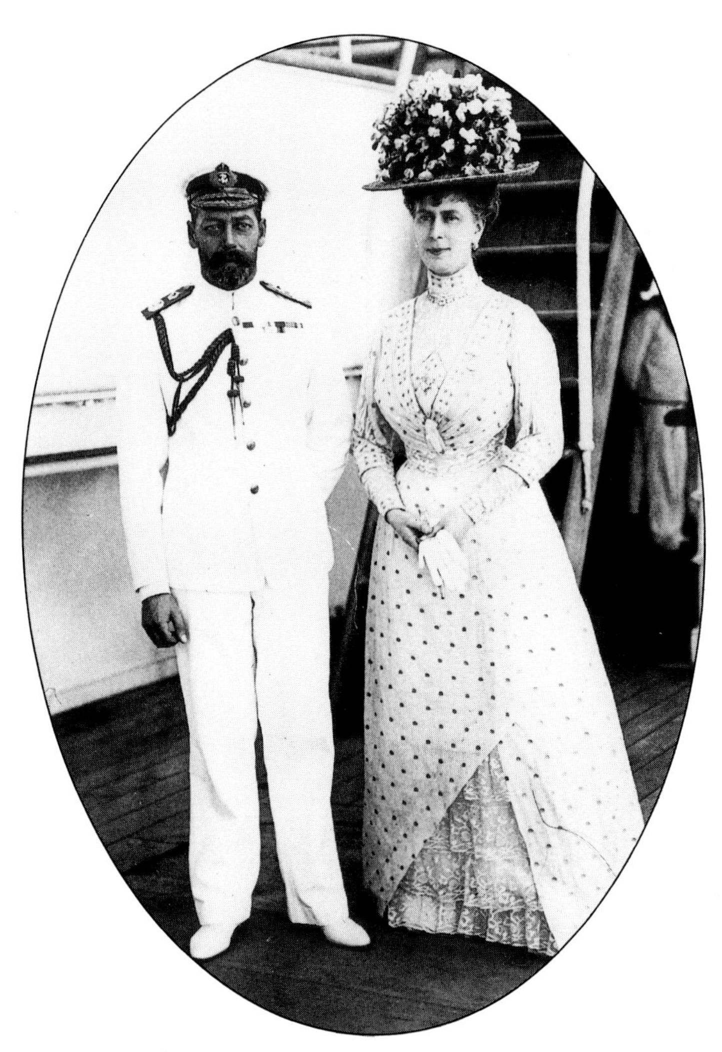

PART THREE

G.R.I.   Mary

India Xmas 1911.

(*Opposite*) KING GEORGE V AND QUEEN MARY WITH THE DUKE AND DUCHESS OF YORK (THE FUTURE KING GEORGE VI AND QUEEN ELIZABETH) ABOARD THE ROYAL YACHT AT COWES, 30 JULY 1935

Edward VII's widow, the Dowager Queen Alexandra, vacated Buckingham Palace with all the reluctance she had displayed at having to leave Marlborough House nearly a decade earlier. Leaving that very same house was for her daughter-in-law, the new Queen Mary, no less of a wrench. But leave it she did, for what she recognized would be a 'more difficult . . . & more ceremonious' life, as the wife and consort of the new King, George V.

This 'ceremonious' life with its traditions and customs, tightly bound by a web of red tape and protocol even more confining than it is today, began with the inevitable coronation ritual which took place in London on 22 June 1911. Dressed in a gown of white satin, heavily embroidered with gold flowers and imperial emblems, Queen Mary took her place beside her husband in the monumental State Coach, built for her great-grandfather George III, on what she described as a 'dull but fine morning'. Drawn by a team of richly-harnessed cream horses, and accompanied by a Sovereign's escort of the Household Cavalry, this spectacular equipage, adorned with tritons, cherubs and other allegorical figures, lumbered off towards Westminster Abbey and what both the King and Queen later referred to as a 'beautiful & impressive' but ultimately 'terrible ordeal'.

Less than a month later, an ordeal of a not dissimilar kind befell the eldest son of King George V and Queen Mary. On 23 June 1910, which happened to be his sixteenth birthday and the day before the one chosen for his confirmation, Prince Edward, or 'David', now Heir Apparent, had been created Prince of Wales. His formal investiture as such – the closest he would ever come to being crowned – took place at Caernarvon Castle on 14 July 1911.

For the people of Great Britain, the summer of 1911 was one long royal cavalcade and, though 'Coronation fever' still hung in the air, the young Prince of Wales viewed his own microscopic 'coronation' with feelings that were not far short of horror. At that time a cadet at the Royal Naval College, Dartmouth, David's embarrassment at the ceremony in prospect was exacerbated by the medieval costume he was expected to wear. Resembling that of a principal boy in pantomime, the Prince's outfit consisted of a belted, velvet tunic trimmed with ermine, satin knee-breeches, silk stockings and patent leather pumps with small heels. 'The ceremony I had to go through with, the speech I had to make, and the Welsh I had to speak were, I thought, a sufficient ordeal for anyone,' he wrote many years later when Duke of Windsor. 'But when a tailor appeared to measure me for a fantastic costume . . . I decided things had gone too far. . . . What would my Navy friends say if they saw me in this preposterous rig?'

During the years that lay ahead of him, there was much this popular and attractive Prince of Wales would find preposterous and unacceptable about the royal way of life and, in time, he would be made to pay the ultimate price for offending the reactionary forces of the British 'Establishment'. In 1911, however, perhaps for the first and last time in both their lives, Queen Mary was able to soothe her son's ruffled pride and persuade him that his contemporaries

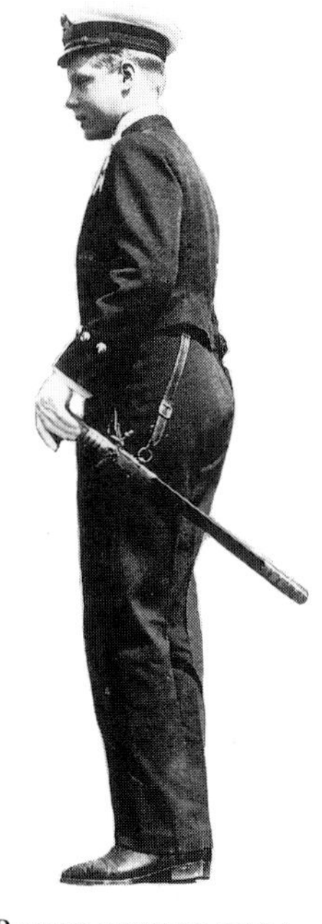

would understand the indignity of the 'rig' designed for his investiture.

Towards the end of that year yet more ceremonial grandeur awaited the King and Queen when, in their royal and imperial capacities, they left England to revisit India. On 11 November their Majesties drove from Buckingham Palace to Victoria Station where fourteen royalties, including Prince and Princess Christian of Schleswig-Holstein, Princess Louise, Duchess of Argyll, Princess Beatrice and her three sons, the Duchess of Albany and Grand Duke Mikhail Mikhailovitch of Russia, waited to bid them *bon voyage*. Led by the prime minister of the day, H. H. Asquith, six members of the Cabinet and their wives were also present to say their farewells, as were no fewer than twenty-eight ambassadors and sixteen other personages, ranging from the Archbishop of Canterbury to the Acting Commissioner of Police.

Once at Portsmouth, where another reception party – led by the Duke of Wellington as acting Lord-Lieutenant of Hampshire – waited to greet them, the King and Queen were joined aboard their ship the *Medina*, a brand-new 13,000-ton liner built for the Penninsula and Oriental Company, by Queen Alexandra, Queen Maud of Norway, the Prince of Wales, Princess Mary and twenty-two other guests – including the then Mr and Mrs Winston Spencer-Churchill – for luncheon. Shortly before 3p.m. the *Medina* slipped anchor just as an almighty storm broke, tossing the tugs which led the ship and her four attendant naval cruisers out to sea, and lashing the flags and bunting of every ship in the Home Fleet, gathered to salute the King and Queen on their departure. For Queen Mary, with her dislike of the sea and her fear of storms, the start of this voyage cannot have seemed a particularly propitious one.

Plagued yet again by tempestuous seas in the Bay of Biscay, the *Medina* eventually entered calm waters around Gibraltar where the royal party disembarked on 15 November. Five days later they landed at Port Said and, on 2 December, finally reached Bombay. On the seventh, the King-Emperor and Queen-Empress entered Delhi for the now famous Durbar, which was held on the plains of the Jumna on 12 December. For this immense spectacle – at the heart of which the King and Queen received the homage of India's princes, rulers of Hyderabad, Baroda, Mysore, Kashmir, Rajputana, Central India, Baluchistan, Sikkim and Bhutan – two concentric amphitheatres, designed to accommodate more than 2,000 spectators, had been built. In the centre of all this was erected the royal dais, a series of marble platforms crowned by a crimson Shamiana (or canopy) above which rose a golden cupola. Within this pavilion were placed two solid silver thrones encased in gold. To a salute of 101 guns, King George and Queen Mary ascended the dais from where they surveyed a glittering scene which encapsulated the very meaning of Britain's sovereign presence in India.

For the Durbar the King and Queen put on their coronation robes once again, he wearing a brand-new crown, specially designed and constructed for this one event, she wearing her 'best diadem' of emeralds and diamonds. Thus arrayed, their Majesties posed for an official portrait photograph but, as with the formal coronation studies taken in London that June (and, indeed, their wedding photographs referred to earlier), it is conspicuously absent from the Queen's private photograph albums.

Four days after the Durbar, the King and Queen went their separate ways. On 16 December George V went off to 'Nepaul [sic] to shoot', while the Queen left Delhi for Agra, Rajputana and Ajmere, spending Christmas week in Bundi – where we see her pictured with the sinister-looking Maharao Rajah, Sir Raghubir Singhji Sahab Bahadur, Chief of Bundi – and Kotah, where she presented a Christmas tree laden with knives, mechanical toys and dolls, which she had bought in London, to what she called 'the native children'.

The King and Queen met up again in Bankipore on 29 December, from where they travelled together to Calcutta, which Queen Mary pronounced 'too European for my taste & not really Indian as the other places I have visited are'. The New Year was seen in at Government House in Calcutta, where they remained until 8 January. Two days later, having stopped off at Nagpur *en route*, the King and Queen arrived back in Bombay to board the *Medina* for the return voyage to England. Travelling via Port Sudan, Port Said, Malta and Gibraltar, the royal party finally arrived at Portsmouth on the morning of 5 February 1912.

From the opulence of the East, King George and Queen Mary turned their sights to the hard-pressed working men of the mining districts of Wales and the North of England. As James Pope-Hennessy wrote: 'The new King and Queen felt more at their ease with British working people than they ever did with members of London society or with foreign royalties.'

It was the royal couple's interest in the welfare of the less privileged that led them to pay a three-day visit to Glamorgan and the Merthyr Valley in June 1912. Together the King and Queen inspected pit-heads, rode in colliery trams, saw the stabling conditions of the little pit ponies and talked freely with the miners themselves. To the surprise of local officials, Queen Mary also insisted upon visiting some of the small, back-to-back colliery houses.

The following month, King George and Queen Mary created as great an impression on the Yorkshire mining community, but it was for their response to one tragic episode in particular that the King and Queen were always to be remembered with affection. During their visit they had not long returned to Wentworth Woodhouse at the end of a long and tiring day, when news was received of a disaster at the Cadeby Colliery, in which several miners perished.

Immediately the King and Queen sent for their car and set off in the direction of Cadeby. 'As she talked to the bereaved families at the pit-head,' wrote her official biographer, 'it was observed that the Queen, whose control over her emotions was usually adamantine, had tears pouring down her cheeks. It was after this incident that the King and Queen were welcomed by the glass-blowers of Stairport singing the refrain: "Kind kind and gentle is she, Kind is my Mary".'

Throughout her long life, Queen Mary always considered herself to be

'English from top to toe'. Yet despite her love for Britain and her unquestionable loyalty and patriotism to the land of her birth, she – like Queen Victoria before her – could only be said to have been 'English' by the very narrowest of margins. Save for a drop of Hungarian blood, inherited from her paternal grandmother, Countess Claudine Rhèdey, the blood which flowed through Queen Mary's veins was predominantly and inescapably German. Her maternal great-grandfather, King George III, who was also the King of Hanover and Duke of Brunswick-Lüneberg, had married Charlotte, Duchess of Mecklenberg-Strelitz, whom, incidentally, Queen Mary always believed she closely resembled. In turn their seventh son and tenth child, Prince Adolphus, had married Princess Augusta of Hesse (a daughter of Friederich, Landgrave of Hesse-Cassel) whose third and last child, born in Hanover, was Queen Mary's mother, Princess Mary Adelaide.

With the start of the Great War in August 1914, however, the Queen, who would one day declare, 'I did not realize that I could really *hate* people as I do the Germans, tho' I never liked them,' spared scarcely a sympathetic thought for the country of her forefathers.

The war years 1914–18, rekindled the organizational skills Queen Mary had learned long before when, as Princess May of Teck, she and her mother had striven to help alleviate poverty and hardship in London's East End. Almost from the very moment war was declared, Queen Mary threw her energies into helping all manner of relief agencies. The Needlework Guild established by Princess Mary Adelaide at White Lodge now became Queen Mary's Needlework Guild, responsible for helping to make shirts, socks, scarves and other comforts for the troops. The Queen was granted the use of the state apartments at St James's Palace for her Relief Clothing Guild, and the National Relief Fund, set up at nearby York House, also benefited from the Queen's direct involvement. In a single day donations totalling a quarter of a million pounds were received from members of the public, following an appeal for funds from Queen Mary and the Prince of Wales.

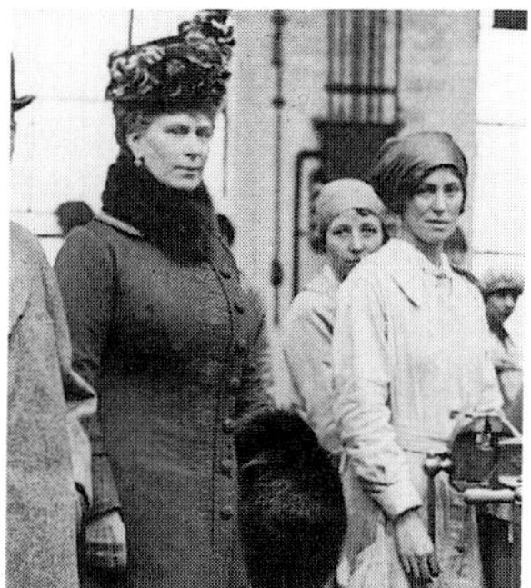

QUEEN MARY VISITING A FACTORY DURING THE WAR

At much the same time, Buckingham Palace announced that the Queen was meeting with 'industrial experts and representatives of working-class women' to discuss a plan she had conceived 'to collect money for schemes of work for women unemployed on account of the war'. This plan swiftly came to fruition as 'The Queen's Work for Women Fund'. At one point there was even talk of turning Buckingham Palace into a hospital, but when that idea was dropped on the grounds that the building was too old-fashioned and too inconvenient for such a purpose, the Queen put the palace garden at the disposal of injured officers, whole-heartedly approved of horses from the Royal Mews being employed for ambulance work, and agreed that the fleet of royal carriages should be used to carry wounded soldiers from railway stations to hospitals.

Towards the end of 1914, the King made the first of several visits to the Front, while at home both he and the Queen undertook innumerable visits to

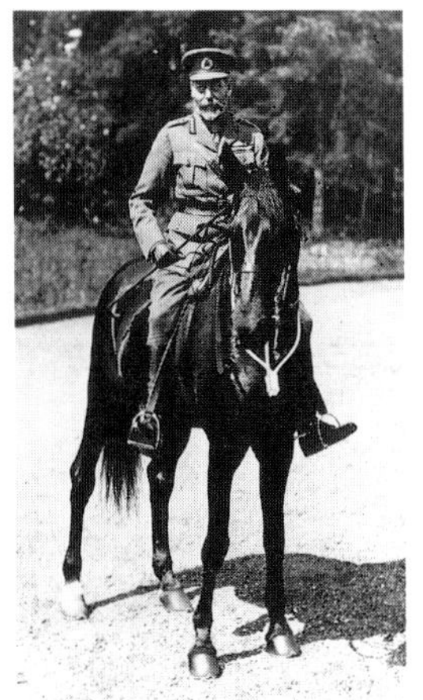

THE KING ON HORSEBACK

military and civilian hospitals, factories, munition works, food centres and canteens the entire length and breadth of the country. The Queen was also a regular visitor to the limb-fitting centre at Gifford House, Roehampton, just outside London, which later became Queen Mary's Hospital and is now world-famous for its limb-fitting and burns units.

In July 1917 the Queen – who reached her fiftieth birthday that May – paid an eleven-day visit to Normandy in order to bring comfort and encouragement to the wounded and to their nurses, to visit aerodromes and casualty clearing stations. Two years earlier, in October 1915, George V had himself become a casualty of the war in France – and had to be brought back to England on a stretcher – when, during an inspection of the Royal Flying Corps at Hesdigneul, his horse reared up and fell back on him. At home it was discovered that the King had sustained a fractured pelvis and, as a result, Queen Mary found her own work-load increased to breaking-point during the King's enforced period of inactivity.

In spite of all the horror of what was called 'the war to end all wars', there were, of course, lighter moments to be caught and savoured. One such, on 6 July 1918, was the celebration of the King and Queen's silver wedding anniversary, marked by a semi-state drive through London to St Paul's Cathedral where a service of thanksgiving was held.

With the eventual dawning of peace there came renewed sadness for the King and Queen Mary, with the sudden death on 18 January 1919 of their youngest child, Prince John, aged thirteen and a half. The prince suffered from epilepsy and it was after one of his attacks that he died at Wood Farm, his home on the Sandringham estate. 'For him it is a great release,' Queen Mary wrote to a friend, 'as his malady was becoming worse as he grew older, & he has thus been spared much suffering. I cannot say how grateful we feel to God for having taken him in such a peaceful way, he just slept quietly into his heavenly home, no pain, no struggle, just peace for the poor little troubled spirit which had been a great anxiety to us . . . ever since he was four years old.'

Three years later, the King and Queen saw the marriage of the first of their five surviving children. In November 1921 Princess Mary became engaged to Henry, Viscount Lascelles, later 6th Earl of Harewood. At thirty-nine, tall and cadaverous, Lord Lascelles was fifteen years older than his bride. 'Mary is radiant,' noted the Queen, '& I am getting *so* fond of him & we get on very well.'

Princess Mary's wedding was arranged to take place at Westminster Abbey on 28 February 1922 and, as the day drew nearer, the bride's brother Bertie (later King George VI) wrote to the Prince of Wales, then touring India, 'As far as I can make out, the 28th is going to be a day of national rejoicing in every conceivable & unconceivable manner. . . .' It was, but both the King and Queen were to miss their daughter's presence at home more than they could have imagined. On the evening of the wedding day itself, for instance, Queen Mary wrote to her eldest son, 'Papa & I felt miserable at parting [from Mary],

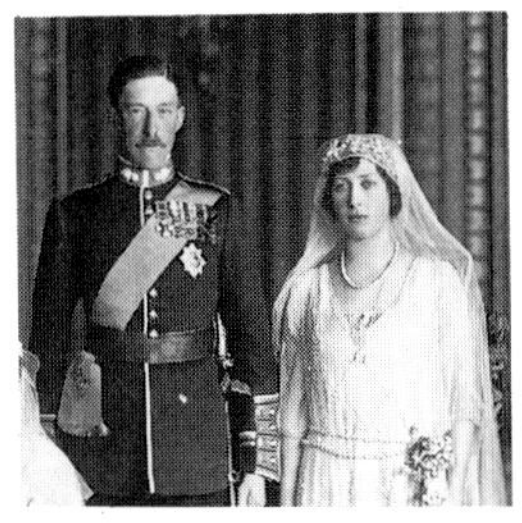

THE WEDDING OF
PRINCESS MARY AND
VISCOUNT LASCELLES,
28 FEBRUARY 1922

poor Papa broke down, but I mercifully managed to keep up as I so much feared Mary wld break down.'

For George V and Queen Mary, the following year was to prove no less emotional or exciting. On 7 February 1923 Princess Mary presented her parents with their first grandchild, the present Earl of Harewood, who at his christening at Goldsborough Hall on 25 March received the names George Henry Hubert.

Then on 26 April their Majesties attended the wedding of their second son, Bertie, by now Duke of York, to Lady Elizabeth Bowes Lyon, youngest daughter of the Earl and Countess of Strathmore and Kinghorne, an ancient Scottish family whose seat, Glamis Castle, had been the setting for Shakespeare's gruesome drama, *Macbeth*. Lady Elizabeth had acted as a bridesmaid at the wedding of Princess Mary and Lord Lascelles and her own wedding was likewise celebrated with all the pomp and splendour of a state occasion at Westminster Abbey. Upon her arrival, to the sound of a fanfare of silver trumpets, the bride, who wore a veil of Flanders lace loaned to her by Queen Mary, stepped forward and, in a spontaneous gesture, laid her bouquet of white roses and heather on the tomb of the Unknown Soldier, consecrated in the presence of the King five years before.

At the beginning of May George V and Queen Mary left London for Rome at the start of their second state visit since the end of the Great War. Their first, in the spring of 1922, had taken them to Brussels as the guests of the popular King Albert and his wife Elizabeth. Then the royal couple had visited British war cemeteries, viewed the battlefield of Waterloo, and laid a wreath on the grave of Nurse Edith Cavell, shot by the Germans for the part she played in providing an escape route for British soldiers.

The Italian state visit was, not least for its magnificent setting, a much more colourful affair. Greeted by King Victor Emmanuel III, Queen Elena and Crown Prince Umberto, their Britannic Majesties were cheered by a vast crowd gathered in the square outside the Quirinal Palace. During their stay King George and Queen Mary toured all the sites of Roman antiquity, met Benito Mussolini, and were received in papal audience at the Vatican, for which the Queen, with her dislike of wearing black, dressed from head to toe in white.

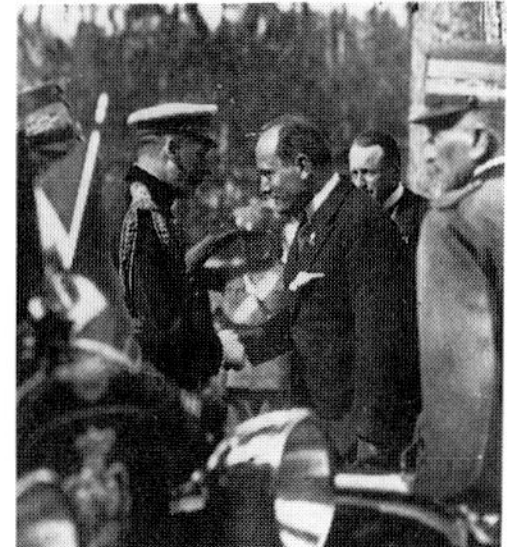

Exactly one year later, the King and Queen of Italy paid a return state visit to England. Among the engagements they kept, like the King and Queen of Romania after them, was a visit to the British Empire Exhibition at Wembley. George V had opened this vast array of pavilions containing products from Britain's colonies and dominions in April 1924, an occasion made yet more memorable by the fact that this was the first time the King had made a public broadcast to his people. To the Queen, the Wembley Exhibition proved so fascinating an enterprise that she made repeated private visits to it and each time took the greatest pride in inspecting 'The Queen's Dolls' House', a unique tribute to Queen Mary herself from some of Britain's finest craftsmen which, through the years, has been seen by millions of visitors to Windsor Castle, where it has been on permanent exhibition since the close of the Wembley venture.

Throughout the decade which preceded his death in January 1936, King George V became increasingly troubled by ill-health. In February 1925, influenza was followed by an attack of bronchitis so severe that his doctors recommended a mediterranean cruise by way of convalescence. That March the King and Queen travelled to Genoa where they boarded their yacht, the *Victoria and Albert*. Over the next five weeks their voyage included visits to Naples and Pompeii in Italy, Syracuse and Palermo in Sicily, but what proved to be the Queen's last overseas visit was ruined by the presence of the King's sister 'Toria'. By now well entrenched in her spinsterly ways and always ready to make much of her own ill-health, whether real or imagined, Princess Victoria was a tiresomely uncultivated woman, whose life had been spent acting as nursemaid and companion to her mother, Queen Alexandra.

Under Toria's influence, the King frequently refused to join his wife on her cultural sightseeing expeditions during this trip or, if prevailed upon to do so, managed to spoil her pleasure by the endless silly jokes and philistine banter in which he and Princess Victoria continually indulged.

As the King's health continued to improve at this time so that of the eighty-one-year-old Queen Alexandra went into its final decline. At Sandringham on 19 November 1925, deaf, lame and with failing sight, 'Motherdear' suffered a heart attack from which she died early the following evening. Six days later, the Queen Dowager's coffin was borne to London where it briefly lay in state at Westminster Abbey before being taken through the early winter snow to its final resting place in St George's Chapel, Windsor.

The following spring happier thoughts again filled the minds of the royal family with the birth of a daughter, the Princess Elizabeth, to the Duke and Duchess of York on 21 April 1926. Known as 'Lilibet', the young princess was a source of enormous happiness to her grandfather, and never more so than when she was permitted to join the King and Queen Mary at Bognor in March 1929. Four months earlier, George V had been taken dangerously ill with an acute form of septicaemia and surgery had been required to drain an abscess in the pleural cavity, eventually located as the seat of the infection. Indeed, so grave had news of the King's illness become that, at one point, a rumour had spread through London that the sixty-three-year-old sovereign was dead.

Towards the end of the year, the King's condition had improved sufficiently for there to be talk of convalescence, and in January a house called 'Craigweil', near the sea at Bognor, was leased for that purpose. On Easter Monday, the King made what amounted to his first public appearance since his operation when he and the Queen sat out in a sheltered spot to listen to the Kneller Hall Band; 'very enjoyable', as Queen Mary noted in her diary. 'A number of people came right up to our "sea-walk" – We went and waved to them . . . & there was great cheering – George looked especially well.'

During the last few years of the King's life, the royal family celebrated a number of special occasions. With two grandsons – George and Gerald Lascelles (the latter born to Princess Mary in August 1924) – to their credit, the

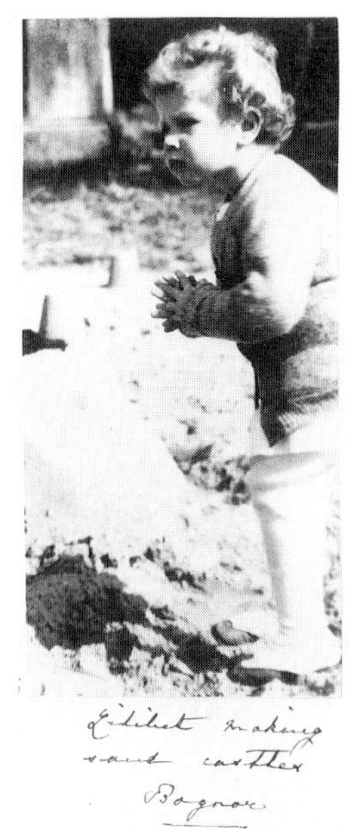

Lilibet making sand castles Bognor

PRINCESS ELIZABETH
AT BOGNOR

Duchess of York presented the King and Queen with their second granddaughter, the Princess Margaret, born at Glamis Castle on 21 August 1930.

Four years later, on 29 November 1934, Prince George, Duke of Kent, youngest surviving son of King George and Queen Mary, was married at Westminster Abbey. His bride was the comparatively unknown Princess Marina of Greece and Denmark, youngest daughter of Prince Nicholas of Greece and his wife, the former Grand Duchess Helen Vladimirovna of Russia. Then, in May 1935, came celebrations marking the twenty-fifth anniversary of the King's accession to the throne, the Silver Jubilee. On 6 May, George V and Queen Mary rode in state through the decorated streets of London to St Paul's Cathedral where, in the presence of the entire royal family and some 2,000 other guests, they attended the nation's service of thanksgiving for the King's reign.

Later that year, on 6 November, the royal couple saw the marriage of their third son 'Harry', by now Duke of Gloucester, to Lady Alice Montagu-Douglas-Scott, a daughter of the 7th Duke of Buccleuch. Originally planned to take place in Westminster Abbey, this particular royal wedding was solemnized in the private chapel of Buckingham Palace. The reason for this was the death of the bride's father only three weeks before the day of the wedding.

The following month, feeling tired and weak, and mourning the death on 3 December of his favourite sister 'Toria', the King, accompanied by Queen Mary, journeyed to Sandringham for the Christmas holiday. From then on, though he managed to go for rides around the estate on his white pony 'Jock', George V's condition deteriorated rapidly until, on 17 January, Queen Mary recognized that her husband was now 'very ill' and summoned his doctor, Lord Dawson of Penn.

Over the next day or two, all the immediate members of the royal family began to assemble at Sandringham and it was there on Monday, 20 January 1936, that the King died. '*Am brokenhearted,*' Queen Mary wrote in her diary that evening, 'at 5 to 12 my darling husband passed peacefully away. . . .'

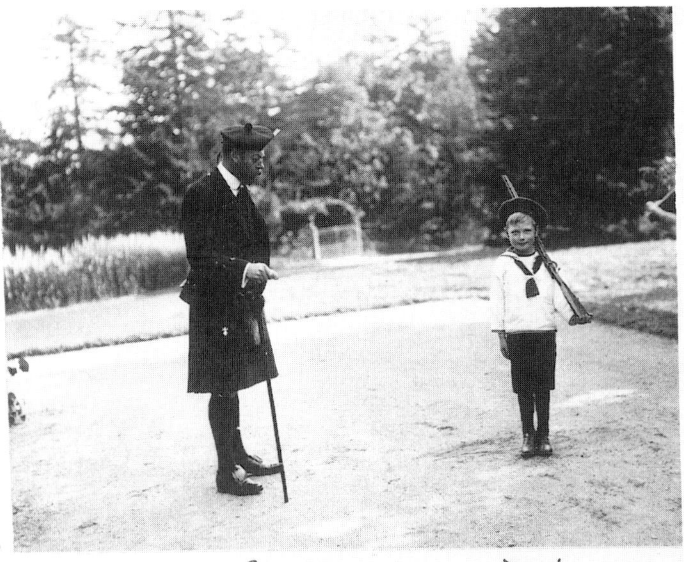

Balmoral
August
&
September
1910 –

G.   *Johnnie*

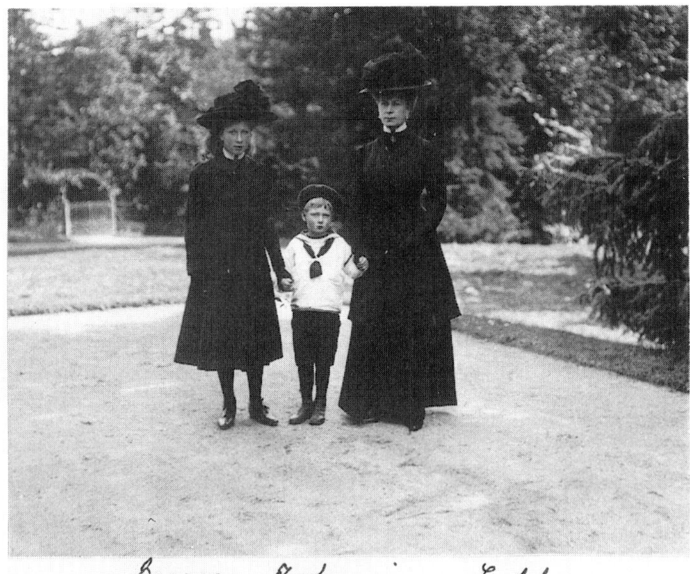

Mary   Johnnie   Self

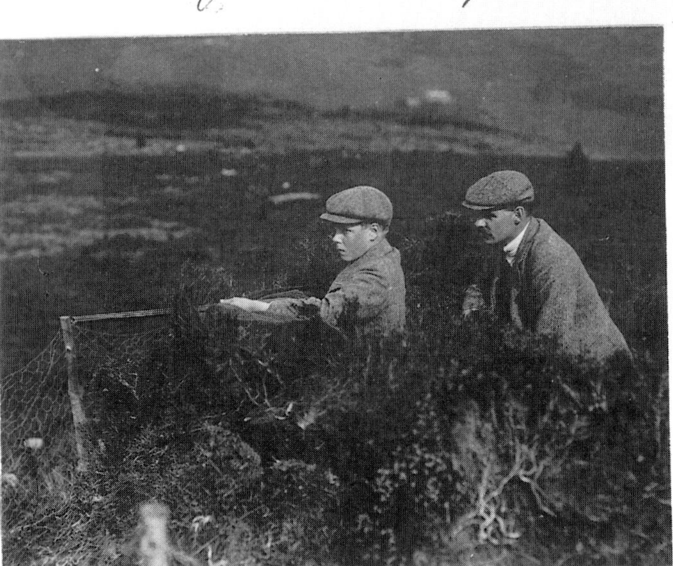

David

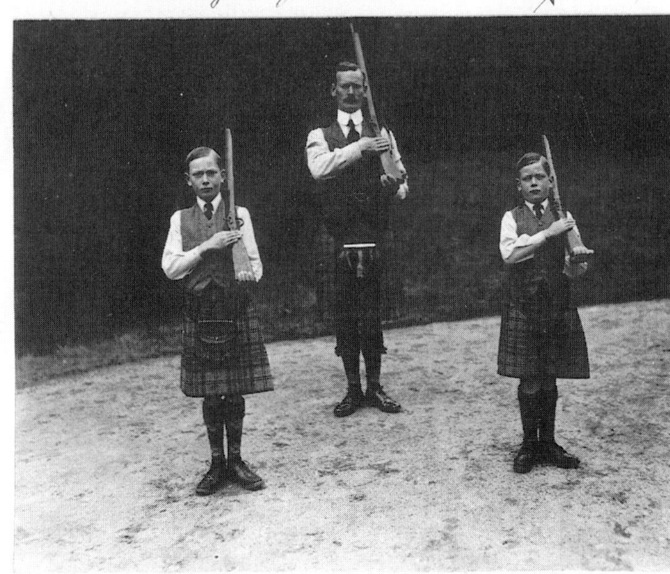

Harry   Forsyth   George

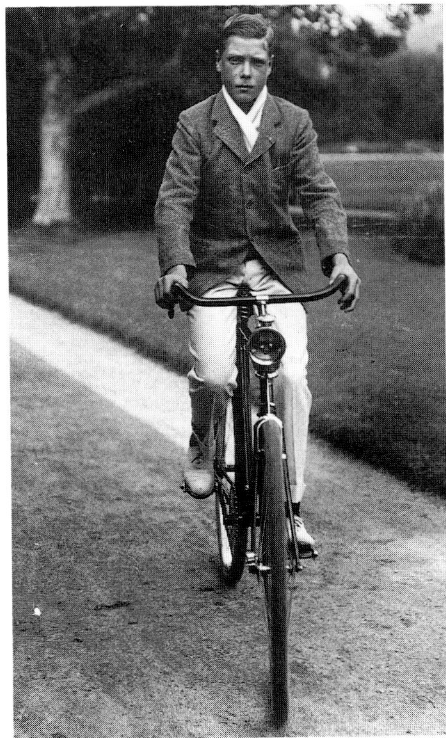

DESPITE HIS PRECARIOUS HEALTH,
JOHNNIE JOINED THE ROYAL FAMILY
ON HOLIDAY WHENEVER HE COULD –
HERE, AT BALMORAL IN THE SUMMER
OF 1910

THE PRINCE OF WALES AT THE AGE
OF SIXTEEN CYCLING AT BALMORAL,
AUTUMN 1910

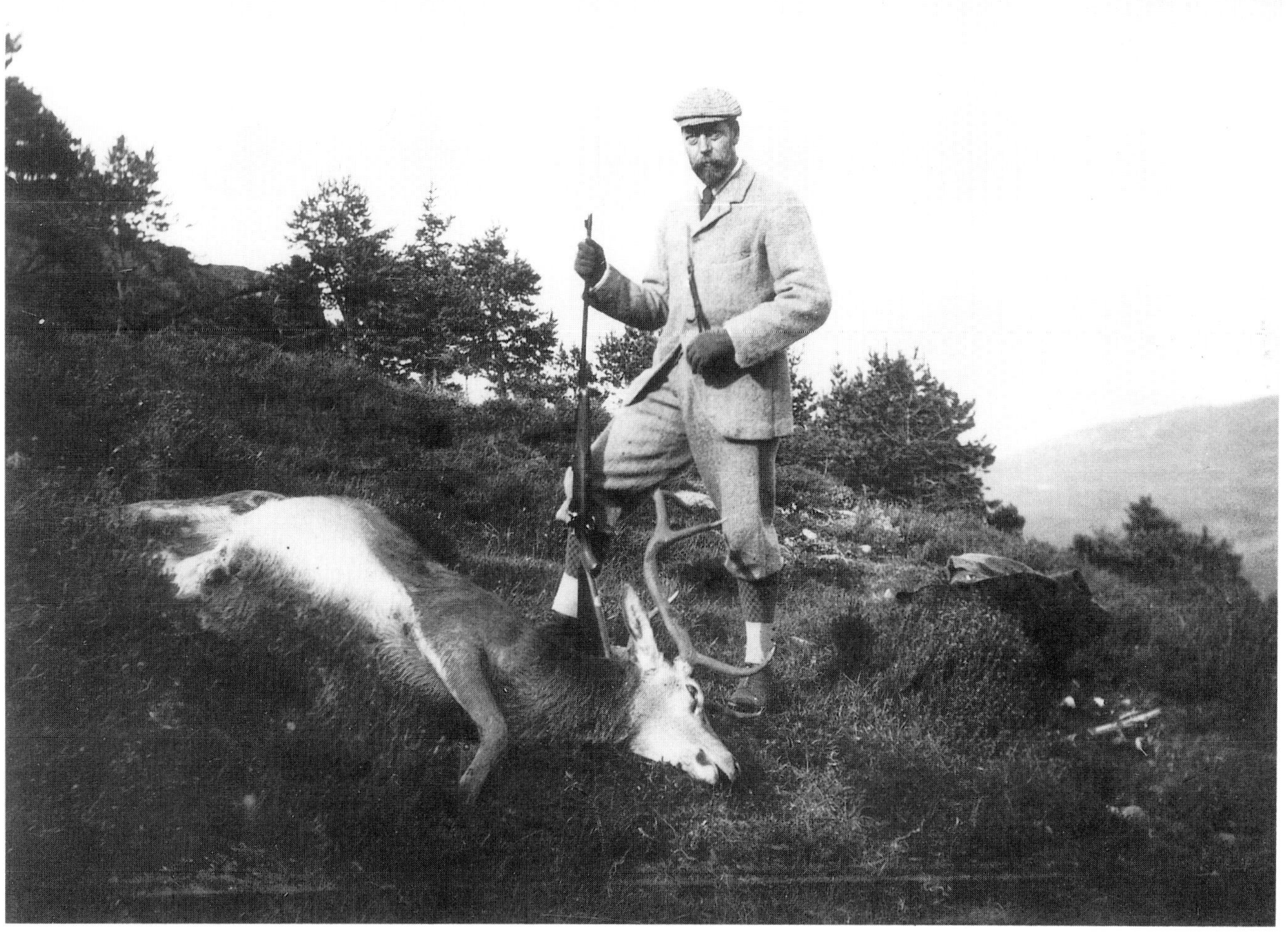

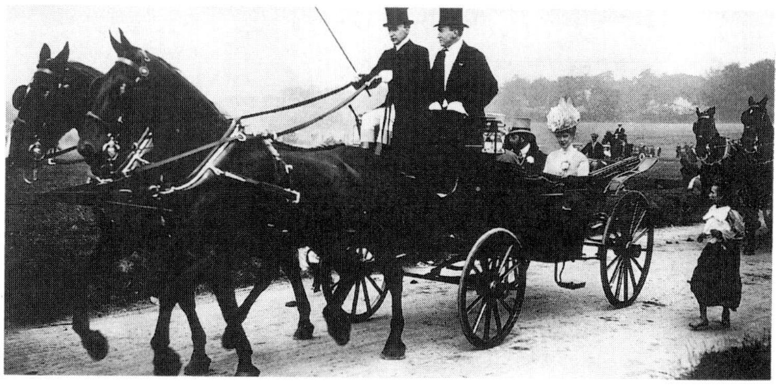

BAREFOOTED, A LITTLE
GIRL RUNS ALONGSIDE THE
ROYAL CARRIAGE TO LOOK
AT THE QUEEN AS SHE AND
THE KING DRIVE TO THE
DERBY ON 31 MAY 1911

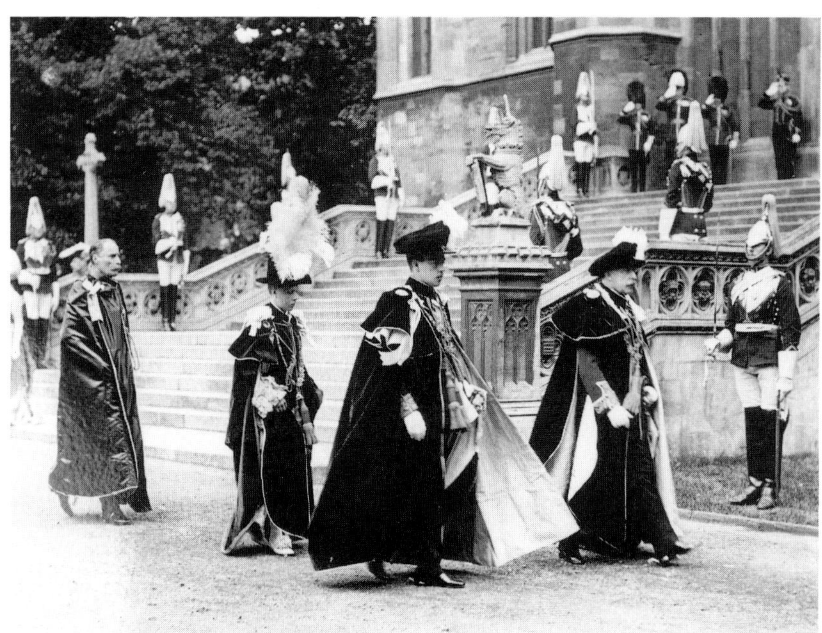

THE PRINCE OF WALES IN GARTER ROBES
FOLLOWS KING MANUEL OF PORTUGAL AND
ARTHUR, DUKE OF CONNAUGHT, FROM THE
PRECINCTS OF ST GEORGE'S CHAPEL, WINDSOR,
ON GARTER DAY, 10 JUNE 1911

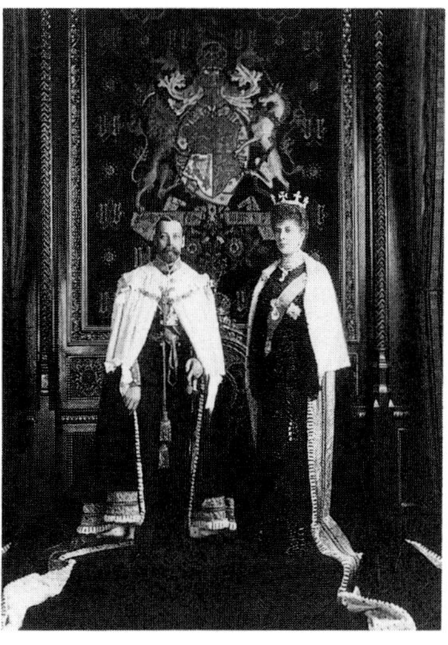

KING GEORGE V AND QUEEN MARY
PHOTOGRAPHED IN THE ROYAL
ROBING ROOM AT THE PALACE OF
WESTMINSTER AFTER THEIR FIRST
STATE OPENING OF PARLIAMENT ON
6 FEBRUARY 1911

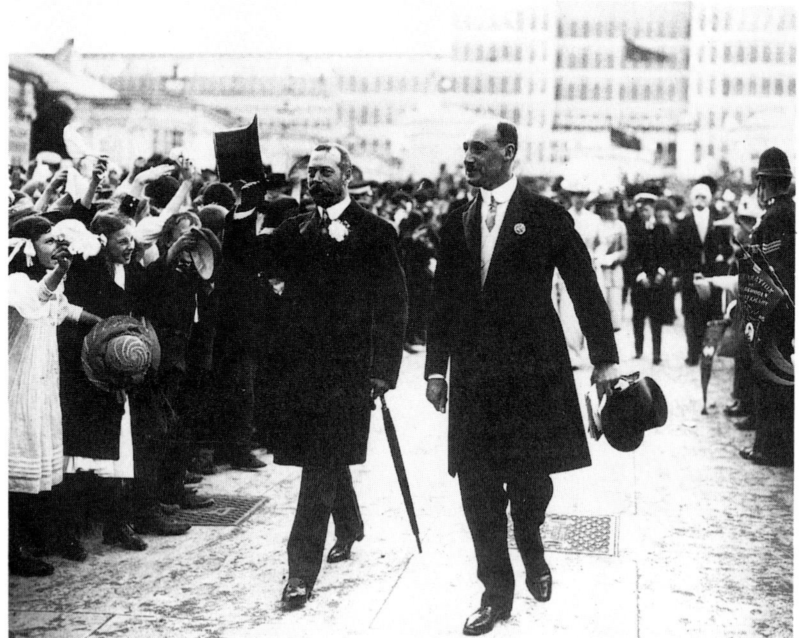

KING GEORGE V DOFFS HIS SILK HAT IN
RESPONSE TO THE CHEERS OF THE CROWD AS HE
AND THE QUEEN (SEEN IN THE BACKGROUND)
ARRIVE AT CRYSTAL PALACE FOR THE
CHILDREN'S CORONATION FÊTE, 30 JUNE 1911

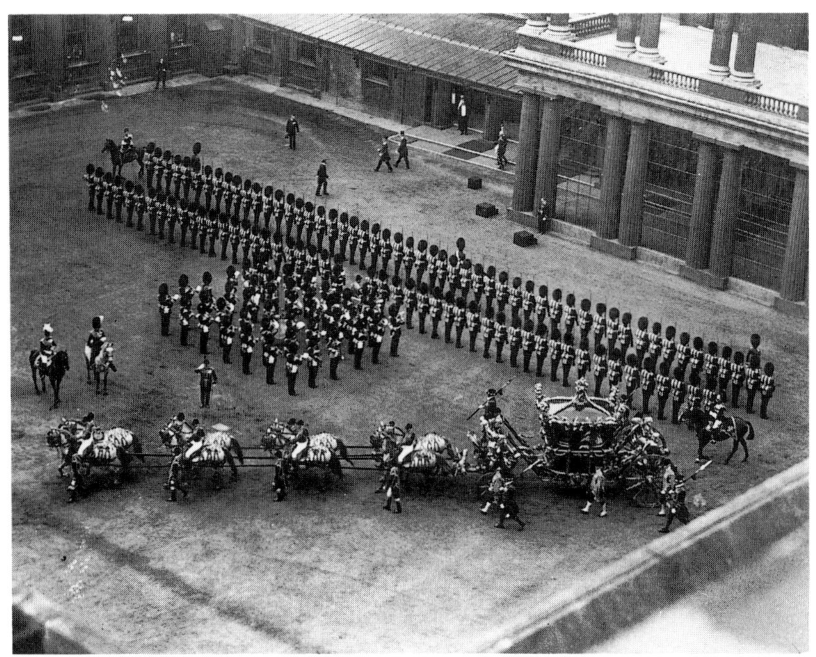

CORONATION DAY, 22 JUNE
1911. THE STATE COACH,
BEARING THE KING AND
QUEEN TO WESTMINSTER
ABBEY, CROSSES THE INNER
QUADRANGLE AT
BUCKINGHAM PALACE

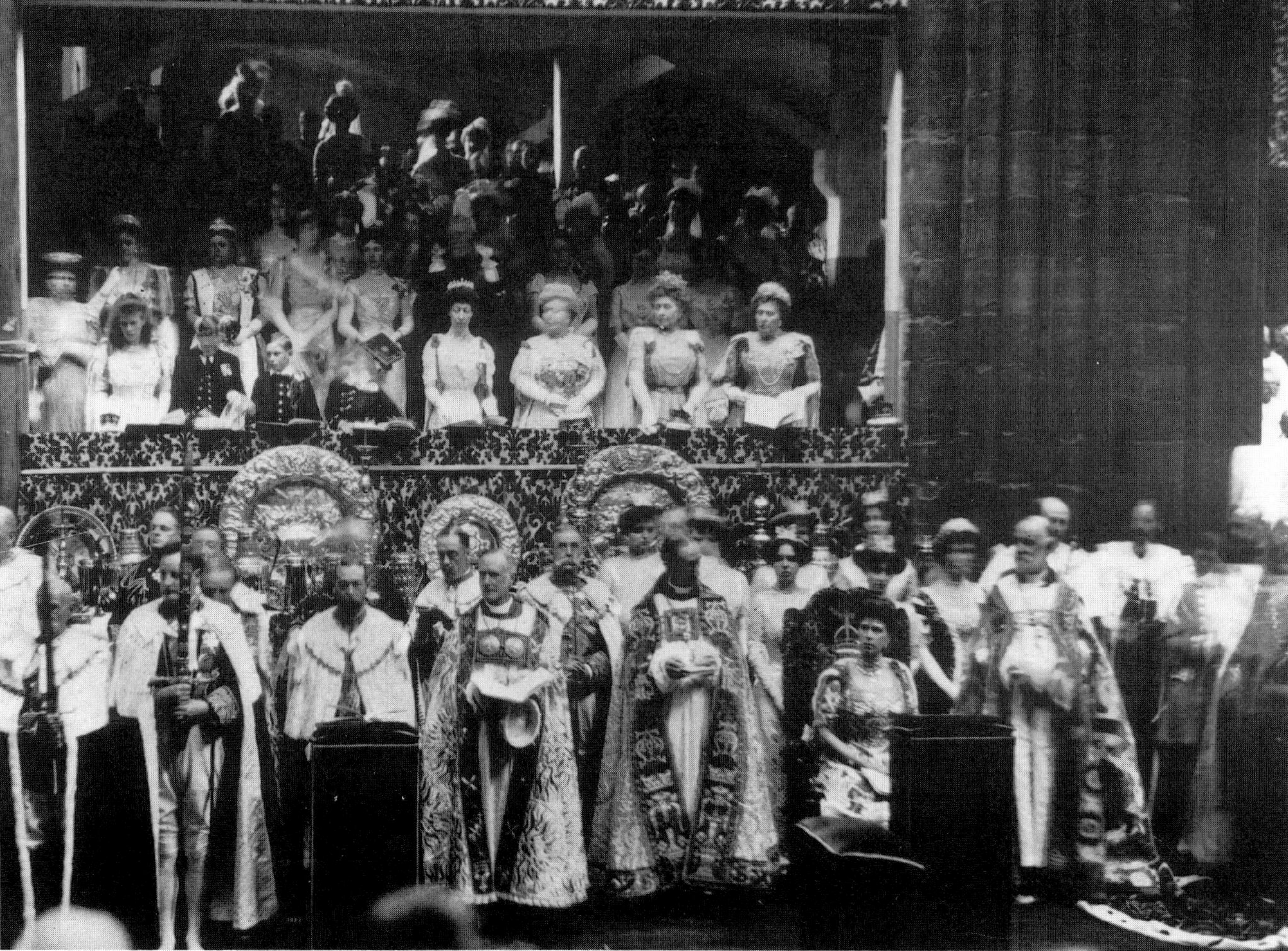

THE ONLY PHOTOGRAPH
OF THE CORONATION IN
QUEEN MARY'S ALBUM IN
WHICH SHE AND THE KING
ARE VISIBLE. HERE THEY
SIT IN THEIR CHAIRS OF
ESTATE BENEATH THE
ROYAL GALLERY IN
WESTMINSTER ABBEY.
PRINCESS MARY, PRINCE
ALBERT, PRINCE HENRY
AND PRINCE GEORGE MAY
BE SEEN IN THE FRONT
ROW, TOGETHER WITH
PRINCESS VICTORIA AND
OTHER ROYAL LADIES

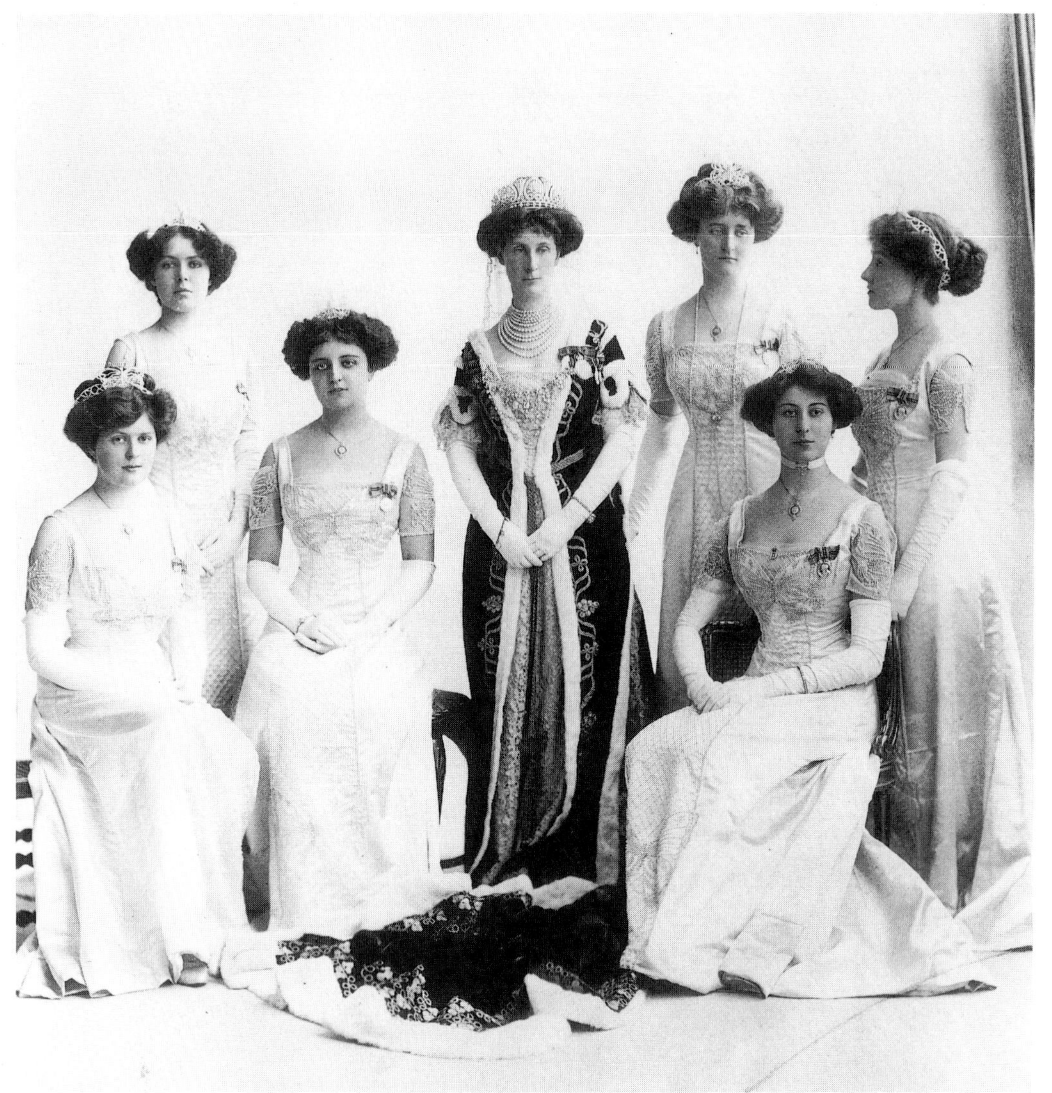

QUEEN MARY'S ATTENDANTS: THE DUCHESS OF DEVONSHIRE, MISTRESS OF THE ROBES, FLANKED BY THE QUEEN'S MAIDS OF HONOUR. LEFT TO RIGHT: LADY VICTORIA CARRINGTON, LADY MABELL OGILVY, LADY MARY DAWSON, LADY DOROTHY BROWNE, LADY EILEEN BUTLER AND LADY EILEEN KNOX

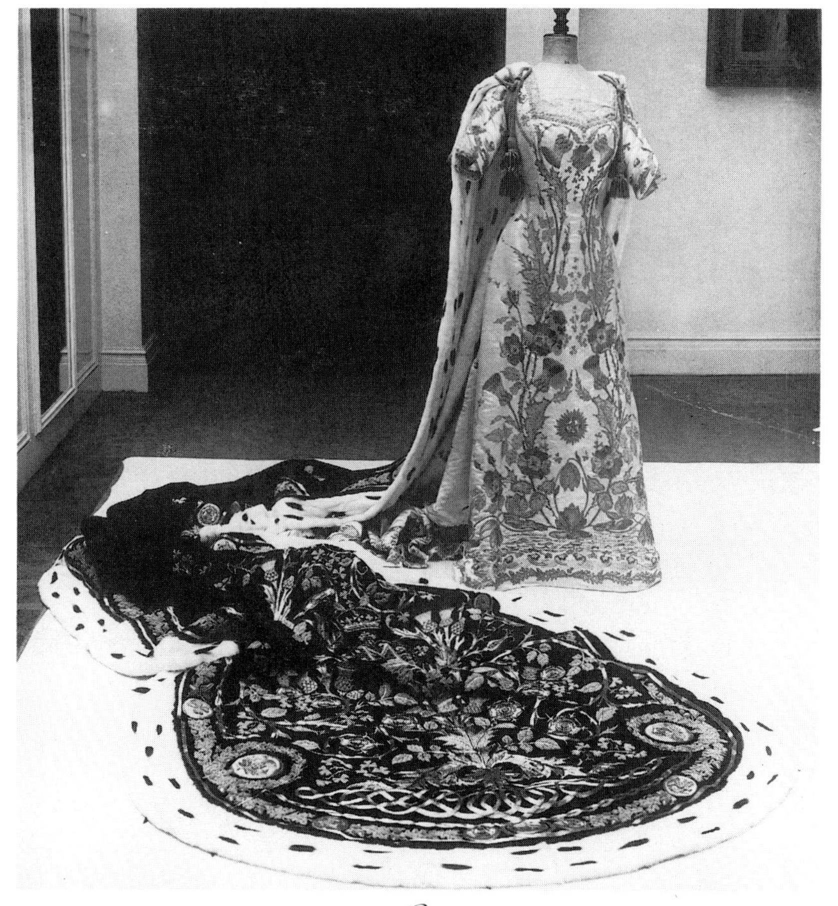

WITH AN EYE TO POSTERITY, QUEEN MARY HAD SEVERAL PHOTOGRAPHS TAKEN OF HER CORONATION GOWN AND TRAIN, THOUGH SHE HERSELF DID NOT MODEL THEM FOR THE CAMERA. INSTEAD, THEY WERE DISPLAYED ON NOTHING MORE REGAL THAN A DRESSMAKER'S DUMMY

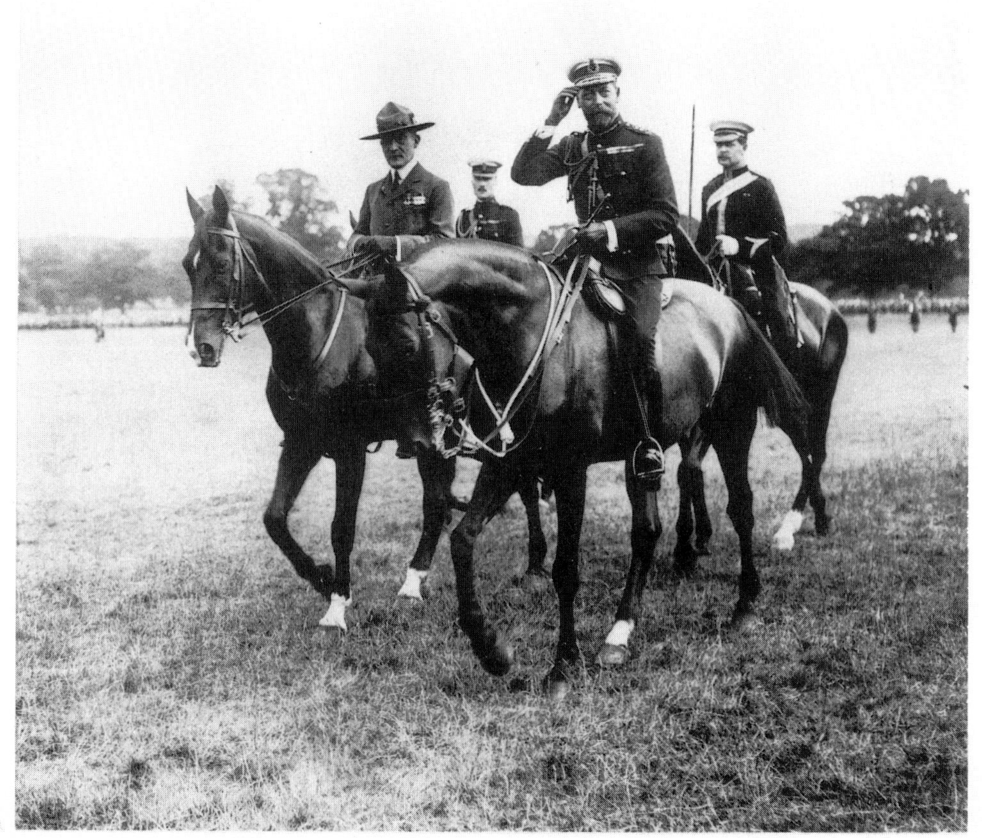

Inspection of boy scouts
July 4th

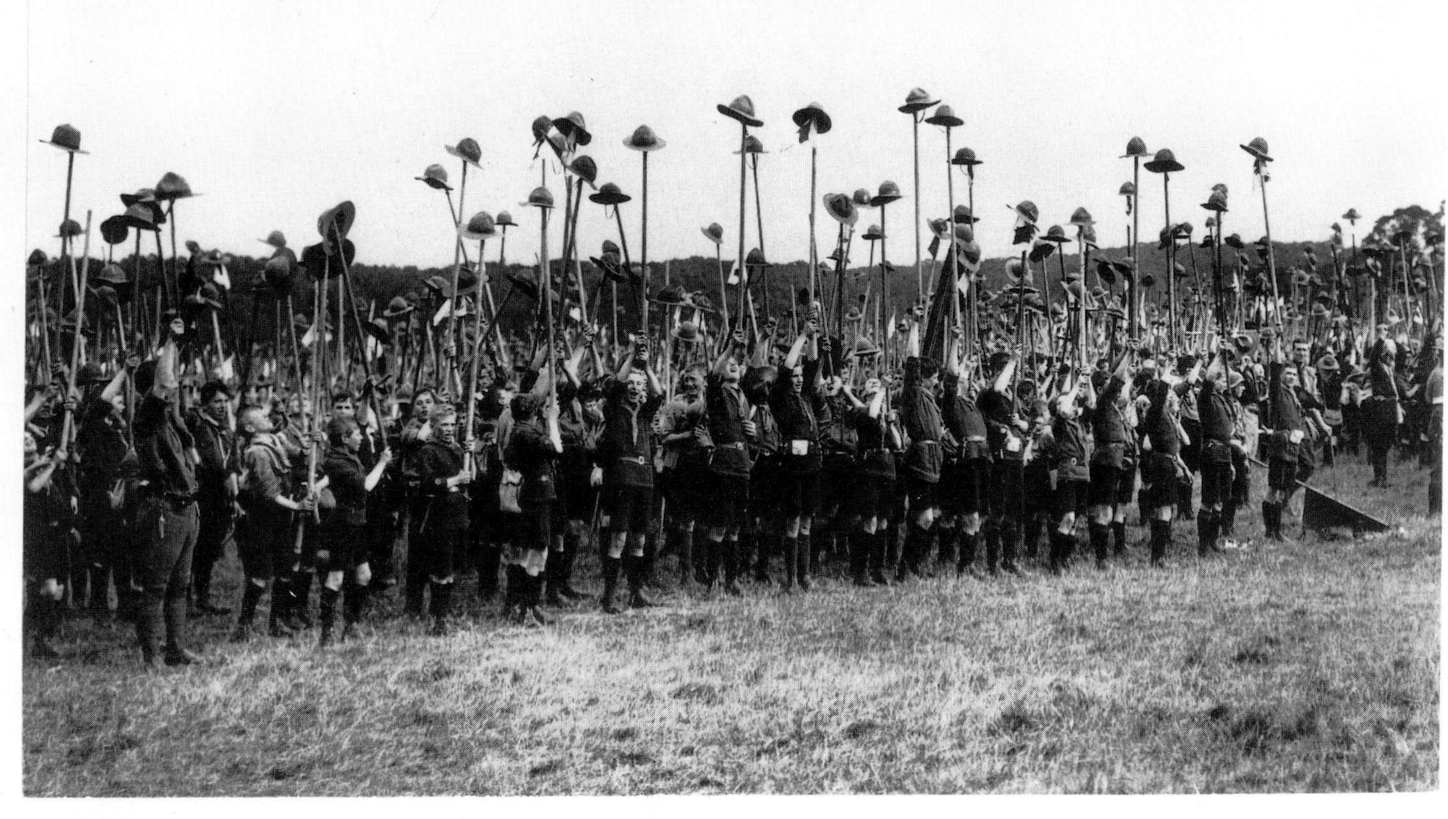

Princess Mary stroking
a penguin at London
Zoo, 4 June 1911

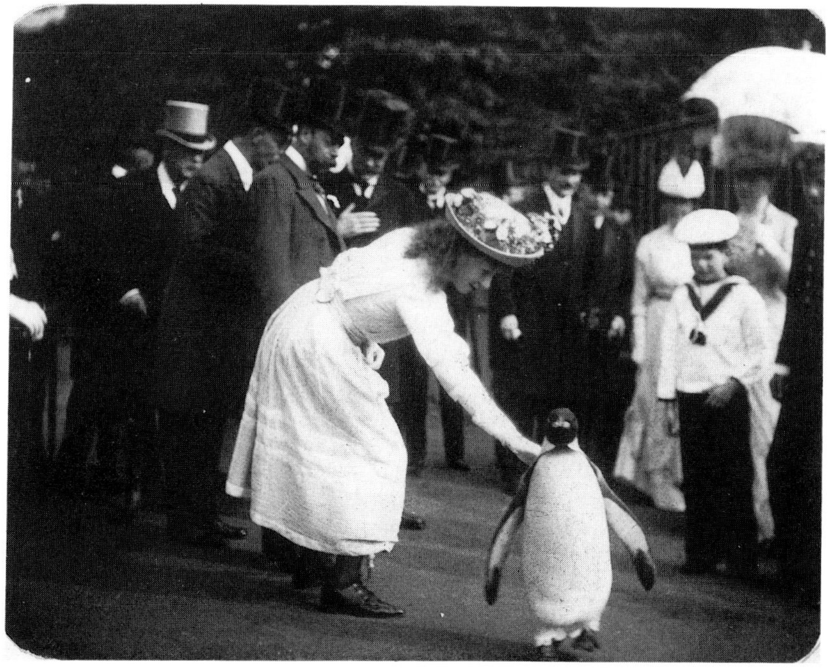

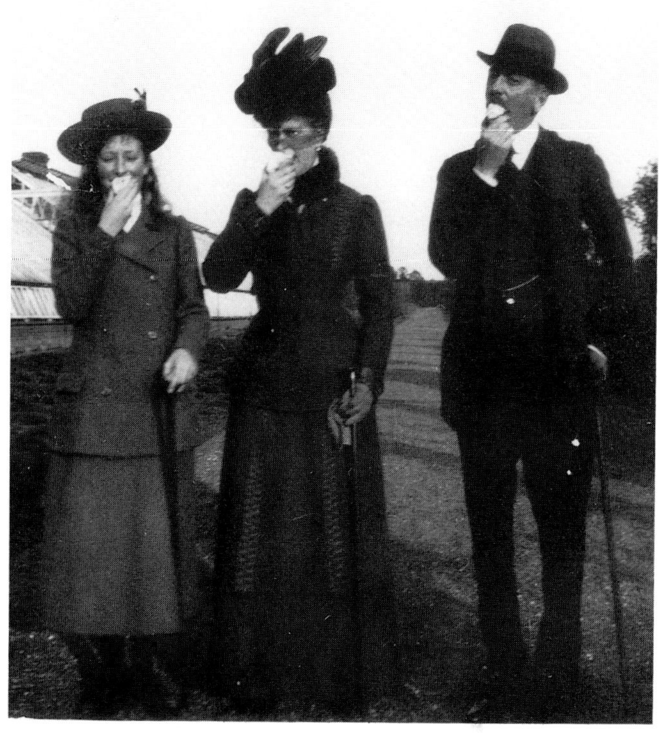

'Coronation fever' ran
high throughout the
summer of 1911. At
Caernarvon Castle on
14 July, David was
formally invested
Prince of Wales and
Earl of Chester

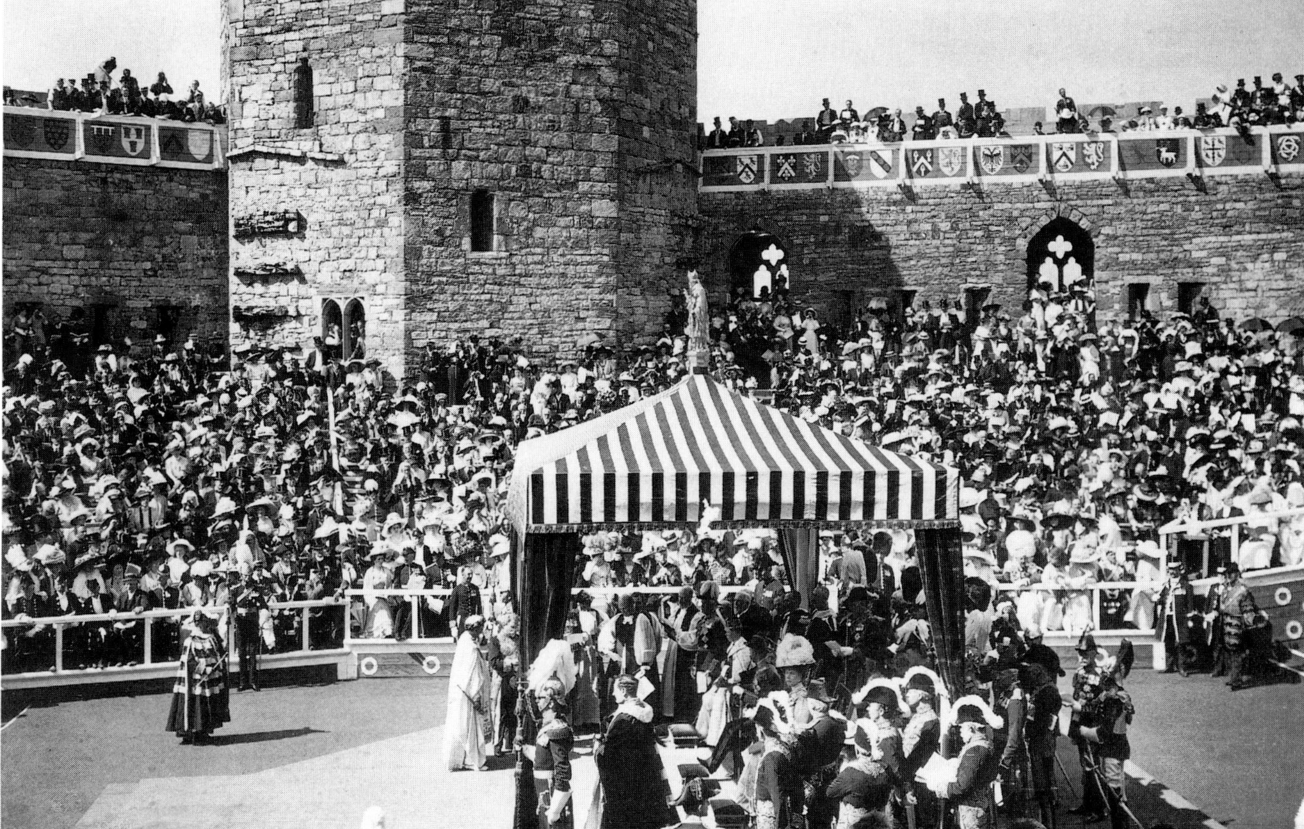

(*Opposite*) The King,
accompanied by Sir
Robert Baden-Powell,
Chief Scout, inspects
Boy Scouts at Windsor
on 4 July 1911

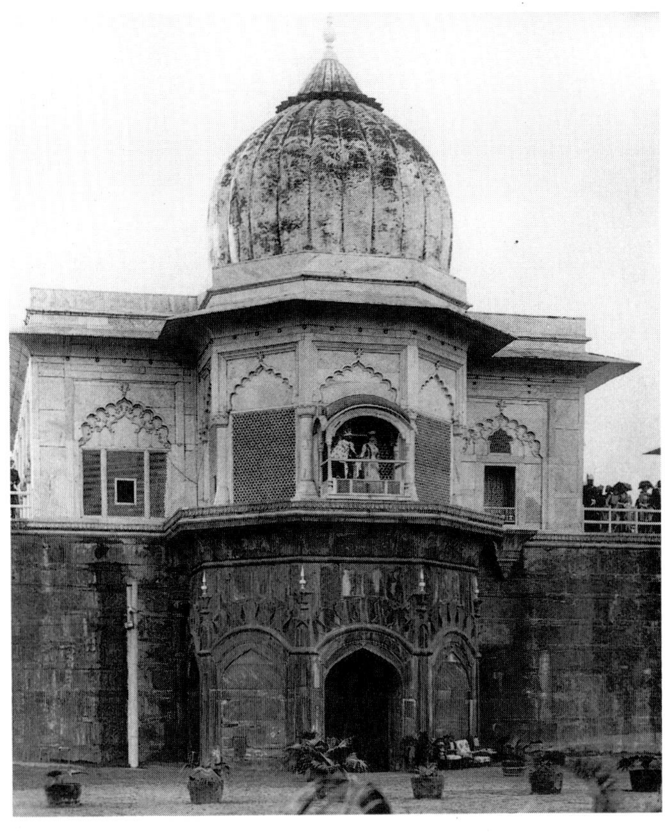

THE DELHI DURBAR, INDIA, 13 DECEMBER 1911. THE
KING AND QUEEN IN THEIR CORONATION ROBES IN
THE JHAROKHA AT DELHI FORT

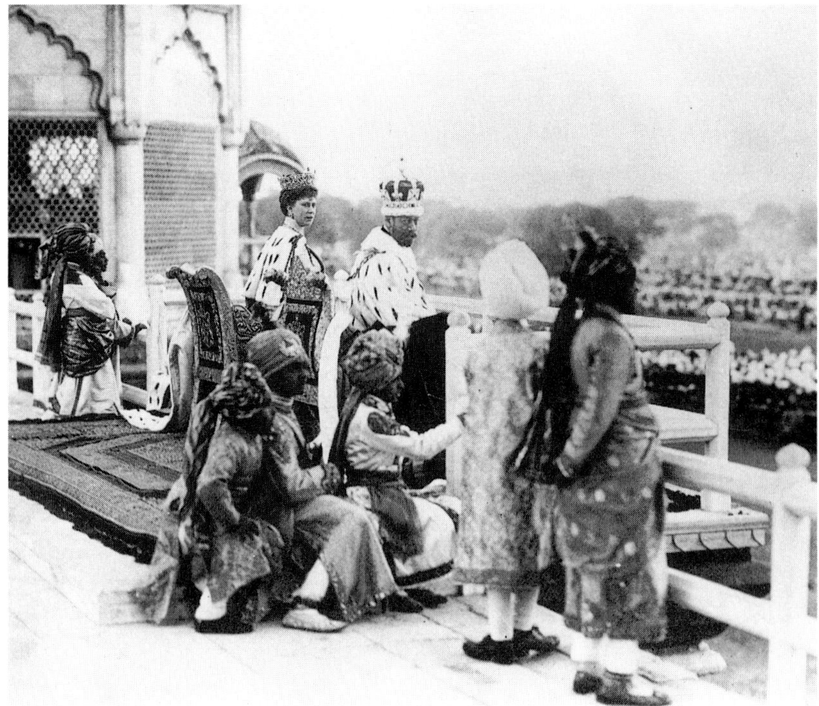

ATTENDED BY THEIR INDIAN PAGES THE KING
AND QUEEN VIEW THE MILITARY PAGEANT AT
THE DURBAR FROM THE FORT

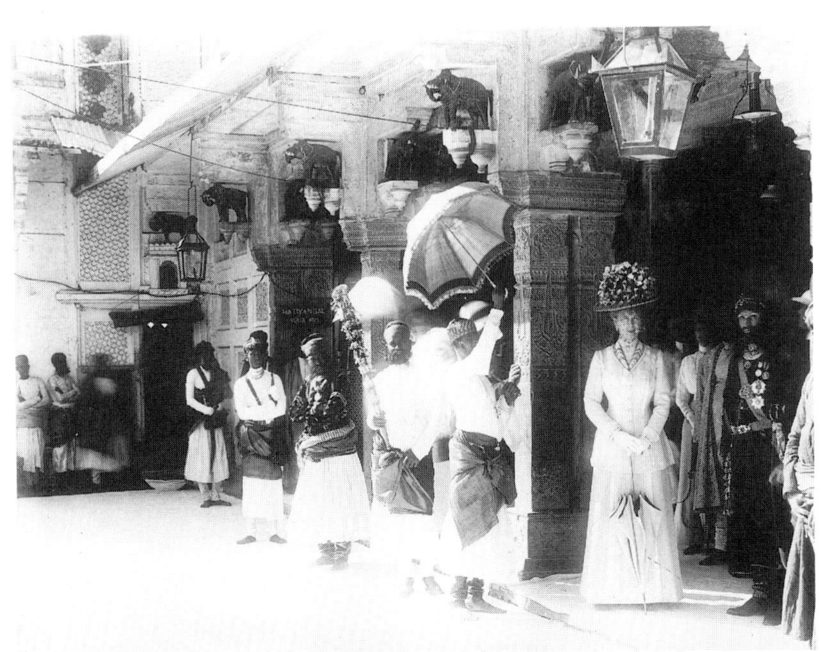

QUEEN MARY IN BUNDI, CHRISTMAS EVE 1911. SHE IS
SEEN WITH THE SINISTER-LOOKING CHIEF OF BUNDI,
THE MAHARAO RAJAH SIR RAGHUBIR SINGHJI SAHAB
BAHADUR

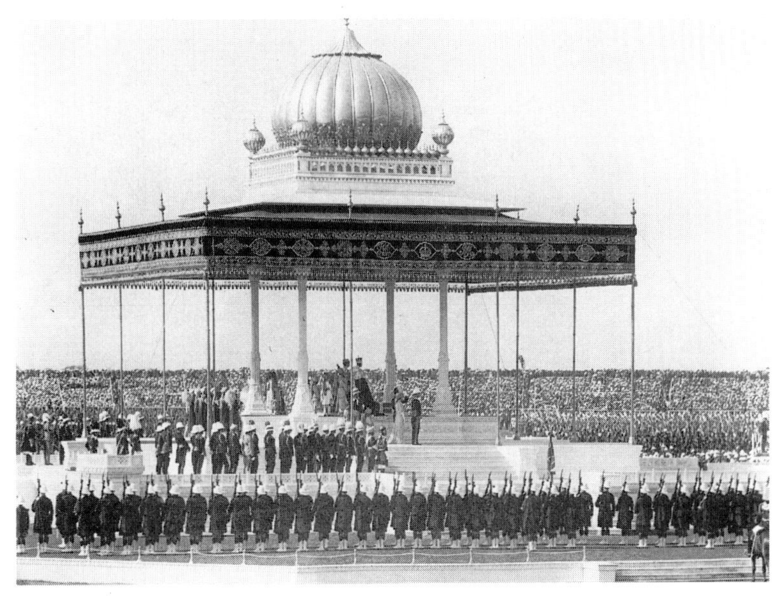

SEATED ON GOLD THRONES ENCASED IN SILVER, THE
KING-EMPEROR AND THE QUEEN-EMPRESS RECEIVE
THE HOMAGE OF INDIA'S RULERS BENEATH THE VAST
CRIMSON AND GOLD SHAMIANA SURMOUNTED BY A
GOLDEN DOME

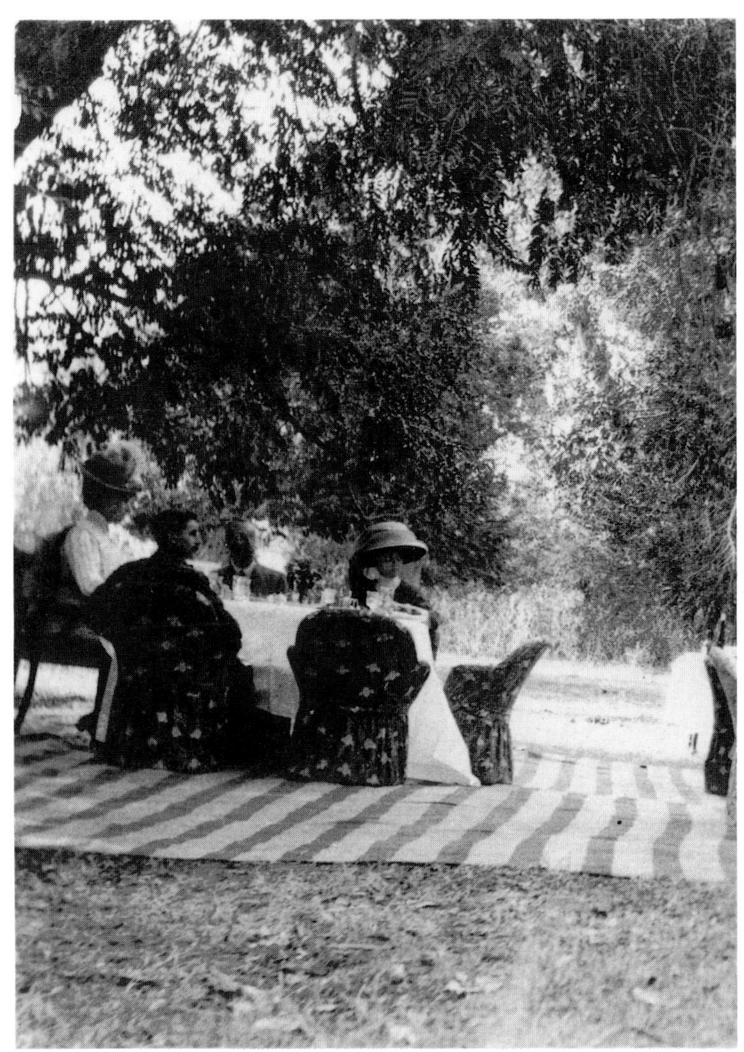

In the Jungle
Kotah
Dec. 27th

Seated comfortably in an armchair set on a
rug, Queen Mary 'in the jungle' at Kotah on
27 December 1911

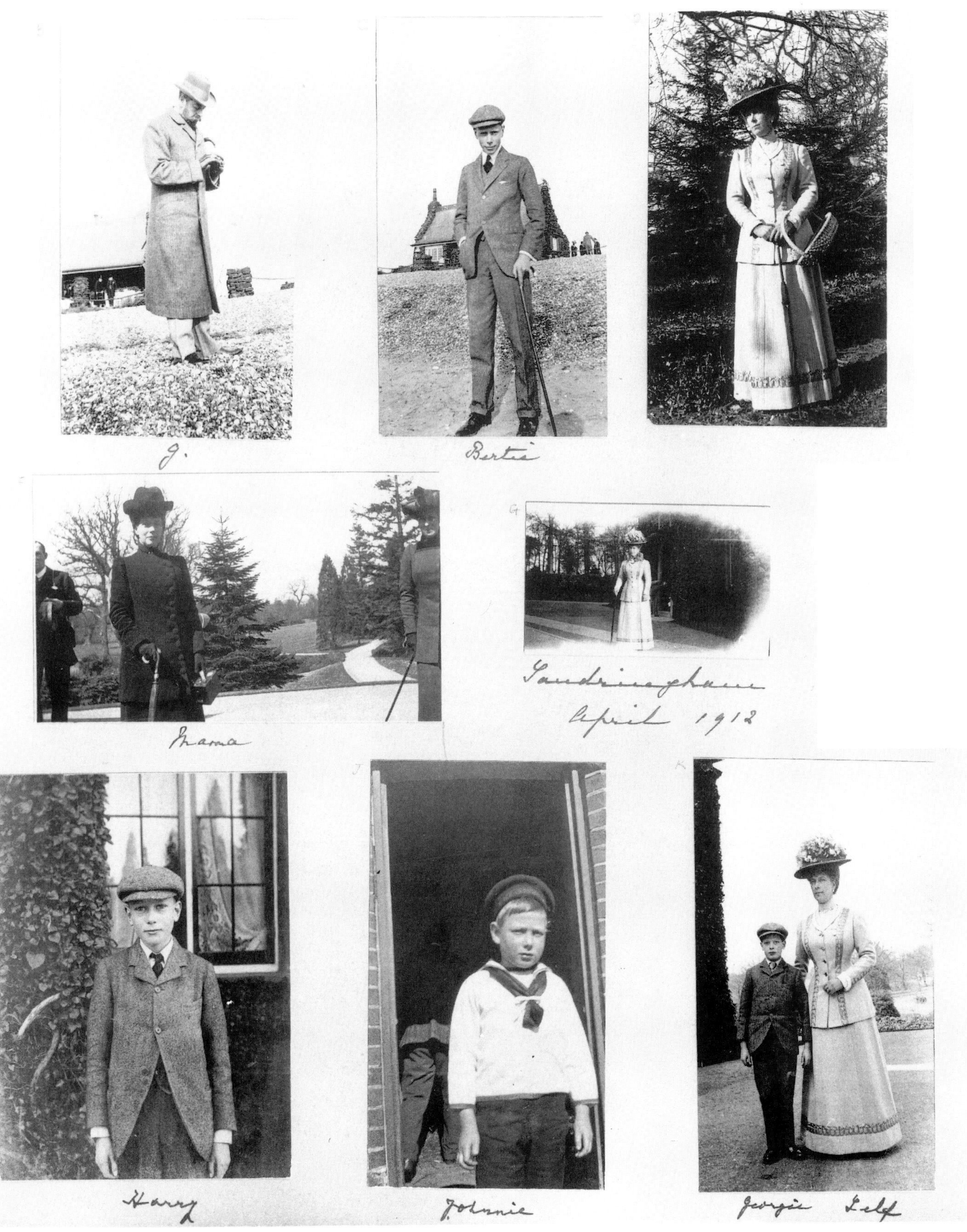

G.
Bertie
Mama
Sandringham
April 1912
Harry
Johnnie
Georgie   Self

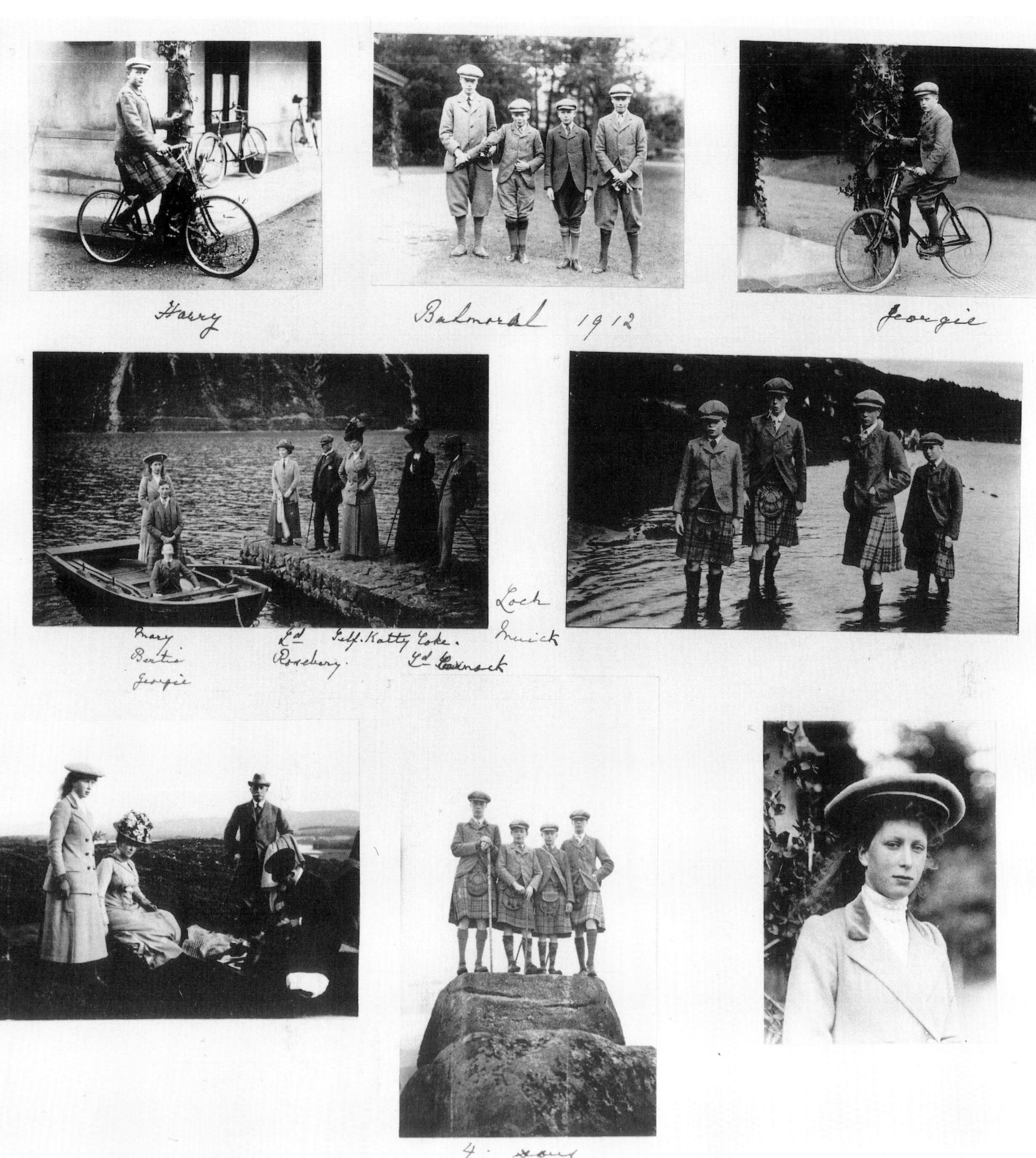
Harry
Balmoral 1912
Georgie
Mary
Bertie
Georgie
Ld
Rosebery.
Self. Katty Coke.
Ld Cadman
Loch
Muick
4. hour

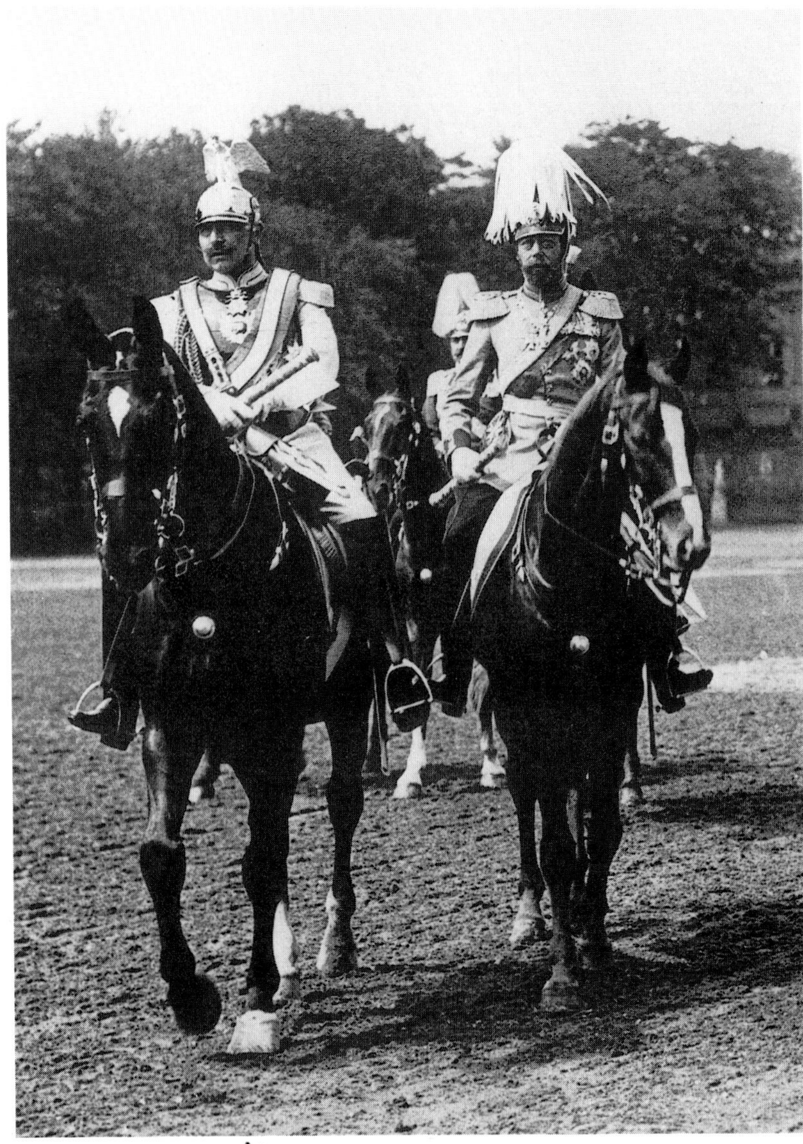

King George V riding with his
cousin, the megalomaniac
Kaiser Wilhelm II of Germany, in
Berlin in May 1913

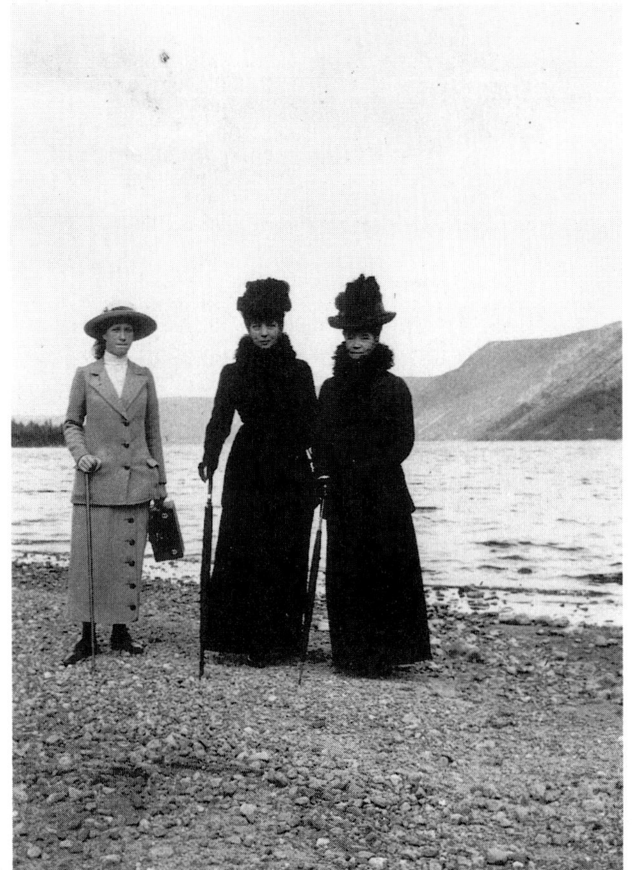

Princess Mary with her
grandmother Queen Alexandra and
'At Minny', the Dowager Tsarina
Marie Feodorovna, mother of the
last Tsar of Russia and Queen
Alexandra's sister, Balmoral 1913

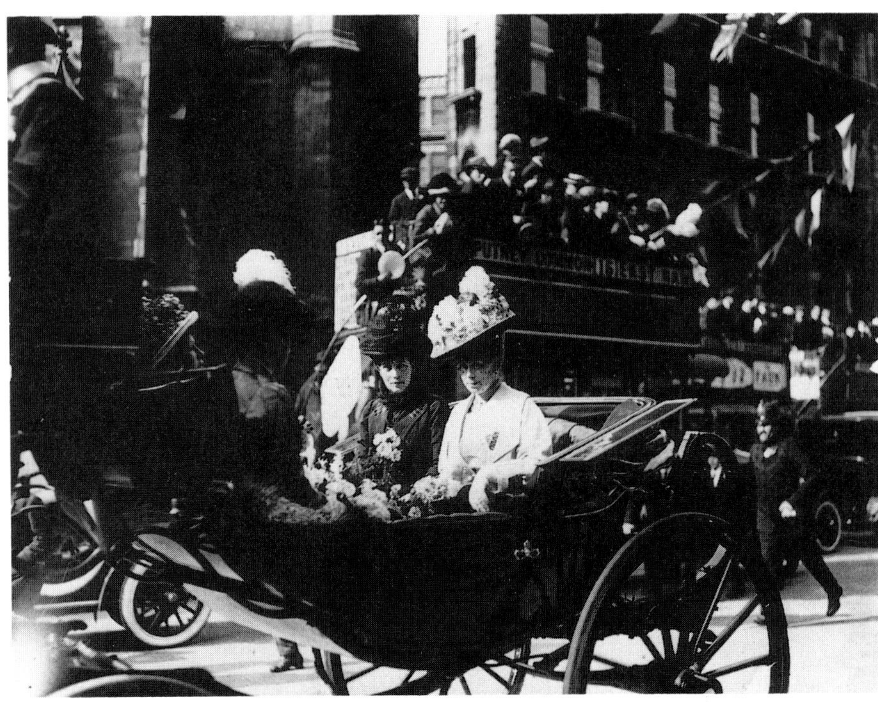

Queen Mary driving with her mother-
in-law, Queen Alexandra –
'Motherdear' – on Alexandra Rose Day,
June 1913

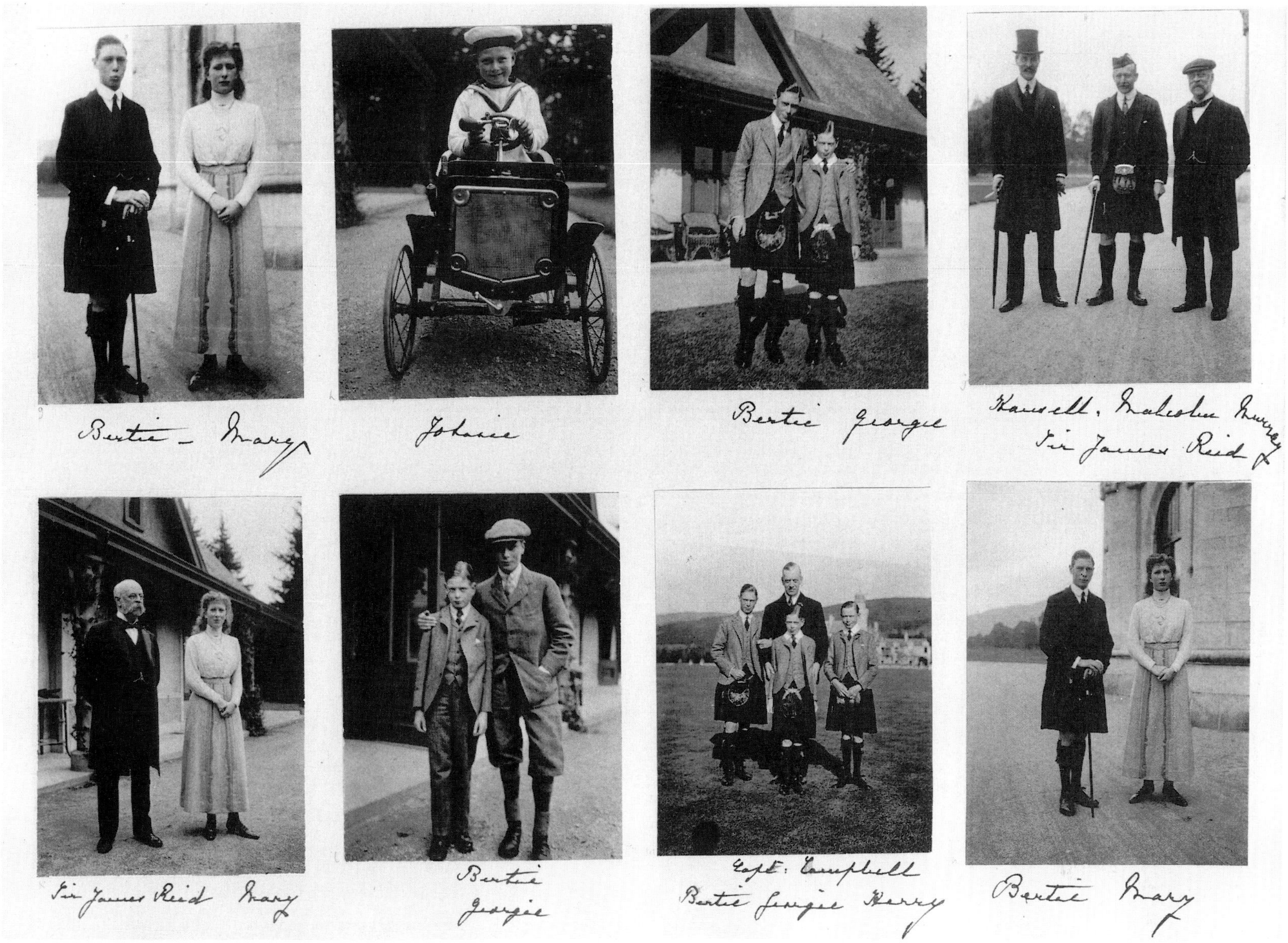

Family snaps taken at Balmoral during August and
September 1913

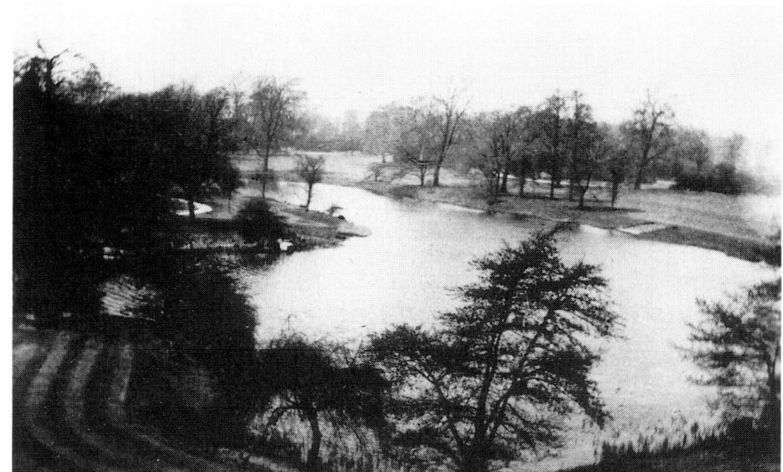

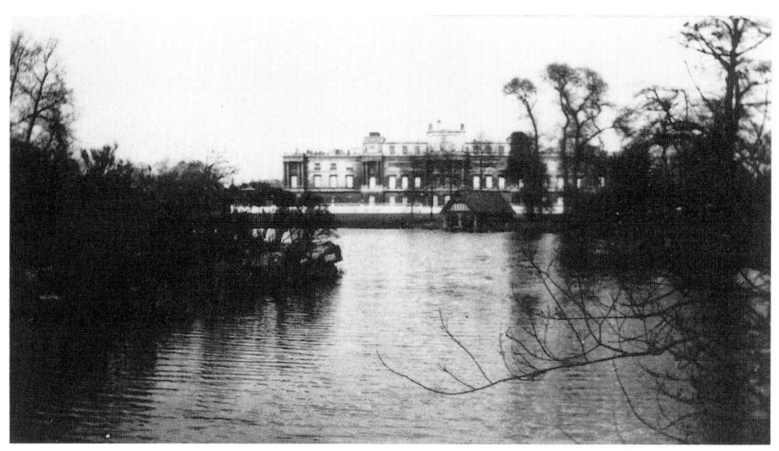

Buckingham Palace and its garden,
photographed in 1914 by Prince Harry

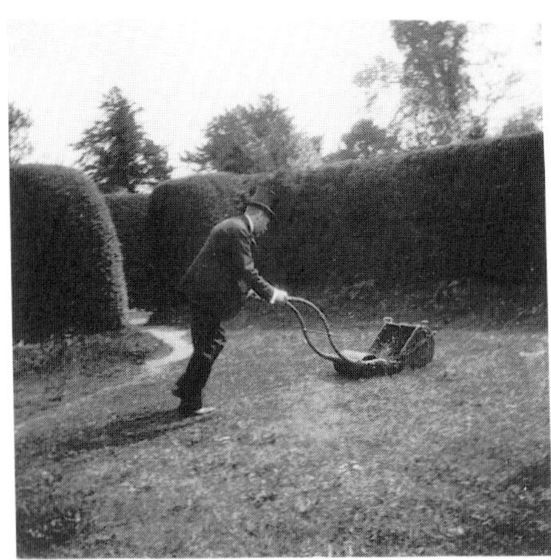

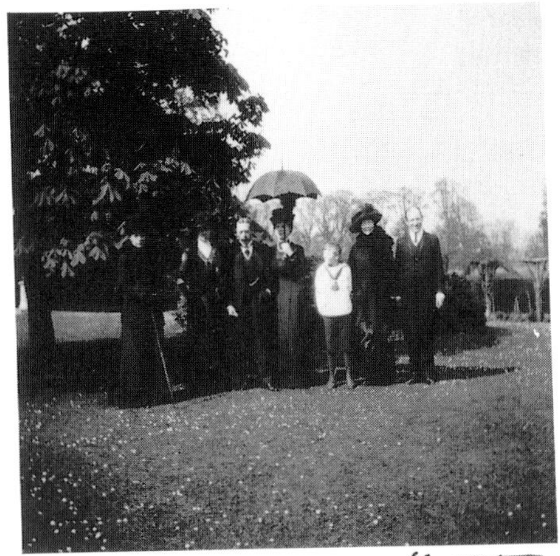

Adelaide Cottage Windsor

G. in tall hat!

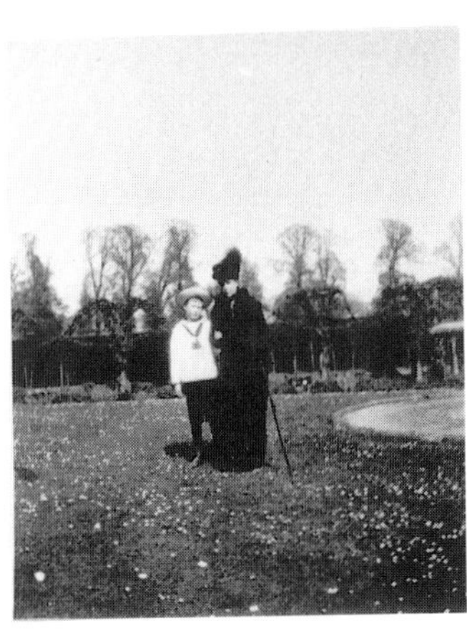

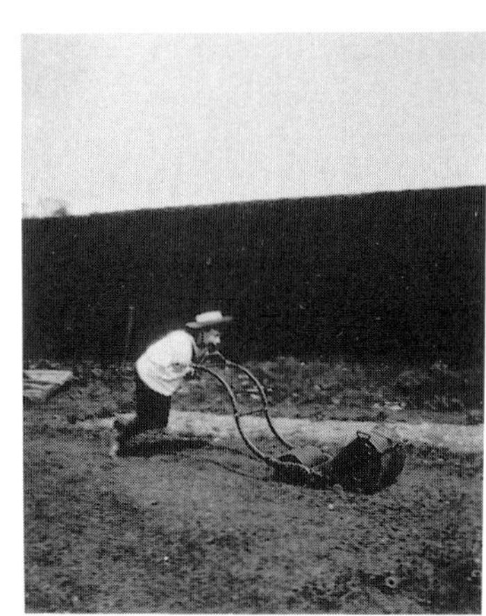

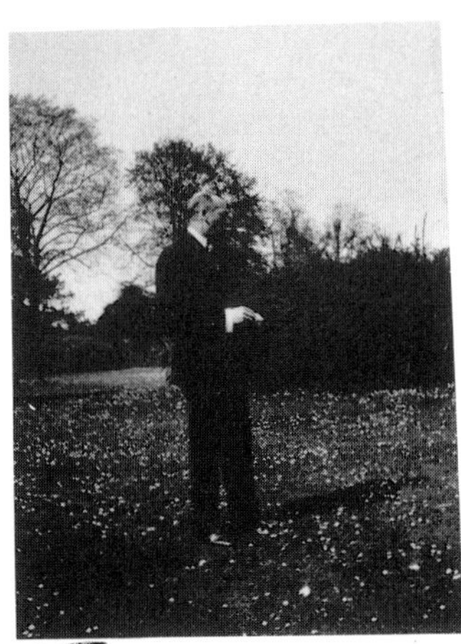

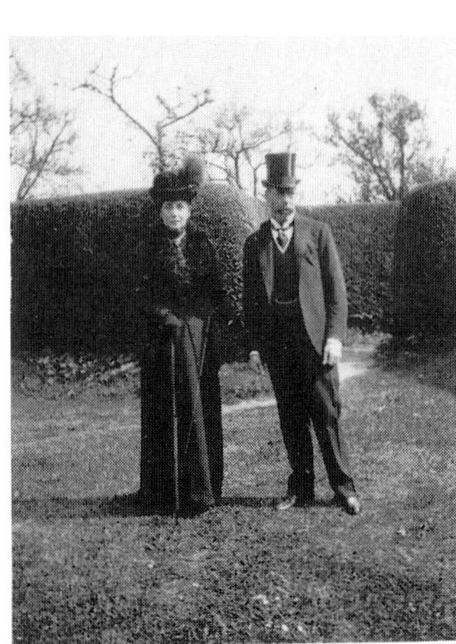

May 6th

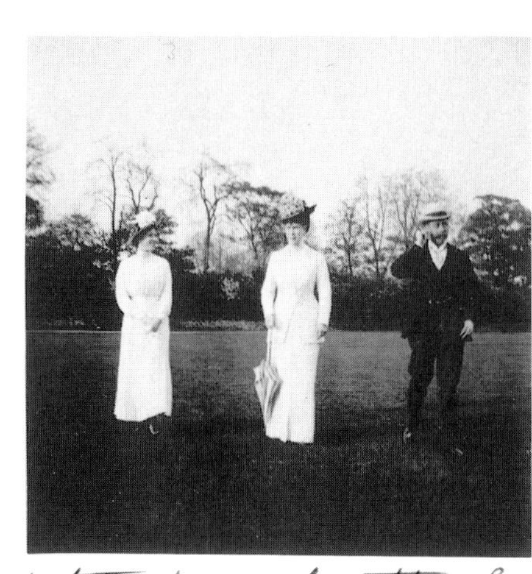

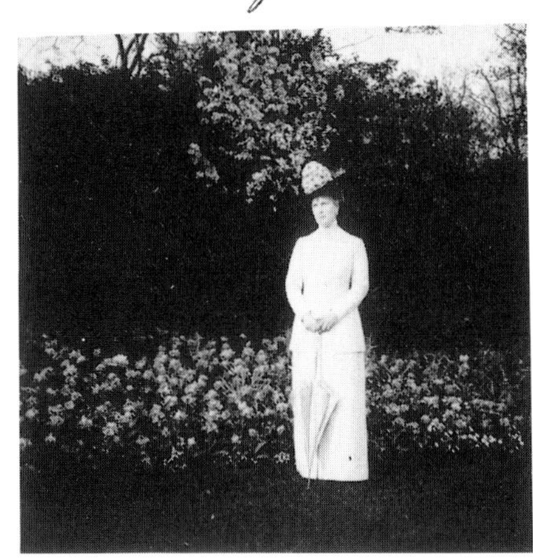

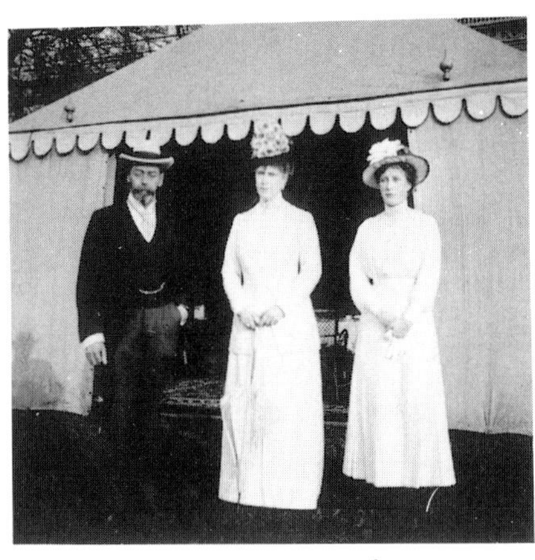

photos done by the Queen of the Belgians

In Buckingham Palace garden

May 7.

GARDENING ROYAL STYLE. KING GEORGE V IN 'TALL HAT' AND TAIL COAT (TOP) MOWING THE LAWN AT ADELAIDE COTTAGE, WINDSOR IN MAY 1915. IN THE MIDDLE ROW JOHNNIE TAKES OVER FROM HIS FATHER. THE LAST TRIO OF PHOTOGRAPHS, SHOWING THE KING, THE QUEEN AND MARY, WERE TAKEN IN THE GARDEN AT BUCKINGHAM PALACE BY ELIZABETH, QUEEN OF THE BELGIANS

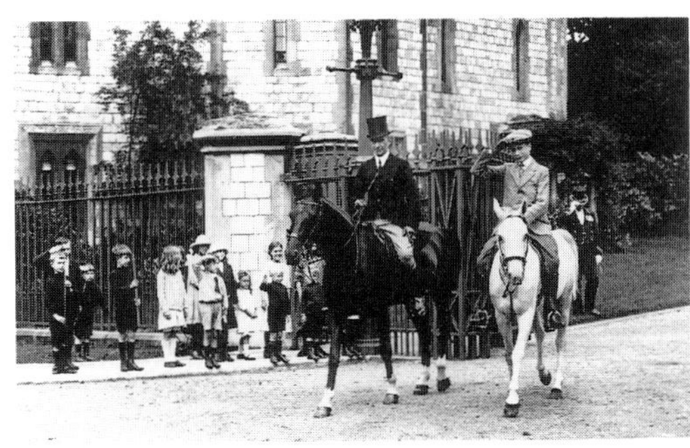

Harry riding at Windsor

PRINCE HARRY RIDING OUT ON TO THE LONG WALK AT WINDSOR IN AUGUST 1915. LOCAL CHILDREN SALUTE THE KING'S SON IN AMUSING FASHION

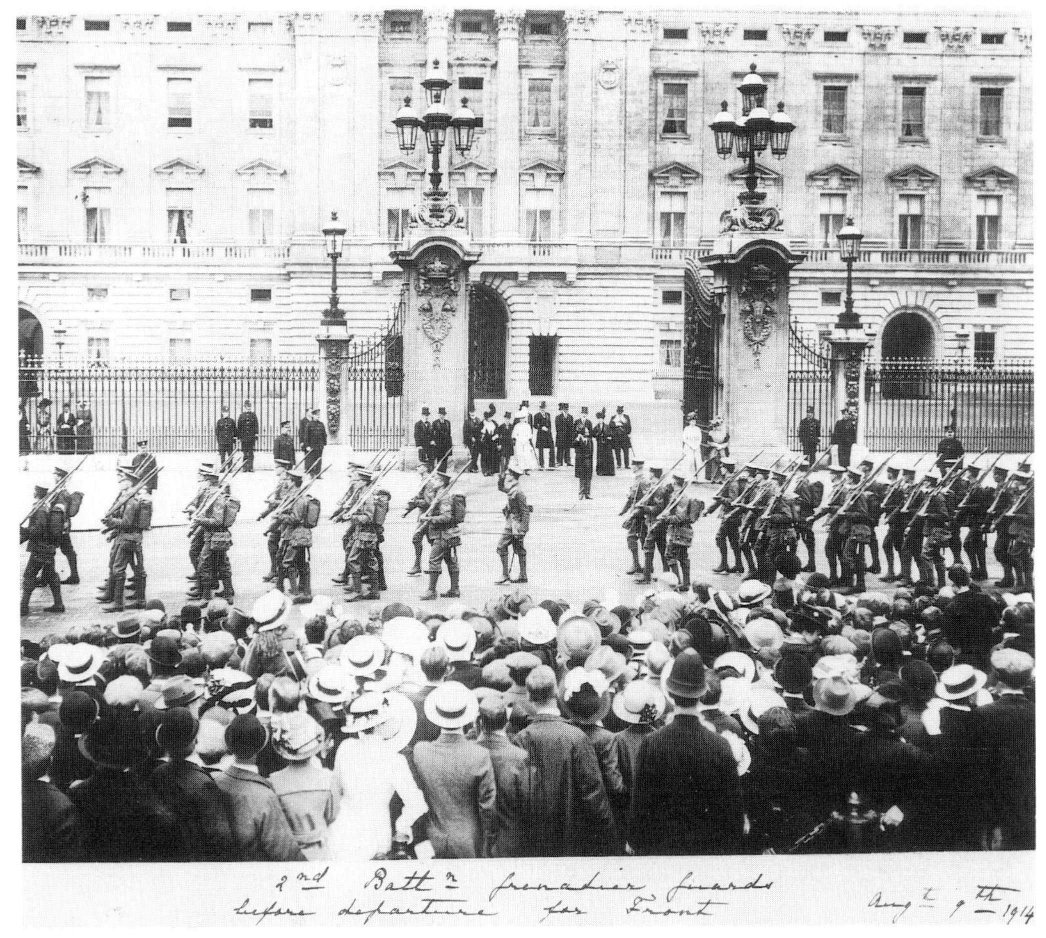

THE GREAT WAR 1914–18. THE KING WITH THE QUEEN AND OTHER MEMBERS OF THE ROYAL FAMILY BIDDING FAREWELL TO THE 2ND BATTALION GRENADIER GUARDS OUTSIDE BUCKINGHAM PALACE ON 9 AUGUST 1914

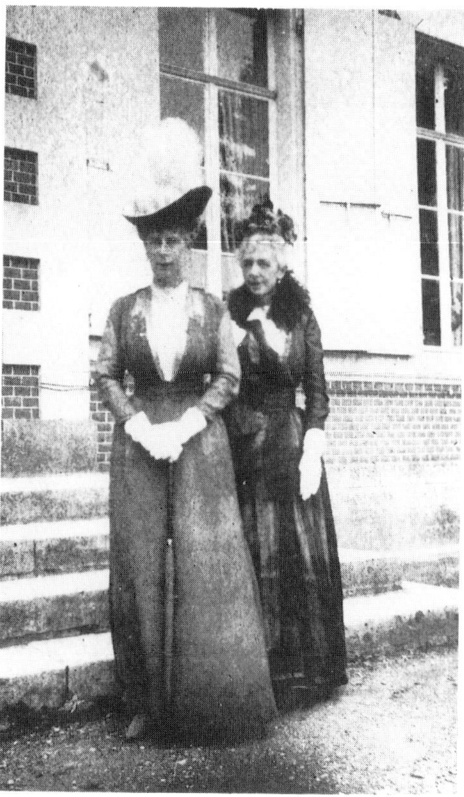

THE QUEEN WITH HER FRIEND AND LADY-IN-WAITING, MABELL, COUNTESS OF AIRLIE, PHOTOGRAPHED BY THE PRINCE OF WALES AT ABBEVILLE ON 10 JULY 1917

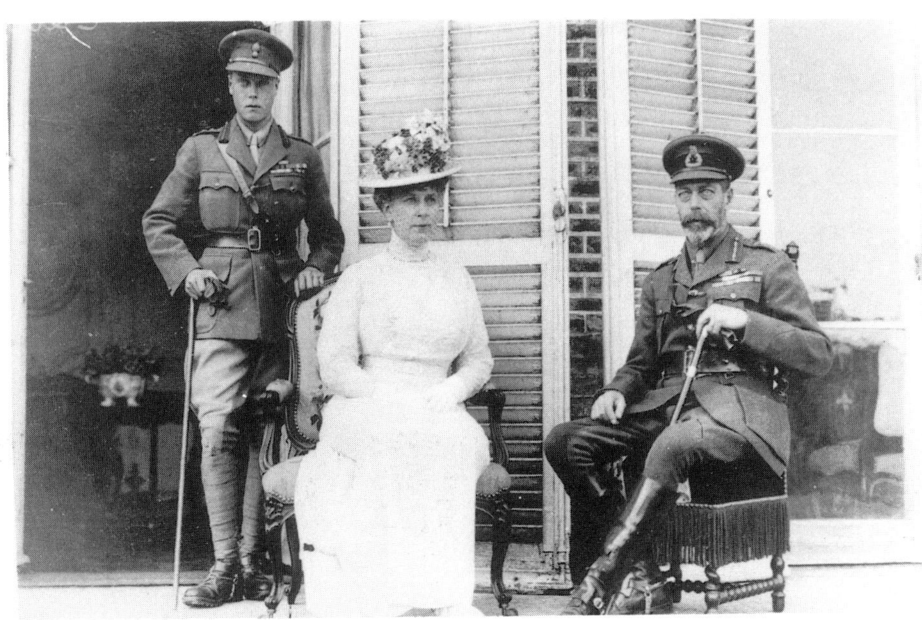

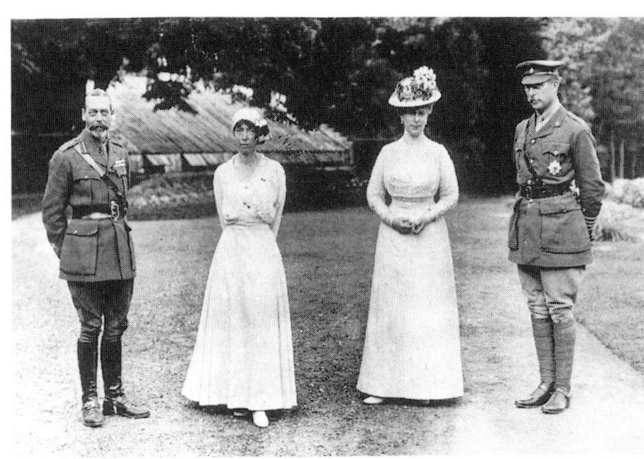

KING GEORGE V AND QUEEN MARY WITH THE PRINCE OF WALES AT THE CHÂTEAU DE TRAMECOURT ON 7 JULY 1917 AND WITH KING ALBERT AND QUEEN ELIZABETH OF THE BELGIANS

THE KING AND QUEEN
VISITING SUNDERLAND'S
MINING COMMUNITY ON
15 JUNE 1917

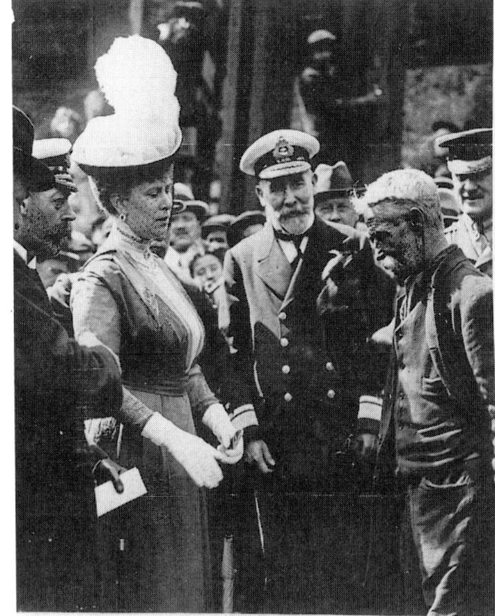
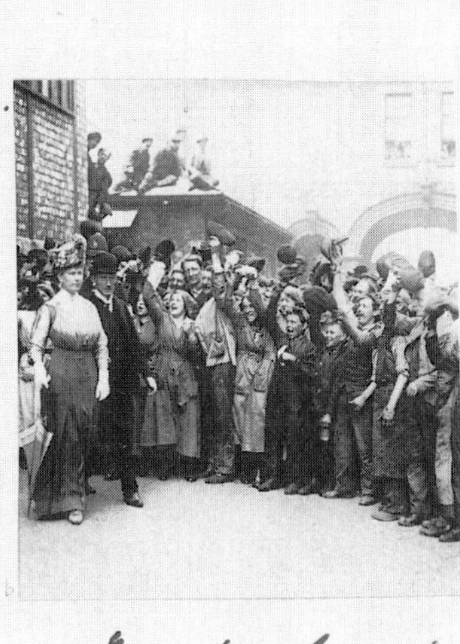

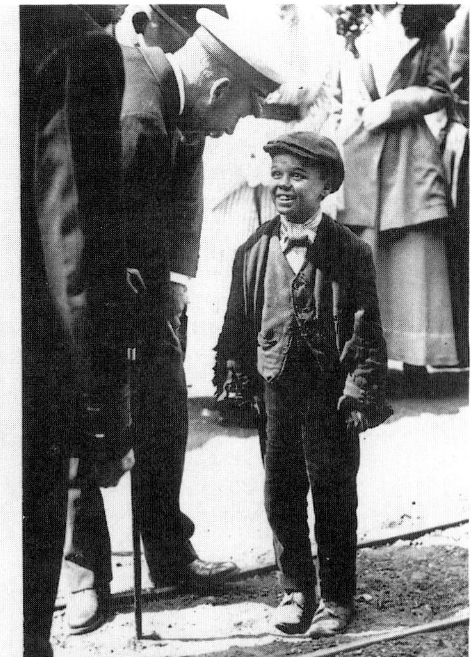

QUEEN MARY VISITING
WOOLWICH BABIES HOME
AND, WITH PRINCESS MARY
AND PRINCESS BEATRICE
(YOUNGEST CHILD OF
QUEEN VICTORIA),
RECEIVING GIFTS FOR
SAILORS AND SOLDIERS AT
ST JAMES'S PALACE IN
JUNE 1917

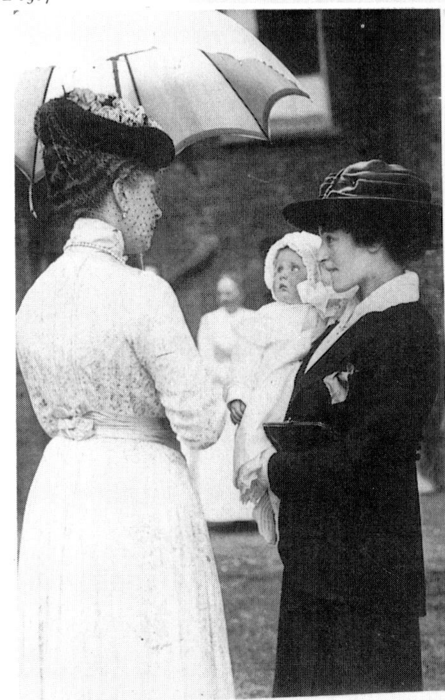
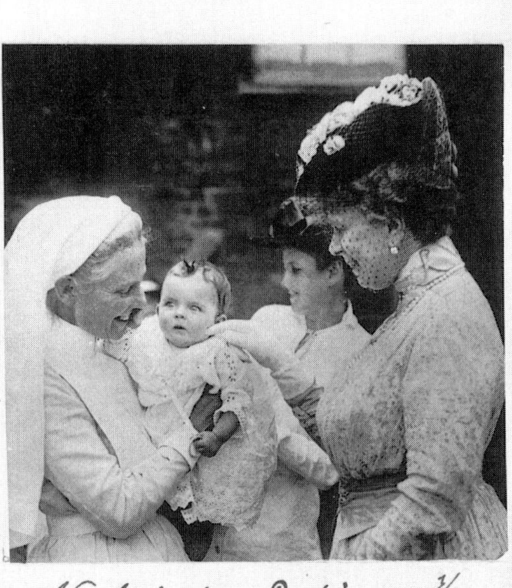
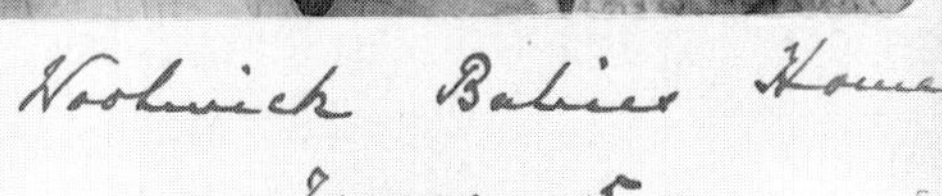

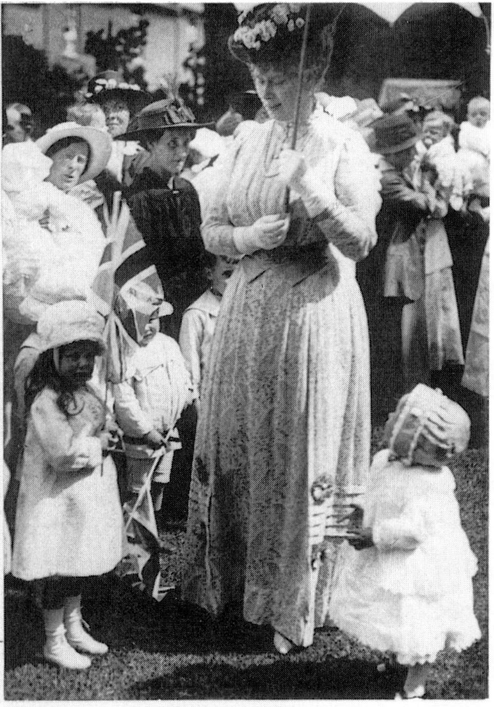

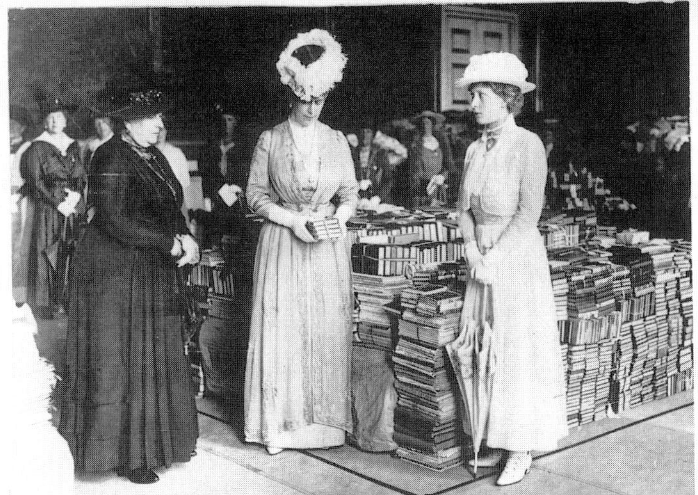
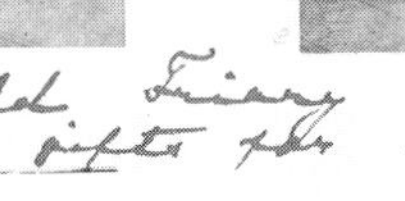

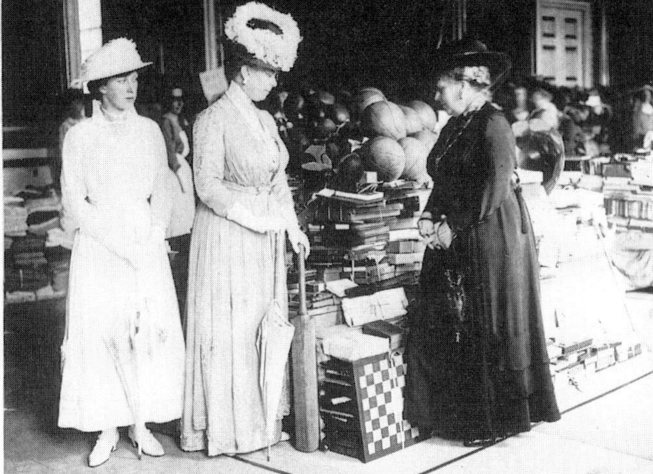

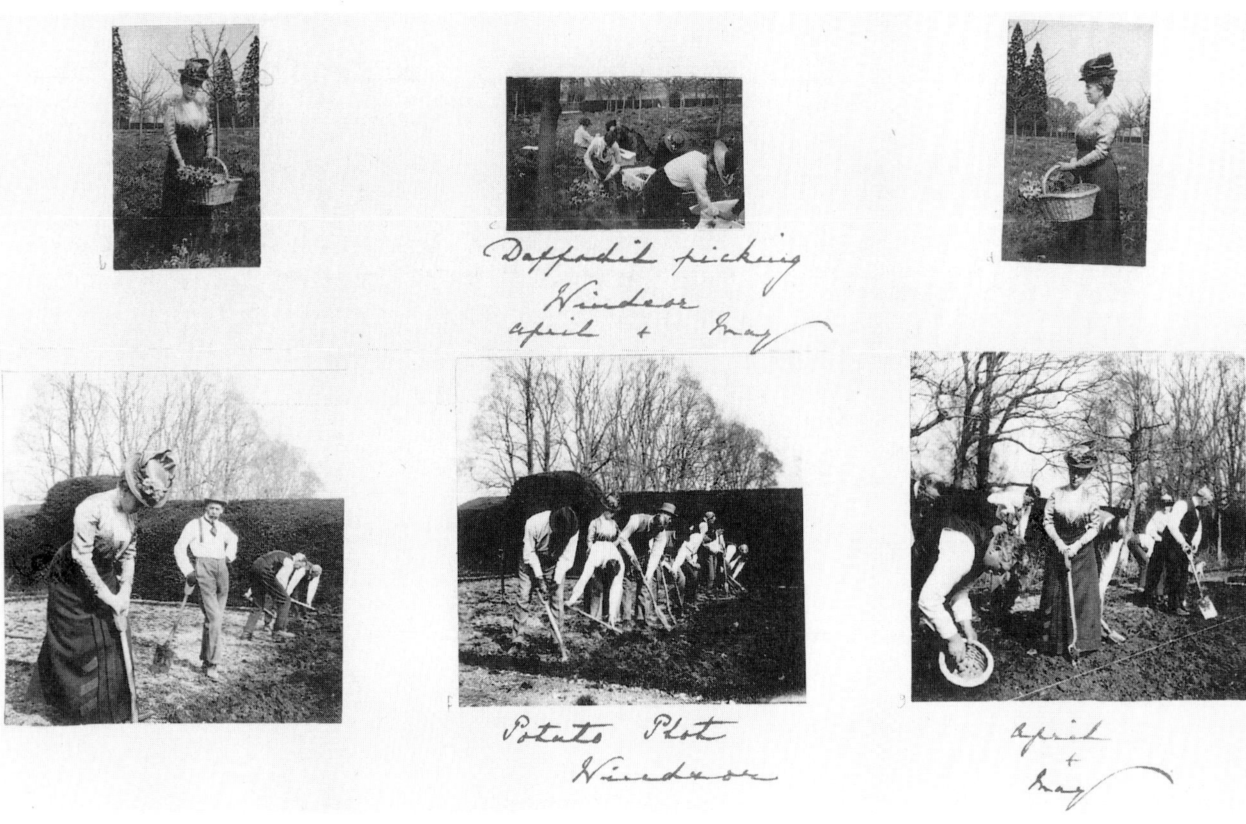

A SERIES OF SNAPSHOTS OF THE KING AND QUEEN AT WINDSOR DURING THE SPRING OF 1917, PICKING DAFFODILS AND WORKING THEIR POTATO PLOT

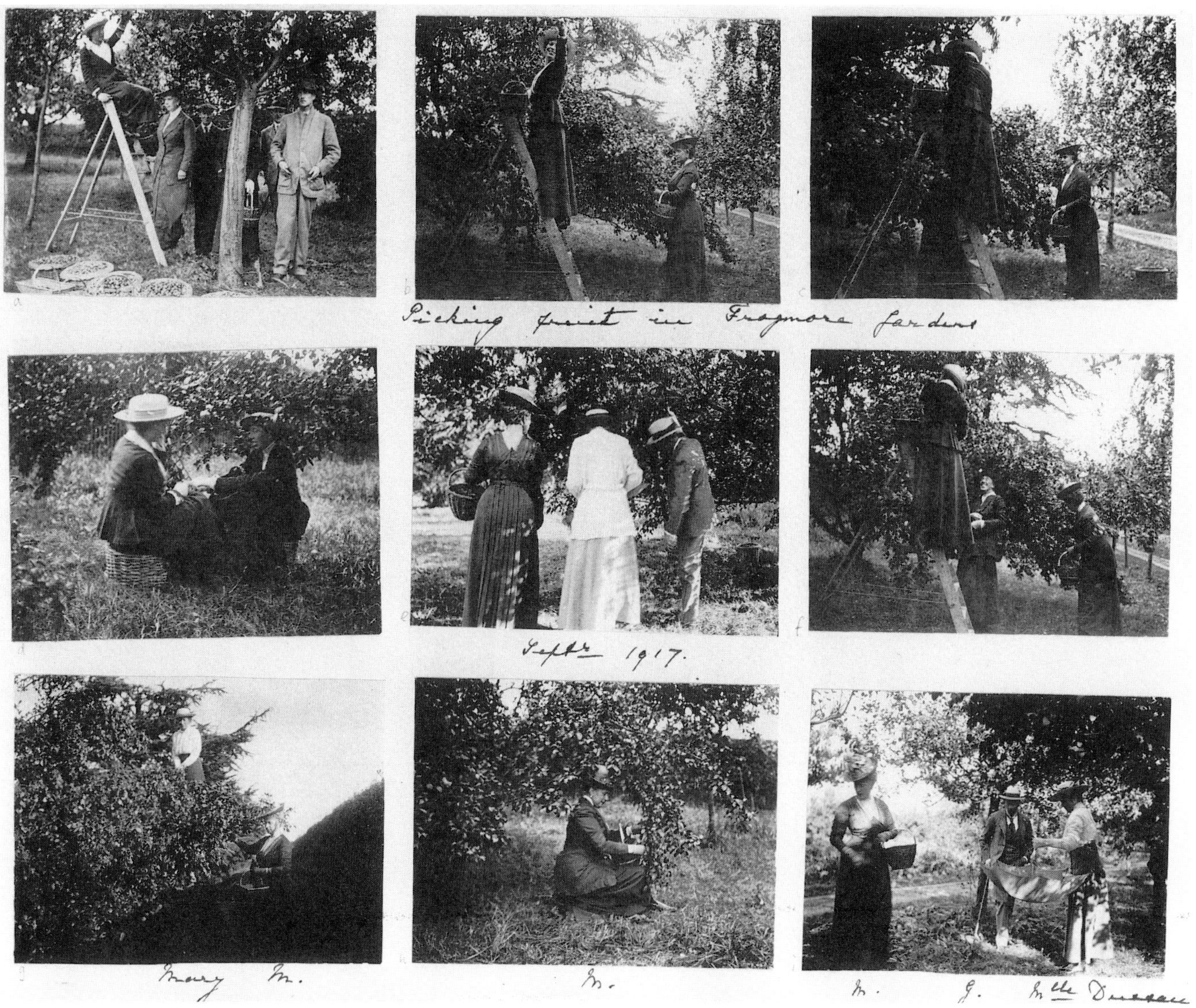

PRINCESS MARY AND HER PARENTS PICKING FRUIT IN THE GROUNDS OF FROGMORE IN SEPTEMBER 1917

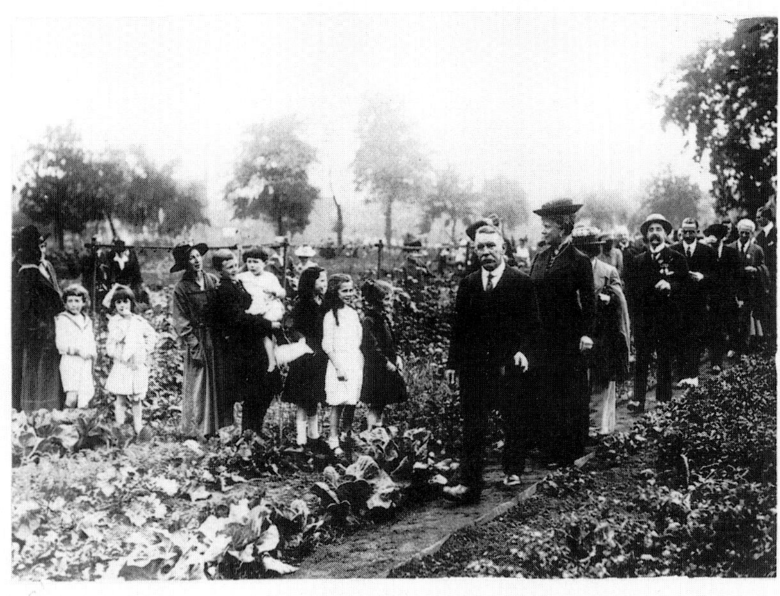

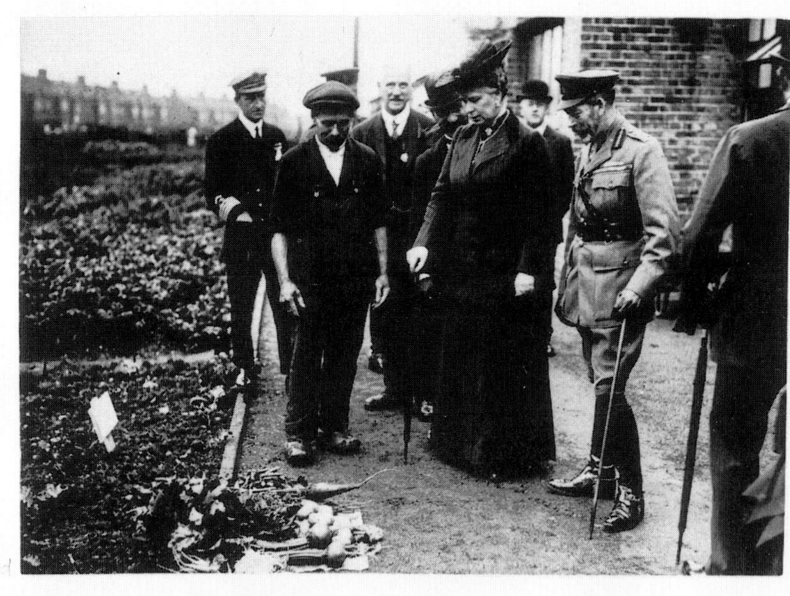

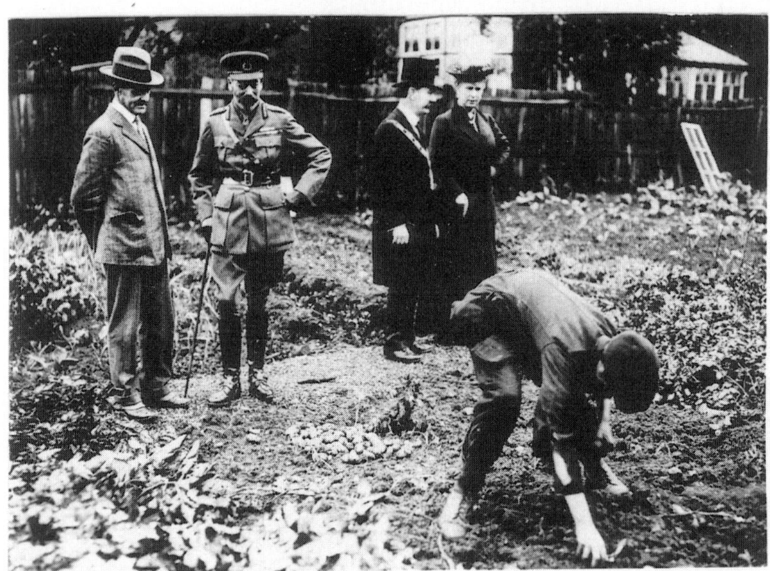

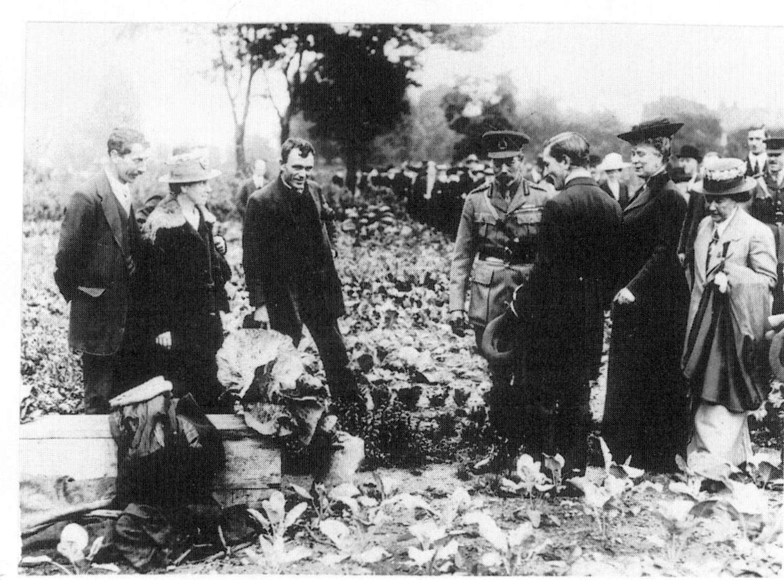

Allotments
round London
July 20th

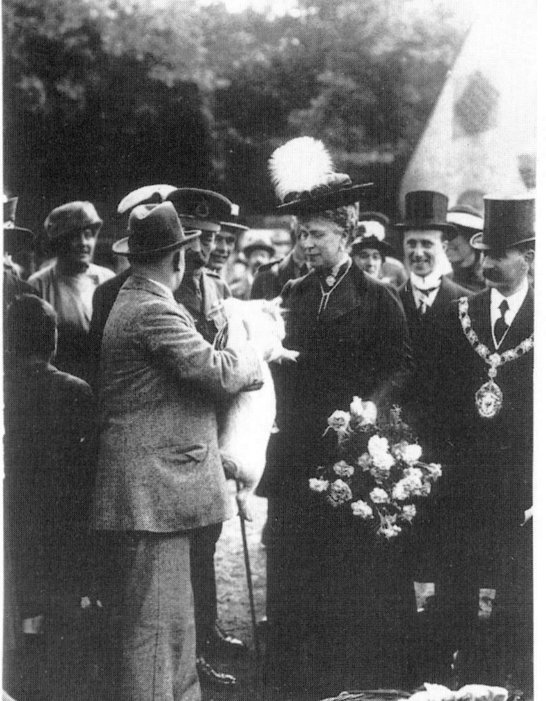

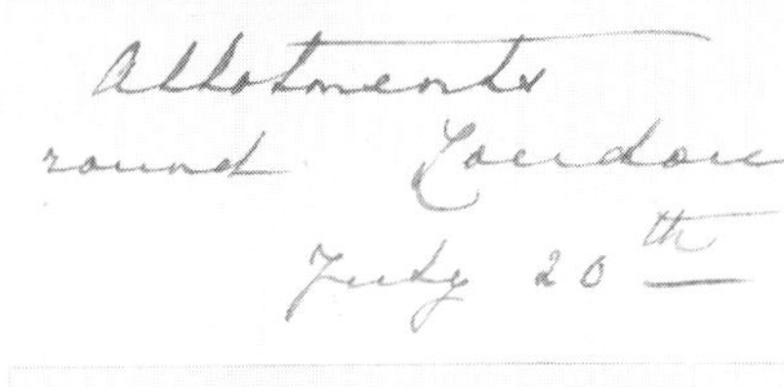

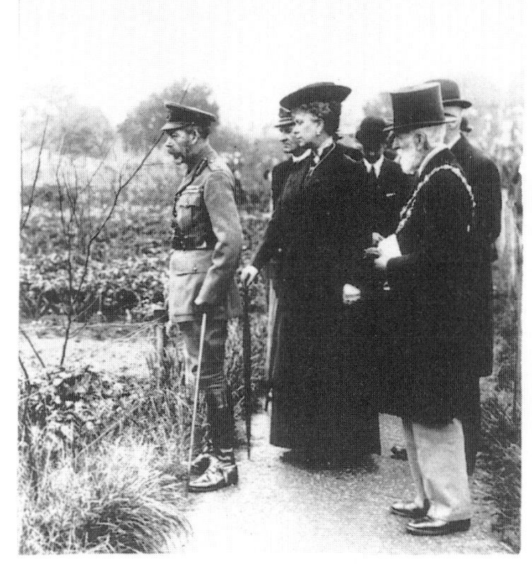

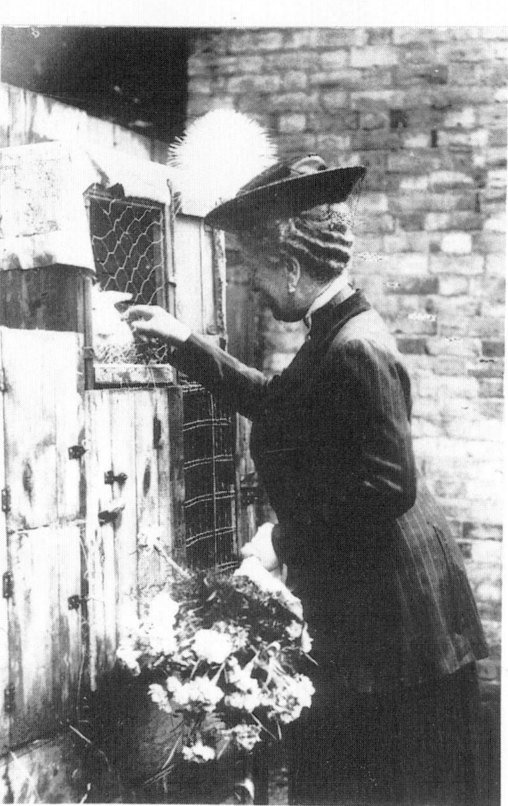

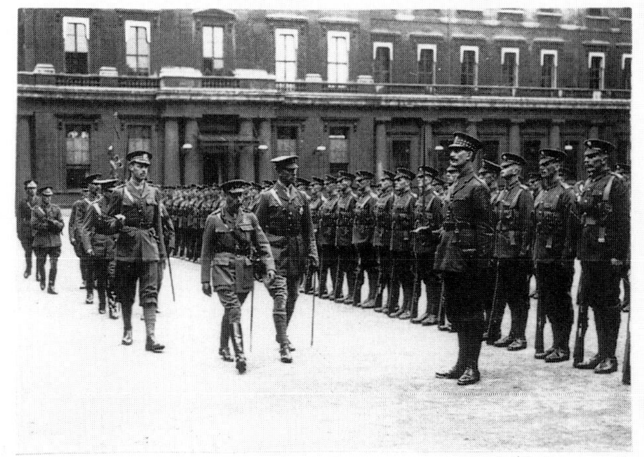
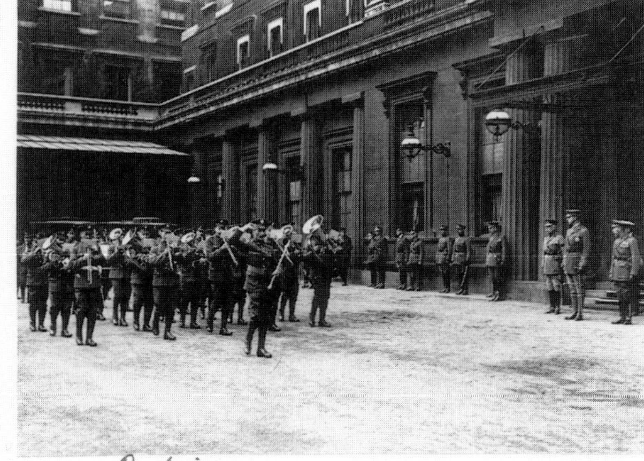

KING GEORGE V AND KING ALBERT OF THE BELGIANS INSPECTING A WARTIME GUARD-OF-HONOUR IN THE QUADRANGLE AT BUCKINGHAM PALACE (TOP). THE KING AND QUEEN POSE WITH SOME OF THEIR CHILDREN ON THEIR SILVER WEDDING ANNIVERSARY (BOTTOM), 6 JULY 1918 – QUEEN MARY WITH A UNIFORMED PRINCESS MARY

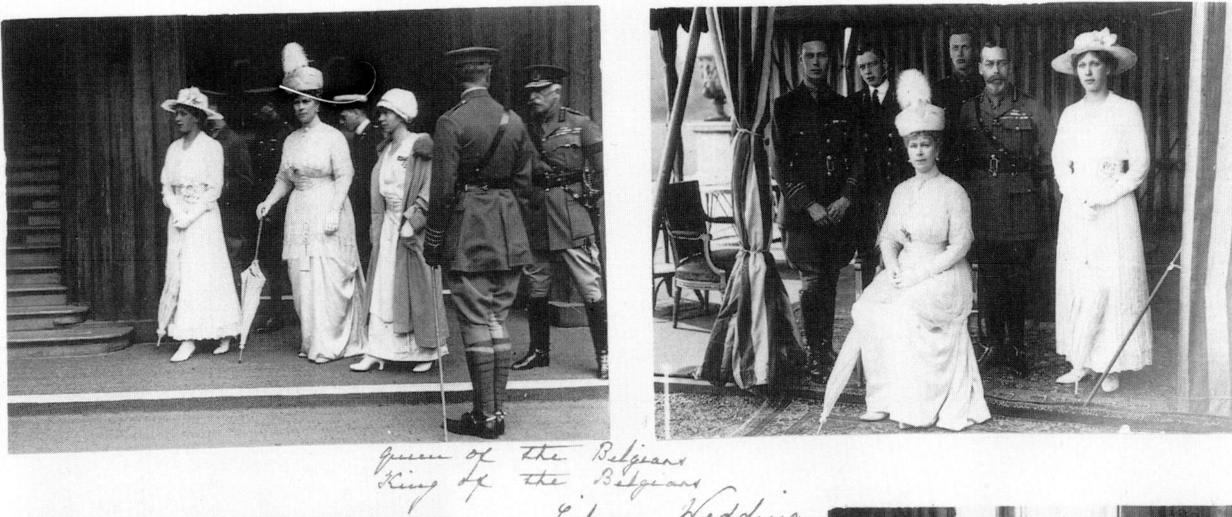

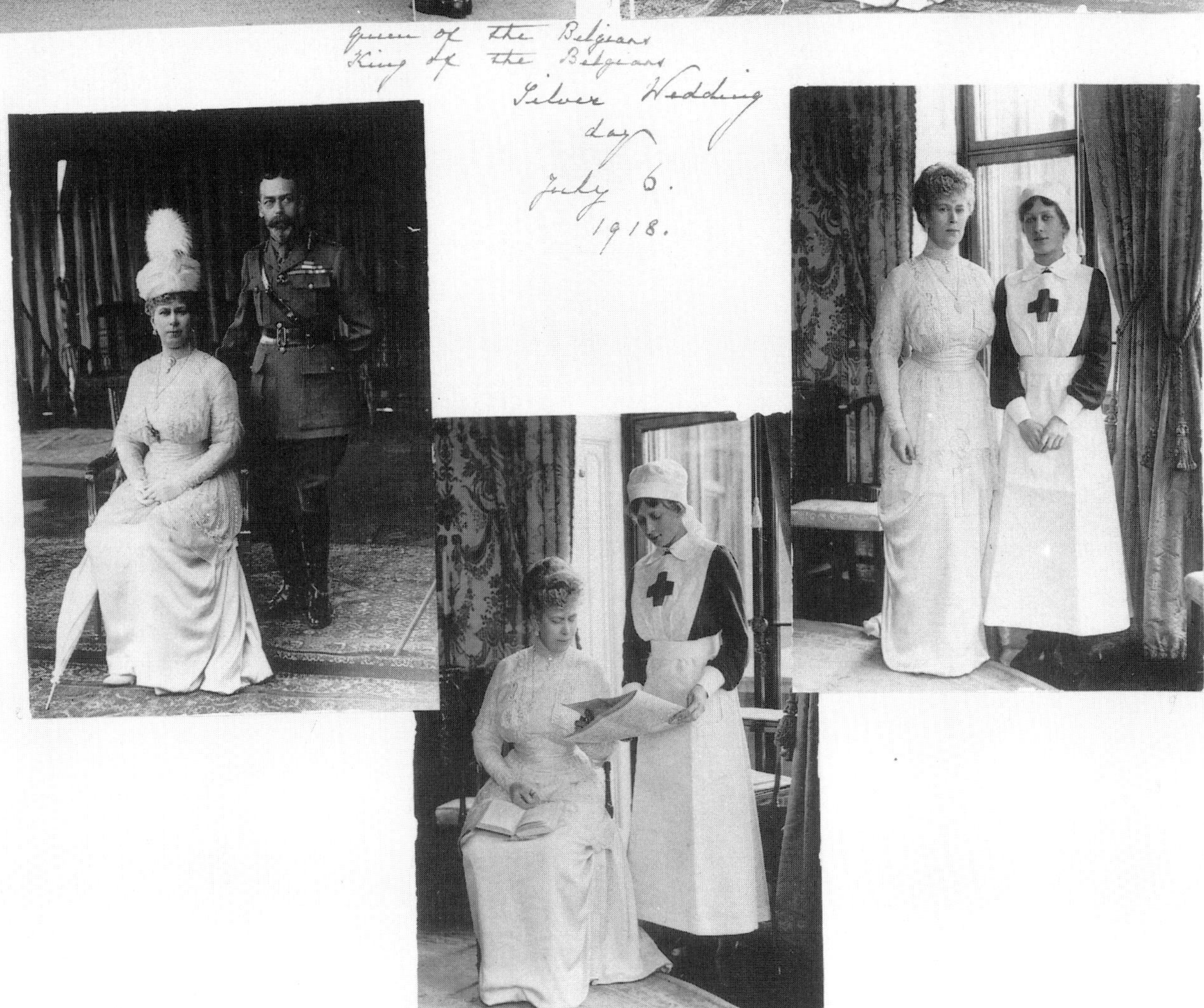

(*OPPOSITE*) THE KING AND QUEEN VISITING ALLOTMENTS AROUND LONDON ON 20 JULY 1918. THE QUEEN ALSO MET A PIG AND A RABBIT IN ITS HUTCH

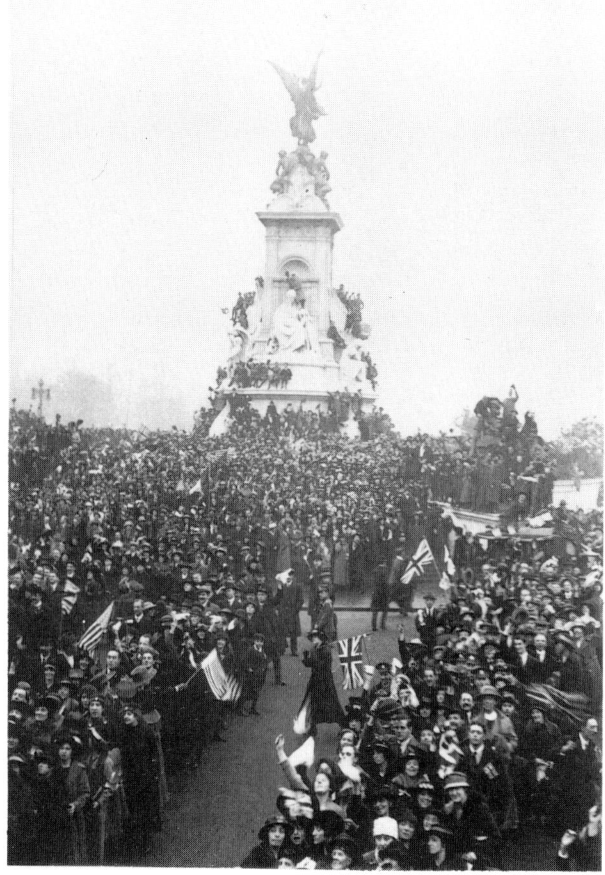

ARMISTICE DAY, 11 NOVEMBER 1918. CROWDS
CHEER THE ROYAL FAMILY FROM THE VICTORIA
MEMORIAL OUTSIDE BUCKINGHAM PALACE

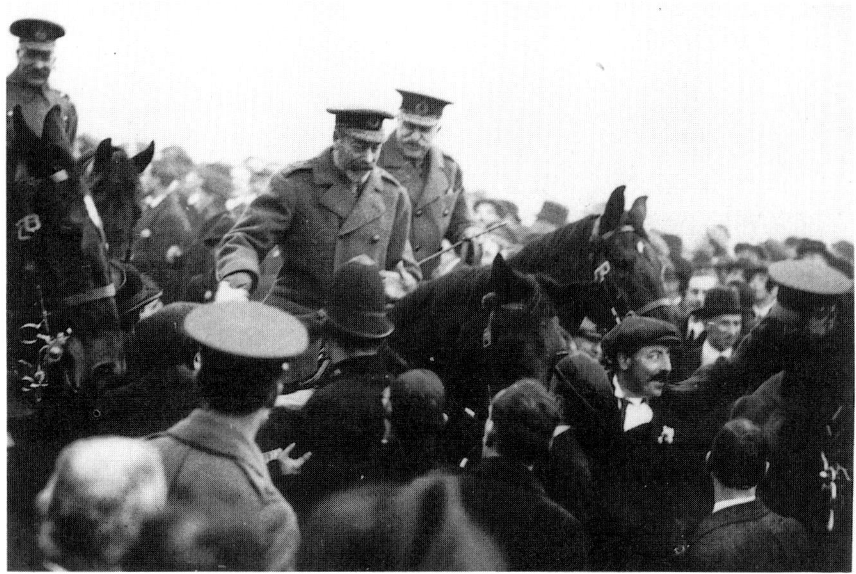
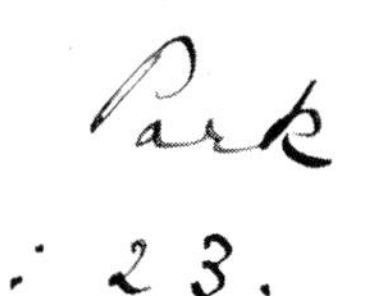

THE KING MEETING SOLDIERS IN HYDE
PARK, 23 NOVEMBER 1918

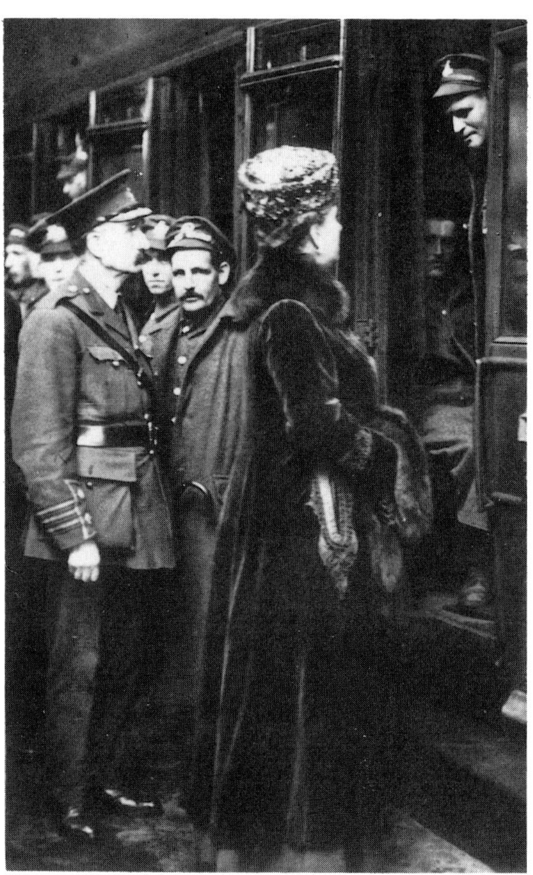

QUEEN MARY GREETING RETURNING
PRISONERS-OF-WAR ON
3 DECEMBER 1918

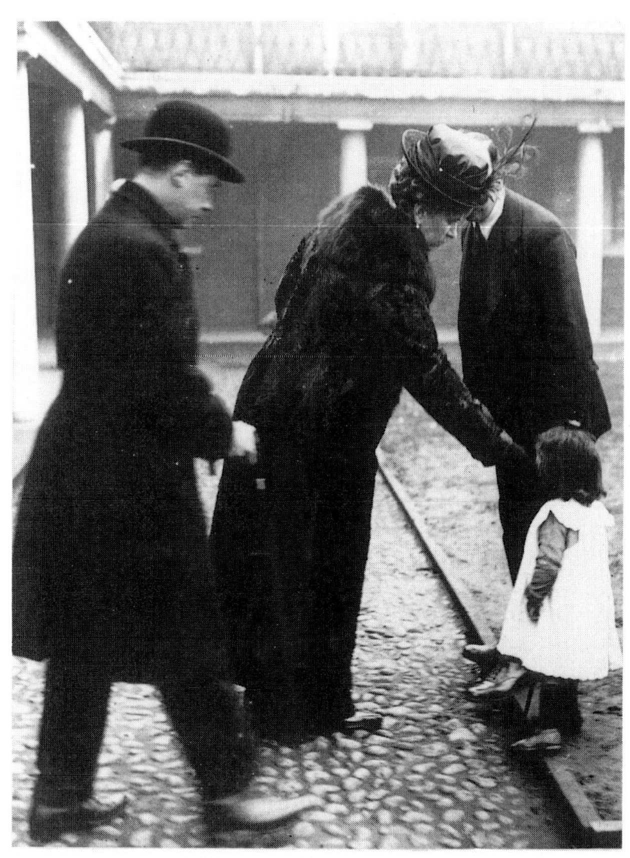

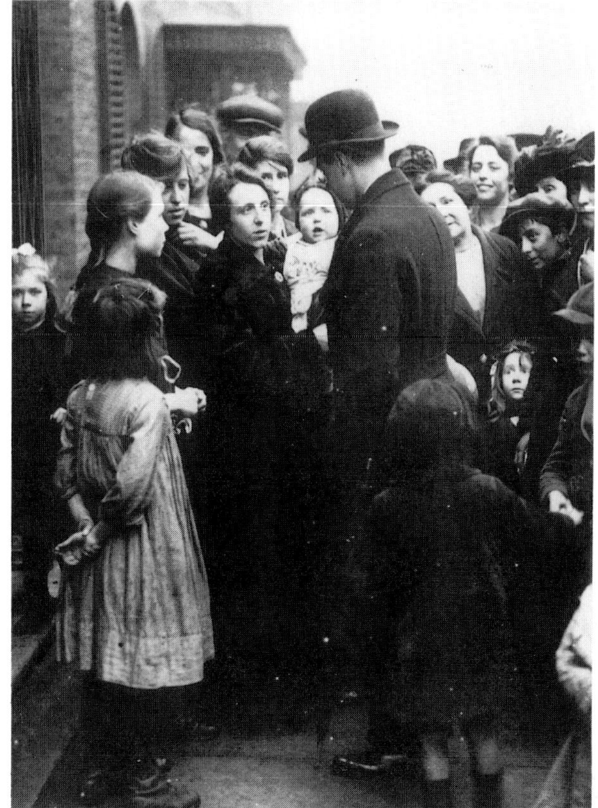

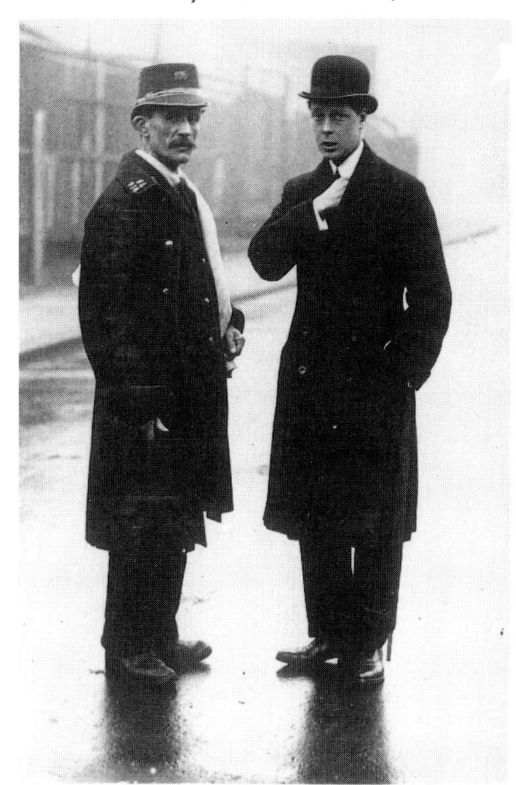

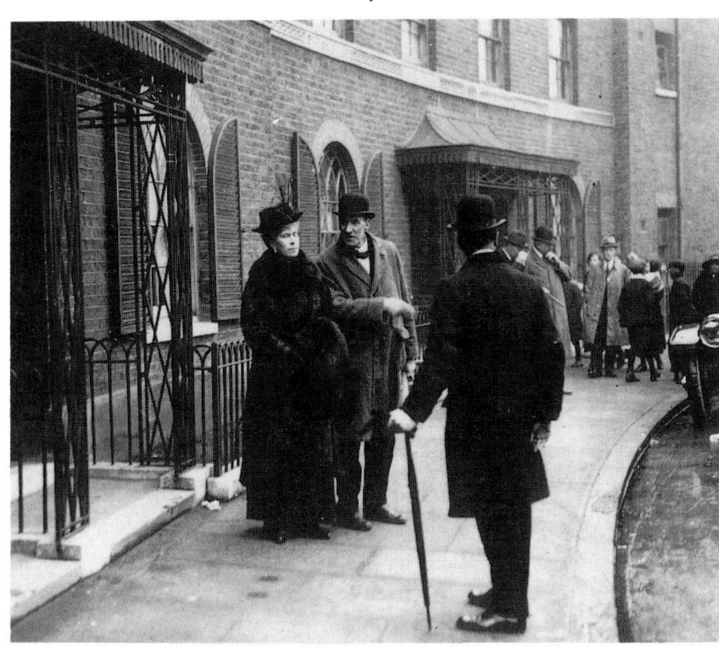

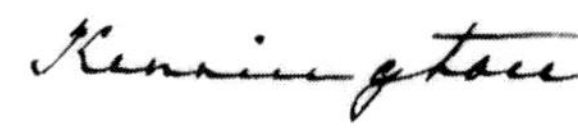

QUEEN MARY AND THE PRINCE OF WALES VISIT
KENNINGTON IN SOUTH LONDON, 10 APRIL 1919

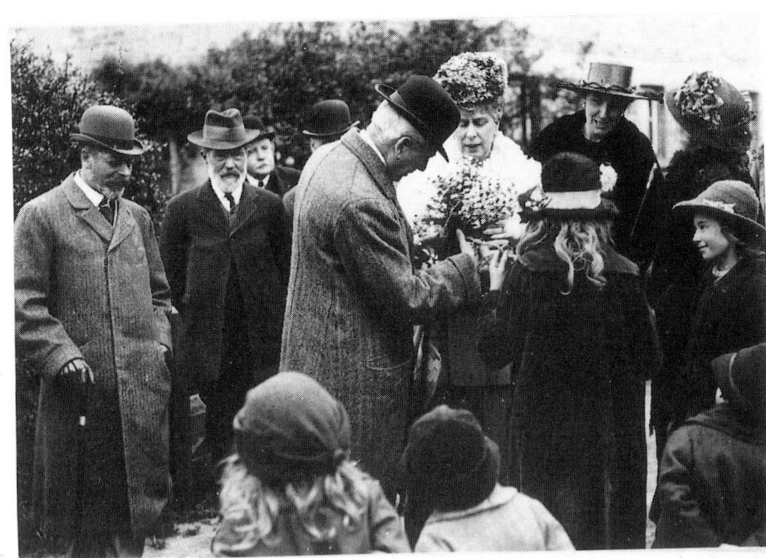 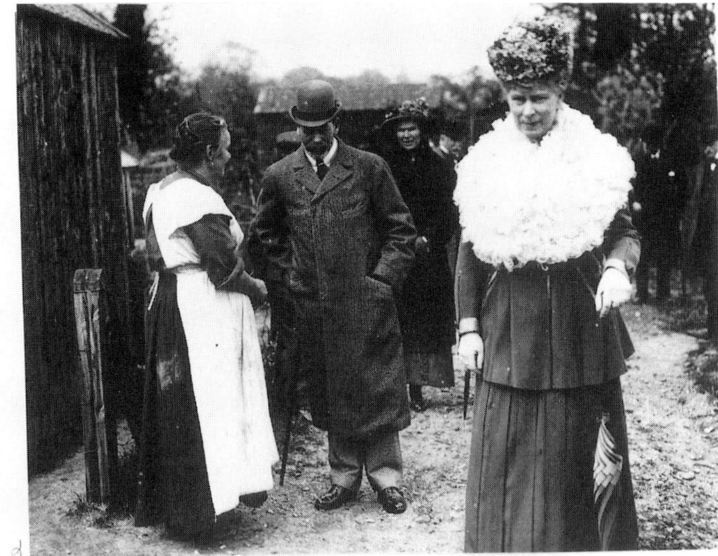

Datchet Cottages   May 7th

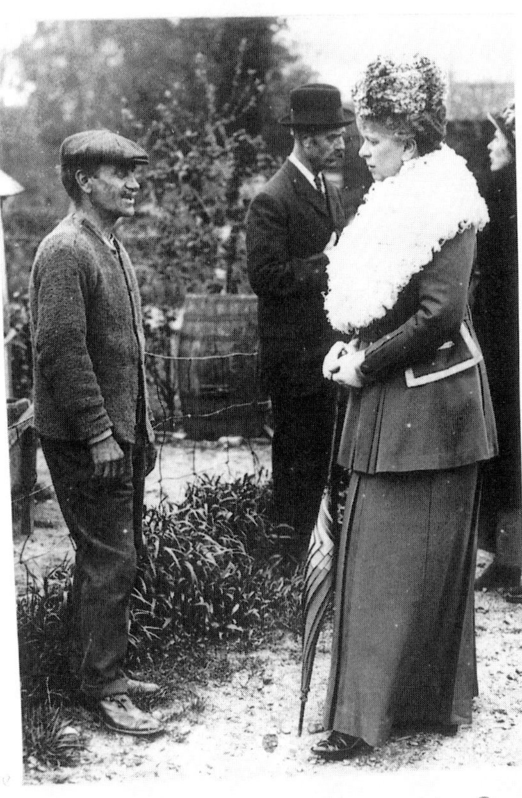 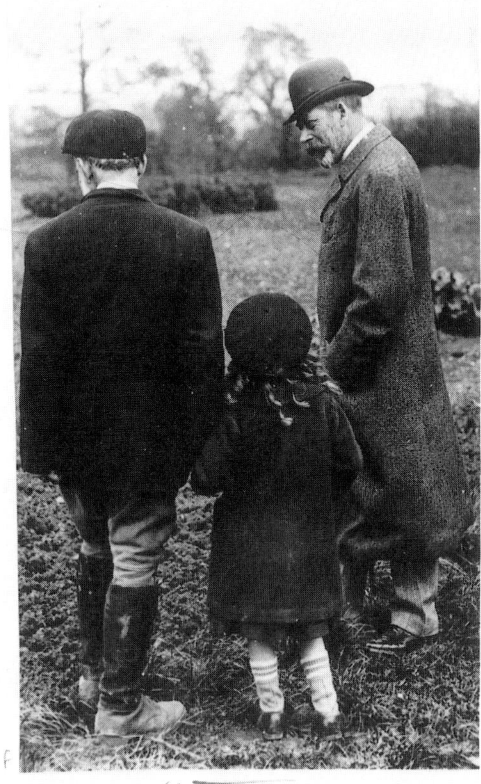 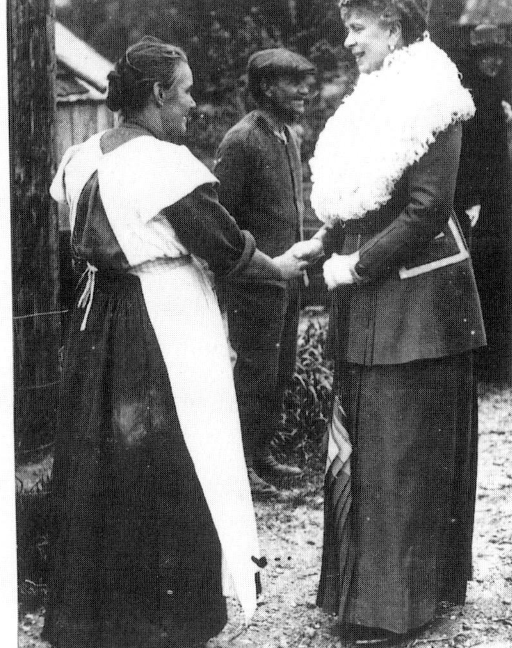

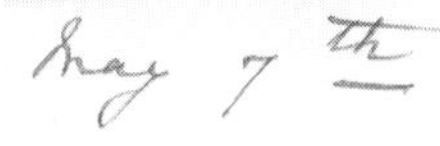

Datchet Cottages   May 7th

THE KING AND QUEEN CHATTING
INFORMALLY WITH THE RESIDENTS OF
DATCHET COTTAGES ON 7 MAY 1919

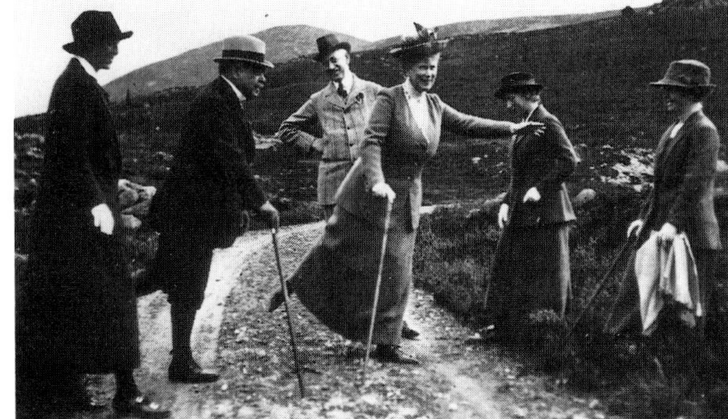 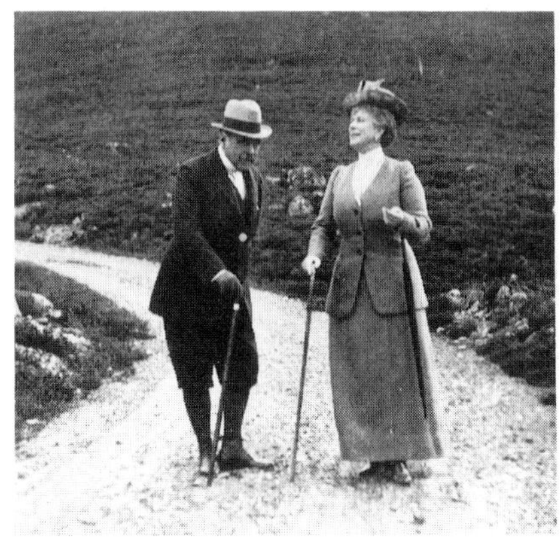

TWO DELIGHTFUL PHOTOGRAPHS OF
QUEEN MARY AT BALMORAL IN
SEPTEMBER 1919. THE QUEEN AND THE
MARQUIS DE SOVERAL APPEAR TO BE
DANCING. PRINCESS MARY MAY BE SEEN
SECOND FROM RIGHT (*FAR LEFT*)

Meet at West Newton.
Jan: 8th 1920.

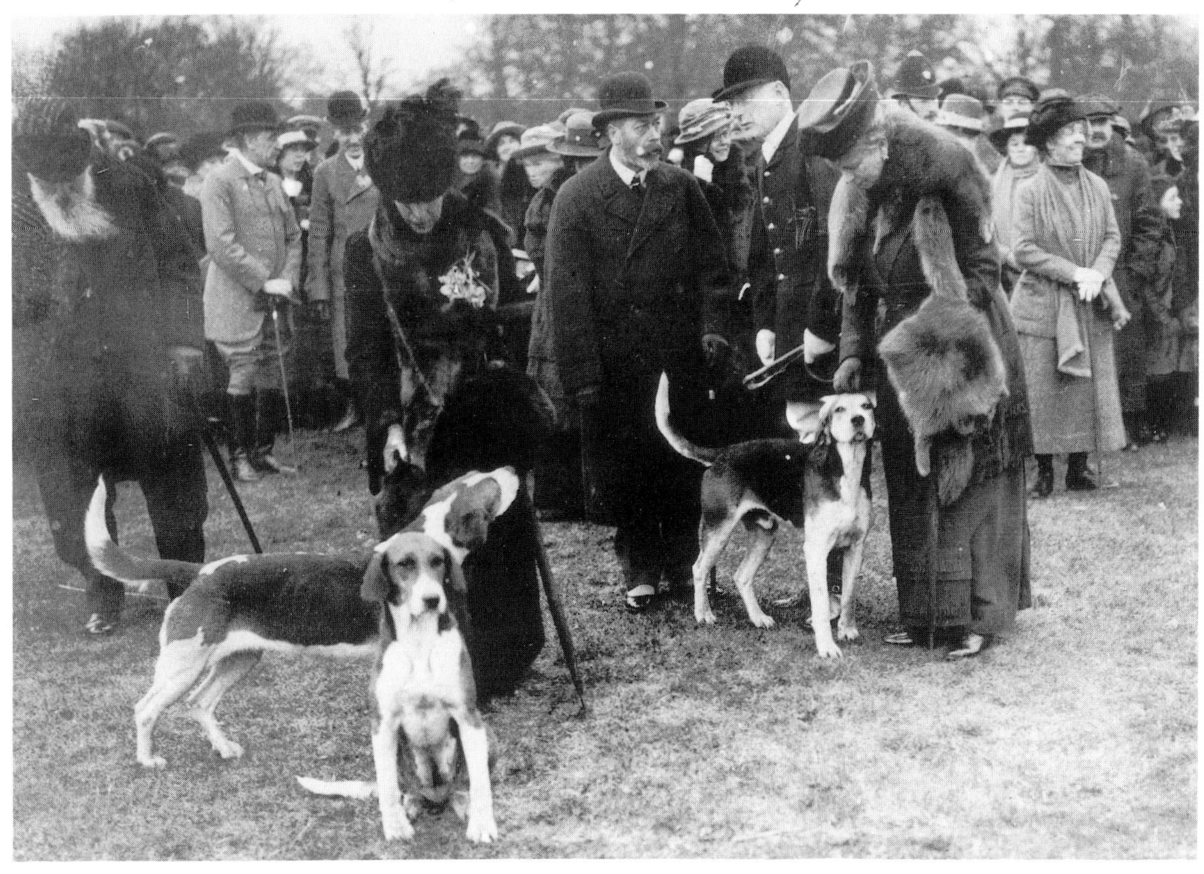

THE KING AND QUEEN AND QUEEN
ALEXANDRA WITH THE HOUNDS AT WEST
NEWTON ON 8 JANUARY 1920

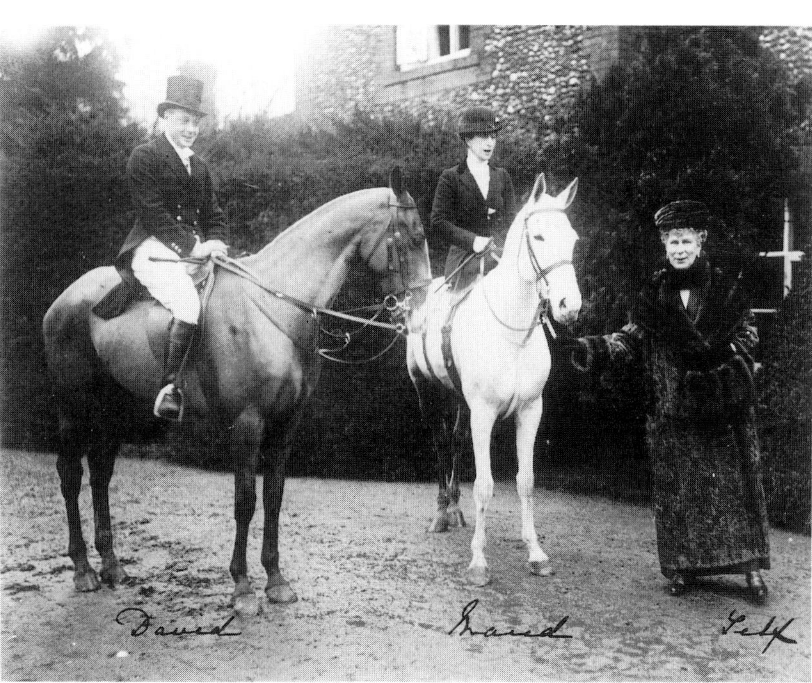

Tittleshall   Decr 27th 1920

THE QUEEN WITH THE PRINCE OF WALES AND HER
FAVOURITE SISTER-IN-LAW, QUEEN MAUD OF
NORWAY. TITTLESHALL, 27 DECEMBER 1920

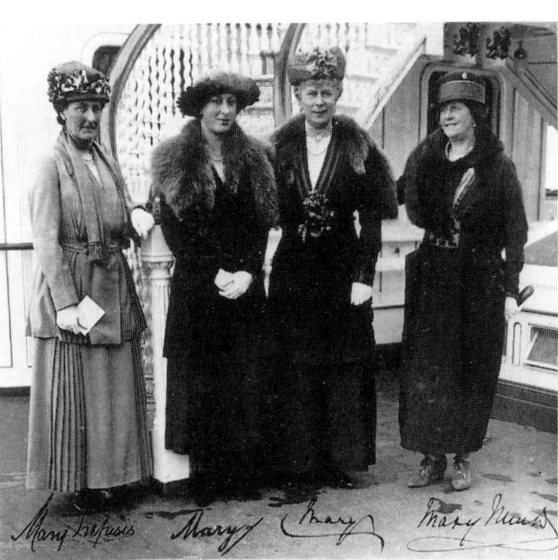

THE '4 "MARIES'''. QUEEN MARY WITH (LEFT
TO RIGHT) LADY MARY TREFUSIS, PRINCESS
MARY AND MARY, COUNTESS OF MINTO,
ABOARD THE ROYAL YACHT *VICTORIA AND
ALBERT*, 10 JULY 1920

4.
"Maries"
July
10th
A. & A.
on
the Clyde

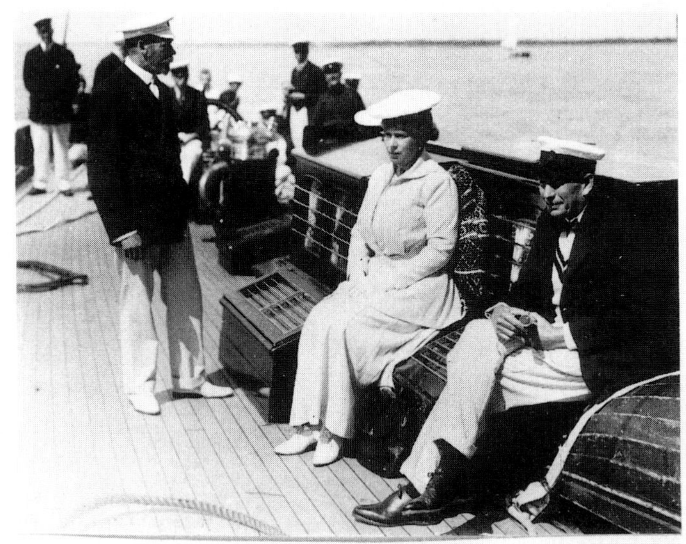 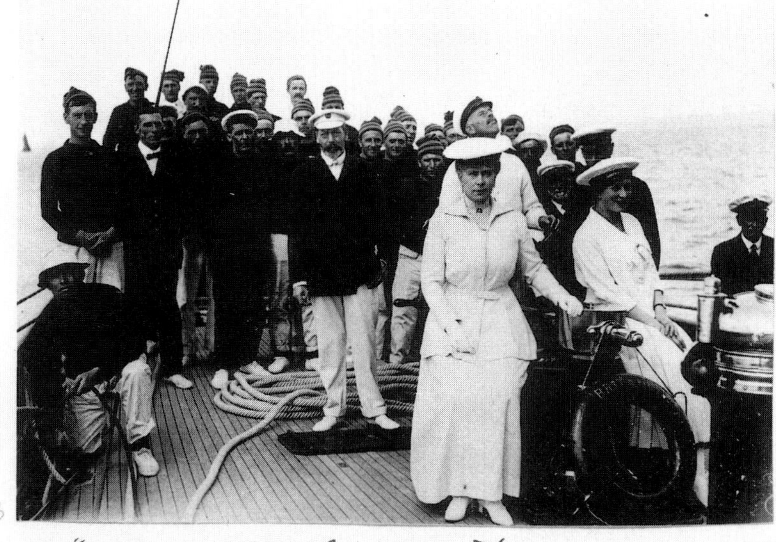

"Britannia" August 1920

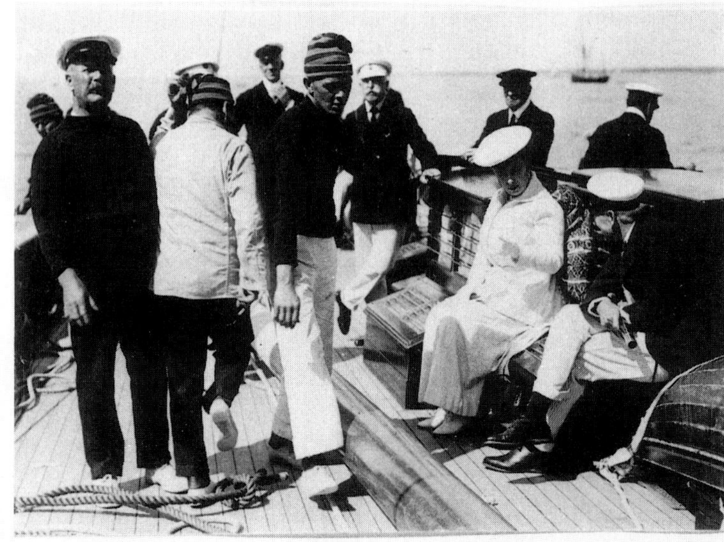 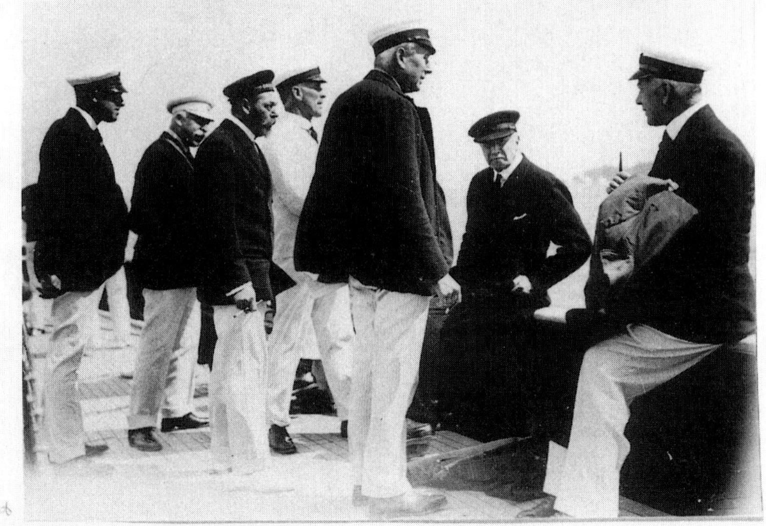

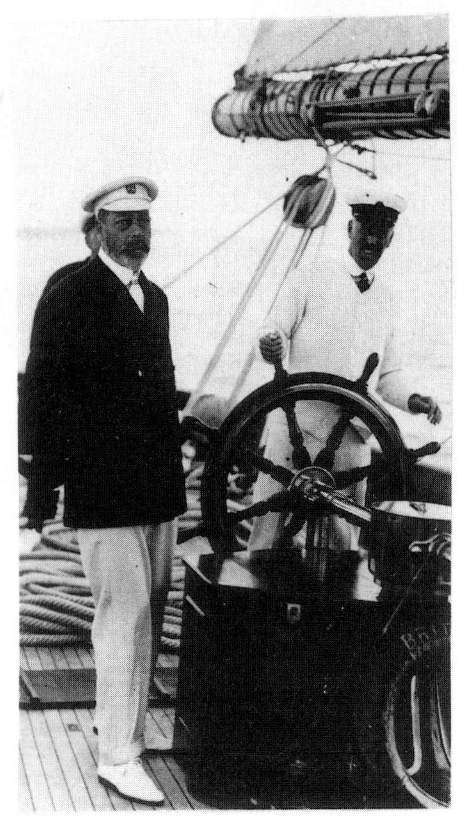 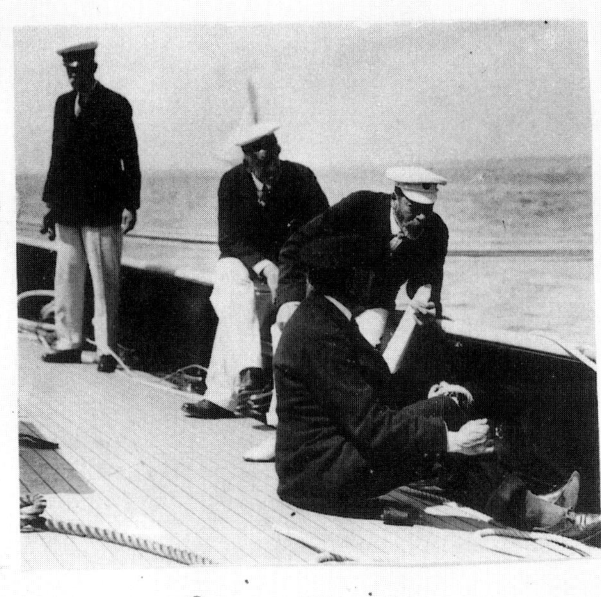 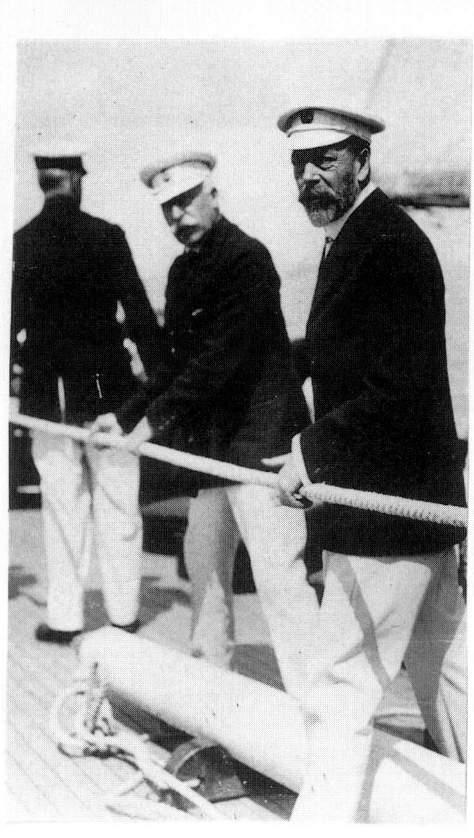

Britannia

1920 -

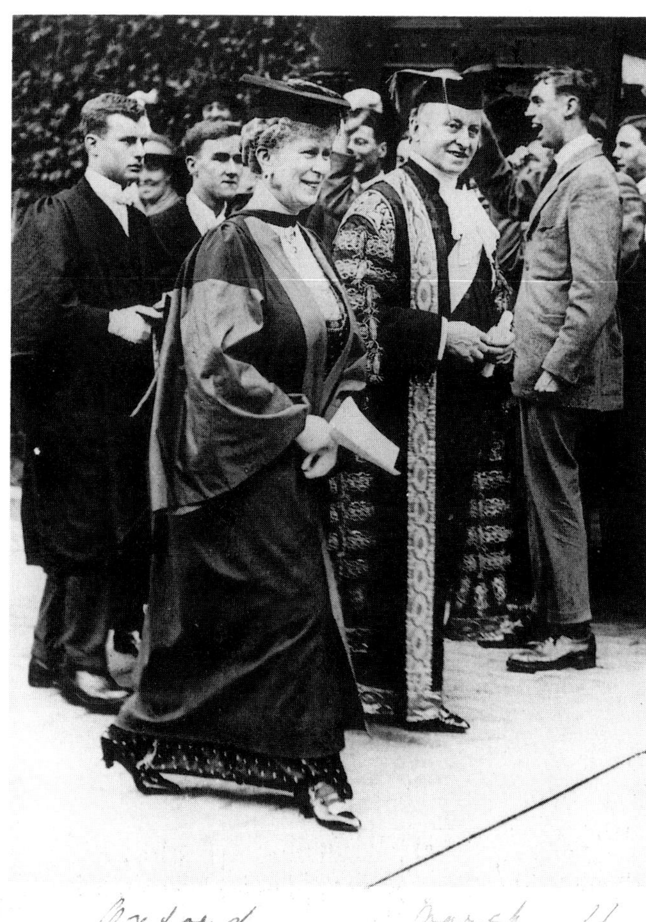

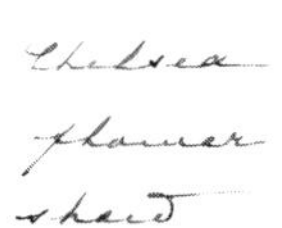

QUEEN MARY AT OXFORD WITH LORD CURZON OF
KEDLESTONE, MARCH 1921

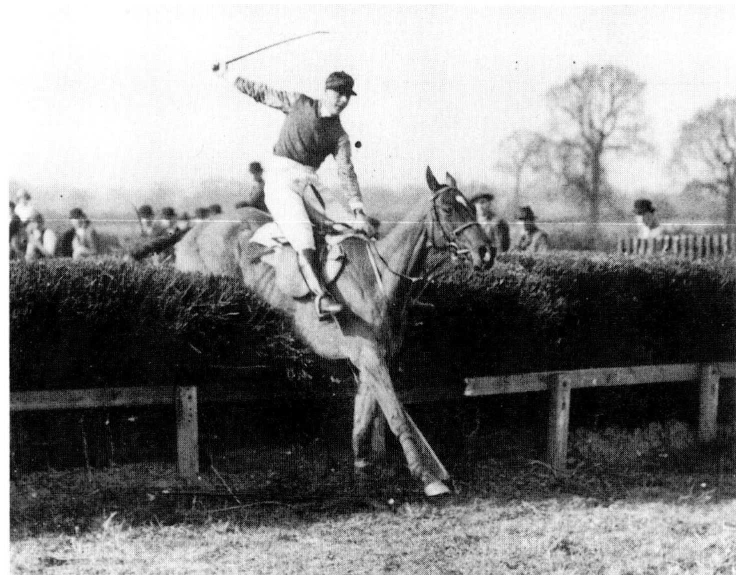

THE PRINCE OF WALES RIDING 'PET DOG' AT
HAWTHORNHILL ON 1 APRIL 1921

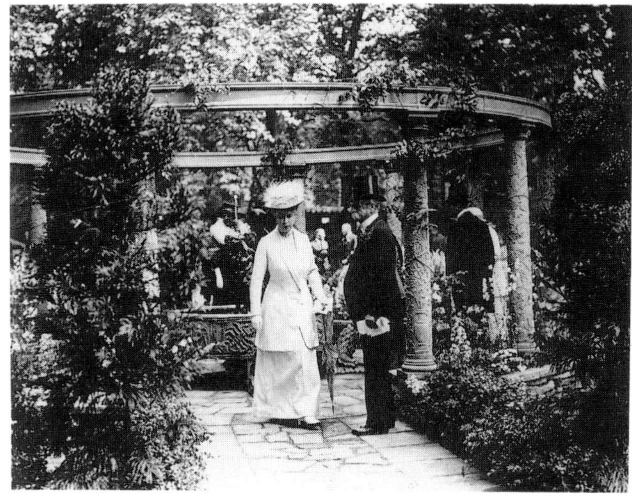

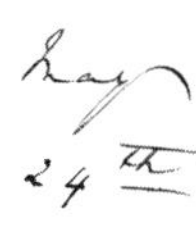

QUEEN MARY AT THE CHELSEA FLOWER SHOW ON
24 MAY 1921

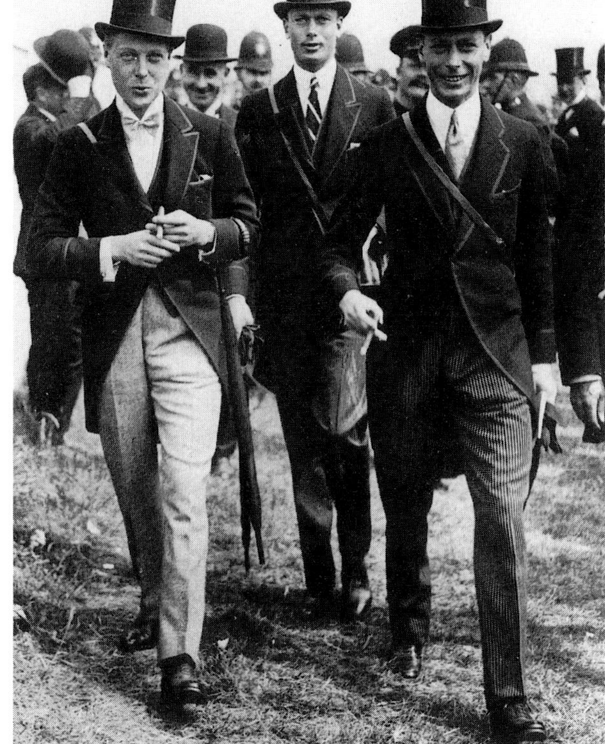

ROYAL BROTHERS: THE PRINCE OF WALES, PRINCE
HENRY AND PRINCE ALBERT ON DERBY DAY,
1 JUNE 1921

WEARING A FULL-LENGTH ERMINE
COAT, QUEEN MARY ARRIVING IN
BELFAST WITH THE KING,
22 JUNE 1921

(*OPPOSITE*) THE WEDDING
OF PRINCESS MARY AND
VISCOUNT LASCELLES ON
28 FEBRUARY 1922

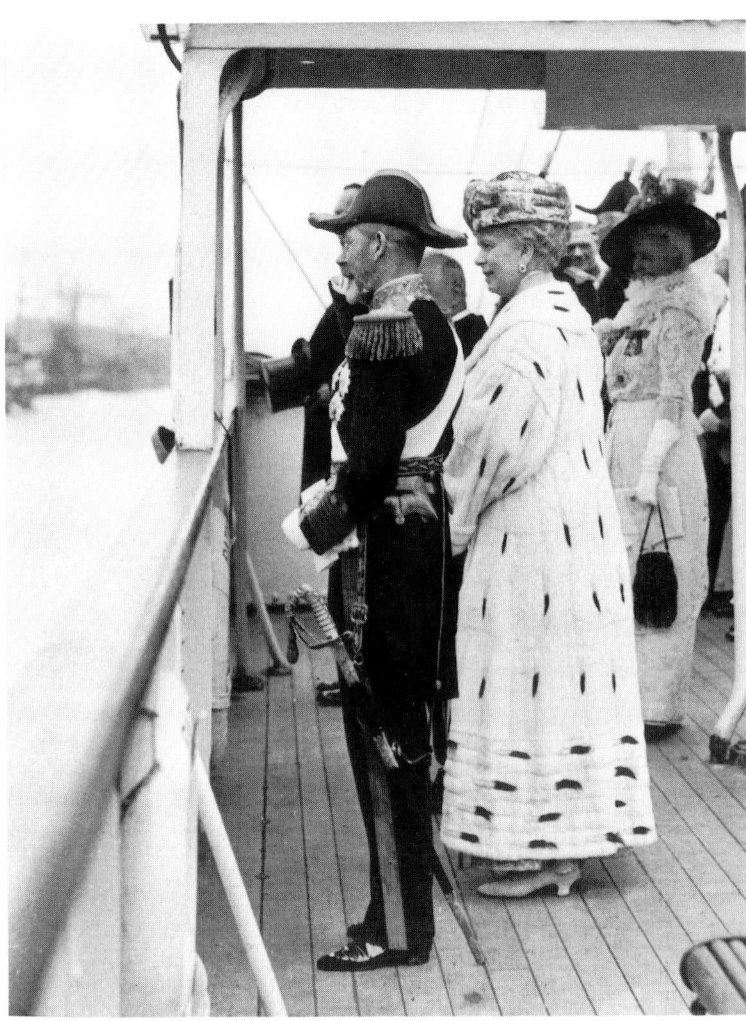

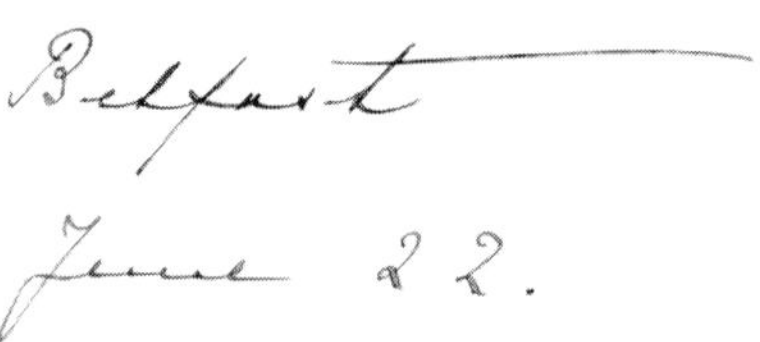

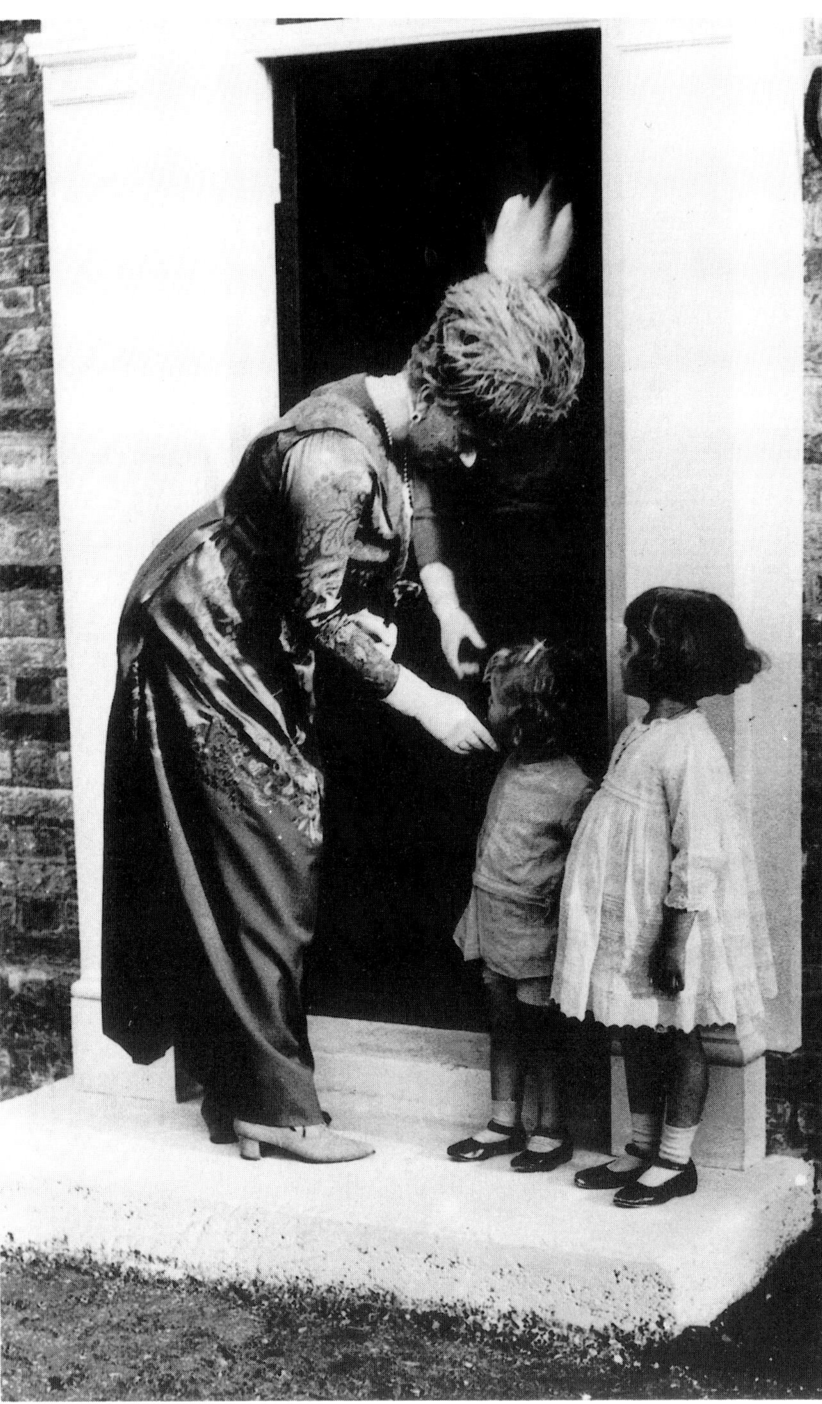

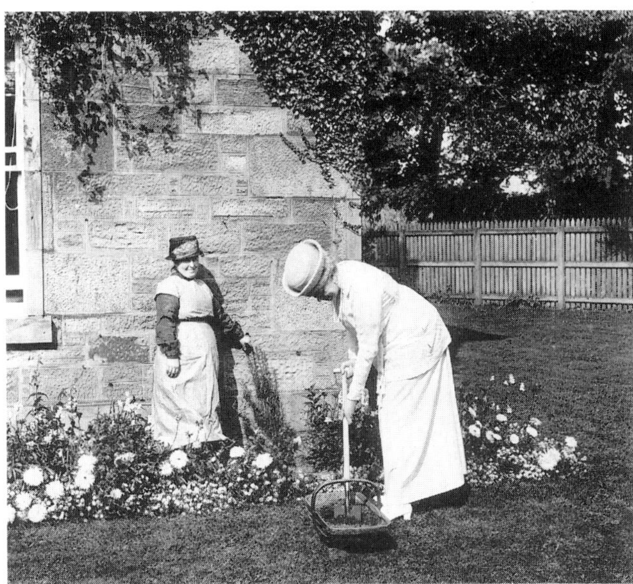

QUEEN MARY TAKING A TURN AT GARDENING
WHILE VISITING KELLY CASTLE IN
SEPTEMBER 1921

THE QUEEN STROKING A LITTLE GIRL'S CHEEK DURING A
VISIT TO THE HOUSING ASSOCIATION FOR OFFICERS'
FAMILIES IN CAMBRIDGE ON 14 OCTOBER 1921

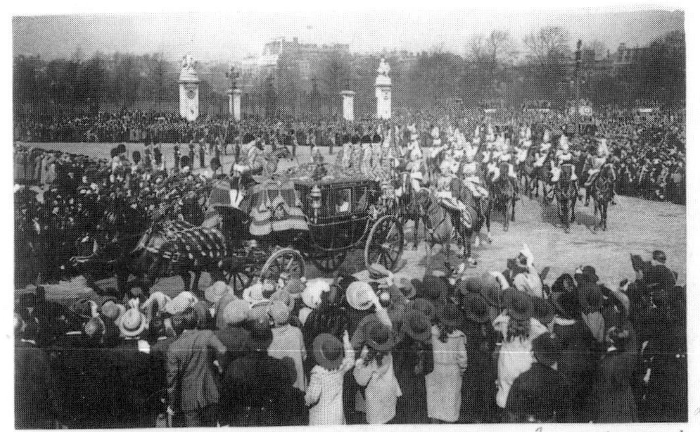
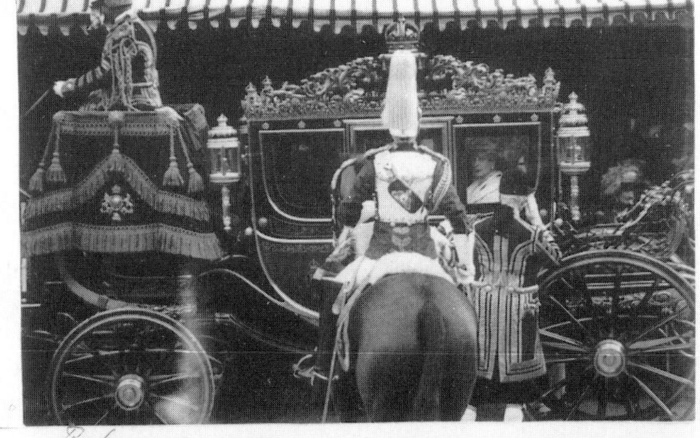

George + I returning to Palace

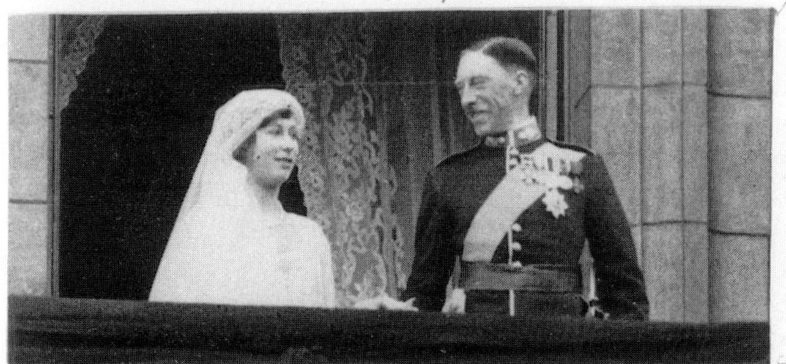
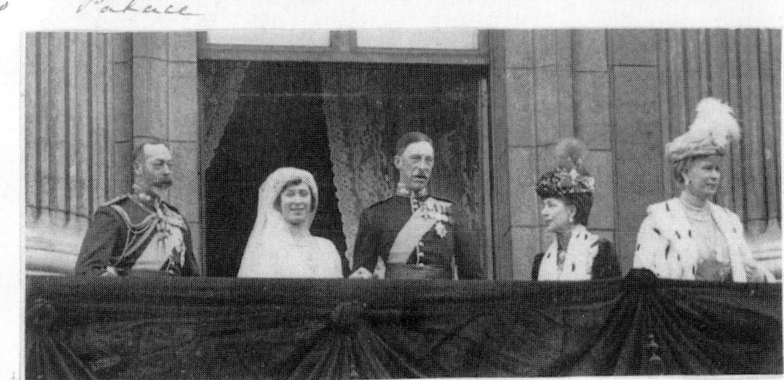

Mary . Harry

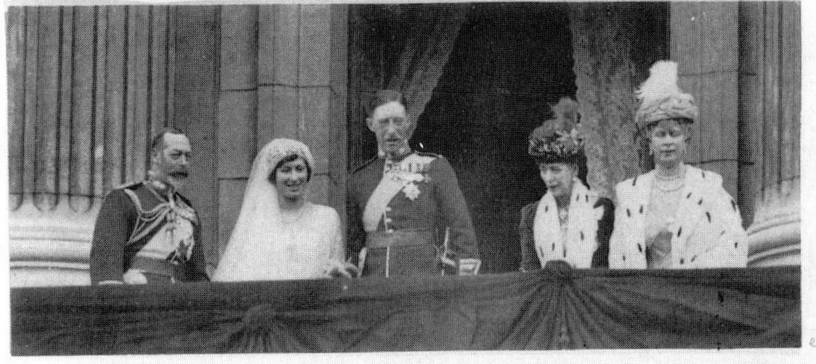
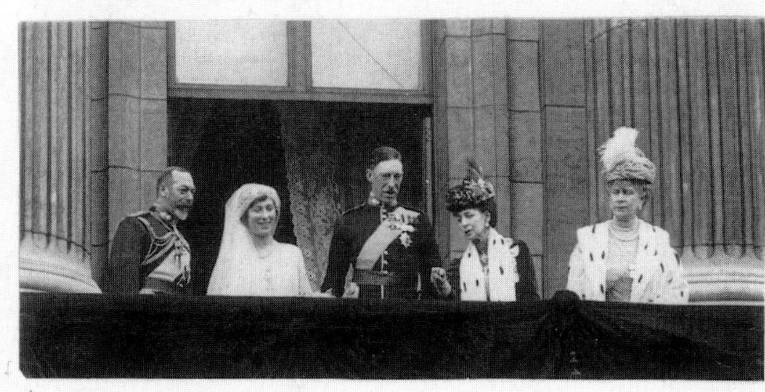

On the balcony

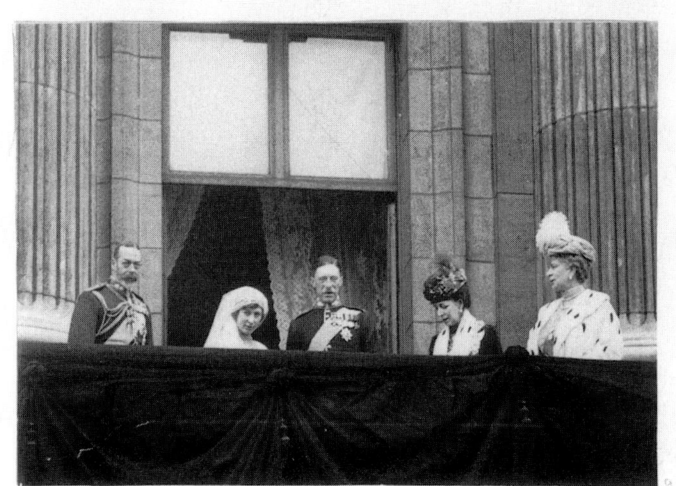
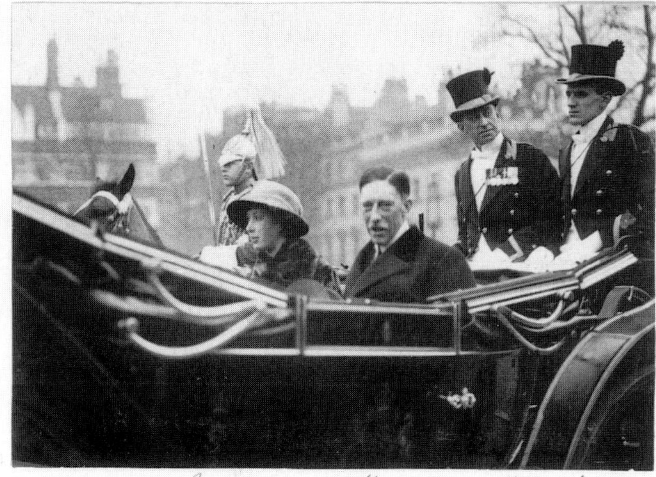

Mary + Harry leaving
for Paddington Station

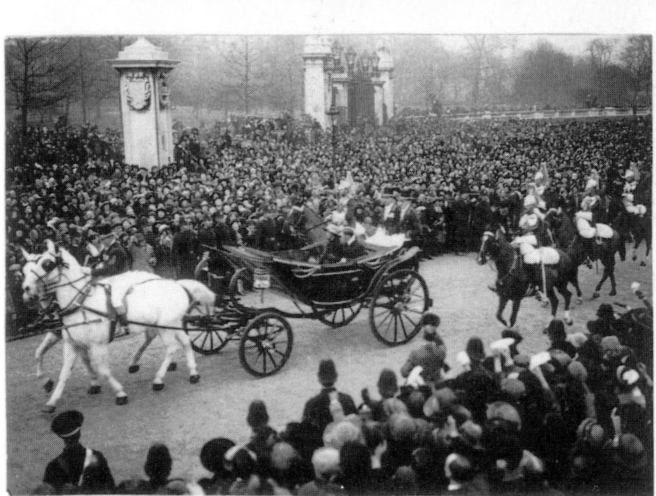
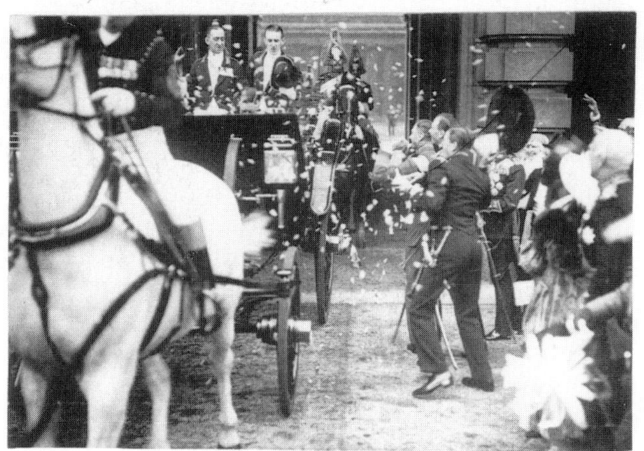

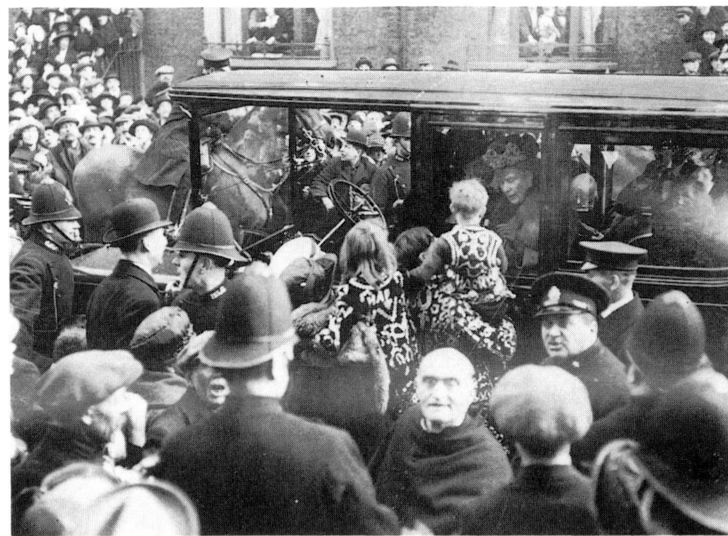
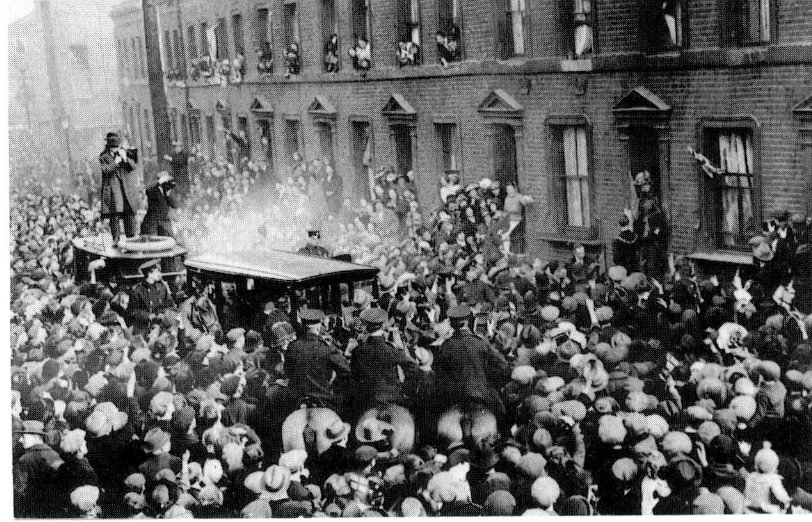

QUEEN MARY VISITING SHOREDITCH IN THE EAST END OF LONDON
ON 18 MARCH 1922. SHE IS SEEN GREETING A 'PEARLY PRINCE' FROM
HER CAR AND (*RIGHT*) EMERGING FROM ONE OF THE HOUSES IN A
STREET CRAMMED WITH CHEERING WELL-WISHERS

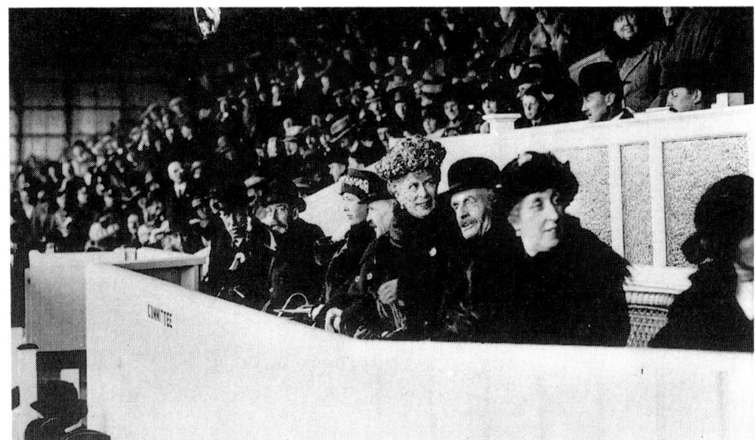

THE ROYAL PARTY AT A
FOOTBALL MATCH IN
ALDERSHOT IN APRIL 1922

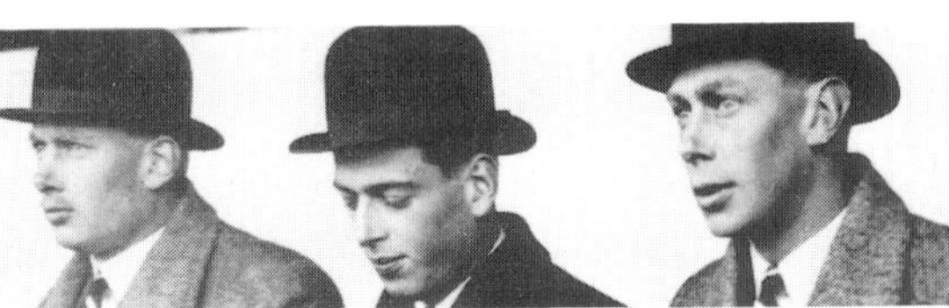
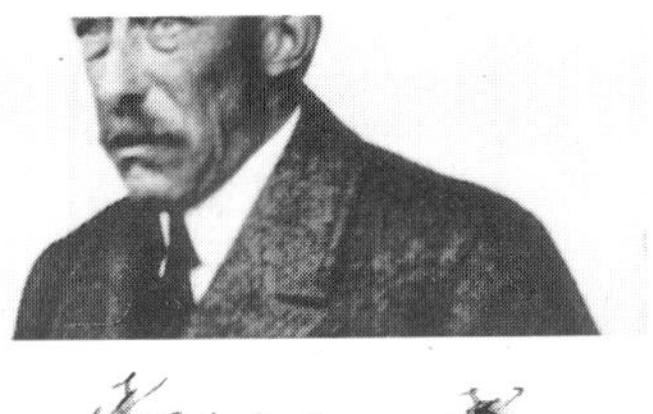

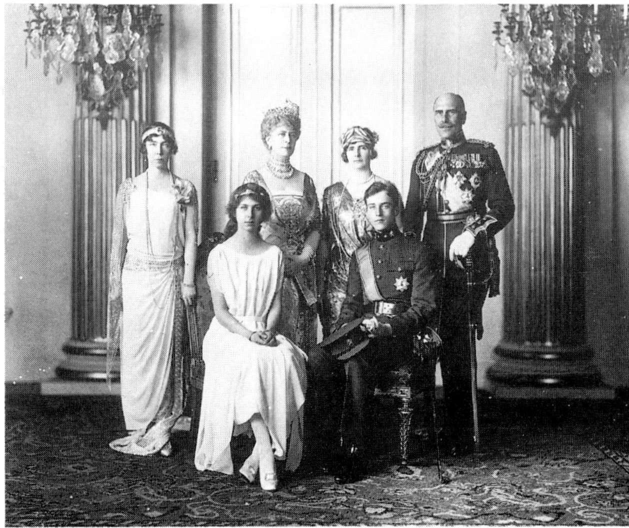

THE STATE VISIT TO BELGIUM IN
MAY 1922. WITH QUEEN MARY ARE
(LEFT TO RIGHT) QUEEN ELIZABETH
OF THE BELGIANS, PRINCESS ALICE,
COUNTESS OF ATHLONE AND THE
EARL OF ATHLONE (QUEEN MARY'S
BROTHER ALGE). SEATED IN FRONT
ARE CROWN PRINCE LEOPOLD OF THE
BELGIANS AND PRINCESS MARIE JOSÉ

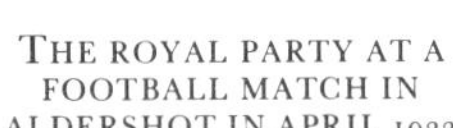

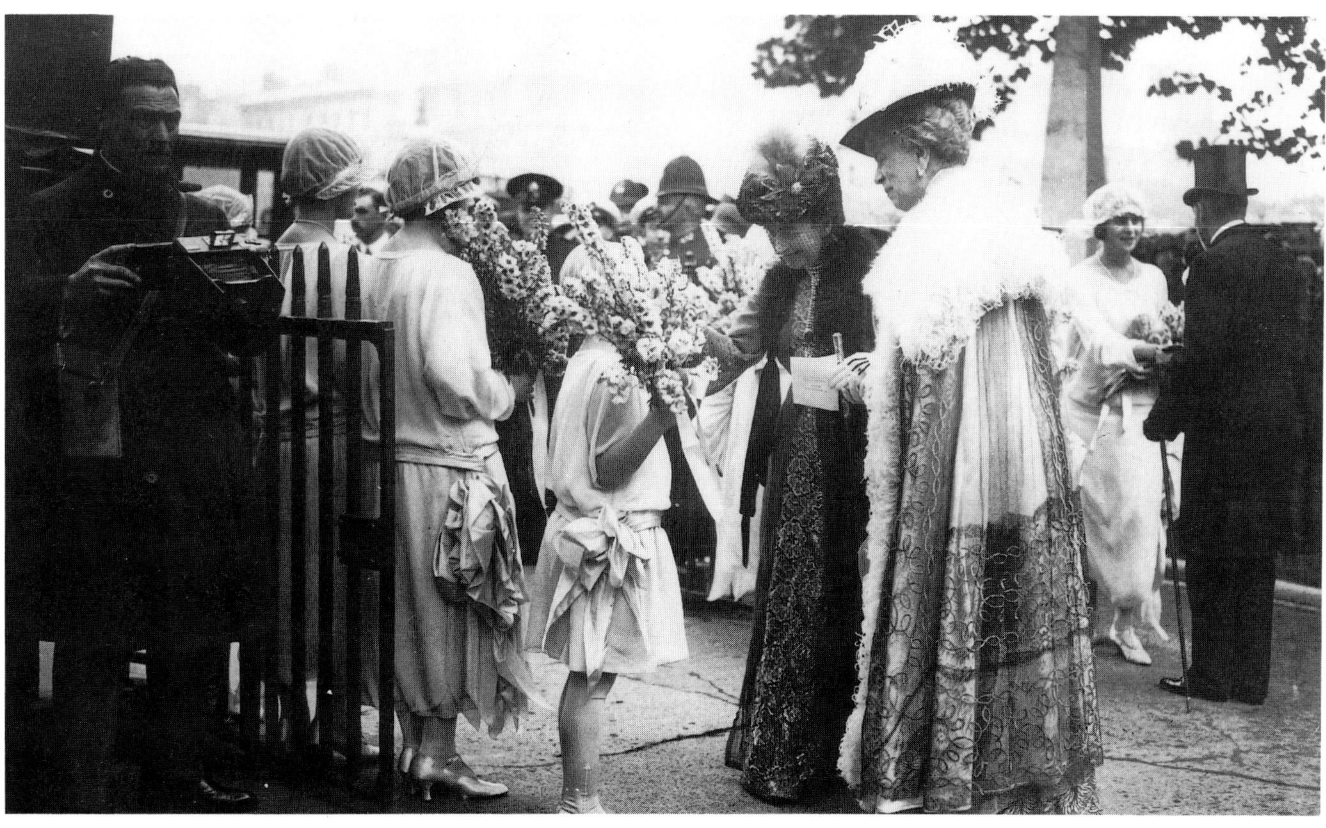

QUEEN MARY AND QUEEN ALEXANDRA TALKING
TO THE BRIDESMAIDS AT ST MARGARET'S CHURCH,
WESTMINSTER, AT THE WEDDING OF LORD AND
LADY LOUIS MOUNTBATTEN ON 18 JULY 1922

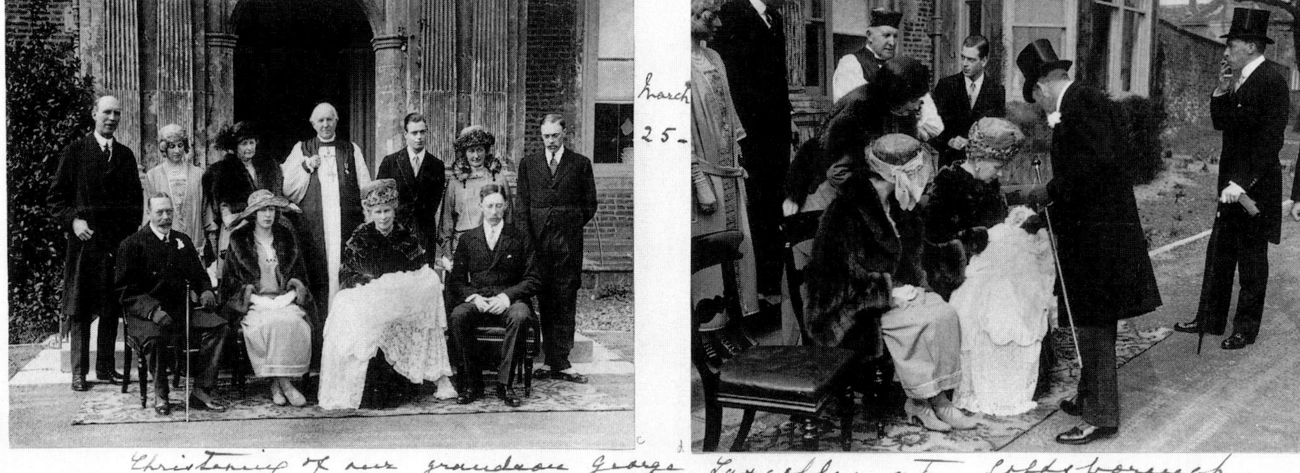

THE CHRISTENING OF THE
HON. GEORGE LASCELLES
AT GOLDSBOROUGH,
25 MARCH 1923. HE WAS THE
FIRST CHILD OF PRINCESS
MARY AND LORD
LASCELLES AND WAS
CHRISTENED BY THE
ARCHBISHOP OF
CANTERBURY, DR LANG

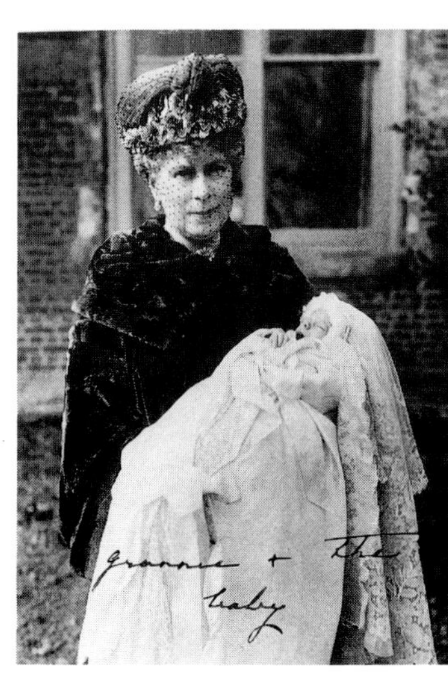

QUEEN MARY CRADLING HER FIRST
GRANDCHILD, GEORGE LASCELLES, THE
PRESENT EARL OF HAREWOOD, ON THE DAY OF
HIS CHRISTENING

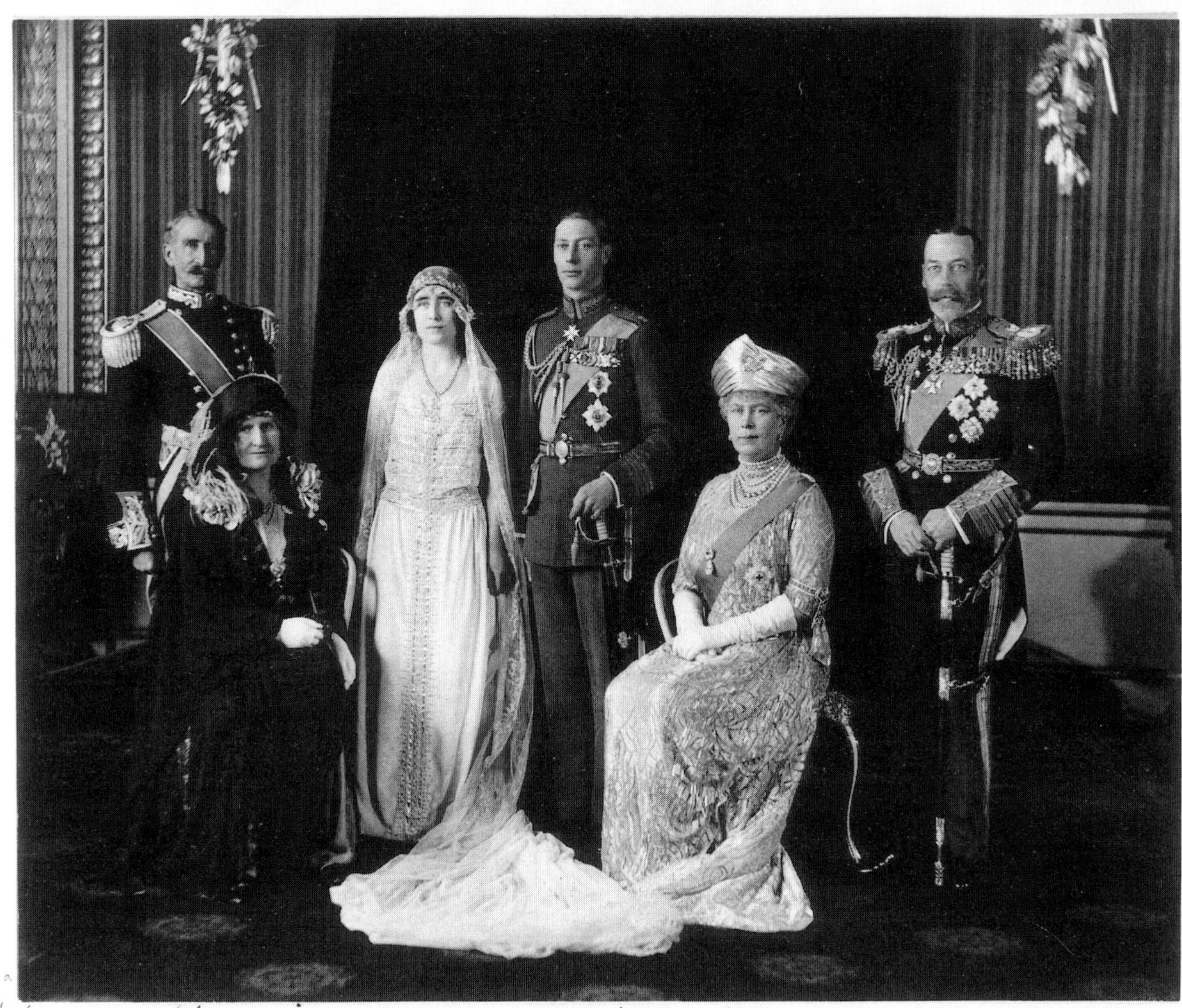

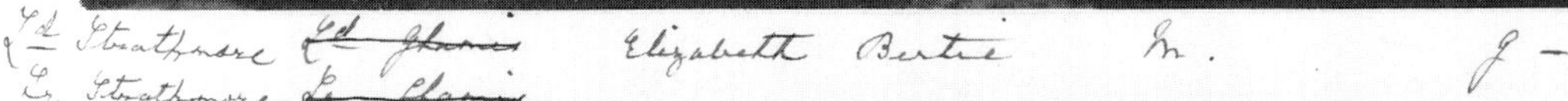
Ly Strathmore   Ld Glamis   Elizabeth   Bertie   M.   G.
E. Strathmore   Ld Glamis

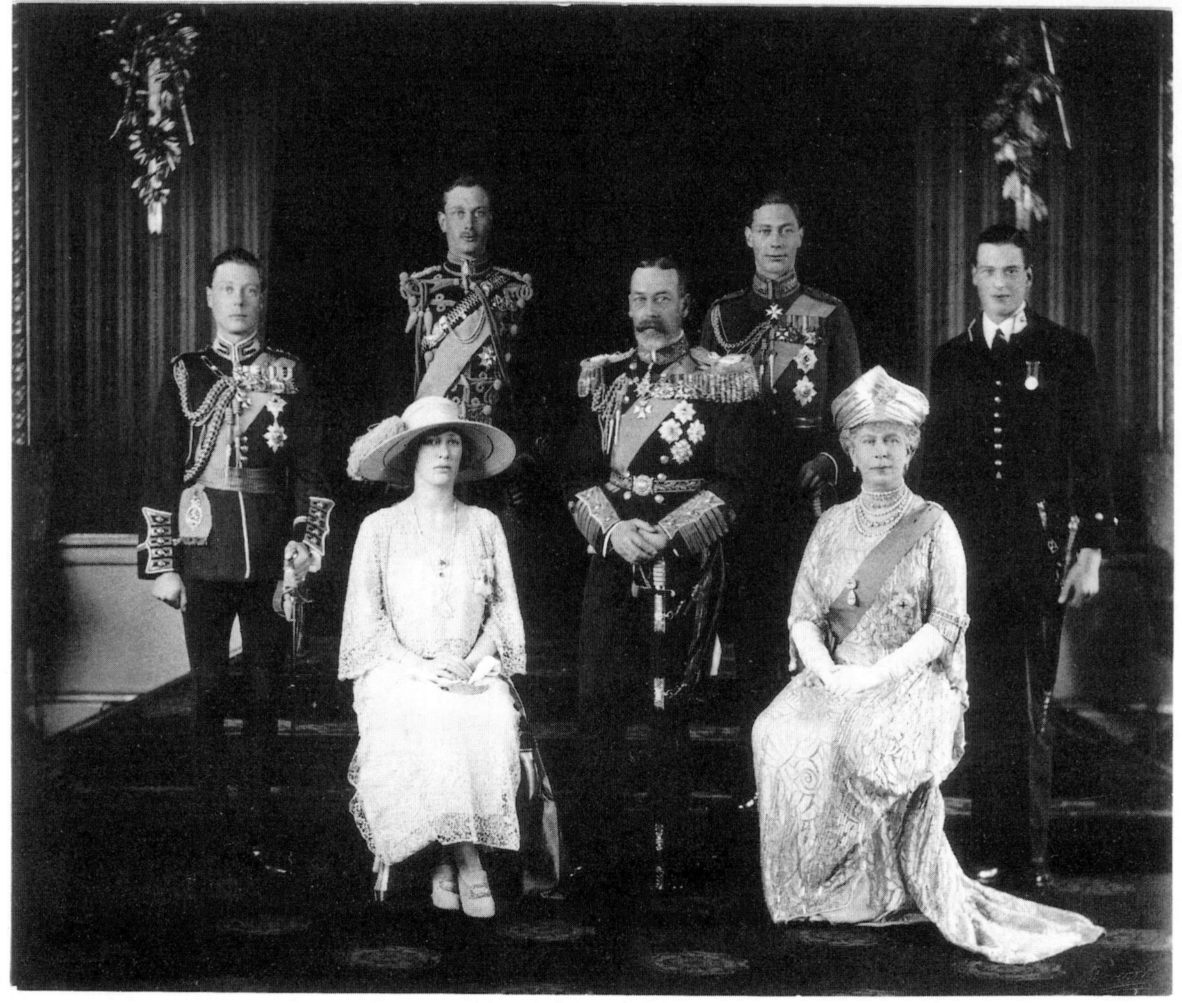

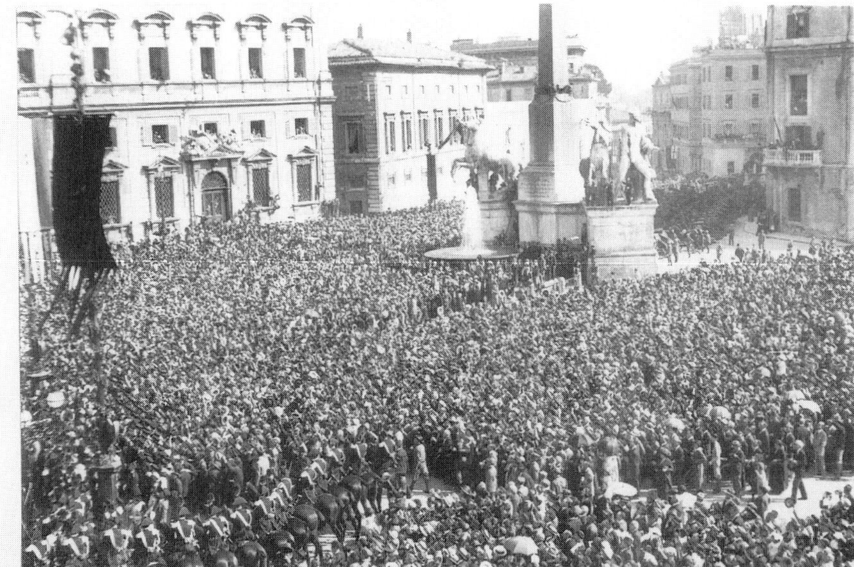

The state visit to Rome, May 1923. The King and Queen were guests of King Victor Emmanuel III and Queen Elena

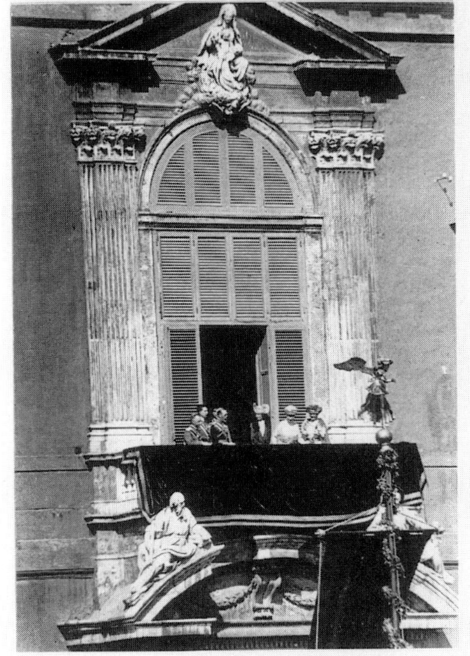

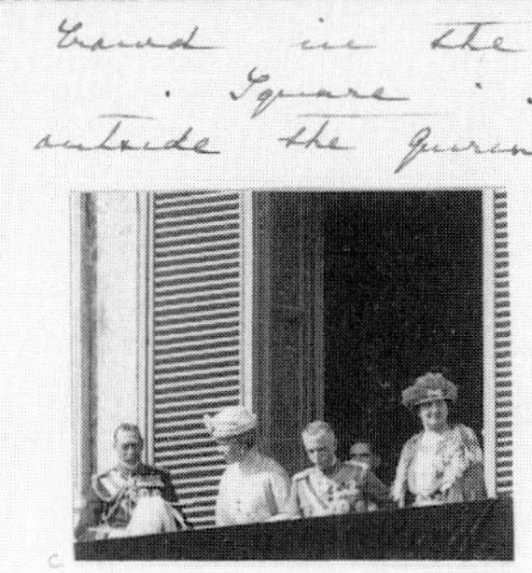

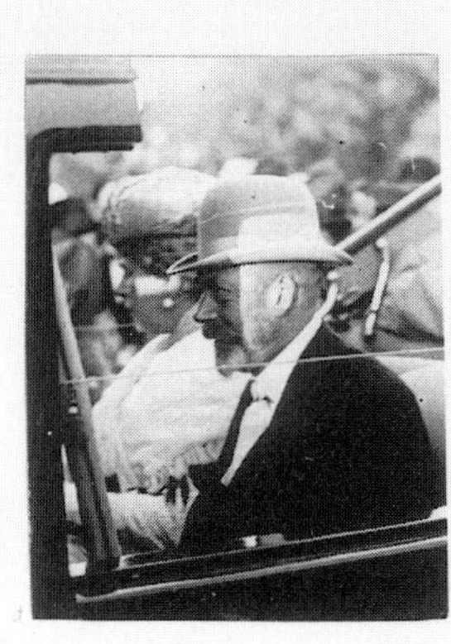

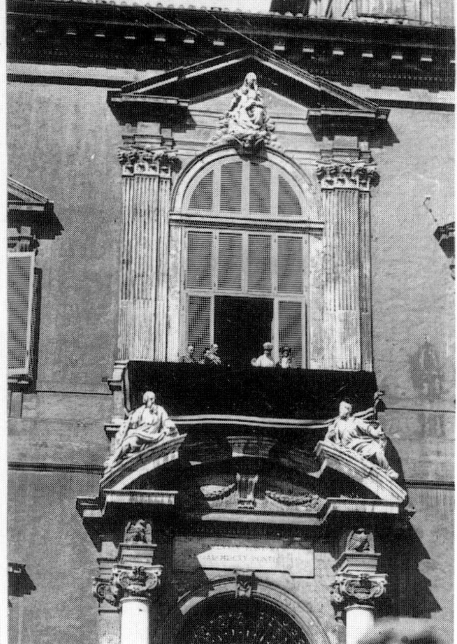

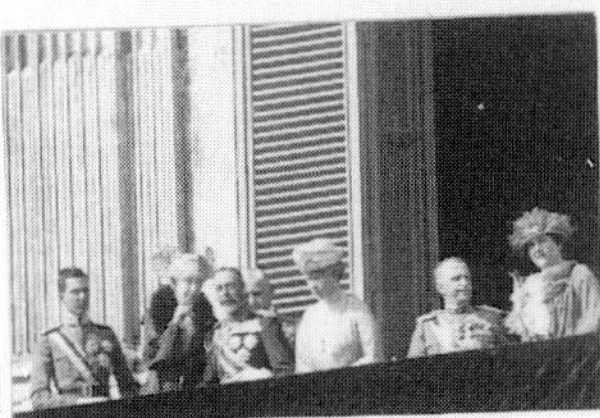

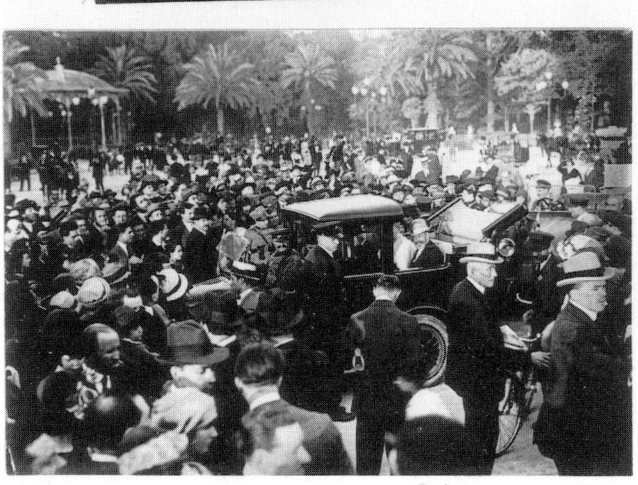

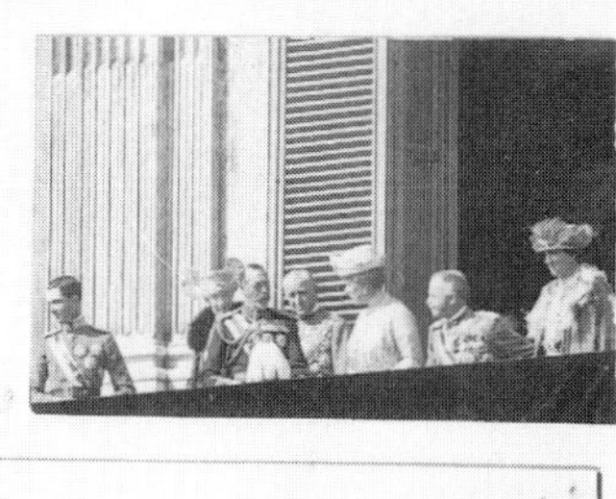

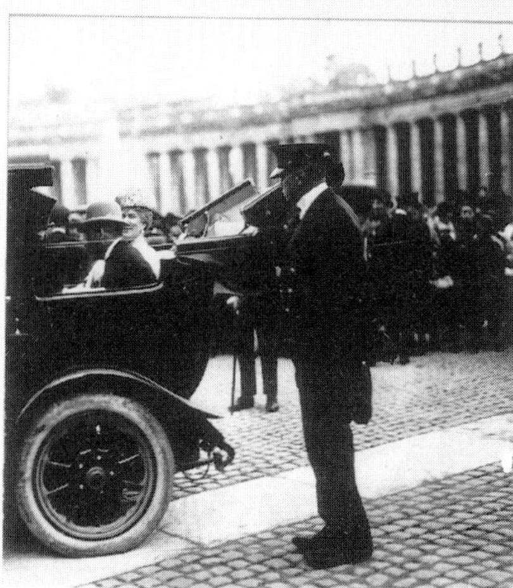

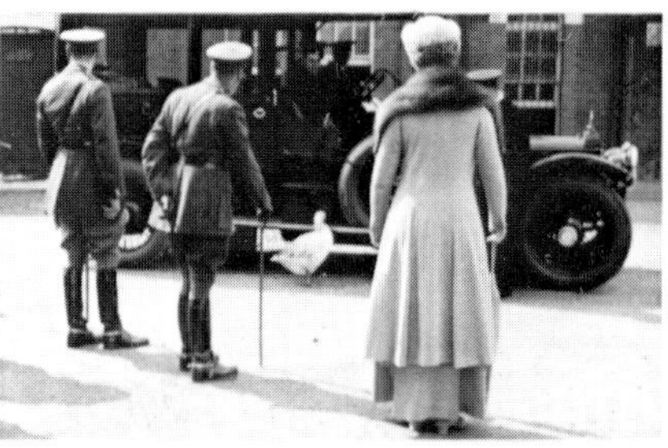

The King and Queen watching a goose inspect their car and Queen Mary attempting to entice the bird, Aldershot, May 1923

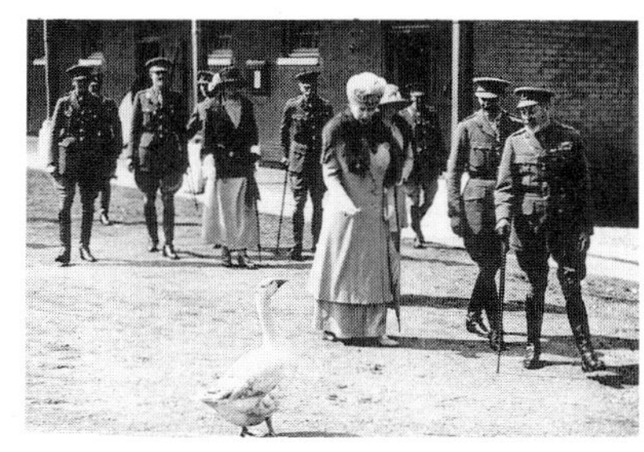

(*Opposite*) The marriage of Prince Albert, Duke of York, and Lady Elizabeth Bowes Lyon, 26 April 1923. Queen Mary made a mistake in the caption for the top photograph – Lord and Lady Glamis were already the Earl and Countess of Strathmore at the time of the wedding. The bottom photograph shows the King and Queen with their five remaining children – Johnnie had died in 1919

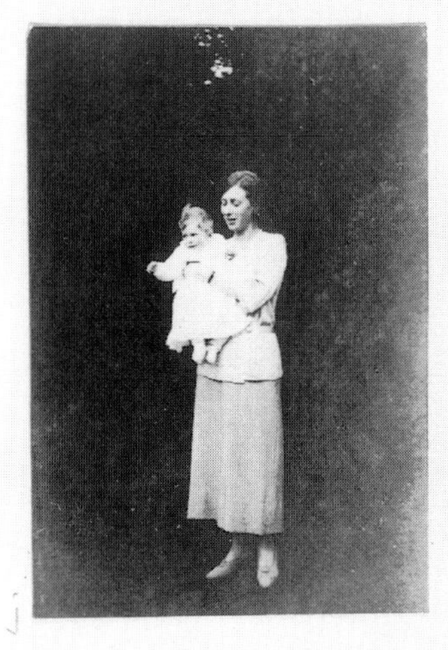 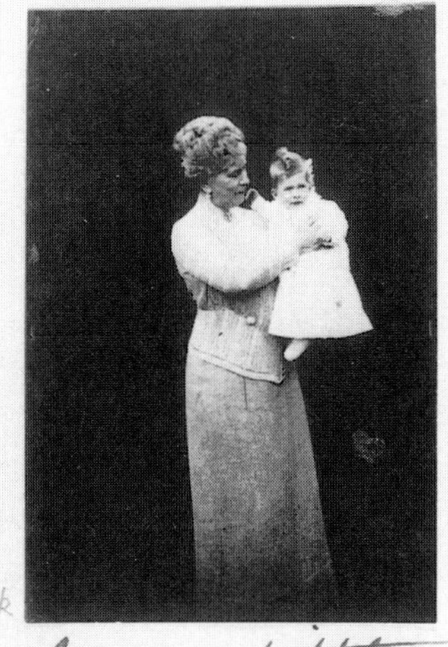 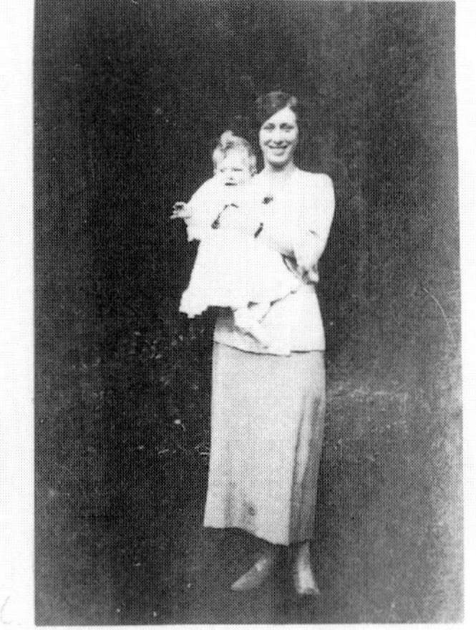

M. & little
George Lascelles
Goldsborough
Aug.

1923 -

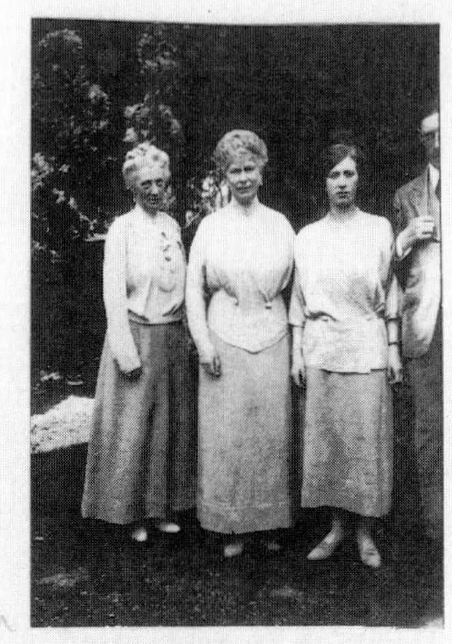 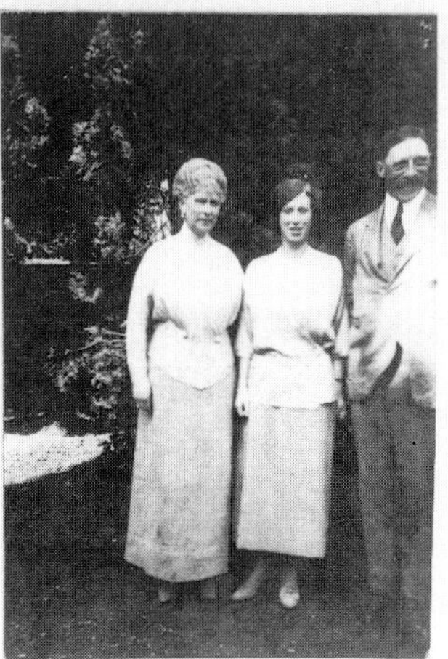

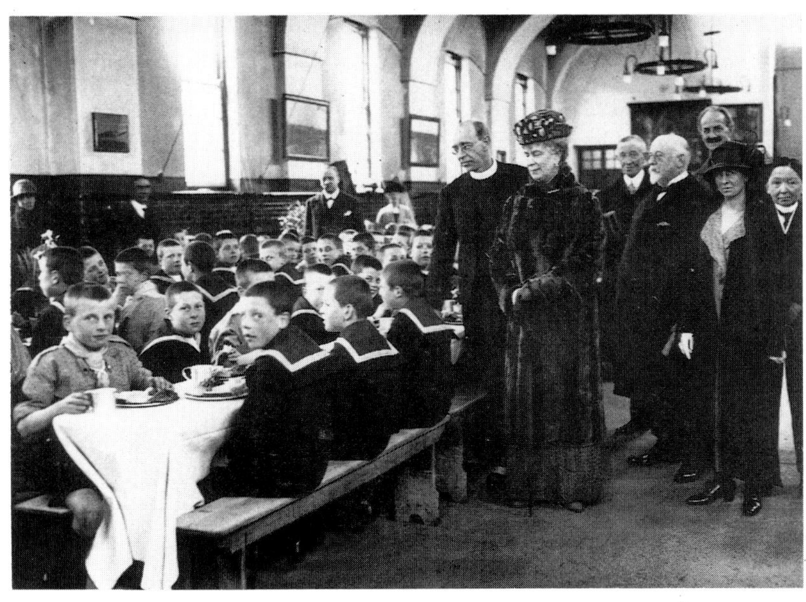 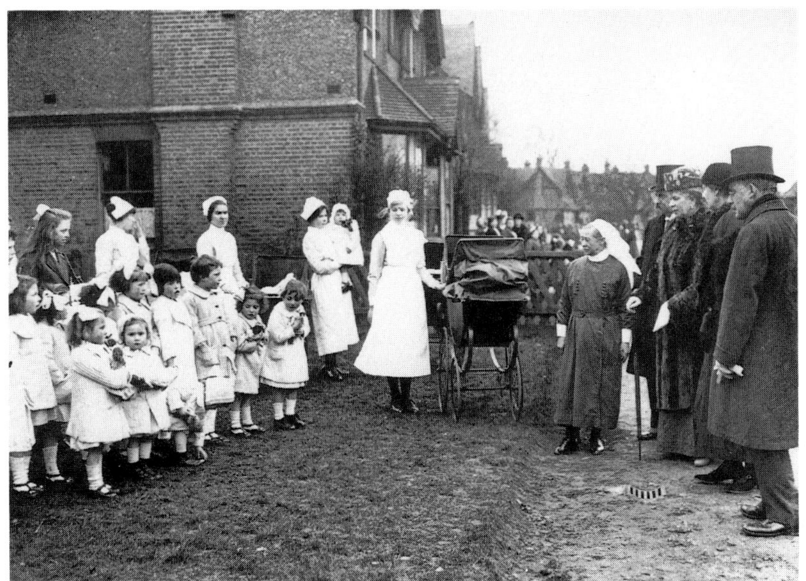

Barnado boys' home. Barkingside
March 27th

QUEEN MARY VISITING THE DR BARNARDO'S
HOME AT BARKINGSIDE ON 27 MARCH 1924

(*OPPOSITE*) QUEEN MARY
AND PRINCE GEORGE
VISITING THE WEMBLEY
BRITISH EMPIRE
EXHIBITION ON 30 MAY 1924

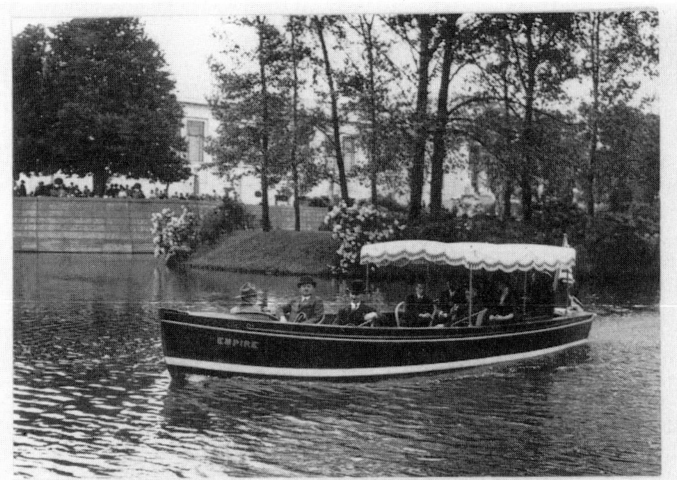

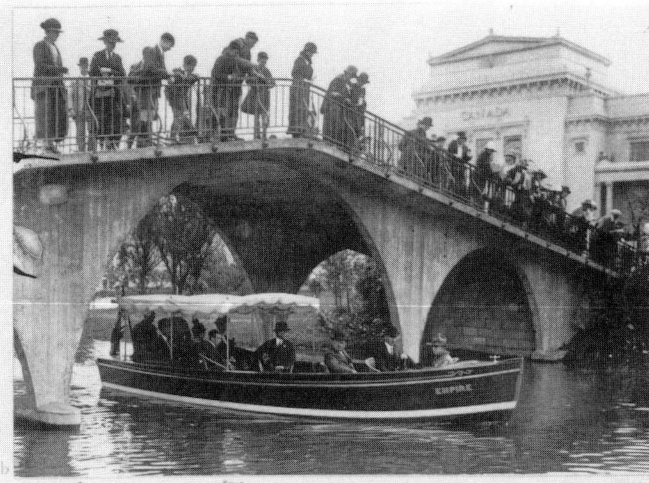

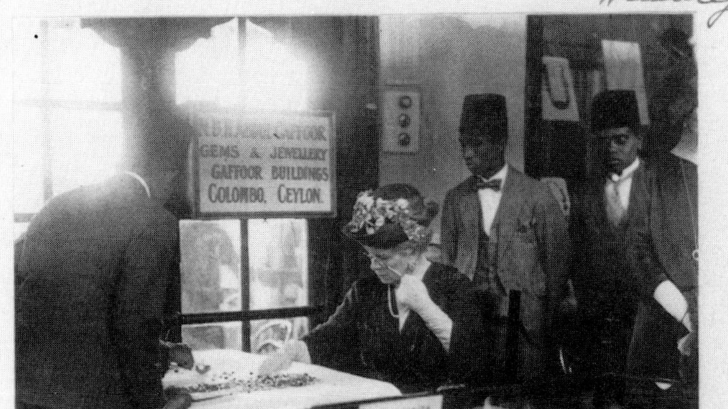

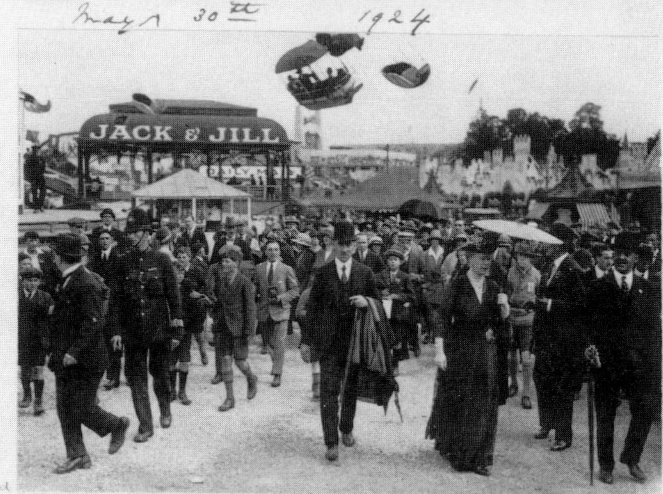

Wembley May 30th 1924

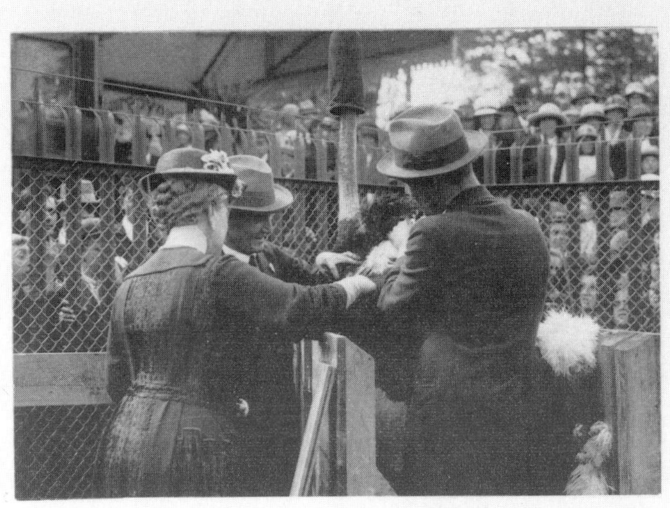

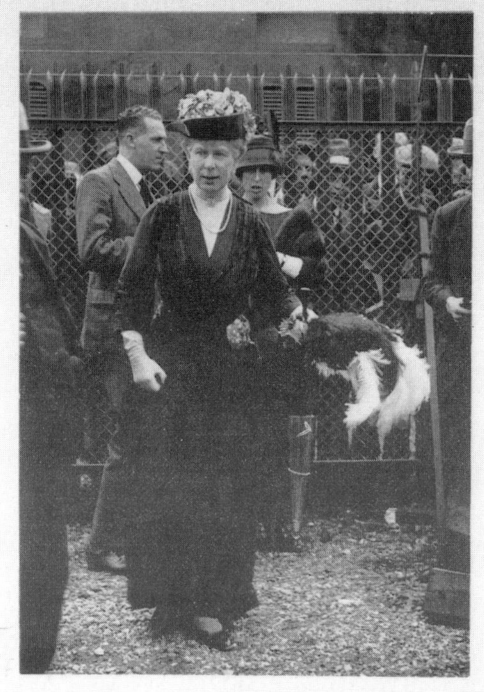

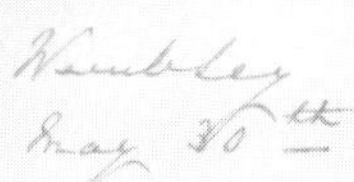

Wembley
May 30th

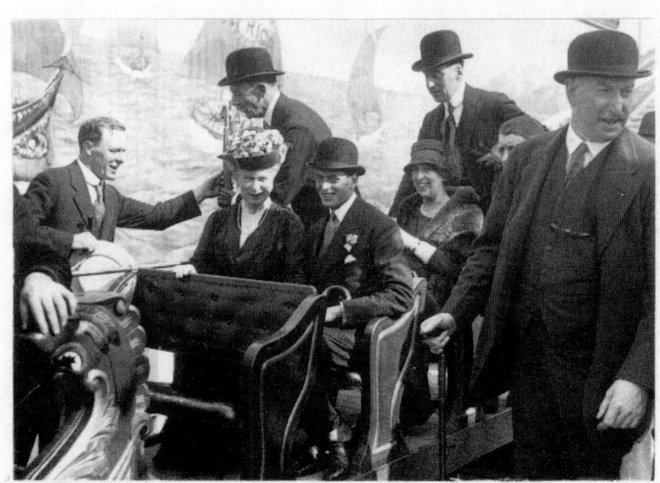

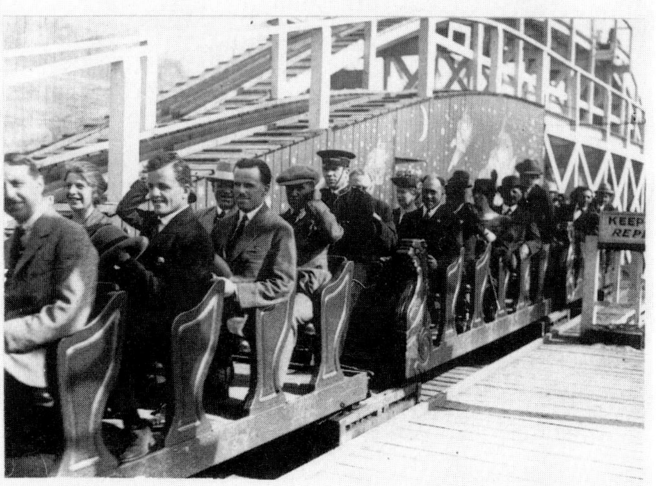

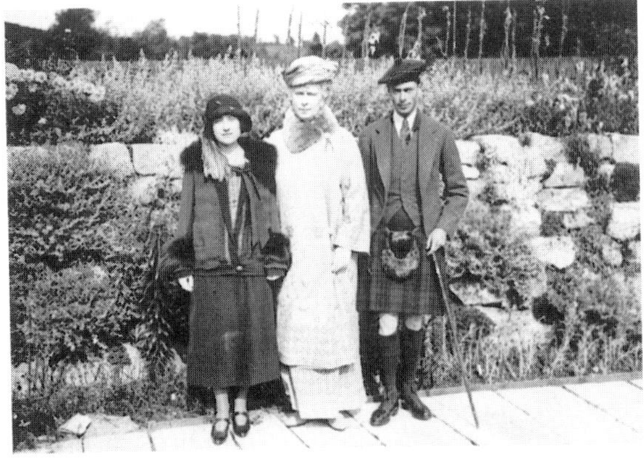

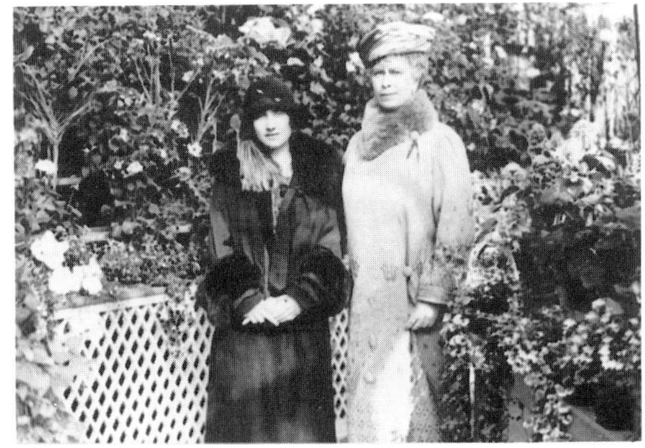

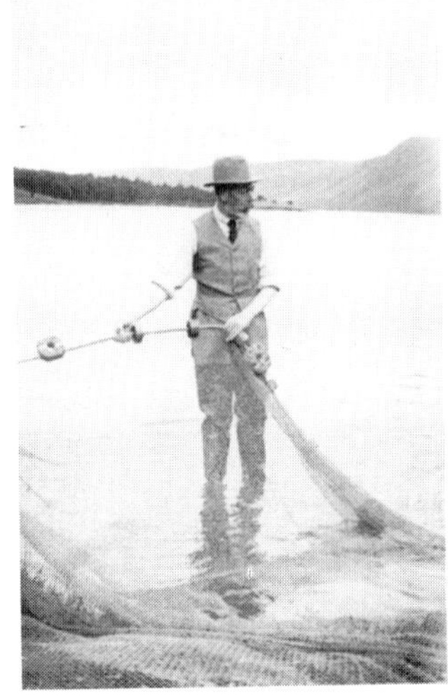

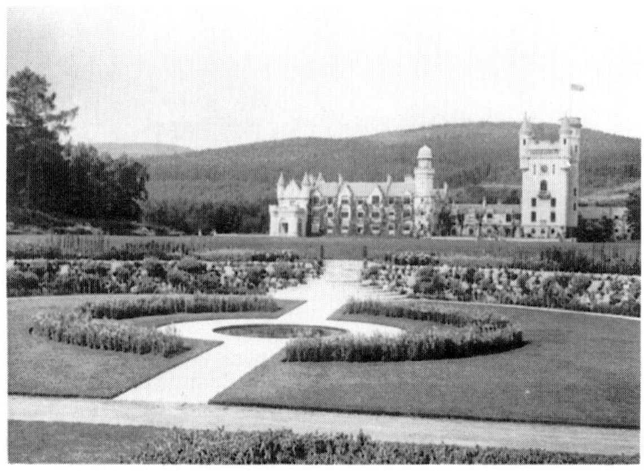

QUEEN MARY WITH BERTIE AND ELIZABETH, DUKE
AND DUCHESS OF YORK, AT BALMORAL IN THE
AUTUMN OF 1924, AND THE KING FISHING THERE

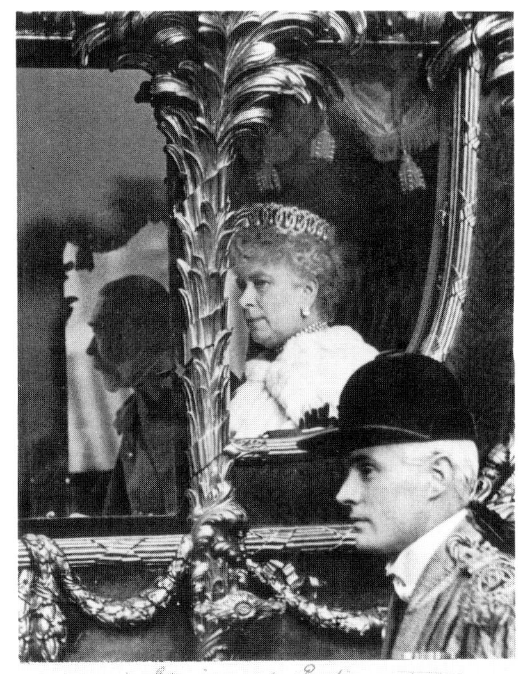

THE KING AND QUEEN
MARY DRIVE TO THE STATE
OPENING OF PARLIAMENT
ON 9 DECEMBER 1924 IN THE
STATE COACH. THE QUEEN
WEARS A TIARA OF
DIAMONDS AND PEARLS
ONCE OWNED BY THE
RUSSIAN GRAND DUCHESS
VLADIMIR (GRANDMOTHER
OF PRINCESS MARINA, THE
FUTURE DUCHESS OF
KENT)

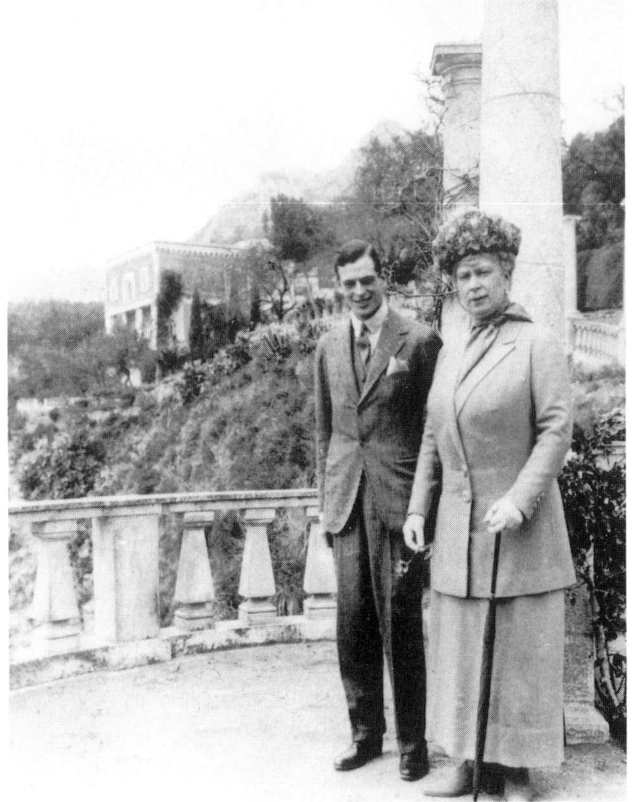

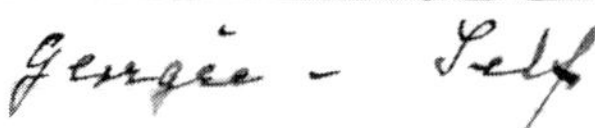

Georgie – Self

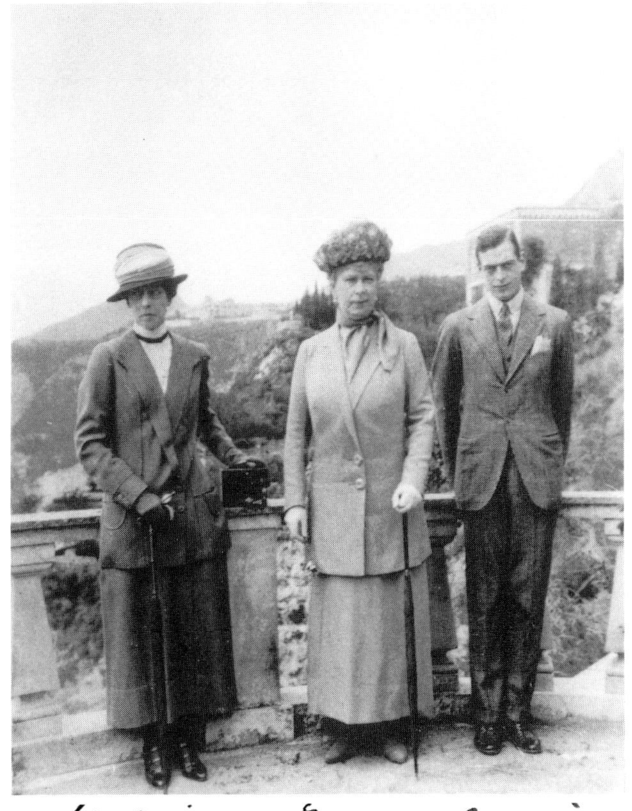

Victoria   Self   Georgie

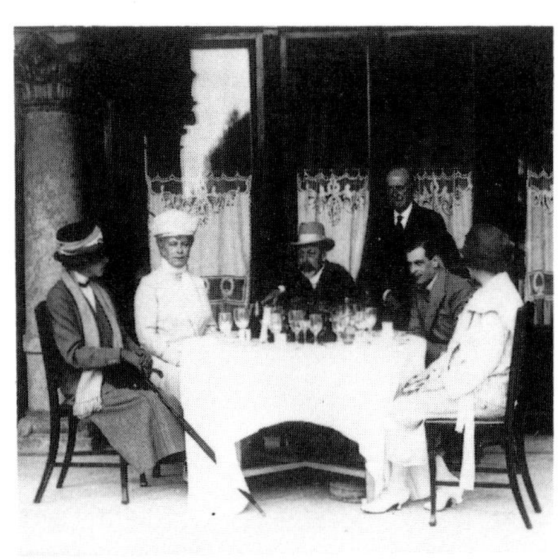

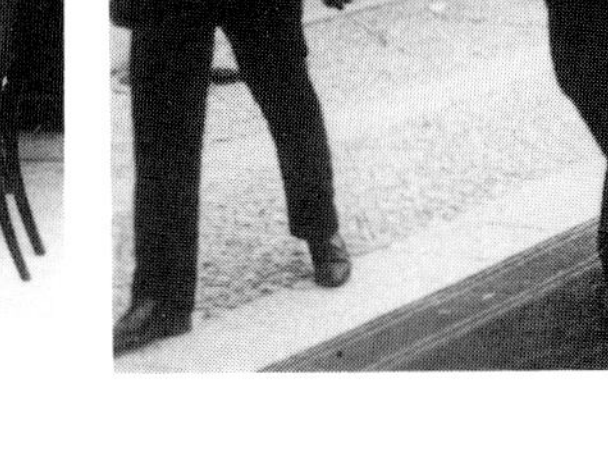

Palermo

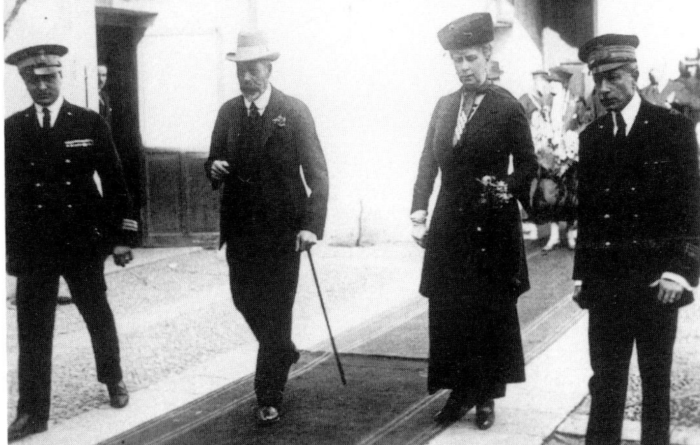

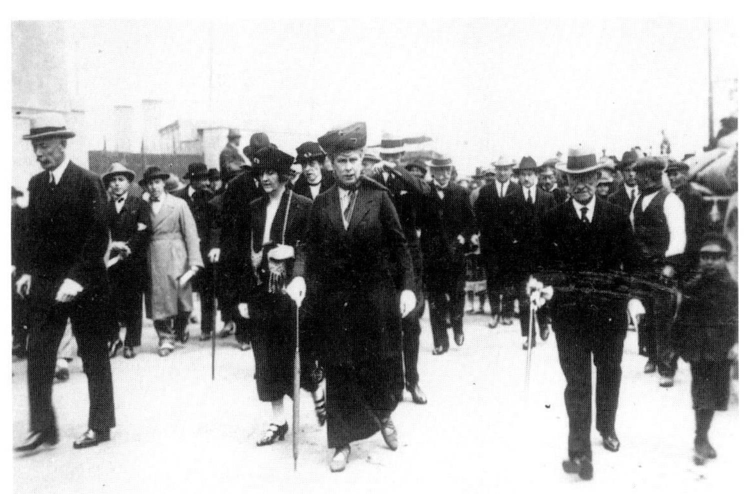

Beloved Mama's funeral
Nov. 1925.

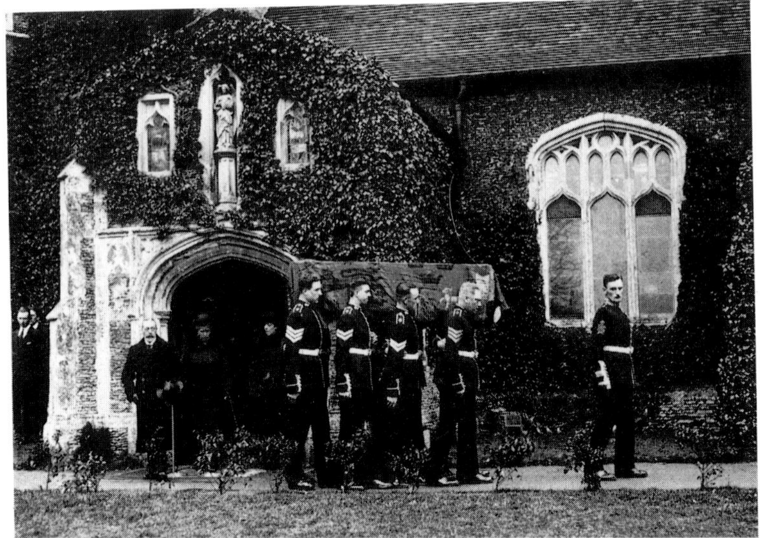

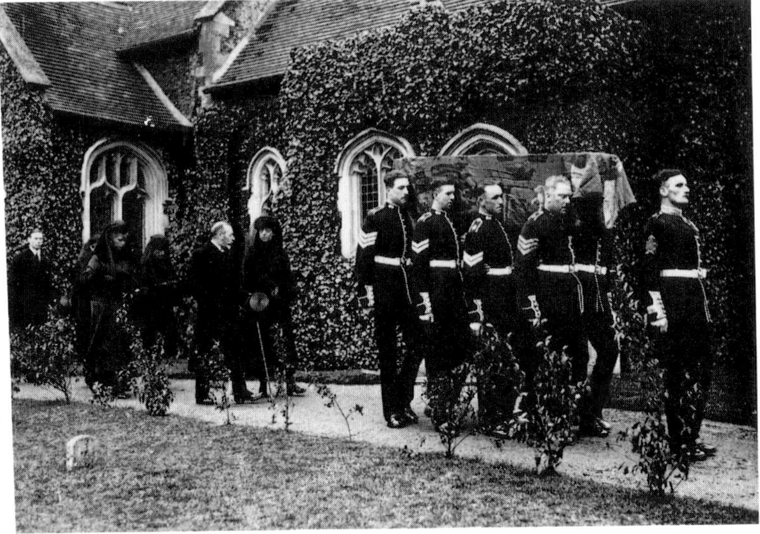

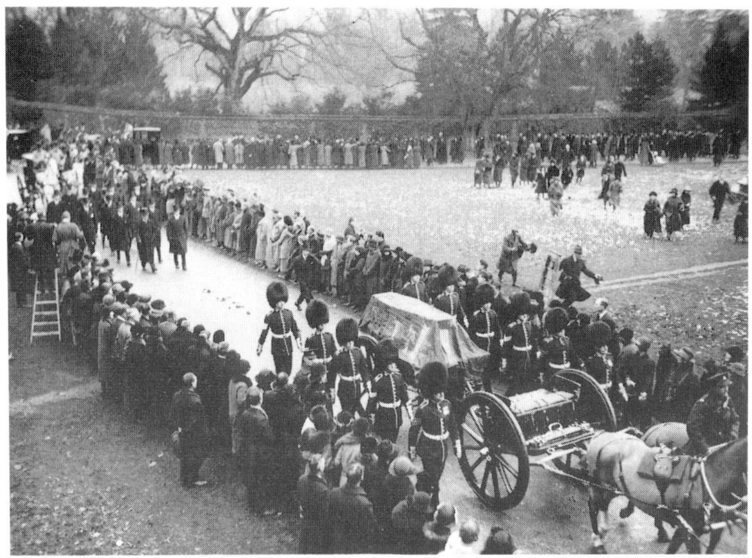

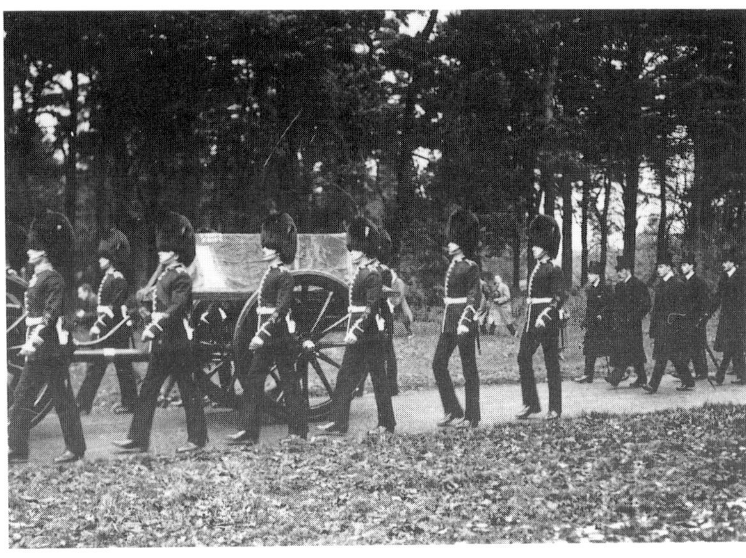

Sandringham

THE DEATH OF QUEEN ALEXANDRA AT SANDRINGHAM IN
NOVEMBER 1925. THE QUEEN DOWAGER'S COFFIN WAS BORNE
FROM NORFOLK TO LONDON, FOLLOWED BY KING GEORGE V,
PRINCESS VICTORIA AND QUEEN MARY

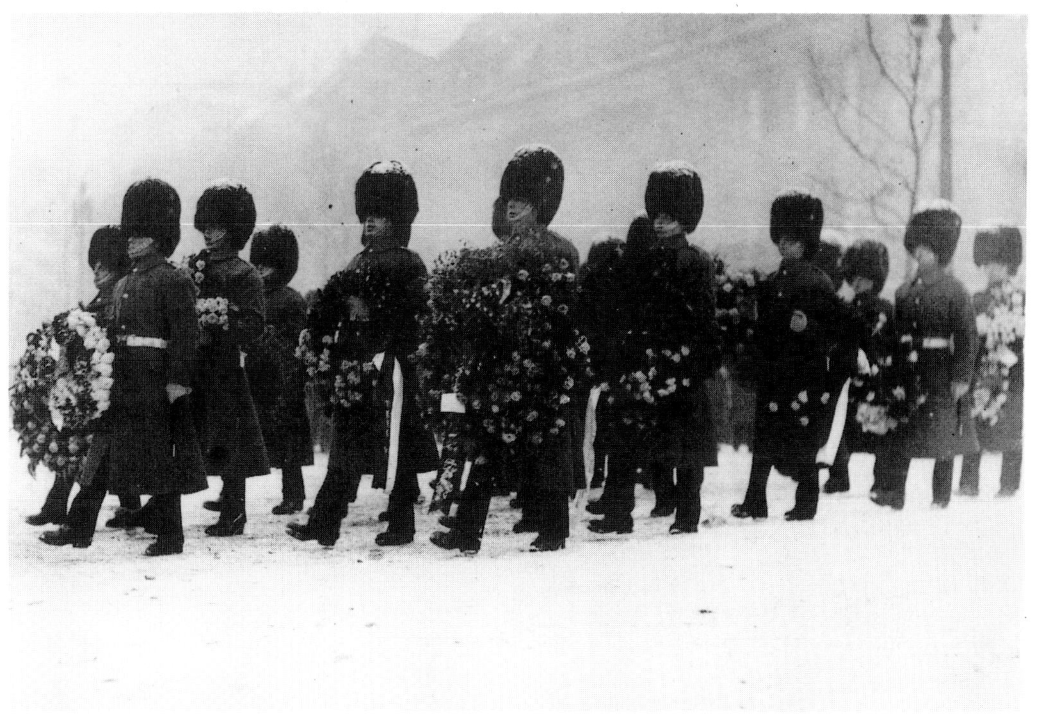

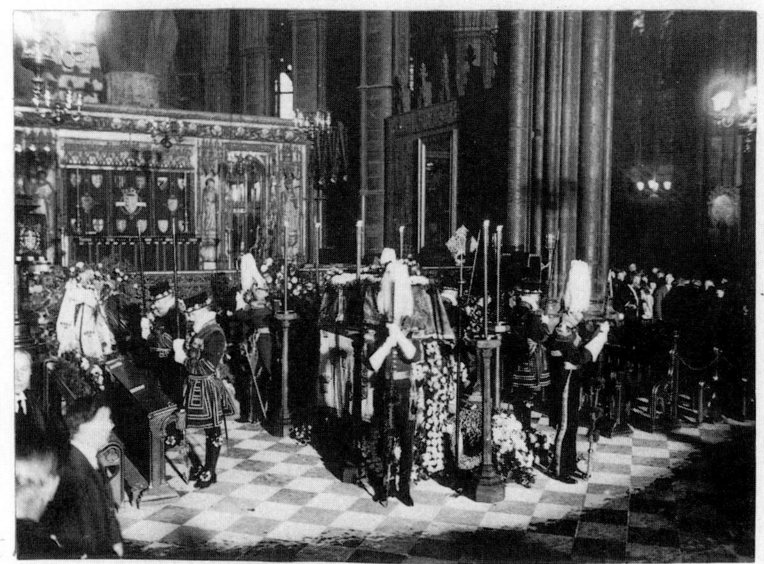

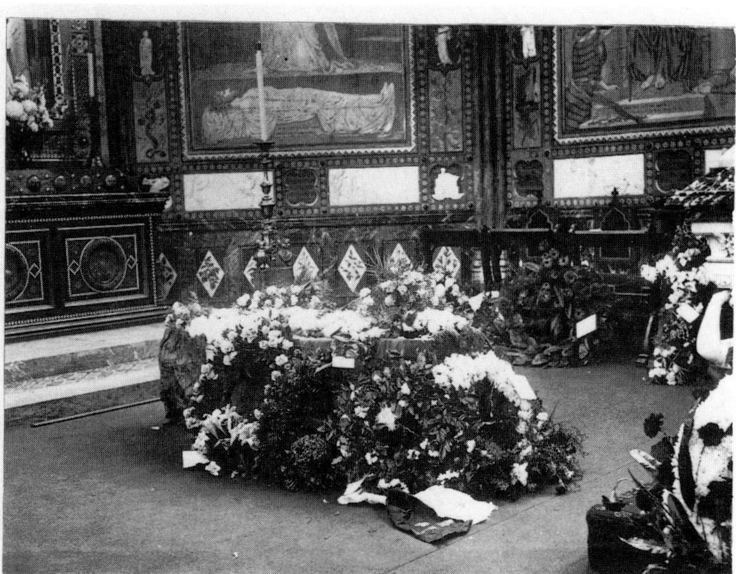

QUEEN ALEXANDRA LAY IN STATE IN WESTMINSTER ABBEY
(LEFT) AND, IMMEDIATELY BEFORE THE FUNERAL SERVICE, IN
THE ALBERT MEMORIAL CHAPEL, ADJACENT TO ST GEORGE'S
CHAPEL AT WINDSOR CASTLE

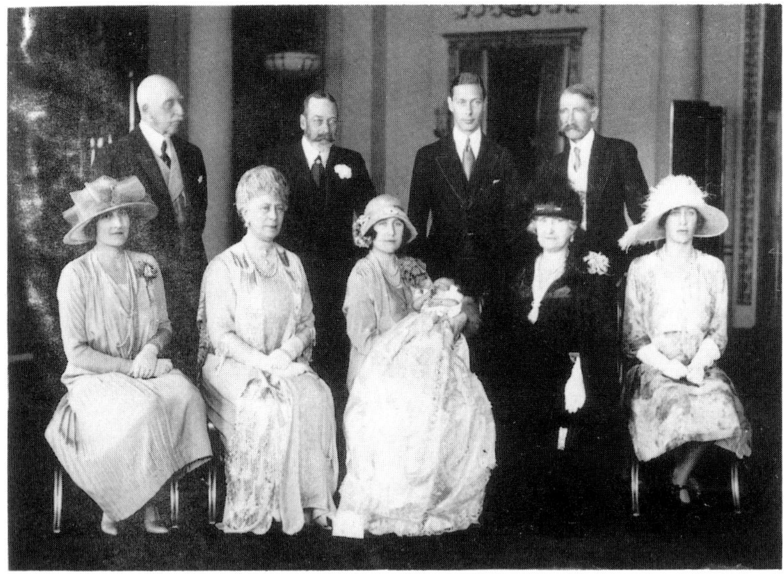

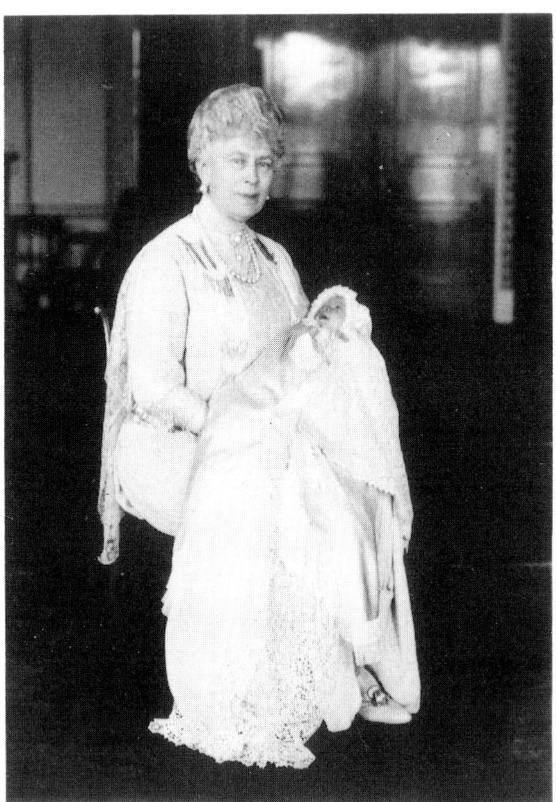

THE CHRISTENING, ON 29 MAY, OF THE KING
AND QUEEN'S FIRST GRANDDAUGHTER,
PRINCESS ELIZABETH OF YORK, BORN ON
21 APRIL 1926. THE GROUP SHOWS (STANDING
LEFT TO RIGHT) ARTHUR, DUKE OF
CONNAUGHT, KING GEORGE V, THE DUKE OF
YORK AND THE EARL OF STRATHMORE. (SEATED
LEFT TO RIGHT) LADY ELPHINSTONE (THE
DUCHESS OF YORK'S SISTER), QUEEN MARY, THE
DUCHESS OF YORK WITH HER DAUGHTER, THE
COUNTESS OF STRATHMORE AND THE PRINCESS
MARY

KING GEORGE V ON HOLIDAY IN SCOTLAND AT
GLASSALT, SEPTEMBER 1926

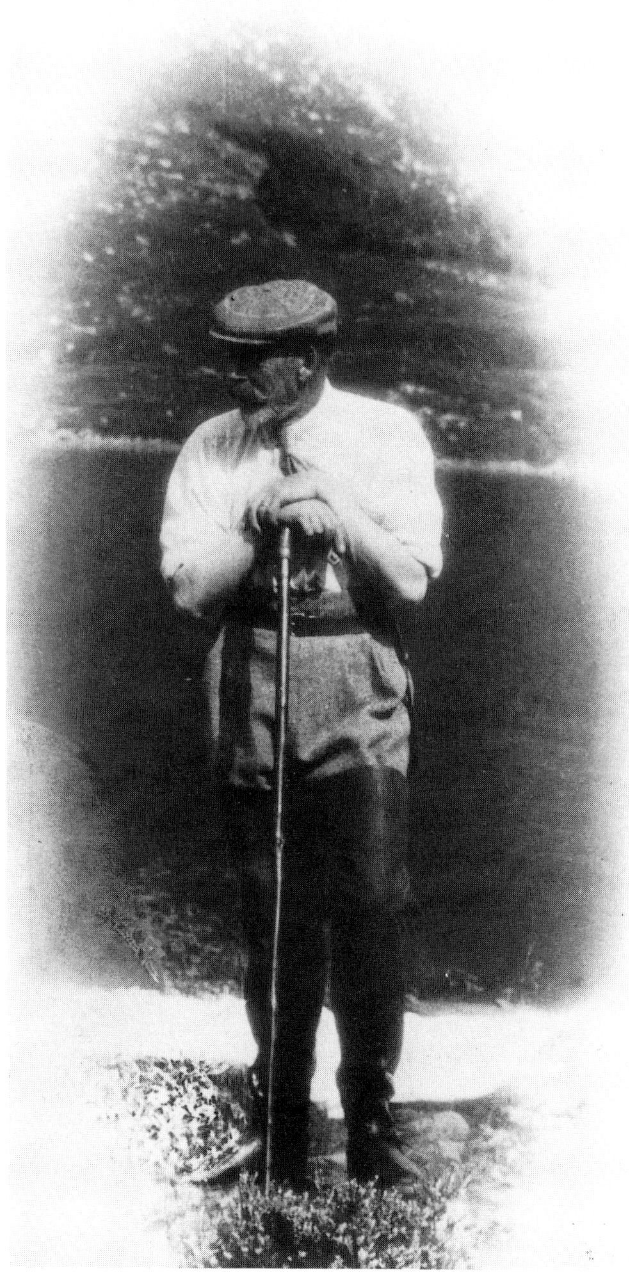

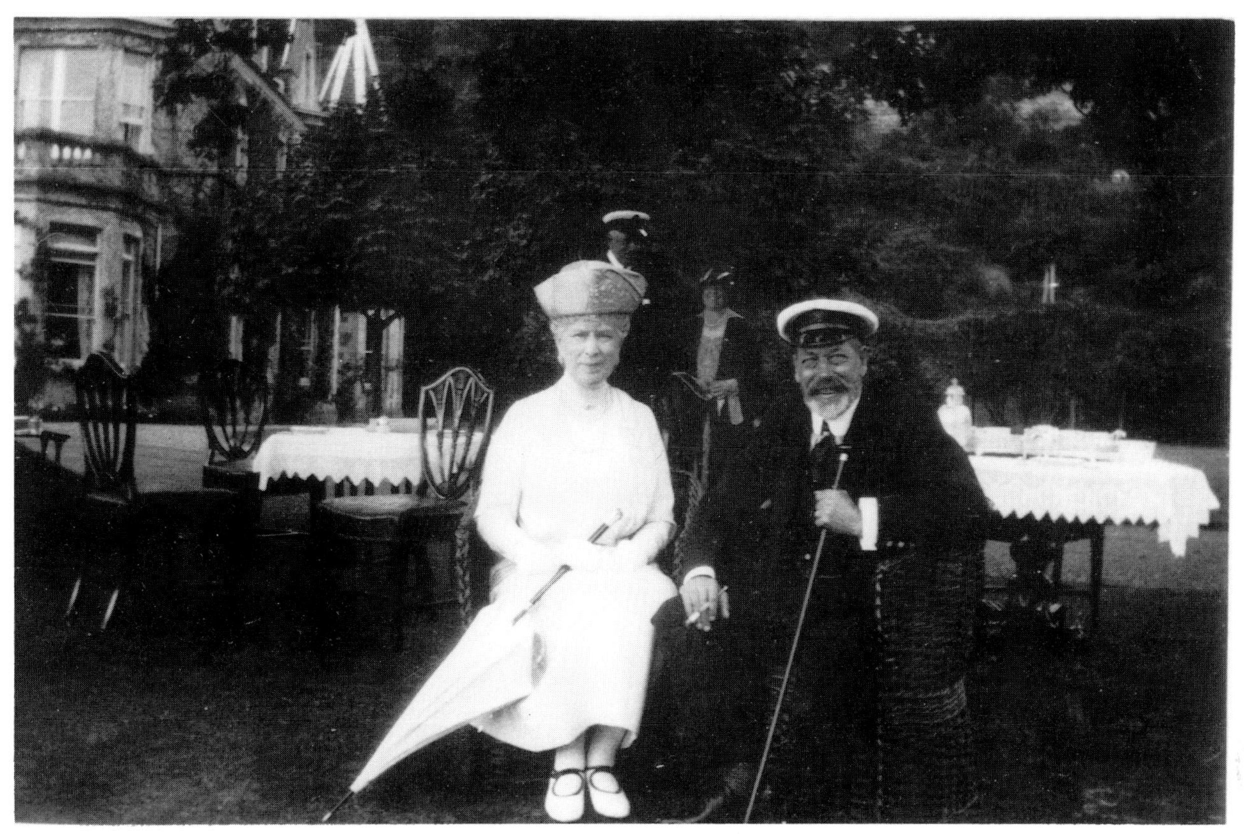

THE KING AND QUEEN AT LORD JELLICOE'S HOUSE (ST LAWRENCE)
ON THE ISLE OF WIGHT, 7 AUGUST 1927

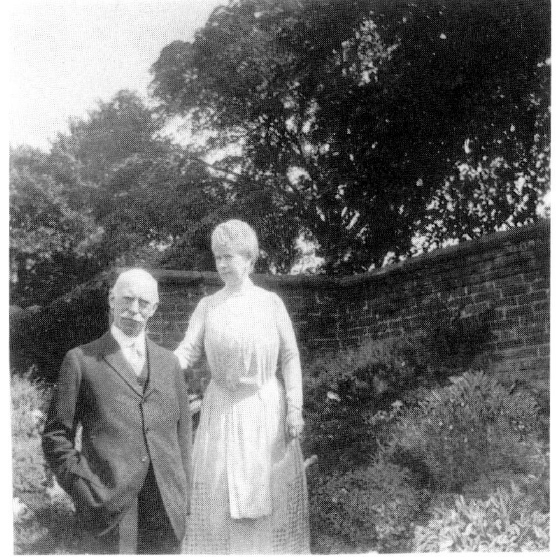

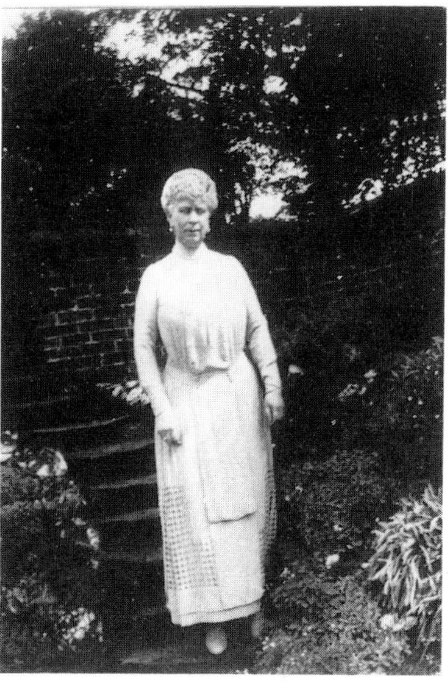

QUEEN MARY WITH HER BROTHER DOLLY AT CASTLE BROMWICH
HALL ON 18 AUGUST 1927

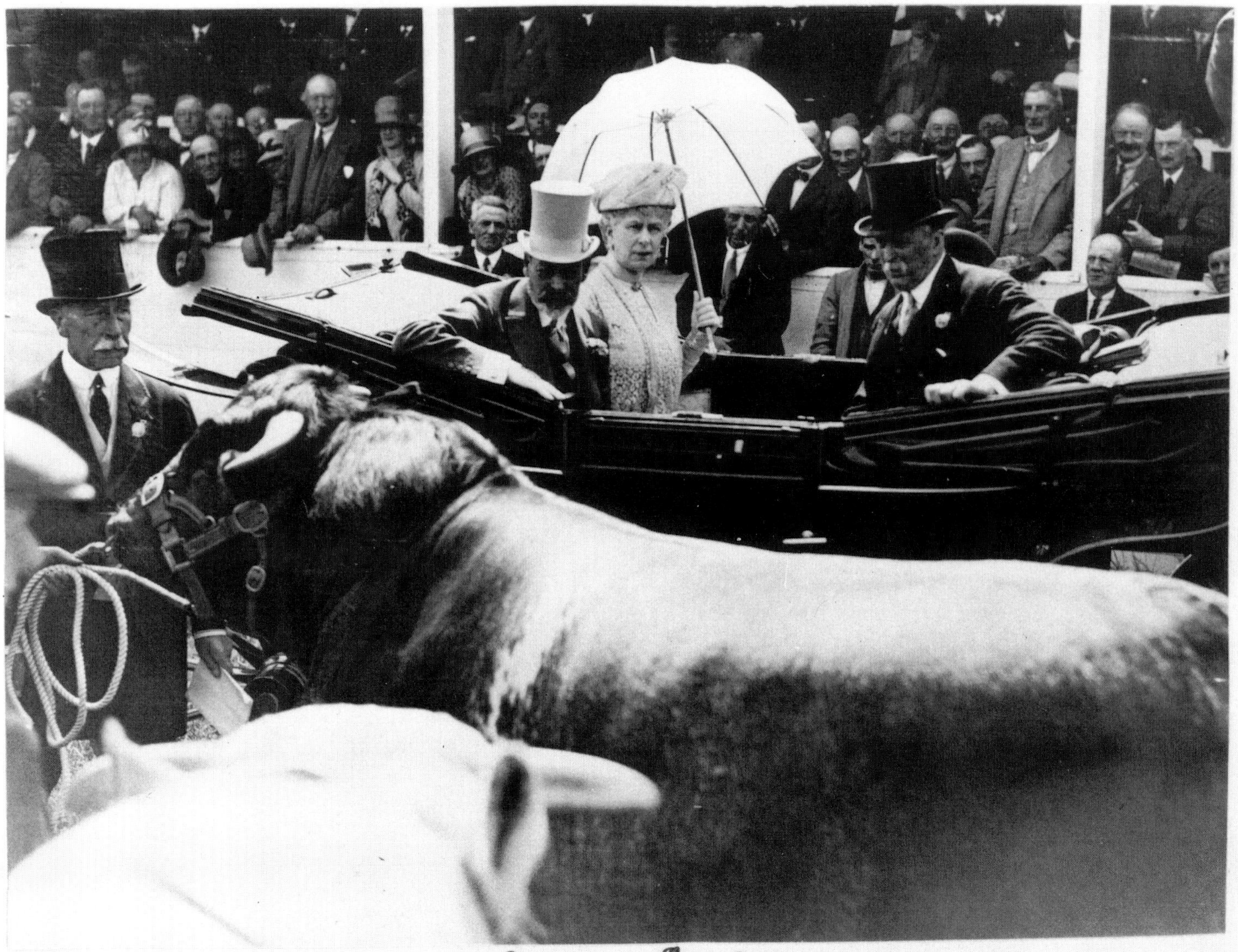

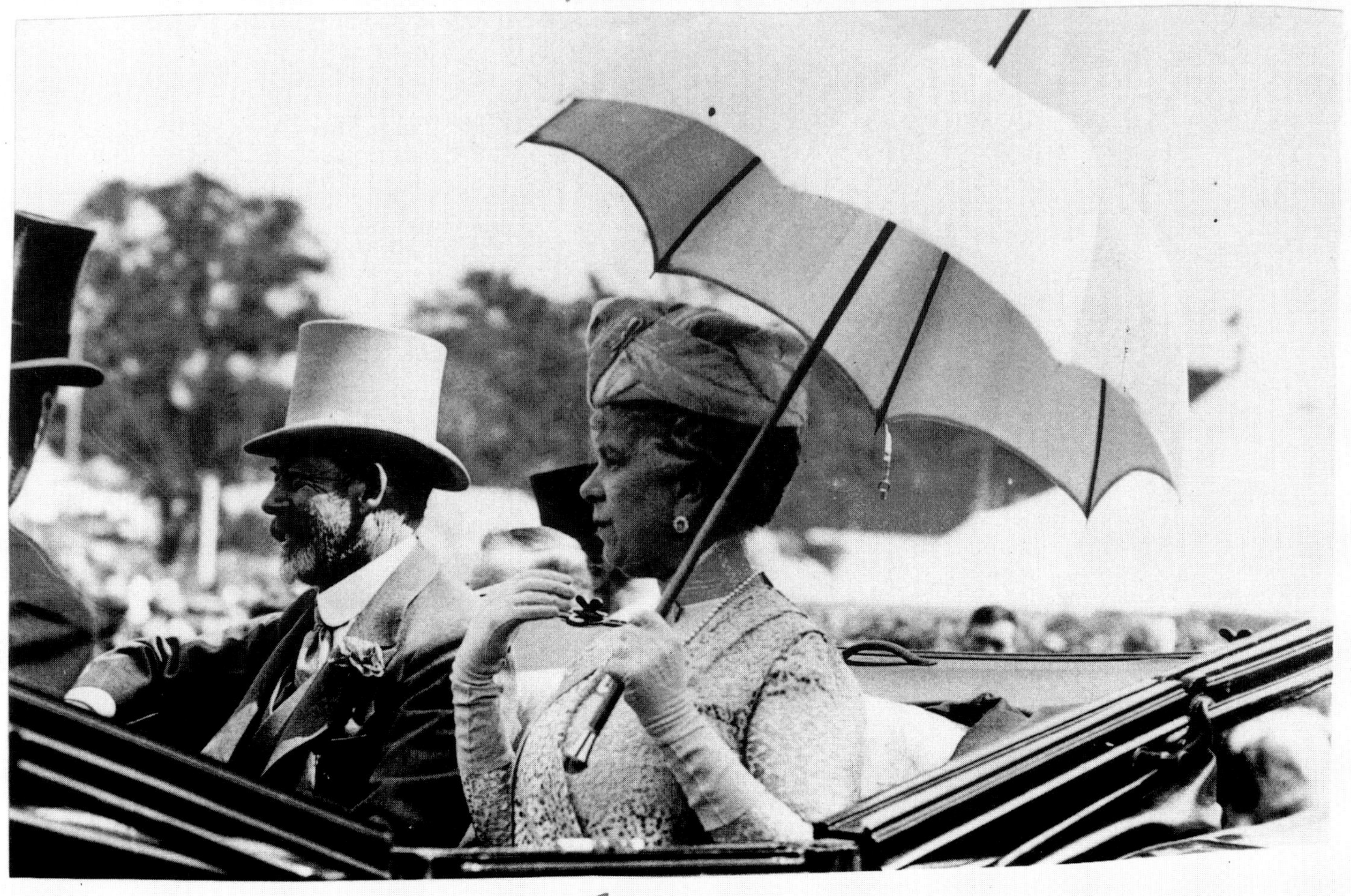

Royal Stand

Nottingham

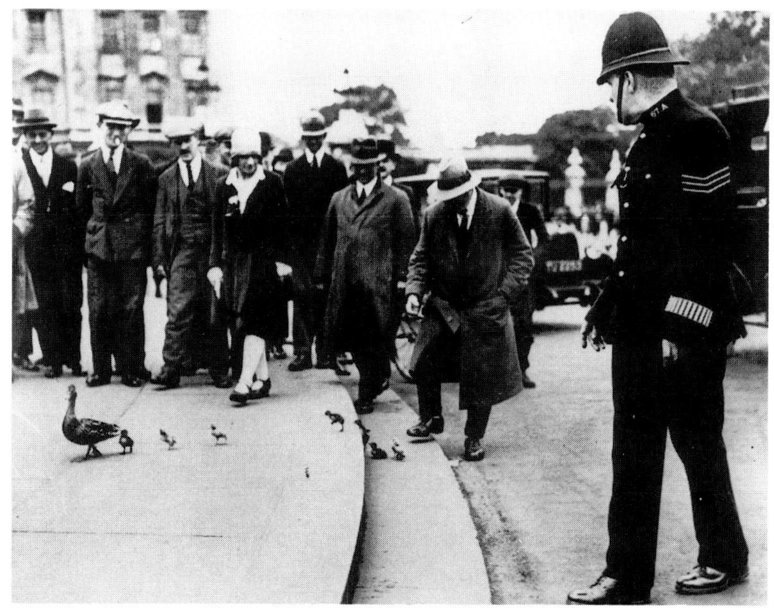

A SCENE OFTEN TO BE WITNESSED TODAY; A DUCK, WITH POLICE ESCORT, CROSSING THE MALL WITH HER YOUNG, EN ROUTE TO ST JAMES'S PARK

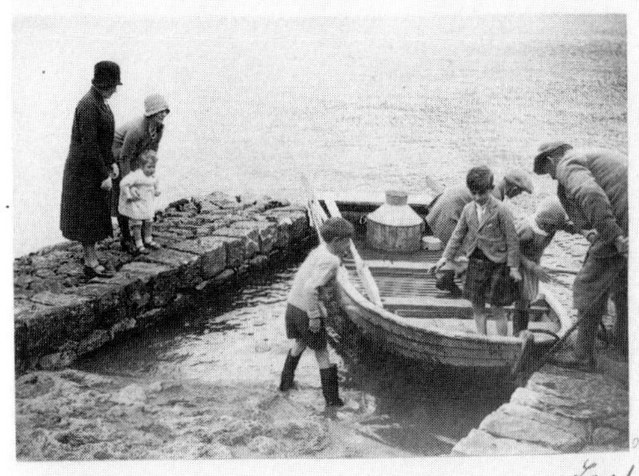
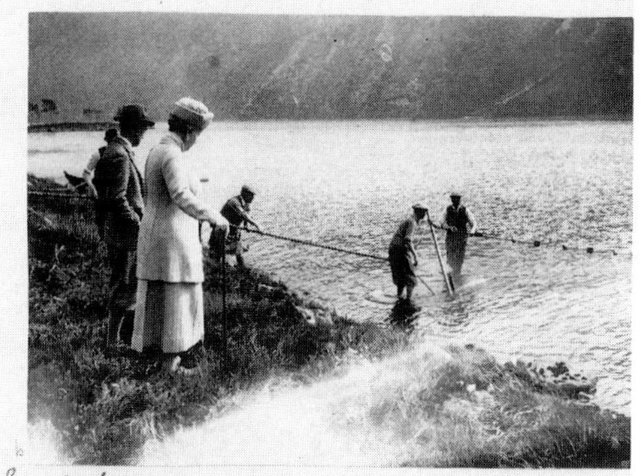

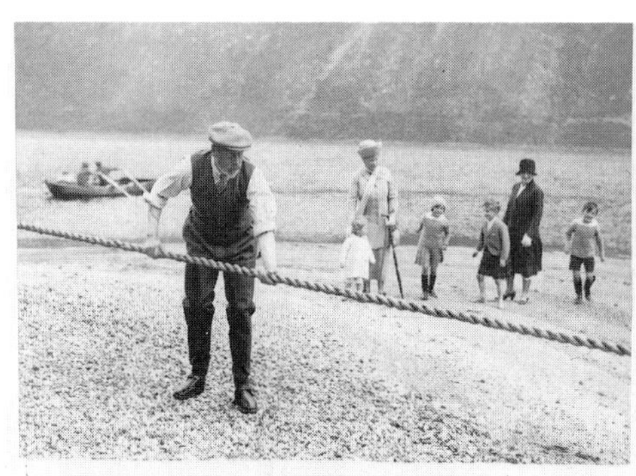
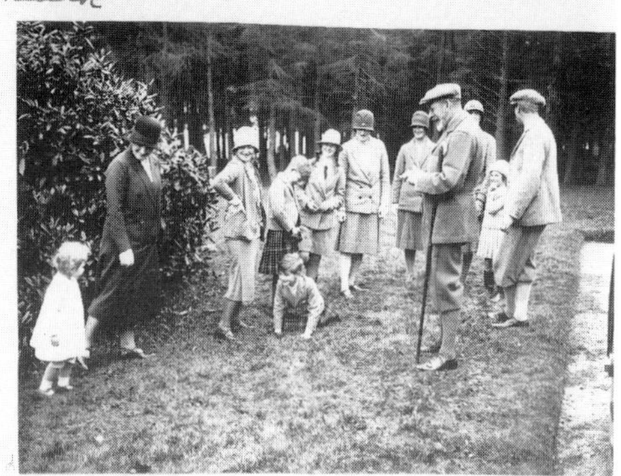

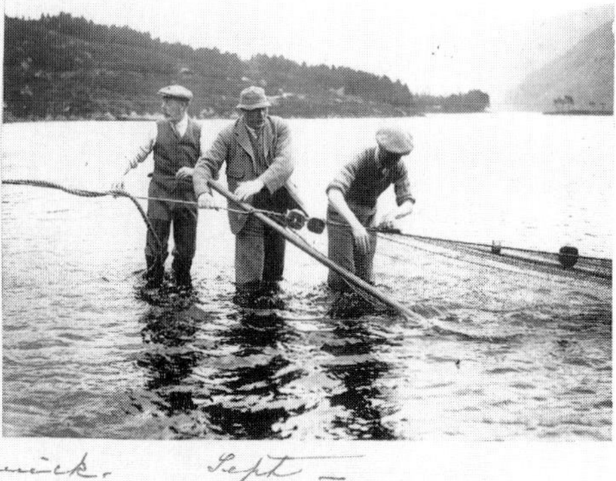

(*OPPOSITE*) KING GEORGE V AND QUEEN MARY VISIT THE ROYAL SHOW AT NOTTINGHAM, JULY 1928

STUDIES OF ROYAL FUN AND GAMES BESIDE LOCH MUICK ON THE BALMORAL ESTATE, SEPTEMBER 1928. THE KING, WEARING A FLAT CAP AND ROLLED-UP SHIRT SLEEVES, HELPS A FISHING ENTERPRISE WATCHED BY THE QUEEN, PRINCESS ELIZABETH, MRS CLARA KNIGHT (THE PRINCESS'S NURSE) AND OTHER COMPANIONS

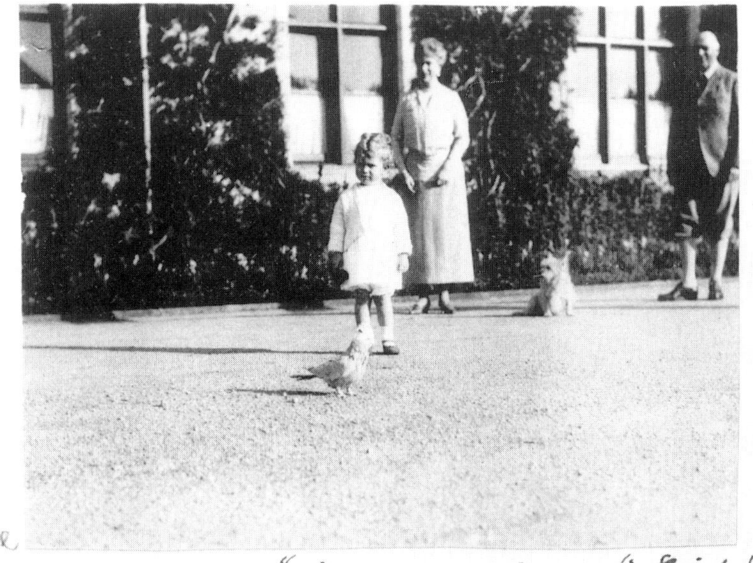

"Charlotte"   "Snip"
The Parrot

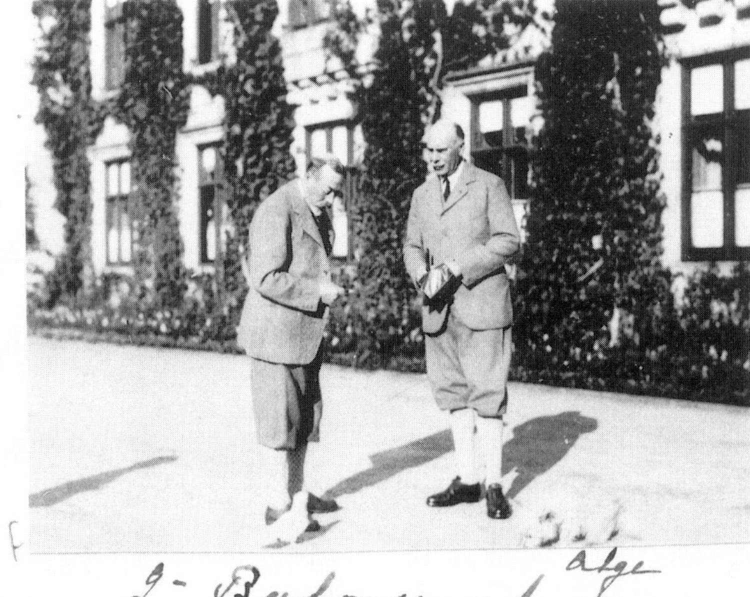

G. Balmoral
Sept. 1928.

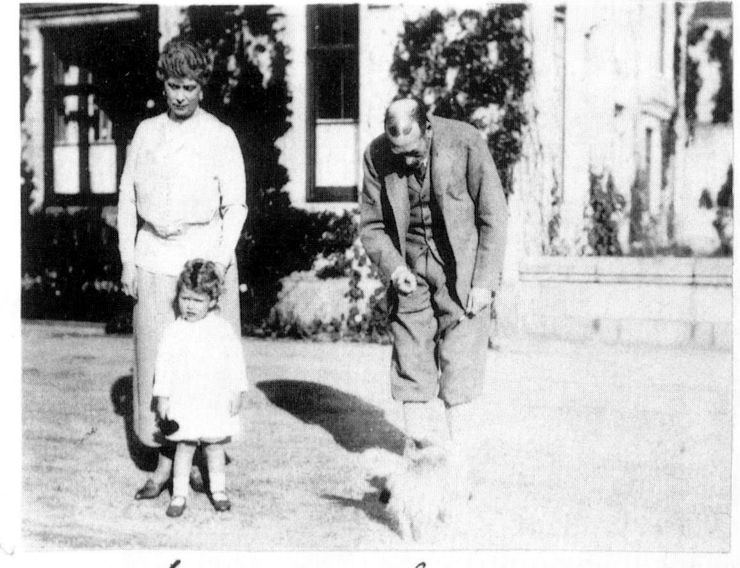

Self   G.
Lilibet   Snip

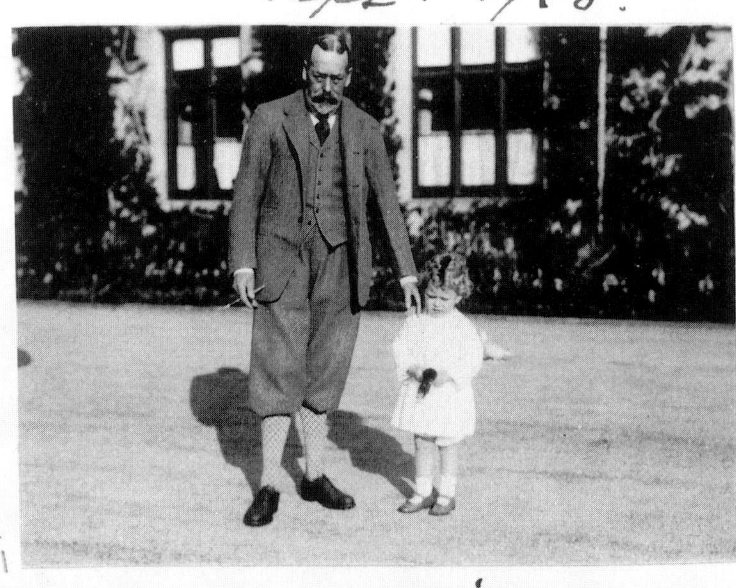

G. + Lilibet

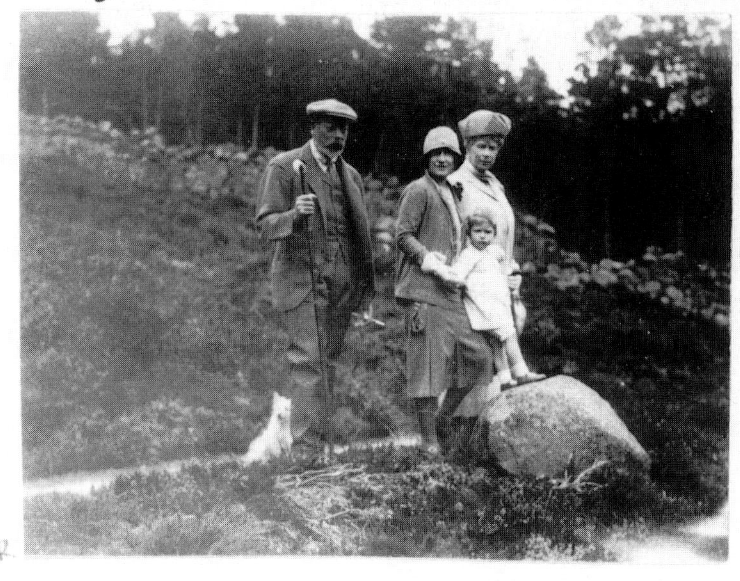

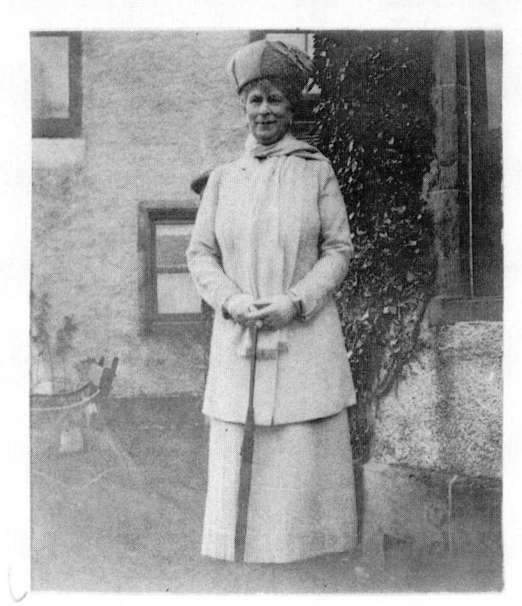

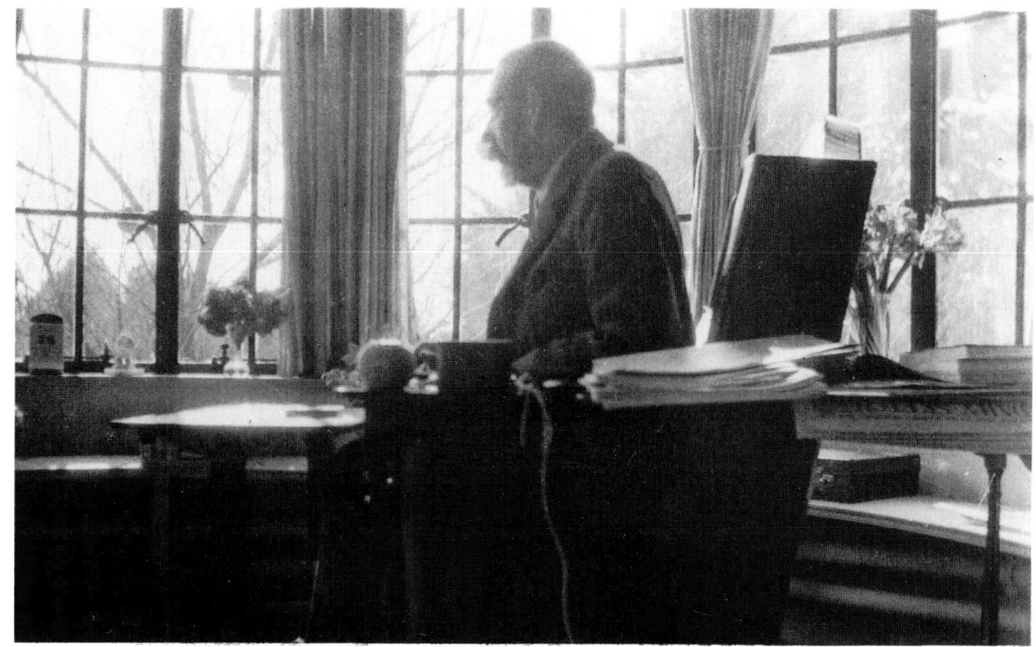

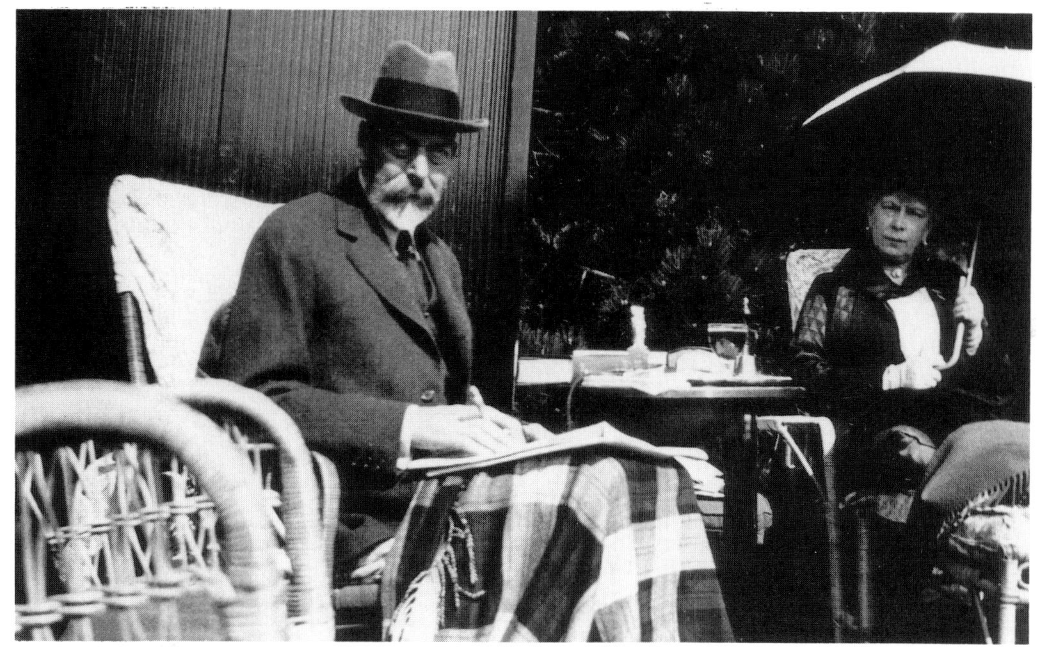

THE KING'S CONVALESCENCE AT BOGNOR IN
MARCH AND APRIL 1929

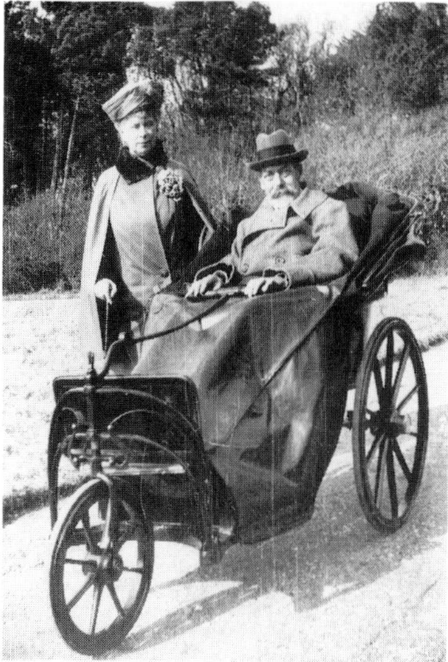

(*OPPOSITE*) A SERIES OF
SNAPSHOTS OF THE ROYAL
FAMILY AT BALMORAL IN
SEPTEMBER 1928. WITH THE
KING AND QUEEN ARE THE
DUCHESS OF YORK AND
PRINCESS ELIZABETH, THE
EARL OF ATHLONE (ALGE),
'CHARLOTTE', THE KING'S
PARROT, AND 'SNIP', HIS
TERRIER

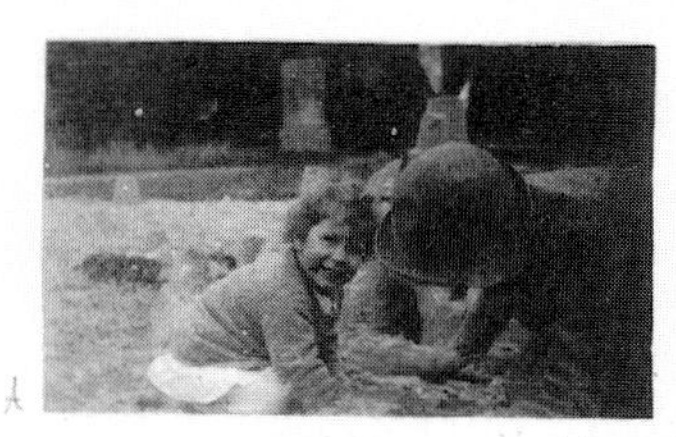

A

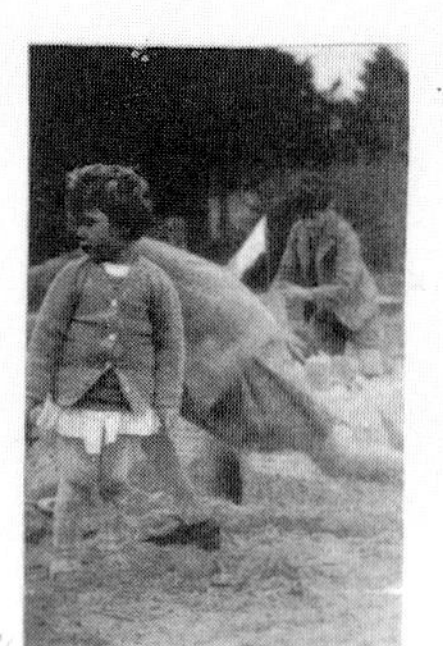

e

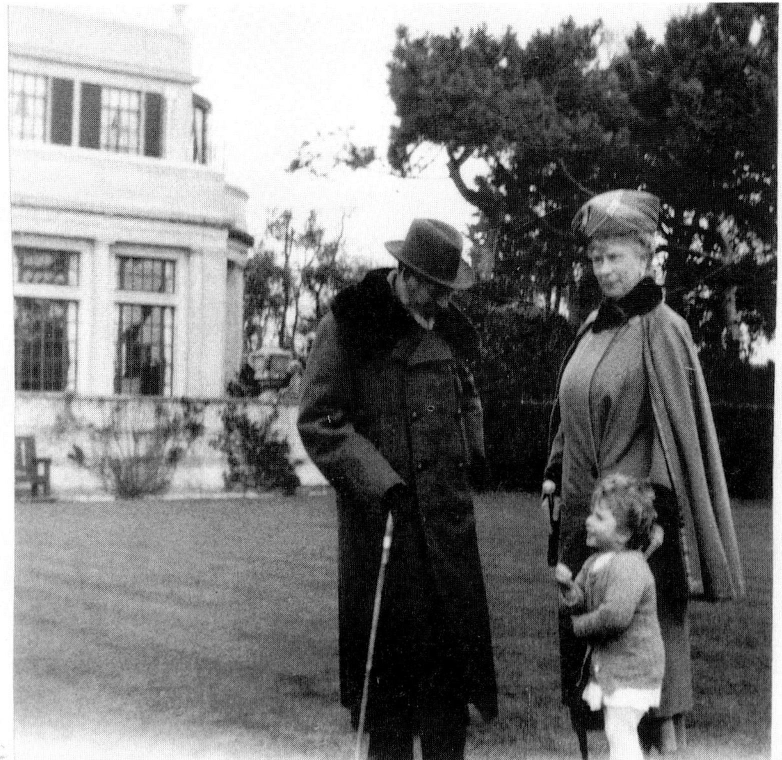

f

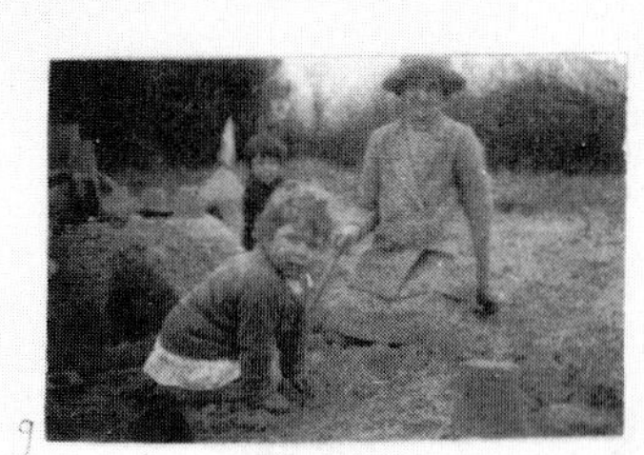

g

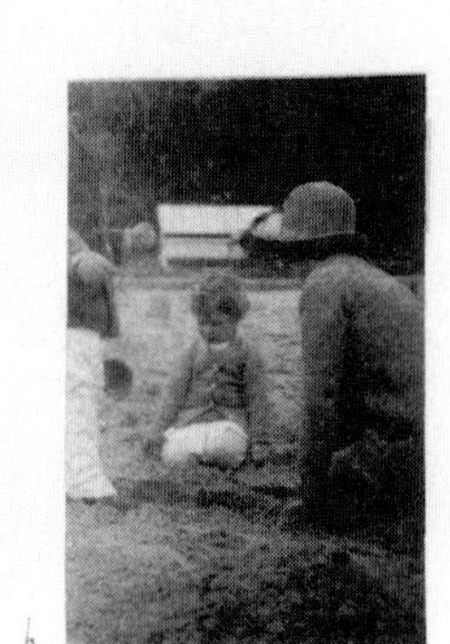

h

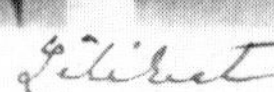

Lilibet

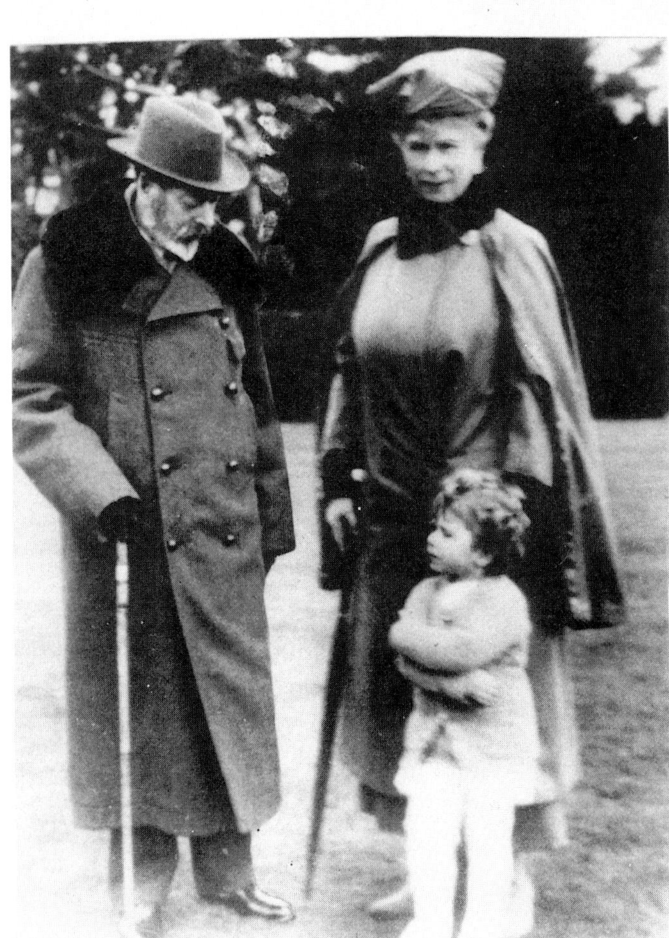

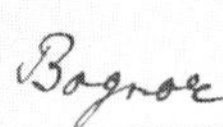

Bognor

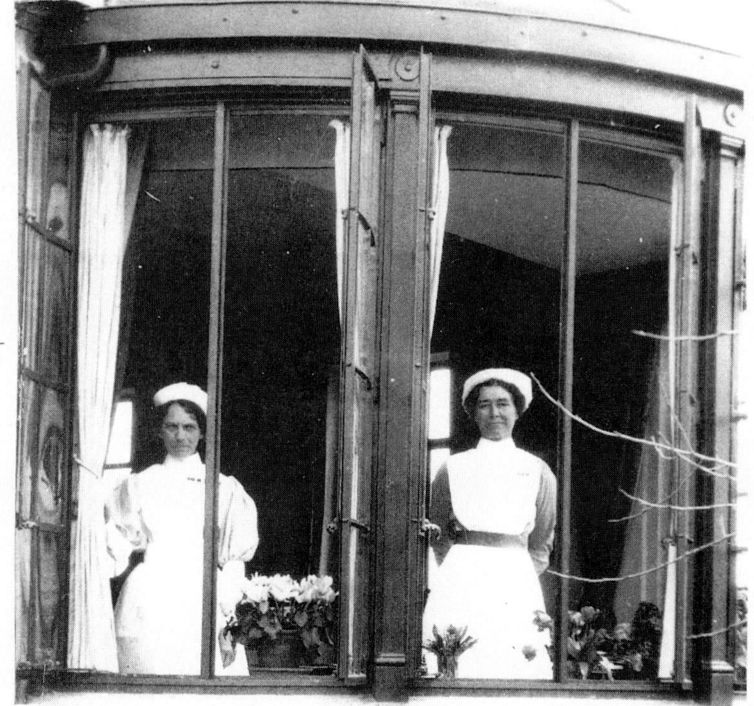

Sister Black . Sister Purdie

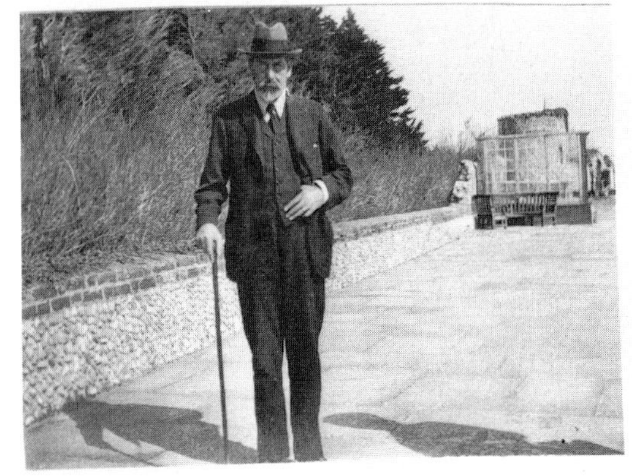

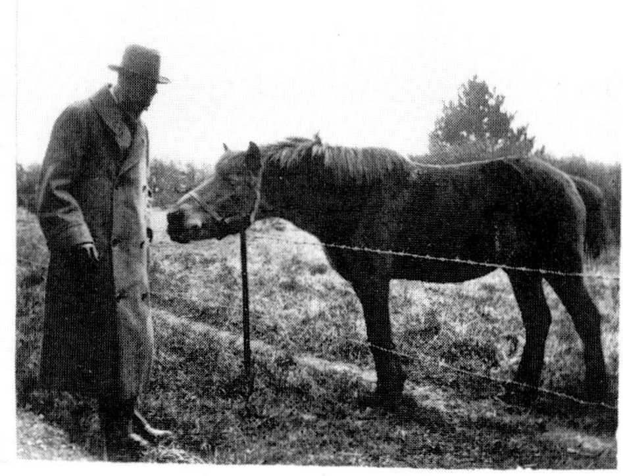

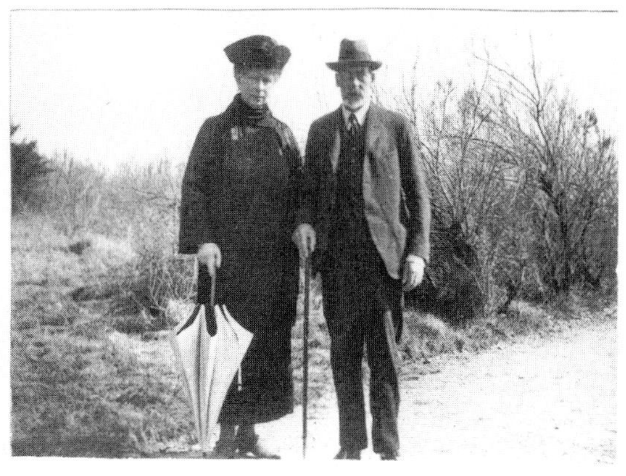

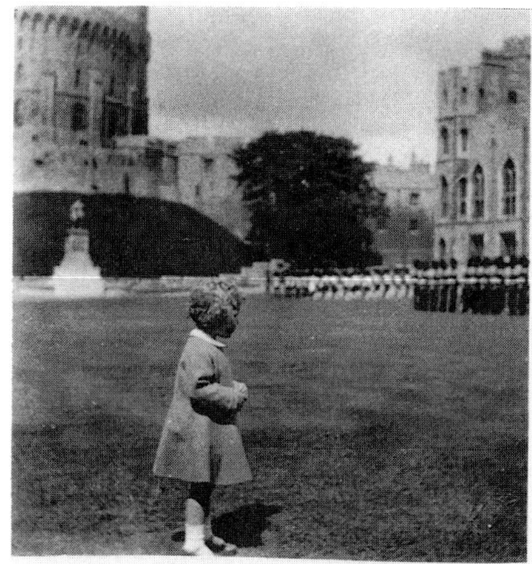

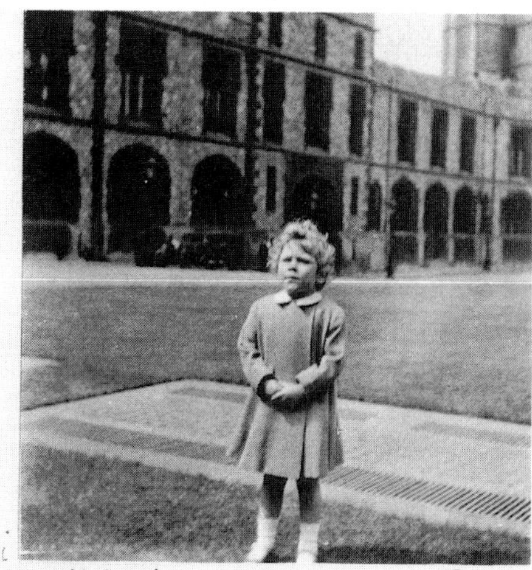

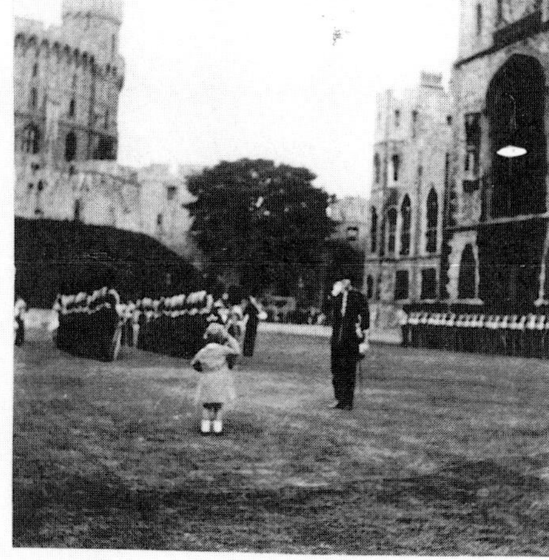

PRINCESS ELIZABETH IN
THE QUADRANGLE AT
WINDSOR CASTLE,
WATCHING A MILITARY
PARADE AND SALUTING
THE COMMANDING
OFFICER, MAY 1929

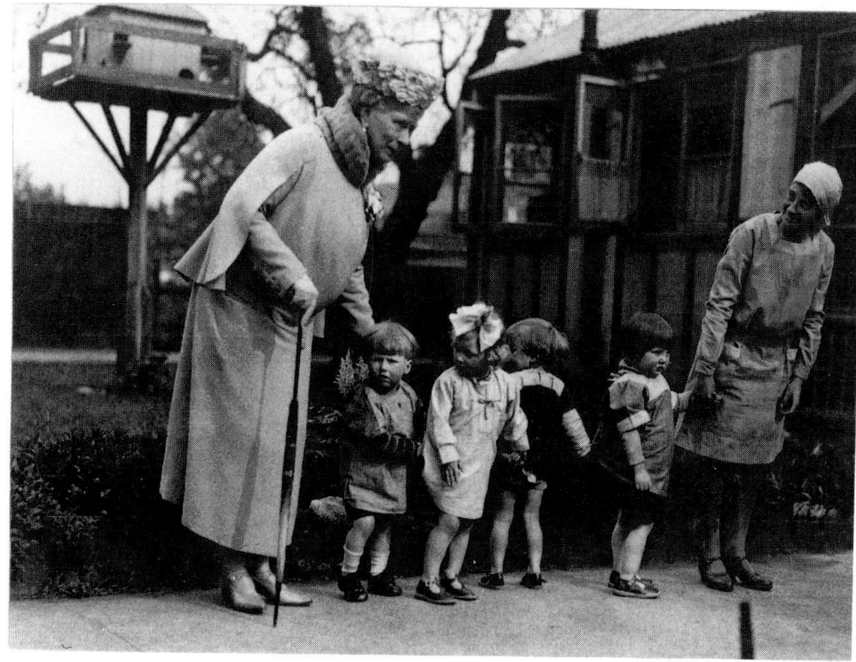

QUEEN MARY VISITING THE
NURSERY SCHOOL AT THE RACHEL
MACMILLAN TRAINING COLLEGE
IN DEPTFORD, LONDON, ON
8 MAY 1930

(*OPPOSITE*) 'LILIBET' WENT TO STAY
WITH HER GRANDPARENTS
AT BOGNOR DURING THE
KING'S CONVALESCENCE.
HER PRESENCE WAS SAID
TO HAVE AIDED HER
GRANDFATHER'S
RECOVERY

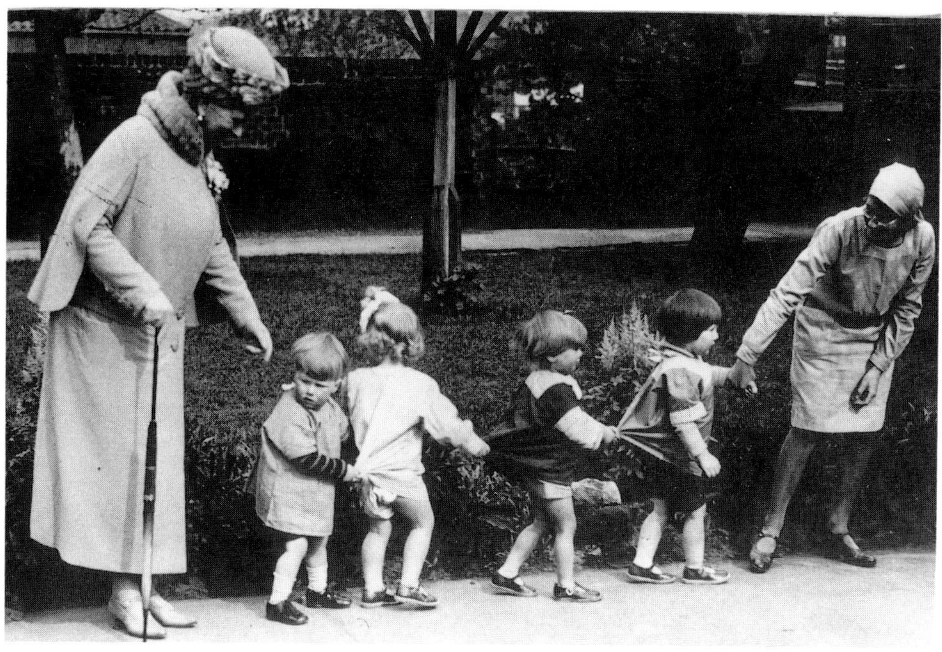

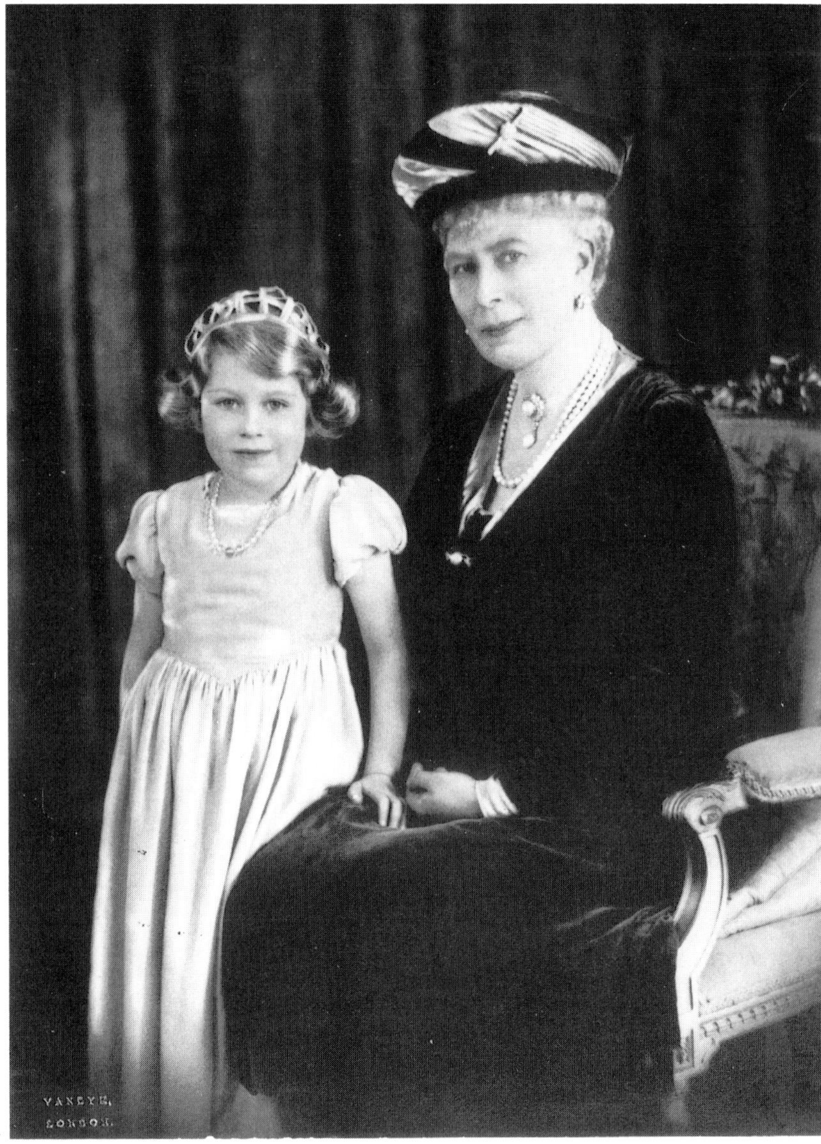

QUEEN MARY WITH HER GRANDDAUGHTER 'LILIBET' AT THE MARRIAGE OF THE QUEEN'S NIECE, LADY MAY CAMBRIDGE TO CAPTAIN HENRY ABEL SMITH, 24 OCTOBER 1931, AND PRINCESS ELIZABETH, WHO WAS A BRIDESMAID, WRAPPED IN A FUR CAPE ARRIVING AT THE WEDDING

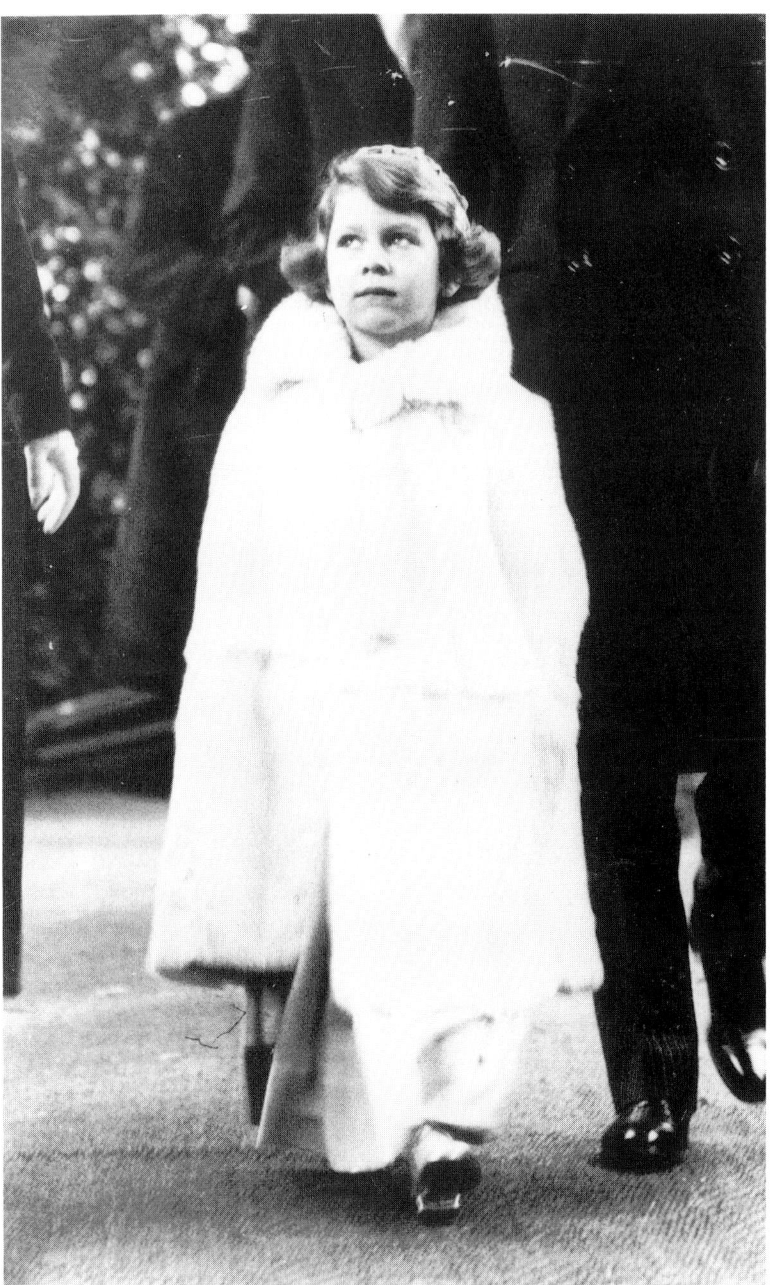

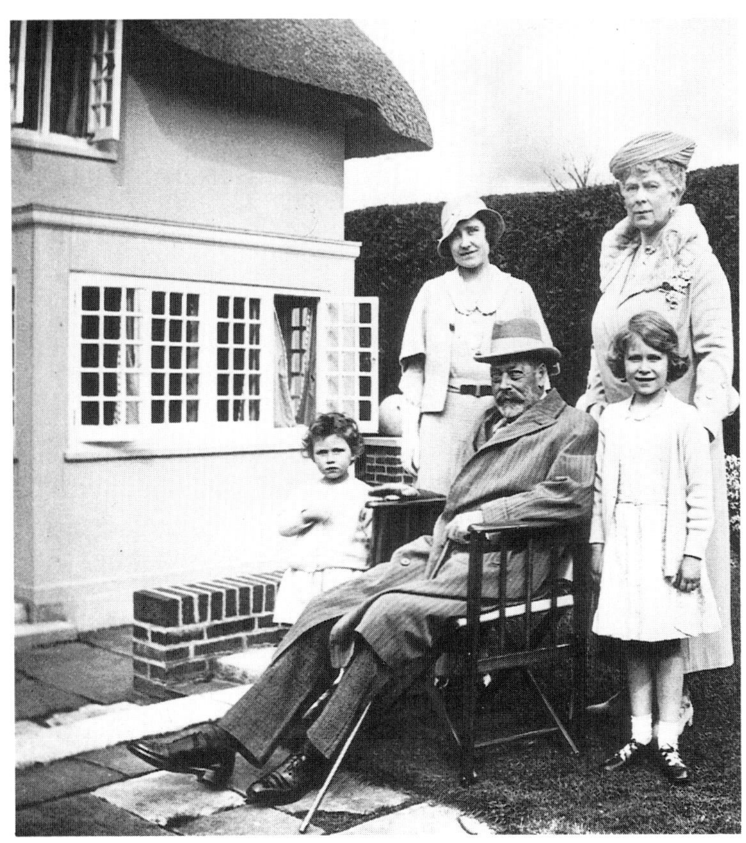

KING GEORGE V, QUEEN MARY AND THE DUCHESS OF YORK WITH THE PRINCESSES ELIZABETH AND MARGARET OUTSIDE 'LILIBET'S HOUSE', Y BWTHYN BACH (A GIFT FROM THE PEOPLE OF WALES), IN THE GROUNDS OF ROYAL LODGE, WINDSOR, MAY 1933

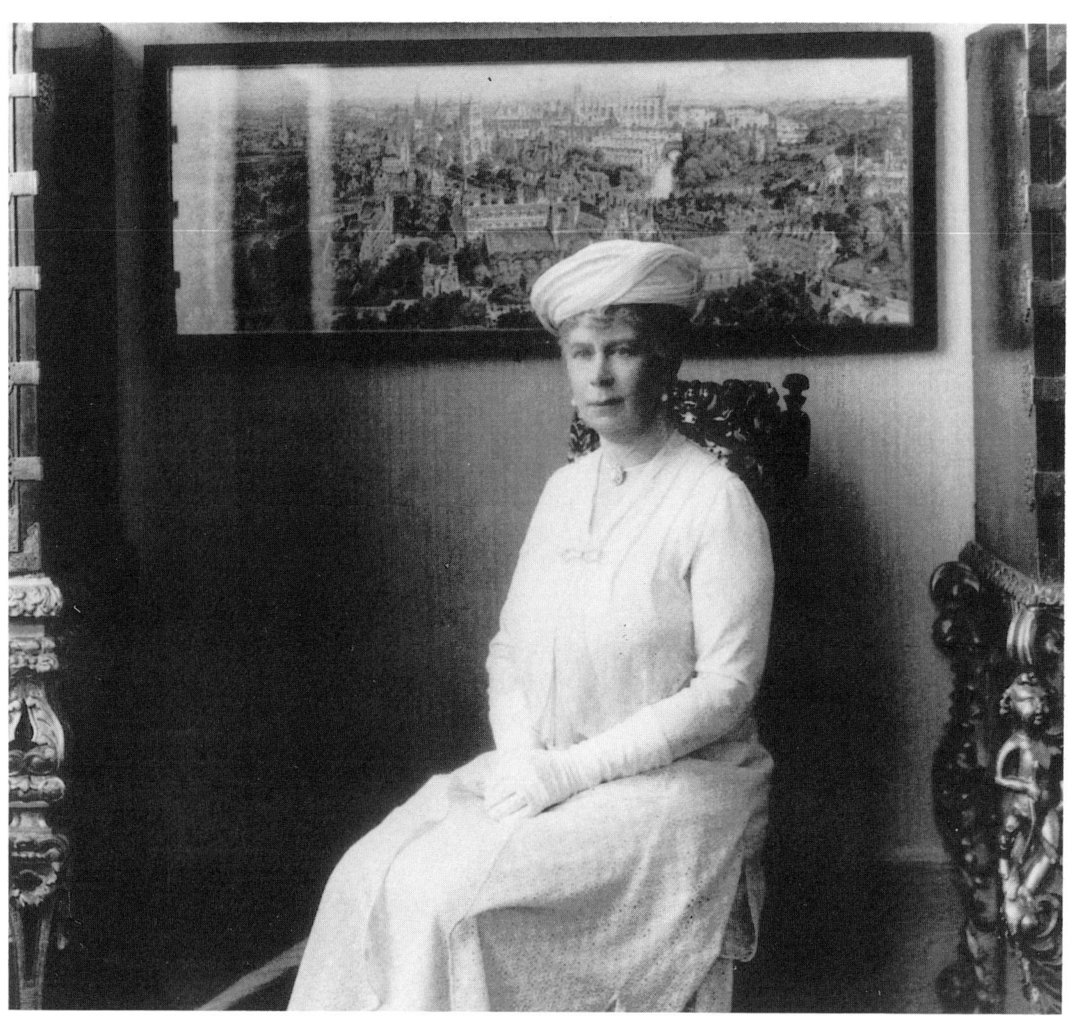

A SERENE PORTRAIT OF
QUEEN MARY AT THE
FITZWILLIAM MUSEUM,
CAMBRIDGE IN JULY 1932.
HER MAJESTY IS SITTING
BENEATH A PICTURE OF
CAMBRIDGE WHICH SHE
GAVE TO THE MUSEUM

July 14th   Cambridge
Fitzwilliam Museum.
Self under picture of Cambridge I gave
to the Museum.

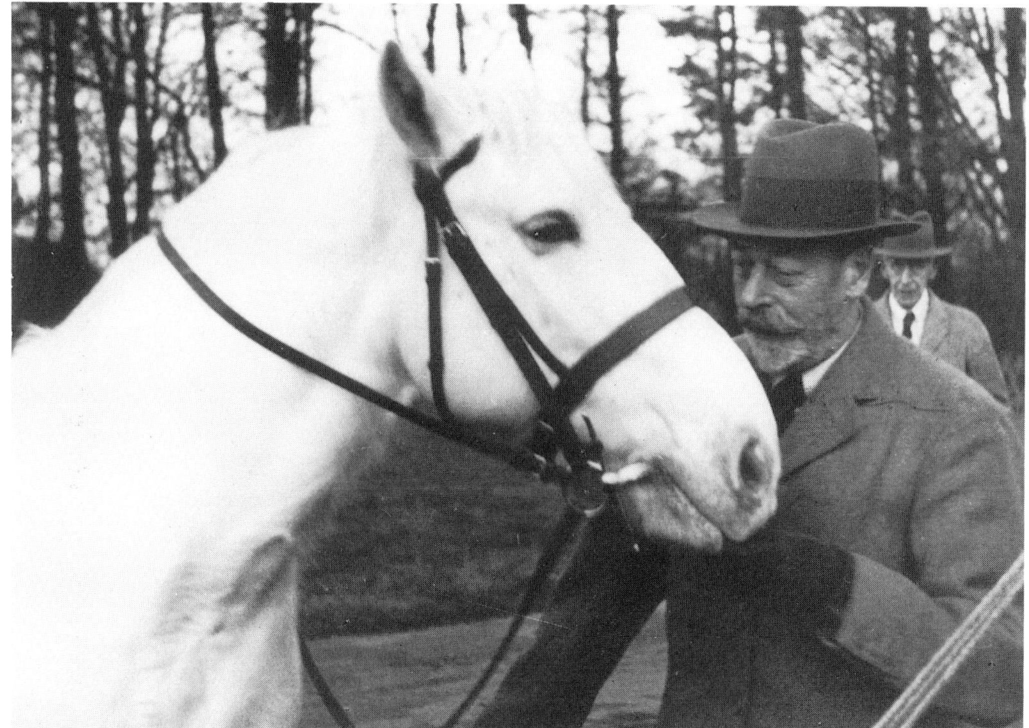

KING GEORGE V WITH HIS
PONY 'JOCK' AT
SANDRINGHAM, 1935

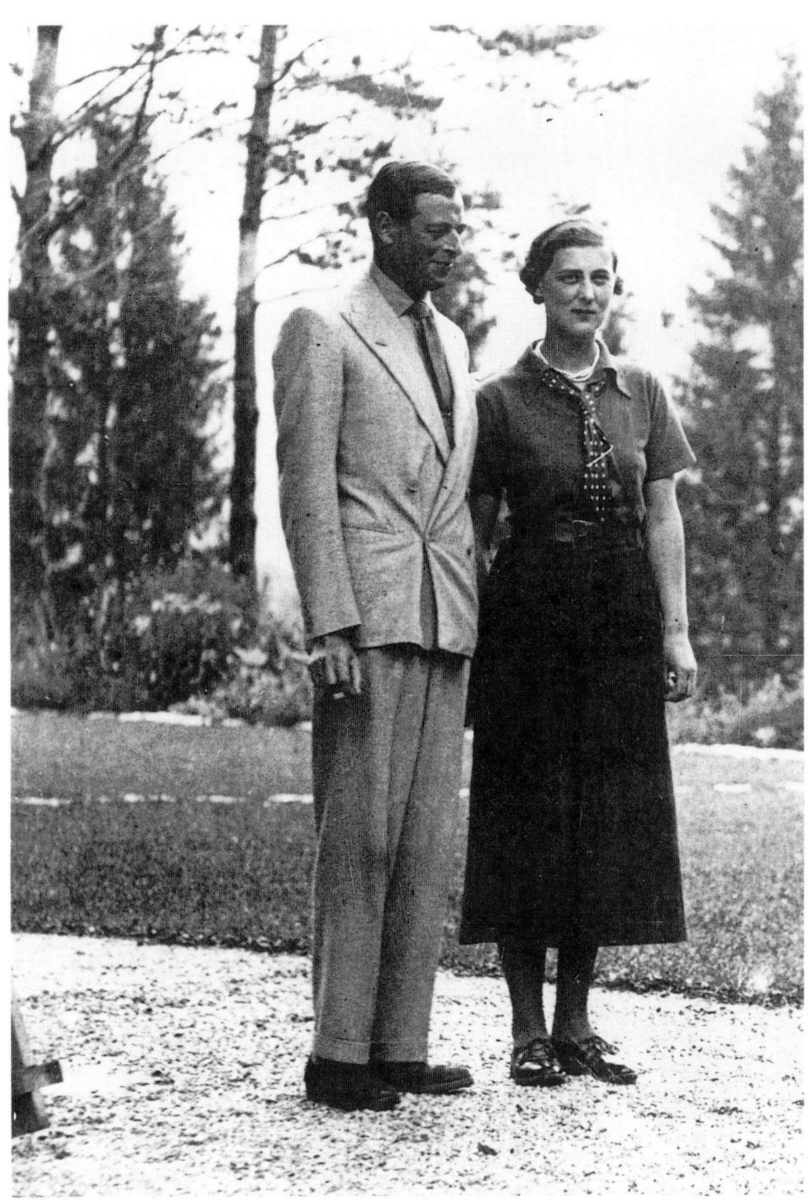

PRINCE GEORGE, DUKE OF KENT, WITH HIS
BRIDE-TO-BE, PRINCESS MARINA OF GREECE
AND DENMARK, IN SEPTEMBER 1934

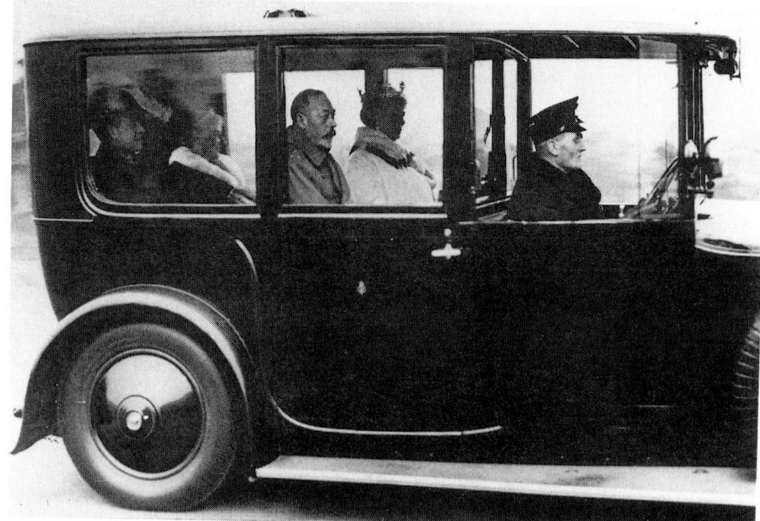

THE KING AND QUEEN ARE DRIVEN BY CAR TO THE
OPENING OF PARLIAMENT, NINE DAYS BEFORE THE
WEDDING OF GEORGE OF KENT AND PRINCESS MARINA,
20 NOVEMBER 1934

PRINCESS MARINA
ALIGHTING FROM A
CLOSED LANDAU FOR HER
WEDDING AT
WESTMINSTER ABBEY ON
29 NOVEMBER 1934

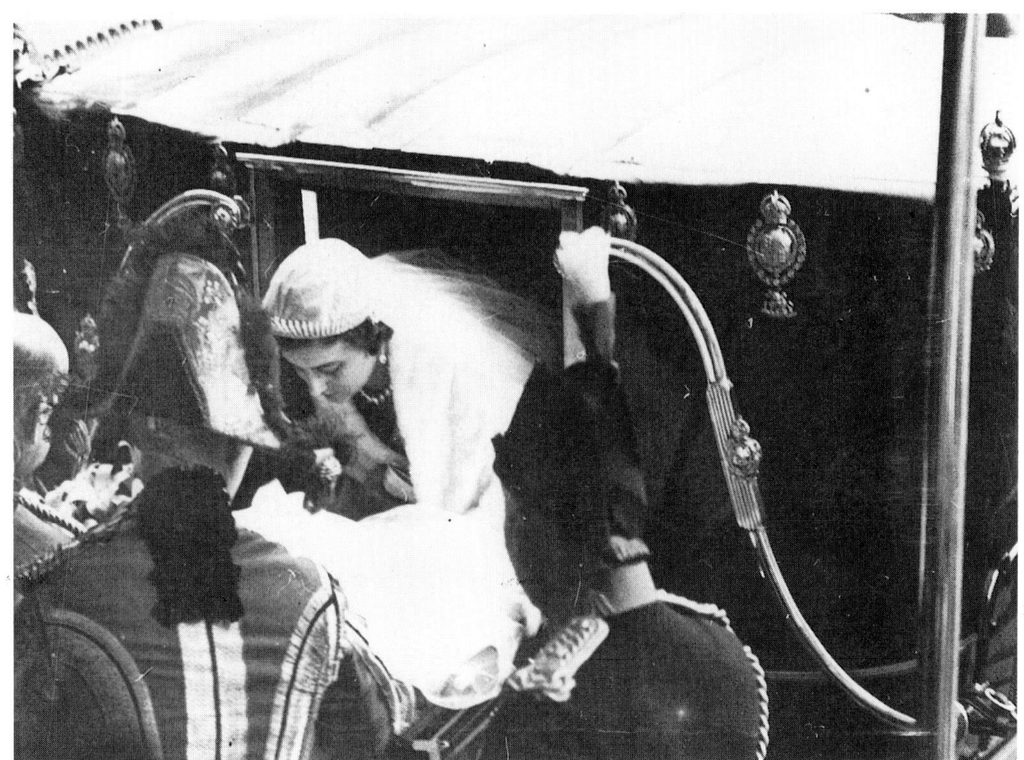

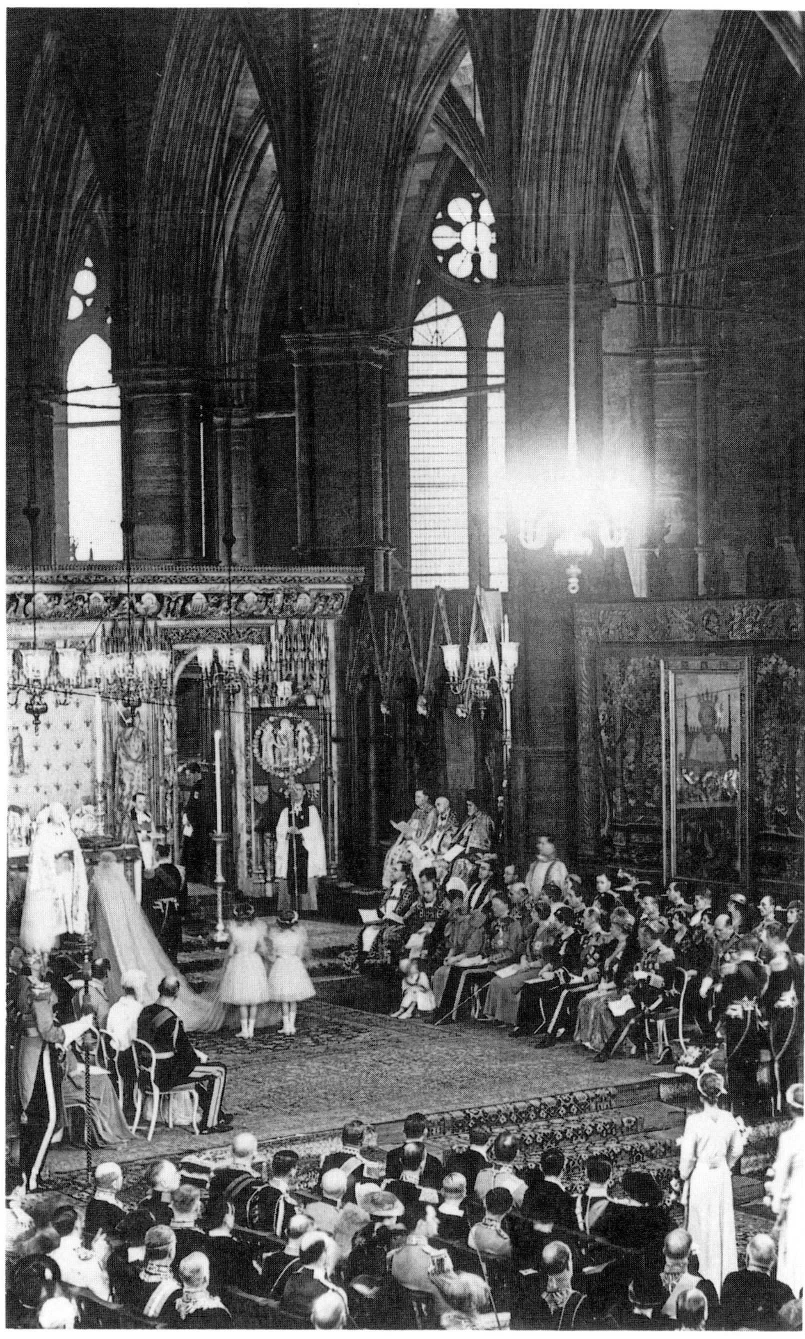

PRINCESS ELIZABETH AND LADY MARY CAMBRIDGE
HOLDING THE BRIDE'S TRAIN WHILE SHE AND THE
DUKE OF KENT KNEEL BEFORE THE ALTAR OF
WESTMINSTER ABBEY. PRINCESS MARGARET CAN BE
SEEN SITTING ON A FOOTSTOOL IN FRONT OF HER
MOTHER

Ceremony

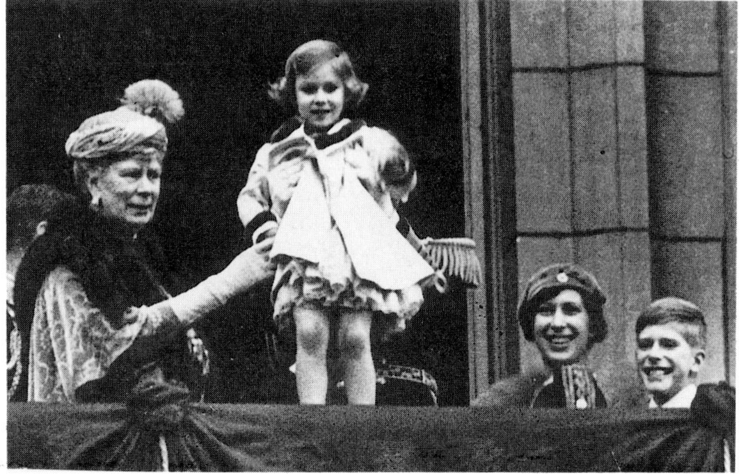

KING GEORGE V HOLDING PRINCESS
MARGARET ON THE BALCONY OF
BUCKINGHAM PALACE AFTER THE KENT
WEDDING. WITH THEM ARE QUEEN
MARY, THE PRINCESS ROYAL AND ONE OF
HER SONS, THE HON. GERALD LASCELLES

Self   Margaret   Mary & Gerald
S. holding her

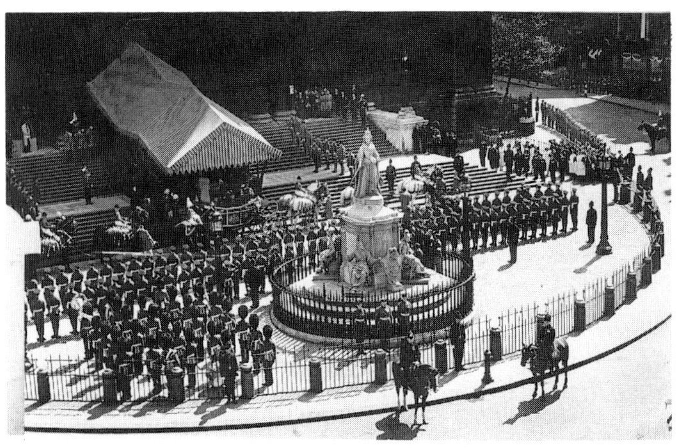

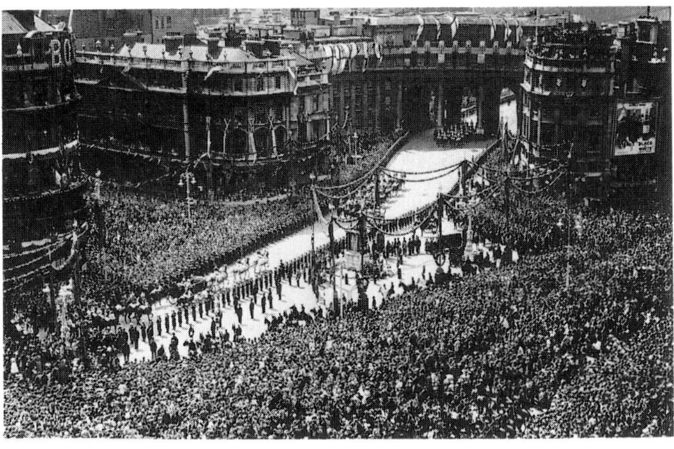

THE OFFICIAL CELEBRATION OF THE SILVER JUBILEE ON 6 MAY 1935.
KING GEORGE V AND QUEEN MARY ARE DRIVEN IN THE SCARLET AND
GOLD 1902 STATE LANDAU TO ST PAUL'S CATHEDRAL

KING GEORGE V SYMBOLICALLY RECEIVING THE SWORD OF LONDON FROM THE LORD MAYOR AT
TEMPLE BAR ON THE WAY TO ST PAUL'S CATHEDRAL

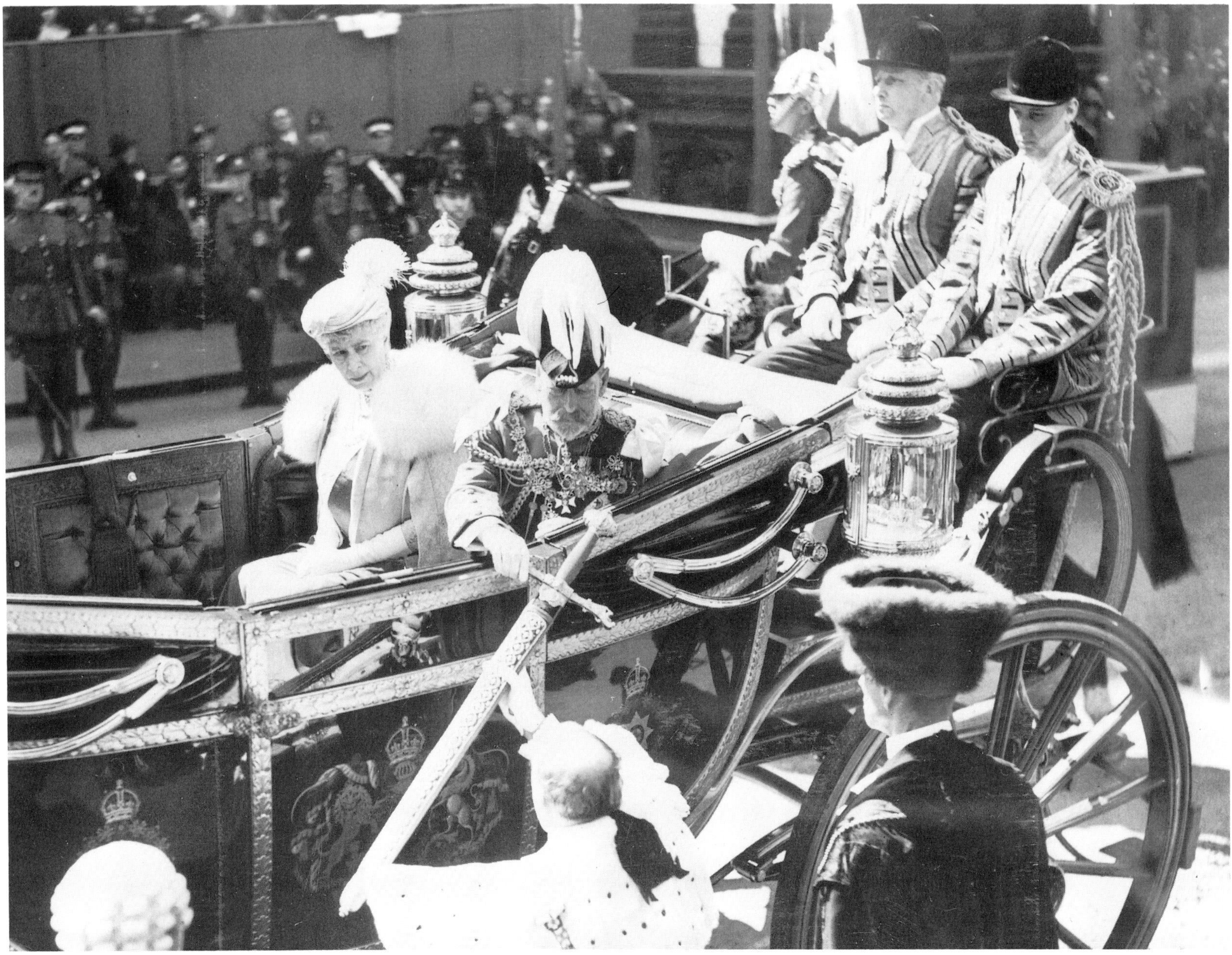

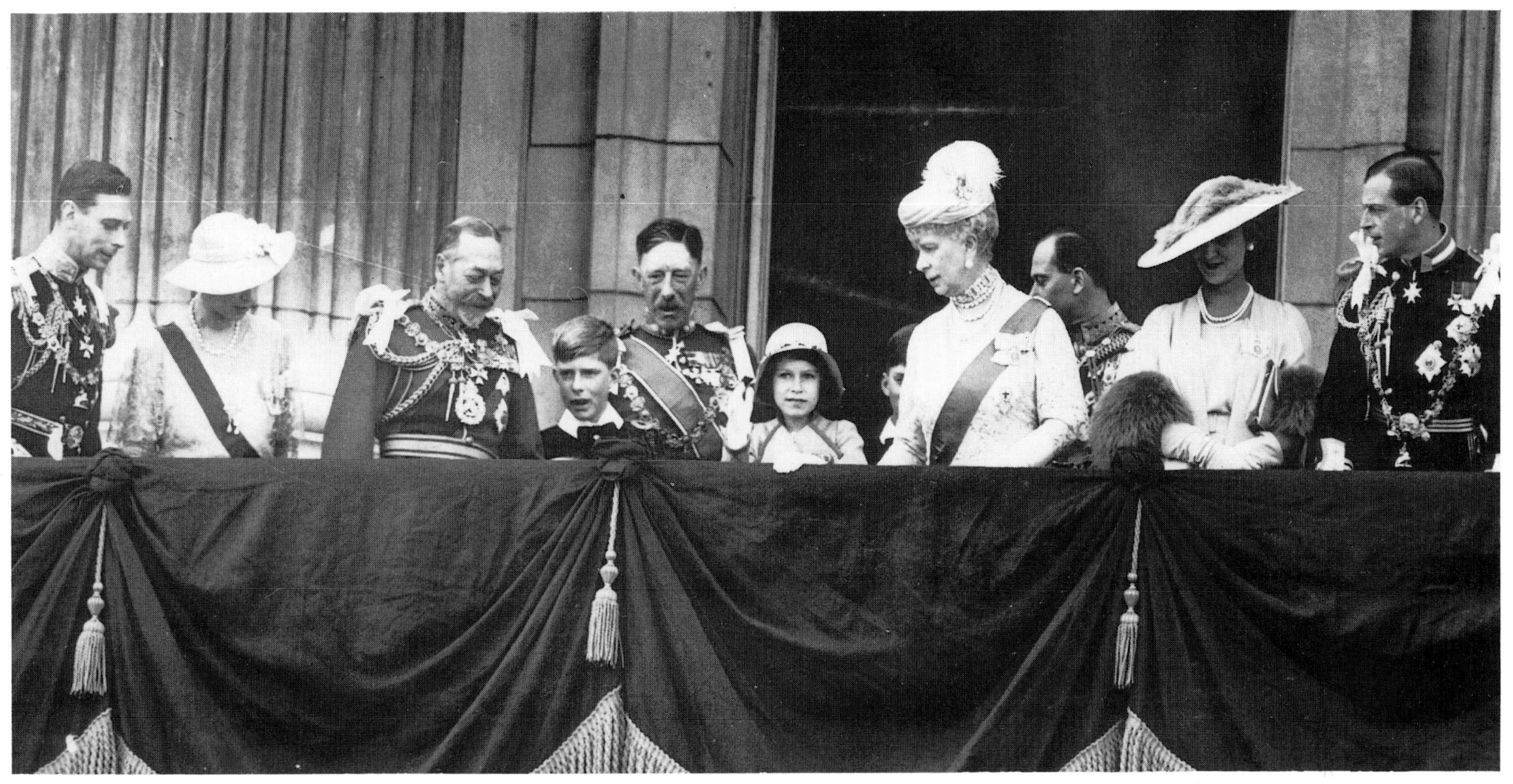

THE ROYAL FAMILY ON THE BALCONY OF BUCKINGHAM PALACE.
FROM LEFT TO RIGHT: THE DUKE OF YORK, MARY, THE PRINCESS
ROYAL, KING GEORGE V, SMILING DOWN AT PRINCESS MARGARET
(UNSEEN), THE HON. GERALD LASCELLES, THE EARL OF HAREWOOD,
PRINCESS ELIZABETH, QUEEN MARY, THE DUKE OF GLOUCESTER AND
THE DUKE AND DUCHESS OF KENT

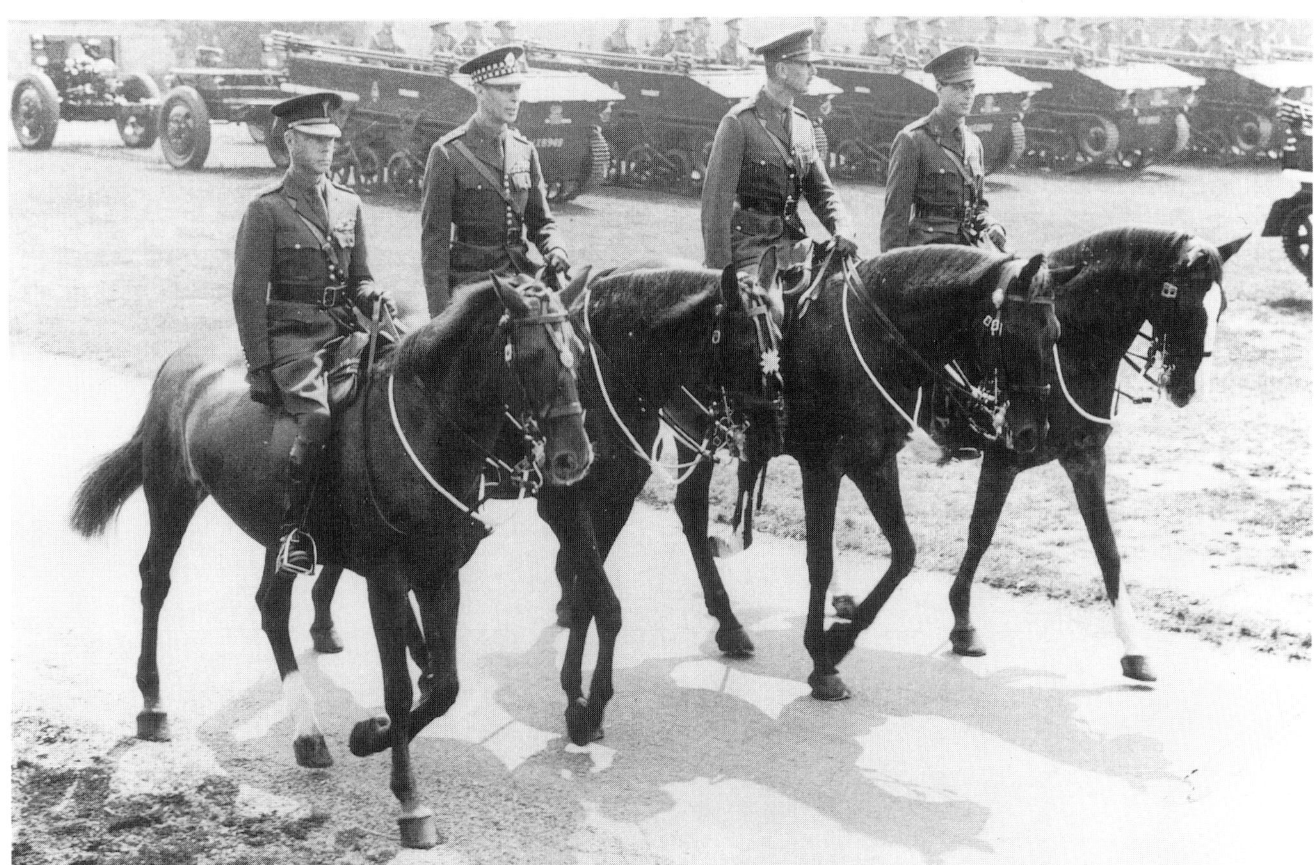

THE PRINCE OF WALES
(LEFT) RIDING WITH HIS
BROTHERS, THE DUKES OF
YORK, GLOUCESTER AND
KENT, AT ALDERSHOT ON
13 JULY 1935

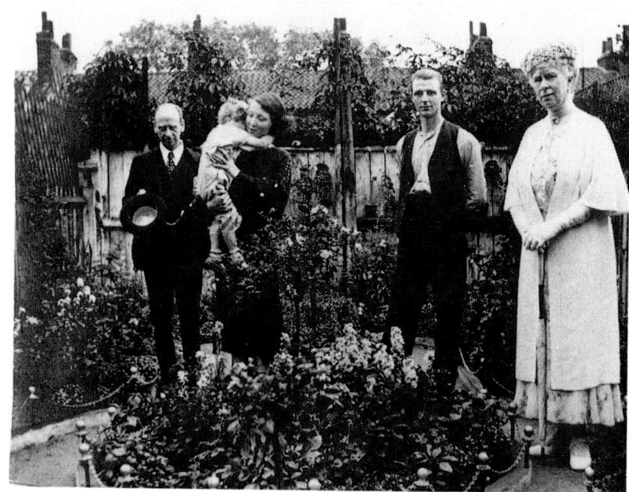

Gardens East End.
10. July

The Queen touring gardens in
the East End of London in July 1935

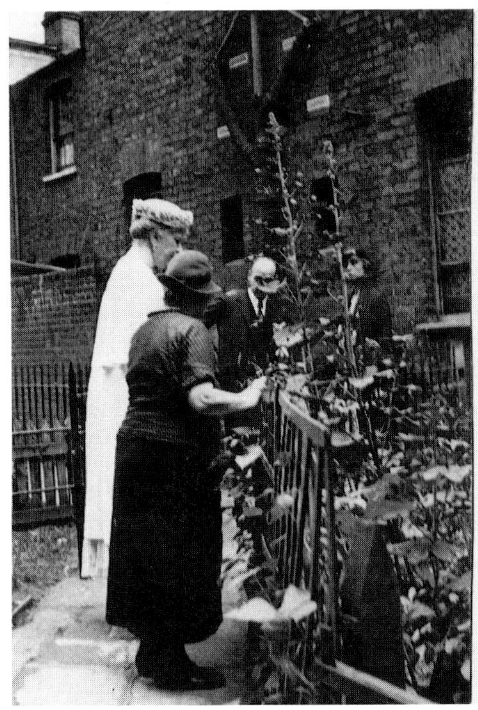

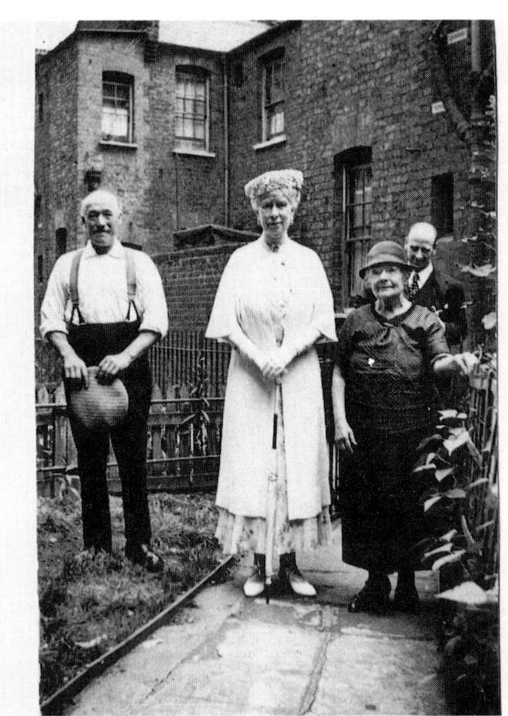

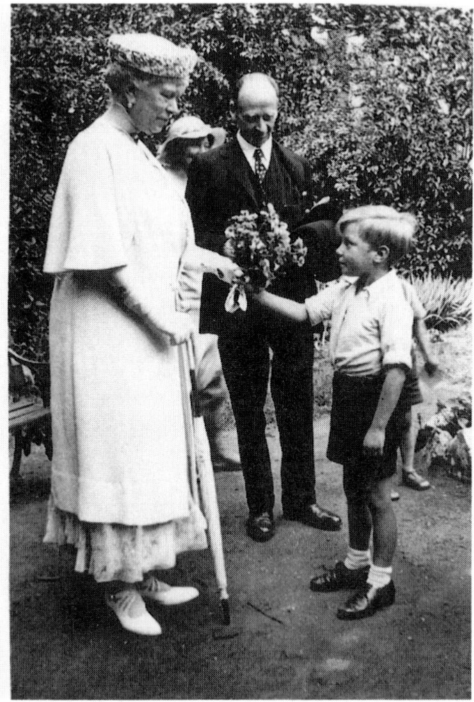

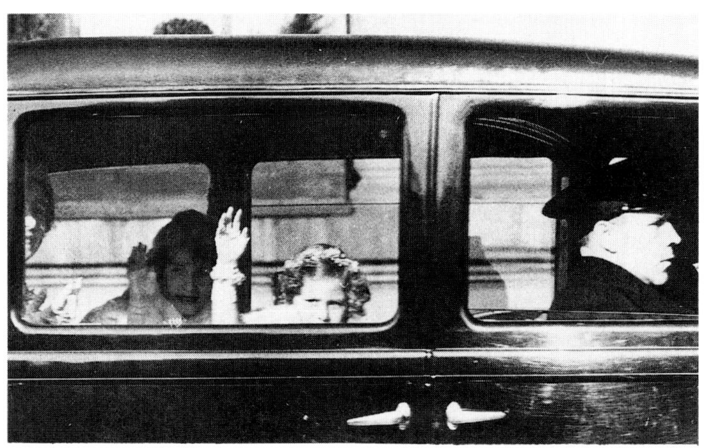

The princesses Elizabeth and Margaret leaving their home at
145 Piccadilly for the wedding of Henry, Duke of Gloucester, and
Lady Alice Montagu-Douglas-Scott at Buckingham Palace on
6 November 1935

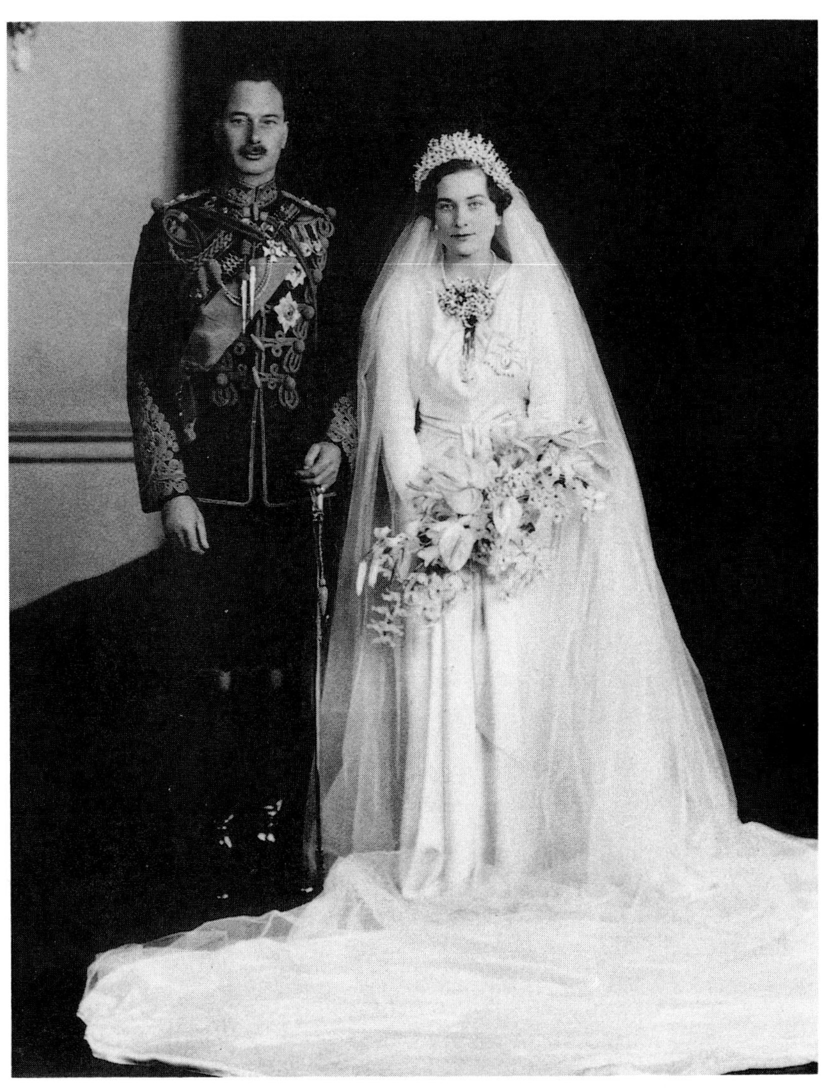

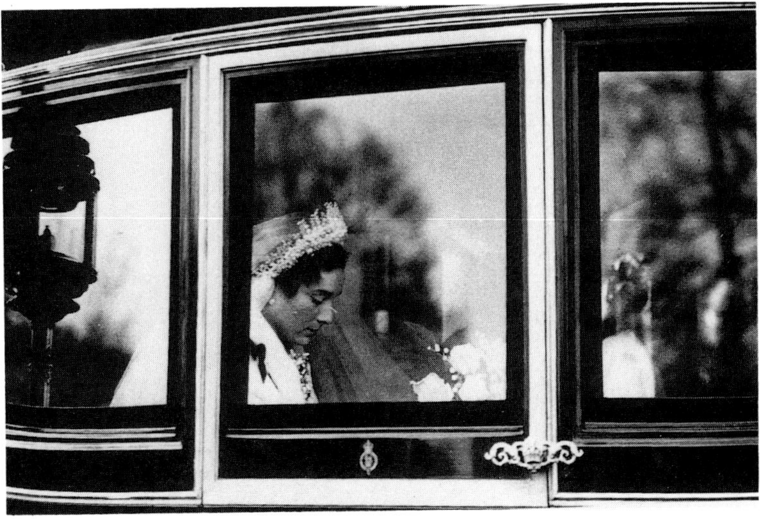

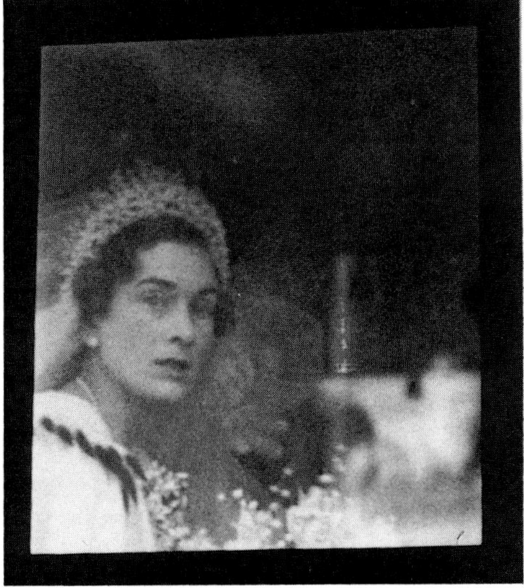

LADY ALICE MONTAGU-
DOUGLAS-SCOTT DRIVING
IN THE GLASS COACH TO
HER WEDDING, ONLY
THREE WEEKS AFTER THE
DEATH OF HER FATHER,
THE DUKE OF BUCCLEUCH

DRESSED BY NORMAN HARTNELL IN PALEST SHELL
PINK, THE NEW DUCHESS OF GLOUCESTER POSES
WITH HER HUSBAND AFTER THEIR MARRIAGE

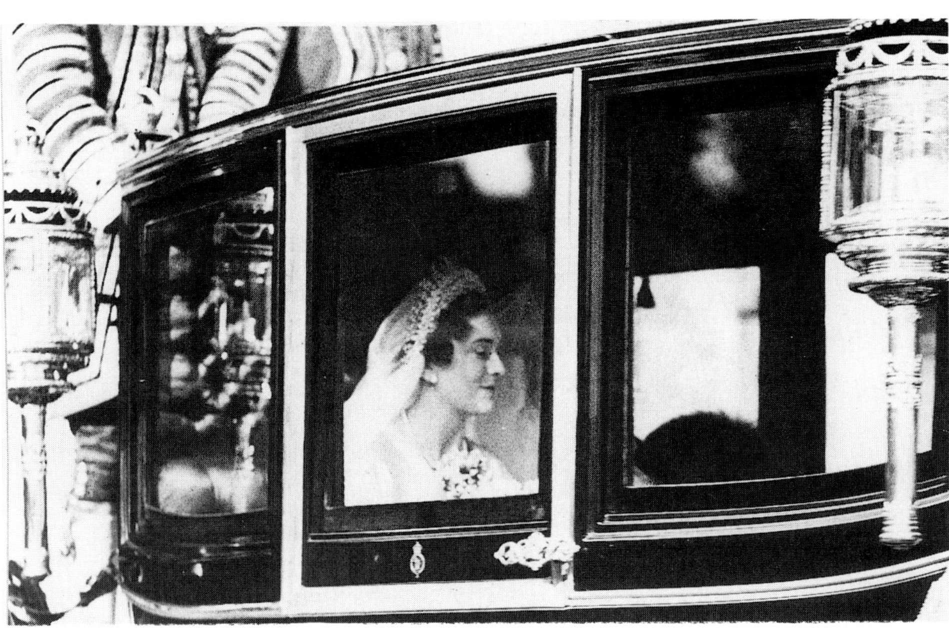

Alice

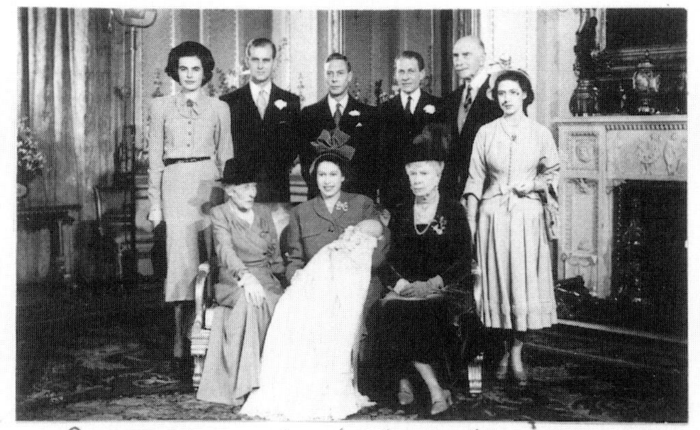

The Godparents

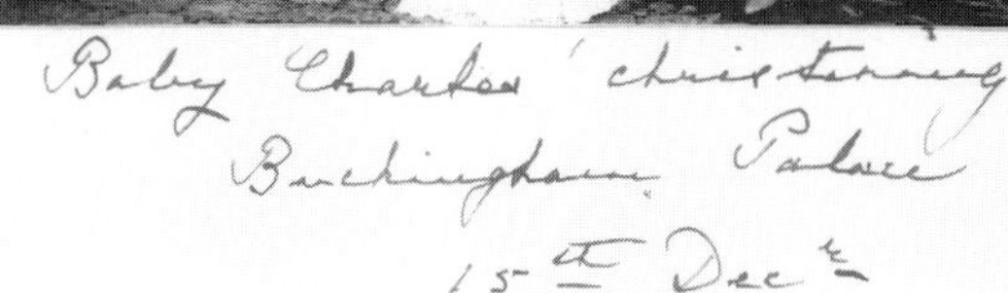

Baby Charles' christening
Buckingham Palace
15th Dec.

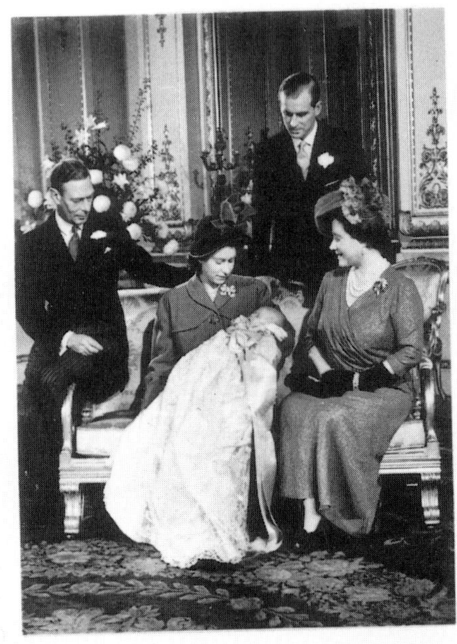

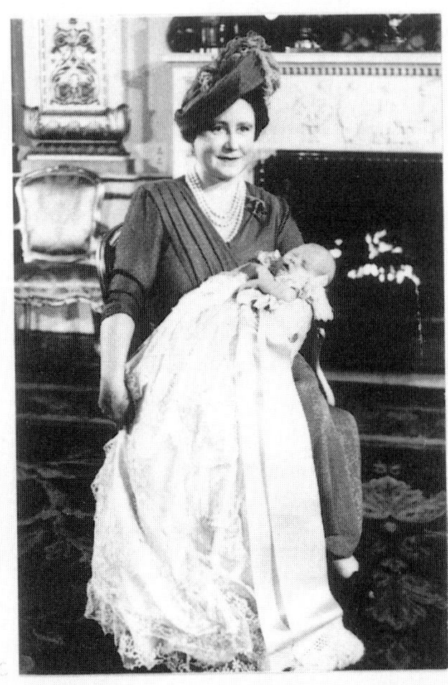

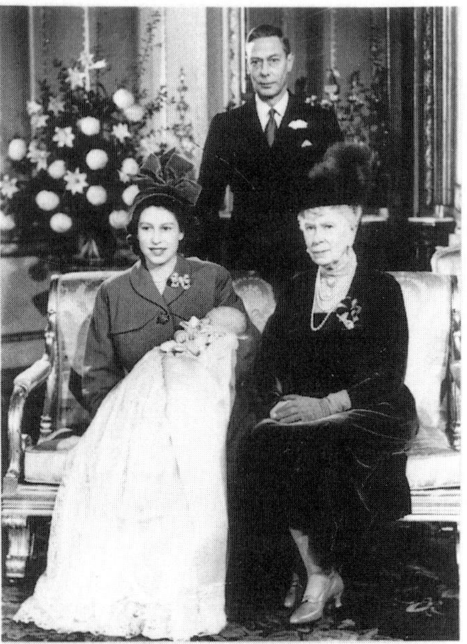

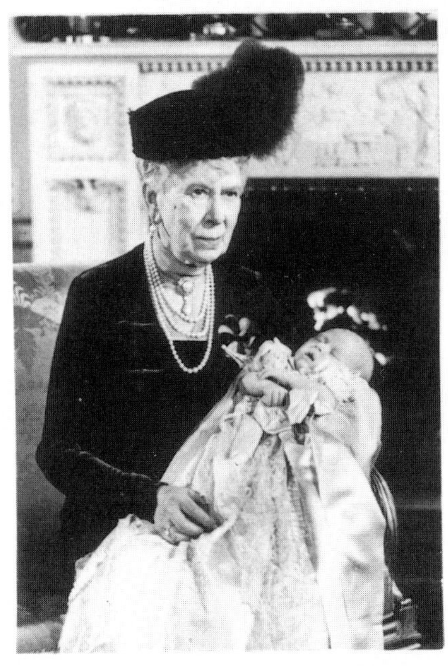

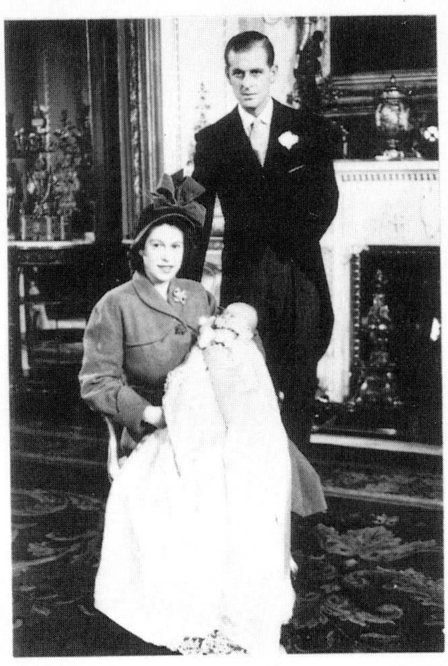

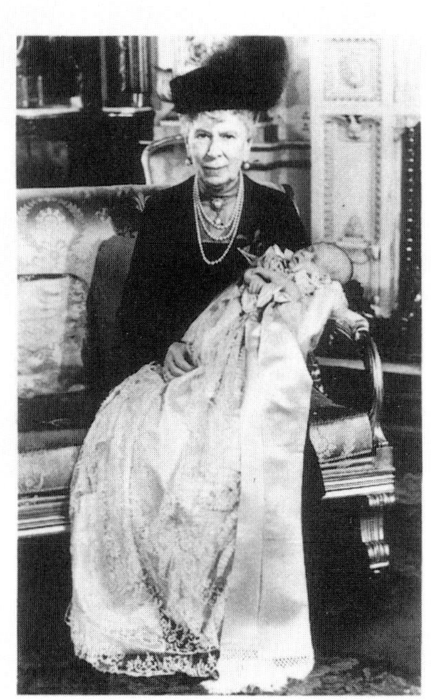

PART FOUR

Mary

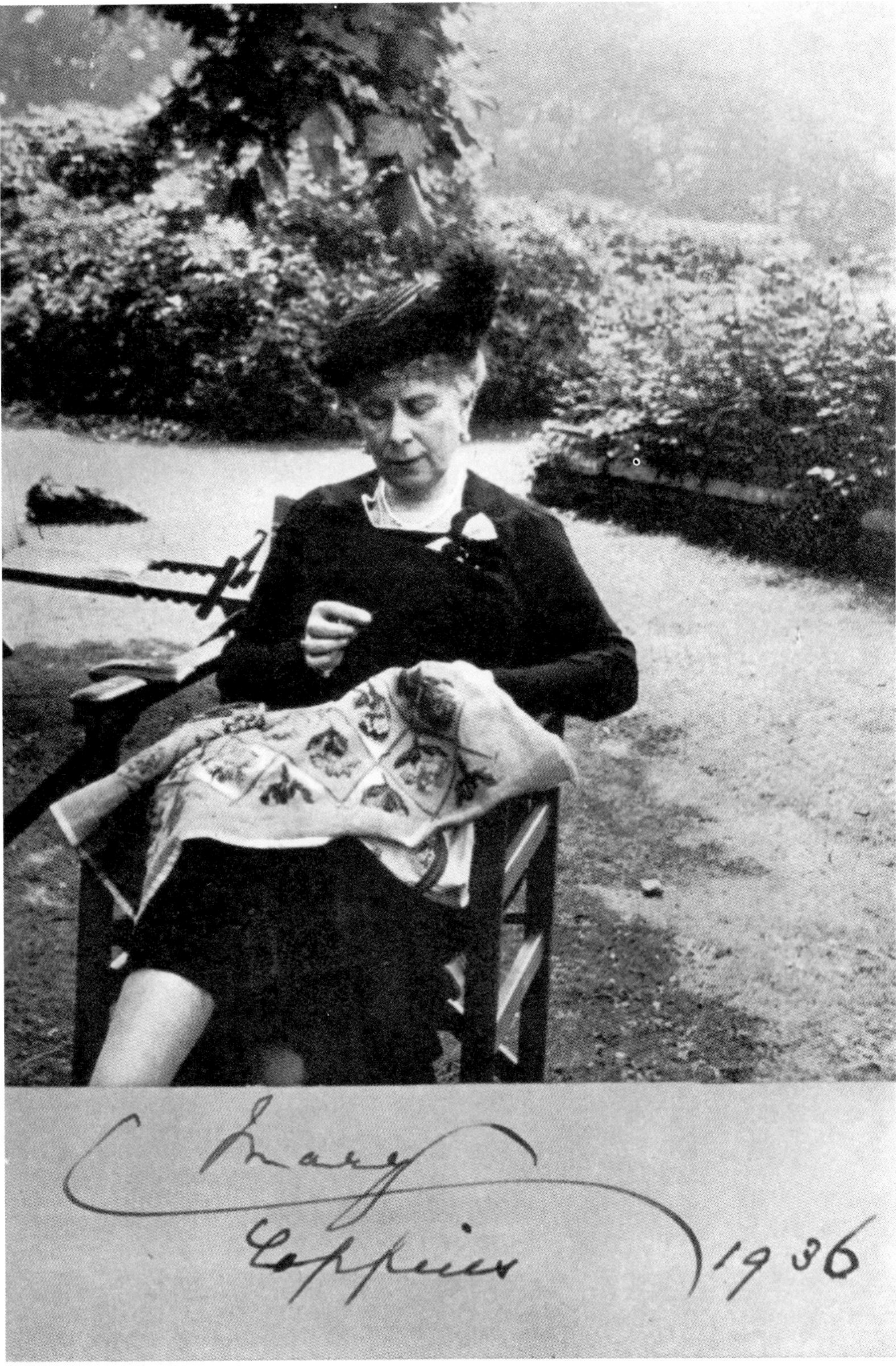

QUEEN MARY IN THE
GARDEN OF COPPINS, HOME
OF THE DUKE AND
DUCHESS OF KENT, JUNE
1936. THE QUEEN DOWAGER
IS SEEN SEWING ONE OF
THE PANELS OF THE
FAMOUS CARPET SHE MADE

(*OPPOSITE*) THE
CHRISTENING OF PRINCE
CHARLES, DECEMBER 1948

If 1935 had been a 'wonderful' year in the life of Queen Mary, 1936 must surely have been the most distressing. The death of her husband and the prolonged state ceremonial surrounding his lying-in-state and funeral; the accession of their eldest son as King Edward VIII and all his thoughts about modernizing the monarchy; together with the prospect of re-establishing herself at Marlborough House, this time alone, must on occasions have seemed overwhelming.

During the early months of her widowhood, the Queen, helped by her daughter Mary, now the Princess Royal, not only began the sad task of going through the late King's possessions, but gradually turned her thoughts towards the refurbishment of the house that had once been her home and to which she would have to return.

As summer approached and the six-month period of Court mourning for George V began to expire, so Queen Mary resumed her round of public appearances. In April she visited the Royal Pavilion at Aldershot to stay with the Duke and Duchess of Gloucester, and in June she drove to Horse Guards Parade to watch David (Edward VIII) take the salute at the ceremony of Trooping the Colour. Three weeks later, before leaving London once more for Sandringham, she again attended a parade at which Edward VIII presented new colours to the Brigade of Guards. All were emotional occasions which brought back vivid memories of George V performing the very same kind of duties, but all were occasions on which Queen Mary's outward composure never once deserted her.

Less easy to cope with as the year wore on, however, were the letters and news reports Queen Mary received from abroad concerning the new King and his American lady-love, the exquisitely elegant Mrs Wallis Simpson. That summer, instead of taking the traditional royal holiday at Balmoral, Edward VIII chartered Lady Yule's steam-yacht, the *Nahlin*, for a leisurely cruise along the Dalmatian coast. Among His Majesty's guests was Mrs Simpson.

At that time informal royal behaviour, as we accept it today, was unknown to the public at large and the King's holiday cruise went virtually unremarked in Great Britain, though newspapers throughout Europe and the United States of America made the most of all they saw. By autumn, speculation about the King's relationship with Mrs Simpson, whom Queen Mary would brand an 'Adventuress', had reached its zenith, particularly in America where, on 26 October, the banner headline of one popular morning newspaper confidently – and accurately for that matter – predicted 'KING TO MARRY "WALLY" – Wedding next June'.

No single episode in the entire history of the British monarchy can have been so thoroughly and consistently documented as 'The Abdication Crisis', and clearly no useful purpose would be served by discussing the events of late 1936 here, save to remind ourselves that Edward VIII's decision to forfeit the throne in order to marry Wallis Simpson so hurt and angered Queen Mary that she never forgave her son for what she regarded as his selfish dereliction of duty.

'You will remember how miserable I was when you informed me of your intended marriage and abdication and how I implored you not to do so for our sake and for the sake of the country,' Queen Mary wrote to the former King, by now Duke of Windsor, in July 1938.

You did not seem able to take in any point of view but your own. . . . I do not think you have ever realized the shock, which the attitude you took up caused your family and the whole Nation. It seemed inconceivable to those who had made such sacrifices during the war that you, as their King, refused a lesser sacrifice. . . . My feelings for you as your Mother remain the same, and our being parted and the cause of it, grieve me beyond words [but] all my life I have put my Country before everything else, and I simply cannot change now.

By royal tradition, no former Queen Consort had ever attended the coronation of her husband's successor. But in May 1937, Queen Mary's presence at Westminster Abbey for the coronation of her second son, King George VI, was widely interpreted as a public gesture of support for the reluctant new sovereign and his wife.

As the new reign became established in the popular imagination and the tremors occasioned by King Edward VIII's abdication subsided, the nation's sympathy and admiration for Queen Mary continued unabated. Wherever she travelled, the affection and esteem in which she was held were manifest in the warmth of the welcome she was always guaranteed to receive. In 1938, for example, the Queen was greeted rapturously by the people of Plymouth and of Trent, by the inhabitants of 'Constable country' in Essex – where she visited picturesque Flatford Mill – and by the citizens of Bath, when she visited the famous Assembly Rooms that September. Each of these visits is commemorated by photographs in Queen Mary's album for that last full year of peace.

The following May, as the political situation in Europe steadily deteriorated, King George VI and Queen Elizabeth set out on a state visit to North America. On 6 May 1939, Queen Mary with the Princesses Elizabeth and Margaret, the Princess Royal, the Duke and Duchess of Gloucester and the Duke and Duchess of Kent, gathered to bid the King and Queen an emotional farewell.

While her son and daughter-in-law were away in America Queen Mary was involved in a motoring accident. On 23 May the Queen Dowager, accompanied by her lady-in-waiting, Lady Constance Milnes Gaskell, and her comptroller, Lord Claud Hamilton, was returning to Marlborough House from an engagement in Surrey, when a lorry laden with steel tubing collided with the royal car as it drove along Wimbledon Park Road in the London suburb of Southfields (not far from the All England Lawn Tennis Club which Queen Mary invariably visited every summer for the Wimbledon tennis championships). In an alarming burst of broken glass and buckled metal, the royal

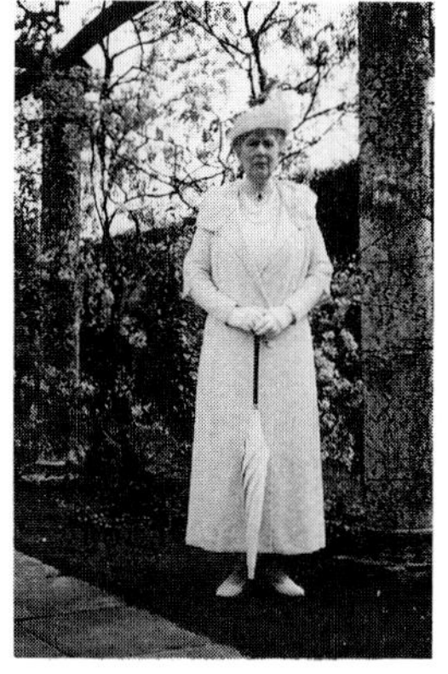

QUEEN MARY AT TRENT IN
MAY 1938

limousine was thrown over on to its side, hurling the seventy-one-year-old Queen and her companions to the floor in a painful heap. 'It was a wonder we . . . occupants were not killed,' Queen Mary remarked afterwards.

Rescued by workmen who were painting a nearby house and who hurried across with ladders – which they wedged through one of the broken windows on the inside while firmly supporting another on the outside – the Queen, muttering 'Oh dear, oh dear!' all the while, was taken to the home of a local vicar and given a cup of tea while her 'big car' was summoned from Marlborough House.

One witness to the Queen's regal descent from her battered Daimler wrote later, 'She climbed up and down those ladders as if she might have been walking down the steps at the coronation. She had not her hat or one curl out of place. . . . The only outward sign of disaster was a broken hat-pin and her umbrella [Queen Mary was famous for her jewel-handled parasols] broken in half.'

Attended by her doctor once she had arrived back home, it was discovered that the Queen had not only sustained severe bruising – her back, she complained, 'hurt abominably' – but that a splinter of glass had 'brushed off the film' of her left eye. Having been persuaded to rest – she reluctantly did so for the following ten days – Queen Mary was up and about again in good time to welcome the King and Queen back home on 22 June, and to attend a garden party at St James's Palace a fortnight later.

On Sunday 3 September, Queen Mary was at Sandringham attending morning service in the church of St Mary Magdalene when she heard that Britain was again at war with Germany. Despite her protests that, like the King and Queen, it was her duty to remain in London for the duration, Queen Mary agreed to leave Sandringham for Badminton, the Gloucestershire estate of her niece, the Duchess of Beaufort ('Dolly's' daughter was married to the 10th Duke). Before the Queen and her entourage – composed of no fewer than sixty-three persons, chiefly made up of Queen Mary's personal staff and their families – stretched a journey by road lasting almost nine hours. At length this unlikely royal caravan of limousines, saloon cars and heavily-laden trucks, swept through the gates of Badminton House during the early evening of 4 September. There Queen Mary would remain until hostilities ceased five years later.

Even in the comparative seclusion of the Gloucestershire countryside, Queen Mary's war was certainly no less active than that of 1914–18 had been and, in spite of her advanced age, scarcely a day passed without the Queen visiting something or somebody. Among the photographs of the war years we see Queen Mary calling upon Princess Juliana of the Netherlands and her baby daughters Beatrix and Irene at Lydney Park, posing with a team of Royal Engineers, who disposed of a bomb that had fallen on Badminton Village, and visiting the Hinnegar Camp for bombed women and children, and the Waifs and Strays Home at Batheaston. We see her at Aldershot with men of her Regiment, The Queen's Own Rifles of Canada, visiting a factory at Brislington Hill, receiving Mrs Eleanor Roosevelt, wife of the then American President, and, posing at their request, with a group of sailors and airmen from the Royal Australian Navy and Royal Australian Air Force whom she encountered while on a visit to Bath in September 1941. Beside this snapshot is a yellowed newspaper cutting reporting this spontaneous meeting.

We also see the Queen with her daughter-in-law Marina, Duchess of Kent, with soldiers of the Gloucestershire Regiment in the Duchess of Beaufort's hut at the YMCA canteen at Badminton. On the same page in the Queen's album are two photographs which, at first glance, simply appear to remind us of Queen Mary's keen sense of humour. The left-hand photograph, captioned 'Fore', shows the Queen from the front, while the right-hand photograph, captioned 'Aft', is a view of her Majesty from the rear. What these two pictures tell us, in fact, is the story of the Gloucestershire Regimental badge, which the Queen is wearing. Eager to learn more about the history of this double cap badge, which Queen Mary was told had originated at the battle of Alexandria in 1801, the royal librarian told her that, because the French had attacked the Gloucestershire Regiment 'in the flank', the rear rank had 'turned their caps to the back to show they were not running away, since when they wear their badge both front & back "fore & aft" . . .'. 'I am allowed to wear the badge,' Queen Mary noted proudly, 'so the aft is pinned at the back of my hat!'

During her stay at Badminton there were three wartime pastimes in which the Queen enthusiastically took part. One was collecting salvage – discarded bottles, tin-cans and scrap-iron – required for the war effort, all of which was dumped into her otherwise majestic Daimler and driven off to some collection depot. The second was leading what was known as the Queen's 'Ivy Squad' – organized to tear down these destructive creepers from buildings, walls and trees. The last activity, in which Queen Mary was joined by her four personal dispatch-riders, John Salmon, Arthur Mellor, Ronald Nunn and Ted Hallett, was 'wooding', involving sawing-up branches and logs, thinning or clearing thickets or spinneys and clearing up woodland debris in general.

Like the 120 men of the Gloucestershire Regiment stationed at Badminton, the Queen's dispatch-riders had not been directed to act as military errand-boys but as her Majesty's personal bodyguards. We are told that these four soldiers had embarked on their royal mission with some trepidation, but 'quickly came to regard the Queen with personal affection', recalling 'the wiles Queen Mary would employ to discover the dates of their birthdays so as to give them surprise birthday presents, or the way in which she handed round cigarettes during the short break in a "wooding" afternoon, chatting to them about her family or theirs as she stood amongst them, herself smoking a cigarette'.

Early in 1942 it is quite likely that Queen Mary told her four 'wooding' stalwarts of the christening of her latest grandchild, Prince William of Gloucester, which she attended in the private chapel at Windsor Castle on 22 February. Born two months earlier, on 18 December 1941, the prince was the first child of the Queen's third son Harry, Duke of Gloucester and Alice, his forty-year-old wife. Prince William's brother, Richard, the present

Duke of Gloucester, was born three years later on 26 August 1944.

On 4 August 1942, which also happened to be Queen Elizabeth's forty-second birthday, Queen Mary again joined members of the royal family at Windsor for the christening of yet another grandchild, this time Prince Michael, third and youngest child of Prince George, Duke of Kent and his wife Marina. Also present at this family gathering were the baby prince's brother, the seven-year-old Prince Edward ('Eddie'), the present Duke of Kent, and their sister, Princess Alexandra, who had been born on Christmas Day 1936, exactly a fortnight after the abdication of their uncle David.

It was at Badminton House on 25 August, just three weeks after the christening of Prince Michael of Kent, that Queen Mary received the shocking news of the death, earlier that day, of Prince Michael's father, and her adored younger son 'Georgie'. That morning Queen Mary had visited Corsham Court to inspect Lord Methuen's picture gallery and upon her return that afternoon had spent a few hours attending to her photograph albums while Lady Cynthia Colville, one of her ladies-in-waiting, sat reading to her. News that the Duke of Kent had perished when the Sunderland flying-boat in which he was travelling to inspect RAF bases in Iceland had crashed into a ridge near Eagle's Rock on the Duke of Portland's Langwell Estate in Caithness, was brought to Queen Mary shortly after dinner. 'I felt so stunned by the shock,' she wrote in her diary, 'I could not believe it.' Early next morning, Queen Mary set off from Badminton to comfort her son's devastated widow, Princess Marina, at Coppins, the Kent family home just outside the village of Iver in Buckinghamshire.

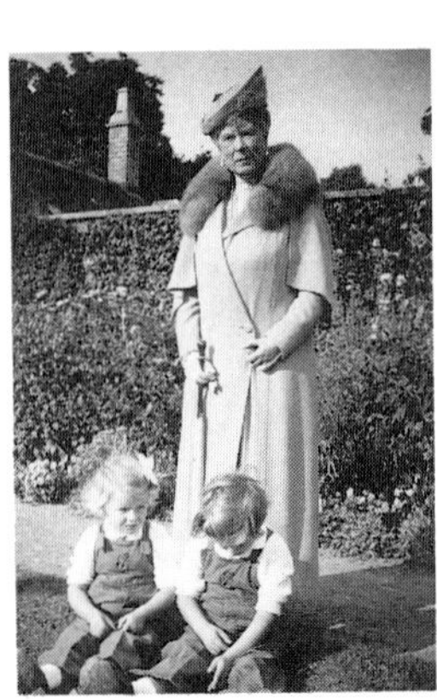

When peace finally came on 'VE Day', 8 May 1945, Queen Mary realized that it was only a matter of time before she would have to return to London and, for the third time in her life, re-establish herself at Marlborough House. For the moment, though, she, like the villagers of Badminton, converged on the Portcullis Club in the local pub to celebrate the end of the war. 'We sang songs, a friendly affair and amusing,' as she wrote later that evening. When finally the day came for her to leave Badminton House, her farewells were tinged with a deep sadness. Indeed, as she presented thank you gifts to members of the Beaufort household, the Queen was in tears. 'Oh, I *have* been happy here!' she was heard to remark. 'Here I've been anybody to everybody, and back in London I shall have to begin being Queen Mary all over again.'

With life in Britain slowly returning to normal – or at least regaining some semblance of normality – so Queen Mary was able to ease herself back into her familiar pre-war routine; visiting art galleries and exhibitions, attending plays, concerts and shows and, in short, looking ahead without the menace of war blighting the horizon as it had done for five long, if not entirely joyless, years.

In 1947 the royal family and the nation as a whole had at least two notable events to celebrate. The first, on 26 May, was the eightieth birthday of Queen Mary herself. Despite grumbling that it was 'so tiresome getting old!!!' she nevertheless entered into the festive spirit of the occasion with great vitality,

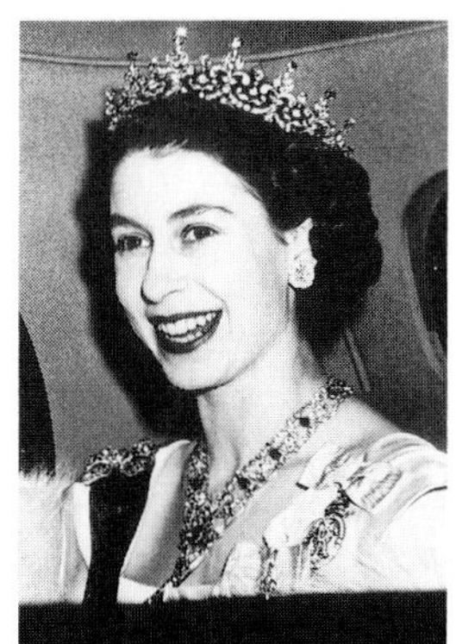

'LILIBET' WEARING A
TIARA GIVEN TO HER BY
QUEEN MARY, MARCH 1950

even hosting an evening party for some of her old friends at Marlborough House. The second event was the wedding at Westminster Abbey on 20 November of her eldest granddaughter 'Lilibet', the Princess Elizabeth, to Lieutenant Philip Mountbatten RN, newly created Duke of Edinburgh, only son of the late Prince Andrew of Greece and Denmark and his wife, the former Princess Alice of Battenberg.

The year 1948 also produced a brace of royal celebrations and at much the same intervals. In April, the silver wedding of King George VI and Queen Elizabeth was officially commemorated by a service of thanksgiving, held once again at St Paul's Cathedral. Seven months later, on 14 November, Princess Elizabeth not only gave her husband an early first-wedding-anniversary present in the form of a son – the present Prince of Wales – but presented her parents with their first grandchild and Queen Mary with her first great-grandchild.

By this time, however, the happiness and satisfaction members of the royal family derived from occasions such as these was overshadowed by concern for the King's health. On 23 November it was announced that George VI was suffering from an obstruction to the circulation of his right leg. The following March a lumbar sympathectomy was performed with satisfactory results, but within two years anxiety was revived when, for what appeared to be a heavy chest cold, King George underwent a bronchoscopy. The result, though the King himself did not know it, revealed cancer of the left lung. On 23 September 1951 surgery was again performed, this time for lung resection, and thereafter, at least in the short term, the King's condition started to improve.

By Christmas George VI was well enough to spend the holiday with his family at Sandringham and, on 31 January 1952, he even felt strong enough to accompany Princess Elizabeth and the Duke of Edinburgh to London Heathrow Airport upon their departure for East Africa. At Marlborough House the day before Queen Mary, who had returned from Sandringham early because the changeable Norfolk weather had upset her rheumatism, took leave of her granddaughter with a feeling of sadness that her tour of duty would keep her away from home until early summer. Scarcely had the Princess and her husband arrived in Kenya, however, than they were recalled. At Sandringham, sometime during the small hours of Wednesday 6 February, George VI had died peacefully in his sleep. Lilibet, not quite twenty-five-years-old, had suddenly become Her Majesty Queen Elizabeth II.

King George VI, 'Bertie', was the third of Queen Mary's six children to have died in her lifetime. His was also the fifth reign through which she had lived. Now Queen Mary prepared herself to greet her new sovereign and late the following afternoon she drove the short distance to Clarence House, home of the former Princess Elizabeth. 'Her old Grannie and subject must be the first to kiss her hand,' she had said.

Accompanied by other members of the royal family, Queen Mary joined her son's widow, now Queen Elizabeth The Queen Mother, and his daughters, the new Queen and Princess Margaret, at Westminster Hall for the formal

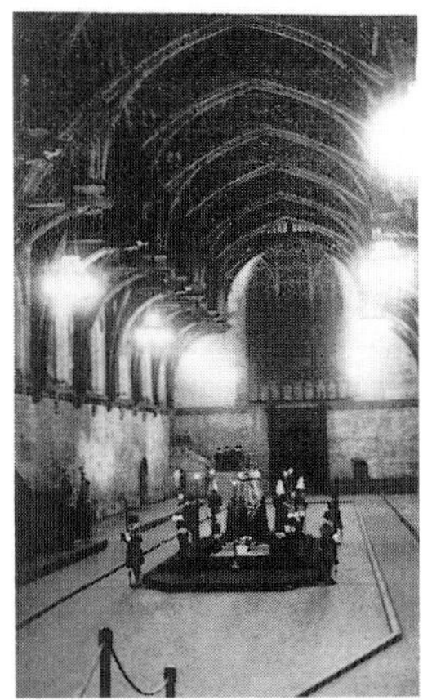

KING GEORGE VI LYING IN
STATE IN WESTMINSTER
HALL

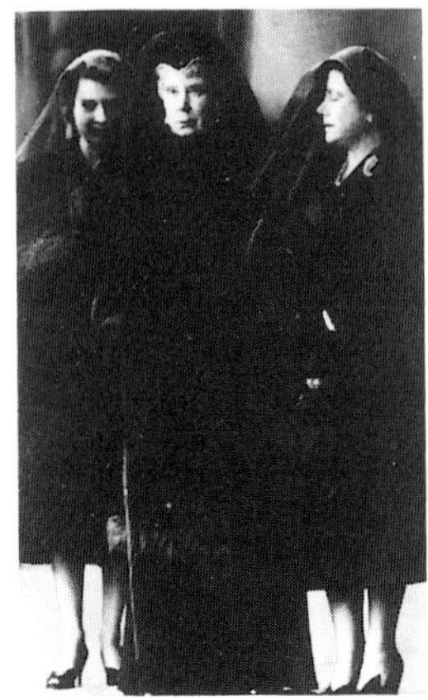

THREE QUEENS AFTER THE
DEATH OF KING GEORGE VI

lying-in-state, but she did not attend the funeral itself, which took place at St George's Chapel on 15 February. That morning, she sat at a window of her room at Marlborough House to watch the funeral procession pass along the Mall on the first part of its journey to Windsor. As the King's coffin, draped with the royal standard and resting on a gun-carriage, came into view, Queen Mary, tall and erect in a long black dress, rose from her chair. 'Here *he* is,' she murmured to her lady-in-waiting. Then, as the cortège passed slowly by, the Queen raised her arm in a silent gesture of farewell to her son.

That April Queen Mary became ill and took to her bed, where she remained for several weeks. By 26 May, her eighty-fifth birthday, she was up and about once more and taking an active interest in the preliminary arrangements for her granddaughter's coronation, set to take place just over one year hence. During the summer of 1952, the Queen Dowager went to Sandringham, where she stayed until 17 September. A photograph of her return to London that day is the last we see of Queen Mary through the treasury of her photograph albums. All the remaining pages in this final volume are blank.

Early in the new year, Londoners caught what was to be their last glimpse of Queen Mary as she drove through the West End to look at the stands already going up for the coronation that June. At the end of February, the Queen was confined to bed once more with a recurrence of gastric trouble and, on 2 March, an announcement released to that effect was the first intimation the public had that Queen Mary was slowly fading. Two weeks later, on 16 March, a bulletin stated that her Majesty had had a 'less comfortable night and a less restful day'. On 24 March four bulletins were issued. The first, at 11.40 that morning, revealed that the Queen's condition was 'causing anxiety'. That issued only two hours later read, 'During the past hours Queen Mary's condition has become more grave. There has been a serious weakening of the heart action which gives rise to increasing anxiety.'

Throughout the day Queen Mary was repeatedly visited by members of her family, the new Queen and the Duke of Edinburgh with Princess Margaret, the Queen Mother, the Duke of Windsor, the Princess Royal, the Duke and Duchess of Gloucester, and the Duchess of Kent and her two elder children. Mabell, Countess of Airlie, both friend and lady-in-waiting for more than half a century, also sat by the Queen's bedside:

> . . . the exquisitely embroidered soft lawn nightgown – the same as she had worn in her youth – the nails delicately shaped and polished a pale pink; the immaculately arranged grey hair. Her face had still a gentle beauty of expression; no trace of hardness as so many faces have in old age, only resignation. As I kissed her hand before leaving her I noticed the extreme softness of her skin.

These were the dowager Lady Airlie's last impressions of the Queen whose service she had entered in 1911.

At 7p.m. on the evening of 24 March 1953, the third bulletin of the day posted outside Marlborough House told the silent crowd waiting for news, 'Queen Mary's strength is ebbing . . .'. Then, little more than four hours later, 'While sleeping peacefully Queen Mary died at twenty minutes past ten o'clock.'

At her own wish, the Queen Dowager's obsequies were dealt with decorously but with the minimum of fuss. Her lying-in-state at Westminster Hall – Queen Mary was the only Queen Consort to have been so honoured within the Palace of Westminster – lasted a mere thirty-two hours; and instead of being borne through the streets of London in the traditional manner thereafter, the Queen's coffin was discreetly taken to Windsor in a motor-hearse. Once there, however, the funeral service in St George's Chapel, on 31 March, lacked none of the grandeur of a state funeral.

Today, Queen Mary lies beside her husband, King George V, just inside the Chapel's great west door, in the comparatively simple, yet still magnificent, sarcophagus of white Clipsham stone, designed by Sir Edwin Lutyens. Sir William Reid Dick's recumbent effigies of the King and Queen, dressed in Garter robes, lie above; a permanent reminder of a sovereign and his Lady who, in life as in death, epitomized the dignity of the British Monarchy.

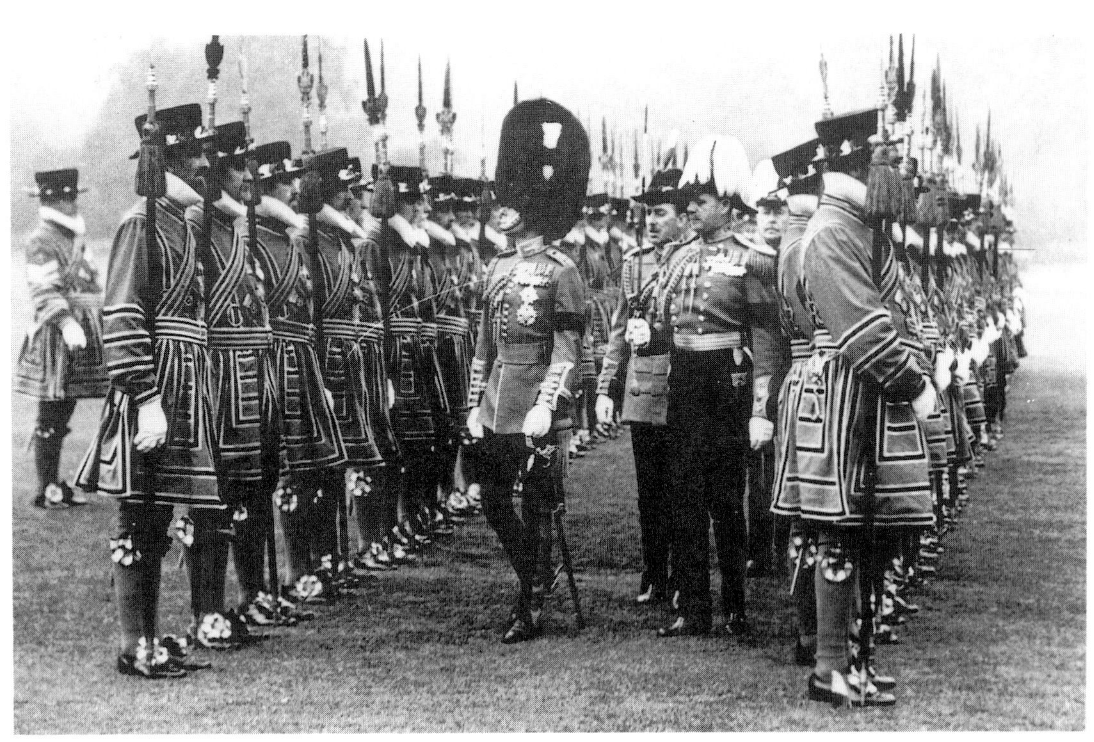

David inspecting the Yeomen of the Guard June 26th 1936

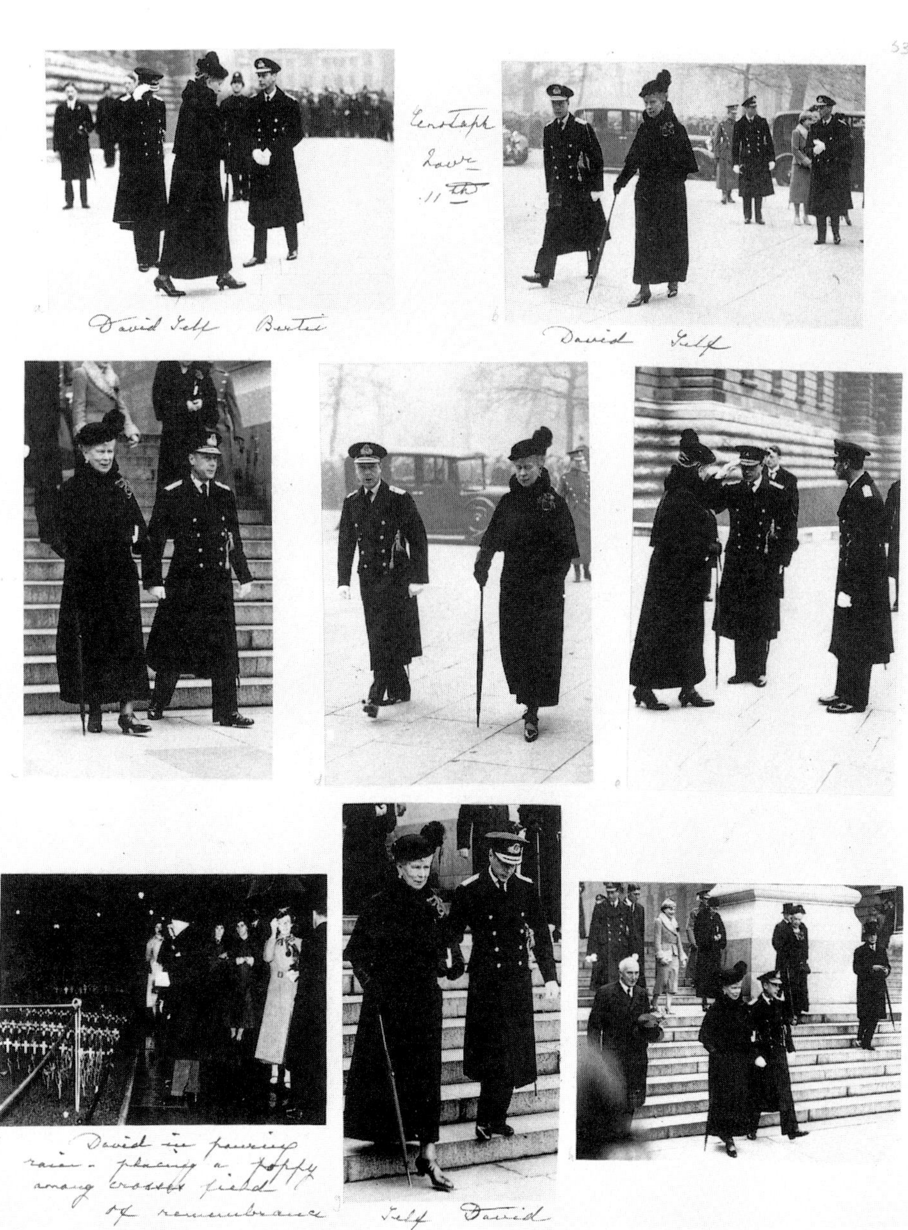

KING EDWARD VIII AND QUEEN MARY ARE ACCOMPANIED BY OTHER MEMBERS OF THE ROYAL FAMILY TO THE ARMISTICE DAY CEREMONY ONE MONTH BEFORE THE ABDICATION, NOVEMBER 1936

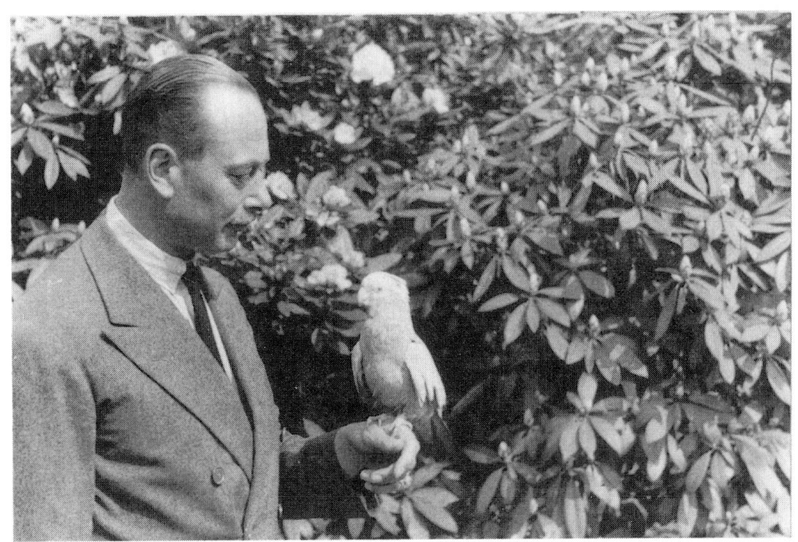

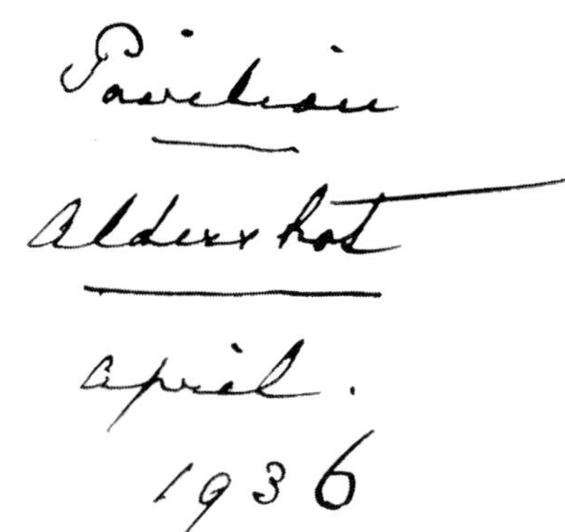

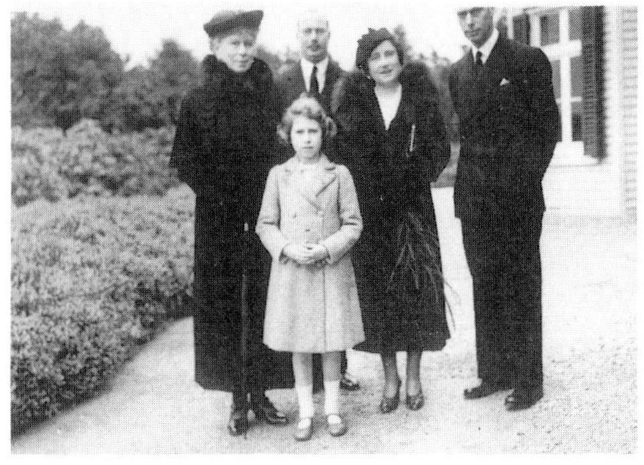

ALDERSHOT, APRIL 1936. THE
DUKE OF GLOUCESTER WITH HIS
LATE FATHER'S PARROT,
'CHARLOTTE', AND WITH QUEEN
MARY, THE DUKE AND DUCHESS
OF YORK AND PRINCESS
ELIZABETH. THE ROYAL FAMILY
ARE STILL IN MOURNING FOR
GEORGE V

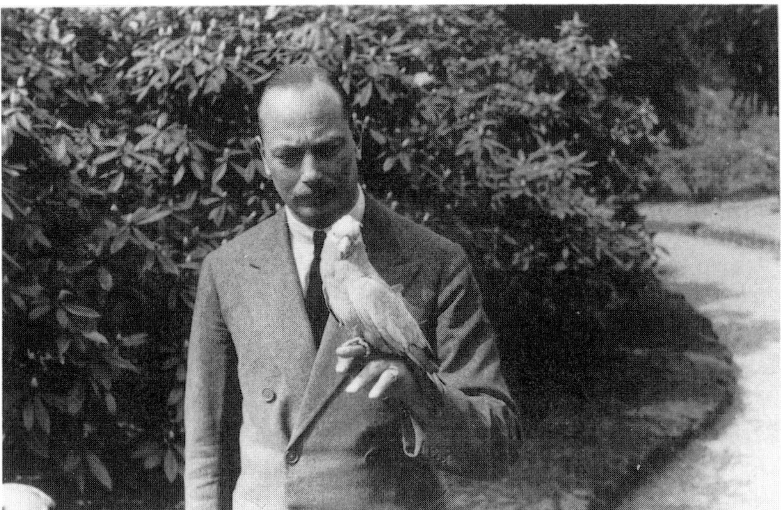

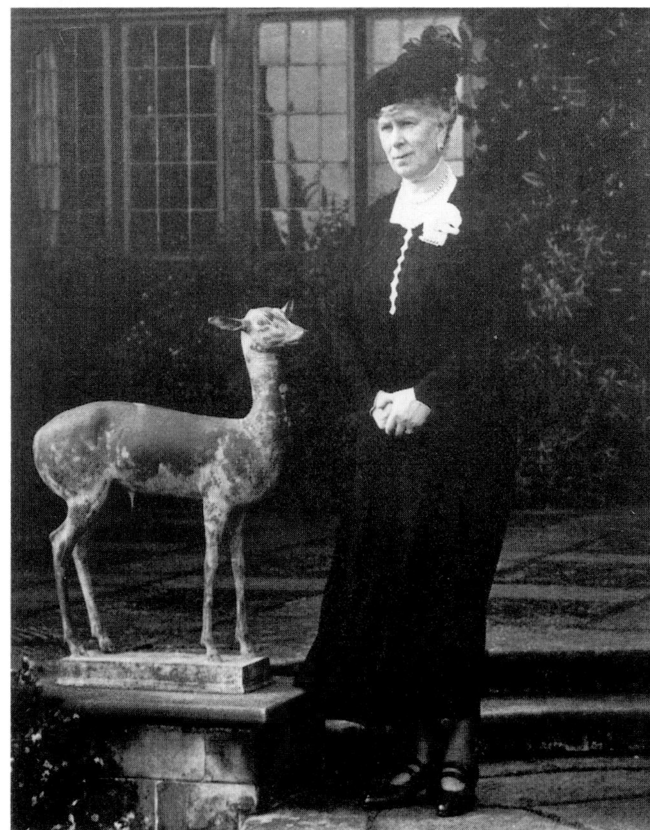

QUEEN MARY, SEPTEMBER 1936

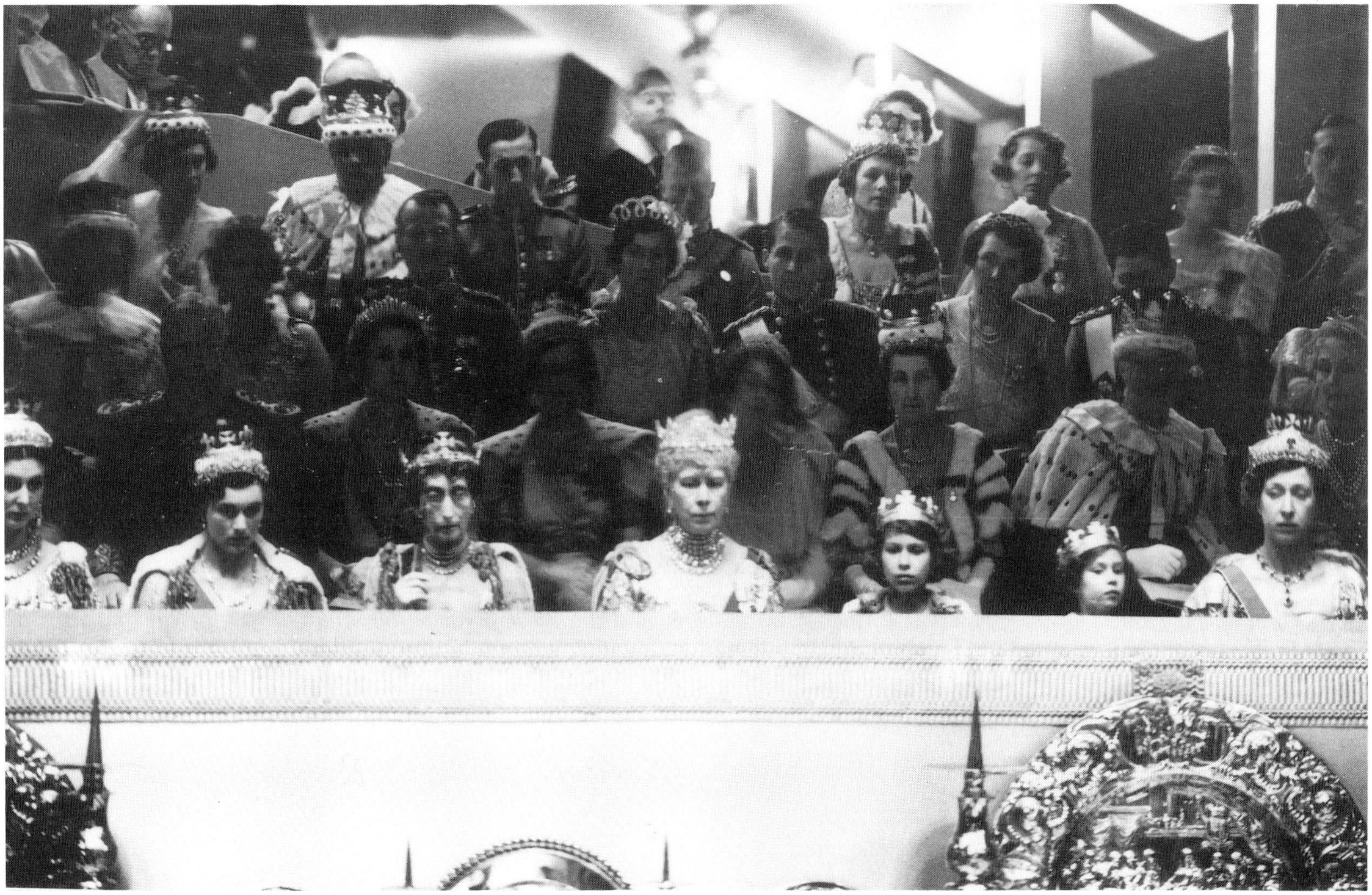

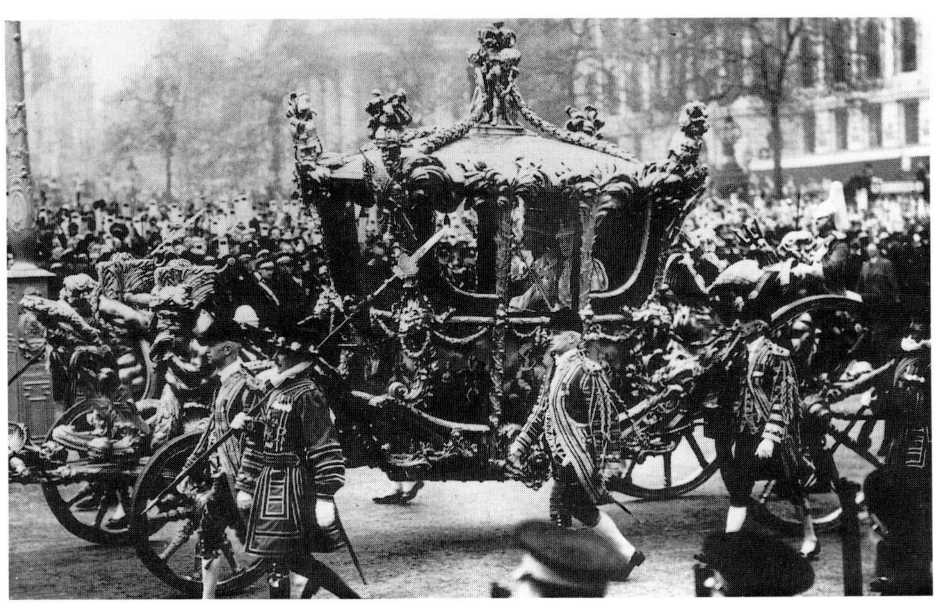

QUEEN MARY IN THE
ROYAL GALLERY AT
WESTMINSTER ABBEY
DURING THE CORONATION
OF KING GEORGE VI AND
QUEEN ELIZABETH, 12 MAY
1937. WITH HER ARE (LEFT
TO RIGHT) THE DUCHESS
OF KENT, THE DUCHESS OF
GLOUCESTER, QUEEN
MAUD OF NORWAY,
PRINCESS ELIZABETH,
PRINCESS MARGARET AND
THE PRINCESS ROYAL

THE NEW KING AND QUEEN
RETURNING TO
BUCKINGHAM PALACE IN
THE STATE COACH

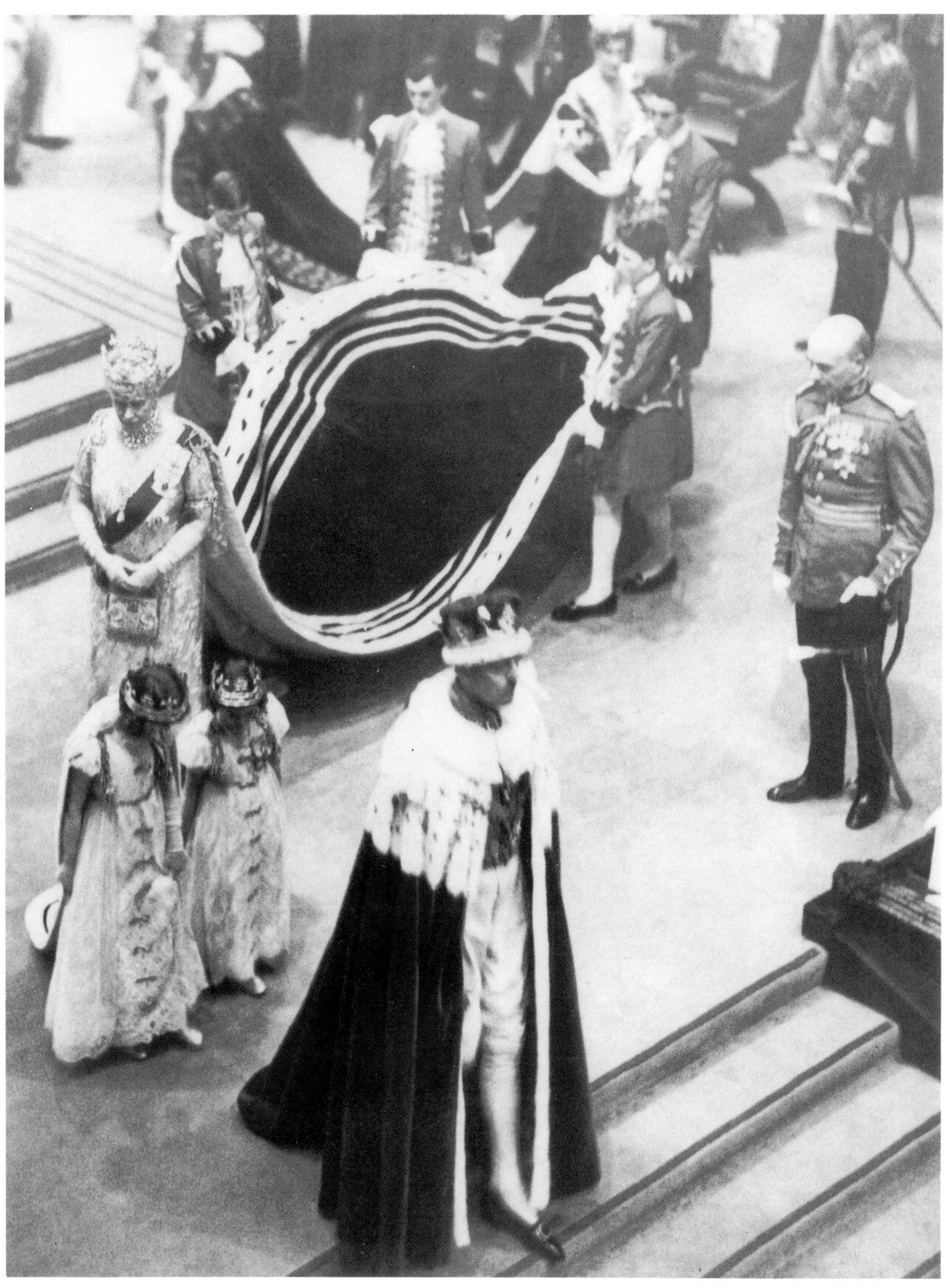

QUEEN MARY LEAVING
WESTMINSTER ABBEY
AFTER THE CORONATION.
SHE IS PRECEDED BY THE
PRINCESSES ELIZABETH
AND MARGARET

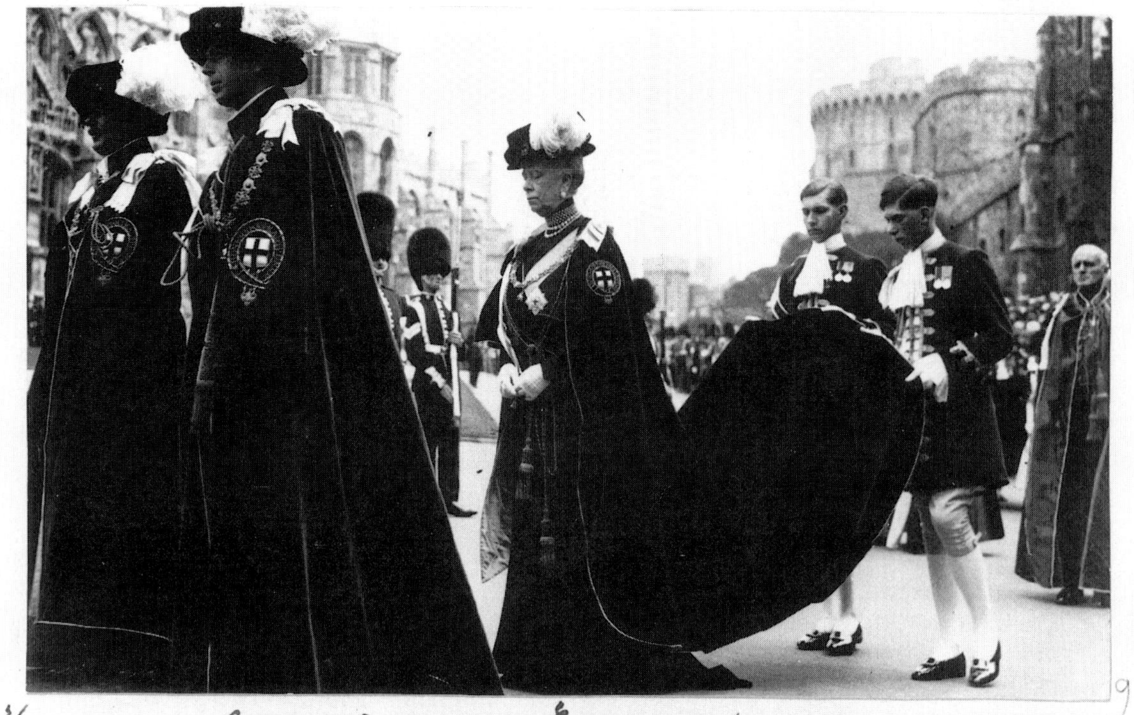

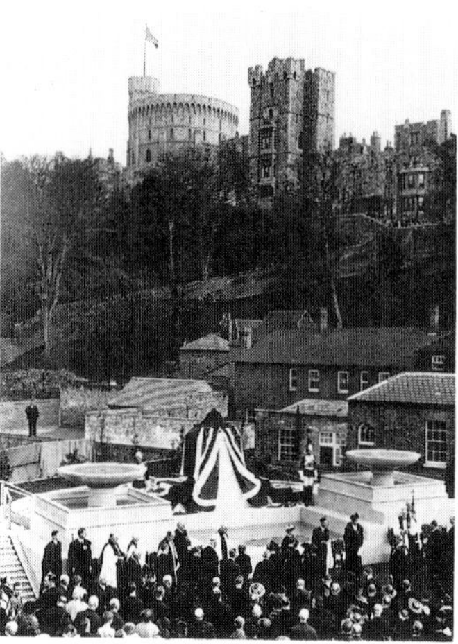

The Royal Family attend the
unveiling of a memorial to King
George V at Windsor on
23 April 1937

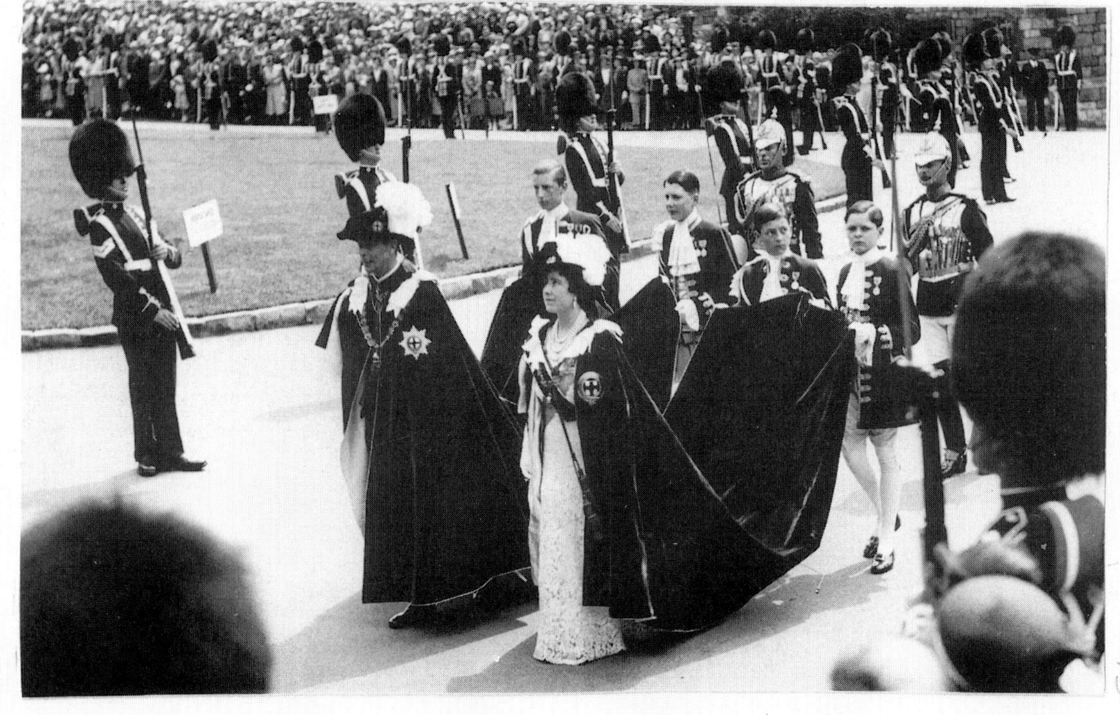

Garter Day at Windsor, 14 June 1937. One of
Queen Mary's train bearers is her
grandson, George, Viscount Lascelles,
now Earl of Harewood

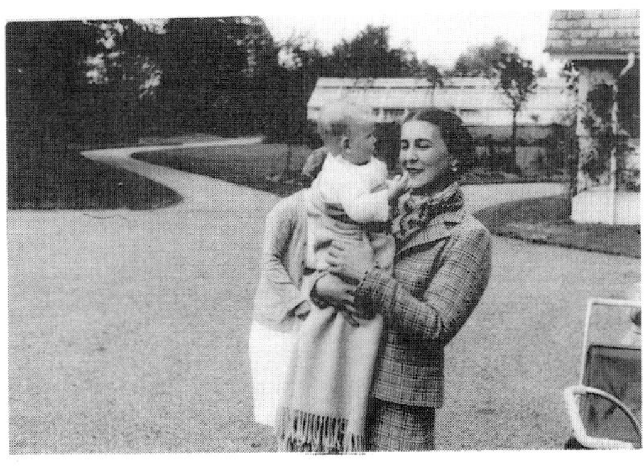

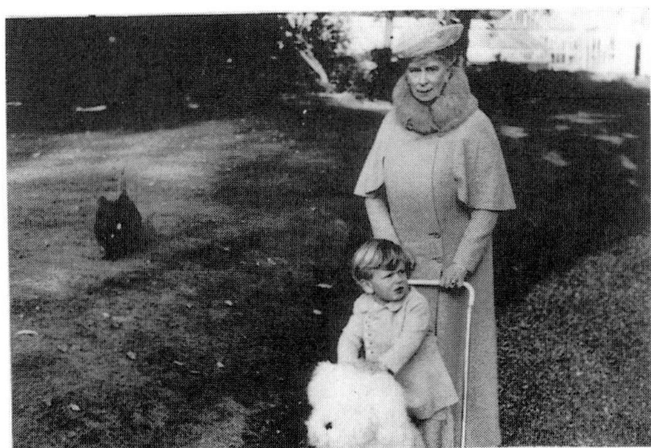

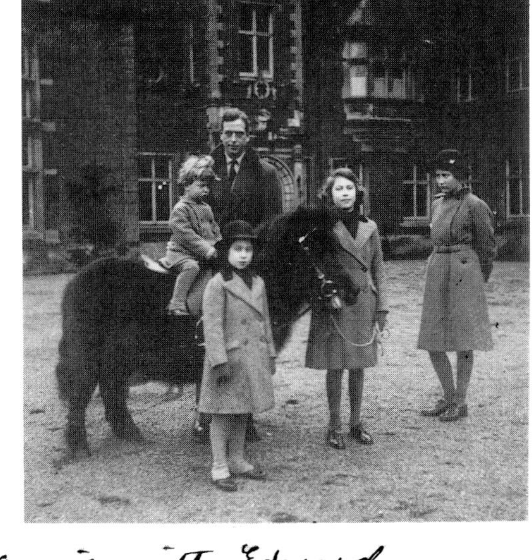

Alexandra. Marina

COPPINS 1937. PRINCESS MARINA, DUCHESS OF KENT, WITH PRINCESS ALEXANDRA AND QUEEN MARY WITH PRINCE EDWARD OF KENT. SANDRINGHAM 1938. PRINCE GEORGE, DUKE OF KENT, WITH HIS SON EDDIE, THE PRINCESSES ELIZABETH AND MARGARET AND LADY MARY CAMBRIDGE

Georgie with Edward Margaret. Lilibet & Mary Cambridge 1938

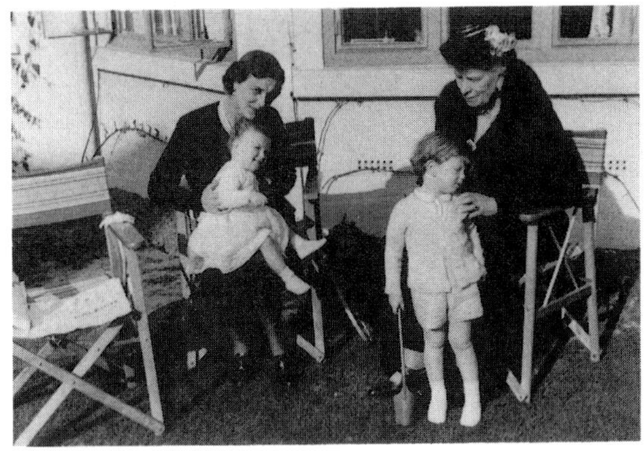

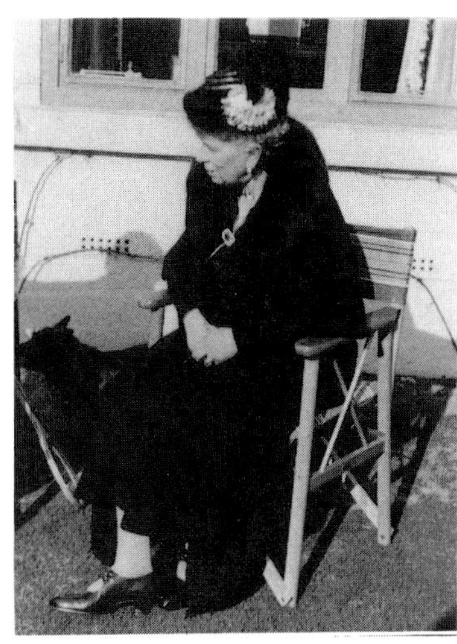

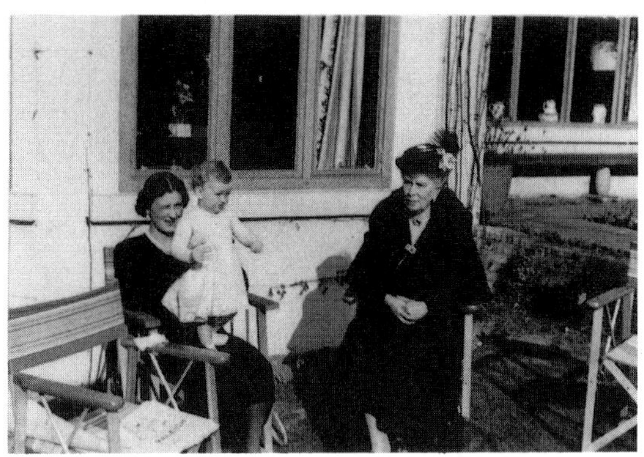

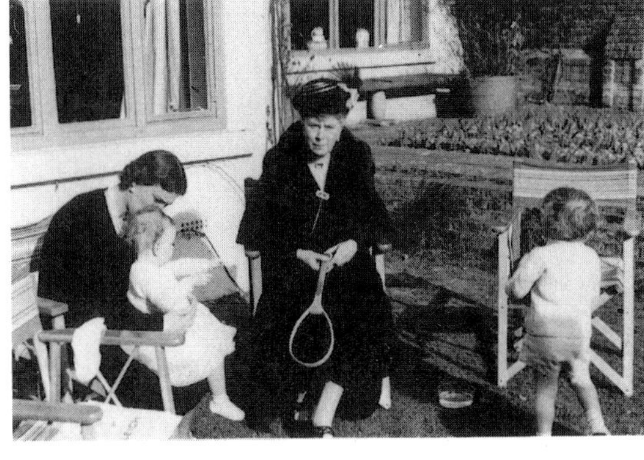

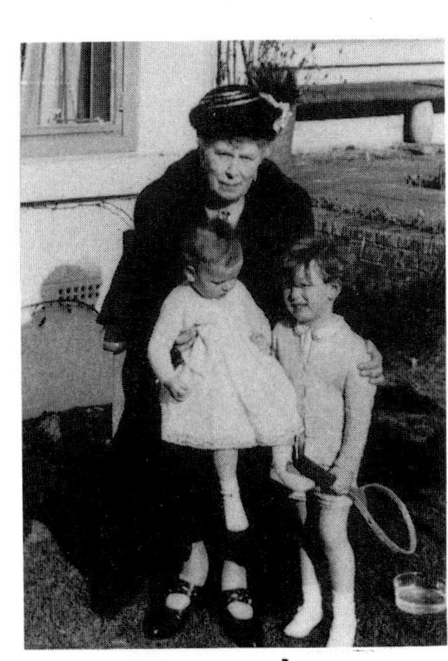

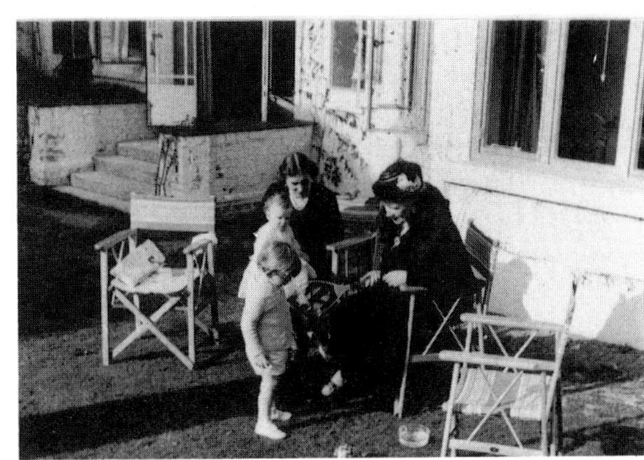

Coppins

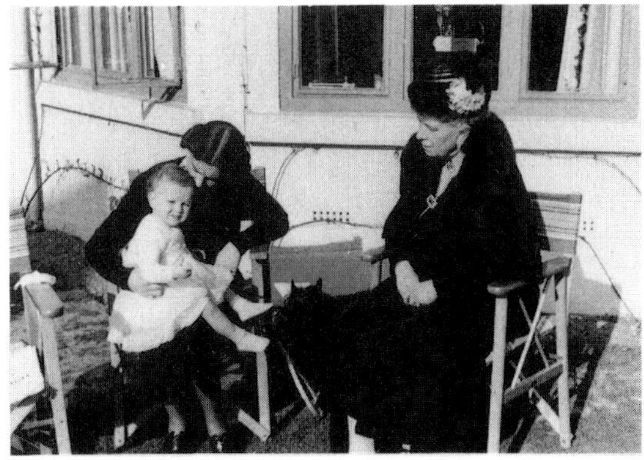

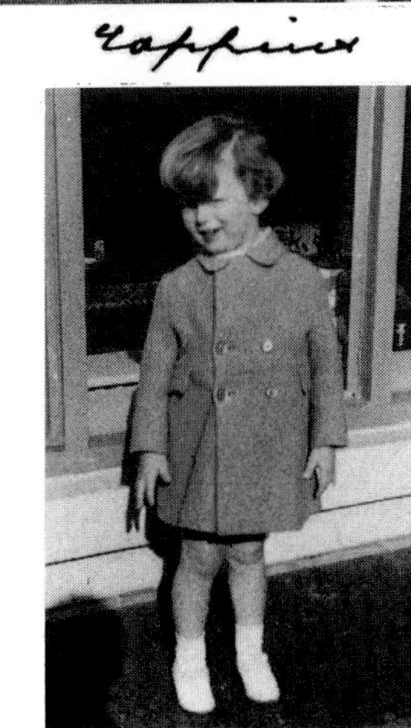

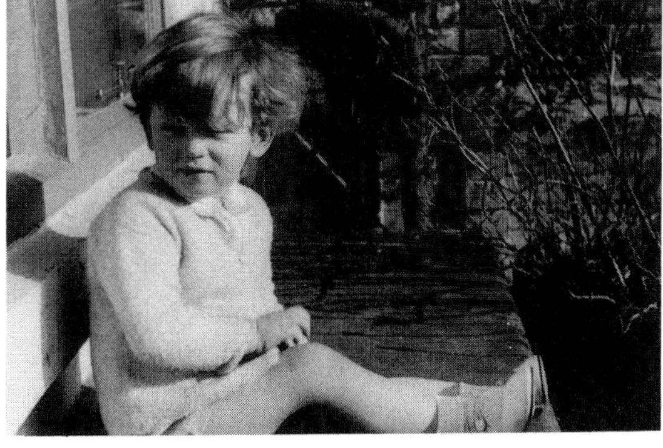

Marina — Self
Alexandra —

A SERIES OF SNAPSHOTS OF QUEEN MARY WITH THE DUCHESS OF KENT AND HER CHILDREN AT COPPINS, MARCH 1938

Edward

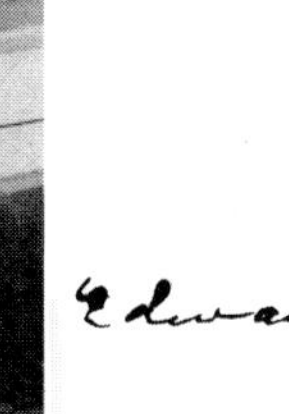

Edward

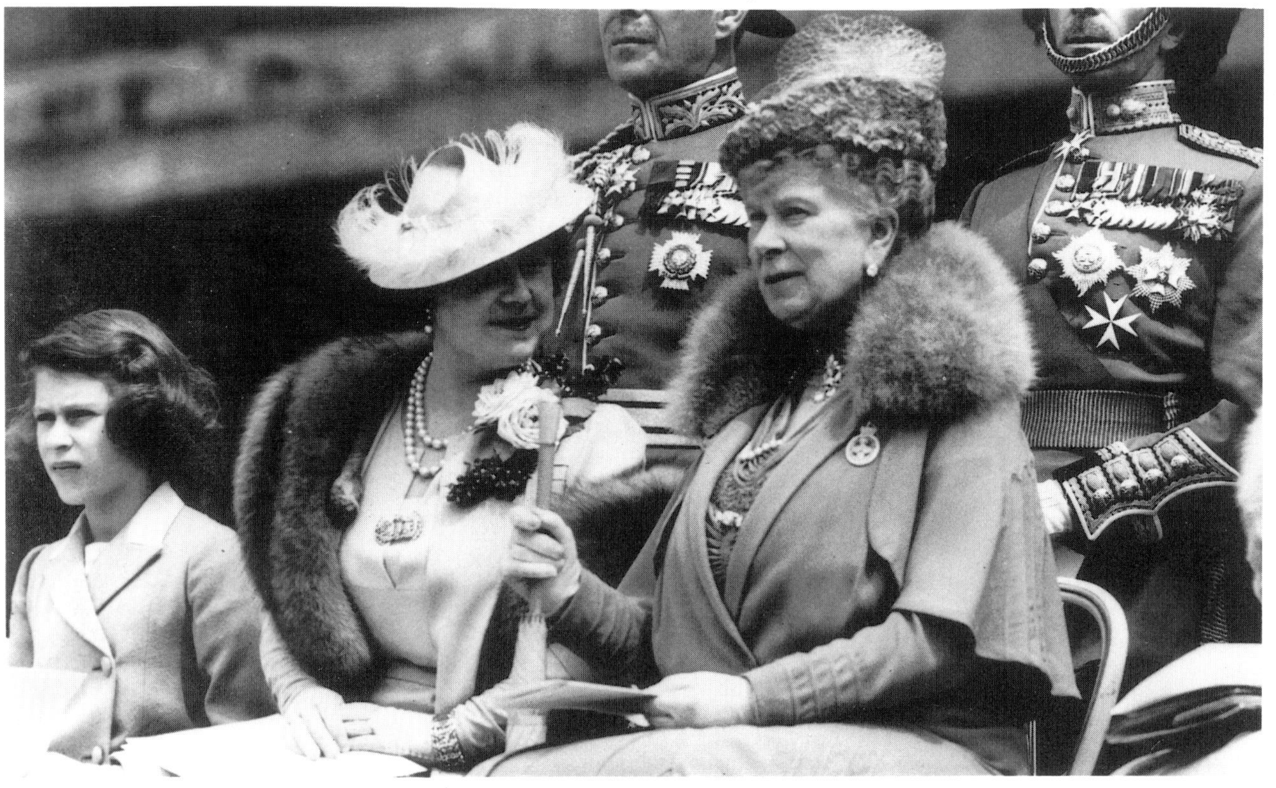

QUEEN MARY WITH THE QUEEN AND PRINCESS
ELIZABETH WATCHING THE KING PRESENT NEW
COLOURS TO THE 2ND BATTALION GRENADIER GUARDS
AT BUCKINGHAM PALACE, 25 MAY 1938

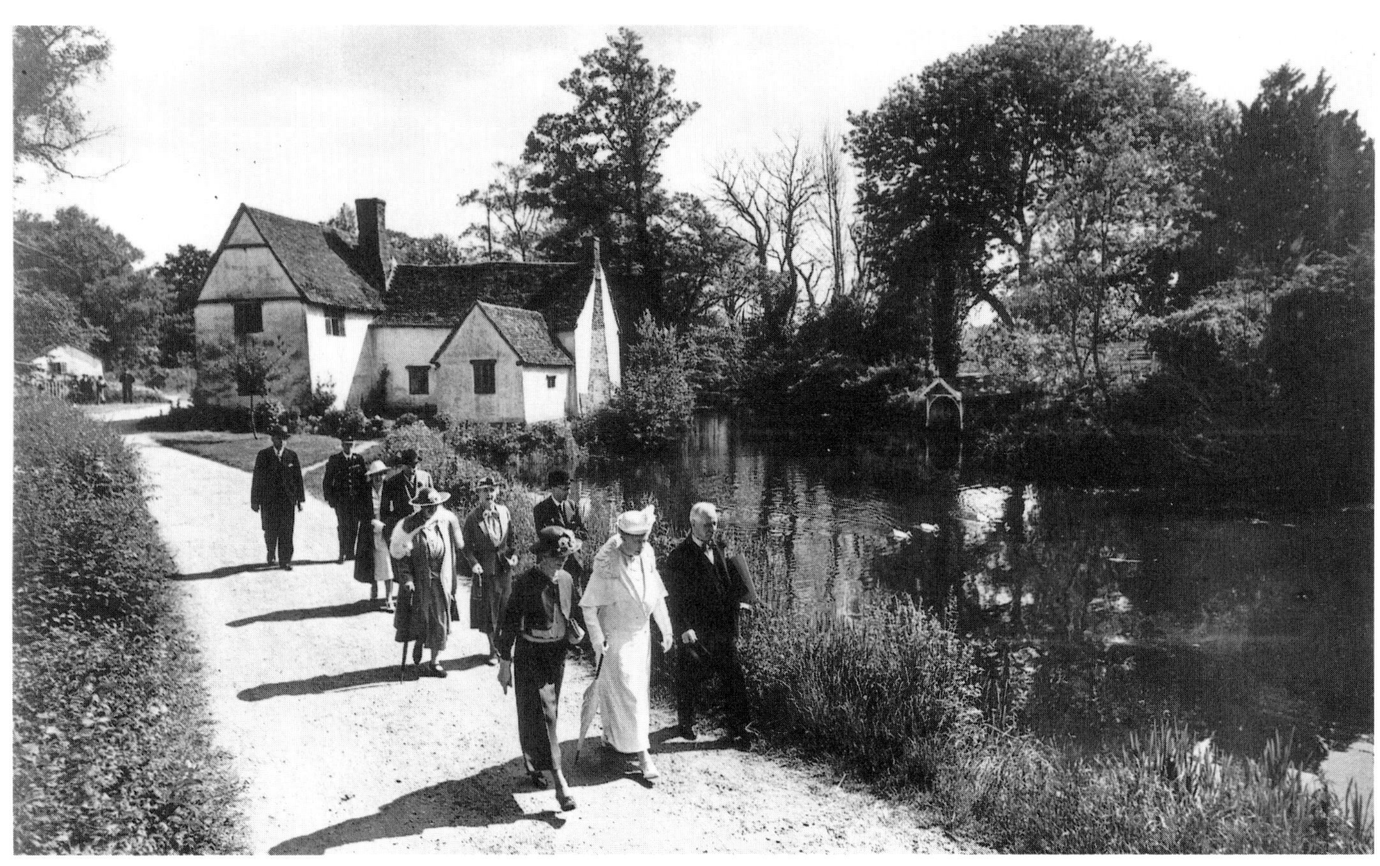

QUEEN MARY AT FLATFORD MILL ON
15 JUNE 1938

QUEEN MARY WENT BY LAUNCH UP THE
THAMES TO ATTEND A GARDEN PARTY AT
THE TOWER OF LONDON ON 13 JULY 1938

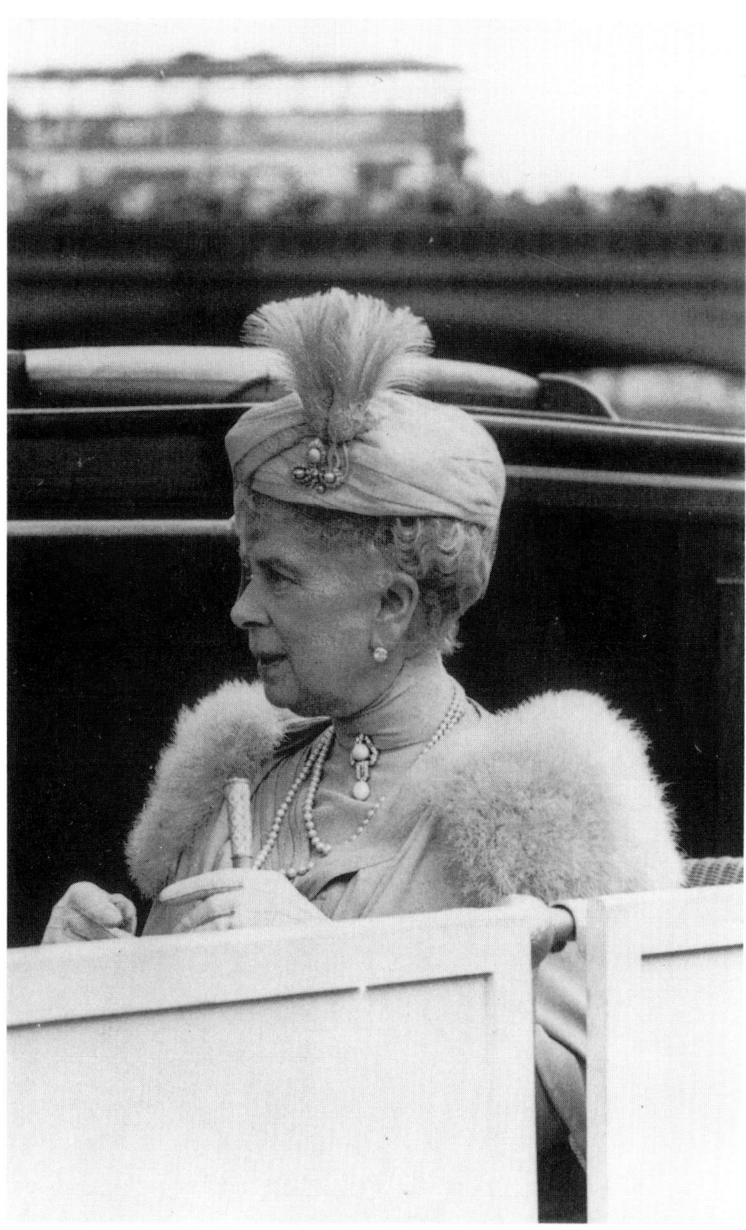

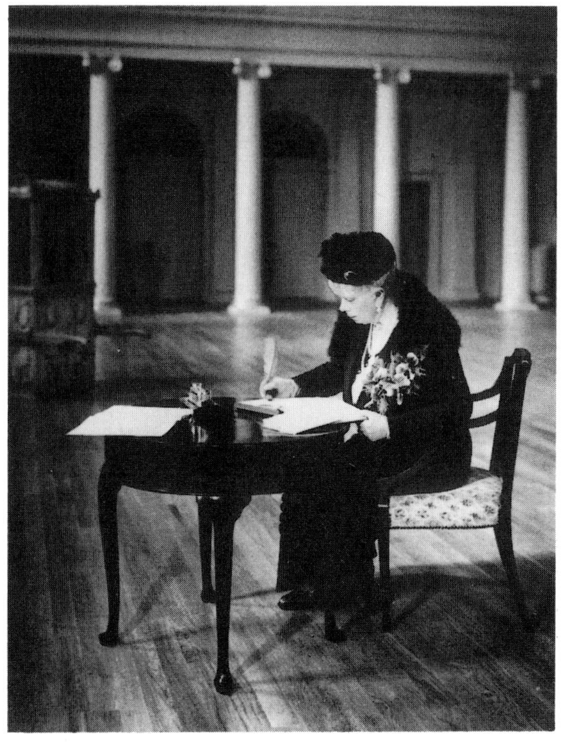

QUEEN MARY SIGNING THE VISITORS' BOOK AT
THE ASSEMBLY ROOMS IN BATH ON
26 SEPTEMBER 1938

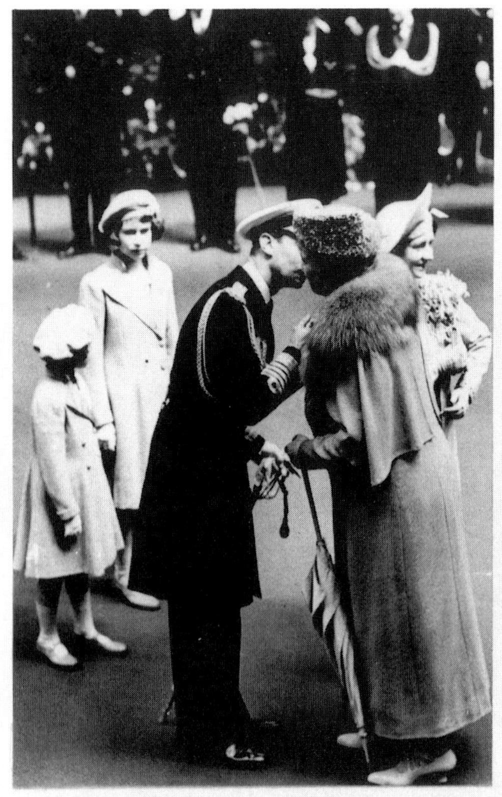

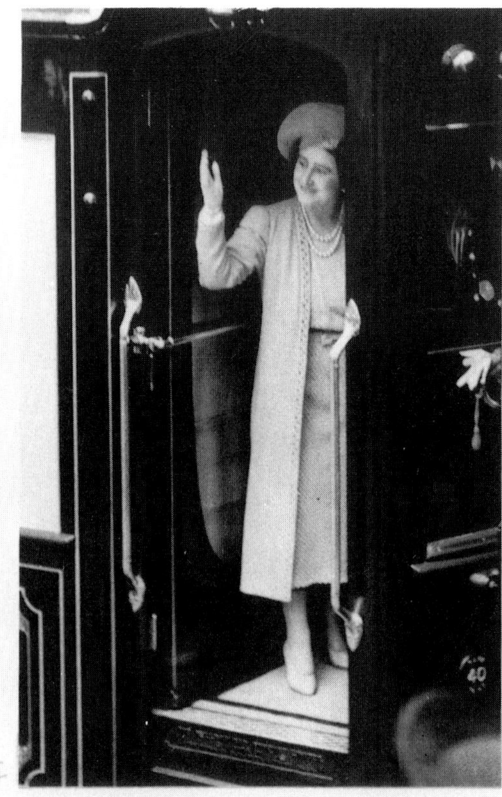

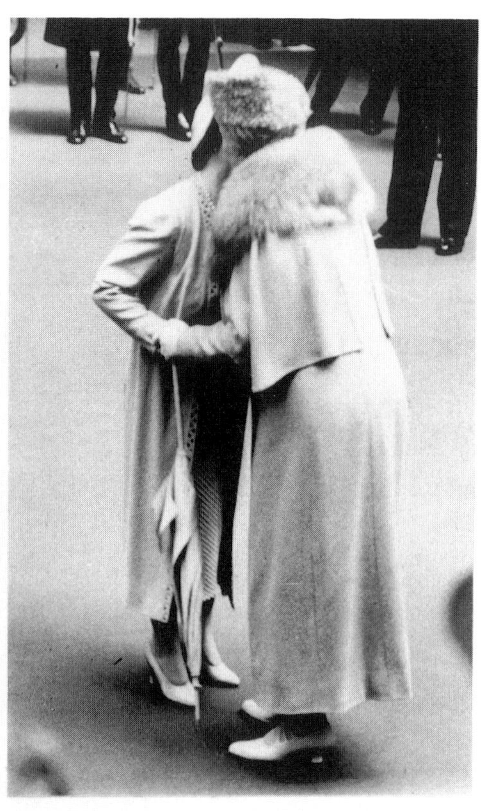

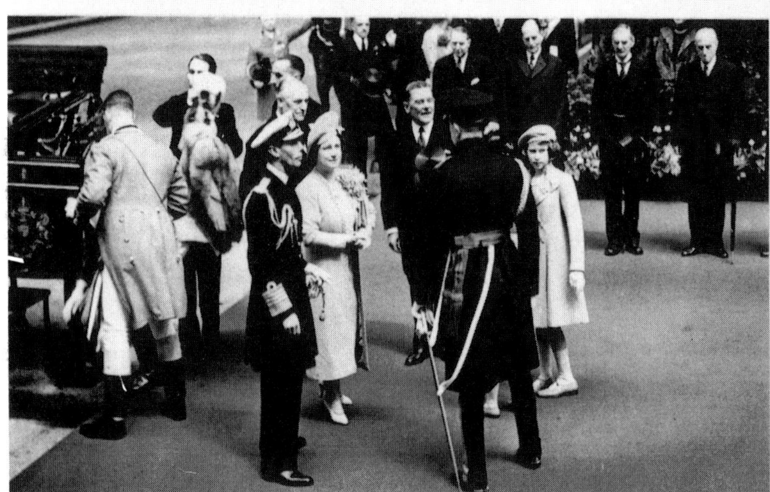

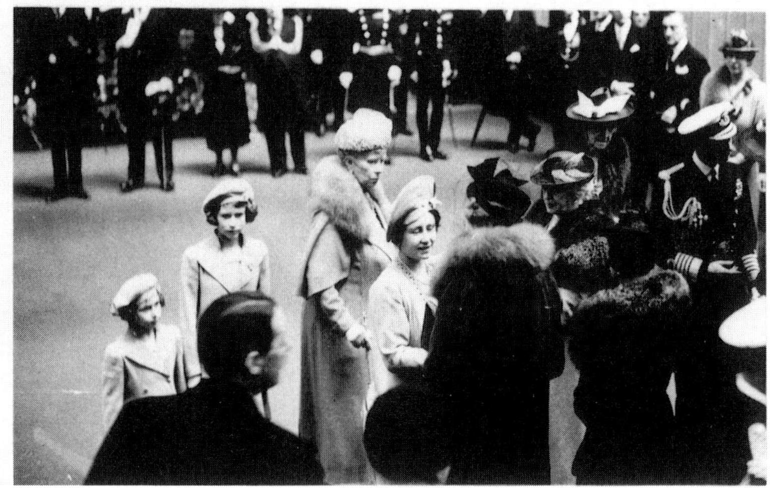

KING GEORGE VI AND QUEEN ELIZABETH
DEPART FOR THE STATE VISIT TO THE
UNITED STATES, 6 MAY 1939

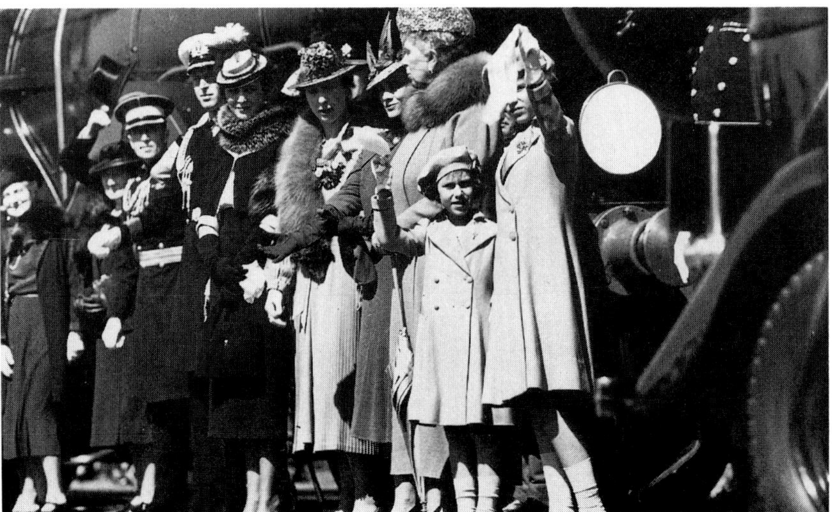

MEMBERS OF THE ROYAL FAMILY WAVING
FAREWELL TO THE KING AND QUEEN AS
THEIR SHIP SAILS

Waving as the ship departed.

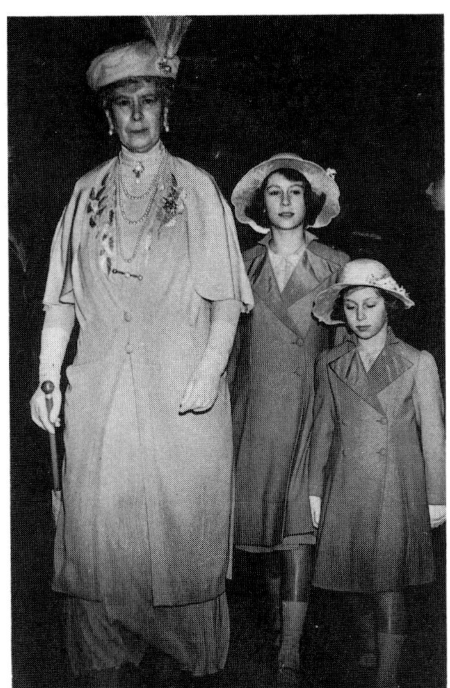

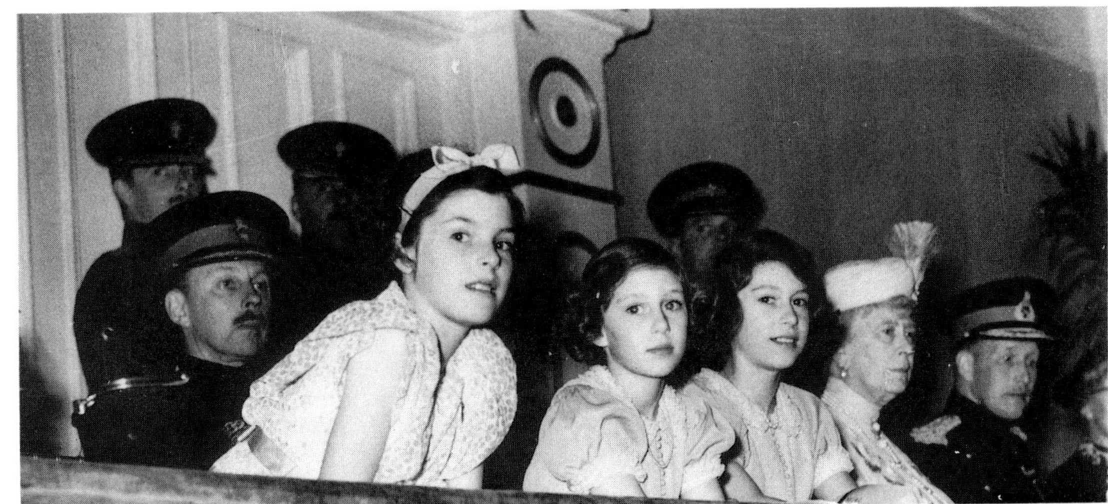

THE QUEEN DOWAGER TAKES HER GRANDDAUGHTERS
TO A PERFORMANCE OF THE ROYAL TOURNAMENT AT
EARLS COURT IN MAY 1939

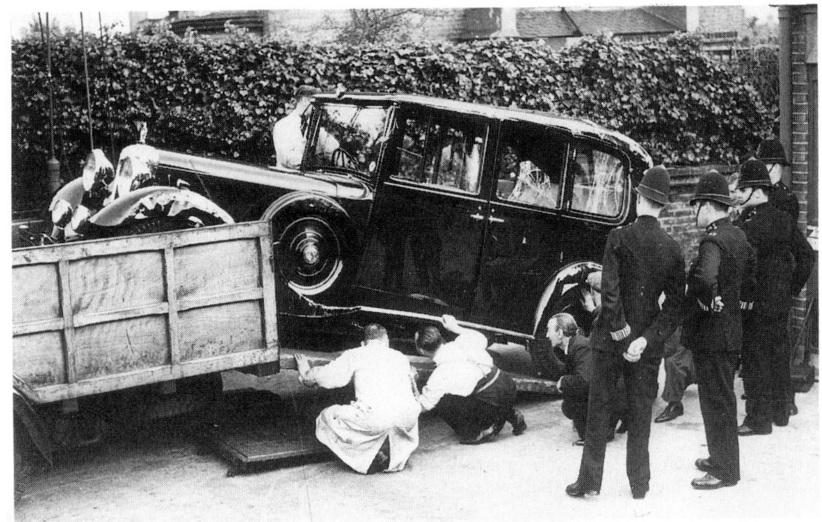

QUEEN MARY'S BATTERED
DAIMLER AFTER IT HAD BEEN HIT
BY A LORRY IN SOUTHFIELDS,
SOUTH LONDON, ON 23 MAY 1939

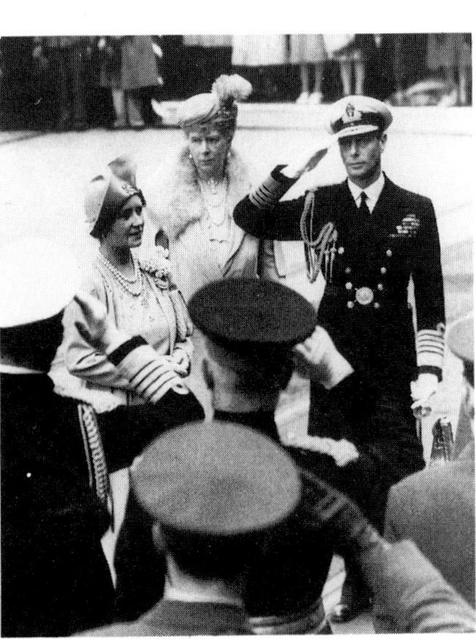
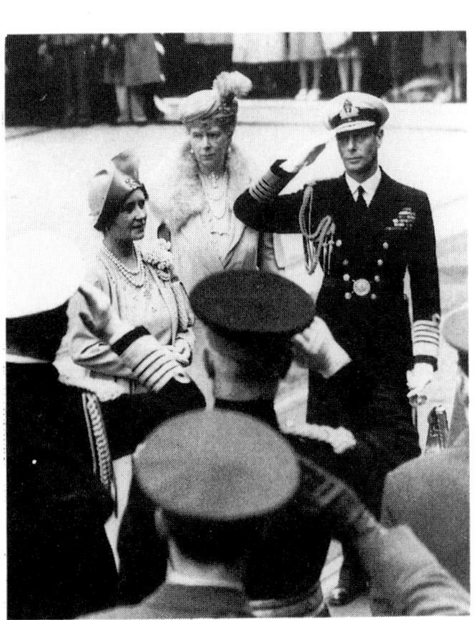

THE KING AND QUEEN ARE
GREETED BY QUEEN MARY UPON
THEIR RETURN FROM THE UNITED
STATES, 22 JUNE 1939

QUEEN MARY RELEASING A BALLOON
DURING A GARDEN PARTY AT ST JAMES'S
PALACE ON 5 JULY 1939

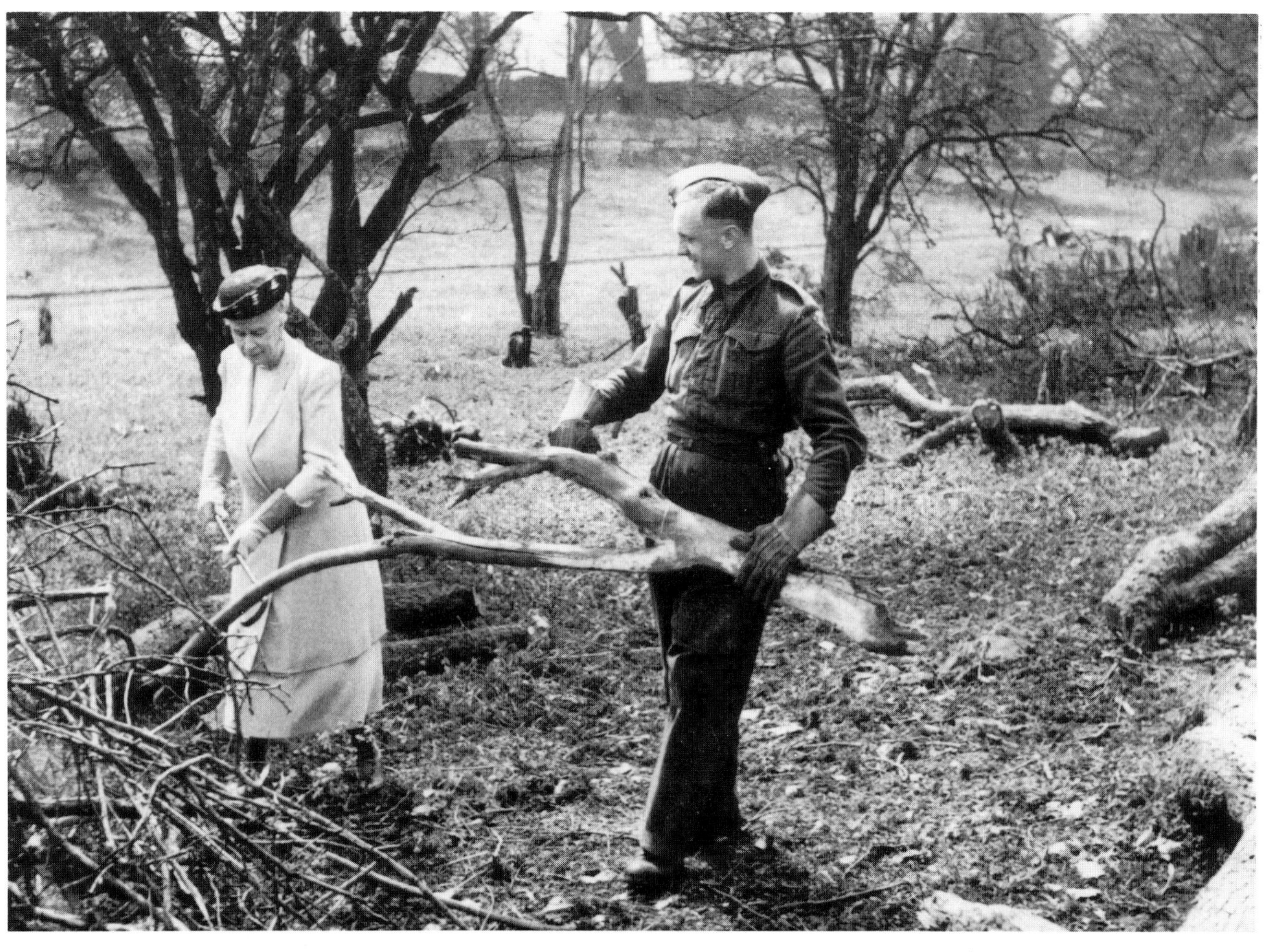

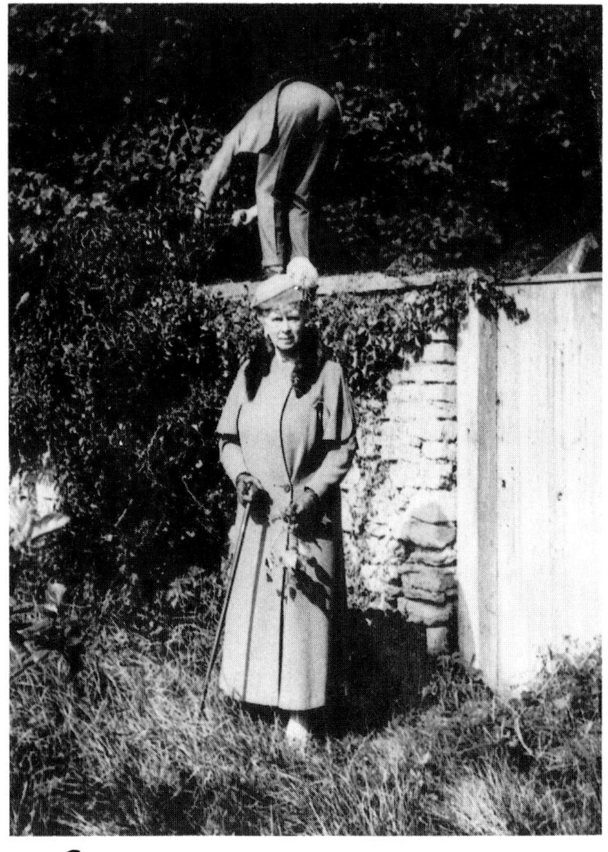

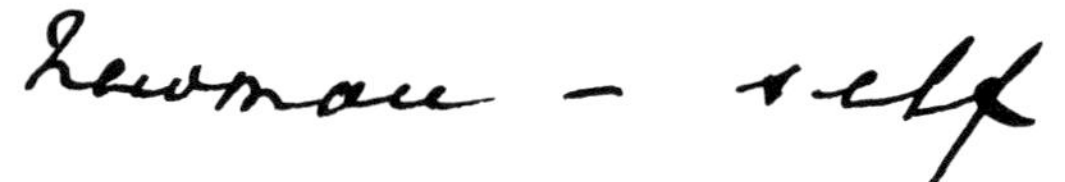

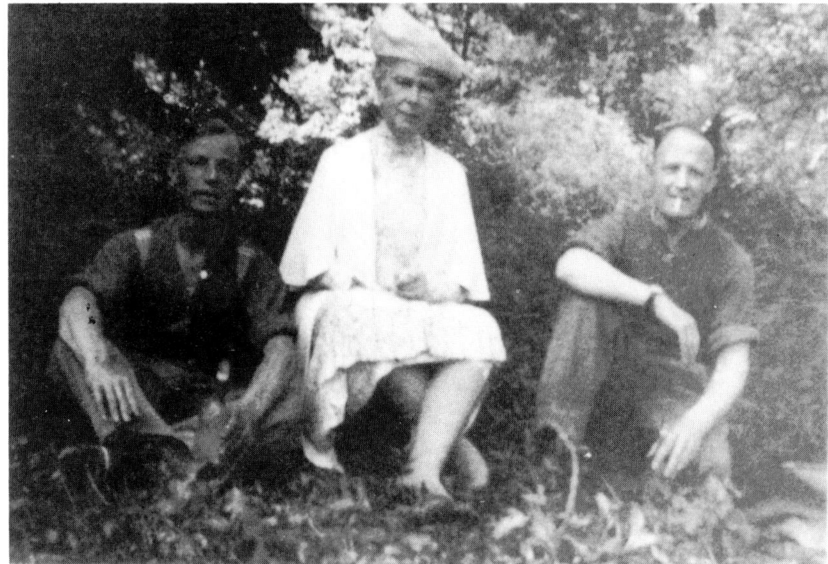

(*ABOVE* AND *TOP*) QUEEN MARY WITH TWO OF HER DISPATCH RIDERS, JOHN SALMON AND RONALD NUNN, 'WOODING' DURING HER WARTIME EVACUATION TO BADMINTON

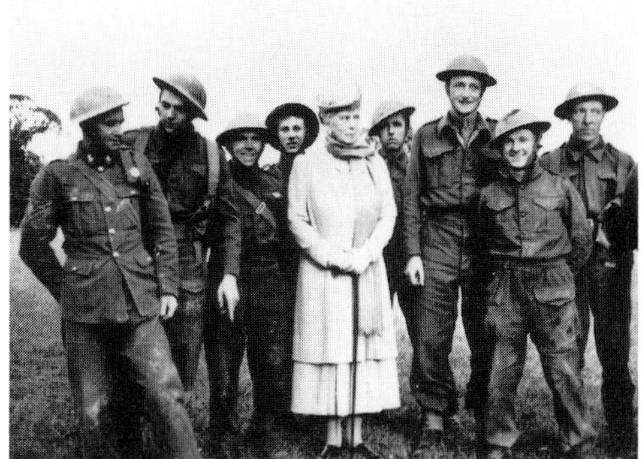

QUEEN MARY POSING WITH A TEAM OF ROYAL ENGINEERS AFTER THEY HAD DISPOSED OF AN UNEXPLODED BOMB WHICH FELL ON BADMINTON VILLAGE ON 9 JULY 1940

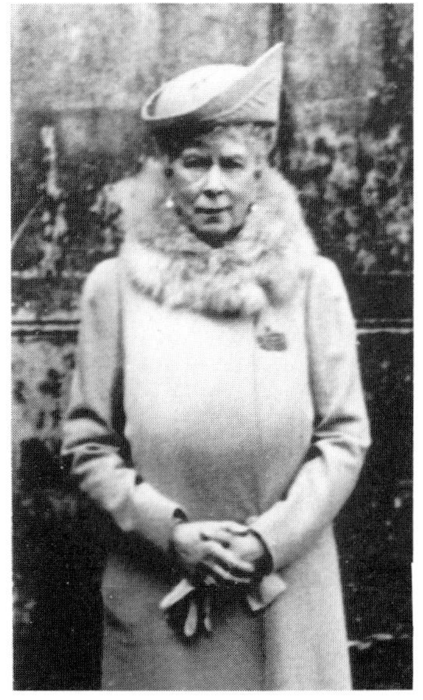
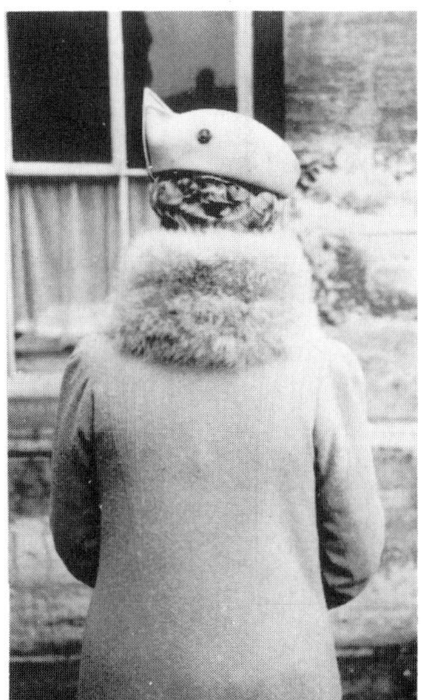

'FORE' AND 'AFT'. QUEEN MARY WEARING THE
BADGE OF THE GLOUCESTER REGIMENT

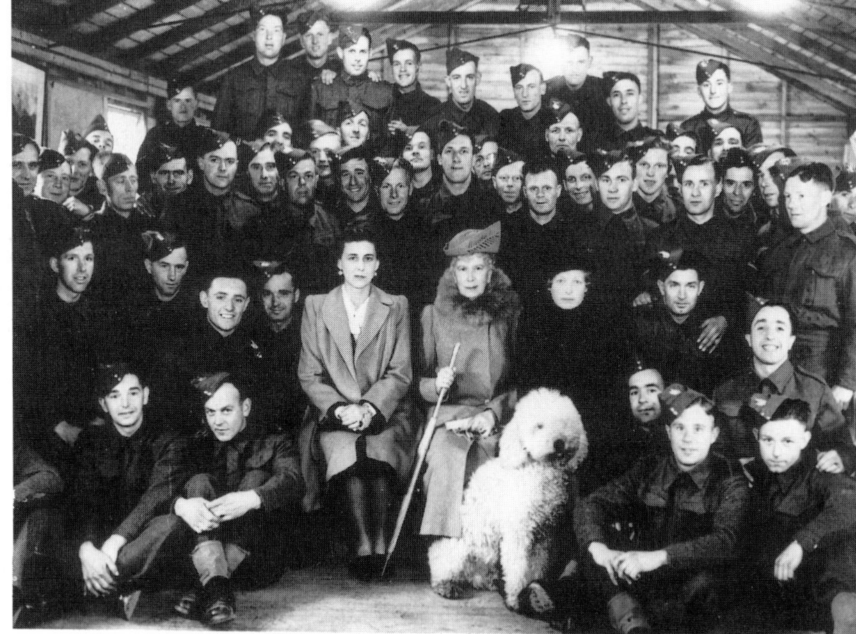

QUEEN MARY AND HER
NIECE MARY, DUCHESS OF
BEAUFORT (RIGHT), AND
THE DUCHESS OF KENT
WITH SOLDIERS OF THE
GLOUCESTERSHIRE
REGIMENT IN THE
DUCHESS OF BEAUFORT'S
HUT AT THE YMCA
CANTEEN AT BADMINTON
IN 1941

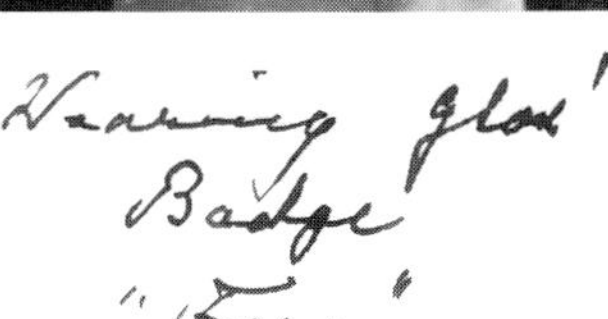

QUEEN MARY AND HER
FOUR PERSONAL DISPATCH
RIDERS, JOHN SALMON,
ARTHUR MELLOR, RONALD
NUNN AND TED HALLETT,
BADMINTON, APRIL 1941

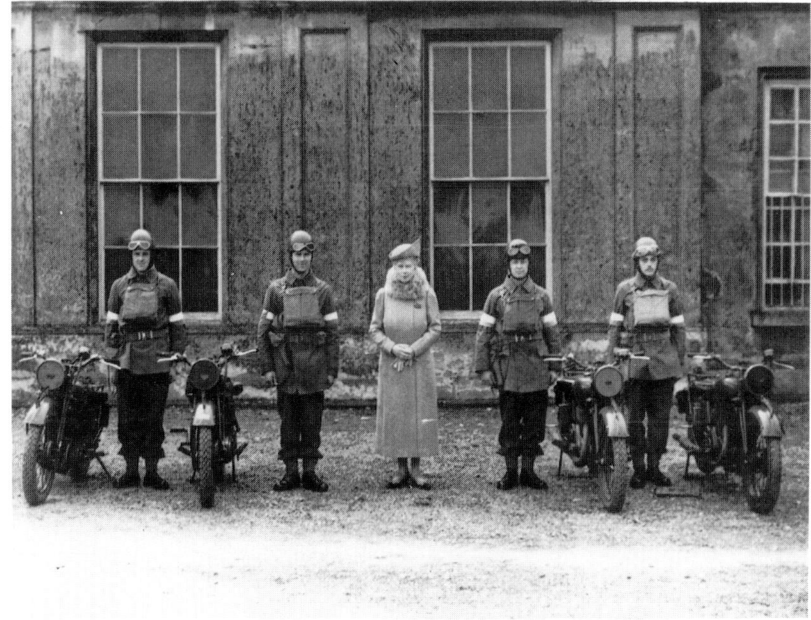

QUEEN MARY WITH STAFF AND
CHILDREN AT THE WAIFS AND
STRAYS HOME FOR BOMBED-OUT
CHILDREN AT BATHEASTON,
AUGUST 1941

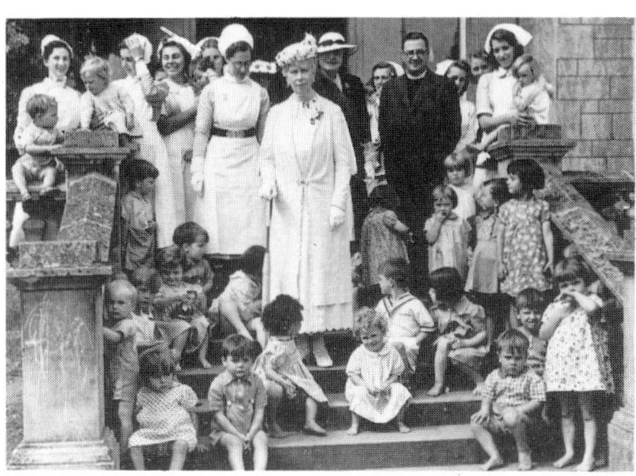

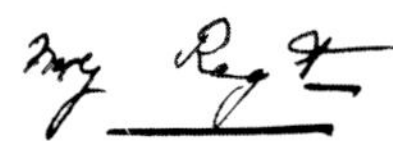

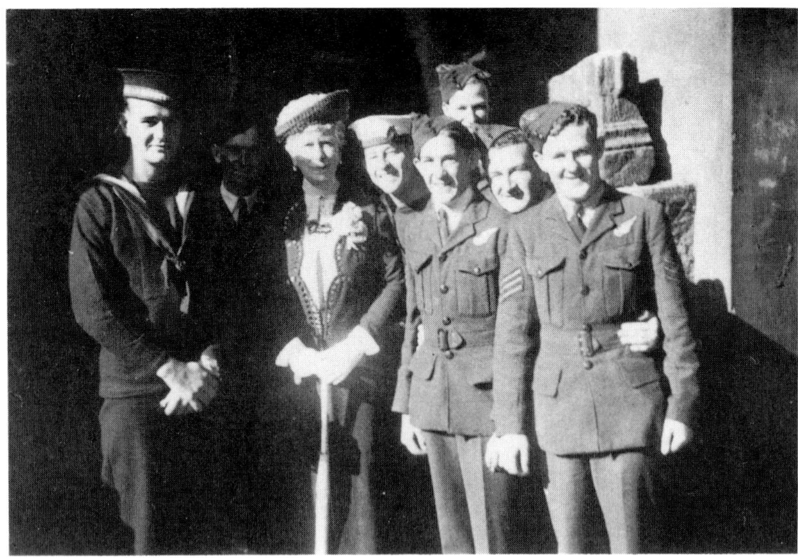

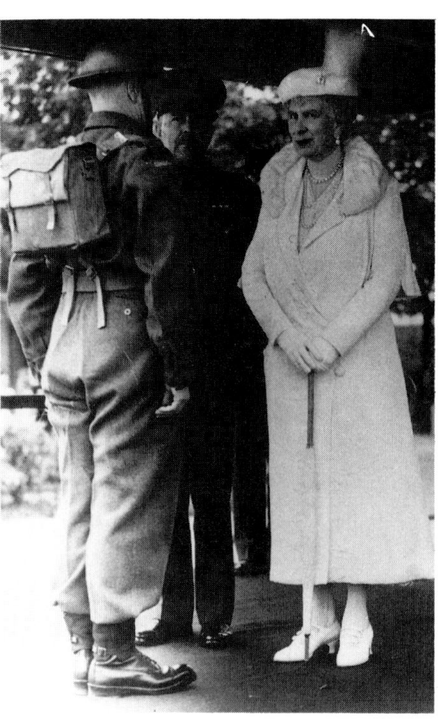

(*ABOVE*) DURING AN IMPROMPTU VISIT TO BATH IN SEPTEMBER 1941, QUEEN MARY ENCOUNTERED A GROUP OF AUSTRALIAN NAVAL AND AIR FORCE PERSONNEL WHO ASKED HER TO POSE WITH THEM. (*RIGHT*) WITH A 'TWINKLE IN HER EYE' QUEEN MARY VISITS HER REGIMENT, THE QUEEN'S OWN RIFLES OF CANADA, AT ALDERSHOT, 10 SEPTEMBER 1941

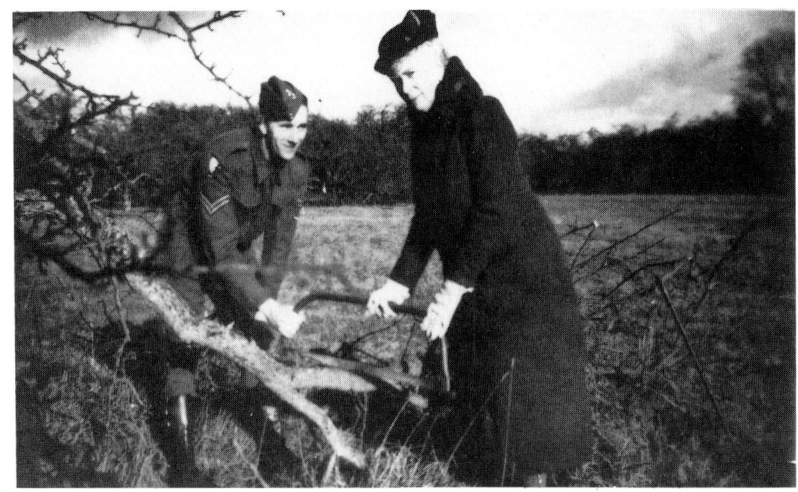

QUEEN MARY AND ARTHUR MELLOR 'WOODING'

QUEEN MARY AND THE DUCHESS OF BEAUFORT VISITING THE HINNEGAR CAMP FOR BOMBED-OUT WOMEN AND CHILDREN, JULY 1941

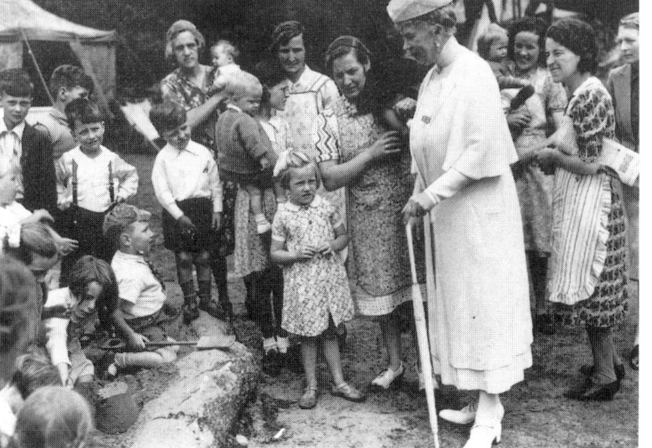

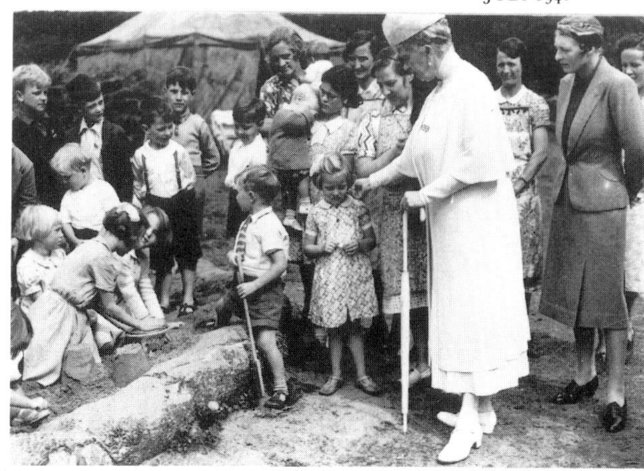

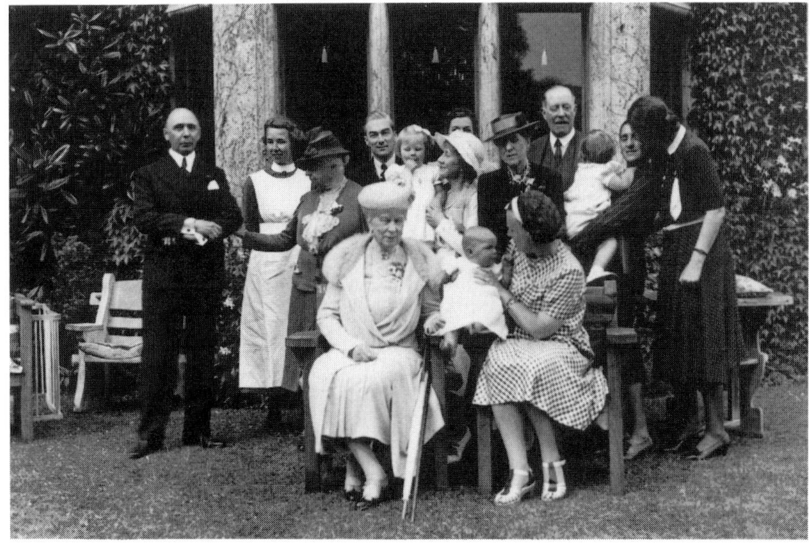

Lydney Pk.
Juliana + her children

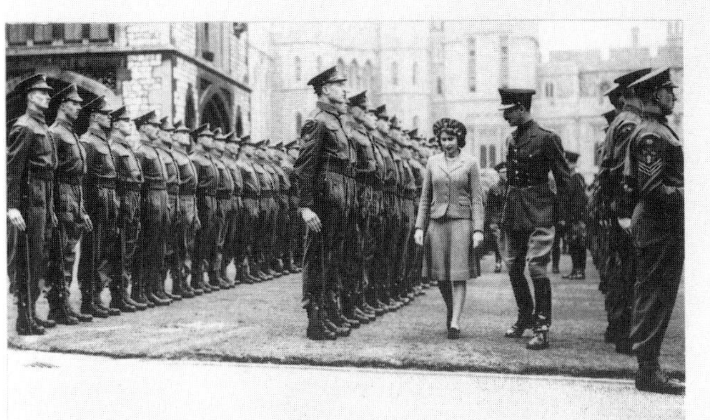

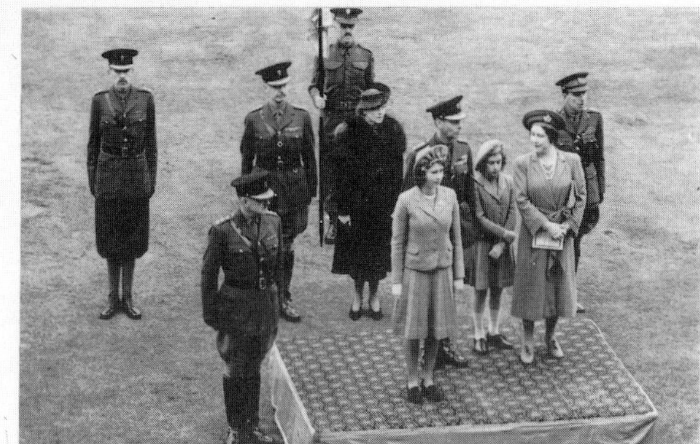

Lilibet inspecting Grenadier Guards as Colonel —   Windsor Castle   21. April

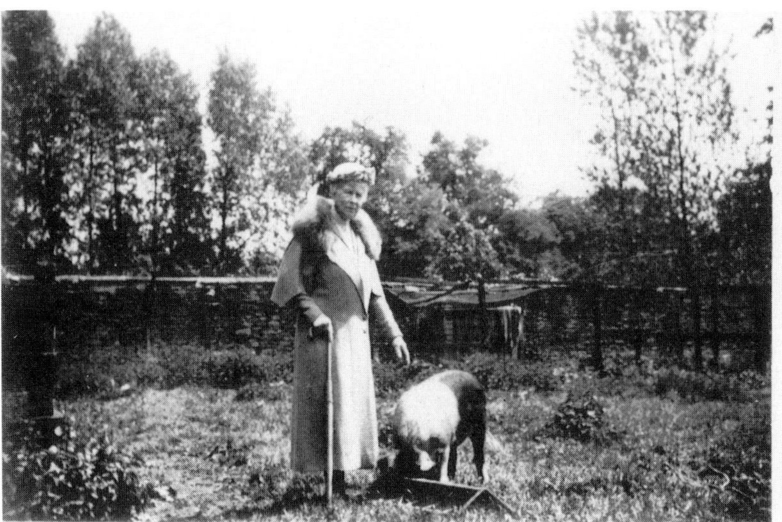

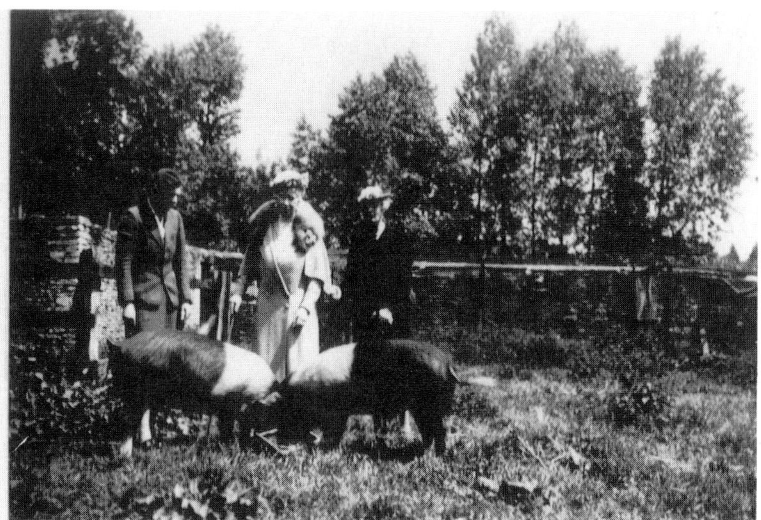

Me + my pig — Badminton
June

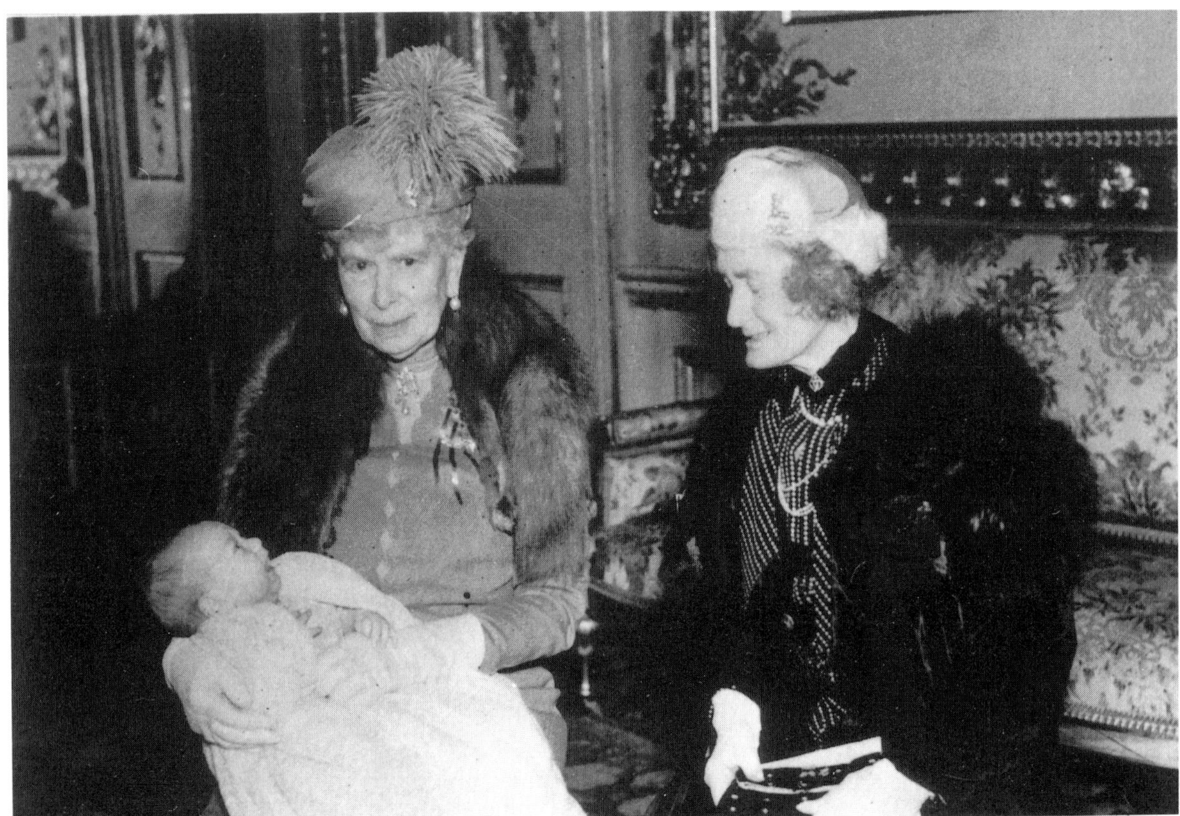

THE CHRISTENING OF PRINCE WILLIAM OF GLOUCESTER AT WINDSOR ON 22 FEBRUARY 1942. WITH QUEEN MARY (*ABOVE*) IS MARGARET, DUCHESS OF BUCCLEUCH (THE DUCHESS OF GLOUCESTER'S MOTHER), AND WITH OTHER MEMBERS OF THE ROYAL FAMILY (*BELOW*) ARE THE DUCHESS OF GLOUCESTER'S BROTHER AND SISTER-IN-LAW, THE YOUNG DUKE AND DUCHESS OF BUCCLEUCH

Self & Margaret Buccleuch the two grandmothers

Christening of Harry & Alice's boy William Henry Andrew Frederick 22. Feb: 1942

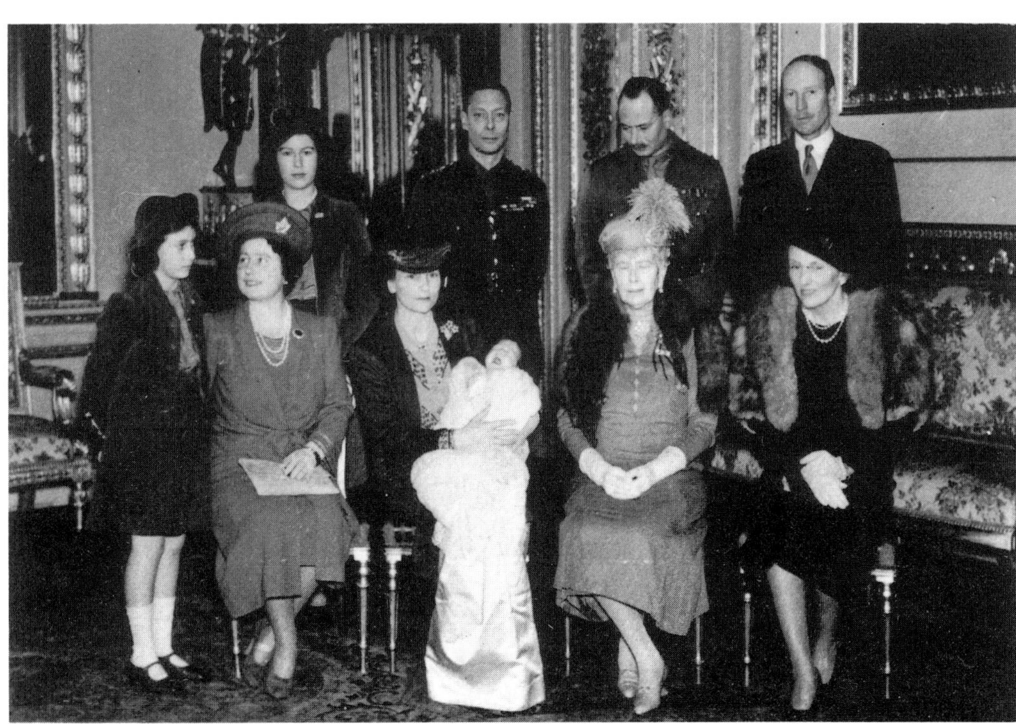

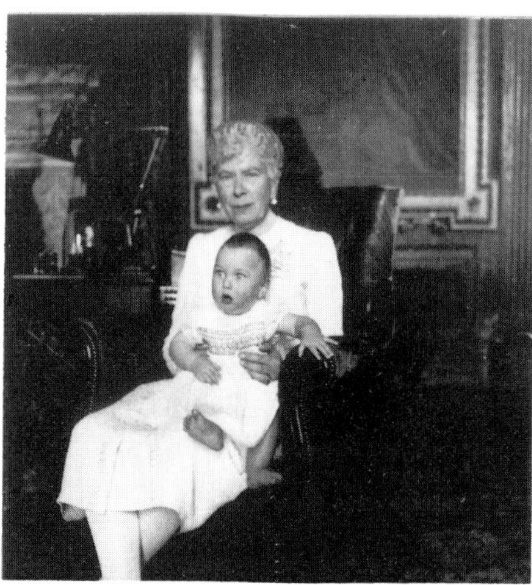

William on my knee. Badminton

Windsor Christening

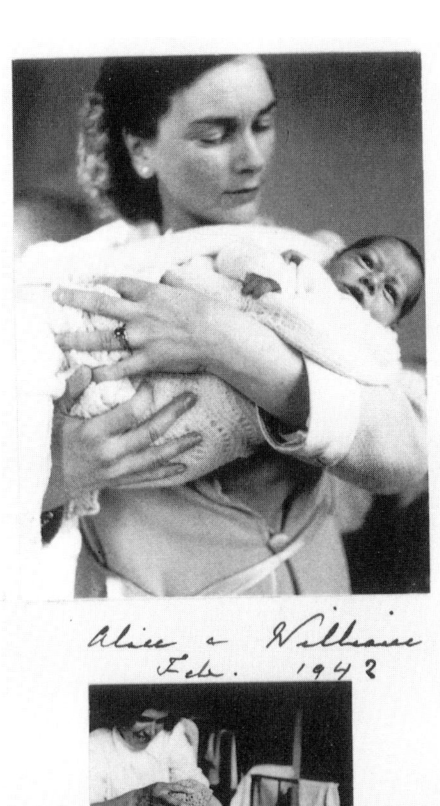

Alice & William
Feb. 1942

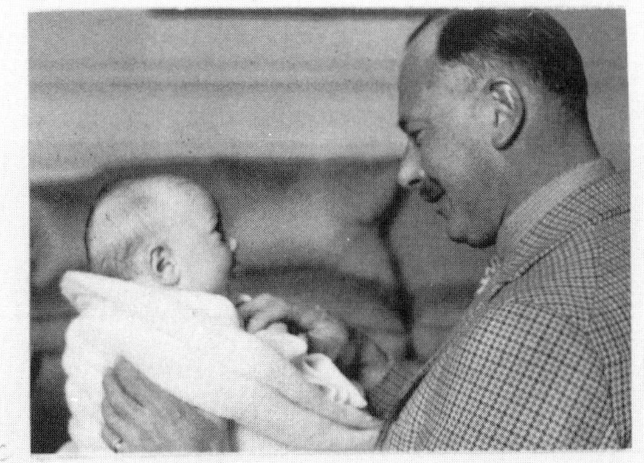

William & Harry
March 1942

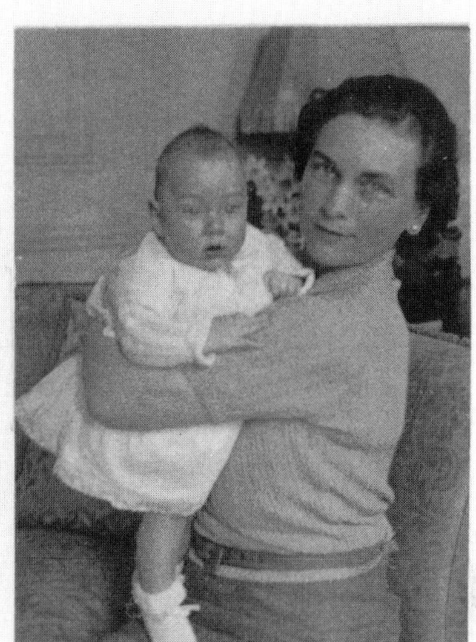

William & Alice
July 1942

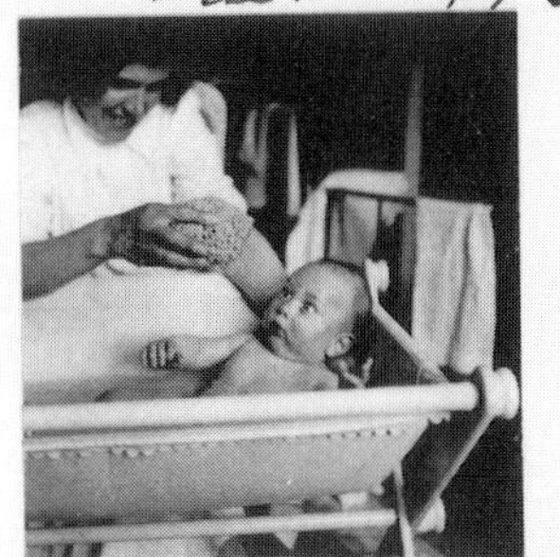

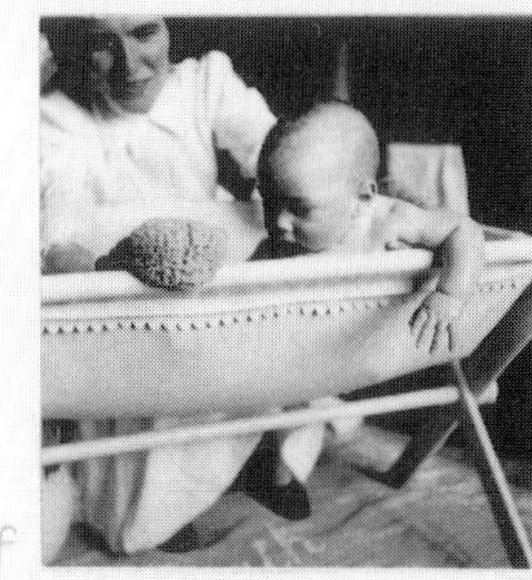

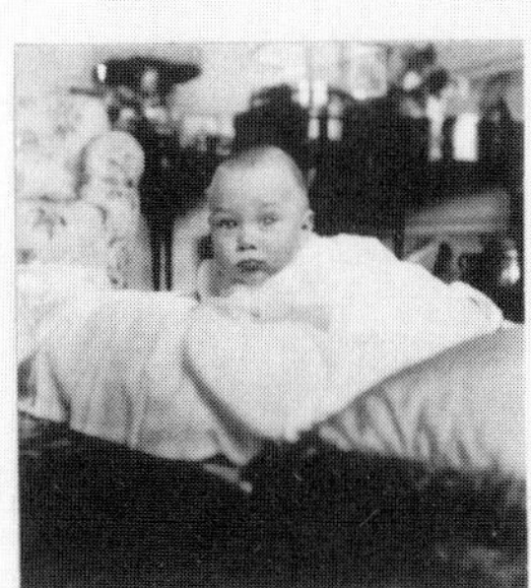

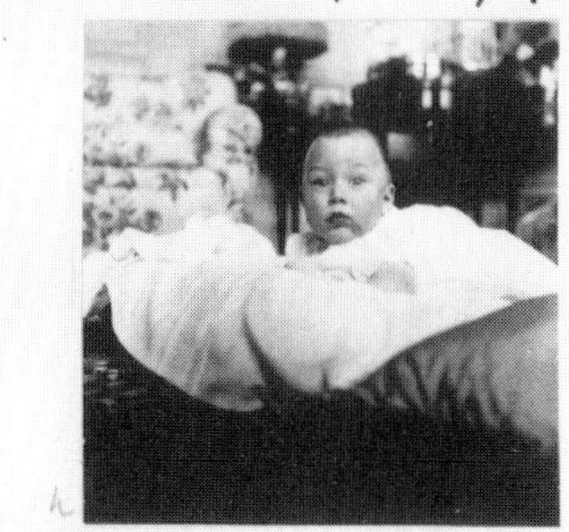

William — Badminton   July 1942

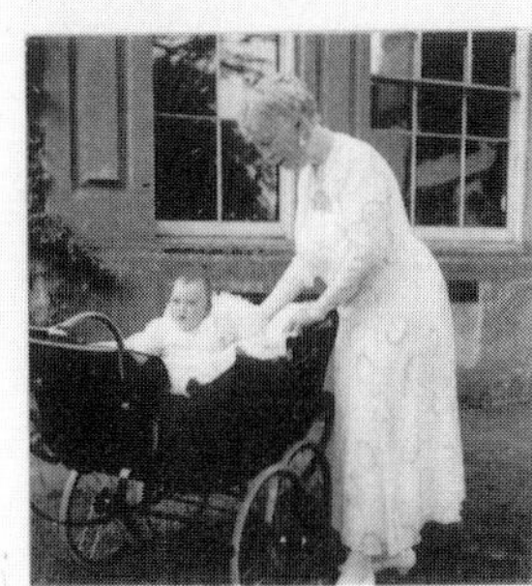

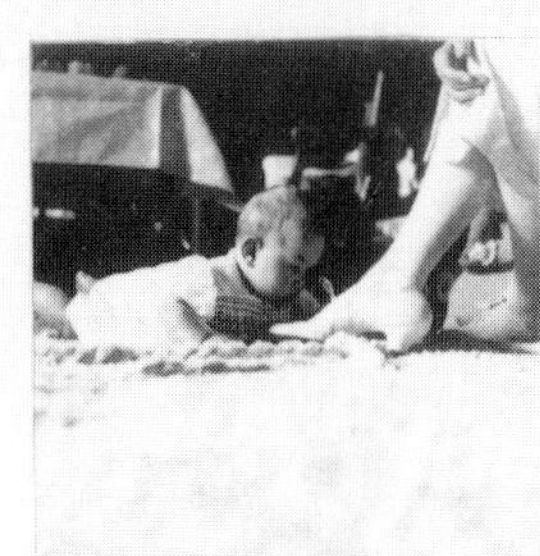

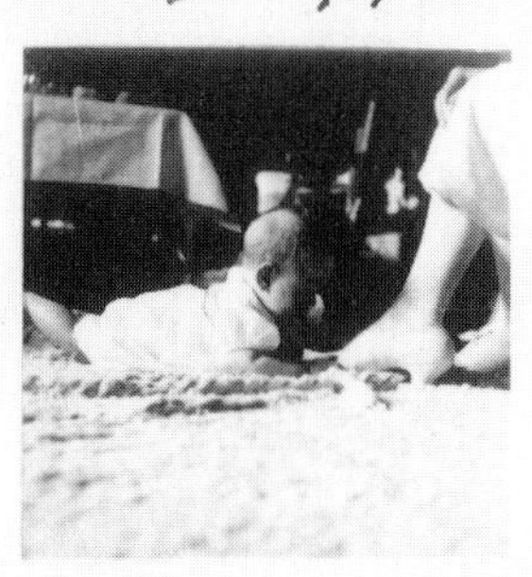

William playing with my shoes!

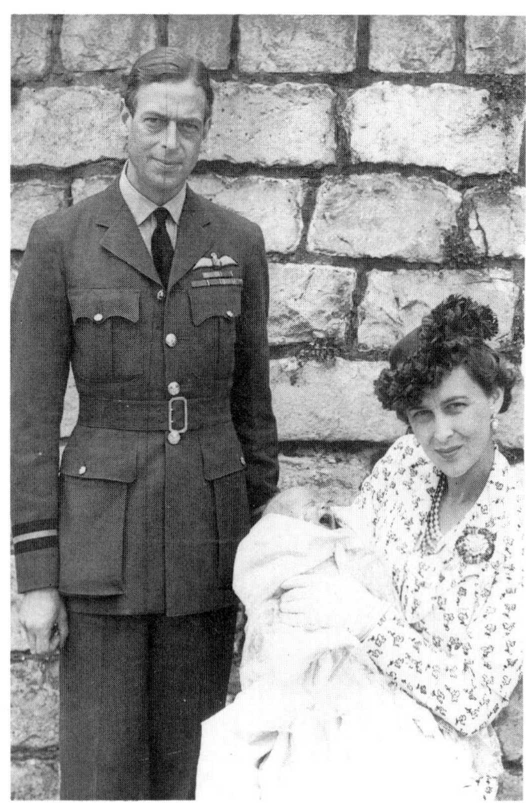

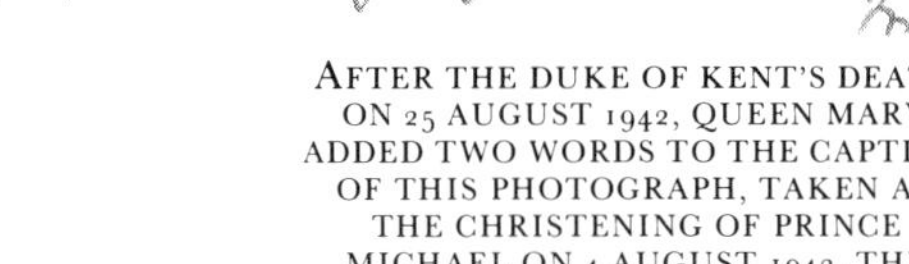

AFTER THE DUKE OF KENT'S DEATH
ON 25 AUGUST 1942, QUEEN MARY
ADDED TWO WORDS TO THE CAPTION
OF THIS PHOTOGRAPH, TAKEN AT
THE CHRISTENING OF PRINCE
MICHAEL ON 4 AUGUST 1942. THE
DUKE REMAINS IDENTIFIED FOR
POSTERITY AS 'MY PRECIOUS
GEORGIE'

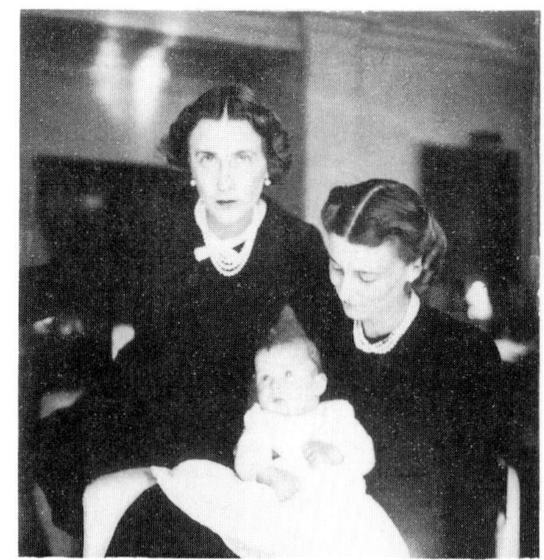

THE WIDOWED DUCHESS OF KENT
WITH HER YOUNGEST CHILD PRINCE
MICHAEL AND HER SISTER OLGA,
PRINCESS PAUL OF YUGOSLAVIA, AT
COPPINS, NOVEMBER 1942

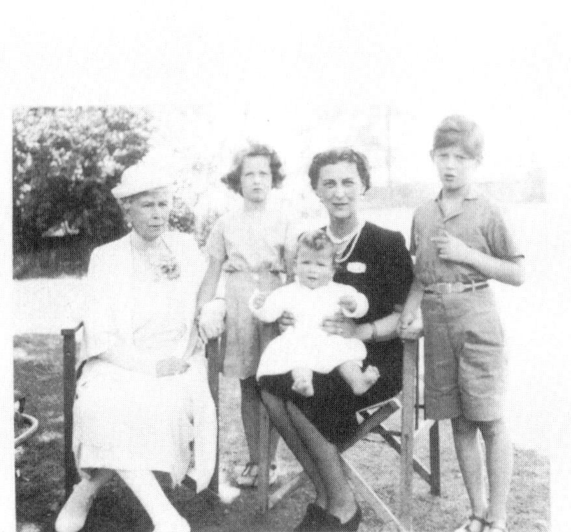

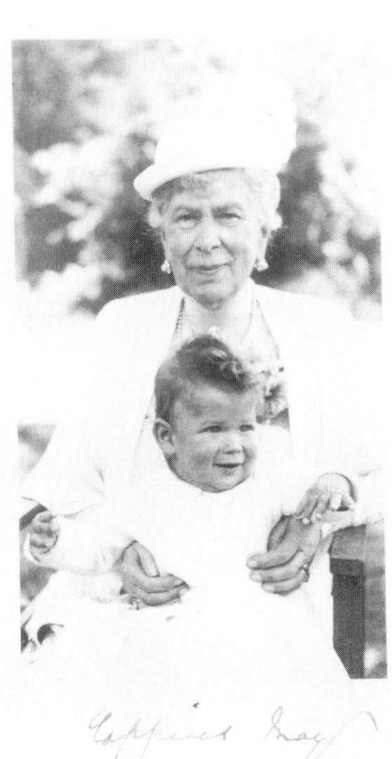

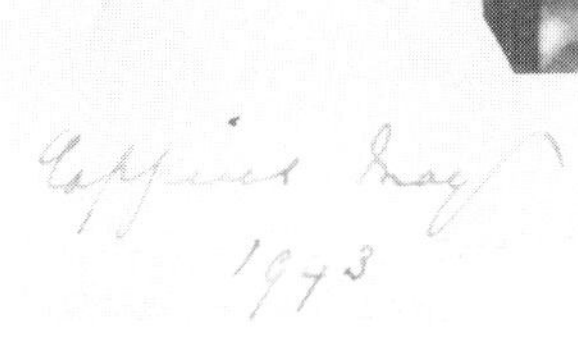

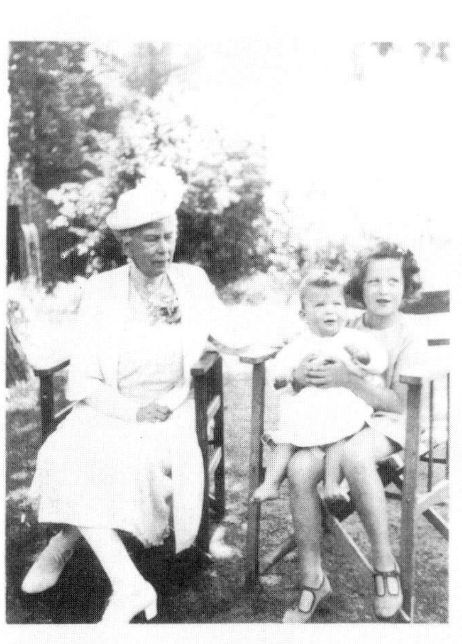

QUEEN MARY, THE DUCHESS OF KENT, EDDIE, THE
DUKE OF KENT, PRINCESS ALEXANDRA AND
PRINCE MICHAEL AT COPPINS IN MAY 1943

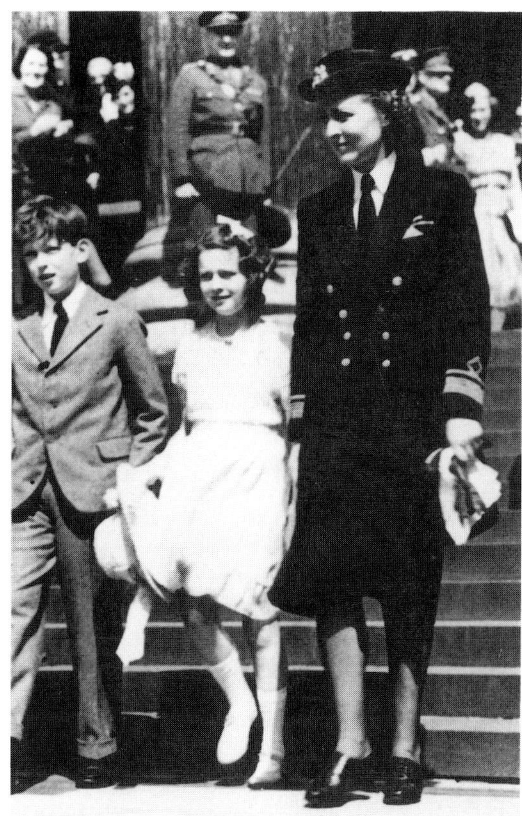

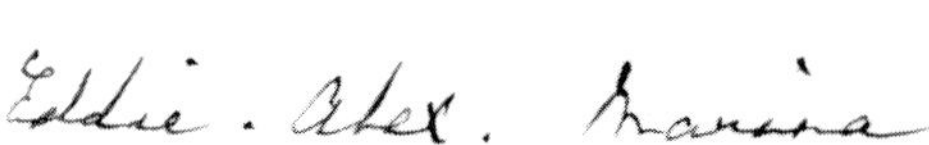

Eddie . Alex . Marina

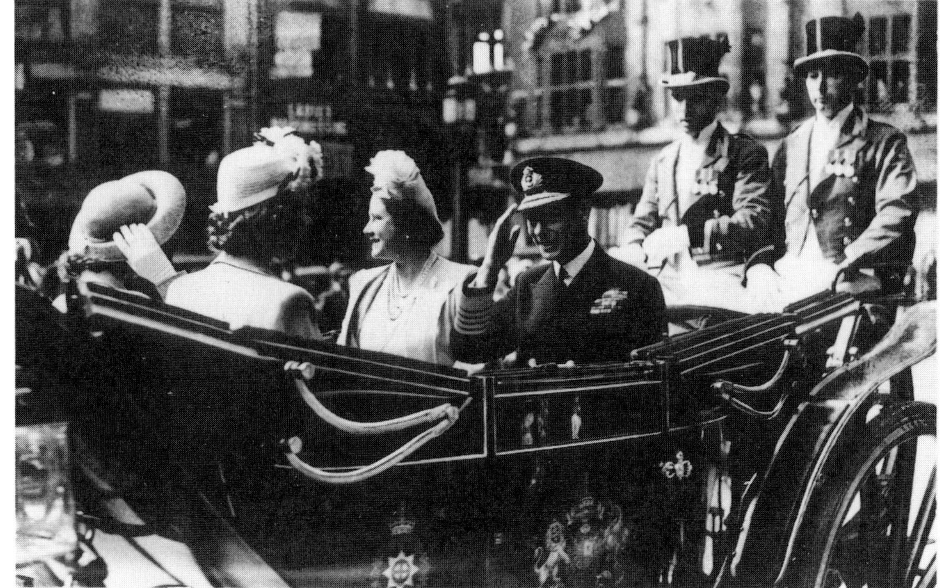

Thanksgiving Service
St Paul's Cathedral
May 13th 1945

THE ROYAL FAMILY
ATTENDING A
THANKSGIVING SERVICE
FOR THE END OF THE WAR
AT ST PAUL'S CATHEDRAL
ON 13 MAY 1945

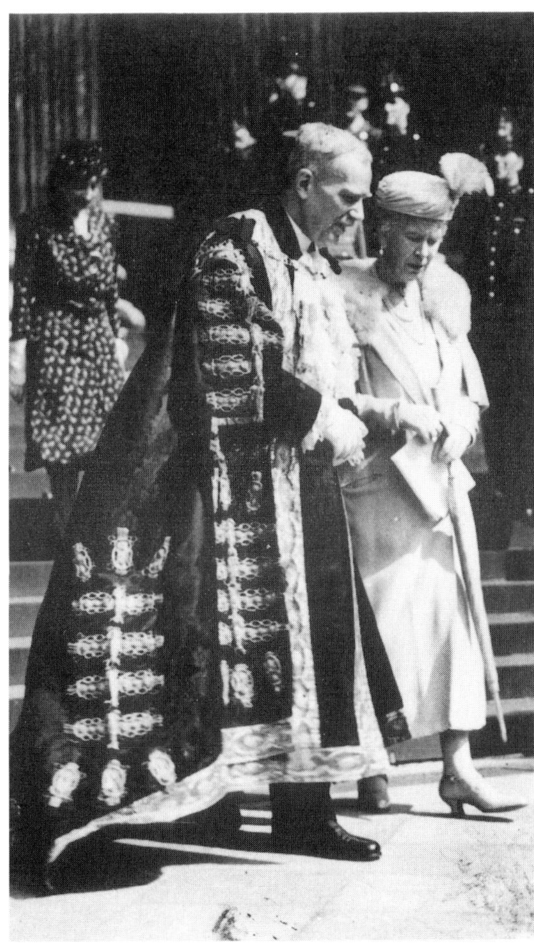

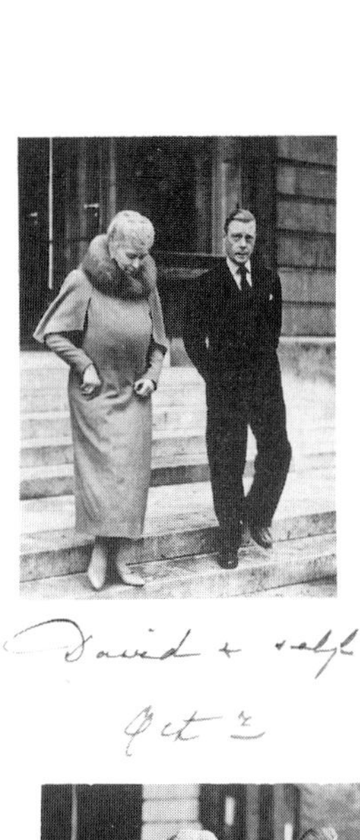

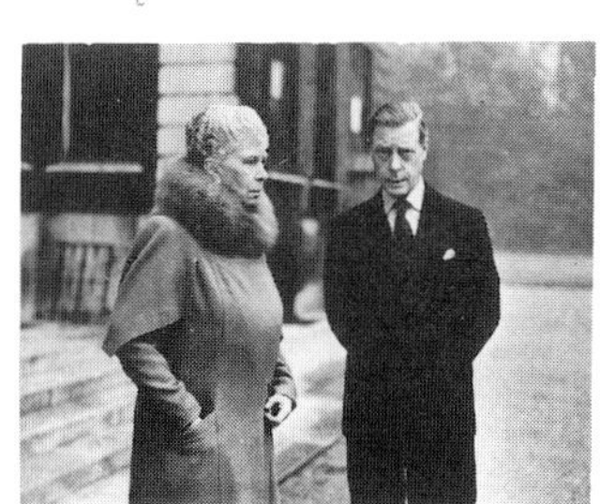

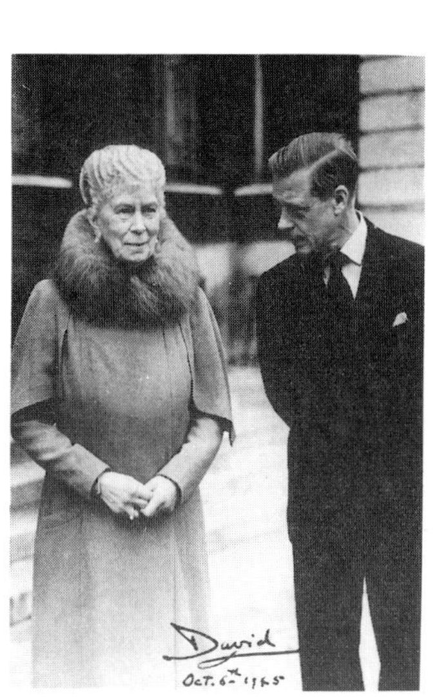

QUEEN MARY WITH THE
DUKE OF WINDSOR IN THE
GARDEN OF
MARLBOROUGH HOUSE,
6 OCTOBER 1945. THIS WAS
THE FIRST MEETING
BETWEEN MOTHER AND
SON SINCE THE
ABDICATION

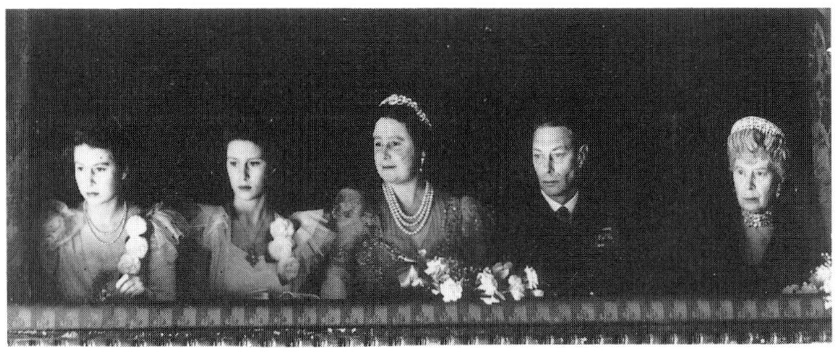

THE REOPENING OF THE ROYAL OPERA HOUSE AFTER THE SECOND WORLD WAR. THE KING AND QUEEN, ACCOMPANIED BY QUEEN MARY AND THE PRINCESSES ELIZABETH AND MARGARET, ATTEND A GALA PERFORMANCE OF *THE SLEEPING BEAUTY*, FEBRUARY 1946

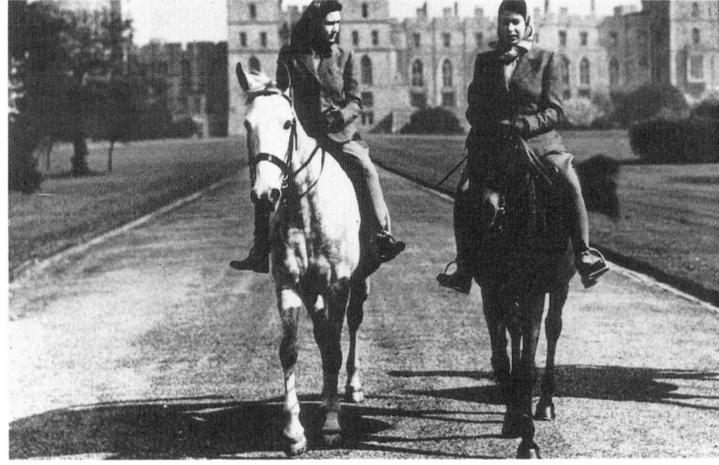

PRINCESS ELIZABETH AND PRINCESS MARGARET RIDING ON THE LONG WALK AT WINDSOR CASTLE IN APRIL 1946

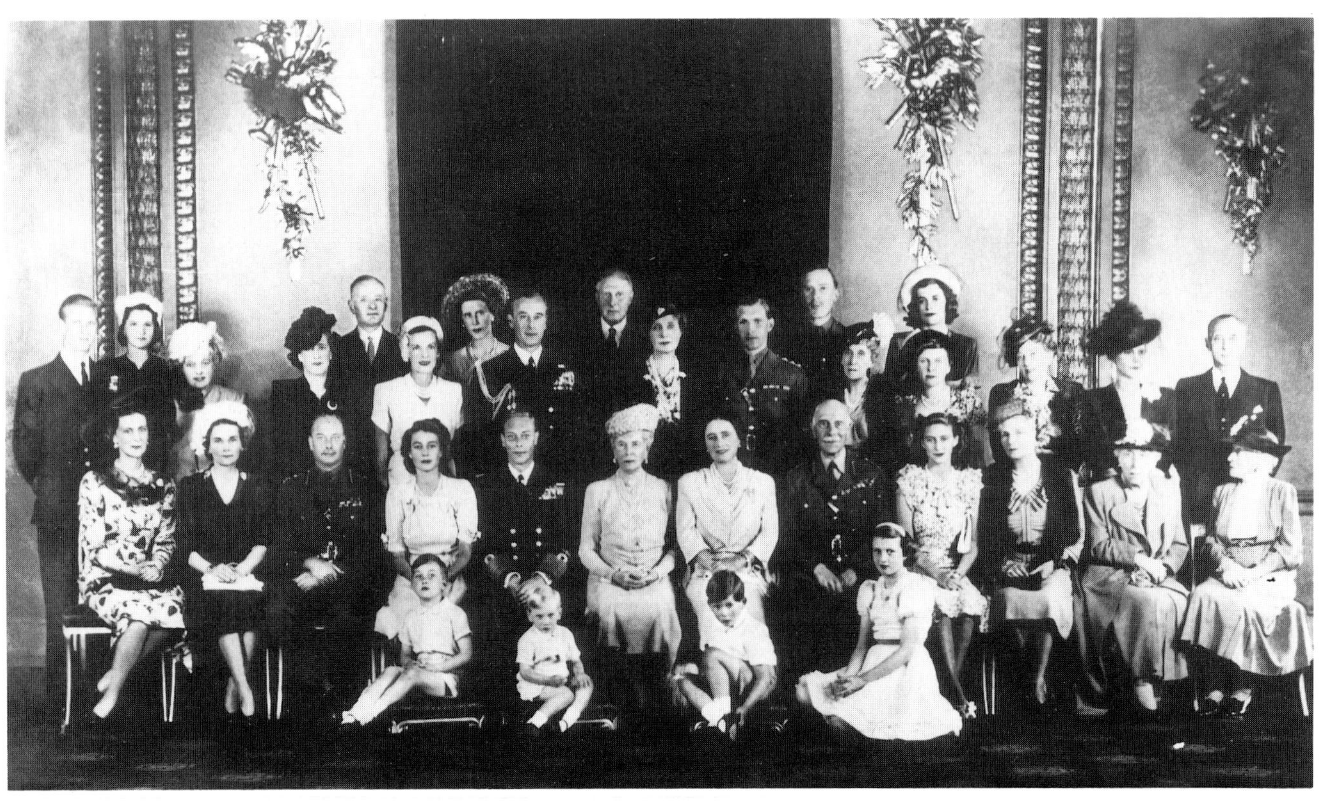

QUEEN MARY'S 80TH BIRTHDAY. A FORMAL FAMILY PORTRAIT TAKEN IN THE THRONE ROOM AT BUCKINGHAM PALACE, 26 MAY 1947

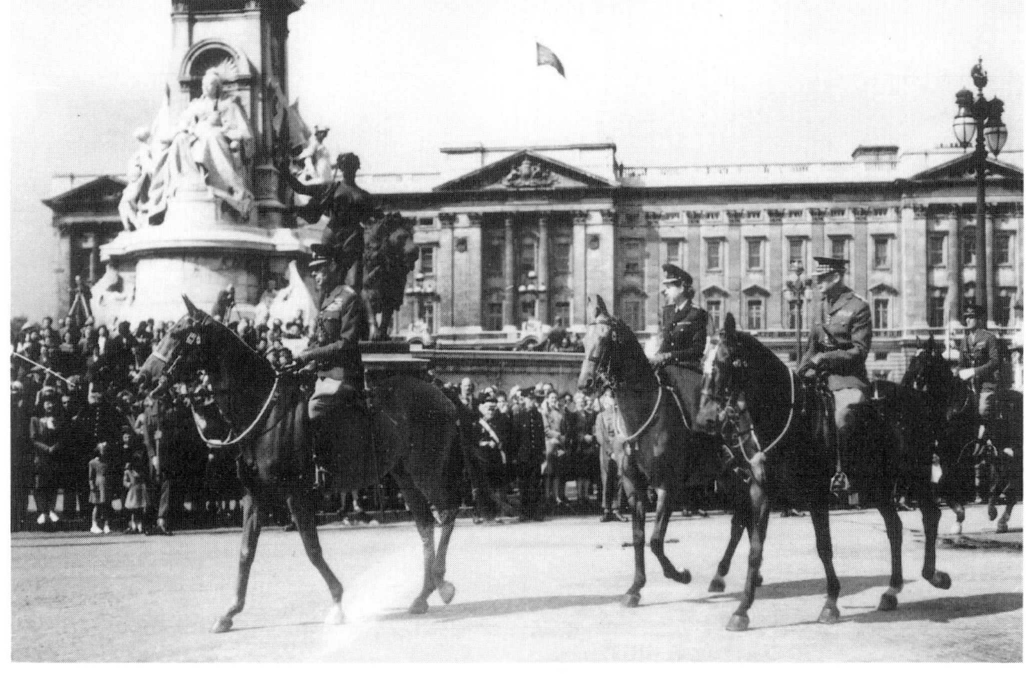

PRINCESS ELIZABETH ACCOMPANIES THE KING TO THE SOVEREIGN'S BIRTHDAY PARADE (TROOPING THE COLOUR), 12 JUNE 1947

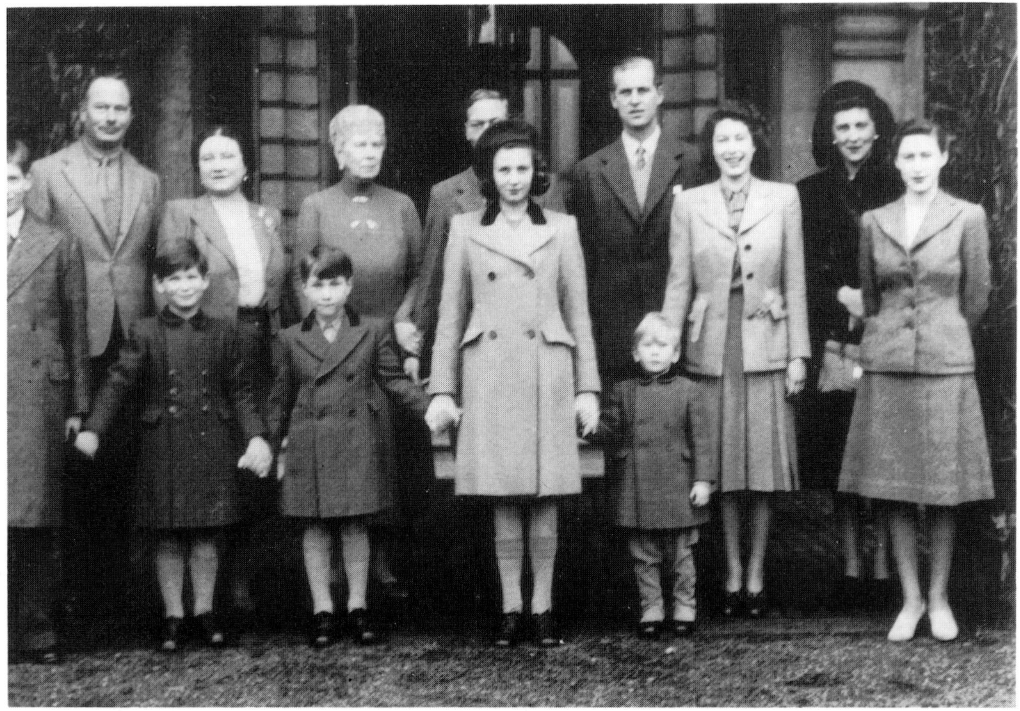

AN INFORMAL ROYAL GROUP AT SANDRINGHAM IN 1948. *BACK ROW:* THE DUKE OF GLOUCESTER, QUEEN ELIZABETH, QUEEN MARY, KING GEORGE VI, THE DUKE OF EDINBURGH, PRINCESS ELIZABETH, THE DUCHESS OF KENT AND PRINCESS MARGARET. *FRONT ROW:* EDDIE, DUKE OF KENT, PRINCE MICHAEL OF KENT, PRINCE WILLIAM OF GLOUCESTER, PRINCESS ALEXANDRA OF KENT, AND PRINCE RICHARD OF GLOUCESTER

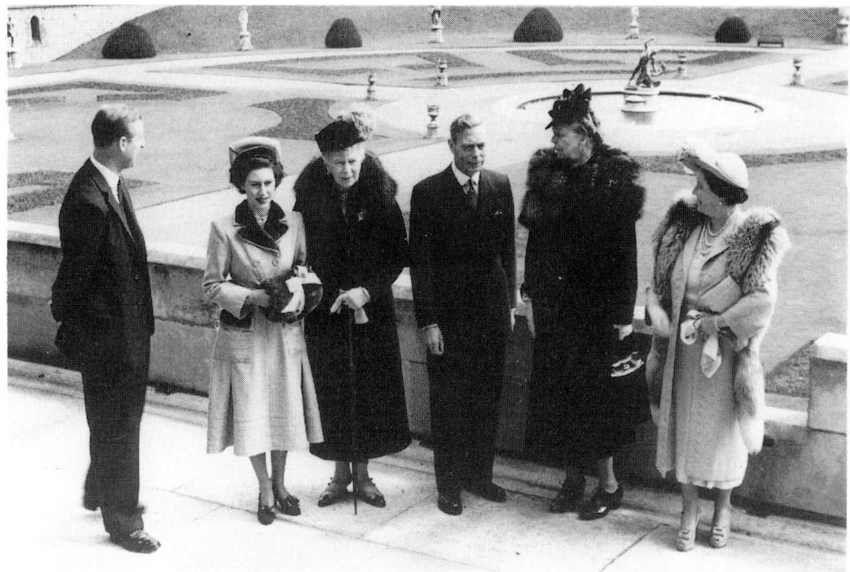

MRS ELEANOR ROOSEVELT AT WINDSOR CASTLE WITH KING GEORGE VI AND QUEEN ELIZABETH, QUEEN MARY AND PRINCESS MARGARET, 4 APRIL 1948

(*OVERLEAF*) THE WEDDING OF PRINCESS ELIZABETH AND THE DUKE OF EDINBURGH WAS CELEBRATED AT WESTMINSTER ABBEY ON 20 NOVEMBER 1947

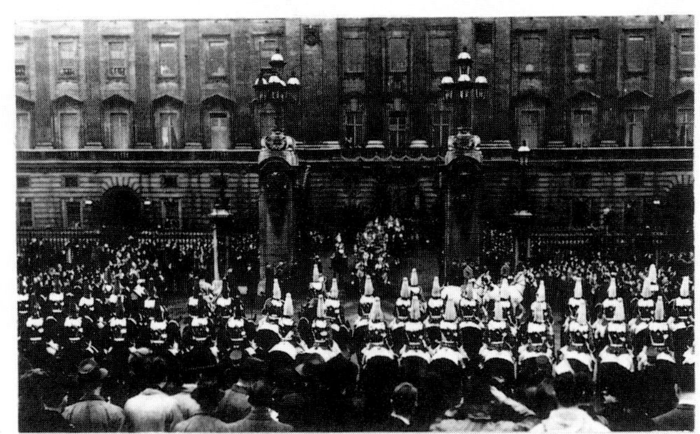
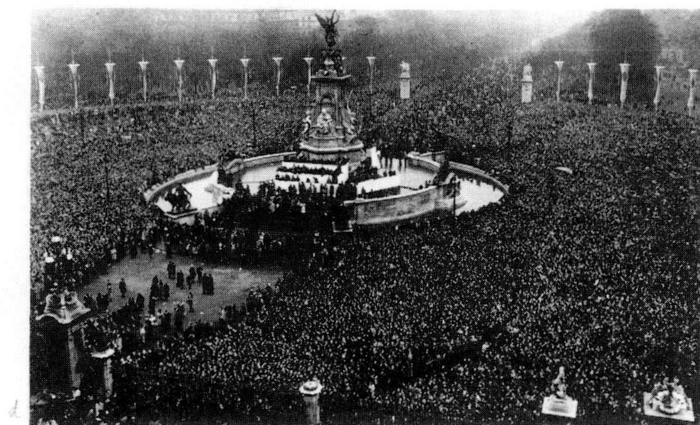

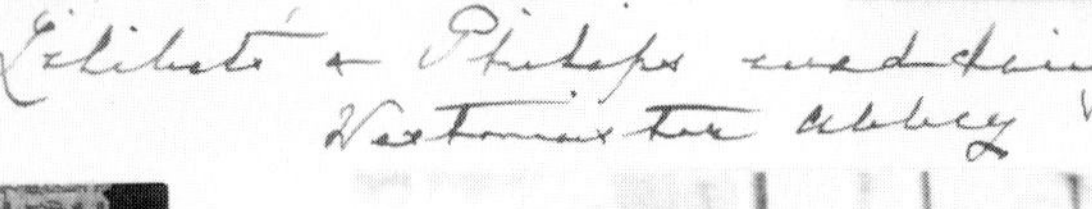
Lilibet & Philip's wedding
Westminster Abbey   Novr 20th 1947

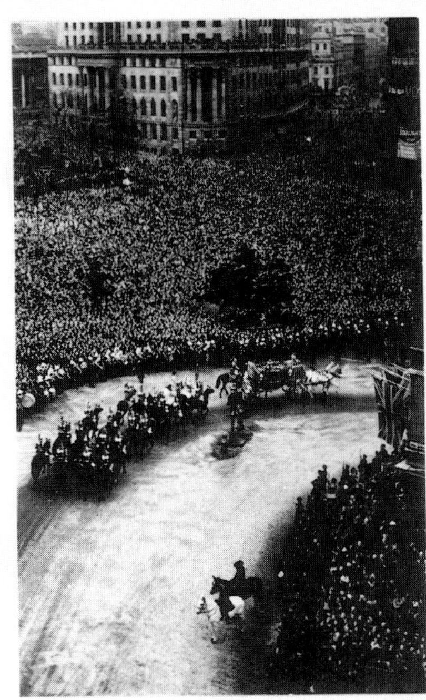
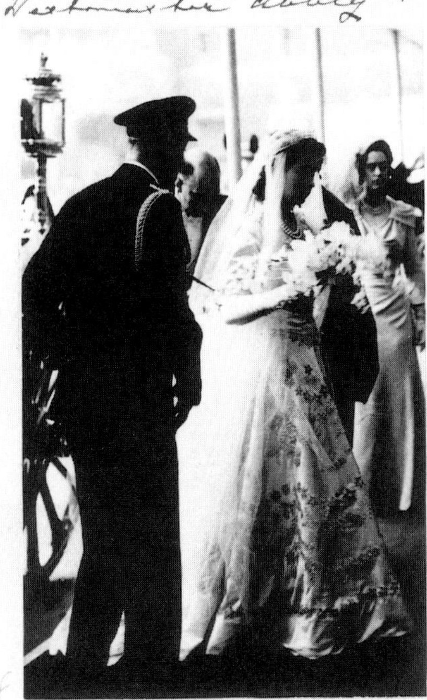
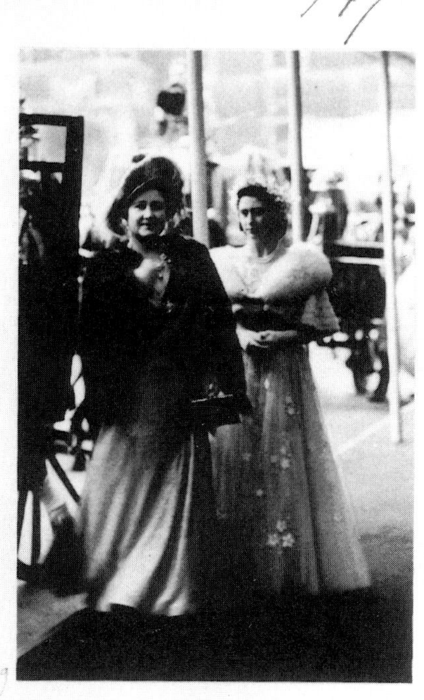

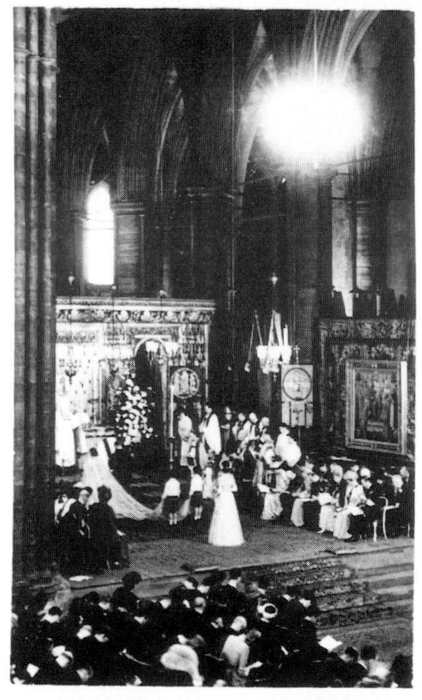
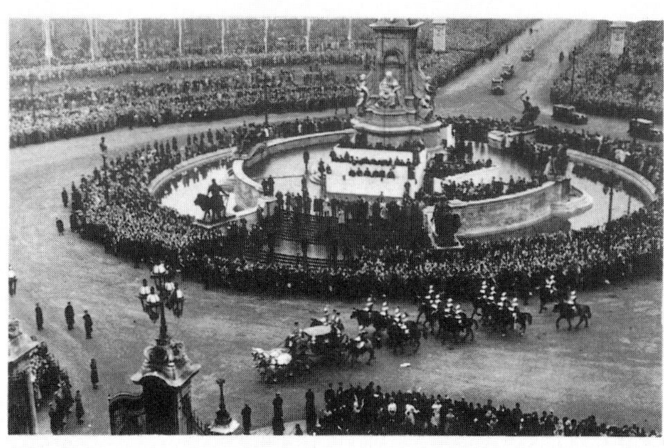
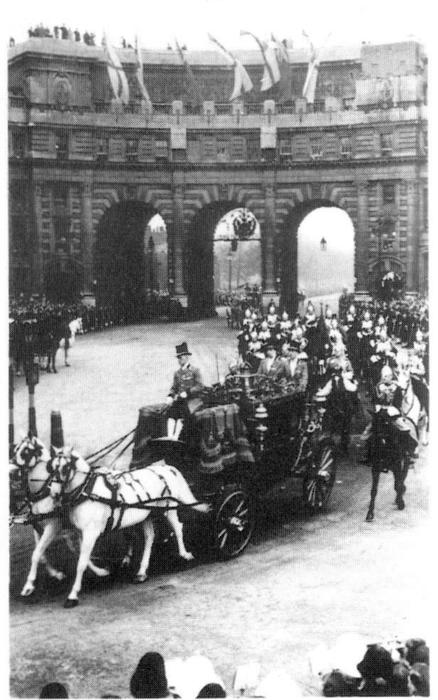

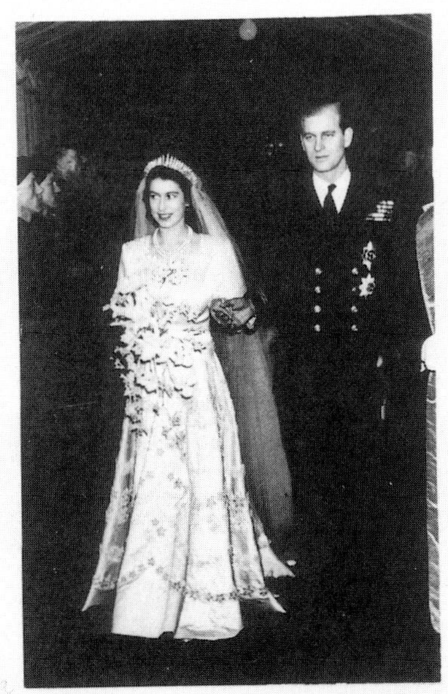
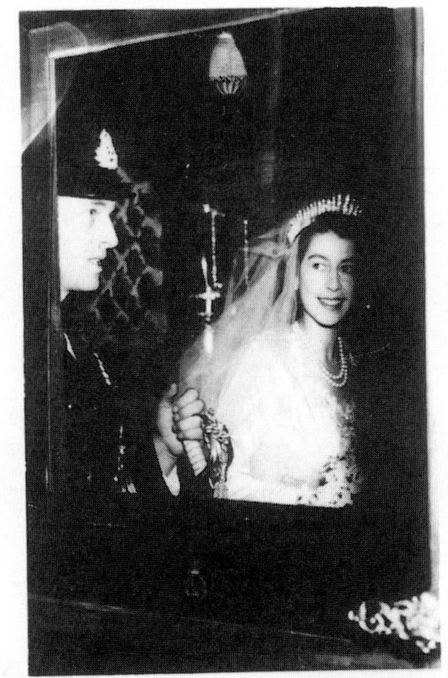
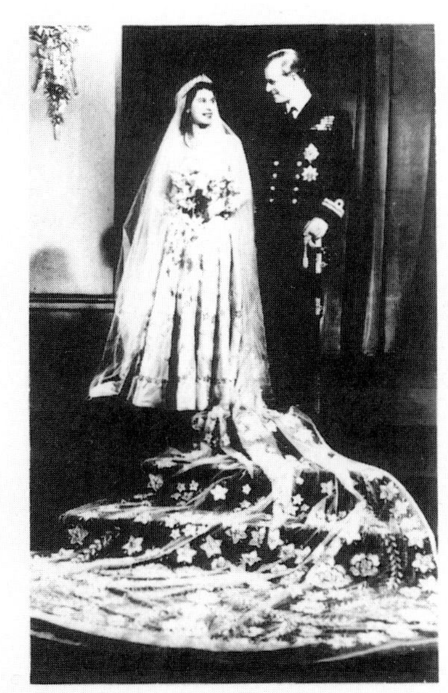

Wedding

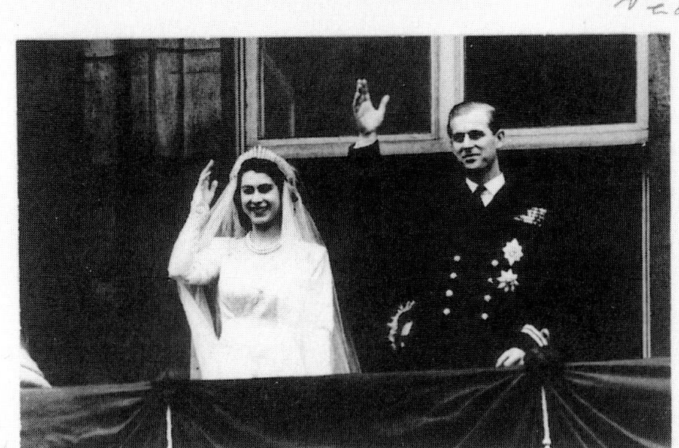
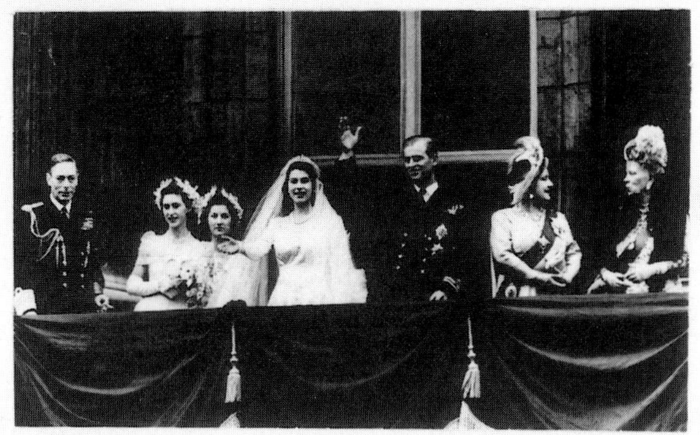
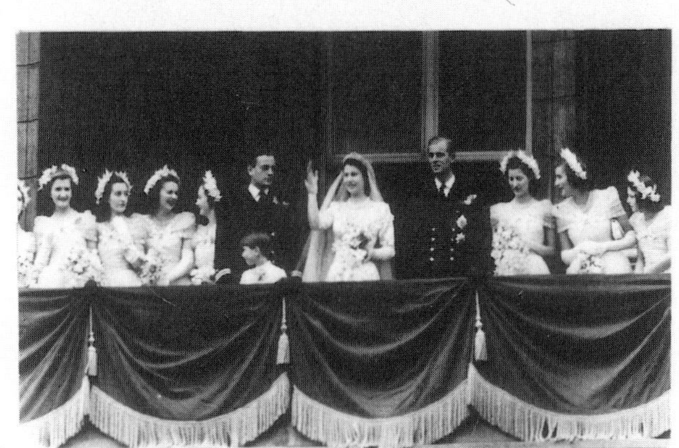
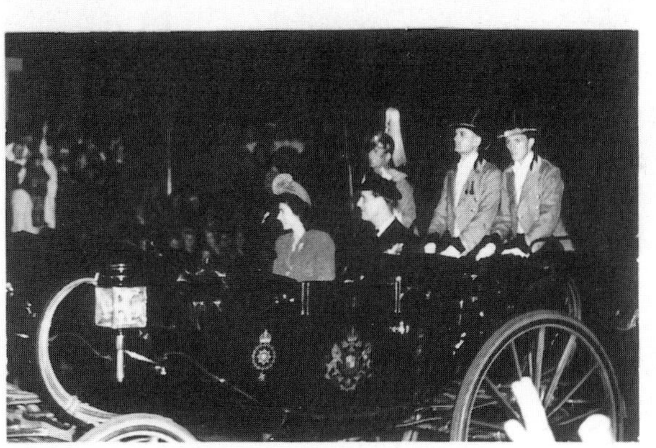
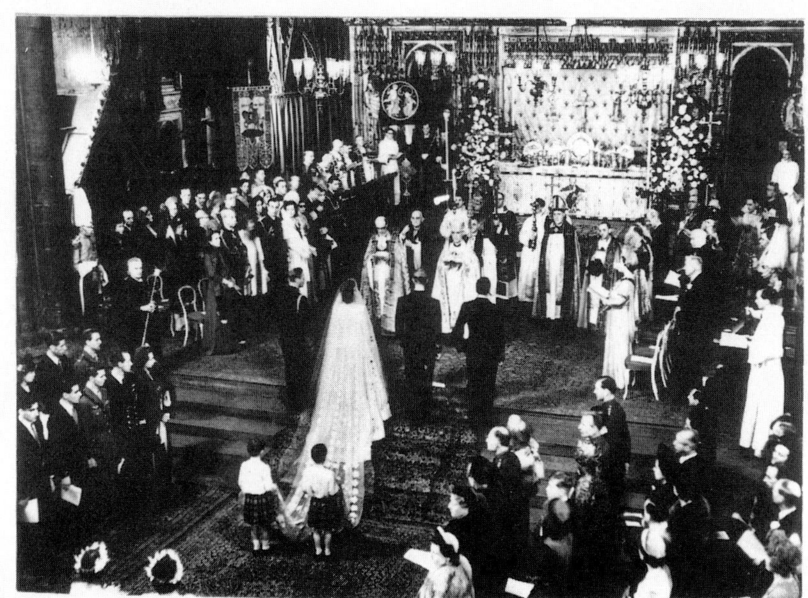

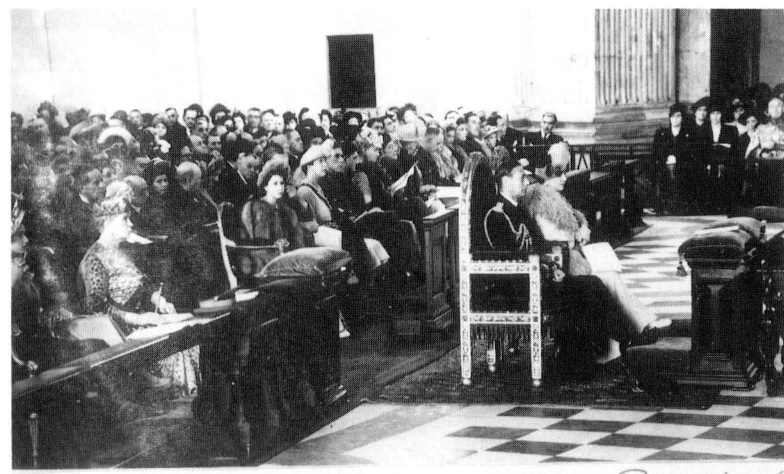

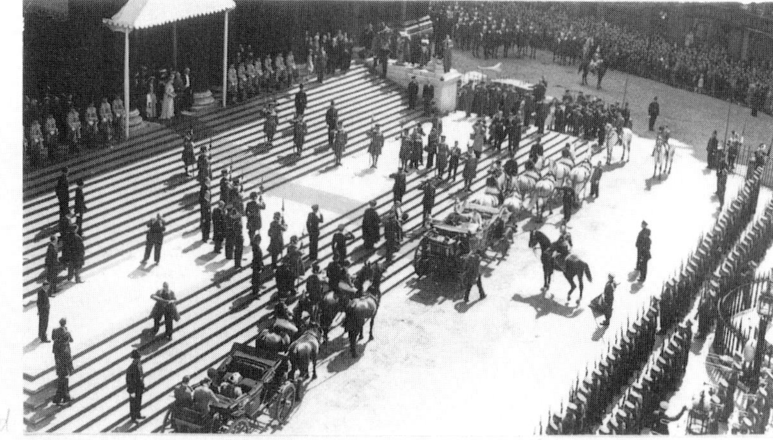

St Paul's Cathedral
Bertie & E's silver wedding day
April 26th
1948

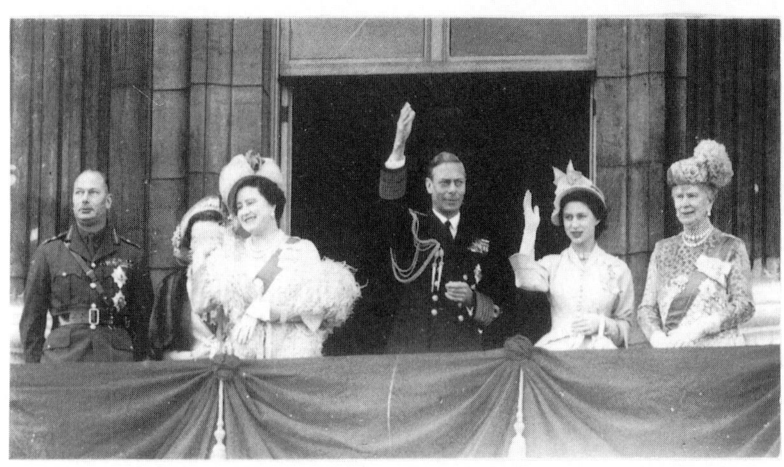

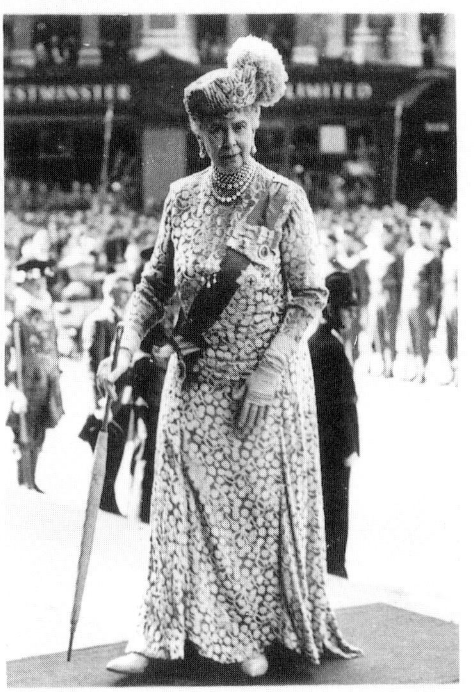

THE SILVER WEDDING ANNIVERSARY OF THE KING
AND QUEEN, A CELEBRATION MARKED BY A
SERVICE OF THANKSGIVING AT ST PAUL'S
CATHEDRAL ON 26 APRIL 1948

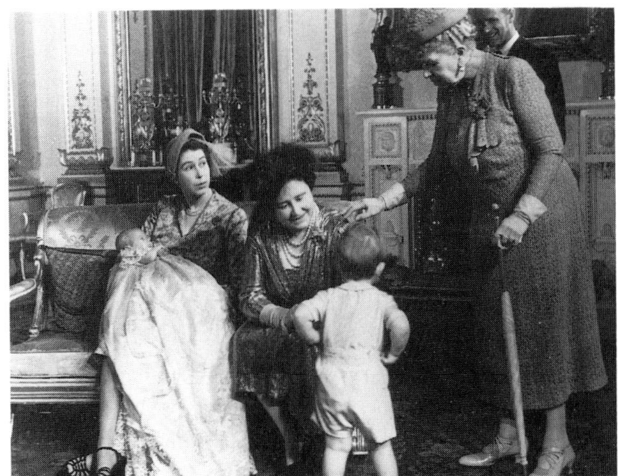

PRINCESS ANNE WAS BORN ON 15 AUGUST
1950 AND CHRISTENED ON 21 OCTOBER.
PRINCE CHARLES SHOWS KEEN INTEREST
IN HIS SISTER

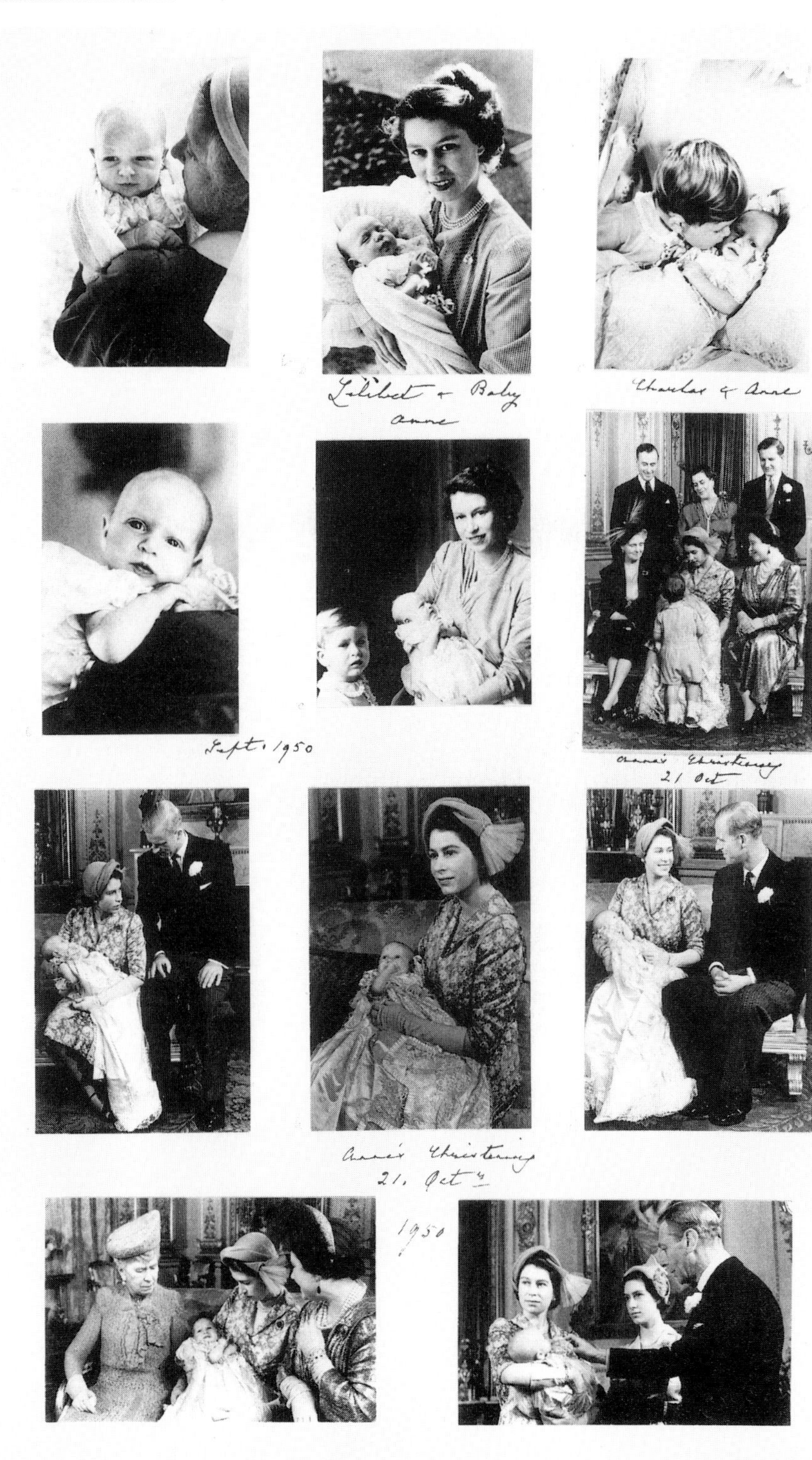

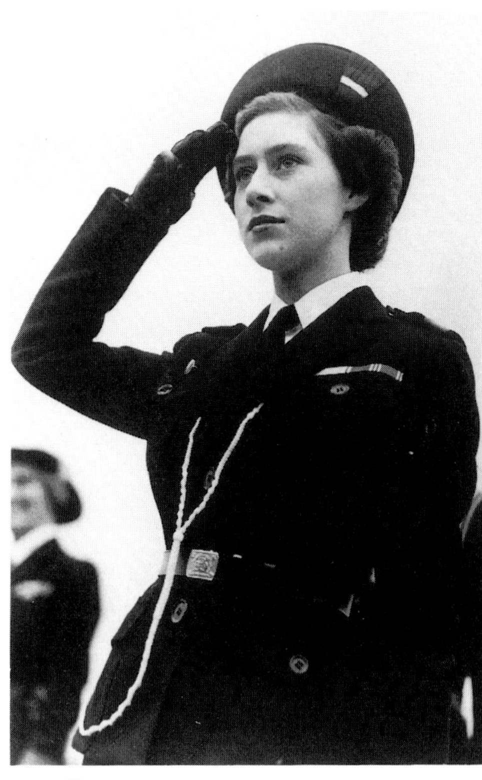

PRINCESS MARGARET AS COMMODORE
OF THE SEA RANGERS IN OCTOBER 1950

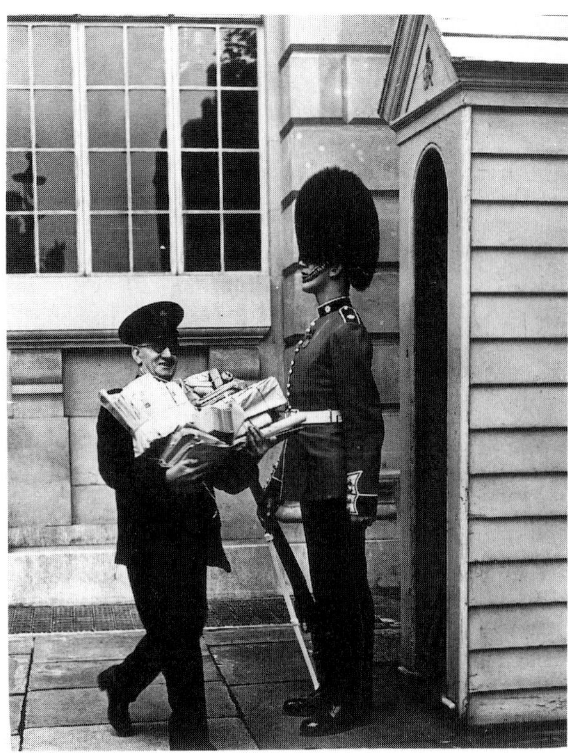

A POSTMAN PASSING THE SENTRY BOX
OUTSIDE MARLBOROUGH HOUSE ON
QUEEN MARY'S 83RD BIRTHDAY IN
MAY 1950

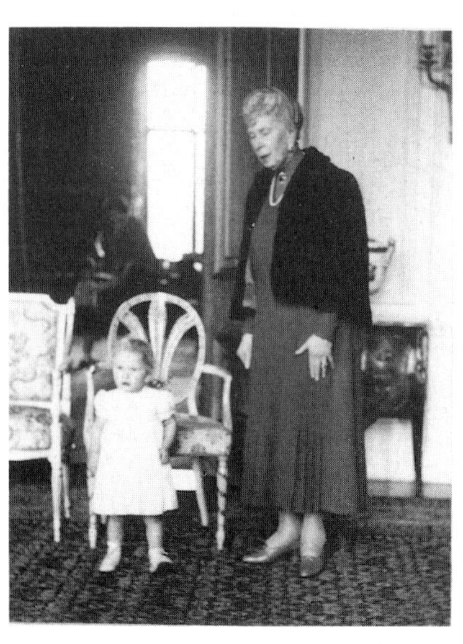

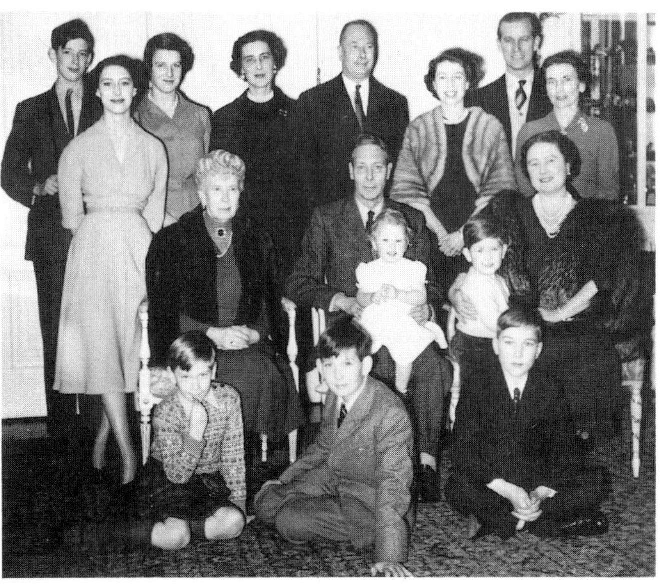

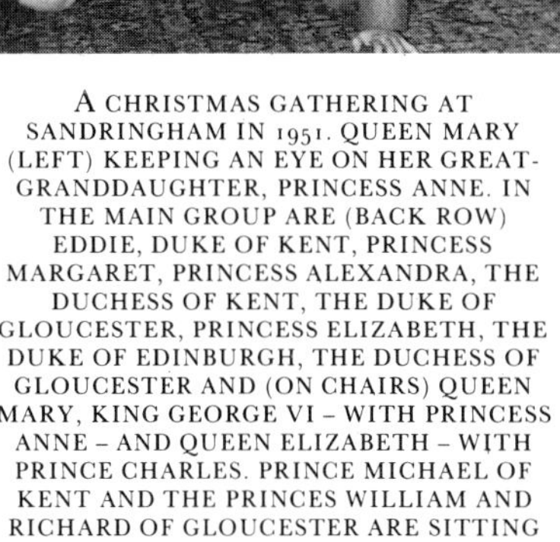

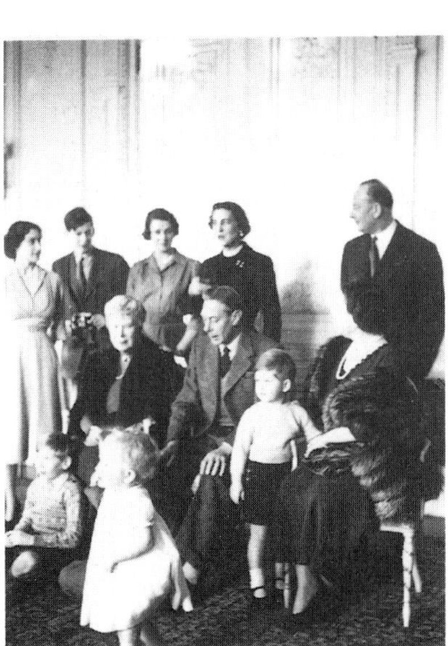

A CHRISTMAS GATHERING AT
SANDRINGHAM IN 1951. QUEEN MARY
(LEFT) KEEPING AN EYE ON HER GREAT-
GRANDDAUGHTER, PRINCESS ANNE. IN
THE MAIN GROUP ARE (BACK ROW)
EDDIE, DUKE OF KENT, PRINCESS
MARGARET, PRINCESS ALEXANDRA, THE
DUCHESS OF KENT, THE DUKE OF
GLOUCESTER, PRINCESS ELIZABETH, THE
DUKE OF EDINBURGH, THE DUCHESS OF
GLOUCESTER AND (ON CHAIRS) QUEEN
MARY, KING GEORGE VI – WITH PRINCESS
ANNE – AND QUEEN ELIZABETH – WITH
PRINCE CHARLES. PRINCE MICHAEL OF
KENT AND THE PRINCES WILLIAM AND
RICHARD OF GLOUCESTER ARE SITTING
ON THE FLOOR

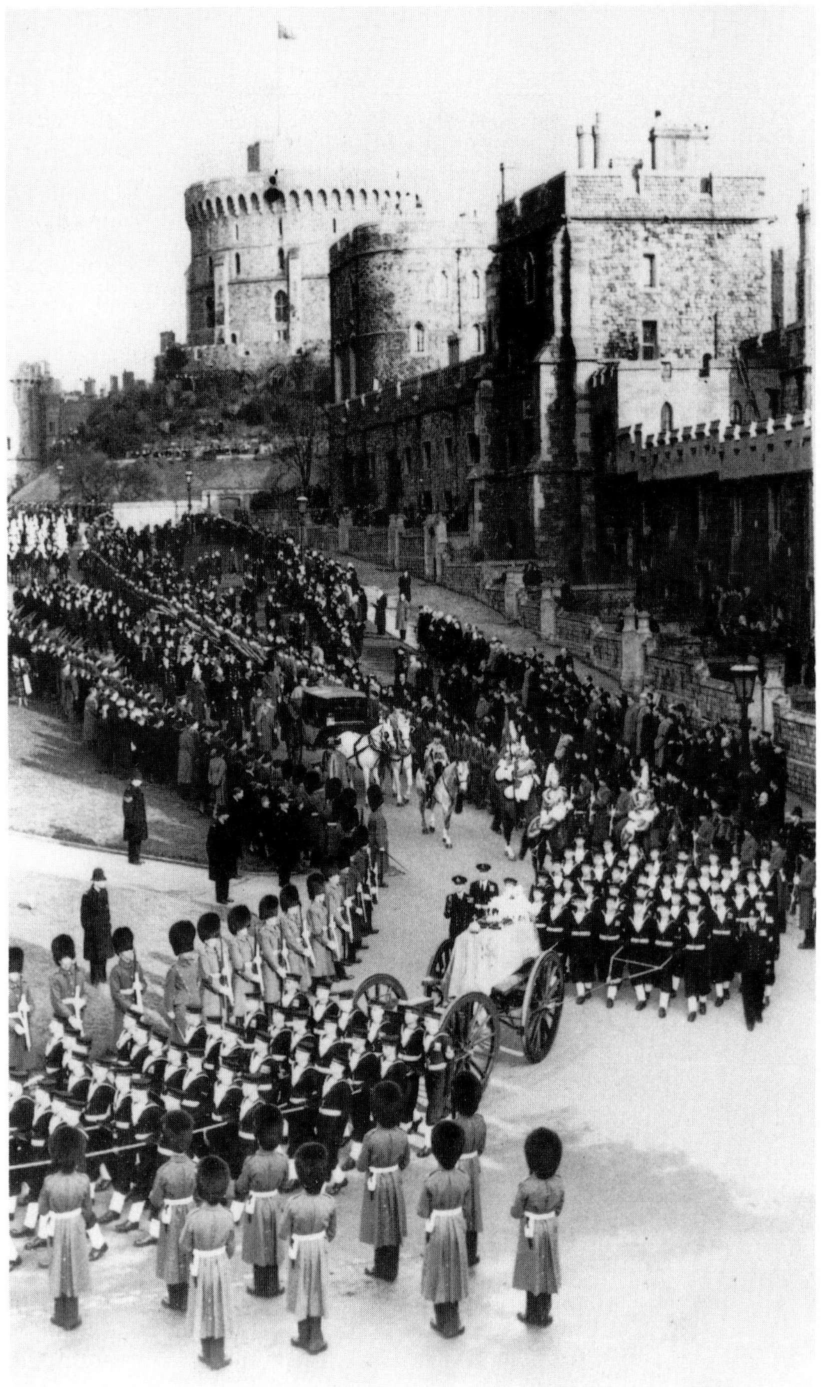

THE FUNERAL OF KING GEORGE VI,
15 FEBRUARY 1952. THE KING'S COFFIN,
BORNE ON A GUN-CARRIAGE, MAKES ITS
WAY THROUGH THE LOWER WARD AT
WINDSOR CASTLE

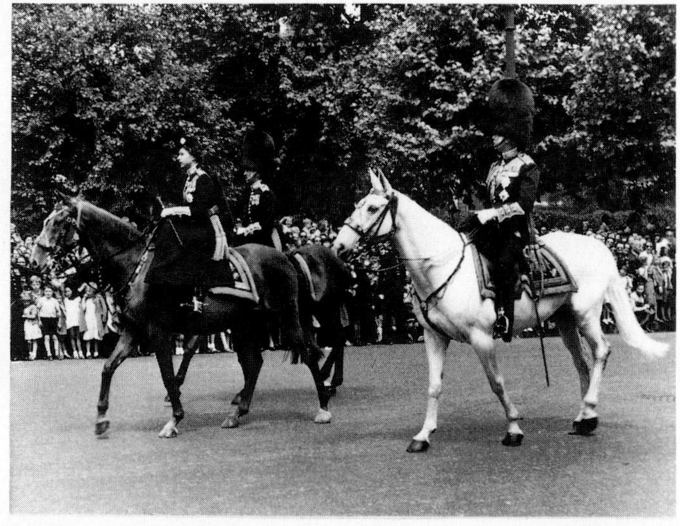

QUEEN'S BIRTHDAY PARADE

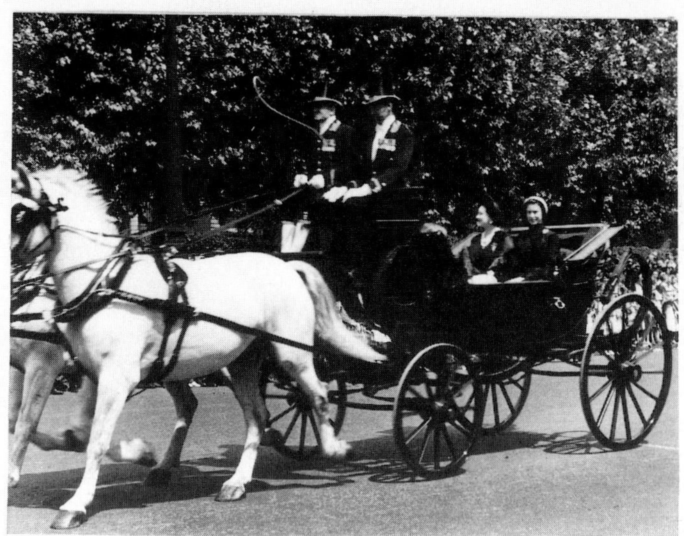

TROOPING THE COLOUR

A NEW REIGN: THE SOVEREIGN'S BIRTHDAY PARADE
ON 5 JUNE 1952. QUEEN ELIZABETH II IS
ACCOMPANIED BY THE DUKE OF GLOUCESTER.
PRINCESS MARGARET AND THE QUEEN MOTHER ARE
STILL WEARING MOURNING FOR GEORGE VI

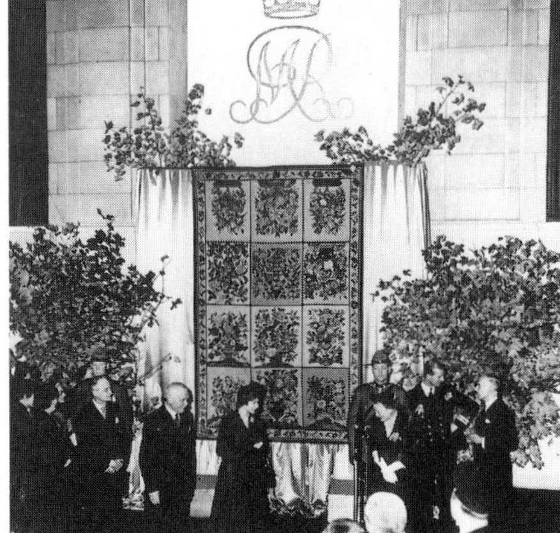

THE TWELVE-PANELLED
CARPET, WORKED BY
QUEEN MARY, BEING
PRESENTED BY PRINCESS
ELIZABETH IN OTTAWA IN
OCTOBER 1951

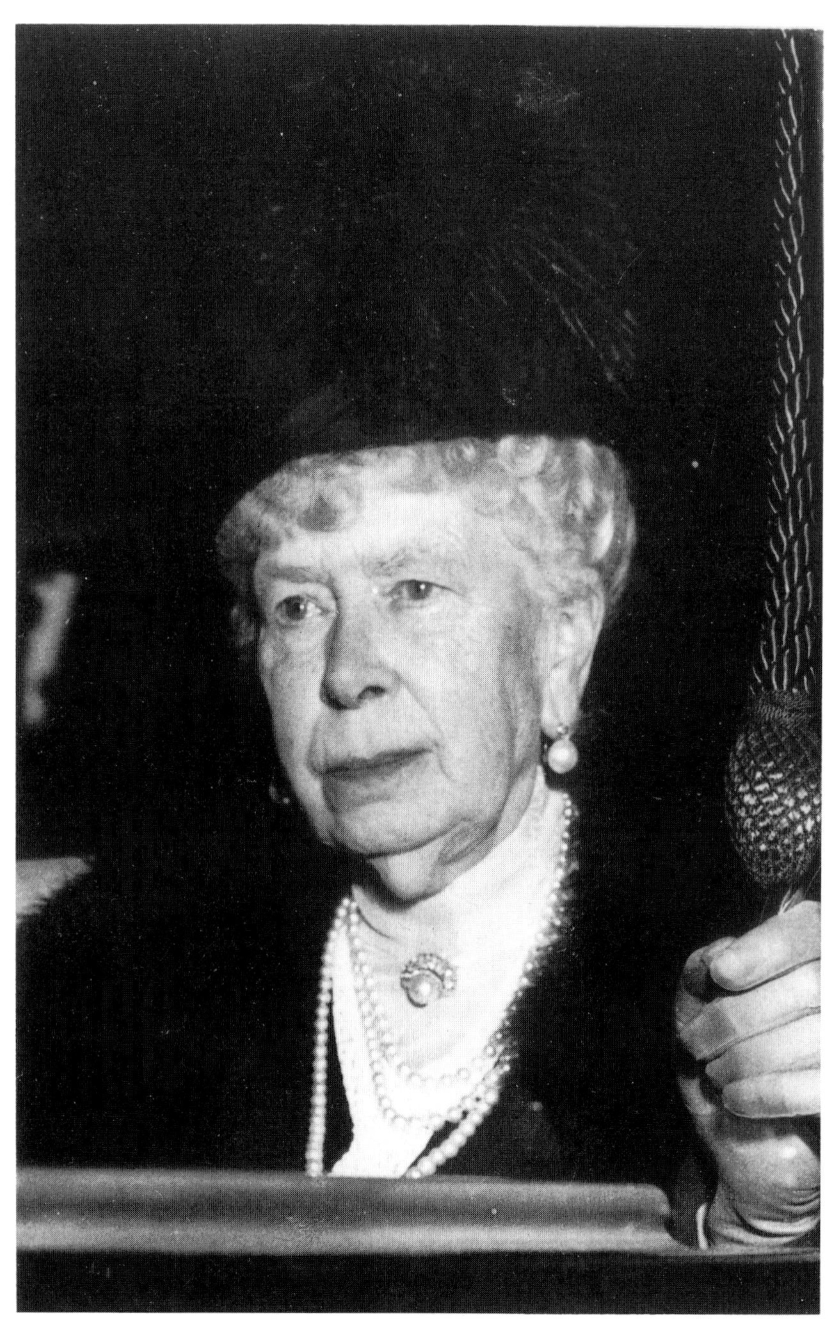

RETURN TO LONDON

17 SEPT., 1952.

THE LAST KNOWN PHOTOGRAPH OF
QUEEN MARY AND THE LAST ONE TO
APPEAR IN HER ALBUMS. TAKEN ON
17 SEPTEMBER 1952